The Incarnate Lord

The Incarnate Lord

A Thomistic Study in Christology

THOMAS JOSEPH WHITE, OP

The Catholic University of America Press

Washington, D.C.

Library of Congress Cataloging-in-Publication Data
White, Thomas Joseph, 1971–
The incarnate Lord : a Thomistic study in Christology /
Thomas Joseph White, OP.
pages cm. — (Thomistic ressourcement series ; Volume 5)
Includes bibliographical references and index.
ISBN 978-0-8132-3009-2 (pbk. : alk. paper) 1. Jesus Christ—
Person and offices. 2. Jesus Christ—History of doctrines—
Middle Ages, 600–1500. 3. Thomas, Aquinas, Saint, 1225?–
1274. I. Title.
BT198.W463 2015
232—dc23   2014043100

In him was life, and the life was the light of men. The light shines in the darkness, and the darkness has not overcome it.

John 1:4–5

The hint half guessed, the gift half understood,
   is Incarnation.
Here the impossible union
Of spheres of evidence is actual,
Here the past and future
Are conquered, and reconciled

T. S. Eliot, *The Dry Salvages*

If you believe in the divinity of Christ, you have to cherish the world at the same time that you struggle to endure it.

Flannery O'Connor, Letter to A., Autumn 1955

I saw, above the many thousand lamps,
a Sun that kindled each and every one
as ours lights up the sights we see above us,
and through that living light poured down
a shining substance. It blazed so bright
into my eyes that I could not sustain it.
O Beatrice, my sweet beloved guide!
To me she said: "What overwhelms you
is a force against which there is no defense.
Here is the Wisdom and the Power that repaired
the roads connecting Heaven and the earth
that had so long been yearned for and desired."

Dante, *Paradiso*, XXIII

Contents

Preface

———:———

I am grateful to many people who made the preparation of this book possible. They may not all agree with everything that is written in it, but they have contributed in various ways to the reflections and convictions that helped to constitute it. In a particular way, I would like to thank Sr. Maria of the Angels, OP, Nicanor Austriaco, OP, Brian Daley, SJ, Emmanuel Durand, OP, Gilles Emery, OP, Jean-Miguel Garrigues, OP, Andrew Hofer, OP, Reinhard Hütter, James F. Keating, Greg La Nave, Matthew Levering, Bruce L. McCormack, Bruce D. Marshall, Chad Pecknold, Trent Pomplun, and Thomas Weinandy, OFM Cap. In addition, Michael Gorman and Guy Mansini, OSB, have been of great help due to their close and insightful readings of the whole text. It has been a privilege to work with Paul Higgins in his fine editing of the text. Likewise I must especially thank Sr. Mary Dominic of the Holy Spirit, OP, for her generous proofreading and her Oxonian defence of the English language. Austin Litke, OP, graciously assisted me on multiple occasions with English translations of Latin texts.

I am grateful to the editors of various journals and presses who have graciously permitted me to make use of previously published essays, in particular, Timothy Bellamah, OP, Bill Eerdmans, Reinhard Hütter, Greg La Nave, Matthew Levering, Joseph Mangina, and the Catholic University of America Press. I am grateful in a particular way to the administration and faculty of the Pontifical Faculty of the Immaculate Conception at the Dominican House of Studies in Washington, D.C., who by their fraternal support and camaraderie have made the work of this study possible.

I would like to dedicate this book in particular to Reinhard Hütter, Matthew Levering, and Bruce Marshall. Their friendship in the study of the theology of St. Thomas Aquinas is a continual source of inspiration.

Acknowledgments

Earlier versions of chapters in this book appeared in the following publications.

Prolegomenon: "Classical Christology after Schleiermacher and Barth: A Thomist Perspective," *Pro Ecclesia* 20 (2011): 229–63.

Chapter 2: "The Pure Nature of Christology: Human Nature and *Gaudium et Spes* 22," *Nova et Vetera* (English edition) 8, no. 2 (2010): 283–322.

Chapter 3: "How Barth Got Aquinas Wrong: A Reply to Archie J. Spencer on Causality and Christocentrism," *Nova et Vetera* (English edition) 7, no. 1 (2009): 241–70.

Chapter 4: "'Through Him All Things Were Made' (John 1:3): The Analogy of the Word Incarnate according to St. Thomas Aquinas and Its Ontological Presuppositions," in *The Analogy of Being: Invention of the Antichrist, or the Wisdom of God?,* ed. Thomas Joseph White, 246–79 (Grand Rapids, Mich.: Eerdmans, 2010).

Chapter 5: "The Voluntary Action of the Earthly Christ and the Necessity of the Beatific Vision," *The Thomist* 69 (October 2005): 497–534.

Chapter 6: "Intra-Divine Obedience in Karl Barth and Nicene-Chalcedonian Christology," *Nova et Vetera* (English edition) 6, no. 2 (2008): 377–402.

Chapter 7: "Jesus' Cry on the Cross and His Beatific Vision," *Nova et Vetera* (English edition) 5, no. 3 (2007): 555–82.

Chapter 8: "Kenoticism and the Divinity of Christ Crucified," *The Thomist* 75 (2011): 1–41.

Conclusion: Some sentences in the chapter are taken from "The Precarity of Wisdom: Modern Dominican Theology, Perspectivalism and the Tasks of Reconstruction," in *Ressourcement Thomism: Sacred Doctrine, the Sacraments, and the Moral Life,* ed. M. Levering and R. Hütter, 92–122 (Washington, D.C.: The Catholic University of America Press, 2009).

Abbreviations of Works of
St. Thomas Aquinas

———— : ————

Comp. Theol.	*Compendium theologiae ad fratrem Reginaldum socium suum carissimum*
Credo	*Collationes super Credo in Deum*
De ente	*De ente et essentia*
De Malo	*Quaestiones disputatae de malo*
De Pot.	*De Potentia Dei*
De Ver.	*De veritate*
De Unione	*De Unione Verbi Incarnati*
Expos. de Trin.	*Expositio super librum Boethii de Trinitate*
In de Anima	*Sententia super De anima*
In de Causis	*In librum de causis expositio*
In Col.	*Super Epistolam ad Colossenses*
In I Cor.	*Super I Epistolam ad Corinthios*
In II Cor.	*Super II Epistolam ad Corinthios*
In de Div. Nom.	*In librum beati Dionysii de divinis nominibus expositio*
In Eph.	*Super Epistolam ad Ephesios*
In Gal.	*Super Epistolam ad Galatas*
In Heb.	*Super Epistolam ad Hebraeos*

Abbreviations

In Ioan.	*Lectura super Ioannem*
In Matt.	*Lectura super Matthaeum*
In Meta.	*In duodecim libros Metaphysicorum Aristotelis expositio*
In Peri Hermeneias	*Expositio libri Peryermenias*
In Post.	*Expositio libri Posteriorum*
In Rom.	*Super Epistolam ad Romanos*
In I Tim.	*Super I Epistolam ad Timotheum*
Sent.	*Scriptum super libros Sententiarum magistri Petri Lombardi episcopi Parisiensis*
SCG	*Summa contra Gentiles*
ST	*Summa theologiae*

The Incarnate Lord

The Biblical Ontology of Christ

Catholic Christianity affirms that Jesus of Nazareth is the Son of God, eternally begotten of the Father, and that he became man and suffered for the redemption of the human race. It also proclaims that this Jesus who was crucified under Pontius Pilate is now alive. He has been raised from the dead and has been glorified in his human body, so as to die no more. These truths, so the Catholic church claims, are of objective significance for all human beings. An understanding of the ultimate meaning of human existence is possible only in light of the mystery of Jesus Christ.

Undoubtedly these are bold claims, scandalous to many. The earliest Christians were put to death for affirming them. They were the subject of intense speculative discussion in medieval Europe, often in dialogue with the objections of non-Christian religious traditions. In the modern age, they have long been considered unfashionable or even despised within important strands of Western culture. They certainly no longer serve as they once did (arguably even until the eighteenth century) as the highest truths of reference in the modern university. Indeed, many philosophical doctrines that have deeply influenced modern culture were developed in direct opposition to the classical dogmatic tenets of Catholicism regarding the person of Christ, original sin, the reality of grace, or the authority of divine revelation.

Nevertheless, whatever the historical criticisms of Christianity, be they ancient, medieval or modern, its teachings regarding the person of Christ remain today a largely unstudied subject. In fact, it could be said without exaggeration that there is very little theological knowledge of Christianity—and of the person of Christ—present in mainstream modern European and American culture. This is as true of academic culture as it is of popular culture. One might object to this kind of claim. After all, are the practices of Christianity not evidenced all around us, throughout the world? Yet such an objection suggests the undetected presence of a confusion between what is to be regarded as generally Christian in human culture (including even the intentional practice of Christianity of some kind) and a deeper historical and systematic *theological* knowledge of Christianity. In our own age, even when the former influence is prevalent, the latter form of learning is encountered infrequently. Indeed, true theological study of classical Christianity in general and of the person of Jesus Christ in particular are rare. This does not mean, however, that they are not valuable.

For theology is not only intellectually interesting, but also profoundly illuminating. It considers reality in light of the Holy Trinity. Consequently, when it is practiced rightly, theology is normally expansive in vision and not enclosed, cosmopolitan and not parochial. Why is this the case? Theology seeks to understand the world in light of God, and God is, among other things, the most expansive horizon of human thinking. Everything else can be understood relative to the mystery of God because God is the first cause and final end of all things. Consequently, theology seeks to explain the world with reference to the most ultimate parameters of human understanding. Medieval theologians rightly noted that just because this is the case, theology can be termed a "science" in its own right, one that has a distinct subject matter: God and all things considered in light of God.[1] At the same time, theology needs to respect and even assimilate the

1. *Summa theologiae*, in *Sancti Thomae Aquinatis opera omnia*, vols. 4–12 (Rome: Leonine Edition, 1888–1906), I, q. 1, aa. 2–3 [hereafter "ST"]. On the doctrine of theology as a *scientia* in the Middle Ages, see Ulrich G. Leinsle, *Introduction to Scholastic Theology*, trans. M. J. Miller (Washington, D.C.: The Catholic University of America Press, 2010), 120–81.

authentic insights of the lesser sciences: the sound conclusions of philosophy, historical study, and the modern sciences.[2] When challenged by the arguments stemming from these disciplines, it should offer patient and reasonable answers. Even if theology has an authentic autonomy of subject matter, it is not for that reason wholly alien to ordinary reason or totalitarian in its epistemological impulses. It is a sapiential, inclusive discipline that seeks to see all true but lesser human learning in relation to the first and ultimate truth about God.

Unlike natural forms of learning, theology is a science based upon the principles of divine revelation. Truth revealed by God is given freely and as such transcends the scope of ordinary human reason. The mysteries of Christianity cannot be proven or disproven, therefore, by philosophical or scientific argumentation.[3] They can be shown, however, to be congruent and beautifully interwoven with the soundest conclusions of philosophical, scientific, and ethical realism.[4] Furthermore, what is revealed by God is pregnant with wisdom, and has its own intrinsic intelligibility.[5] The mysteries of Christianity are densely intelligible, if numinous, and so they can be studied and understood for their own sake. In this vision of things, the study of theology is primarily speculative in nature, rather than practical.[6] It certainly provides practical orientation to human prudence. (Why do we exist? What ought we to do? How ought we to live?) More fundamentally, however, theology aims to make sense of reality in light of what is most ultimately real. It is about the first and last truth, the Alpha and the Omega. It is because theology is so speculatively inclined

---

2. As already noted by Aquinas in ST I, q. 1, a. 6, ad 2.

3. This principle is underscored in a thematic way by the First Vatican Council—see *Dei Filius* (1870). It is reiterated and developed in the Second Vatican Council document, *Dei Verbum*, paras. 2 and 17. See also the *Catechism of the Catholic Church* (English Edition) (New York: Doubleday, 1995), paras. 51–53 and 153–65. See the treatments of divine revelation in Ambroise Gardeil, *Le donné révélé et la théologie*, 2nd ed. (Paris: Cerf, 1932), 41–76, and Jean-Hervé Nicolas, *Synthèse dogmatique: De la Trinité à la Trinité* (Fribourg: Éditions Universitaires, 1985), 191–98. All citations to and translations from the Second Vatican Council in this book are taken from *Vatican Council II: Vol. I, The Conciliar and Post Conciliar Documents*, ed. A. Flannery (Northport, N.Y. / Dublin: Costello Publishing / Dominican Publications, 2004).

4. *Dei Filius*, ch. 3; see Gardeil, *Le donné révélé*, 252–318.

5. *Dei Filius*, ch. 4; see *Dei Verbum*, para. 2.

6. ST I, q. 1, a. 4.

that it is also so eminently practical.[7] Theology invites us to make all our basic decisions in light of what is most ultimately the case.

ONTOLOGICAL CHRISTOLOGY

This is a book of speculative theology. It is about Jesus Christ and the fundamental affirmations of Catholic theology regarding his person. The goal of the work is to understand what the mystery of the incarnation is and how that mystery reveals who God is to us. I will examine, for example, the personal identity of Christ (the hypostatic union), his divine and human natures, and his divine and human knowledge. The book is also a study of the mystery of the redemption. What does it mean to say that Christ was humanly obedient, that he suffered and died for the sake of the human race? How should we understand Christian claims regarding the descent of Christ into hell and the resurrection of Christ from the dead? In treating these diverse topics, I am greatly indebted to the theological insights of St. Thomas Aquinas and the subsequent Thomist tradition. At the same time, I engage a range of influential modern theological and non-theological positions. In other words, this is a Thomistic study in Christology that seeks to understand in a speculative fashion what it means to say that God became a man and that this man who is God died by crucifixion and rose from the dead for the salvation of the human race. There is a concern in the argument of the book to understand what Thomism has taught about these subjects historically, but also so as to argue about what is in fact perennially true with respect to the mystery of Jesus. Consequently, the book engages a range of possible contemporary opinions in view of a defense and presentation of Thomistic Christological wisdom. A presupposition of the book is that there exists a perennial Thomistic theological science that is of enduring value down through time, of as much relevance today as it was in the age of St. Thomas Aquinas. At the same time, much of what I consider "Thomist" herein is sometimes equally upheld by other scholastic authors—Alexander of Hales, Bonaventure, Albert the Great. Many themes in this book will resonate soundly, then, with students of other great scholastic authors.

7. ST I-II, q. 1, aa. 3–4; q. 2, a. 8.

The basic argument of the book is that Christology has an irreducible ontological dimension that is essential to its integrity as a science. Christology is in some sense intrinsically ontological because it is concerned with the being and person of Christ, and with his divine and human natures and actions. By this definition, it can be said unequivocally that without the ontological study of the person, being and natures of Christ, Christology ceases to be an integral science. It loses sight of its proper object, which is God the Word made man. This is by no means a trivial or uncontroversial claim, since modern Christology has often looked askance upon traditional, ontological ways of speaking of Christ, or has openly contested them.[8] I will argue in the course of this study that Catholic theology certainly can undertake intellectually compelling forms of discussion of the ontological aspects of the mystery of Christ. Furthermore it should do so. For only in doing so can it renew unceasingly its contact with classical forms of thinking that are doctrinally normative in Christian thought. I am thinking here in particular of the accounts of Christ given by the Councils of Nicaea, Ephesus, Chalcedon, and Constantinople III. Without a robustly metaphysical form of thinking about Jesus, the truth of these councils becomes obscured. In addition, however, this approach to Christology is also future-oriented and is full of perennial promise and vitality. Why is this the case? Because classical, orthodox Christology has a unique and irreplaceable capacity to illumine in depth our understanding of who God is, and what human beings are. It casts a unique light upon the ultimate sense of the human condition.

In speaking here of ontology I am drawing no real distinction between "metaphysics" and "ontology."[9] By the use of both terms I mean to denote the same thing: the study of what exists or of what

8. Regarding the influence of Immanuel Kant's "post-metaphysical" critical philosophy upon modern, liberal Protestantism, see Karl-Heinz Menke, *Jesus Ist Gott Der Sohn* (Regensburg: Friedrich Pustet, 2008), 335–50, and Gerhard Ludwig Müller, *Katholische Dogmatik: Für Studium und Praxis der Theologie* (Freiburg: Herder, 2005), 265–71.

9. *Pace* the oft-cited Heideggerian distinction that is sometimes made between the two. See in this respect Martin Heidegger, "The Onto-theo-logical Constitution of Metaphysics," in *Identity and Difference*, trans. Joan Stambaugh (New York: Harper and Row, 1969), 42–74. Nevertheless, the words "metaphysics" and "ontology" are used with overlapping significations in the majority of Heidegger's writings.

has being. However, in speaking of ontological *Christology*, I am referring not to a subject of philosophy as such, or to philosophical reflection on Christ (for example, Aristotelian-inspired analysis of the person of Christ). Rather, I am referring specifically to a biblical mystery: Christ is revealed in scripture as a person who truly exists. The *personal being* of Christ is subject to theological investigation. The mystery of God made man has an inward "form" or ontological determination. On the one hand, this subject eludes explanation by recourse merely to the ordinary categories of human experience and philosophical forms of ontological analysis. On the other hand, this mystery is luminous and has a certain internal intelligibility. It can be studied for its own sake and considered in itself in a properly theological manner. Such a study has always had a distinctively ontological character to it.[10] What does it mean to say, for instance, that Christ is a divine person, or to speak of the union of his divine and human natures in one hypostasis? How can we understand the relation between his human and divine natures, in their real distinction and necessary inseparability? How ought we to understand the fact that Christ possesses an individual human nature, and consequently both an organic body and a spiritual soul? How are all these truths at play when we consider the human knowledge of Christ, or his human action? What are the knowledge and action of Christ that are present in the redemption and in his experience of the crucifixion?

Are these questions alien to scripture itself? Some would say that they are. The most famous modern example of such skepticism is found in the work of Adolf von Harnack, the early twentieth-century historian of church dogma, and archetypal representative of modern liberal Protestantism.[11] For Harnack the dogmas of the Councils of Nicaea and Chalcedon were developed in relative independence from the teaching of the New Testament itself. They are extrinsic "Hellenistic" accretions, speculations accidental to the message of Jesus

10. See on this point, Charles Journet, *Introduction à la Théologie*, ch. 2, in *Oeuvres Complétes* (Paris: Éditions St. Augustin, 2007), 9:977–92.

11. Adolf von Harnack, *Lehrbuch der Dogmengeschichte*, 3 vols. (Freiburg: J. C. B. Mohr, 1886–89). The English translation by N. Buchanan was made from the 1909 third edition (7 vols.), *History of Dogma*, reprinted in 4 vols. (New York: Dover Publications, 1961).

and the earliest Christians. It is their ontological dimension in particular that marks them out as decidedly non-Judaic and even post-biblical.[12] Where there is speculation regarding the person and natures of Christ as God and man, there we stand outside the threshold of authentic scriptural theology. Scripture, we might say, is a world apart from metaphysics. According to this influential way of thinking, a biblical, ethical Christology (deeply influenced in Harnack's case by Kantian philosophy and ethics) must be distinguished from a philosophical, ontological Christology (that which we find in the church fathers and the scholastics).[13]

This is a poignant claim with an alluring simplicity, but from a historical and biblical point of view it can be shown to be untenable. I will offer arguments below for why I take this to be the case. To state things in so gentle a way, however, is in fact already to concede too much. For if Harnack is in error on this point (which I take to be the case), then we should be concerned not merely to establish *the right* of the interpreter to consider the ontological dimension of the mystery of Christ, as if this were one way of reading scripture among others. Rather, we must say that unless we study the mystery of Jesus ontologically, we fundamentally cannot understand the New Testament. For generally speaking the Bible is deeply concerned with the ontological structure of reality and its dependence upon God. The New Testament in particular, however, is concerned *above all and before all else* with the ontological identity of Christ and the fact that

12. See, for example, Harnack, *History of Dogma*, "On the Conception of Pre-Existence," 1:318–31.

13. Consider the analysis of Pope Benedict XVI in his Regensburg Address of September 12, 2006 (*Faith, Reason and the University: Memories and Reflections*): "Fundamentally, Harnack's goal was to bring Christianity back into harmony with modern reason, liberating it, that is to say, from seemingly philosophical and theological elements, such as faith in Christ's divinity and the triune God. In this sense, historical-critical exegesis of the New Testament, as he saw it, restored to theology its place within the university: theology, for Harnack, is something essentially historical and therefore strictly scientific. What it is able to say critically about Jesus is, so to speak, an expression of practical reason and consequently it can take its rightful place within the university. Behind this thinking lies the modern self-limitation of reason, classically expressed in Kant's 'Critiques,' but in the meantime further radicalized by the impact of the natural sciences." http://www.vatican.va/holy_father/benedict_xvi/speeches/2006/september/documents/hf_ben-xvi_spe_20060912_university-regensburg_en.html

he is both God and man. No teaching is more central. It is the truth that underlies all other scriptural affirmations regarding Jesus. Consequently, to study the New Testament realistically *at all* is to study the being and person of Christ—his two natures and operations, divine and human, as they are manifest in and through his life, death and resurrection. I will argue throughout this book that this is in fact the case. In some real sense it is true to say: ignorance of ontology is ignorance of Christ. The understanding of the Bible offered by the fathers and the scholastics, then, is not merely something that can be justified as one possible form of reading among others (defensively, as against a post-critical anthropological turn in modern philosophy). Rather, it is the only form of reading that attains objectively to the deepest truth about the New Testament: a truth concerning the identity of Christ as the God-man. By the same measure, only this reading of scripture can attain to a proper understanding of the subject of biblical theology as such. Everything else remains lodged in the merely accidental, and for that reason is, from the point of view of theological realism, a mere shadow of the truth.

THE BIBLICAL ONTOLOGY OF
THE NEW TESTAMENT

The whole of this book is concerned with the claim that the study of Christ must be undertaken ontologically, or metaphysically, in various ways. To introduce this idea, however, I would like to signal four motifs in the New Testament that are basic to the teaching of early Christianity and which demonstrate the inevitability of metaphysical inquiry into the person of Christ for a right understanding of scripture itself. Let us consider in turn, briefly and by way of initiation, the following themes: (1) the pre-existence of Jesus Christ and the notion that he is the creator, (2) the Lordship of Christ, (3) the form of his human nature, and (4) the use of the communication of idioms. In each case we find in the New Testament itself the seeds of ontological reflection concerning Christ, and we can begin to see that such reflection is in fact unavoidable for any true science of the person of Jesus.

Pre-existence and the Notion
of Christ as Creator

It is commonly observed within modern biblical scholarship that various passages of the New Testament refer unambiguously to the "pre-existence" of the person of Jesus. In Colossians 1:15–20, for instance, we read:

He is the image of the invisible God, the first-born of all creation; for in him all things were created, in heaven and earth, visible and invisible, whether thrones or dominions or principalities or authorities—all things were created through him and for him. He is before all things, and in him all things hold together. He is the head of the body, the Church; he is the beginning, the first-born from the dead, that in everything he might be pre-eminent. For in him all the fullness of God was pleased to dwell, and through him to reconcile to himself all things, whether on earth or in heaven, making peace by the blood of his cross.[14]

Christ is portrayed in this passage as a personal agent who stands at the beginning of all things, and who has attributed to him the power of creation, a power that is proper to God alone according to ancient Israelite theology.[15] In addition, however, Christ is the one who is God dwelling among men, and who died in the crucifixion ("in him all the fullness of God was pleased to dwell"). When we speak of the "pre-existence" of Jesus, then, we refer to the common New Testament teaching that the Son existed personally as God prior to his historical life as man.[16] He who is God has become human by "descending" into the human condition.

This idea plays a prominent and thematic role in the New Testament. It does not appear as a merely peripheral idea in the theology of the early Christian movement, nor as something accidental that developed in subsequent years. It is, on the contrary, a predominant, consistent theme of the New Testament in light of which all

---

14. Translations of the Bible in this introduction are taken from the Revised Standard Version, which I have occasionally slightly modified.

15. See the argumentation in Richard Bauckham, *God Crucified: Monotheism and Christology in the New Testament* (Grand Rapids, Mich.: Eerdmans, 1998).

16. See the arguments of Gordon D. Fee, *Pauline Christology: An Exegetical-Theological Study* (Peabody, Mass.: Hendrickson Publishers, 2007), 88–94, 304–13.

else is meant to be understood.[17] We might think here of a number of well-known examples. Paul's letter to the Philippians, by all accounts one of the earliest Christian epistles, speaks of the pre-existence of Jesus who "was in the form of God," but who took upon himself the "form of a servant" (Phil 2:6–7).[18] Galatians 4:4 speaks of "God [sending] his Son, born of a woman, born under the law."[19] John 1 frames the fourth Gospel with reference to the incarnation: "In the beginning was the Word … and the Word was God.… All things were made through him, and without him was not anything made that was made.… And the Word became flesh and dwelt among us" (Jn 1:1, 3, 14).[20] The Gospel of Mark is introduced by the notion that Jesus is the "Son of God," a creedal statement pronounced also by the gentile centurion who seems to confess the divinity of Christ at the term of the book (Mk 1:1, 15:39). Confession of the sonship of Christ thus "frames" this Gospel from beginning to end.[21] The prologue of the epistle to the Hebrews states that "in these last days, [God] has spoken to us by a Son, whom he appointed the heir of all things, through whom also he created the world. He reflects the glory of God and bears the very stamp of his nature, upholding the universe by his word of power" (Heb 1:2–3).[22]

The point of listing these references is not merely to show that the pre-existence of Christ is a normative doctrine found in many key texts of the New Testament. The point is that it is a framing issue which is meant to give the right perspective on all else that is presented in the apostolic testimony. The authors of these various works take it as a theological given that the historical life, death, and resurrection of Jesus cannot be properly understood except in reference to

17. On this point, see Martin Hengel, *The Son of God: The Origin of Christology and the History of Jewish-Hellenistic Religion*, trans. J. Bowden (Philadelphia: Fortress, 1976).

18. See the analysis of this controversial text by N. T. Wright, *The Climax of the Covenant: Christ and the Law in Pauline Theology* (Minneapolis, Minn.: Fortress, 1993), 56–98.

19. See Simon J. Gathercole, *The Pre-existent Son: Recovering the Christologies of Matthew, Mark and Luke* (Grand Rapids, Mich.: Eerdmans, 2006), 28–29.

20. See Rudolf Schnackenburg, *The Gospel according to St. John*, 3 vols., trans. C. Hastings et al. (New York: Seabury Press, 1980–82), 1:481–93.

21. The textual issues surrounding this interpretation are highly debated. See the helpful essay by Tommy Wasserman, "The 'Son of God' was in the Beginning (Mark 1:1)," *Journal of Theological Studies* 62, no. 1 (2011): 20–50.

22. See Bauckham, *God Crucified*, 32–34.

his pre-existent identity as the Son through whom the Father created the world. It is not clear at all that this transcendent unity of God
and Jesus arises as the *conclusion* of an early Christian trajectory of
thought.[23] In the New Testament, or much of it, the pre-existence
and divinity of Christ as creator seem to be understood as the *precondition* for any right form of theological thinking.

Commentators commonly note that there is a clear Jewish precedent for the form of pre-existence that the early Christian movement
ascribes to Christ. It is found in the sapiential literature of the Old
Testament.[24] There, the "wisdom" of God is commonly portrayed as
a pre-existent principle identical with God or emanating from God,
in which and through which all things are created.[25] The wisdom of
God is anticipatory, as it were, of all that is to come about in creation,
by a kind of transcendent exemplary causality. "For [wisdom] is a reflection of eternal light, a spotless mirror of the working of God, and
an image of his goodness.... She reaches mightily from one end of
the earth to the other, and she orders all things well" (Wis 7:27, 8:1).
In the Gospels of Luke and Matthew, Jesus seems at times to attribute
the power of this wisdom to himself (Lk 7:35; Mt 11:28–30, 23:37–
39).[26] Paul even speaks of Christ crucified in this way, calling him the
"power of God and the wisdom of God" (1 Cor 1:24).[27] As a final example, we might consider the virginal conception of Jesus as it is recounted in the nativity sequences of Matthew and Luke. Some scholars have not hesitated to see herein an idea of the pre-existence of the
Son as the wisdom of God, who takes flesh in the womb of the Virgin
Mary.[28] On this reading, we are not considering any form of Greek

23. Contrary to the speculations of Wilhelm Bousset, *Kyrios Christos: Geschichte des Christusglaubens von den Anfängen des Christentums bis Irenaeus* (Göttingen: Van-denhoeck & Ruprecht, 1913), and as argued forcefully by Larry W. Hurtado, *Lord Jesus Christ: Devotion to Jesus in Earliest Christianity* (Grand Rapids, Mich.: Eerdmans, 2003).

24. See Menke, *Jesus ist Gott der Sohn*, 168–89.

25. Job 28:20–28; Prov 8:22–36; Sir 24:1–12; Wis 7:22–30, 8:1, 9:1–10.

26. See André Feuillet, "Jésus et la Sagesse divine d'après les Évangiles Synoptiques: Le 'Logion johannique' et l'Ancien Testament," *Revue Biblique* 62 (1955): 161–96, as well as the critical reflections of Gathercole, *The Pre-existent Son*, 203–9.

27. James D. G. Dunn, *The Theology of Paul the Apostle* (Grand Rapids, Mich.: Eerd-mans, 1998), 274, argues for pre-existence in this passage; see, however, the critical con-cerns of Fee, *Pauline Christology*, 102–6.

28. See Gathercole, *The Pre-existent Son*, 284–89.

mythological speculation (which would treat the deity anthropomorphically), but a specifically Jewish notion of the creator who freely
takes on the form of the creature without ceasing to be the creator.
The virginal conception occurs by way of the unique power of God,
and in that sense, it is a miraculous sign that the one who is conceived
in the womb of Mary is the very one who sustains all things in being. For he who is conceived is "Emmanuel," "God with us" (Mt 1:23,
Is 7:14 [LXX]).[29]

What do we mean, however, when we speak of "wisdom"? It is
well and good to test the genealogical hypotheses and consider historically with reasonable probability how Jewish monotheistic terms
for God's pre-existent wisdom *might* have come to be ascribed to Jesus of Nazareth. But the deeper question is, what do we mean ontologically by speaking of divine wisdom? In fact, to pass into this deeper understanding of scripture itself, we are required to begin to think
in distinctively ontological terms. For Aquinas, the biblical term "wisdom" denotes knowledge as well as love. The wise person is one who
knows that which is worthy of love and is one who loves intelligent-
ly and prudently.[30] On this reading of scripture, divine wisdom is
God's own self-knowledge but it is not a morally indifferent form of
knowledge. It is knowledge of God's own divine goodness, imbued
with God's ecstatic, non-egotistical love of his own goodness.[31] Furthermore, this loving knowledge that God has of himself stands at
the foundation of his gifts in the order of creation and in the order of
grace. That is to say, divine wisdom is knowledge capable of creating
and of bestowing the life of grace. It is knowledge that is itself effusive
of divine goodness.[32]

Undoubtedly, in speaking of wisdom in this way, we have already
begun to think in starkly ontological terms about God and about

29. Already Ignatius of Antioch connects the miracle of the virginal conception of
Jesus to his ontological status as Son of God in the flesh (*Ad Smyrn.* 1–2): "You are firmly
convinced about our Lord, who is truly of the race of David according to the flesh, Son of
God according to the will and power of God, truly born of a virgin … he was truly nailed
to a tree for us in his flesh under Pontius Pilate … he truly suffered, as he is also truly ris-
en." *Apostolic Fathers*, ed. J. B. Lightfoot (London: Macmillan, 1889), II.2:289–93.

30. ST I, q. 1, a. 6, corp. and ad 3; q. 20, a. 1; q. 22, a. 2, sed contra and corp.

31. ST I, q. 19, a. 2, corp. and ad 2.

32. ST I, q. 20, a. 2, corp. and ad 1; q. 44, a. 4.

the reality of creation. And in fact, this is all only an initial ground-clearing. For if the Son of God is the wisdom of God, then what does it mean to say that he pre-exists? And what exactly does he pre-exist? In short, we might ask, how is the pre-existent Son distinct from the creation that depends upon him? Negatively, we might say that the Son of God prior to the incarnation does *not* exist as a creature. Biblically speaking, a creature is anyone or anything that can come into being or cease to be, and that exists uniquely by virtue of immediate causal dependence upon God as the actual cause of its being. But the Son necessarily does not exist in this way, for the Son exists eternally, and is he through whom all things come to be, upon whom they depend for their existence. Furthermore, any temporal and physical being in our world comes to be in a certain manner, through physical generation or corruption, and in simultaneous causal dependence upon the activity of other physical beings. But the Son pre-exists our state of being. Seemingly, then, if the Son is eternally begotten of the Father as his "Word" before all ages (Jn 1:17), this does not mean that the Son exists eternally in the same way as creatures that are material, physical, and temporal. On the contrary, he must proceed eternally from the Father in some other, very distinct way, one that implies no temporal or physical begetting.[33]

Furthermore, as we can see, the ascription to the Son of creative *causality* is entailed by the attribution to him of a notion of divine wisdom. The Son as the wisdom through whom God creates must not come into existence as a creature from the creator, for he is the cause of the coming into being of creatures. "All things were created through him and for him" (Col 1:16). Positively, this means that the Son exists in a higher and other way than creatures, as God exists, as the Father exists, he by whom all things were made. The Son exists, however, not as the person of the Father, but as one who is personally distinct from the Father and as he who is one with the Father. The Son is he *through* whom all things were made.

To say all this is to suggest that once we begin to think seriously about the notion of Jesus's pre-existence as well as his personal distinction from the Father, we are already well on our way to a no-

33. ST I, q. 27, aa. 1–2; q. 45, aa. 5–6.

tion of God as Trinity. The Son is eternally distinct from the Father and the Holy Spirit but he is also truly God, eternally one with the Father and the Holy Spirit. As was noted above, however, the pre-existence of the Son is a notion that is fundamental to reflection on the New Testament as such. Consequently, belief in the Holy Trinity is required for any correct reading of the New Testament. Reflection on Jesus's ontological identity is foundational for any right reading of the apostolic witnesses, and is a necessary element of any well-framed interpretation of the text of scripture.

The Lordship of Christ

The biblical concept of Christ as the pre-existent principle of creation invites us to think about the Lordship of Christ in terms of "efficient causality." All things come to be in and through the Word and Wisdom of God. However, we might also think of the identity of Christ by direct reference to his *incarnate* Lordship. Here the Bible invites us to consider the personal identity of Jesus of Nazareth. "Who do men say that I am?" (Mk 8:27) is answered throughout the New Testament canon with recourse to the Greek Septuagint title *Kyrios*, a term that often explicitly denotes divinity. Jesus is "Lord" in just the same way as the God of Israel is the Lord.[34] He is that Lord now incarnate.

We can note this theological motif, for example, in Matthew 25:31–46, the parable of the last judgment, where the Son of Man separates the sheep and the goats based on their responses to the needs of the poor, the sick, and the imprisoned. The sheep and goats in turn ask the Son of Man (whom Matthew clearly understands to be Jesus): "Lord, when did we see thee hungry or thirsty or a stranger or naked or sick or in prison?" (Mt 25:44). The authority of eschatological judgment that Israel normally reserves to God alone is now recognized as being present in the Son of Man, Jesus who is the "Lord."[35] For the authors of scripture, it is presumably in this spirit that we are to understand the imperfect but real apprehensions of the authority of Jesus by those who encounter him in his apostolic life: "Lord, if

34. See Hurtado, *Lord Jesus Christ*, 108–18, 178–85.
35. See Frank J. Matera, *New Testament Christology* (Louisville, Ky.: Westminster John Knox, 1999), 27.

you will, you can make me clean" (Mt 8:2). "Lord, I am not worthy to have you come under my roof; but only say the word, and my servant will be healed" (Mt 8:8). Christ bears within himself a power and authority akin to that of God. He can perform actions that are normally reserved to God alone. We see this in the opening chapters of Mark, when Jesus forgives sins by his own authority, to which the Pharisees respond: "Who can forgive sins but God alone?" (Mk 2:7–10). Mark seemingly would have us understand that Jesus himself has the authority to forgive sins that is proper to the Lord of Israel.[36]

The early Christian movement, then, did not hesitate to attribute to the risen Christ the title of Lord. Furthermore, there is widespread evidence in the New Testament that they worshiped Christ, a practice reserved in Second Temple Judaism to God alone under pain of serious sin.[37] We see in the Acts of the Apostles, for example, that as Stephen is being stoned, he prays directly to Christ as Lord, saying, "Lord Jesus, receive my spirit" (7:59). Some chapters later, when Saul is addressed by Christ on the road to Damascus, he responds: "Who are you, Lord?" He receives the answer, "I am Jesus, whom you are persecuting" (Acts 9:5). He who once lived among us as a mortal man and who died is understood to be alive now in the resurrection. Yet he is also understood to have *always* been the Lord, even in his human life, crucifixion, and death.[38] Consequently, St. Paul can say, "But far be it from me to glory except in *the cross of our Lord* Jesus Christ, by which the world has been crucified to me, and I to the world" (Gal 6:14).

As we see in Luke's portrayal of the conversion of Saul, there is also the notion that the disciples of Christ are somehow "in" the Lord.[39] Those who persecute the church, persecute Christ. This New Testament theme of incorporation into the Lord manifests clearly the notion of his deity. By grace, we can be incorporated into Christ and so into the life of God. "The grace of the Lord Jesus Christ be with

36. See the careful, speculative treatment of this by Hurtado, *Lord Jesus Christ*, 406, 287–88.

37. Ibid., 27–78.

38. Ibid., 108–26, 184–85, 197–206.

39. See the analysis of C. F. D. Moule, *The Origin of Christology* (Cambridge: Cambridge University Press, 1977), esp. 57, 86–89.

your spirit" (Phil 4:23); "Wives, be subject to your husbands, as is fitting in the Lord" (Col 3:18); "See that you fulfill the ministry which
you have received in the Lord" (Col. 4:17); "For now we live, if you
stand fast in the Lord" (1 Thes 3:8). There is a collective identity of
Christ that can incorporate others into itself, because Christ is the
"Lord" in whom the disciples reside as a gift of grace.[40] Ultimately, the
orientation of this form of thinking is eschatological. We can die "in
Christ" (1 Cor 15:18–20). The book of Revelation portrays God the Father and the Lamb together as "the Lord" in whom the blessed make
their home. "I saw no temple in the city, for its temple is the Lord
God the Almighty and the Lamb" (Rev 21:22). Seeing all in the light
of Christ, the blessed "need no light of lamp or sun, for the Lord God
will be their light, and they shall reign forever and ever" (Rev 22:5).[41]

What we confront inevitably in all these passages is the question: what is it that we mean when we say that Jesus of Nazareth is the
Lord, the God of Israel? We can appropriately restate the question in
such a way as to refer explicitly to the personal subject of Christ: what
does it mean for the Lord God personally to be human? Notice that
here we are speaking no longer of the Son as the cause of the creation,
but of the Son in the flesh. How is it that Christ is both God and human? To ask this question is to touch upon a central mystery of the
New Testament, the mystery that subsequent theology would designate helpfully as "the hypostatic union." The title of "Lord" as it is applied to the personal subject of Christ in primitive Christianity contains the seeds of this theology. It pushes us to examine the personal
unity of Christ as one who is both God and man, as the Lord who is
one with the Father, and as the Lord who is crucified. Nothing short
of a Christology that looks directly into ontological questions is capable of such a reflection, and yet failing such a reflection, the New Testament itself remains fundamentally unintelligible.

The Form of Human Nature

The New Testament is concerned not only with the divinity of Christ,
but also with the integrity of his human nature, its development and

---

40. Ibid., 54–69.
41. Ibid., 89.

activities. The Gospels and epistles take seriously the reality and structure of the human nature of Christ. Philippians 2:6–7 speaks of him
who is in the "form of God" taking upon himself the "form of a servant," denoting thereby the human form that is shared by both Adam
and Christ. Whereas Adam in his original sin refused to serve God,
Christ has come in the form of the suffering servant (Is 53:11–12) to
repair or restore human nature, thereby reversing the disobedience
of Adam that cast human beings into a fallen state.[42] The presupposition of the narrative, then, is that Christ shared in some way in what
is common to Adam and all other human beings, the natural form or
essence that is possessed by each. The Council of Chalcedon did not
hesitate to read the passage cited above in just this way:

[This synod] … opposes those who conceive of a confusion or mixture in
the case of the two natures of Christ; and it drives out those who foolishly
think that the "form of a slave" which was assumed by him from among us is
of a heavenly, or some other essence; and it anathematizes those who make
up the teaching that before the union there are two natures of the Lord, but
imagine that after the union there is one.[43]

The theories of both Apollinarius and Eutyches are being revoked
here, each of whom conceived in different ways of the unity of the divine and the human in Christ according to a singularity of nature.[44]
In upholding the distinction of natures, the Council noted rightly the
biblical witness to the integrity of the human nature of Christ. But
this affirmation of two natures in one person in turn raised profound
questions of an ontological nature: what is the relationship between
the essential properties of human nature and individual personhood?
What relation are we to understand (ontologically and logically, in
turn) between the individual characteristics of a given personal subject (Peter, Paul, Jesus) and the nature that is common to each? In
what does the latter consist? Here we touch upon speculative issues
that lie at the heart of New Testament Christology, and that can only
be engaged by an overtly metaphysical reflection on scripture.

42. Fee, *Pauline Christology*, 373–401.
43. Translation by Richard A. Norris Jr., in *The Christological Controversy* (Philadelphia: Fortress, 1980), 158.
44. Aloys Grillmeier, *Christ in Christian Tradition: From the Apostolic Age to Chalcedon (451)*, trans. J. S. Bowden (New York: Sheed and Ward, 1965), 469–74, 481–87.

Nor is this issue important for speculative reasons alone. Christological reflection on the normative content of human nature is integrally related to New Testament reflection on the practical form of human redemption. For one of the core presuppositions of the early Christians is that human beings typically fail to understand adequately what they are. They are unable in their fallen condition to see ultimately what they are made for, and find it impossible to orient themselves toward God as their true last end (Rom 1:18–32).[45] Correspondingly, only Christ can fully reveal to the human person what he or she is, and what he or she is ultimately made for, in light of the mystery of filial adoption by grace.[46] This also means, however, that the revelation of Christ must serve to correct multiple errors of the human intellect, both practical and speculative, that tend to corrupt fallen human thinking regarding what it means to be a human being. If this is the case, then the salvation of the human person depends in large part upon a Christological and theocentric recentering of one's understanding of human nature. The study of the human nature of Christ is ontological, but it also has an eminently practical purpose for right understanding of the sense of human existence.

Ultimately, a Christological study of the meaning of human nature must also look at the kind of life undertaken by Christ: his actions and sufferings. These actions stem from the love of Christ, his obedience and lowliness of heart. These depend in turn upon the unique form of prophetic understanding that characterizes Jesus's acts of knowledge. Christ sees the good and pursues it freely in a uniquely perfect way. His thinking and acting as man therefore are illuminating for us. They reveal a human nature that is radiant with spiritual and moral perfection, "full of grace and truth" (Jn 1:14).[47] This revelation of human perfection reaches its apogee in the Paschal mystery. Here Jesus is subject to excruciating suffering and death, which he embraces in charity, but he is also conformed to a new life of glo-

---

45. See Aquinas's reflections on the matter in ST I-II, q. 109, aa. 3–4.

46. The argument is underscored vividly in Athanasius, *De Incarn.*, 3–13. All citations of Athanasius in this volume are taken from *Nicene and Post-Nicene Fathers*, vol. 4, trans. J. H. Newman, ed. A. Richardson (New York: Charles Scribner, 1903).

47. Aquinas argues from this verse in ST III, q. 7, a. 9, that Christ as man possesses a plenitude of grace, and that this grace flows through him to the human race.

ry in the mystery of the resurrection. In the words of the Second Vatican Council, "it is only in the mystery of the Word made flesh that the mystery of man really becomes clear. For Adam, the first man, was a type of him who was to come, Christ the Lord.... Whoever follows after Christ, the perfect man, becomes himself more of a man."[48] How, then, are we to understand the physical body and immaterial soul of Christ in and through his passion, death, and resurrection? How do these events in turn invite us to understand our own human nature in a Christological mode? Christology leads inevitably into eschatology, but by that same measure it invites us to ask fundamental and ultimate questions about the natural structure of the human person and our ultimate destiny.

The Communication of Idioms

The communication of idioms begins in the New Testament. "But we impart a secret and hidden wisdom of God, which God decreed before the ages for our glorification. None of the rulers of this age understood this; for if they had, they would not have crucified the Lord of glory" (1 Cor 2:7–8). Paul here signifies that the Lord was crucified and so affirms implicitly that all of the human attributes and sufferings of Christ must be attributed to the Lord as subject. By the same logic, the divine attributes that pertain to Christ as God must also be attributed to the same subject, for Christ is one person, both human and divine. So we see in the aforementioned "Christological hymn" of Philippians 2:6–11:

Though *he* was in the form of God, [*Jesus*] did not count equality with God a thing to be grasped, but emptied *himself*, taking the form of a servant, being born in the likeness of men. And being found in human form *he* humbled himself and became obedient unto death, even death on a cross. Therefore God has highly exalted *him* and bestowed on *him* the name which is above every name, that at the name of Jesus every knee should bow, in heaven and on earth and under the earth, and every tongue confess that *Jesus Christ is Lord*, to the glory of God the Father.

The passage begins with the pre-existent subject, the Son of God, who takes on himself the form of a servant (human nature) and who

---

48. *Gaudium et Spes*, nos. 22 and 41.

in his human actions humbles himself and is obedient. This same person is passively subject to crucifixion, death, and exaltation, but also to the public manifestation of his identity as Lord. It is the same subject, the Lord Jesus Christ, who came into the world, who is obedient and crucified, and who is exalted in his resurrection.

My reading of the passage is admittedly controversial, though it does represent on the central textual issues the majority position of exegetes, both ancient and modern. The key point for our purposes, however, concerns the question of the resolution to the subject. However one understands the sequence here regarding a potential pre-existence of Jesus and an eventual recognition of his divine identity, it is unambiguously clear that there is only one subject to whom all is attributed. It is Christ who is both in the form of God and the form of a servant. He is both subject to death and exalted and given the name above every other name, the name of the God of Israel. Consequently, it is clear that both divine and human properties are attributed to his one person.

We should be hesitant, therefore, to see the development of a tradition of the communication of idioms (the attribution of divine and human properties to the one person of Jesus) as the extrinsic projection of an alien "patristic Greek theology" back onto the New Testament. The Council of Ephesus, for example, insisted that there are not two subjects in Christ, one human and the other divine.[49] Consequently, it is correct to say that the Virgin Mary is the "Mother of God" or *Theotokos* because the human being to whom she gave birth is the person of the Word made flesh. Likewise, we can and must speak of Jesus of Nazareth as "God crucified" because the man who was crucified under Pontius Pilate is in fact God the Son.[50] Christ

49. Council of Ephesus, anathema 4: "If anyone distributes between the two persons or hypostases the expressions used either in the Gospels or in the apostolic writings, whether they are used by the holy writers of Christ or by him about himself, and ascribes some to him as to a man, thought of separately from the Word from God, and others, as befitting God, to him as to the Word from God the Father, let him be anathema." Translation by N. Tanner, *Decrees of the Ecumenical Councils*, ed. N. Tanner, 2 vols. (London / Washington, D.C.: Sheed and Ward / Georgetown University Press, 1990), 1:59.

50. Council of Ephesus, anathemas 1 and 12: "If anyone does not confess that Emmanuel is God in truth, and therefore that the holy virgin is the Mother of God (for she bore in a fleshly way the Word of God become flesh), let him be anathema...."

was crucified in his human body and suffered physically and spiritually *by virtue of his human nature*. But it is the Word himself, Jesus Christ, who is the true subject of the suffering. Are these affirmations non-biblical? Clearly not. The Gospel of Matthew portrays the gentile "wise men" from the East finding the child Jesus "with Mary his mother," and adds "they fell down and worshiped him" (Mt 2:11). The subject who is worshiped is God, and Mary is the human mother of that person. Likewise Elizabeth in the Gospel of Luke: "Why is this granted me, that the mother of my Lord should come to me?" (Lk 1:43). Mary of Nazareth is portrayed here indeed as the mother of the Lord. As for the crucifixion of God, it is evident from the quotation from Paul with which we started this section: Jesus is the "crucified … Lord of Glory" (1 Cor 2:8). John's Gospel presents a similar theology. In John 8:28, Jesus says to his skeptical interlocutors, "When you have lifted up the Son of Man, then you will know that I am." Here the "I am" of Jesus's self-designation (*ego eimi*) refers implicitly to the divine name of the Lord as it is represented in the Old Testament.[51] It is the Lord who is raised up on the cross. It is God who is crucified.

What all these passages point us toward is a deeper ontological mystery. How is it that God the Son and Word subsists as a human being, having a human nature, even while he retains the prerogatives of his divine identity and nature? Christ is able to cure the sick, raise the dead, and even forgive sins. Christ is also subject to human suffering, death, and resurrection from the dead. The subject who acts is one, but he acts always both as God and as man, simultaneously able to do what only God can do, and able to suffer what only a human being can suffer. To approach this mystery in its depth is to approach the heart of New Testament teaching. But this approach can only be one grounded in a distinctively metaphysical mode of Christological reflection.

If anyone does not confess that the Word of God suffered in the flesh and was crucified in the flesh and tasted death in the flesh and became the first born of the dead, although as God he is life and life-giving, let him be anathema" (Tanner, *Decrees*, 59, 61).

51. Particularly in the Septuagint translation of passages such as Isaiah 43:10, 25 and 45:18. See Hurtado, *Lord Jesus Christ*, 370–73.

A THOMISTIC STUDY IN
CHRISTOLOGY

This book seeks to answer a series of fundamental Christological and biblical questions. What does it mean to say that Christ is the Son of God made man? What does it mean to say that we ascribe to Christ a complete human nature? What is the ontological relation between the human and divine natures in Christ, and how does this specific correlation relate to the analogy of being between created human nature and the creator? Does a realistic theology of the incarnation require some form of implicit recourse to natural theological reflection? Can we say that Christ as man knew that he was God, and if so, how? Did his human will correspond always to the inclinations or operations of his divine will? What does it mean to say that Christ was obedient to the Father? Did the Father abandon Jesus in the passion? What does it mean to say that Christ "emptied himself" in the passion (Phil 2:7)? Does this mean that he surrendered some characteristic of his deity? What does it mean to say that the Son of God experienced human death and "descended into hell"? Did Christ suffer damnation? How does the resurrection of Christ cast light upon the whole of the human condition, and so reveal the meaning of human existence to us?

The answers to these questions are related to a set of common ontological themes: the notions of divine person or hypostasis, divine and human nature, human material body and immaterial soul, grace and the beatific vision, divine and human intellect, and the coordination of the two wills of Christ. The use of these notions is meant to instantiate the central thesis of the book: that scholastic Christology is of perennial importance for a right understanding of central mysteries of the New Testament, those of the incarnation and redemption. These notions are employed, therefore, in discussion with prevalent themes in modern Christology, precisely so as to underscore how profoundly the Thomistic heritage is able to engage in the consideration of the person of Christ. Aquinas's permanent relevance to Christology can be shown ably against the backdrop of modern Christological discussions.

The order of the book follows, in an approximate way, the order of Christological inquiry developed by Thomas Aquinas in the third part of his *Summa theologiae*. There Aquinas begins with the question of "why God became a man," so as to study the central motives or "reasons of fittingness" for the incarnation (ST III, q. 1). He then goes on to consider the person of Christ and the ontology of the hypostatic union, as well as the fact that this union occurs in two natures, the divine and the human (qq. 2–6). The central point for our purposes is that the hypostatic union is for Aquinas the first principle from which the study of Christology takes its point of departure, and in light of which it gains the deepest form of intelligibility. Who is Christ? He is the Lord incarnate, God the Word become fully human, without ceasing to be God.

The next section of the *Summa* considers the grace of Christ as man (qq. 7–8) and the ways that this grace affects his human operations of knowing and willing (qq. 9–16, 18–19). How does Christ as man know what pertains to his mission as the redeemer of the human race? What does it mean for his human will as man to accord fully with the intentions of his divine will as God? How are we to understand the obedience and prayer of Christ? (qq. 20–21). This order of inquiry makes perfect sense, for as Aquinas says, *agere sequitur ad esse*: action follows upon being.[52] The activity of a given being is derivative from its subsistence as a given kind of being. A rational animal produces acts of rational deliberation and choice making. Analogously, the Word made flesh, Jesus, who is both God and man, acts as one who is both divine and human. He can touch the face of the blind man, and he can effectively heal him of his malady. His actions are, in just this sense, "theandric" or divine-human, the acts of the God-man.[53] But they are these kinds of acts due to who Christ is. Ontology is the ground of activity.[54]

It is fitting that after his treatment of Christ's ontological composition and action, Aquinas should take up the subject of his historical

---

52. *Summa contra Gentiles,* in *Sancti Thomae Aquinatis opera omnia,* vols. 13–15 (Rome: Leonine Edition, 1918–30), III, c. 69, para. 20 [hereafter "SCG"].

53. ST III, q. 19, a. 1, corp. and ad 1.

54. For a similar interpretation of Aquinas's order of reflection in the ST III, see John F. Boyle, "The Twofold Division of St. Thomas's Christology in the *Tertia pars,*" *The Thomist* 60 (1996): 439–47.

life. He begins with the conception and birth of Jesus (qq. 31–36), and considers in detail the apostolic life (qq. 38–45). His study reaches its apex in the examination of Christ's crucifixion, death, burial, and resurrection (qq. 46–59). The mysteries of the life of Christ are derived from his person and are expressive of his identity. However, these mysteries also occur in and through historical time, and are manifest in and through the genuine developments of Christ's human life. The ontology of Christ's person and the inner meaning of the Paschal mystery are therefore mutually interrelated. It is precisely in his fully human development—and especially in his Paschal mystery—that Christ's divine identity and the ultimate purpose of his mission are fully made manifest.

The argument of the book follows this pattern of thinking in a selective and particular way. The book is divided into two parts: the first concerns the mystery of the incarnation, and the second concerns the mystery of the redemption. The book also has a prolegomenon and a conclusion that serve as a coherent frame for the work. The prolegomenon introduces the book by asking "what does it mean to speak about a *modern* Thomistic Christology?" What are the key factors that characterize modern Christology, and how might a Christological investigation of Thomistic inspiration situate itself—critically and creatively—in relation to these? Here I take Friedrich Schleiermacher and Karl Barth as two very different but interrelated proponents of modern theology and propose in response to each of them a set of key theses regarding the ontological and historical character of Christology. This introduction sets the stage for the larger theological and metaphysical form of argument found in the book. In differentiation from Schleiermacher and Barth, modern Christology should articulate a form of Chalcedonian Christology that fully respects the ontological dimensions of Christ's mystery as the Son of God subsisting in two natures, as both divine and human. It should be able to do so in ways that take fully into account the legitimate contributions of modern historical-critical reflection on the person of Jesus of Nazareth within his historical setting.

The first part of the book, then, follows up this aim of recovering a genuinely ontological form of reflection about Jesus, in critical conversation with various strands of modern and contemporary Christology. Chapter 1 treats the hypostatic union and the grace of Christ in an overt recapitulation of Aquinas's own starting point. Who is Jesus Christ? To treat this question one must consider the mystery of the hypostatic union. Here I make the argument that Karl Rahner's treatment of the hypostatic union is in fact deeply problematic. Rahner's thought has had a deep impact on modern Roman Catholic Christology, but at the same time, it in fact resembles in key ways medieval, scholastic forms of thinking that Aquinas himself deemed "Nestorian." Is it possible that a genuinely Nestorian tendency of thought has had a predominant influence in various strands of contemporary Catholic Christology? I argue that this is the case, and that Aquinas's ontology of the hypostatic union helps us to diagnose and correct the problematic character of Rahnerian thinking on this subject.

The second chapter of the book looks into the question of the human essence or nature of Christ. The Second Vatican Council, in *Gaudium et Spes* no. 22, proclaimed that the mystery of human existence can only be fully understood in light of the incarnation and the Paschal mystery of Jesus of Nazareth. What is the correlation, then, between a metaphysical understanding of the human essence all human beings share, and a historical and Christological understanding of Christ's human essence? Here I take issue with the historicist ontologies of Karl Rahner and Marie-Dominique Chenu in order to argue that only a metaphysics of human nature that understands there to be perennial characteristics of the human being through time can permit a historical theology of the divine economy that underscores the unique saving perfections of the human nature of Christ. Christology and metaphysics are mutually reinforcing, not mutually incompatible.

The third chapter of the book considers the analogy of being. In particular, how does the human nature of Christ resemble by ontological similitude his divine nature? Here the book enters into an ecumenical engagement with the criticisms of Aquinas's metaphysics articulated by Karl Barth and his disciple Eberhard Jüngel. They argue that a Thomistic metaphysics of the analogy of being places a necessary obstacle to a proper understanding of Jesus Christ and of the creative causality of God. I argue in turn that Aquinas's understanding of analogy and ontological similitude is the necessary condition for a proper safeguarding of the divine transcendence that Barth and Jüngel wish to uphold.

The fourth chapter of the book continues this theme. Catholic theologians such as Gottlieb Söhngen and Hans Urs von Balthasar responded to Barth's criticisms of the Catholic practice of philosophical theology. They argued that an authentic natural theology can be articulated within and as an intrinsic dimension of a Christology of the two natures of Christ. Christology is the presupposition of natural theology, but the latter has its own integrity as an authentic form of reasoning. Without accepting or contesting this presupposition of Söhngen and Balthasar, I argue in turn that a corollary to their proposition is necessarily the case. *If* we are capable of thinking theologically by grace about the reality of the incarnation, then a necessary presupposition of this fact is that we are naturally capable of thinking philosophically about the creator by way of analogical terms drawn from the creation. In other words, orthodox Christology is in no way reducible to natural theology, but it is also not possible without it.

The fifth chapter of the book considers the human noetic and voluntary acts of Christ. Did Jesus as man know that he was God, and if so, how was this the case? Here I engage contemporary critics of Aquinas's position. Aquinas held that Jesus of Nazareth possessed the beatific vision in his earthly life. Based upon his principles, I argue that the vision is a prerequisite for a right understanding of the mystery of Christ's knowledge of his own divine identity, his voluntary action, his human obedience, and his prayer. How is it the case that Christ possessed both a divine and a human will, and that there existed a profound concord of the two at all times? How might we understand the true human historicity and developmental "consciousness" of Jesus in light of the classical affirmation of the two wills of Christ?

The second half of the book examines the mystery of the redemption. If the "structure" of the incarnation is examined in part 1, the mystery of the passion, death and resurrection of Jesus is considered in part 2. Here, the study begins in chapter 6 with an examination of the obedience of Christ. The notion of obedience has been central to modern Christologies, from those of Barth and Balthasar to Moltmann and Pannenberg. These theologies all attribute some form of obedience not only to the human will of Christ, but to his divine nature as such. In this way they wish to argue that what happens in the passion is expressive of what God is eternally in himself. Christ in his deity is eternally obedient to the Father. What does it mean to say this? Can we affirm such a position and yet maintain the core tenet of divine unity as it is proclaimed in the Council of Nicaea? Here I offer a critique of this Christological theme of "divine obedience" in modern theology. I argue that Aquinas's treatment of Christ's human obedience allows us to attain a more nuanced position. The human actions of Jesus in his historical life and passion are indicative of his divine identity and of his eternal relation to the Father, just as he is one who receives everything from the Father. However, it is only metaphorically and not literally true to say that the Son of God *as God* is obedient to the Father. The distinction of natures must be maintained even when we affirm unambiguously that the Trinity is revealed in and through the actions and sufferings of the sacred humanity of Jesus.

Chapter 7 examines the passion of Christ and in particular the cry of dereliction. What does it mean for Christ to exclaim from the cross, "My God, why have you abandoned me" (Mk 15:34)? Is this affirmation compatible with the equally Biblical affirmation that "God was in Christ, reconciling the world to himself" (2 Cor 5:19)? Is it compatible with the traditional Catholic teaching that Christ in his earthly life possessed the beatific vision? Here the goal is to see the organic unity of a theology of the hypostatic union and a theology of the cross. The two are not rightly understood if they are seen as standing in necessary juxtaposition or dialectical tension with one another. Rather, they are organically interrelated and mutually complementary ways of understanding who Jesus Christ is.

Chapter 8 examines the mystery of the death of Jesus with particular reference to the concept of Christ's "kenosis" or self-emptying. Modern kenotic theology has argued that the death of Jesus touches upon the identity of God in such a way as to affect his very deity. God himself is subject in some real sense to death in the mystery of the crucifixion. I examine diverse accounts of this idea taken from Wolfhart Pannenberg, Eberhard Jüngel, and Hans Urs von Balthasar. In contradistinction to aspects of their views, I argue that the Son of God as God undergoes no form of ontological diminishment or self-relinquishment in the course of his passion. A comparison of the modern kenotic "tradition" and the classical account of Christ's death offered by Aquinas allows us to see how two very different forms of Christological reflection emerge, and why the soteriological repercussions of these varying viewpoints are of great importance for theology.

Chapters 9 and 10 examine respectively the descent of Christ into hell and his resurrection from the dead. In the first of these two chapters I undertake a comparison of the theology of Hans Urs von Balthasar and that of Thomas Aquinas on the subject of Christ's descent into hell. What are the key motivations undergirding the theologies of each on this topic? How does each understand the separation of body and soul that takes place in death? What is "hell" in each case, and what soteriological function is the descent into hell seen to play? I argue in this chapter that Balthasar's absence of a clear doctrine of the immaterial soul affects his articulation of this mystery in very acute ways. The descent into hell becomes something trans-temporal, or in some real sense, ahistorical. In a way, then, Aquinas has a much more profound and coherent doctrine of the descent of Christ into hell, and one that assigns to that mystery a classical soteriological function of universal import with regard to all those who died in a state of grace prior to the time of Christ's historical existence as man.

Chapter 10 concludes this study of Christ's historical life by considering the mystery of his resurrection from the dead. What does it mean to say that Jesus not only underwent death, but also that he experienced the reconciliation of body and soul after death, and that his body was transformed in a glorified, resurrected state? How does the resurrection reveal Christ's perfect humanity and his perfect divinity? Here I engage two influential modern theologies. Rudolph Bultmann's theology of the resurrection seeks to demythologize the event, removing from it any appeal to the physical resurrection of Jesus. Karl Rahner's theology sees death as the total annihilation of the human person (body and soul), and resurrection as a kind of total re-creation of the person, following immediately upon death (so-called death-in-resurrection theory). Joseph Ratzinger offers important criticisms of both these lines of thinking, particularly with recourse to the hylomorphic theory of Thomas Aquinas. In this chapter, then, I follow Ratzinger in exploring the eschatology of Thomas Aquinas. How does the physical resurrection of Christ illumine the meaning of the human condition? How does Christ reveal himself as the Son of God precisely through the activity of his resurrected humanity?

The final chapter serves as a kind of extensive conclusion to the book. The first half of the book examines the mystery of the incarnation and the second half the mystery of the redemption. Both halves argue for the centrality of metaphysical realism for a right appreciation of the heart of the mystery of Christ. The conclusion recapitulates this argument by engaging the postmodern turn in modern Christology. Here I undertake an analysis of the historicist, hermeneutical Christology of Eduard Schillebeeckx. I argue that his attempt at a modern reinterpretation of Christological dogma is vulnerable to the anti-metaphysical critiques of modern academic narrative offered by Friedrich Nietzsche and Michel Foucault. Against Schillebeeckx, Nietzsche, and Foucault, I argue that the metaphysical tradition of Aristotle and Aquinas is of perennial value and that it permits us to articulate a Christological science that is of enduring value as well. Christology is not primarily, then, a historical science, though it does take account of a variety of historical reflections. It is above all a science and a wisdom regarding the truth about God and about the nature and destiny of human beings understood in light of God. If this is the case, then Christology is ontologically structured through and through, because it peers into the mystery of God, the mystery of man and the mystery of the God-man.

We rightly identify Aquinas as a "scholastic" theologian. What characterizes scholasticism, however, is not merely the dialectical comparison of diverse sources. It is, rather, the scientific examination of the very causes of being. If this is the case, then *theological* scholasticism is at its heart the consideration of the inner structure or form of the mystery of God. Scholasticism is inevitable, therefore, whenever theology becomes truly itself. For theology seeks above all to peer into the mystery of God himself. This book seeks, in its own modest way, to consider who God is, in light of the incarnation. Jesus is the incarnate Lord. Consequently, his life, death, and resurrection offer us a profound understanding of who God is, and of ourselves as the creatures of God, offered redemption in the blood of Christ. This redemption is our shelter and our home. It is luminous, for he who died for us is the Word of God, whose light shines even amidst the darkness of this world, and who enlightens all human beings (Jn 1:4–5).

PROLEGOMENON

-----:------

Is a Modern Thomistic Christology
Possible?

At the start of our study of Thomistic Christology, we might first ask: is there such a thing as a *modern* Thomistic Christology? Behind this question there are a number of substantive issues. For example, what is does it mean to be modern? What constitutes "Thomism"? What is the relation between Thomistic thought and characteristically modern philosophy and theology? These are of course immense topics. Without pretending to ignore their importance, however, it is permissible to narrow the scope of our inquiry if we refocus the initial question posed here in a twofold way by asking: what are the particular defining features of Christology as it is articulated in modernity, and what distinctive contributions or theories is Thomism able to provide within the context of the modern conditions of debate on this subject?

This initial chapter is intended to serve as a prolegomenon to the rest of the book. It introduces several themes that traverse the chapters that follow. For each is in some way concerned with the way we might pursue Thomistic Christology within a contemporary theological context. In the first half of this opening chapter I would like to describe briefly what I take to be the two most important challenges of modern Christology, and to examine in turn two typical conundrums to which these challenges give rise. For the sake of this presentation, I will employ examples from Friedrich Schleiermacher and Karl Barth, respectively, to illustrate diverse ways in which antinomies are present in modern Christology, conflicts or contradictions that remain (at times) unresolved or inadequately treated. In the second half of the chapter, I will sketch out what I take to be two ways that Aquinas's Christology, especially as read by some of his modern interpreters, provides a set of cathartic distinctions that can help us to resolve tensions in modern Christology, and to propose a potentially more complete treatment of the mystery of Christ taken on modern terms, or at least developed in response to modern challenges. These reflections help set the stage for the larger study that ensues.

TWO MODERN CHALLENGES TO CHRISTOLOGY AND TWO LINGERING CHRISTOLOGICAL ANTINOMIES

Identifying Two Challenges of Modern Christology

The classical Chalcedonian doctrine of faith affirms that Christ is one person, the Son of God, who subsists in two natures as both God and man. In essence, one can characterize the challenges of modern post-Enlightenment thought to classical Christology and Chalcedonian doctrine in a twofold way. On the one hand, at least since Hermann Reimarus and Gotthold Lessing, the modern theological interpretation of the person of Jesus Christ has repeatedly confronted the question of the relationship between the historical Jesus and the New Testament doctrinal presentation of Jesus as Christ, Son of God and Lord.[1] Lessing, for example, envisaged the historical Jesus as pri-

---

1. See Hermann Samuel Reimarus, *Apologie oder Schutzschrift für die vernünftigen Verehrer Gottes,* ed. Gerhard Alexander, 2 vols. (Frankfurt-am-Main: Insel, 1972); Gotthold Ephraim Lessing, *Lessing: Philosophical and Theological Writings,* ed. H. B. Nisbet (Cambridge: Cambridge University Press, 2005). The argument that there is a profound discontinuity between the Jesus of history and the Christ of the New Testament was originally developed by Spinoza and the English deists, and subsequently formulated more explicitly by Reimarus and Lessing. See the historical discussion by Jonathan Israel, *Radical Enlightenment: Philosophy in the Making of Modernity 1650–1750* (Oxford: Oxford University Press, 2001), 197–229, 447–76.

marily a moral sage, a precursor to Enlightenment philosophical doctrine. The New Testament projected back onto his historical life the theological overlay of Christological ontology and dogma. The unavoidable question such speculations raised subsequently was: what is the relationship between the Christ of the New Testament and subsequent church dogma, on the one hand, and the modern historical reconstructions of the figure at the origin of the early Christian movement on the other? In one sense, this is to ask the question of whether naturalistic explanations of the origins of Christianity succeed in overturning the potential rational and historical intelligibility of classical doctrinal and creedal statements. How should classical Christianity defend itself "apologetically" with respect to its modern historicist critics? However, in another (and distinct) sense, to respond to this question is also to grapple with a more integrally theological question: what importance (if any) should the hypothetical construal of the historical Jesus have within a modern Christology that bases itself upon the New Testament understanding of the significance of Christ? How should modern theology speak of the life of Jesus, and particularly of revelatory events such as the transfiguration or the ascension, in which the very mystery and being of the person of Christ are unveiled? What are the historical-critical conditions for a *theological* rather than merely apologetic discussion of these events as revelatory of Christ?

Second, in light of Immanuel Kant's critique of classical metaphysics and the subsequent Hegelian and Heideggerian reformulations of ontology in a modern, historical mode, what is the importance of the longstanding metaphysical tradition that was employed classically to articulate the meaning of the incarnation in theological terms: "one in being with the Father," "one person in two natures," "two wills and operations," and so on?[2] Do these expressions retain the full weight of their classical expression in a post-metaphysical age,

---

2. On Kantian and Heideggerian notions of classical metaphysics as "ontotheology" and the respective criticisms of classical metaphysics by these thinkers, see Olivier Boulnois, *Être et representation: Une généologie de la métaphysique moderne à l'époque de Duns Scot (XIIIe-XIVe Siècle)* (Paris: Presses Universitaires de France, 1999); Thomas Joseph White, *Wisdom in the Face of Modernity: A Study in Thomistic Natural Theology* (Naples, Fla.: Sapienta Press, 2009).

and if so, how can this be?[3] Are we invited or required in modernity to reinterpret Chalcedonian doctrine in a post-Kantian, post-onto-
theological way, and if so, what shape should this interpretation take?[4]
Correspondingly, what difference should Christ make to our modern
contemporaries, who admittedly inhabit a culture of distinctly empir-
icist hue? In what sense is contemporary Christology obliged to sal-
vage, or to radically reformulate, classical ontological definitions concerning the person and natures of Christ, if Christianity is to present
itself as an authentic knowledge of God in the modern world?

These are of course vast questions, and in this context, they are
being asked only in order to paint a background in very broad brush
strokes concerning two ways in which modern Christology has developed responses to these challenges, at least in two of its most important representatives: Schleiermacher and Barth (who admittedly cannot by any typological configuration be said to represent all modern
Christological development).[5] My argument is that in both of these

3. Is our age truly "post-metaphysical?" Certainly contemporary analytic philosophy is quite concerned with metaphysical questions, classical and otherwise (consider
Kripke, Plantinga, Searle, or Swinburne). However, such considerations do not contribute a normative form of discourse to the broader university culture the way that metaphysical references of thought did in the pre-modern age. In the broader academy, em-
piricism and postmodernism remain the prevalent modes of unifying philosophical
discourse. Furthermore, whatever one makes of the contemporary revival of metaphysics in analytic philosophy, this development has affected post-Kantian Protestant and
Catholic theology very little (while such theology has tended to adopt its central philosophical principles from continental philosophy).

4. Bruce McCormack in *Karl Barth's Critically Realistic Dialectical Theology: Its Genesis and Development, 1909–1936* (Oxford: Clarendon Press, 1995) argues that the Kantian critique of metaphysics stands in the background of the development of much of
Barth's early work. He develops this idea in relation to Barth's later work in "Karl Barth's
Version of an 'Analogy of Being': A Dialectical No and Yes to Roman Catholicism," in
The Analogy of Being: Invention of the Antichrist or the Wisdom of God?, ed. Thomas Joseph White (Grand Rapids, Mich.: Eerdmans: 2010). Alternative post-Kantian and
"post-metaphysical" Christologies are developed by Eberhard Jüngel, *God as the Mystery
of the World: On the Foundation of the Theology of the Crucified One in the Dispute between
Theism and Atheism*, trans. D. L. Guder (Grand Rapids, Mich.: Eerdmans, 1983), and Jürgen Moltmann, *The Crucified God: The Cross of Christ as the Foundation and Criticism of
Christian Theology*, trans. R. A. Wilson (San Francisco: Harper and Row, 1974).

5. In English-speaking scholarship, Schleiermacher and Barth are commonly treated as two distinct paths of negotiating modern theological problems. However, it is
also frequently acknowledged that they share common premises. See in particular
Hans Frei's *Types of Christian Theology*, eds. George Hunsinger and William C. Placher

historically significant thinkers there are contrasting options taken regarding the problems mentioned above, but the thought of each of them remains markedly inadequate in certain key ways. In fact, these inadequacies suggest commonalities between them—structures of thought—that are deeper than the contrasts, and which merit to be challenged in turn by some Thomistic reflections.

Historical Jesus Studies: Alternative Solutions
of Schleiermacher and Barth

Let us consider, then, two contrasting ways of being a modern theologian in light of the two challenges mentioned above. The first contrast between Schleiermacher and Barth concerns the way in which each articulates the relationship between historical Jesus studies and classical Christological doctrine. For the purposes of my argument, I am concerned primarily with the revelatory epistemology and theological method of each.

In Schleiermacher one sees the emergence of a methodology in modern German Christology that will in turn evolve within liberal Protestantism from thinkers like Albrecht Ritschl and Wilhelm Hermann to Adolf von Harnack.[6] Succinctly stated, Schleiermacher correlates post-Enlightenment studies of the history of Jesus with a decidedly post-Chalcedonian stance of interpretation regarding classical (pre-modern) Christological ontology. Fundamentally, he embraces a primitive version of the modern Enlightenment historical study of the Jesus of history (as distinct from the Christ of scripture), but claims against both German Lutheran orthodoxy and Enlighten-

---

(New Haven, Conn.: Yale University Press, 1992), where Frei arranges the two thinkers—despite their differences—together under a common "type" of theology. A extensive list of works on the interrelations of the two thinkers can be found in the bibliography of Matthias Gockel, *Barth and Schleiermacher on the Doctrine of Election* (Oxford: Oxford University Press, 2006).

6. Friedrich Schleiermacher, *Der christliche Glaube* (Berlin: G. Reimer, 1821–22); *The Christian Faith*, 2 vols., eds. H. R. Mackintosh and J. S. Stewart (New York: Harper and Row, 1963); Albert Ritschl, *Die christliche Lehre von der Rechtfertigung und Versöhnung*, 3 vols. (Bonn: A. Marcus, 1870–74) and *Theologie und Metaphysik: zur Verständigung und Abwehr* (Bonn: A. Marcus, 1887); Wilhelm Herrmann, *Die Religion im Verhältniss zum Welterkennen und zur Sittlichkeit: eine Grundlegung der systematischen Theologie* (Halle: M. Niemeyer, 1879); Adolf von Harnack, *Das Wesen des Christentums* (Leipzig: J. C. Hinrichs, 1900).

ment secular historians that the historical-critical method can be employed profitably to identify rationally the enduring *theological* significance of the historical figure of Jesus. Chalcedonian doctrine has to
be radically reinterpreted theologically in light of modern historical
studies. Behind this approach lies the presupposition that there exists
no sharp differentiation between the natural world and the supernatural activity of grace. What is "given" in Christ ("by grace") is what is
always already coming into being through the natural religious orientation of human nature: a perfection of human religious consciousness.[7] The true Jesus of history shows us what it means to be a perfectly religious human being.

The central concern of theology, then, must be to recapture
through a *historical-critical discernment* the original religious consciousness and sentiments of the founder of Christianity in their unalloyed
beauty, as distinct from the later overlay of scriptural and ecclesial symbols and doctrines which are in fact "accidental" to a theological doctrine of Christ as such. In a qualified fashion, Schleiermacher numbers
among such accidental features classical doctrines such the virgin birth,
the prophecies attributed to Christ in the New Testament, and at least
some of his miracles, the resurrection, the ascension, and the final judgment.[8] This approach makes historical Jesus studies in some real sense

7. Schleiermacher, *The Christian Faith*, 1:64: "It must be asserted that even the more
rigorous view of the difference between Him and all other men does not hinder us from
saying that His appearing, even regarded as the incarnation of the Son of God, is a natural fact. For in the first place: as certainly as Christ was man, there must reside in human
nature the possibility of taking up the divine into itself, just as did happen in Christ.…
But secondly: even if only the *possibility* of this resides in human nature, so that the actual implanting therein of the divine element must be purely a divine and therefore an
eternal act, nevertheless the temporal appearance of this act in one particular Person
must at the same time be regarded as an action of human nature, grounded in its original constitution and prepared for by all its past history, and accordingly as the highest
development of its spiritual power."

8. Ibid., 2:419–20: "Belief in these facts, accordingly, is no independent element in
the original faith in Christ, of such a kind that we could not accept Him as Redeemer
or recognize the being of God in Him, if we did not know that He had risen from the
dead and ascended to heaven, or if He had not promised that He would return for judgment. Further, this belief is not to be derived from those original elements; we cannot
conclude that because God was in Christ, He must have risen from the dead and ascended into heaven, or that because he was essentially sinless He must come again to act as
Judge. Rather they are accepted only because they are found in the Scriptures; and all

foundational for the discernment of what constitutes (or does not constitute) properly theological knowledge of Christ. Historical judgments about the real Jesus are to be distinguished from later apostolic presentations of the mystery of Christ given in scripture. Schleiermacher is clear about this at least with respect to basic discernments about what is essential to the Gospel as opposed to what is "accidental." For example, the reader of scripture is invited to determine for himself if the non-essential doctrines of the resurrection or ascension are to be considered historical (presumably through both modern exegetical study and theological pondering of their fittingness), and if so or if not, what underlying theological repercussions there might be for one's doctrine of Christ.[9] However, the answer to this particular question *cannot determine* as such the intrinsic content of a doctrine of Christ, which is integral with or without the belief in the historical and physical resurrection and exaltation of Jesus. The proper object of theological faith is recalibrated in critical dialogue with modern historical criticism and this occurs in such a way that the latter defines the content of the mystery of faith at least negatively, if not constructively, in significant ways.

On the other hand, for Schleiermacher, the Chalcedonian metaphysics of Christ as both God and man (one person subsisting in two natures) is reinterpreted in terms of the "original experience" of God in Christianity, as first instantiated in the life of Jesus (in his God-consciousness), and as transmitted to his disciples, who in turn codified this experience in doctrinal terms.[10] Historical study of Jesus in what is presupposed to be a post-metaphysical age permits us to recover anew the truth of Christianity that lies behind the artifices of ontological doctrine, a truth foundational to the existence of authentic Christianity. Unsurprisingly, it is this same pre-doctrinal, primitive truth that is simultaneously most relevant to our post-doctrinal contemporaries.

that can be required of any Protestant Christian is that he shall believe them insofar as they seem to him to be adequately attested." The judgment concerning proper attestation seems to permit a rational-historical inquiry to determine whether these are to be considered historically based doctrines. Yet their importance is already ancillary as they have, as doctrines, been shifted outside of the proper scope of the object of "the original faith in Christ."

9. Cf. Schleiermacher, *The Christian Faith*, 2:420.

10. Ibid., 2:385–87.

Barth initially seems to be at the antipodes of this epistemological stance. His doctrine concerning the historical Jesus resembles in key respects the doctrine of Martin Kähler, in his famous work of 1892, *The So-Called Historical Jesus and the Historical Biblical Christ*.[11] In that work, Kähler had proposed that modern "biographies" of the historical Jesus, if we judge them by the canons of modern historiography, are not really scientifically warranted works. They only serve, therefore, as a distraction to a proper understanding of the object of theology: the person of Christ as presented in Scripture, and as interpreted in distinctly theological terms by the later ecclesial community.[12] The latter community is itself primarily subject by faith to knowledge of the resurrected and glorified Christ who is alive, rather than the questionable and always conjectural human reconstructions of historians concerning the "Jesus of history," a past figure whose real historical life now completely evades us.[13]

11. Martin Kähler, *Der sogenannte historische Jesus und der geschichtliche, biblische Christus* (Leipzig: A. Deichert, 1892); *The So-Called Historical Jesus and the Historical Biblical Christ*, trans. Carl E. Braaten (Philadelphia: Fortress, 1964).

12. Kähler, *So-Called Historical Jesus*, 54–56: "Obviously we would not deny that historical research can help to explain particular features of Jesus' actions and attitudes as well as many aspects of his teaching. Nor will I exaggerate the issue by casting doubt on the historian's capacity to trace the broad outlines of the historical institutions and forces which influenced the human development of our Lord. But it is common knowledge that all this is wholly insufficient for a biographical work in the modern sense. Such a work is never content with a modest retrospective analysis, for in reconstructing an obscure event in the past it also wishes to convince us that its *a posteriori* conclusions are accurate. The biographical method likes to treat that period in Jesus' life for which we have no sources and in particular seeks to explain the course of his spiritual development during his public ministry. To accomplish that something other than a cautious analysis is required. Some outside force must rework the fragments of the tradition. This force is nothing other than the theologian's imagination—an imagination that has been shaped and nourished by the analogy of his own life and of human life in general.... In other words, the biographer who portrays Jesus is always something of a dogmatician in the derogatory sense of the word."

13. Ibid., 66–67: "The real Christ is the Christ who is preached. The Christ who is preached, however, is precisely the Christ of faith. He is the Jesus whom the eyes of faith behold at every step he takes and through every syllable he utters—the Jesus whose image we impress upon our minds because we both would and do commune with him, our risen, living Lord. The person of our living Savior, the person of the Word incarnate, of God revealed, gazes upon us from the features of that image which has deeply impressed itself on the memory of his followers ... and which was finally disclosed and perfected through the illumination of his Spirit." See the similar, contemporary proposals of Luke Timothy Johnson, *The Real Jesus* (New York: Harper Collins, 1996).

Like Kähler, Barth treats the problem of modern reconstructions of the historical Jesus by a creative reappropriation of the classical Lutheran adage: *Sola Fide*; *Solo Christo*; *Sola Gratia*. Modern Jesus of history studies are conjectures of mere human reason, hypothetical, inherently uncertain, and potentially deeply flawed.[14] The root of the epistemological problem is the failure to realize what kind of book the New Testament is: not one from which we justify the warrant of our own beliefs through historical-critical reconstructions of the figure of Jesus, but rather a book through which the Word of God is communicating itself, setting up *its own preconditions* in the hearer for an authentic knowledge of God in Christ.[15] Barth's methodological neutralization of the *theological* importance of the historical-critical life of Jesus studies is almost the inverted mirror image of Schleiermacher (a logical contrary in the same genus). For Schleiermacher, modern historical reconstructions have the power to provide a more accurate portrait of Christ and to deliver us from overdependence on the historically outdated doctrinal scaffolding that covers over Jesus. For Barth, historical reconstructions stand outside of the proper object of Christology, and that object has an intrinsically doctrinal content that is in turn alien to all merely human speculation about Jesus based upon conjectural constructions by modern historians.[16]

14. Karl Barth: "Thousands may have seen and heard the Rabbi of Nazareth. But this 'historical' (*historisch*) element was not revelation. The 'historical' element in the resurrection of Christ, the empty tomb as an aspect of this event that might be established, was not revelation.... As regards the question of the 'historical' certainty of the revelation attested in the Bible we can only say that it is ignored in the Bible itself in a way that one can understand only on the premiss that this question is completely alien to us, i.e., obviously and utterly inappropriate to the object of its witness." *Church Dogmatics*, trans. and eds. G. W. Bromiley and T. F. Torrance, 4 vols. (Edinburgh: T. & T. Clark, 1936–75), I, 1, 325 [hereafter "CD"].

15. Barth, CD I, 1, 109: "The fact that God's own address becomes an event in the human word of the Bible is ... God's affair and not ours. This is what we mean when we call the Bible God's Word.... If the word imposes itself on us and if the Church in its confrontation with the Bible thus becomes again and again what it is, all this is God's decision and not ours, all this is grace and not our work."

16. Barth, CD I, 1, 399–406. See the criticisms of Bultmann and Dibelius (402): "The essential understanding is threatened if one agrees with M. Dibelius (RGG2 Art. 'Christologie') in formulating the problem of the New Testament Christology as the way in which 'knowledge of the historical figure of Jesus was so quickly transformed into faith in a heavenly Son of God.' The question is whether one can presuppose that knowledge of a historical figure came first and a transforming of this into faith in the

While they are contrary to one another in a specific respect, generically both these views share a common problem. Neither instructs us as to how, if at all, we might reasonably seek explicitly to integrate methodologically the content of modern studies of Jesus of Nazareth in his historical context with a modern defense of the classical doctrine of Chalcedon. In accord with what has been discussed above, this deficit can be characterized in a twofold fashion. Let us presume for the sake of argument (on the basis of theological faith) that Christ is truly God incarnate, and that this historical and ontological mystery of the Son of God made man was in some real sense accurately portrayed and interpreted in the New Testament (under the influence of divine inspiration). How, then, should we respond to the doubts of Christians themselves concerning the claims to historicity when they are confronted with alternative narratives of Christian origins, specifically those that deny the historicity of the New Testament? Is an apologetic construal of the "Christ of history" a possible or even necessary element of a responsible modern Christology, even if reconstructions of the historical Jesus remain only conjectural and relatively probabilistic (or improbabilistic)? And in a related but distinct sense, when one presumes the historicity of the incarnate Word and begins from the premises of faith in the basic historicity of the Gospel interpretation of Christ, what *constructive* theological meaning should questions of *how* the life of Christ unfolded in its historical context have? For surely it is one thing to expound a dogmatic theology of the mystery of the person of Christ and the significance of the redemption, and another thing to expound a conjectural, reconstructed web of theories of how Jesus could have expressed himself originally and been perceived historically within his cultural-linguistic context. But should we have to choose between these two objectives that seemingly are not intrinsically opposed, even if the two are clearly not identical? In fact, is the question of their possible harmonization not an unavoidable challenge set before modern Christology in the face of its Enlightenment critics?

---

heavenly Son of God came second, so that we have then to ask in terms of the history of thought how this came about. We see no possibility of this road ending anywhere but in a blind alley."

Post-Kantian Ontology and Christology: Alternative
Solutions of Schleiermacher and Barth

There are in Schleiermacher and Barth contrasting responses to the
Kantian critique of the classical metaphysical heritage. And yet, simultaneously, their respective approaches to this issue are not altogether
dissimilar. For Schleiermacher, as I have already noted, Chalcedonian
ontology is reinterpreted radically with reference to Jesus's God-consciousness, his exemplary religious experience of God. Schleiermacher's theory depends upon a notion of pre-categorical awareness of
God that precedes all creedal or doctrinal formulations in theology. This idea has been subject to intense criticism in light of Wittgenstein's philosophical notions of linguistic world-articulation.[17] George
Lindbeck has argued against the "experiential expressivism" of Schleiermacher that language and cultural contexts of interpretation are always intrinsic to the ways in which one understands experience and
its meaning, and that these explanations are even in some real sense
generative of the latter experiences. In other words, doctrinal cognition precedes and gives an internal form to religious experiences of
any kind. Given the reality of the societal character of most human
knowing, and its irreducibly linguistic mode of transmission, Schleiermacher's notion of a pietistic sentiment of absolute dependence
that is pre-conceptual (and therefore pre-dogmatic) appears as naïve
and philosophically problematic. Speaking in a more Thomistic vein,
we could say that it is simply too anti-intellectual, in that it denies any
necessary conceptual "in-formation" to the act of human judgment, an
act which must be present in the heart of any spiritual experience, including the apprehension of one's ultimate dependence upon God.

However, for the purposes of my argument here, the criticisms of
Lindbeck and others, true though they may be, are of secondary importance. The more fundamental issue pertains to the nature of the
union of God and man in Christ. For Schleiermacher, in truth, abandons the *ontological* locus of divine-human union as it is conceived

17. See especially, George Lindbeck, *The Nature of Doctrine: Religion and Theology in
a Post-Liberal Age* (Louisville, Ky.: Westminster John Knox, 1984); Fergus Kerr, *Theology
after Wittgenstein* (Oxford: Blackwell, 1986); Bruce D. Marshall, *Trinity and Truth* (Cambridge: Cambridge University Press, 2000).

classically in Chalcedonian Christology. For him the union of God
and man in Christ no longer occurs in the personal subject as such
(the hypostatic subject of the Son existing as man) but rather within the world of human consciousness, and specifically within the human consciousness of Christ. Christ is united with God through his
self-awareness. The problem is that, ontologically speaking, any process of human consciousness—while it truly exists or has being—
cannot be said to be all that a person is, for it is only an "accidental"
characteristic of a substantial human being, albeit a quite important
characteristic.[18] This holds true also in the case of Christ. His thinking and willing, no matter how significant, are not all that he is, but
are merely "accidental properties" of his subsistent, personal being.
Consequently, such operations are not hypostatic and cannot adequately substitute as an authentic locus of divine-human unity in the
incarnation.

Here we return in fact to classical Christological considerations.
For the theology of the hypostatic union as it emerged historically
(particularly in the theological writing of Cyril of Alexandria) was
understood to concern the very substance of the man Jesus, his being as flesh and soul, and not simply his conscious self-awareness,
consciousness of God, self-expression, or linguistic communication.
God became man—that is to say, united a human nature to himself
hypostatically—such that God subsists in the flesh as the man Jesus
Christ.[19] For Aquinas, in particular, this theology of substantial union

18. Were this not the case, (were the operations of knowledge or consciousness
what we are essentially) then the activity of knowledge or consciousness would have to
be the unifying principle of all the other powers of the soul, acting in and through them.
Biological digestion, then, would be an act of human knowledge, and would depend
formally itself in some way upon an act of thinking. Clearly such is not the case. Again,
consciousness would also have to serve as the unifying principle of the body (which
is substantial in the human person). The simple act of being of the living human body
would be an act of consciousness. But this too is plainly false, since we remain embodied persons even when unconscious. Instead, acts of knowledge and love are accidental
properties of the embodied person, but are not themselves what the person is substantially. Meanwhile, God alone simply is his knowledge. Cf. Aquinas, ST I, q. 77, a. 1, corp.
and ad 1.

19. St. Cyril of Alexandria, *On the Unity of Christ*, trans. John A. McGuckin (Crestwood, N.Y.: St. Vladimir's Press, 1995), 80: "If, as they [the Nestorians] say, one [the
Word] is truly the Son of God by nature, but the other [the man Christ] has the sonship

is what characterizes the understanding of the hypostatic union at the Councils of Ephesus and Chalcedon, in differentiation from Nestorian and *homo assumptus* forms of Christological interpretation.[20] (I will treat this issue in depth in the next chapter.) The latter Christologies presuppose an accidental union of God and the human being Jesus through a coordination of the wisdom and will of God and the wisdom and will of the man Jesus. They inevitably reduce the union of God and man in Christ to one that is moral rather than substantial, and thereby undermine any capacity to speak in exacting terms of God "existing" or subsisting as a human being.[21]

Against the backdrop of classical theology, then, Schleiermacher's Christology introduces something novel and represents a rupture. He undertakes what amounts to a "transfer" of the locus of divine-human unity from the realm of the substantial to that of the accidental. The locus of divine-human unity in Christ is no longer conceived of primarily by appeal to Christ's substantial personhood and hypostasis (as ontological categories). Structurally, it is the consciousness of Christ that now becomes important for identifying the transforming power of his historical life, and this is evidently a theological decision that

---

by grace and came to such dignity because of the Word dwelling within him, then what more does he have than us? For the Word also dwells in us.... And so if we have been granted the same dignity by God the Father, our position is in no way inferior to his. For we too are sons and gods by grace, and we have surely been brought to this wonderful and supernatural dignity since we have the Only Begotten Word of God dwelling within us." Although Schleiermacher does not hold to a traditional understanding of the distinction of persons in the Trinity (and therefore neither a pre-existent Logos nor a distinction of natures in Christ), the *kind* of union he proposes is analogous to the position Cyril is criticizing here.

20. ST III, q. 2, a. 6. The teaching of Aquinas on this matter has also recently been reexamined quite helpfully by Jean-Pierre Torrell, in *Le Verbe Incarné* I (Paris: Cerf, 2002), Appendix II, 297–339.

21. Aquinas, SCG IV, c. 34, para. 3: "For, in that position, the Word of God was united to that man only through an indwelling by grace, *on which a union of wills follows*. But the indwelling of God's Word in a man is not for God's Word to be made flesh. *For the Word of God and God Himself have been dwelling in all the holy men since the world was founded*.... And this indwelling, for all that, cannot be called incarnation; otherwise, God would have repeatedly been made flesh since the beginning of the world. Nor does it suffice for the notion of incarnation if the Word of God or God dwelt in that man with a fuller grace, for 'greater and less do not diversify the species of the union.' Since the Christian religion is based on faith in the incarnation, it is now quite evident that the position described removes the basis of the Christian religion" (emphasis added).

affects Christology at a more profound level than differing conceptions of *how* the accidental world of "consciousness" is construed or
structured (pre- or post-Wittgenstein). In post-Cartesian philosophy,
the last place of refuge for personal identity typically is consciousness,
a locus intensified by Kant, as introspective moral conscience. After
Schleiermacher it is the introspective moral conscience of Christ that
retains an importance for us in a scientific age, after the collapse of the
culture of traditional metaphysics. While this interpretation of Christ
gave rise to the great "ethical" Christologies of nineteenth-century liberal Protestantism, they in turn have provided the basis for a transition
into the Christologies of "religious pluralism" in the twentieth century,
in which Christ's unity-of-consciousness with God (or "Ultimate Reality") is understood in terms of his capacity to articulate and symbol-
ize within a particular culture and language the communion with God
that he possessed in an exemplary way. [22]

Initially it might seem that Barth's Christology is entirely different from that of Schleiermacher. First, Barth clearly rejected Schleiermacher's basic project through his sustained polemic and overt criticisms of "human religion" as conceived within liberal Protestantism.
Correspondingly, he systematically refused to speculate on the nature
of Jesus's religious and historical consciousness. Second, Barth is certainly post-Kantian in his theological methodology, but he understands the prohibition on metaphysics in modernity very differently
from Schleiermacher.[23] Schleiermacher perceives the Kantian limitation of speculative reason as an opening for emphasis on religious experience, Christian ethical practices, and the religion of piety. Barth
sees in this same speculative limitation the specter of fallen humanity, which is unable by its own powers to resolve basic questions about
religion, the existence and nature of God, or the content and mean-

22. One can think here of thinkers like John Hick and Jacques Dupuis. I take up a
consideration of their views in the following chapter.

23. Simon Fischer discusses the influences of Marburg neo-Kantianism on the development of Barth's thinking in his early, liberal phase in *Revelatory Positivism: Barth's
Earliest Theology and the Marburg School* (Oxford: Oxford University Press, 1988). Bruce
McCormack discusses Barth's Kantianism (formulated against neo-Kantian postulates
that he considered excessively idealist) in the post-World War I, neo-Orthodox phase of
his thought in *Karl Barth's Critically Realistic Dialectical Theology*, 43–49, 129–30, 155–62,
218–26, 245–62.

ing of human nature and ethics. Christology emerges, therefore, dialectically over against the limitations of human philosophical knowledge. Rather than reinterpret Christ in light of modern philosophical
presuppositions, fitting him into the procrustean bed of rationalism,
Barth seeks to reinterpret the enigma of the modern (post-Kantian)
human subject from the perspective of revelation given in Christ.
Kant's methodological agnosticism is maintained as a structural feature of Barthian anthropology, but this is now transposed into a higher, Christocentric key. The crisis of the identity of the modern subject
is resolved only in and by the revelation given in the Lord.[24] Against
Schleiermacher's anthropology, Barth posits a Christocentric theology.

Third and last, in differentiation from Schleiermacher, Barth pursues an overtly Trinitarian and Christological form of theological reflection that is distinctly ontological in character. He reintroduces
Nicene and Chalcedonian themes into post-Kantian theology, not
without influence from classical sources, as well as event-ontology
that is marked by the influence of Hegel.[25] His mature work seeks to
recover an ontology of the hypostatic union and of the distinct "essences" of Christ as one who is both divine and human.[26] This ontology is not one provided for by natural reason, but is made available to
us uniquely through divine revelation as expressed in the New Testament.

Despite all of these differences, which are far from trivial, there

24. Barth, CD I, 1, 236: "But as faith has its absolute and unconditional beginning in
God's Word *independently of the inborn or acquired characteristics and possibilities of man*,
and as it, as faith, never in any respect lives from or by anything other than the Word, so
it is *in every respect* with the knowability of the Word of God into which we are now en-
quiring. We cannot establish it if, as it were, we turn our backs on God's Word and contemplate ourselves, *finding in ourselves an openness, a positive or at least a negative point of
contact for God's Word*. We can establish it only as we stand fast in faith and its knowledge, i.e., as we turn away from ourselves" (emphasis added).
25. For a presentation of Barth that emphasizes the traditional character of his
Christological ontology, see George Hunsinger, "Karl Barth's Christology: Its basic
Chalcedonian character," in *The Cambridge Companion to Karl Barth*, ed. John Webster
(Cambridge: Cambridge University Press, 2000), 127–42. On the influences of Hegelian
ontology, however, see Bruce McCormack, "Seek God Where He May Be Found: A Response to Edwin Chr. van Driel," *Scottish Journal of Theology* 60 (February 2007): 62–79.
26. CD IV, 2, 70–112.

are still important points of similarity between Schleiermacher and Barth. As noted above, Barth adamantly rejects the liberal Protestant understanding of the human being as a historically religious entity, and in doing so seeks to purge Christology of any dependence upon an "a priorist" human anthropology or natural theology. He does share with Schleiermacher, however, a common conviction concerning the Kantian critique of all possible speculative natural knowledge of God. Barth seeks (over against liberal Protestantism) to develop an ontological reflection on God in light of election (CD II, 2), to reflect Christologically upon the being of man (CD III, 1), and to reflect upon the being of Christ and his human and divine essences (CD IV, 1 and 2). All along, however, he also insists that speech concerning the very being of God is only made possible Christologically, and not naturally or philosophically. In other words, he retains with Schleiermacher a prohibition on the intellectual accessibility of God by way of speculative reason. It is significant and not merely accidental, then, that he continues to maintain persistent reservations concerning the Catholic *analogia entis* throughout his life.[27] Barth intends to fashion a theology to permit us to surmount the problem of the radical secularization of the human intellect in modernity. His own way of doing this is to re-read Kant's speculative agnosticism as something "normal" when one considers the fallen character of human knowledge outside of Christ. Barth revives the Lutheran critique of any possible *theologia gloriae*, or human speculative theology, in favor of a unique *theologia crucis*, of the unique revelation of God in Christ.[28]

The problem with this is that, as Schleiermacher rightly intuited, one cannot articulate a genuine Chalcedonian metaphysics without a simultaneous commitment to classical metaphysics in general. Chalcedon must face the same fate as all other forms of pre-modern ontology. If the latter is defensible, then classical Christology may be as well. If it is not, then the traditional Christian doctrine of the church

27. See CD I, 1, 238–47 (and many other places in this volume); II, 1, 310–21 and 580–86; III, 3, 89–154. In CD IV, 1 and 2 Barth develops in various ways the notion of a Christologically centered analogy between God and man, established through the graced event of Jesus Christ. I do not think this is meant to imply a reversal of any of his earlier positions. I will attempt to show where and how Barth seriously misinterprets Aquinas's thought on the metaphysics of analogy below in chapter 3.

28. See CD I, 1, 14–17 and 167–69.

is endangered. If this presupposition is true, then Barth fails to confront the deeper problem. How do we respond critically to the Kantian prohibition on speculative thinking about God in general? If we have no philosophical (natural) capacity for speaking about God's presence in the world generally, then a theological treatment of the ontology of Christ is prohibited as well.

Kant himself—in response to Hume—did attempt to leave adequate conceptual space for speculative consideration of the problem of God in distinction from empirical reality, and did so by defending the possibility of an analogical concept of God derived from empirical realities. In this he appealed to a theory of proportional analogy.[29] He also insisted, however—in logical consistency with his own epistemological principles—that any appearance of God *within history* would need to be interpreted in pure continuity with the forms of natural phenomena as they appear to us (strictly in terms of natural causality), or as existing in dialectical opposition to these forms (supernatural thinking as magical thinking). Any gratuitous "revelation" of God is either necessarily reducible to the sphere of pure rationality, or in fact illusory.[30] If one loyally follows through to the consequence of such a prohibition of speculative thinking about God's presence in history, then the *transcendence* of God incarnate as it is understood *to be revealed in Christ* is in fact something the mind simply does not have the capacity to entertain intellectually. We can only conceive of the presence of the divine *in this world* univocally, in terms of the natural forms of our world. The reality of the deity of Christ present historically in the flesh is a truth which is inherently unintelligible given the constraints of Kantian reason.

Of course, if one adopts these epistemological presuppositions, there are serious consequences for Christology. Insofar as God is

29. Immanuel Kant, *Prolegomena to Any Future Metaphysics*, trans. P. Carus (Indianapolis, Ind.: Bobbs-Merrill, 1950), §58 (357–61). Kant makes clear that he wishes to argue against Hume that the notion of God as a primary cause of the world is not unintelligible or literally inconceivable, but that this conception is only useful for our thinking about the world we encounter sensibly as potentially caused, and tells us nothing about God in himself.

30. This is a major theme in *Religion within the Boundaries of Mere Reason*. See the edition translated and edited by Allen Wood and George di Giovanni (Cambridge: Cambridge University Press, 1998), especially 6:63–64 and 190. I return to this issue below in chapter 3.

conceived in Christ, he is conceived in terms that are strictly natural-istic. Schleiermacher seems to undertake this kind of transposition in a fluid way: it happens through a reduction of the mystery of Jesus to the world of human religious feeling and ethics. What is important about Jesus is not the claim that he performed miracles, or the ontol-ogy of the incarnation, or the historical event of the resurrection. In-stead, it is the evolution of his religious consciousness. When human nature becomes most perfect in its own natural religious trajectory (in Jesus of Nazareth), then it is divine.

Barth seemingly rejects such an approach. However, he does not provide us with a satisfying alternative. For in his own way, Barth also seeks to understand the deity and being of Christ uniquely with re-course to intra-worldly categories, based upon human actions and historical events. Here we see in a strange way the shadow of Kant: human thought cannot rise speculatively above a consideration of the forms of this world, and so God by condescension takes on the form of our being in his own deity as a way of showing us what God is in himself. Consider, for example, Barth's attempt (in CD IV, 1) to inter-pret all Trinitarian theology and Christology in light of Christ's hu-man act of obedience. On this account, we find God in history only in Christ's humanity, and specifically in Christ's human actions of obedience. How can Christ's human actions reveal to us *what God is*? For Barth, God has created this world so that the human essence of Christ might reveal to us what the deity of God is, from all eternity. Consequently, the event of Christ's obedience unto death is expres-sive of the very life of God the Son, in its eternal constitution. What the cross reveals to us is that God the Son is eternally obedient to the Father.[31] The argument is then developed further: the event of the passion in time is in fact an event in the life of God himself. God in his very deity obeys and suffers. The very deity of God can be sub-

---

31. Barth, CD IV, 1, 200–201. Bruce McCormack has recently analyzed this section of the CD very accurately. See Bruce McCormack, "Karl Barth's Christology as a Re-source for a Reformed Version of Kenoticism," *International Journal of Systematic Theol-ogy* 8, no. 3 (2006): 243–51, as well as his essay "Divine Impassibility or Simple Divine Constancy? Implications of Karl Barth's Later Christology for Debates over Impassibil-ity," in *Divine Impassibility and the Mystery of Human Suffering*, eds. James F. Keating and Thomas Joseph White (Grand Rapids, Mich.: Eerdmans, 2009), 150–86. I return to this issue in chapter 7 below.

ject to death and the regaining of eternal life. This, at least, is how disciples like Moltmann, Jüngel, and Jenson interpret Barth (arguably rightly), so as to present a historicized portrait of the deity of God.[32]

Such a perspective is clearly very different from that of Schleiermacher. The problem, however, is that it too fails to preserve a classical form of Chalcedonian thought. What does it mean to say that God personally "exists" as a human being among us? How should we understand the difference between Christ's human nature and his divine nature? Both these questions point us toward the need for a metaphysics of the analogy of being. In one case, hypostatic existence needs to be understood analogically: how is the existence of the person of the Word different from our own? In the other case, we must examine different senses of the word "nature": how is it attributed to Christ's human essence as distinct from his divine essence? In seeking to recover Chalcedonian ontology "after Kant" without a commitment to classical metaphysics, the Barthian "tradition" cannot answer these questions adequately. It has produced answers that are creative, but which are also of a highly ambivalent nature.

In keeping with this criticism, we can note that there is an irony to Barth's particular focus upon the human operations of Jesus as expressive of his deity. Barth clearly rejects the liberal Protestant conception of our human religious consciousness as the locus of the divine-human encounter, yet he also seeks to place the "site" of the hypostatic union in an odd location: the transcendent identity of God is revealed in a voluntary act of the human Christ (the free and willing submission of Christ to God). Therefore, as with Schleiermacher's pietistic God-consciousness (the sentiment of absolute dependence), an "accidental" feature of the human being of Christ (conscious self-determination in freedom) becomes the privileged locus of divine-human unity. Barth wants to retrieve a sense of the classical Christological ontology over against liberal Protestantism, but he arguably ends up projecting an element of created human life onto the deity anthropomorphically.

32. This is one of the points of Erich Przywara's critique of Barth's thought as "theopanism" that has recently been reemphasized by David Bentley Hart. See David Bentley Hart, "No Shadow of Turning: On Divine Impassibility," *Pro Ecclesia* 11 (Spring 2002): 184–206.

We might summarize the argument, then, in this way: Schleier-macher rejects metaphysics and resorts to consciousness, while Barth rejects human metaphysics and resorts to a sort of revealed Christo-logical metaphysics. But Barth's strategy, seemingly designed to avoid falling into Schleiermachian reductionism, ends up (ironically) being an application of human categories after all, and (even more ironical-ly) these turn out to be categories of consciousness. One can avoid these problems by accepting the possibility of a natural capacity in human beings for metaphysical reflection, so long as this metaphysics is endowed with a sense of analogy, so that divine things are not re-duced to human ones.[33]

Classical Chalcedonian theology could respond, then, to both Barth and Schleiermacher by asking the following questions. Is the unity of God and man in Christ assured first and foremost by his ac-tions of obedience or by something more fundamental: his person-al identity as the Word made flesh? Does Christ obey and suffer by virtue of his divinity, or uniquely by virtue of his humanity? In the divine nature are there properties distinct from the divine essence that allow it to undergo a "history" of development through actions of obedience? Following the mainstream patristic and scholastic tra-dition, we could argue that Barth fails to recognize the doctrine of the pure actuality of God.[34] God in his incomprehensible deity is not composed of potency and act. Therefore, he is not subject to acciden-tal development or progressive enrichment.[35] Consequently, if we are

---

33. I am greatly indebted to Michael Gorman for this summation of the argument.

34. Thomas Aquinas, *Scriptum super libros Sententiarum magistri Petri Lombardi epis-copi Parisiensis* (vols. 1–2), ed. P. Mandonnet (Paris: P. Lethielleux, 1929) and vols. 3–4, ed. M. Moos (Paris: P. Lethielleux, 1933–47), d. 8, q. 4, a. 3 [hereafter "*In I Sent.*"]; SCG I, c. 23; *De potentia Dei*, ed. P. M. Pession, in *Quaestiones disputatae* (vol. 2), ed. R. Spi-azzi (Turin: Marietti, 1965), q. 7, a. 4 [hereafter "*De Pot.*"]; ST I, q. 3, a. 6; *Compendium theologiae ad fratrem Reginaldum socium suum carissimum*, vol. 42 of *Sancti Thomae de Aquino opera omnia* (Rome: Leonine Edition, 1979), c. 23 [hereafter "*Comp. Theol.*"].

35. SCG I, c. 23, para. 3: "Furthermore, what is present in a thing accidentally has a cause of its presence, since it is outside the essence of the thing in which it is found. If, then, something is found in God accidentally, this must be through some cause. Now, the cause of the accident is either the divine essence itself or something else. If some-thing else, it must act on the divine essence, since nothing will cause the introduction of some form, substantial or accidental, in some receiving subject except by acting on it in some way. For to act is nothing other than to make something actual, which takes place through a form. Thus, God will suffer and receive the action of some cause—which is

to attribute accidental features of human thinking or willing to God (even licitly) these must be rethought analogically when ascribed to the eternal life of God, precisely in order to preserve a sense of the divine transcendence.[36]

In appealing to the doctrine of God as pure actuality, I am not presuming that Aquinas's metaphysics is necessarily correct, or that a particular version of classical metaphysics must be embraced if any modern Christian theology is to succeed. I am only suggesting that despite their otherwise laudable intentions, neither Barth nor Schleiermacher settles adequately the issue of how or to what degree classical ontology is a necessary feature of any real commitment to Chalcedonian Christology. Can we really retrieve this tradition if we do not make use of traditional ontological categories and concepts to speak about God in just such a way that many a post-Kantian thinker would in fact reject? If the mystery of Christ must be understood in ontological terms, then perhaps modern Christology must retrieve in an overt way the right use of the "metaphysics of being," and the language of analogical predications ascribed to God, even if this stands over against the prohibitions of Kant. (I will make this argument below, in greater detail, in chapters 3 and 4.)

Such a reconsideration of the "analogy of being" allows us to overcome the problematic opposition that emerges in modern Christology between the excessively anthropological focus (represented typologically by Schleiermacher), and the uniquely Christological focus (represented by Barth). Aquinas's metaphysics proposes that the human mind is meant ultimately to transcend history, attaining its complete perfection only through the knowledge of God and the analogical consideration of the divine names.[37] This natural openness to

---

contrary to what we already established. On the other hand, let us suppose that the divine substance is the cause of the accident inhering in it. Now it is impossible that it be, as receiving it, the cause of the accident, for then one and the same thing would make itself to be actual in the same respect. Therefore, if there is an accident in God, it will be according to different respects that He receives and causes that accident, just as bodily things receive their accidents through the nature of their matter and cause them through their form. Thus, God will be composite. But, we have proved the contrary of this proposition above [c. 18]." In cc. 22 and 23, Aquinas cites as patristic testimony St. Hilary, De Trinitate VII, 11; Augustine De Trinitate V, 4, and Boethius, De Trinitate II.

36. ST I, q. 13, a. 5.

37. See, for instance, Aquinas, ST I, q. 12, aa. 1 and 12; I-II, q. 3, a. 2, ad 4; a. 6.

the transcendence of God is seen as a *sign* that the human intellect is capable of being elevated gratuitously into the order of supernatural grace, even unto the beatific vision.[38] On such an account, there is no dialectical opposition between the Christological revelation of God the Trinity and our authentic anthropological fulfillment. Theology of the human person and Christocentric theology are not opposed methodologically, but are related in a hierarchical way. God unveils who he is in Christ so that we might become like him through the contemplation of his mystery. In discovering God in Christ, we also find ourselves. "The Word of Life … was made manifest and we saw it … the eternal life that was with the Father …. It does not yet appear what we shall be, but we know that when he appears we shall be like him, for we shall see him as he is" (1 Jn 1:1–2; 3:2).

THOMISTIC REFLECTIONS ON THE CONDITIONS OF MODERN CHRISTOLOGY

Two Thomistic Reflections

The first half of this chapter has been etiological, while the second half is meant to be prescriptive. In what follows, I would like briefly to consider two ways that Aquinas's Christology provides resources for avoiding the two speculative antinomies I have identified above, each of which tends to influence greatly modern Christological thought. To do so I will take up key distinctions of Aquinas as they are interpreted by modern Thomists. First, then, I will consider the issue of the potential harmonization or integration of historical life of Jesus research and Chalcedonian doctrinal reflection. Second, I will consider Chalcedonian Christology and the metaphysics of being and divine naming. The reflections offered here are evidently very partial, but are meant to designate distinctions found in St. Thomas Aquinas's writings that speak eloquently to the problems described above. They indicate ways that a Thomistic Christology can be envisaged under modern conditions. As such, they serve in turn as preparations for the chapters that are to follow.

38. ST I-II, q. 3, a. 8.

The Historical Son Incarnate: Formal
and Material Objects of Faith

To address the first question, then, let us appeal to a well-known Thomistic distinction (found for example in the ST II-II, q. 1. a. 1) between the "formal object" of faith and the "material object" of faith. Aquinas writes in this article:

The object of every cognitive habit includes two things: first, that which is known materially, and is the material object, so to speak, and secondly, that whereby it is known, which is the formal aspect of the object. Thus in the science of geometry, the conclusions are what is known materially, while the formal aspect of the science is the means of demonstration, through which the conclusions are known.

In speaking of the epistemological act of faith, the material object is the reality we believe in by the grace of faith and that we tend toward in hope and love. That material object is, ultimately, God himself, in whom we believe and who has been made manifest to us in Christ. The formal object, meanwhile, is the medium through which or by which we have access to God and to Christ in the supernatural habit of faith. The formal object, simply speaking, is God revealing himself, the gift of knowledge of God that comes to us through the event of Christ, and subsequently through the conveyance of divine truth in scripture, tradition, and the ecclesial magisterium.[39] In faith we know the Trinity and the Word incarnate who has lived a human life among us for our salvation. In faith we know this *by* the medium or formal object of God revealing himself.

In his *Commentary on Boethius's De Trinitate*, as well as in the *Summa theologiae*, Aquinas employs this distinction to explain how it is that we might know God both through the formal medium of revelation *and* through the distinct formal medium of philosophical speculation simultaneously.[40] The two forms of knowledge attain to the same material object (who is God) but they in no way conflict with one another, as they approach God in distinct ways (and in differing

---

39. ST II-II, q. 1, aa. 9–10.
40. *Expos. de Trin.*, q. 2, a. 2; ST I, q. 1, a. 1, ad 2. See also ST II-II, q. 2, aa. 3–4; SCG I, cc. 4–5.

degrees of imperfection).[41] Even though the two forms of knowledge are distinct, however, they do not remain merely alien to one another. For, as Aquinas points out in the beginning of the *Summa theologiae*, knowledge of God by grace permits us to make use of the grammar of metaphysical reflection upon God—assimilating the truths of this discourse into a greater sapiential totality that is distinctly theological. Sacred doctrine can make use of philosophy to illustrate theological truths, just as (analogically) the science of politics can make use of military knowledge to defend the citizens and material goods of the state.[42] Human metaphysical reflection upon God's simplicity, goodness, unity, knowledge or will, for instance, may be employed within a context that is specifically theological, serving therein to articulate in more profound and numinous terms the mystery of the triune God.[43]

41. *Expos. de Trin.*, q. 2, a. 2: "Now the knowledge of divine things can be interpreted in two ways. First, from our standpoint, and then they are knowable to us only through creatures, the knowledge of which we derive from the senses. Second, from the nature of divine realities themselves, and although we do not know them in their own way, this is how they are known by God and the blessed. Accordingly, there are two kinds of science concerning the divine. One follows our way of knowing, which uses the principles of sensible things in order to make the Godhead known. This is the way the philosophers handed down a science of the divine, calling the primary science 'divine science.' The other follows the mode of divine realities themselves, so that they are apprehended in themselves. We cannot perfectly possess this way of knowing in the present life, but there arises here and now in us a certain sharing in, and a likeness to, the divine knowledge, to the extent that through the faith implanted in us we firmly grasp the primary Truth itself for its own sake." In ST II-II, q. 1, a. 5, ad 4 Aquinas speaks not of distinct "formal objects" but rather of the same object considered under distinct aspects (in reference to Aristotle's *Posterior Analytics* I, 33, 89b2), and applies this to the distinction between revealed and natural knowledge of God.

42. ST I, q. 1, a. 5, corp. and ad 2.

43. *Expos. de Trin.*, q. 2, a. 3: "The gifts of grace are added to nature in such a way that they do not destroy it, but rather perfect it. So too the light of faith, which is imparted to us as a gift, does not do away with the light of natural reason given to us by God.... Accordingly we can use philosophy in sacred doctrine in three ways. First, in order to demonstrate the preambles of faith, which we must necessarily know in [the act of] faith. Such are the truths about God that are proved by natural reason, for example, that God exists, that he is one, and other truths of this sort about God or creatures proved in philosophy and presupposed by faith. Second, by throwing light on the contents of faith by analogies, as Augustine uses many analogies drawn from philosophical doctrines in order to elucidate the Trinity. Third, in order to refute assertions contrary to the faith, either by showing them to be false or lacking in necessity."

This distinction between the two formal objects—attaining the same material object in two different ways—is the starting point for a modern development of Thomistic thought undertaken at the beginning of the twentieth century by the French Dominican Ambroise Gardeil. In response to the so-called modernist crisis, Gardeil applied Aquinas's analysis to the relationship between faith and history.[44] This was a reflection that he in turn passed on to his student, Yves Congar, and which we find presented anew in Congar's classic work *Tradition and Traditions*.[45] In the distinction between formal and material objects, Gardeil perceived the basis for several important claims concerning the relationship of faith to history.

First, modern rational historical study, with its conjectural reconstructions concerning the historical Jesus or the winding paths of past development of ecclesial doctrine, approaches the subject of Jesus Christ or church doctrine from a different vantage point (under a different objective formality) than does the scriptural and ecclesial deposit of faith as such. The former study, even when it takes into account the claims of scriptural revelation or significant philosophical truths about man, proceeds on the basis of rational historical speculation that begins from empirical certitudes of historical facts and attempts to infer from these facts probable connections of cause and effect that explain historical developments.[46] The mystery of Christ as understood by scripture and the church, meanwhile, has a different objective formality. The subject of its study is no less concrete in nature. (There is nothing more concrete than the incarnation and resurrection of Christ.) However, this form of reflection attains to depths of reality and to divinely caused historical occurrences at levels that the senses and mere empirical reason cannot perceive, and that the reconstructions of historical reason (no matter how philosophically informed) can neither demonstrate nor verify. The theological knowledge of the mysteries of faith is much closer to the form of natural knowledge that is properly metaphysical, or ontological, than it is to mathematics or to the observational sciences. Being, essence, unity,

---

44. See Ambroise Gardeil, *La crédibilité et l'apologétique* (Paris: J. Gabalda et Fils, 1928), and *Le donné révélé et la théologie*, esp. 196–223.

45. Yves Congar, *La tradition et les traditions*, 2 vols. (Paris: A. Fayard, 1960–63).

46. Often only natural causes and effects.

and goodness are present throughout all created reality, after all, but
are not merely reducible to the objects of sense experience. The mystery of God revealed in Christ is like this. We cannot see the divinity
of Christ with our eyes, but we can touch it by way of an intellectual
judgment. Formally speaking, this mystery utterly transcends the domain of natural reason as such (including metaphysical knowledge)
and is properly supernatural. Therefore the methodology of modern
historical-critical study of the life of Jesus cannot be employed to provide the foundations for accepting the truth of the Christian faith as
such. These foundations can only be received supernaturally by grace,
and understood in that light.[47]

We might note that the supernatural character of the "science" of
theology is something Kähler and Barth both rightly understood and
defended in conflict with liberal Protestantism's seeming attempt to
derive foundational principles of Christology from the modern study
of history. (Analogous criticisms were posited by the Catholic John
Henry Newman against Anglo-Catholicism's attempt to derive the
norms of Catholic doctrine from one's personal study of the history
of doctrine).[48] However, the acceptance of such supernatural realism
does not imply that the material object of faith (in this case the mys-

47. Gardeil, *La Crédibilité et L'Apologétique*, 221–22: "Tradition and Scripture alone
contain the revelation and constitute the theological loci that are *fundamental*. The
Church has no other role than to determine with an infallible authority what is contained
in Tradition and Scripture. Logically speaking, the Church comes after Tradition and
Scripture [and is subordinate to these]. If, then, one begins treating the theological loci
with a consideration of the theological loci of the Church, this could be based on a decision of a practical order that is pedagogically useful but in no way necessary. But what
one cannot do without acting against the proper character of the theological principles of
faith as such is to attempt to *found* their authority upon the authority of the Magisterium
of the Church *in so far as this authority results from rational proofs* of rational apologetics
[such as historical-critical reasons in favor of the faith]. This is to interpret reductively the
theological loci which are the foundation of theology and must be the starting points in
faith from the beginning. Between these starting points and the goal pursued in a rational apologetical argument on behalf of the faith, there is a gulf that can only be crossed
by the total and definitive adhesion to the Catholic faith, and with this the apologetical
arguments are finished. There is a discontinuity between the science of rational defense
of the credibility of faith and the science of theology. In the interval between the two is a
psychological act of faith, free and supernatural.... It is the faith and not the conclusions
of apologetics that stands at the origins of theology 'quae procedit ex principiis fidei.'" All
translations from French are my own unless otherwise stated.

48. See Congar, *La tradition et les traditions*, 1:244, 268–70.

tery of Jesus Christ) cannot be also understood in complementary
fashion with recourse to the "formal medium" of the historical study
of Jesus, the historical study of the eventual formation of the New
Testament canon, of ecclesial doctrine, etc. On the contrary, such
forms of knowledge *might contribute* to a better understanding of the
material object of consideration (Jesus of Nazareth himself) but only
as enriching the original "givens" of divine revelation, *illustrative* of
the principles of theological science and not as *demonstrative* of these
principles.[49] Historical study can serve after the fact, so to speak, in
the service of theological faith to further research as to *how* the principles of faith were unveiled, given, or received in subsequent historical contexts.[50] Historical reflection can also render us more sensitive

49. Aquinas teaches that arguments for the rational credibility of Christian faith
(such as those based upon sound argumentation for the historicity of the Gospels)
cannot procure the faith but do allow one to defend in a fashion the proper principles
of faith, according to a mode that is distinctly rational. ST II-II, q. 1, a. 4, ad 2: "Those
things which come under faith can be considered in two ways. First, in particular; and
thus they cannot be seen and believed at the same time, as shown above. Secondly, in
general, that is, under the common aspect of credibility; and in this way they are seen by
the believer. For he would not believe unless, on the evidence of signs, or of something
similar, he saw that they ought to be believed." In this sense, the arguments in question,
insofar as they do enrich the intellect's apperception of the object, can rightly be said
not only to have a genuine apologetic (rational defensible) value, but also to illustrate
more deeply something of the truth of the material object under consideration. Such
argumentation occurs, however, in formal distinction from revelation as such, and ultimately only in the service of the mystery of faith. Gardeil's thought is influenced in part
by the analysis of apologetics by Reginald Garrigou-Lagrange, in his *De Revelatione*, 2
vols. (Rome and Paris: Ferrari and Gabalda, 1921), 1:41–44.

50. Or, in the more nuanced formulation of Gardeil, historical or philosophical
study of Christianity might demonstrate its reasonableness, even in a rationally compelling fashion, but such "apologetic argumentation" will not provide immediate access to
the divine mystery itself. *Le Donné Révélé*, esp. 204–5: "A scientific faith [or belief] produced by the evidence of certain motives of credibility, or acquired faith [stemming from
study of history], which is human and natural, provides a certain correspondence between [Christian] theology and the science of God [the knowledge that God has of
himself], because such an apologetic demonstrates rigorously that God speaks in His
Church and that all the dogmas of the Church are, from a human point of view, worthy
of belief by divine faith. But it is clear that the certitude that these arguments give is only
an incomplete certitude, a certitude in waiting, that is ordered towards the certitude of
the divine faith itself.... A sub-alternated science has to be able to join back up with the
principles that are its foundation, so as to participate fully in their certitude.... Yet the
only means by which theological science as such can rejoin effectively the object known
by divine science is ... supernatural faith, which allows us to believe, with an assurance

to dimensions of the life of Jesus of Nazareth, and such knowledge can in turn invite us to further theological reflection. The ontological mystery of the incarnate Word has historical-cultural conditions as dimensions of its being that can be studied rationally, and likewise, knowledge of the empirical, historical-cultural conditions of Christ can invite us to a deeper reflection about the mystery of the incarnate Word. Ultimately, however, none of the conditions of Christ's life can be fully understood except by recourse to supernatural faith, for only at this level of reflection do we attain to the deepest ontological core of his person. Therefore historical study as such cannot allow us to determine what is held in faith, even if it can help us to clarify what is and is not reasonable to believe concerning the *historical mode* in which a given mystery was unveiled historically.

Allow me to illustrate this argument by means of a brief Thomistic consideration of the theories of N. T. Wright concerning the "sacrificial intentionality" of the historical Jesus on the eve of his death.[51] As everyone knows well, the sacrificial system of Jesus's own time revolved around the application of Levitical and Deuteronomical precepts of physical sacrifice within the context of the Second Temple and its vast cultic, political, and economic sociology. And yet within a generation after Jesus's death, Christians who composed the writings of the New Testament considered the death of Jesus a "sacrifice" of a unique and ultimate kind.[52] Using Old Testament sacrifice imagery to describe the significance of his death, they claimed that this event displaced in some way the economy of Temple sacrifices and had redemptive effects for the entirety of humanity. They also claimed (arguably) that the eucharist both signified and rendered present the sacrificed body and blood of Christ.[53]

---

caused directly in us by God, that which God himself knows and reveals to us." It should be noted that Gardeil here seems to reduce Aquinas's conception of *sacra doctrina* in ST I, q. 1, to "theology" as distinct from and exclusive of revelation, which is a problematic interpretation of Aquinas on this point, but this is immaterial to the argument at hand.

51. See especially the discussion of Jesus's self-interpretation of his impending death in N. T. Wright, *Jesus and the Victory of God,* (Minneapolis, Minn.: Fortress, 1996), 540–611.

52. Albert Vanhoye offers a helpful study of the emergence of the early Christian concept of the priesthood of Christ in his *Old Testament Priests and the New Priest,* trans. Bernard Orchard (Petersham, Mass.: St. Bede's Press, 1986).

53. See the brief scriptural argument to this effect by Charles Journet in *The Mass:*

But even if all this is the case, can we simply remain content to develop a theology of sacrifice from the New Testament if Jesus of Nazareth, himself a first century Jew, may never have conceived of his own death in sacrificial terms? Clearly the formal object of the faith is the significance of the death of Jesus as it is presented and understood in faith and for faith as God has revealed through scripture. Furthermore, the New Testament attributes to Christ himself in numerous instances a willingness to offer his life "sacrificially" for the multitude. However, this does not render irrelevant the question of how we might explain the origin of this belief historically in the life of Jesus himself, within the context of Second Temple Judaism, or the question of how his own Jewish mode of self-expression in this historical context might have illustrated *his own conviction* of the "sacrificial" and soteriological significance of his death. It is this kind of probabilistic and conjectural argument that Wright, for example, provides through the formal medium of historical speculation, following scholars like Martin Hengel[54] and George Caird,[55] upon whom his work builds.[56]

If, for example, we can trace back the eucharistic institution narrative to the earliest Palestinian Christian community ("this is the blood of the covenant, which will be shed for the many"), then we have evidence of a primitive theology of the death of Jesus that can reasonably be seen (by recourse to historical-critical modes of argumentation) to have originated with Christ himself. This theology of

The Presence of the Sacrifice of the Cross, trans. Victor Szczurek (South Bend, Ind: St. Augustine's Press, 2008), 30–32.

54. Martin Hengel, *The Atonement: The Origins of the Doctrine in the New Testament*, trans. J. Bowden (Philadelphia: Fortress, 1981).

55. See C. B. Caird and L. D. Hurst, *New Testament Theology* (Oxford: Oxford University Press, 1994).

56. See, for instance, *Jesus and the Victory of God*, 257: "The crucial thing is that for Jesus this repentance, whether personal or national, *did not involve going to the Temple and offering sacrifice.* John's baptism, as we saw earlier, already carried this scandalous notion: one could 'repent,' in the divinely appointed way, down by the Jordan instead of up in Jerusalem! In just the same way, Jesus offered membership in the renewed people of the covenant god *on his own authority and by his own process.* This was the real scandal. He behaved as if he thought (a) that the return from exile was already happening, (b) that it consisted precisely of himself and his mission, and hence (c) that he had the right to pronounce on who belonged to the restored Israel." Likewise, see E. P. Sanders, *Jesus and Judaism* (Philadelphia: Fortress, 1985), 203, 206.

Jesus of Nazareth itself in turn refers to the foundational covenant sacrifice of Exodus 24 (where the phrase "blood of the covenant" originates), and that is seen in Exodus to have established the twelve tribes in contractual communion with the Lord of Israel. If Jesus not only foresaw his death, but interpreted it in advance as a radical renewal and completion of the covenant of Exodus 24, even a universalization of the covenant "for the many" (cf. Is 53:10–12), and if he signified this for his followers by the prescription of a new mode of sacrifice that now takes place outside of the Temple, then we begin to understand how Christ in history was conscious of articulating the sacrificial character of his death in distinctly Jewish terms, and yet simultaneously interpreted his own life and mission as having an entirely singular, authoritative significance.[57]

A collage of such illustrations of Christ's self-consciousness could suggest in greater and richer depth *how* the incarnate Word conceived of himself, his identity and authority, within the context of the first century Judaism of his time, even while suggesting plausibly how the words and gestures of the historical Jesus gave rise to the subsequent beliefs about him that were promulgated in the New Testament writings. Do such historical conjectures *determine* the content of the object of faith, or prove its truthfulness? For example, if it can be shown merely from the principles of natural reason to be historically probable that Jesus of Nazareth interpreted his oncoming execution in sacrificial terms, does this demonstrate that the death of Jesus should be considered theologically to have been a sacrifice? Of course not. Such

---

57. I am leaving to one side N. T. Wright's account of how Jesus acquires the insights of his self-understanding. Wright believes that any attribution of higher prophetic illumination given to the human intellect of Christ that would account for Christ's extra-ordinary self-understanding would entail a form of theological docetism that undercuts a sufficient realism concerning Christ's historical, fully human consciousness. Does Wright believe then that Jesus's self-understanding was obtained only through natural causes? He suggests that Jesus knew something of his own deeper identity as the Son and agent of YHWH through an obscure faith in his own mission, without clear certitude, articulated only by recourse to the resources of contemporary Jewish symbols and traditions that he creatively reformulated (see *Jesus and the Victory of God*, 648–53). Is this degree of self-understanding sufficient soteriologically for the moral intention that Christ must have had in order to make the sacrifice of the cross a saving act, by giving *his own life* on behalf of all? Despite the many advantages of his work, Wright's interpretation on this point seems to me to be based on naturalistic theological suppositions, and to be problematic soteriologically.

knowledge is given to human beings by grace alone, by the activity of the Holy Spirit teaching us through the medium of scripture, tradition, and the living proclamation of the church. Do such historical reflections permit us to envisage theologically *how* the historical life of God the Son *might* have unfolded in its historical context, and to defend a plausible historical account of Jesus *apologetically* over and against secular historical constructions that would contradict the testimony of the New Testament doctrine itself? Yes they do, or at least, yes they can in principle. The historical science of modern rational historical investigation (more modest in certitude than many other sciences, but capable of some demonstrative conclusions) can be placed in the service of the faith, so as to attempt to decrypt a more perfect understanding of its material object, the Son made man, even while it remains clear that this historical study does not provide or obtain the radical access to the mystery of Christ that comes through faith alone, through the mediating formal object of faith. Schleiermacher's confusion or blending of the two formal objects obscures the supernatural mystery of Christ and confines his meaning to the reductionist speculations of historical-critical scholars and their conjectures. Barth expurgates (or at least severely curtails) the possibility of such conjectures being used meaningfully in the service of the object of faith as a form of historical reason in the service of revelation. Gardeil seeks to distinguish in order to unite. He acknowledges the distinct contribution of historical-critical reflection as a lesser science of reason, a science that can be assimilated sapientially to the superior (and irreducibly integral) science of divine revelation. It is from the latter science alone, however, that theology receives its first principles.

Chalcedonian Christology and Metaphysical Knowledge of God: Primary and Secondary Actuality

The second topic discussed above concerns the relationship between classical Chalcedonian ontology and the modern philosophical prohibition on speculative knowledge of God. Can we really articulate theologically the redemption of the modern human self either by an experience of absolute religious dependence, or by a revelatory actualism that alone makes accessible an ontological reflection on the depths of God if from the beginning the human mind is always, already bound to consider transcendent realities only from within the scope of intra-worldly univocity? In other words, must all Christology be subject to the constraints of a post-Kantian philosophical naturalism?

I have intimated that a recovery of the metaphysics of being and of the divine names is an integral part of a renewed Chalcedonian Christology. Here I would like to suggest two ways in which Thomistic reflection on the being of Christ invites our modern secularized intellects to a remedy; not a cure from Wittgenstein, but rather, one from the Aquinate. That is to say, not a rethinking from ordinary language we already know, but a rethinking *from within Christology* about our *natural* capacities for knowledge of God. What does Christ himself teach us about ourselves, and about the transcendent capacities and teleological meaning of the human mind? In answering to this question, let us consider first a point in response to Barthian concerns, and then one in response to Schleiermacher.[58]

These two points can be elaborated around another central Thomistic distinction, this one not being epistemological, but metaphysical: the distinction Aquinas (following Aristotle) makes between primary actuality and secondary actuality.[59] Primary actuality, for Aquinas,

58. In making this argument, I am indebted in part to the thinking of Hans Urs von Balthasar in his seminal work *Karl Barth: Darstellung und Deutung Seiner Theologie* (Köln: Verlag Jakob Hegner, 1951), trans. E. Oakes as *The Theology of Karl Barth: Exposition and Interpretation* (San Francisco: Ignatius Press, 1992), esp. 267–325. Balthasar makes the case that a natural ontology and metaphysical theology are possible and even necessary within the framework of a Christological doctrine of the God-world analogy and a Catholic consideration of the relations of nature and grace. I am suggesting here something potentially complementary but distinct, and more classically Thomistic: because an analogical ontology of creation and God are possible and necessary within Christology, therefore a natural theology is necessary that is distinguishable from Christology. And without a distinct metaphysical reflection on God that is philosophical in kind, true Christological reflection becomes intrinsically impaired. I develop this argument more extensively below.

59. See, for example, Aquinas, *De Ver.*, q. 21, a. 5; ST I, q. 48, a. 5; q. 76, a. 4, ad 1; q. 105, a. 5; I-II, q. 3, a. 2; q. 49, a. 3, ad 1; *In IX Meta.*, lec. 5, 1828; lec. 9, 1870; *In de Anima* II, lec. 1, 220–24. The distinction is found originally in Aristotle, particularly in *Metaphysics* IX, 6, 1048b6–9, and 8, 1050b8–16. He specifically applies the distinction to operations of the soul as accidental properties of the substance ("second acts") in *On the Soul* II, 1, 412a17–29.

pertains to the substantial being of a thing, its being in act as a certain whole with an essential determination.[60] To be in act, in this primary respect, is to exist, simply, as a unique being of a certain kind. For example, we may say that from the time she is conceived an embryonic person is a new human being, and this being will eventually develop in various ways, but retains continuity of substance over time. She always exists in act. The second mode of actuality, secondary act, pertains to operations, for example, operations of conscious knowledge and reflective reason, or of deliberation or choice that progressively develop and manifest themselves. Such operations occur in human persons in habitual ways that make their behavior predictable and subject to normative descriptions (for example, in the form of virtues and vices). These secondary acts of the person (such as operational acts of piety or obedience) are accidental properties of the substance, secondary acts relative to that primary act that is substantial.[61]

It is important for our purposes, then, to consider the union of God with human nature according to these two respective modes of being in act. The incarnation, in which God exists as a human being, takes place primarily in the first of these modes: God subsists personally as a human being. By contrast, *our union* with God takes place primarily in the second mode, through human operations. By the working of grace, we can come to know God and to love him, so as to be united with him by our human actions.[62] The distinction is important, then, because it allows us to see clearly the true "locus" of the incarnation that is particular to Christ. It does not take place in the human consciousness of Jesus or in his human operations of obedience. It takes place in the very substance of Christ's person.

60. ST I, q. 48, a. 5: "Act is twofold; first and second. The first act is the form and integrity of a thing; the second act is its operation."

61. *In de Anima* II, lec. 1, 224: "The difference between accidental form and substantial form is that whereas the former does not make a thing simply be, but only makes it be in this or that mode—e.g., as quantified, or white—the substantial form gives it simple being [*facit esse actu simpliciter*]. Hence the accidental form presupposes an already existing subject; but the substantial form presupposes only potentiality to existence, i.e., bare matter. That is why there cannot be more than one substantial form in any one thing; the first makes the thing an actual being; and if others are added they confer only accidental modifications, since they presuppose the subject already in act of being."

62. ST III, q. 6, a. 6, ad 1–2.

According to Aquinas's way of stating this point, then, the union of God and man in Christ is substantial and not accidental. It takes place within the subsistent person of the Word, and not in the accidental operations of the man Jesus. The Son unites to himself a human nature in his own person. Consequently, the man Jesus Christ is the second person of the Trinity.[63] Accordingly, the Word exists as man in such a way that his body and soul subsist by virtue of his very *esse* (the being in act of the Word himself). Or, to say the same thing slightly differently, the human nature of the incarnate Word subsists in his person by virtue of his being in act as God.[64] Therefore, all that occurs to Jesus by virtue of his human nature, from the time of his conception until the moment of his death, is properly ascribed to God himself, as when we say, for example, that the Son of God wept, or that the Son of God was crucified.[65] We can also say that God obeyed as man, or that God suffered in his human nature. But if we do so we are saying this due to the hypostatic subsistence of the Word in a human nature, and not because of a transposition of human attributes onto the divine nature. If we locate the union of God and man in the hypostasis of the Son, we must still distinguish

63. ST III, q. 2, aa. 2–3.

64. ST III, q. 17, a. 2: "Now being [*esse*] pertains both to the nature and to the hypostasis; to the hypostasis as to that which has being, and to the nature as to that whereby it has being.... But the being which belongs to the very hypostasis or person in itself cannot possibly be multiplied in one hypostasis or person, since it is impossible that there should not be one being for one thing. If, therefore, the human nature accrued to the Son of God, not hypostatically or personally, but accidentally, as some maintained, it would be necessary to assert two beings in Christ—one, inasmuch as He is God—the other, inasmuch as He is Man.... [But] since the human nature is united to the Son of God, hypostatically or personally as was said above [ST III, q. 2, aa. 5–6], and not accidentally, it follows that by the human nature there accrued to Him no new personal being, but only a new relation of the pre-existing personal being to the human nature, *in such a way that the Person is said to subsist not merely in the Divine, but also in the human nature*" (emphasis added). In a late disputed question on the union of the incarnate Word (*De Unione*, a. 4) Aquinas does consider the possibility of a human, created *esse* in Christ. Based on this text, the twentieth-century Thomist Herman Diepen famously posited an "integration" theory of *esse* in Aquinas's thought. Even if one adopts Diepen's interpretation, the personal subsistence of Christ is one and its unity stems from his divine *esse* as the eternally existent Son. Consequently, what I am claiming here about the unity of Christ's personal divine existence has no direct bearing upon the truth or falsehood of Diepen's interpretation.

65. *Comp. Theol.* I, c. 210.

adequately the human and divine natures of Christ, and his human and divine operations.

Notice, then, that being-in-act (*entelecheia*) is understood by Aristotle and Aquinas to be denoted analogically and to have similar but not identical modes of realization. We can be-in-act substantially, or accidentally-operationally.[66] Thus we are speaking of an *analogia entis* or analogical realization of created human being that is distinct from the question of an analogical knowledge of God based upon natural knowledge of creatures (natural theology). Neither Barth nor Schleiermacher, however, grasps adequately this analogical distinction, and so both think *univocally* about the being-in-act of operations (Jesus's consciousness of religious dependence, Christ's human obedience) as in some way equivalent with or susceptible to signifying formally the being in act of substantial being (the subsistent person of Christ in his unity of being with the Father). This is what leads each of them, in two very different ways, to seek to locate the divine-human union in Christ in the human actions of Jesus. In addition, then, Barth does not identify accurately what distinguishes the operations of the divine and human natures of Christ. Human operations become direct windows into the operation of the deity itself, as if the two were somehow equated.

I have suggested above that the underlying problem that has to be confronted is whether Chalcedonian Christology depends in part upon our acceptance of some form of classical ontology. If we turn the question around, we might also ask whether a robust form of Chalcedonian Christology has implicit recourse to analogical thinking about God in metaphysical terms. Consider, for example, the discourse concerning "existence" that the Chalcedonian speculations of Thomas Aquinas entail. They require that we can say that Christ, this existent man, is God, and that God exists as this man.[67] This notion of the existence of the Word made flesh is assuredly only accessible to us within the mystery of faith, and again, through the medium of the formal object revealed in scripture. Nevertheless, since it requires

66. Aristotle, *Metaphysics* IX, 6, 1048b6–9: "But all things are not said in the *same sense* to exist actually, but only by analogy—as *A* is in *B* or to *B*, *C* is in *D* or to *D*; for some are as movement to potentiality, and others as substance to some sort of matter." All translations of Aristotle in this book are taken from W. D. Ross in *The Complete Works of Aristotle*, 2 vols., ed. Jonathan Barnes (Princeton, N.J.: Princeton University Press, 1984).

67. Aquinas, ST III, q. 16, a. 9.

of us to speak of a relation between the existence of God the creator and that of his creation (for it is the *existent* creator who *exists* as man) such language also implies that the concept of the incarnation *is not itself wholly alien to our ordinary human way of knowing*. As knowledge it does not fall naturally within our ordinary scope of understanding, and it has to be revealed to us, in faith, and by scripture, but when this occurs, the truth is not something so extrinsic to our thought that it remains unintelligible. On the contrary, we can undertake a graced act of faith in an intellectually *intrinsic* way, in what we truly are as cognitive human beings. If this were not the case, we would be no more subject to receiving divine revelation than is a stone.

What this line of argument suggests is significant. From within the natural frontier of our ordinary human knowing, we are in the possession of a *way of thinking about existence* that is intrinsically open to God, and open even to the possibility of speaking about God *existing* as one of us that does not fail to acknowledge at the same time that *God's existence* as the creator of the world cannot be univocally identified with our mode of existence, *even when God the creator exists as human*. There is an analogy of being that is implicitly present within Christology, *pace* Kant, Schleiermacher, and Barth. The recognition of the presence of God's transcendence in Christ, even in the midst of his immanence as one of us, requires, then, that we as creatures are naturally open to reflection about the metaphysical transcendence of God and can relate to his existence through conceptual thinking that is analogical. This form of Christological thinking does not reduce our understanding of God to that of the world. The goodness of Christ as God is not identical with his goodness as man. His obedience as man is not identical with his divine willing as God. Such analogical thinking avoids the reduction of the deity of Christ to the naturalistic forms of this world. All of this suggests that if human beings *can* believe in the incarnation (by grace), then they are also capable of natural, analogical thinking about the transcendent God. That is to say, Christology makes implicit use of natural theology.[68] If we believe in the incarnation, we need to be committed to the retrieval of some form of classical metaphysics.

---

68. I take up this argument in greater detail in chapter 4 below.

What should we say, then, about "secondary actuality"? Of what value are the operative actions of Christ as a revelation of the Son of God, and as a revelation to us of what it means to be authentically human? Here I wish to shift the point of emphasis from Barth to Schleiermacher. I have argued above that Barth wishes to recover a robust Chalcedonian ontology in modernity but that he fails to identify sufficiently the locus of divine human unity in Christ (in the subsistence of the Word made flesh). This is due in part to a mistaken rejection (or misuse) of the metaphysics of being. Schleiermacher, meanwhile, seeks to appeal to the human religiosity of Jesus as the model of our encounter with God, but substitutes this treatment of Christ for a Chalcedonian Christology. In a rightly ordered Christology, however, we should not be obliged to choose between an ontology of the hypostatic union and an anthropological theology that focuses upon the human actions of Christ.

To illustrate this claim, I will appeal to a soteriological point made by Jacques Maritain in his work *On the Grace and Humanity of Jesus*.[69] Maritain's book contains an analysis of Christ's knowledge, and specifically of Christ's beatific vision in his earthly life, that is to say, of his immediate, intuitive knowledge of his own identity, and of the Father and the Holy Spirit. As commentators on Aquinas such as Maritain have noted, according to Aquinas, the historical Jesus did not believe that he was God by faith, but knew who and what he was by a kind of higher immediate insight.[70] And he knew as well that he had come into this world to save us. This is a classical Thomistic doctrine (and the teaching of the ordinary magisterium of the Catholic church).[71] What Maritain points out in this respect is that there is a double referentiality or we might say "relativity" to the human knowledge of Christ, to his "secondary acts" of consciousness, as extraordinary as they are.[72] On the one hand, the actual consciousness of Christ by which he knows of his own identity as the Son is relative to the being of the Son, the primary actuality just discussed. That is to say, Christ

69. Jacques Maritain, *On the Grace and Humanity of Jesus* (New York: Herder and Herder, 1969).

70. ST III, q. 9, aa. 2–3.

71. See *Catechism of the Catholic Church*, paras. 472–74.

72. See Maritain, *On the Grace and Humanity of Jesus*, 14–27, 52–53, 62–67.

knows as man that he is one with the Father and he wishes to communicate knowledge of this unity to his disciples, in and through the
event of his passion and death (Jn 17:11). On the other hand, his consciousness reveals the final good of our human nature. Because we
are intellectual creatures, we are made to see God face to face by the
grace of the beatific vision, which alone can ultimately satisfy the human heart and its longing for ultimate truth and undiminished goodness (Jn 17:24).[73]

If we accept this twofold conception of the consciousness of Christ,
we can overcome some of the difficulties in modern theology inherited from Schleiermacher's thought. Against the liberal Protestant tendency, a Thomistic Christology of the consciousness of Christ cannot absolutize the consciousness of Jesus as the unique locus wherein
his unity with God is formed or measured. On the contrary, it sees the
self-awareness of Jesus as itself measured by and as a witness to the
deeper ontological ground of unity between Christ and the Father.
Barth is rightly concerned that any theology which places an emphasis
on the religious acts of Christ can entrap us within a reductive form of
anthropocentricism, or a generic "philosophy of religious ethics." However, a Thomist account of the consciousness of Christ as "secondary
action" avoids this danger and invites us to a theology of the human
person that is theocentric in the most Trinitarian of manners. For according to Aquinas, Christ as man is aware in a human way of his own
divine identity by virtue of the beatific vision. Consequently, he can reveal to us in his own human actions and teachings who God truly is.
Moreover, if the vision of the triune God alone will ultimately satisfy
and in fact redeem the human person, then Christ also reveals humanity to itself by possessing as man that immediate knowledge of God to
which we are called. He has come to us in human nature to reveal to us
the inner life of God the Trinity, and to call us to himself in the eventual vision of the divine essence, and in the direct unveiling of God to the
human mind.

If what I have argued above is the case, then Thomistic theolo-

---

73. This is why Aquinas will argue that it is necessary for Christ to have the beatific
vision: in order as man to be the Savior, and not one who is himself saved (ST III, q. 9, a.
2). I return to this argument in subsequent chapters.

gy invites us to overcome a problematic modern opposition between Christological ontology and the anthropological dimension of theology. Aquinas makes very clear in the questions on beatitude at the beginning of *Summa theologiae* I-II that we attain to complete happiness and thus become fully ourselves only through the vision of God, which is a form of knowledge that transcends all historical objects, and that we are naturally open to or capable of, but which we also cannot procure for ourselves.[74] This being-turned radically toward the Trinitarian God, into the vision of God, only occurs by the grace of God given in Christ. All things are centered, therefore, on Jesus, who is the way to the Father and who is himself the eternal Word who proceeds from the Father, and who with the Father spirates the Holy Spirit. We are called to know God in the eschaton, in ecstatic joy, by which the intellect is taken out of preoccupation with itself and into the unique contemplation of the Trinity. St. Thomas insists that in charity we love God for God's own sake, *only for the goodness of God's own self*, through a love and admiration of God that place him above every other good, even our own good of eternal happiness.[75] There is no rivalry, then, between a theology of the human person and a theocentric theology. Under grace, the redeemed human person can become conscious of his or her dependence upon God for salvation, but this is a salvation that comes through knowledge of the very being and life of the Word incarnate who has dwelt among us, God himself living among us as a human being.

CONCLUSION

What has this prolegomenon sought to establish? We began by considering a juxtaposition of two modern theologians, Schleiermacher and Barth. I have argued that despite their differences, they share in a common set of predicaments, as their ingenious theologies fail to answer adequately certain essential questions. Can the Council of Chalcedon be harmonized with a well-employed use of modern biblical studies regarding Jesus of Nazareth? Can the ontology of the incarnation

74. ST I-II, q. 5, aa. 1 and 5.
75. See ST I-II, q. 3, a. 1; II-II, q. 27, a. 3.

be understood rightly without recourse to core elements of the "pre-Kantian" metaphysical tradition? I have suggested that there are problems with the respective answers of Schleiermacher and Barth to these two central questions. One places the accent upon modern historical studies of Jesus and a post-Kantian philosophical anthropology. The other places the accent upon the biblical portrait of Christ and a uniquely theological ontology. As such, neither resolves sufficiently the question of how we might reconcile the biblical portrait of Christ and modern historical studies of Jesus. Nor do they provide us with an adequate understanding of the relationship between Chalcedonian ontology and a realistic philosophical metaphysics that acknowledges our capacity for analogical discourse concerning the transcendent God.

One condition for a coherent modern Christology is that it promote a Chalcedonian theology that is based fundamentally in the revelation of the scriptures and the dogmatic tradition, but which also makes judicious use of modern historical-critical approaches to the figure of Jesus. Another condition is that modern theology challenge the Kantian prohibition on speculative knowledge of God. Any sufficiently profound exploration of the person of Christ—of God existing among us in history—must make use of our human capacity to speak of the divine attributes of God. This metaphysical accent in theology is also necessary so that we might rightly identify in what way Christ is (and is not) to be understood as a model of human perfection in his human operations of knowledge and love, or, to use the modern terminology, in his "religious consciousness" of God.

A modern Thomistic theology, then, needs to be attentive to both the personal being of Christ and his operations or activities. Who is Christ as a person? What is the hypostatic union, and how are we to understand the fact that the Word subsists in a human nature? These are questions I take up in chapters 1 and 2 below. In light of the mystery of the incarnation, I then consider the relationship between this mystery and the analogy of being in chapters 3 and 4. Subsequently, I proceed to a reflection on the human operations of Christ's knowledge and voluntary action in chapter 5. These considerations serve as a foundation for the study of the second half of the book, in which the salvific action of Christ is considered in his life, death, and resurrection. It is to the theology of the hypostatic union, then, that we now should turn.

Part One

The Mystery of the Incarnation

1

The Ontology of the Hypostatic Union

The first part of this book is concerned with the mystery of the incarnation. What does it mean, from a Thomistic point of view, to hold that God the Word, the second person of the Trinity, became man and lived a true, human life in a historical place and time? To ask this question is to touch upon a significant theological topic: the ontology of the hypostatic union. What is the union of God and man that takes place *in the very person* of the Word? What does it mean to say that God the Word subsists personally as a human being?

In asking the question this way, we are of course presupposing that Jesus of Nazareth is God made man. And historically (both in antiquity and modernity) this is easily the most contested of Christian beliefs. However, the presupposition of its truth is basic to the science of theology. This is only reasonable, because the affirmation of the incarnation is not the subject of rational demonstration or of disproof. This is the case because the reality of the incarnation is a truth of divine revelation, and not a truth of natural human reason. By this very fact, it is the kind of truth that utterly transcends the mere capacity of human reason to ascertain by its own powers. It is, we might say, a truth that is given to human reason to explore and understand, but not one that can be procured by the human intellect operating from within the speculative horizon of its own native first principles and final conclusions. It does not contradict those principles and conclusions, and it is a truth complementary with all that the human intellect can discover naturally. It is even a truth that the human intellect is naturally capable of receiving, presuming the initiative of grace, and which is congruent in many ways with the observations and insights of natural human reason. But it is, when all is said and done, a truth known only by way of divine revelation. Why, then, speak in the first place about the mystery of the incarnation, if it is such a given?

The reason is that the credibility of the incarnation—literally, the fact of its being subject to intelligibility and notional assent—is bound up with a theological analysis of the contours or content of the mystery. No one can demonstrate the existence of the mystery, but how might one *rightly affirm theologically* the character of the mystery? And here it is to be noted that the incarnation is a subject fraught with potential difficulties and divisions among Christians down through the ages. For it is one thing to hold that God became a man, and quite another to maintain a normative doctrine and sound theological theory of how this is the case (or how it is not).

In the prolegomenon to this book I implicitly raised a stark question. Is it possible that the primary models for human comprehension of the incarnation in Protestant modernity have failed in some basic way to grapple with the essence of the mystery? Are we led onto stray paths, or off into false visions, by aspects of the thinking of Schleiermacher and Barth? To ask this question is to suggest the possibility that well-known tendencies of thought in modern theology might be very influential, but simultaneously ultimately ill-equipped to grapple with the heritage of the church's Christological reflection on Jesus. But what if this is the case not only in various strands of modern Protestantism, but also within influential strands of modern Roman Catholic thought? What if Catholic theology has gone in directions similar to those explored above, and with greater consequences of its own kind? The argument of this opening chapter is that there exists at work in modern Catholic theology a subtle but real obscuration of the deeper mystery of the hypostatic union. This theology merits consideration from the start of our inquiries, precisely so that we might begin by trying to achieve a balanced understanding of the mystery of the incarnation. We can rightly begin the consideration of Jesus, therefore, with a reflection on the hypostatic union. What does it mean to say that the person of the Son is a divine person, who took upon himself a human nature within the horizon of human history?

ESTABLISHING THE QUESTION: THE HYPOSTATIC UNION AND MODERN "NESTORIANISM"

To speak about the theology of the hypostatic union as I have done above presupposes that there is such a thing as Christian truth. If this is the case, however, then there is also such a thing as error in Christian doctrine, and by that same standard, there must also be such a thing as heterodoxy, or heresy. The notion of a heterodox teaching, however, is quite complex. Ideas such as "Arianism" or "Nestorianism" are intellectual tropes that had their genesis in a particular historical context. They were employed by critics to characterize actual positions (those of Arius or Eunomius, Nestorius or Theodore of Mopsuestia), but they may have characterized such positions accurately or imperfectly. Aloys Grillmeier famously argued, for instance, that Nestorius's own Christology was compatible with that of the Council of Chalcedon, despite what his critics said (though this is perhaps too generous an assessment).[1] Whatever one makes of such claims, however, and independently of initial context, types of heresies (such as Nestorianism) were subsequently employed to examine later, novel positions that emerged, in order to consider their organic continuity with the Catholic faith, or lack thereof. Consider the Christology of the Tome of Leo: in the fifth-century Byzantine empire it was considered "Nestorian" by Severus of Antioch and others. The document was subsequently defended and vindicated at the Third Council of Constantinople in 680–81. Analogously, Aquinas in his own day took a prominent theory of the hypostatic union to be heretical and laced with Nestorianism (the first of three "common

1. Aloys Grillmeier, *Christ in Christian Tradition Volume One: From the Apostolic Age to Chalcedon (451)*, 2nd ed., trans. J. Bowden (Atlanta: John Knox Press, 1975), 447–63, 501–19, 559–68.

opinions" presented by Peter Lombard in the *Sentences*). His opinion
of that doctrine remains disputed. Meanwhile, in the 1940s, the Bene-
dictine Thomist Herman Diepen accused theologians like Déodat de
Basly and Léon Seiller of promoting implicitly Nestorian conceptions
of the incarnation.[2] His critical view was vindicated by Pope Pius XII
in 1951 in the encyclical *Sempiternus Rex*. The point is this: "Nestorianism" as a doctrinal idea is inherently complex. Most importantly, it
has a theoretical content that subsists independently of the original
ideas of Nestorius and is employed by the church for the purpose of
her own doctrinal self-definition. In its progressive use, however, the
term is employed in analogical and novel ways, and such usage, while
licit, is also often controversial. Such controversies can sometimes be
misguided, but they can also facilitate progressive doctrinal clarification. It is not necessarily simplistic or counter-productive, then, to ask
whether such an appellation rightly applies to a given theology.

The argument I will develop below is that there exists a tendency in modern Christology that is of a decidedly Nestorian character,
and that this tendency derives from the mature Christological thinking of Karl Rahner. I do not mean by this, as will be seen below, that
Rahner is simply Nestorian in the most unambiguous sense of the
word (positing two subjects in Christ). I also do not mean by this that
he denies the creedal definitions of Chalcedon. That would be ridicu-
lous, since Rahner is quite explicit about his intention to teach that the
Word of God, consubstantial with the Father, became human for our
sake. What I am claiming is that Rahner locates the ontological union
of God and man in Christ in the same place where Nestorianism typically locates it: uniquely in the spiritual operations of the man Jesus,
particularly as they are conformed by divine indwelling to the mystery
of God in himself. Just in this way, then, he makes the basis for the hy-

2. In 1950, Herman Diepen analyzed the significance of this teaching in Aquinas
with regard to emergent problems in modern Roman Catholic consciousness theories
of Christology, theories that were not wholly dissimilar from that of Schleiermacher.
See his "La critique du baslisme selon saint Thomas d'Aquin," *Revue Thomiste* 50 (1950):
82–118 and 290–329, and "La psychologie humaine du Christ selon saint Thomas
d'Aquin," *Revue Thomiste* 50 (1950): 515–62. This controversy has been studied in depth
by Philippe-Marie Margelidon, *Les Christologies de l'*Assumptus Homo *et Les Christologies du Verbe Incarné au XXe Siècle. Les enjeux d'un débat christologique (1927–1960)*, Bibliothèque de la Revue Thomiste (Paris: Parole et Silence, 2011).

postatic union a union of "mere" moral cooperation between the man Jesus Christ and God (something found analogously in saints or in human persons made holy by grace). In fact, it can be shown that this is precisely what Rahner intends to argue, as he repeats the idea explicitly at various points. In spite of Rahner's affirmations to the contrary, however, such a theory is unable to yield adequate recognition of the most fundamental truth of the incarnation: that the person of the Word assumed a human nature such that the Word subsists hypostatically as man. On Rahner's model, the "grace of union" has been in effect reduced solely to a union of "habitual grace."

Rahner has reasons for his theoretical decision: he is worried about an overly mythological concept of the pre-existence of the Word that is metaphysically inaccessible to the modern human being. He wishes to show, therefore, how God is made manifest in the personal religious history of Jesus of Nazareth as a being in whom total transparency to the transcendent mystery of God is present. Consequently he focuses upon the habitual acts of Christ as expressive of his being-in-relation to God. However, one can rightly affirm the foundational importance of the grace of union (as Aquinas does), and respond to Rahner's worries about classical accounts of the incarnation without succumbing to the mythological form of thinking he fears.

To make sense of what is at stake Christologically in this dispute, I will begin by considering Thomas Aquinas's analysis of what "Nestorianism" consists in, particularly as he contrasts this with a scriptural understanding of the ontology of the incarnation. Second, I will present certain key views of Rahner in summary fashion. To underscore their contemporary theological and ecumenical relevance, I will also note how they resemble views found in the Christologies of Friedrich Schleiermacher and John Hick, as well as those of Jacques Dupuis and Jon Sobrino. Finally, I will return to core ideas about the incarnation of the Word as elaborated by Aquinas in order to suggest ways in which his understanding of the ontology of the incarnation is of permanent value. In particular, how does it allow us to respond to several of Rahner's modern concerns about the historical realism of the incarnation without forfeiting scriptural, ontological realism regarding the personal uniqueness of Jesus Christ as the Son and Word of God?

AQUINAS ON "NESTORIANISM"

Thomas Aquinas was born in 1225 and died in 1274. In the middle of his teaching career—between 1261 and 1265—he spent time in Orvieto, Italy, where he had access to the papal archives.[3] It is thought that during this time Aquinas carefully read (in Latin) the Councils of Ephesus and Chalcedon, as well as Constantinople II and III. As a result he became sensitive to the importance of Cyril's single-subject Christology in a way few of his medieval Latin theological contemporaries were, and he developed a more focused analysis and critique of Nestorianism as a form of heterodoxy.[4] This development is reflected in the works of his mature period as a theologian, particularly in *Summa Contra Gentiles* IV, *Summa theologiae* III, the *Commentary on the Gospel of John*, and the *De Unione Verbi Incarnati*.

Aquinas on Nestorianism and
the Hypostatic Union

For our purposes, it is helpful to consider Aquinas's treatment of Nestorianism in two textual locations in particular: ST III, q. 2, a. 6, and *De Unione*, a. 1. We can do so in two stages. First, we might ask: how does Aquinas understand Chalcedonian Christology in differentiation from Nestorianism and Monophysitism? Relatedly: What does he take the form of union that Nestorianism posits to consist in? Second, how does this impact his interpretation of theories of the incarnation that were prevalent in his time?

We can begin with the first question. Aquinas claims that the teachings of the councils of Ephesus and Chalcedon advance an ontology of Christ that falls between two contrary extremes. In doing so, he follows a typology established by the Second Council of Constantinople.[5] On one extreme lies the teaching of Apollinarius and Eutyches.

3. Jean-Pierre Torrell, *Saint Thomas Aquinas, Vol. I, The Person and His Work*, trans. R. Royal (Washington, D.C.: The Catholic University of America Press, 2005), 117–41.

4. See Martin Morard, "Thomas d'Aquin lecteur des conciles," *Archivum Franciscanum Historicum* 98 (2005): 211–365, and "Une source de saint Thomas d'Aquin: le deuxième concile de Constantinople (553)," *Revue des Sciences Philosophiques et Théologiques* 81 (1997): 21–56.

5. ST III, q. 2, a. 6, corp. Aquinas cites Constantinople II, can. 4 and 5.

Each of these figures posited a union of God and man *in the nature of Christ* ("There is only one nature after the union").[6] Consequently, they did rightly uphold that the union in question is substantial, not accidental: Christ the God-man is one being and not two hypostatic subjects related merely by shared properties. Both theologians maintain the existence of a substantial unity in Christ, but at a high price, for they envisage it also as a union of essence or nature. Christ is not only one being or "thing," he is also one *kind* of thing. Consequently, according to these thinkers, in the incarnation the real distinction between the divine and human natures of Christ is seemingly dissolved.

At the other end of the spectrum there is the theory of Nestorius, in which the human nature and the divine nature of Christ are clearly identified as distinct. In this respect, Nestorius is clearly correct over against the Monophysites. However, it seems that he also affirms that each nature subsists in some real sense in a distinct hypostatic subject or *suppositum*. It would follow from this that there are two beings in Christ and in fact two personal subjects: the man Jesus and the eternal Word and Son. Such an understanding is implied by Nestorius's use of the communication of idioms. The Council of Ephesus affirmed that all attributes of Jesus are to be ascribed to the unique *suppositum* of the Word, whether those attributes be human or divine. It is the Lord who is born of the Virgin Mary and suffers death on the cross, and it is the Lord who heals the blind and raises the dead.[7] Human suffering and divine power are both proper to the Son of God. By contrast, for Nestorius, human characteristics are attributed to the man Christ (as a distinct subject, or in Aquinas's terminology, *suppositum*), while divine characteristics are attributed to the subject or *suppositum* of the Logos. Nestorius insisted that the Virgin Mary be called the mother of Christ, but not the mother of God, because she gave birth to the man Jesus Christ and not to the

6. This formula was employed by Eutyches as a way of interpreting Cyril's Christology. The formula originated (in slightly different language) with Apollinarius, and was falsely attributed to Athanasius by later generations. See J. N. D. Kelly, *Early Christian Doctrines*, 5th ed. (London: A. & C. Black, 1977), 293–94, 319, 330–34. See the criticisms of Eutyches's notion by Aquinas in ST III, q. 2, a. 1, corp. and ad 1.

7. See, for example, the famous fourth anathema of Cyril, from his *Third Letter to Nestorius*, which was reaffirmed by the Council of Chalcedon.

person of the Word. Why is it false or even impious, to Nestorius's mind, to say that God was born of a woman or that God suffered and died on the cross? The reason would seem to be that, like Apollinarius (against whom he is reacting), Nestorius presumes that a unity of hypostatic subsistence implies a unity of nature, and vice versa. If both human and divine properties are attributed to one person, then they must also be attributed to one nature. Consequently, he objects to such affirmations because they would imply not that the Son existed hypostatically in two natures, both human and divine, but that the Son existed in one nature only. But in this case, since the Logos has a nature subject to birth, suffering, and death, therefore the deity itself (the divine nature) is subject to these characteristics.[8] Such a conclusion is, of course, forcefully denied by Cyril and the subsequent conciliar tradition (that is, the Council of Chalcedon), which maintained the impassibility of the divine nature of the Incarnate Lord.[9]

What kind of union does Nestorianism posit, then, if it refuses a union in the nature of Christ *and* a union that is hypostatic (in which there is one subject of attribution)? Aquinas notes quite rightly that the only other option available is a union that is not substantial (of one personal entity or being) but "accidental" (of two entities sharing common properties). On this model, Christ is in fact two subsistent entities joined or united by a kind of operational union, a moral synergy. The union in question is based on habitual relations in Christ that are common to the human being that is assumed and the Word that is assuming:

The heresy of Nestorius and Theodore of Mopsuestia ... separated the persons. For they held the person of the Son of God to be distinct from the

8. Consider in this respect the arguments of Nestorius's *Second Letter to Cyril* in Norris, *The Christological Controversy*, esp. 139. See the helpful analysis of Nestorius's theological concerns by Paul L. Gavrilyuk, *The Suffering of the Impassible God: The Dialectics of Patristic Thought* (Oxford: Oxford University Press, 2004), 135–51.

9. To take just one example from Cyril: "God's Word is, of course, undoubtedly impassible in his own nature and nobody is so mad as to imagine the all-transcending nature capable of suffering; but by very reason of the fact that he has become man, making flesh from the Holy Virgin his own, we adhere to the principles of the divine plan and maintain that he who as God transcends suffering, suffered humanly in his flesh." *De symbolo* 24, trans. L. Wickham, *Cyril of Alexandria: Select Letters* (Oxford: Clarendon Press, 1983), 123.

person of the Son of Man, and said these were mutually united: first, "by indwelling," inasmuch as the Word of God dwelt in the man, as in a temple; secondly, "by unity of intention," inasmuch as the will of the man was always in agreement with the will of the Word of God; thirdly, "by operation," inasmuch as they said the man was the instrument of the Word of God; fourthly, "by greatness of honor," inasmuch as all honor shown to the Son of God was equally shown to the Son of Man, on account of His union with the Son of God; fifthly, "by equivocation," i.e. communication of names, inasmuch as we say that this man is God and the Son of God. Now it is plain that these modes imply an accidental union.[10]

Aquinas here gives five examples of ways that accidental union might be established: by mutual indwelling, shared intentions, coordinated operations, participation of one in the honor of the other, and verbal equivocations. All of these trace back in some way to the moral unity of wills: Christ as man thinks and acts in coordination with the wisdom and will of the Word of God. The union is accidental to each hypostasis or subject because it characterizes or qualifies that subject but is distinct from the subject itself. Does this theory explain why Christians adore or worship the man Jesus? According to Nestorius, the man Jesus partakes of the honor and dignity of the Word, and just for that reason he can be adored.[11] The dignity and honor of the Word are attributed to the man Jesus, however, as accidents or properties that qualify him as a human subject. They are not attributed to him as the very person of the Word. Likewise, the Word himself cannot be said to suffer or die.[12]

---

10. ST III, q. 2, a. 6.

11. "I revere the one who is borne because of the one who carries him, and I worship the one I see because of the one who is hidden. God is undivided from the one who appears, and therefore I do not divide the honor of that which is not divided. I divide the natures, but I unite the worship" (Nestorius, *First Sermon against the Theotokos* [Norris, 130]). On Nestorius's doctrine of the worship of Christ, and the criticisms lodged against it by Cyril, see Henry Chadwick, "Eucharist and Christology in the Nestorian Controversy," *Journal of Theological Studies* 2 (1951): 145–64.

12. "To attribute to him, in the name of this association, the characteristics of the flesh that has been conjoined to him—I mean birth and suffering and death—is, my brother, either the work of a mind which truly errs in the fashion of the Greeks or that of a mind diseased with the insane heresy of Arius and Apollinarius and the others" (Nestorius, *Second Letter to Cyril* [Norris, 139]). In ST III, q. 2, a. 6, corp., Aquinas cites the fourth canon of Constantinople II which characterizes such statements as heretical.

In fact the two positions being considered (Monophysitism and Nestorianism) differ by extremes but share a common premise. The premise is that a hypostatic union presupposes a union of natures. If Christ is one concrete subject and being, then he must be one in nature. But this means one must choose between two extremes. Either there is a substantial union and one nature in Christ or there is an accidental union of two subjects and a distinction of natures in Christ. Aquinas shows, then, that the true position lies between the extremes. With the first position and against the second, Christ is one subject and person and so one must affirm in Christ a substantial union of God and man. The Word incarnate is one entity. With the second position and against the first, however, Christ is truly God and truly man. Thus the two natures remain distinct, without mixture or confusion, and the union must not occur *in the nature* of Christ. In short, even though the union is substantial, it is not a union in the nature. Even though there is a distinction of natures, there is not a distinction of persons or *supposita*. Positively speaking, this substantial, non-natural union is *hypostatic*. It is a union in the person. In the Word made flesh there is one concrete, individual person and hypostasis subsisting in two natures.

It is impossible that a nature perfect in itself might receive the addition of another nature; or rather, if it did receive it, it would no longer be the same nature, but another. But the divine nature is sovereignly perfect; likewise, human nature also possesses the perfection of its species. It is impossible, then, that one would be united to the other in a natural union .... And in that case Christ would be neither man nor God, which is unacceptable. It remains, then, that the human nature be united to the Word, not accidentally, nor essentially, but substantially [*neque accidentaliter neque essentialiter, sed substantialiter*], that is to say, hypostatically and personally, insofar as the substance signifies the hypostasis.[13]

Does such a concept defy our ordinary capacity for understanding? Does it have any intelligibility? Aquinas gives two ways of thinking about this union based on analogies from creatures. One is from the distinction one finds in human beings between the nature and the

---

13. *De Unione*, a. 1, corp. The Latin text can be found in *Question Disputée L'Union Du Verbe Incarné*, ed. M.-H. Deloffre (Paris: Vrin, 2000); translations from this text into English are my own.

person. True, a person is an individual of a rational nature. Our human nature thus enters into the definition of human personhood. But no one can equate his or her unique personhood with the essence of human nature as such, as if to say, "Socrates is human nature as such." And, likewise, human nature subsists in each human person in a unique mode. Peter, for example, is a distinct individual as compared to Paul, and while human nature is common to each of them (one is not less a human being than the other) there is a difference in the way or mode in which human nature subsists in Peter as distinct from Paul. Similarly, Christ is a particular individual man, alongside Peter and Paul. Unlike them, he is a human individual who is God.

Likewise, there is an analogy, Aquinas argues, from the body-soul composite, as Athanasius himself pointed out. The soul is the form of the body while the Word is surely *not* the form of the body. The hypostasis of the Word does *not* replace the human soul of Christ, contrary to the views of Apollinarius. However, just as in man the body is the instrument of the soul, so in the incarnate Word the human nature of Jesus is the instrument of the Word. In both cases, the instrumentality is *intrinsic* to the agent, not extrinsic. And it is substantial, not accidental. That is to say, while the hammer is not united to the very being and substance of the carpenter, the body is united to the soul such that they are substantially one being. Likewise, the humanity of Jesus is united to the Word as an intrinsic, "conjoined instrument." The being of the man Jesus is the being of the Word.

All this being said, Christ is not a human person subsisting alongside Peter and Paul like other human persons, nor is his human nature a conjoined instrument exactly like the human body is an "instrument" of the soul. Rather, in Christ there is no autonomous human personhood or human personality. He is the person of the Son and Word made human, subsisting in a human nature. This hypostatic union then pertains to personal subsistence, but it is the personal subsistence not of a human person, but of God made man and of the person of the Son existing in human nature. He is particularly distinct, then, from other persons, because he is a divine person. Likewise, the conjoined instrument in this case is not a human body but the human body *and soul* of Christ. This body-soul composite is united to the person of the Son hypostatically. The Son of God therefore acts in and through the instrumentality of his human nature. He does so through his human rational deliberation and human choice-making, in true human spontaneity and historicity.

While the hypostatic union is not unintelligible, then, it is also not an instance of something we find elsewhere in nature. Furthermore, it is a mystery without pure analogy in the order of sanctifying grace. For Christ cannot be understood adequately even by comparison with saints or holy persons who possess by grace a most perfect degree of human union with God. Such union is real: sanctifying grace does permit moral cooperation with God and the indwelling presence of God in the soul of the human person. It does not, however, constitute a substantial or hypostatic union, as if by grace a human being might "become" a subsistent divine person. Consequently, there is no perfect analogy either in the order of nature or in the order of grace for the hypostatic union. It is something accomplished by the infinite power of God, who can do something new that does not occur elsewhere in creation.

All of the [comparisons] of this kind are deficient, for the union of an instrument [to a person] is accidental. But this is a singular sort of union, superior to all other modes of union that we know. In effect, just as God is goodness itself, and his own existence, so also he is unity by essence. Consequently, just as his power is not limited to those modes of goodness and being that are found in creatures, but can make new modes of goodness and being unknown to us, so also, by the infinity of his power, he can make a new mode of union: such that the human nature be united to the Word personally, not accidentally, even while we do not find an adequate example in creatures.[14]

Aquinas on the Grace of Union and Habitual Grace

St. Thomas is not interested in the ontology of Nestorianism merely so as to avoid intellectual problems of the early Christian period. Medieval lecturers in theology were regularly asked to comment on a passage of Peter Lombard's *Sentences* in which three different ontological explanations of the hypostatic union were presented.[15] These are typically called, in turn, the *homo assumptus* theory, the subsis-

14. *De Unione*, q. 1, corp.
15. Peter Lombard, *Sentences* III, d. 6, c. 2.

tence theory, and the *habitus* theory. In the mature phase of his career, Aquinas became convinced that two of these (the first and the
third) were inherently doctrinally problematic, to such a degree that
they could both be classified as Nestorian and heterodox. Consider, then, the third opinion given in the *Sentences* (the so-called *habitus* theory). Thirteenth-century authors generally took this theory
to be problematic. This opinion held in effect that the humanity of
Christ could not be "something" (*aliud*) substantial as distinct from
the Word. In that respect the theory seemed to wish to avoid Nestorianism: the humanity is not a substantial thing alongside and different
from the Word. To underscore this idea, however, the theory in fact
denied that the body and soul of Christ were united in substantial
unity, as they are in human beings generally. Rather, both the body
and the soul are said to accrue to the person of the Word "accidentally" as qualities or properties of the Word, but without subsistence in
the Word. Also, then, they are not united substantially to one another, but are rather related to one another accidentally. Aquinas notes
that this doctrine wishes to safeguard the unity of person in Christ,
against Nestorius, but that it is implicitly Nestorian in that it does so
by positing merely an accidental union between the Word, the human body, and the soul. A plethora of distinct beings emerges. This is,
in its own way, even worse than Nestorianism classically conceived,
because it does not even acknowledge that the humanity of Christ (as
body and soul united) is one in being.[16]

The position just outlined was not commonly proposed at the
time of Aquinas because it (or some version of it) had been condemned by Pope Alexander III in 1177.[17] Specifically, the Pope condemned the idea that the humanity of Christ *cannot* be called *aliquid*
or "something," and so consequently the theory is typically labeled
"Christological nihilism" because it seems to deny this premise.[18] In
his commentary on the *Sentences* Aquinas takes Alexander's teaching

16. ST III, q. 2, a. 6, corp.
17. In the letter "Cum Christus," in Henry Denzinger, *Enchiridion Symbolorum*, 36th
ed. (Freiburg im Breisgau: Herder, 1965), 393/750.
18. See the study by Marcia L. Colish, "Christological Nihilianism in the Second
Half of the Twelfth Century," *Recherches de Théologie et Philosophie Médiévales* 63 (1996):
146–55.

to mean that the humanity of Christ is something substantial (*aliquid*) as a unity of body and soul in the Word but that this substantial human nature is not a human person (*aliquis*).[19] Christ is "someone" divine and as a human being, he is "something" human.

The first opinion in the *Sentences*, meanwhile, was held more commonly, even in Aquinas's own time. This view was developed in reaction to the one just noted. If the humanity of Christ is something real and substantial, then it has to have its own concrete reality distinct from that of the Word. Therefore, we may speak of the Word assuming the humanity of Jesus and of the man being assumed (*homo assumptus*). In this theory there is only one person (*persona*) in Christ, but we might speak of two hypostases or even two *supposita* in this one person just as there is a true humanity (*aliquid*) and a true divinity. How is the unity of person maintained, then? One argument advanced at the time was that "personal dignity" is a quality that is communicated from the person of the Word to the human nature that it assumes.[20] The union is one of shared quality. The personal dignity of the Word made human is a common accident of both the humanity and divinity of Christ. Aquinas unsurprisingly sees this theory as tending toward Nestorianism because it inevitably posits not a substantial but a merely accidental unity of the Word and the humanity assumed.[21]

What we see, then, is that Aquinas is beginning to refine his concept of Nestorianism in the analysis of these later positions so as to apply it even to theories that seek explicitly to uphold a unity of person in Christ. The problem with such theories is that they share a common theme with classical Nestorian ideas. This is the theme of the merely accidental union of two subsistences or substances by means of a shared quality or set of habitual relations. The union is not

19. *III Sent.* d. 6, q. 2, a. 1; see also d. 6, q. 3, a. 1.

20. Aspects of this form of thinking occur in the Christology of Alexander of Hales. See the analysis of Walter H. Principe in *Alexander of Hales' Theology of the Hypostatic Union* (Toronto: Pontifical Institute of Medieval Studies, 1967), 98–99, 106–7, and in particular, 117–23.

21. ST III, q. 2, a. 6. See *Alexander of Hales' Theology of the Hypostatic Union*, 123. Principe shows how Alexander can consider the human nature of Christ to be a distinct hypostasis while not having a unique personhood, since the latter is a characteristic that the assumed humanity acquires from the divine hypostasis.

in the individual subsistent person of the Word strictly speaking, or otherwise said, the union is not hypostatic.

Positively, this critical turn in Aquinas's thinking is mirrored by a development in his understanding of the hypostatic union as a mystery of grace. What is the grace that is proper to the humanity of Christ insofar as it is the humanity of God the Word? How does his grace compare with that of other saints or holy persons? Here the first thing to note is that Aquinas makes a fundamental distinction between what he terms the "grace of union" and the "habitual grace" that is proper to Jesus as man.[22] The grace of union is that grace (or "gift") bestowed upon the human nature of Christ by virtue of the incarnation, such that it is the human nature of the Son of God. "For the grace of union is the personal being that is given *gratis* from above to the human nature in the person of the Word, and is the term of the assumption."[23] St. Thomas underscores that this grace is infinite because the human nature of the Lord is united to the person of the Word hypostatically, and that person is infinite.[24]

Habitual grace, meanwhile, is that gift which pertains to all the saints insofar as they receive sanctifying grace from God. As such it is something created and finite which elevates the spiritual creature to share truly but imperfectly in the life of God.[25] This occurs chiefly through operations of the soul, in which the spiritual powers of the soul (the intellect and the will) are united to God by knowledge and by love.[26] Because the process of spiritual operations in the human person occurs habitually (by operations that move from capacity to activity), the grace that enlivens these faculties is called "habitual." Under grace, the saints are given the capacity to move themselves freely to know and love God. Without grace given perpetually to inspire and sustain them in this, such acts are impossible.

Does such habitual grace exist in the soul of Christ? Aquinas argues that it must, not least because scripture affirms that Christ is the source of all sanctifying grace in other human beings (Jn 1:16–17):

---

22. ST III, q. 2, a. 10; q. 6, a. 6; q. 7, a. 11.
23. ST III, q. 6, a. 6.
24. ST III, q. 7, a. 11.
25. ST I-II, q. 110, a. 4; q. 111, aa. 1 and 5.
26. ST III, q. 2, a. 10, corp. and ad 2.

"And of his fullness we have all received, and grace for grace. For ... grace and truth came through Jesus Christ."[27] In ST III, q. 7, a. 1, Aquinas offers multiple reasons why Christ must necessarily possess not only the grace of union, but also a plenitude of sanctifying grace. The first is due to the proximity of the human nature to the Word: because this human nature is intimately united to the Word, even hypostatically, it must receive the overflowing effects of grace that will sanctify it interiorly, even in its own spiritual actions of knowledge and love. Second, the saving mission of the Word transpires in and through his human nature and life among us. Consequently, the knowledge and love of Christ as man must be infused with the habitual graces of understanding and charity that allow him to accomplish his mission on behalf of others. Finally, we all come to partake of the grace of Christ, but if this is the case, then he must have an abundance of habitual grace from which all others can receive. In Jesus Christ, then, there is not only the grace of union, but also sanctifying or habitual grace, which is poured into his soul.

For our purposes, the subtleties arise when Aquinas examines the relation between these two forms of grace. What is the order between them? Is the grace of union the foundation for habitual grace, or is the habitual grace something given to the humanity of Jesus by way of disposition in view of the grace of union? The background to this question is, unsurprisingly, related to the first opinion regarding the incarnation in Peter Lombard's *Sentences*. For example, Aquinas's near contemporary, Alexander of Hales, had endorsed a qualified version of the first opinion regarding the incarnation: the humanity of Christ is that of a "man assumed" (*homo assumptus*), substantial in itself and conjoined to the Word by way of a shared quality, that of personal dignity. Likewise, Alexander seems to have held that habitual grace is given to the human nature of Christ as a necessary precondition or disposition in view of the hypostatic union.[28] One can

27. ST III, q. 7, a. 1. See also q. 2, a. 11; q. 6, a. 6.

28. *Glossa Alex* III, 7, 27 (L), in *Magistri Alexandri de Hales Glossa in Quatuor Libros Sententiarum Petri Lombardi*, ed. PP. Collegii S. Bonaventurae, 4 vols. (Florence: Quaracchi, 1960). See Principe, *Alexander of Hales' Theology of the Hypostatic Union*, 163–65, 171–73. Philip the Chancellor holds this view even more overtly; see *De Incarn.* 2, 19, and Walter H. Principe, *Philip the Chancellor's Theology of the Hypostatic Union* (Toronto: Pontifical Institute of Medieval Studies, 1975), 116–17.

see here at least a faint analogy with classical Nestorianism: the human nature of Christ receives grace such that it might operate in con-
junction with the Word, and this operation is of such an intensity that
there is a set of common properties shared by the Word and the human nature. Nevertheless, on such a model, the difference between
Christ's union and our own appears merely to be one of degree, rather than of kind.

In his mature work, Aquinas sees this difficulty and proposes a
very different theory, one meant to underscore that the hypostatic union is the foundation for the sanctity of Christ, and not the inverse. In SCG IV, Aquinas claims boldly that human nature is susceptible to being assumed ontologically into the hypostatic union not
through the medium of sanctifying grace, but *naturally*, just because
of the spiritual character of the human being. "Although the Word of
God by His power penetrates all things, conserving all that is, and
supporting all, it is to the intellectual creatures who can properly enjoy the Word and share with him, that from a kind of likeness He can
be both more eminently and more ineffably united."[29] It follows from
this that God can unite a human nature to himself hypostatically *immediately* and not through the medium of created grace. More to the
point, this is the only way he can do so, because habitual grace is only
a property of a human soul (however crucial that property may be!).
The grace of union, meanwhile, pertains to the whole substance of
the human nature of Christ, insofar as it is united to the Word hypostatically. There is only one concrete being in Christ, the person
of the Word subsisting as man. Only this form of thinking allows us
to take seriously that the Word was united to human nature directly,
not only in the spiritual operations of the soul, but also in the flesh:
"Habitual grace is only in the soul; but the grace ... of being united
to the divine person belongs to the whole human nature, which is
composed of soul and body. And hence it is said that the fullness of
the Godhead dwelt corporeally in Christ because the divine nature is
united not merely to the soul, but to the body also."[30]

Consequently, we see that the ontological order proposed by Alexander must be inverted in order to safeguard the realism of the in-

29. SCG IV, c. 41, para. 13.
30. ST III, q. 2, a. 10, ad 2.

carnation. It is not the case that an intensive degree of habitual grace prepares the humanity of Christ adequately for its union with the Word. Rather, habitual grace flows forth from the hypostatic union as a result of that union, and not as its precondition. Aquinas, in effect, is refining yet again the analysis of "Nestorianism" analogically conceived, considering a subtle form of the error present in his own time. This variant is present in any theory that posits the basis for the hypostatic union of God and man in Christ in the habitual grace Christ possesses as man. That grace is itself accidental, and so necessarily any union grounded in that grace is itself accidental. It must follow, then, that a certain kind of hypostatic dualism is implicit in such thinking, even if this is unintended.

Our union with God is by operation, inasmuch as we know and love Him; and hence this union is by habitual grace, in as much as a perfect operation proceeds from a habit. [But] the union of the human nature with the Word of God is in personal being, which depends not on any habit but on the nature itself.... The soul is the substantial perfection of the body; grace is but an accidental perfection of the soul. Hence grace cannot ordain the soul to personal union, which is not accidental.[31]

What we see at the conclusion of our consideration of Aquinas, then, is that he approaches "Nestorianism" from various angles, but basically characterizes it in two distinct, interrelated ways. In its more overt form, Nestorianism is an error that arises whenever one treats Christ as two distinct entities or subjects. Certain attributes are predicated of God (the Word) and others of a human being, but these attributes are not all predicated of one subject, the incarnate Word. There are, then, two subjects in Christ that are united accidentally by a kind of moral union or cooperation. Against this, one must posit a theology of the hypostatic union.

In addition, however, a more subtle form of Nestorianism arises when one attempts to articulate a theory of the hypostatic union by appeal to merely operational modes of union—for example, by appeal to the work of habitual grace alone. Here one might have *the intention* to affirm a single personal subject in Christ. However, just because operational actions under grace are "merely" properties of a

31. ST III, q. 6, a. 6, ad 1 and ad 2 (emphasis added).

given subject and not the substantial entity per se, such theories are necessarily inadequate. They end up positing the unity of one entity (the human being Jesus) with another entity (God) through the medium of sanctifying grace. This implies in effect that there are two substances or entities present. Thus the more "subtle" form of Nestorianism that Aquinas perceived in some of his contemporaries cannot really evade its intrinsic ties to the more overt form of Nestorianism, as he himself pointed out. On the contrary, it perpetuates an ontology that lays the groundwork for the return of the more overt kind. As we shall see shortly, a very similar pattern of thinking to the one Aquinas criticizes is found in the mature Christology of Karl Rahner, and this form of thinking has permitted the development in modern Catholic theology of a more overt form of Nestorian Christology.

KARL RAHNER ON THE
HYPOSTATIC UNION

Early Questions about the Traditional Account

Like Alexander of Hales, Karl Rahner affirms unambiguously the truth of the Catholic doctrine concerning Christ. In 1954 Rahner published a major essay on Christology, entitled, "Chalkedon—Ende oder Anfang?"[32] It was later republished in the first volume of the *Theological Investigations* under the English title, "Current Problems in Christology." In this early work he states unambiguously: "What faith really makes profession of is a substantial, lasting, indissoluble, hypostatic unity, the belonging of the two natures to one and the same Person as its very own in virtue of its being the selfsame."[33] Throughout his career, Rahner never changed his position, affirming perpetually the fundamental truth of Chalcedonian principles. In addition, in the early work of the aforementioned essay, he also insists that the hypostatic union can only be substantial and not accidental in form.[34] He favors the use of the term "hypostatic unity" (*hypostatische Einheit*)

32. Karl Rahner, "Chalkedon—Ende oder Anfang?," in *Das Konzil von Chalkedon. Geschichte und Gegenwart*, eds. A. Grillmeier and H. Bacht (Würzburg: Echter, 1954), 3:3–49.

33. Karl Rahner, "Current Problems in Christology," *Theological Investigations* I, trans. C. Ernst (Baltimore, Md.: Helicon Press, 1963), 175.

34. "Current Problems in Christology," 181, n. 1.

rather than the customary "hypostatic union" (*hypostatische Vereini-gung*). This linguistic decision emphasizes the unity of existence (*esse*) in Christ, thus favoring—in one respect at least—a Thomistic under-standing of the hypostatic union.

All this being said, one can find seeds of the later evolution of Rahner's thinking even in this first major Christological essay. For here already he expresses difficulties or criticisms directed at the the-ology of the hypostatic union of "the schools," by which he means, no doubt, the modern scholasticism of his epoch, but also, to some extent, classical scholasticism as well. We can note two criticisms in particular that are of special importance for Rahner, each of which serves as a stimulus to the development of his later opinions.

The first concerns the danger of what he calls "mythology" in classical scholastic thinking about the incarnation. When Rahner re-fers to mythology in scholastic Christology he is not denoting the idea of projections of anthropomorphic, narrative features upon the divine, as one finds in Greco-Roman religious myths of antiquity. Nor does Rahner mean to align himself with Rudolf Bultmann by in-dicating a supposed New Testament "mythology." For Bultmann the program of "demythologization" is based upon a Neo-Kantian philo-sophical objection: there are no physical, miraculous, or supernatural forms of divine intervention in history, or at any rate such events are unintelligible to us. Biblical claims regarding such events might sym-bolize inward events or existential stances. Therefore the deeper exis-tential significance of the New Testament can be identified through a modern reinterpretation of such supernatural features. Rahner is basically opposed to Bultmann's program, but also believes that the Lutheran theologian's position stems in part from reaction to exces-sively Monophysite readings of the Christian tradition. Such Mono-physitism exists in classical scholasticism, and it is this feature, in par-ticular, that he opposes, deeming it "mythological."

Mythology in this connection could be defined as follows: The representa-tion of a god's becoming man is mythological, when the 'human' element is merely the clothing, the livery, of which the god makes use in order to draw attention to his presence here with us, while it is not the case that the human element acquires its supreme initiative and control over its own actions by the very fact of being assumed by God. Looked at from this point of view a single basic conception runs through the Christian heresies from Apollinarianism to Monothelitism, sustained by the same basic mythical feeling.[35]

It is noteworthy that this criticism would apply well to the third opinion in Peter Lombard's *Sentences* ("*habitus* theory"), which compared the humanity of Christ to an element of clothing one wears habitually. But where Aquinas saw this opinion as Nestorian due to the accidental union that results, Rahner calls it Monophysite because of the denial of an integral human nature. Implicitly, he is rejoining the affirmation of Alexander III who affirmed that there is a real humanity in Christ that is "something" (*aliquid*).[36] However, Rahner also wishes to advance this criticism in a modern key, and in doing so he takes aim in particular even at traditional subsistence theories of the incarnation.

Basically, Rahner's chief concern is that Christology take seriously the human freedom and initiative of Christ, which are akin to that which one finds in other human beings as *created human persons*.[37] Two presuppositions are at work here. First, Rahner takes it as given that creaturely freedom serves as a basis for the development of human beings in their very identity as persons. Therefore, only if Christ has something of this kind is he able truly to be human as we are.[38] Second, this development of personal identity is historical, and so if Jesus is truly human, there must be some way to speak about the human development of his personality through time.[39] Classical scholastic presentations, meanwhile, are incapable of promoting such a dynamic, historical vision of the humanity of Christ. The reason is that they treat the humanity of Christ as the "instrument" of the divinity. In doing so they implicitly deny the reality of the human agency of Christ, its sufficient autonomy and historicity.[40] Instead, Christ's personhood is expressed in uniquely ahistorical terms due to the eternity of the Word. The "history" of Christ appears, then, more as an outward expression (in human nature) of what is always already true in the immutable person of the Word. This ahistorical metaphys-

---

35. Ibid., 156n1.
36. Rahner seems clearly to allude to the "*habitus* theory" and the teaching of Alexander III in ibid.

37. Ibid., 161.   38. Ibid., 162–63.
39. Ibid., 167.   40. Ibid., 155–57.

ical thinking is what Rahner in fact deems "mythology" because it makes the human history of Jesus seem unreal. If we take seriously this basic truth of the developmental human freedom of the person of Christ, what, then, are the implications for our theology of the hypostatic union?

A second criticism is related to the first one. It has to do with relational consciousness. Jesus of Nazareth, Rahner underscores, is depicted in the synoptic Gospels as a human being who stands before God as his Father, and who relates actively to God in his own human life and history. How then can we understand Christologically this relation between Jesus and God?[41] How might the human consciousness and historical choices of Jesus tell us something pertaining to the identity of Christ as God? Ontological theories of the hypostatic union do not allow us to acknowledge sufficiently Jesus's human actions of dependence and relationality toward God. But Catholic theology should be able to say, with Schleiermacher and others in the liberal Protestant tradition, "Jesus is the man whose life is one of absolutely unique self-surrender to God," if that phrase is properly understood.[42] How should we do this coherently, then, given our commitments to Chalcedonian Christological principles?

Development of New Answers

Rahner would seek to develop answers to the questions posed above in subsequent essays that appeared in the *Theological Investigations*.[43] A synthetic overview of this Christology (taken in large part from the essays) was eventually published in his 1976 work, *Foundations of Christian Faith*.[44] In these various locations, then, we find the mature

41. Ibid., 158–59, 171–72.
42. Ibid., 172.
43. See in particular, "On the Theology of the Incarnation," *Theological Investigations* IV, trans. K. Smith (London: Darton, Longman & Todd, 1966), 105–20. "Christianity within an Evolutionary View of the World," and "Dogmatic Reflections on the Knowledge and Self-Consciousness of Christ," *Theological Investigations* V, trans. K.-H. Kruger (London: Darton, Longman & Todd, 1966), 157–92 and 193–215, respectively.
44. *Foundations of Christian Faith: An Introduction to the Idea of Christianity*, trans. W. V. Dych (New York: Seabury, 1978), 176–321. The German original was *Grundkurs des Glaubens: Einführung in den Begriff des Christentums* (Freiburg im Breisgau: Herder, 1976).

Christology of Rahner. This Christology contains two key themes that
should be considered in turn. First, there is the notion that the hypostatic union is manifest to us through Christ's human consciousness
and freedom. Second, there is the notion that Christ's absolute creaturely relationality toward God *just is* the formal constituent of his filial identity.

The first of these themes emerges plainly in Rahner's essay from
1958, "On the Theology of the Incarnation."[45] Here Rahner begins
with the supposition that knowledge of the Word and knowledge of
the incarnation are in some way co-extensive for us. We know what
the Word is by looking at the historical humanity of Christ. It is here
that God most perfectly "speaks" his own immanent identity outside
of himself within the economy of his creation.[46] What, however, is
human nature, that God should become human? It is in the answer to
this question that the central idea of Rahner's Christology comes to
light, for Rahner will underscore that the nature of the human being
is mysterious precisely because man is inherently open (in the transcendental reaches of human spiritual freedom) to the incomprehensible, infinite mystery of being. This mystery is God himself. Thus the
human being can only be understood as an inchoate desire for or tendency toward the absolute mystery of God, to which man is capable
of surrendering himself fully, in conscious freedom.[47]

Two further claims unfold from this initial starting point. First,
Rahner examines the Thomistic notion that any feature of human
consciousness, including our moral orientation toward God, is an accidental property of the human person. He thinks that this idea taken
in itself is insufficient. Human self-orientation toward God must be
something more than a mere property of human nature, even one of a
privileged kind. Rahner notes here the argument of Thomism that he
knows full well: that the spiritual faculties of the human person (intellect and will) are properties of a rational person, but are not identical

45. The German original, "Zur Theologie der Menschwerdung," was published in
Catholica 12 (1958): 1–16, and subsequently in *Schriften zur Theologie* IV (Einsiedeln:
Benzinger, 1961), 137–55.

46. "On the Theology of the Incarnation," 106–7. See similar themes to those presented in this essay in Rahner's work *The Trinity*, trans. J. Donceel (London: Burns and
Oates, 1970), 21–33.

47. "On the Theology of the Incarnation," 109–10.

with the very essence or substance of the being of man as such. For if (for example) the human intellect were substantial, the body would not pertain to the substance of the human being. The body would be a property of the intellect! Furthermore, faculties of the person such as the will, the emotions, and so forth, would also be properties of the intellect. The truth, then, is that because the intellect is only one faculty among others, it cannot be the very substance or unique essence of the human being per se. To this Rahner responds, however, that the human act of self-surrender to God is in fact the perfect realization of the very act of being by which God sustains the creature in being. This is a striking claim, since it would suggest that the act by which we exist as such simply is the act of free self-realization. "This 'act' of self-surrender is of course primarily the 'act' of the Creator in making human nature .... The action [of self-surrender] is consequent upon the nature, in such a way that (unlike that of sub-spiritual beings) man is called in his action to confront his nature, cause it to 'come to' itself and realize itself."[48] The language here is admittedly ambiguous. Rahner might seem merely to be saying that our human, rational nature unfolds through free acts, which is undoubtedly true. Against this benign scholastic reading, however, Rahner insists that he is making an innovative claim. If that is the case, then what he clearly seems to be intimating is that the free, conscious decisions of a human being in history are the *essential content* of the human person. This does not mean that man is a self-creator: his being in freedom depends upon God. But it does mean that man's free acts are not mere properties of his rational nature but in some sense the very essence of his human nature. The free creature, then, can voluntarily accept his act of receiving being from God, and in turn surrender to God, or it can refuse this gift and fall into ontological oblivion.[49] This idea is not traditional, nor is it easy to defend metaphysically. It does take on more cogency, however, once we see where it is leading, as Rahner treats the specific instance of the unique freedom and religious consciousness of Christ.

The second basic idea, then, is that Christ himself fulfills in plenary fashion this universal human potency for free surrender to God,

48. Ibid., 109n1.
49. Ibid.

and it is precisely in doing so that *his* act of being human is an act of God being among us. "The incarnation of God is therefore the unique, *supreme*, case of the total actualization of human reality, which consists of the fact that man *is* in so far as he gives up himself."[50] Jesus of Nazareth, then, knows the Father in his human life, and is completely abandoned to his Father in his own *human* history as a man. As such he is the perfect exemplar of what it means to be human. At the same time, however, by this very way of being human unto God, he is also the presence of God's being among us.[51] It is in Christ's own historical surrender to the Father that we discover the self-communication of God to us in Christ.

> To grasp the proper nature of this particular [hypostatic] unity, it is not enough simply to say that ... the human reality must be attributed in all truth to the divine subject of the Logos. For this is precisely the question—*why* is this possible? ... This "assumption" and "unification" has the nature of a self-communication; there is "assumption" so that God's reality may be communicated to what is assumed, viz. the human nature (and in the first place the human nature of Christ). But this very communication which is aimed at by this "assumption" is *the* communication by what we call grace and glory—and the latter are intended for all.... Hence, if we may put it this way, the Hypostatic Union does not differ from our grace by what is pledged in it, for this is grace in both cases (even in the case of Jesus). But it differs from our grace by the fact that Jesus is our pledge, and we ourselves are not the pledge but the recipients of God's pledge to us.[52]

Of course what seems to be implicit in such a statement is the idea that the hypostatic union consists formally, in some sense, in the "habitual graces" of knowledge and love that are given to the human nature of Christ. The "grace of union" (to use the classical terminology) flows forth from the habitual, sanctifying grace of Christ. What then makes Jesus unique as the God-man? He is a distinct, highest instance of the realization of man's union with God. In him as precursor, there is the first instantiation of that which God wishes to accomplish in the rest of the human race.

---

50. Ibid., 110.
51. Ibid., 111.
52. "Christianity within an Evolutionary View of the World," 182–83.

The theologian who puts the question in this way can first of all take note of the fact that the Hypostatic Union takes effect interiorly *for* the human nature of the Logos precisely in what, and really only in what, the same theology prescribes for *all* men as their goal and consummation, viz. the direct vision of God enjoyed by Christ's created human soul … we implicitly envisage this Hypostatic Union at the same time as we see the history of the cosmos and of the spirit arriving at the point at which are found both the absolute self-transcendence of the spirit into God and the absolute self-communication of God to all spiritual subjects by grace and glory. Hence the thesis towards which we are working purports to show that, even though the Hypostatic Union is in its proper nature a unique event, and when seen in itself, is certainly the highest conceivable event, it is nevertheless an intrinsic factor of the whole process of the bestowal of grace on the spiritual creature in general.[53]

Such a claim, *prima facie*, is ambiguous. Does Rahner intend to say that Jesus of Nazareth is a unique instance of God existing as a human being (utterly different from all other human beings in this way), and that as a human being he is also the exemplar of the realization of sanctifying grace in history? Or, by contrast, does he mean to say that the grace of the hypostatic union is only the grace of Christ's conscious union with God in freedom, and that this mystery is the highest instance of a more general, universal process transpiring in all human beings? Rahner's statements *can* be read as distinguishing the sanctifying grace of Christ from the grace of union (and thus the hypostatic union as such).

The problem, however, is that he has in effect purposefully evacuated from his theology of the hypostatic union *any other criteria* by which to denote this union *other than* that of habitual, sanctifying grace. Rahner is discarding the traditional language of the "instrumentality" of the sacred humanity of Christ (because he takes it to be implicitly Monophysite and mythological). Furthermore, he almost never speaks either of the hypostatic "subsistence" of a divine person in a human nature or of the union of two natures in a divine person. Instead, it is now the human history of Christ that is seen as a "self-communication" of God to man, and this self-communication of God being united with man acquires its *intrinsic* form through Christ's hu-

---

53. "Christianity within an Evolutionary View of the World," 180–81. See likewise, *Foundations of Christian Faith*, 200–201.

man knowledge of God and free obedience toward God. Otherwise said, the human nature of Jesus of Nazareth acting in history under grace has become the unique locus in which to identify the presence of the hypostatic union—its "formal content," so to speak.

It is not surprising, in light of this approach, that Rahner should place such insistence upon the fact that the human nature of Christ possessed the beatific vision, or the "immediate vision" of God, during the course of Christ's earthly life.[54] For it is precisely Christ's elevated consciousness of God, and the free, loving union with God that it facilitates, that dictate the terms of God's self-communication in Christ, and subsequently, God's gracious self-communication to the rest of the human race.

After all, it is easy to see that such a Hypostatic Union cannot be conceived as a merely ontic connection between two realities conceived of as things, but that—as the absolute perfection of the finite spirit as such—it must of absolute necessity imply a ... "Christology of consciousness"; in other words, it will then be easily seen that only in such a subjective, unique union of the human consciousness of Jesus with the Logos—which is of the most radical nearness, uniqueness and finality—is the Hypostatic Union really present in its fullest being.[55]

What should we say, then, about this account of the incarnation? Clearly Rahner wishes to emphasize to a maximal extent the human history of Jesus of Nazareth and the exemplarity of Christ as a man united with God. Furthermore, he sees in Jesus a unique, unrepeatable instance of God's presence in humanity. The hypostatic union is affirmed. But as with a thinker like Alexander of Hales, the insistence on the unity of person in Christ is marked by ambiguities for two reasons. First, the human nature seems to have a quasi-distinct ontological reality of its own: Rahner does not tell us "how" the Word exists or subsists as human, except by reference to the inherent presence of sanctifying grace in the soul of Christ. The human nature assumed and the Word assuming co-exist in unity, but this unity seems to be constituted primarily by what Aquinas would term the accidental quality of habitual grace. Second, and related to this, there exists in the man Jesus a uniquely intensive *degree* of habitual grace and it

54. "Dogmatic Reflections," 203–5.
55. Ibid., 206–7.

is in some sense *because* of this plenitude of sanctifying grace that we may affirm a hypostatic union, and not the inverse. For Aquinas, Christ possesses a plenitude of sanctifying grace because of the hypostatic union. The habitual graces follow from the grace of union. For Rahner, however, the human nature of Christ is united to God in the beatific vision and in the act of human self-surrender, and in this way, he is the most perfect historical expression of God present among us, communicating himself to us. The formal content of the incarnation, then, seems to consist principally in the created graces of the soul of Christ: the graced acts of knowledge and love by which God communicates himself to the human race. It is not surprising, then, that in an interview in 1974, Rahner should admit a penchant in his thought toward what he termed "orthodox Nestorianism."[56]

Analogous Interpretations

It is helpful to consider the ramifications of Rahner's theology by comparing it with other positions, some of which it has helped to inspire. Here I would like to connect the argument developed thus far in this chapter to the analysis offered in the prolegomenon above. From a Thomistic perspective, why should we say that Rahner's Christology resembles that of Schleiermacher in key ways? Similarly, in what way has Rahner bequeathed to modern Roman Catholic theology a set of ideas not wholly unlike those one finds in certain strands of modern liberal Protestantism? I have argued above that there exists for Aquinas a more subtle form of Nestorianism and a more overt form, but that they are inherently related forms of thought. Both conceive of the union between Jesus and God in exclusively operational, moral terms, rather than substantial terms. One form attempts to maintain a unity of ontological subject in Christ (in an inherently problematic fashion), while the other affirms explicitly the existence of a distinction of subjects, the Logos and the man Jesus. In what follows I will suggest that the theologies of Rahner and Schleiermacher resemble one another as "subtle" forms of Nestorianism, which each influence the subsequent articulation of "overt"

---

56. *Karl Rahner in Dialogue*, eds. P. Imhof and H. Biallowons, trans. H. D. Egan (New York: Crossroad, 1986), 127.

forms. The overt forms I will consider are those of John Hick, Jacques Dupuis, and Jon Sobrino.

The association of these authors is not accidental. The thought of John Hick develops with explicit reference to that of Schleiermacher, while Dupuis and Sobrino are influenced very deeply by Karl Rahner, but also (especially in the case of Dupuis) by Schleiermacher and Hick. In other words, these disciples of Rahner develop themes in his thought that I have sought to identify, in coordination with a modern Protestant tradition that merits clear examination. I will seek here only to analyze briefly key features of the positions of these four thinkers, and will not offer a developed textual defense of these interpretations. In each case, I would claim, one can see a structural similarity with Rahner under three aspects. For, as in Rahner's mature Christology, each of these related positions makes no clear distinction between substantial union as opposed to accidental/operational union, or if one does find such a distinction, it is employed in order to eschew the former mode of union as a way of explaining the uniqueness of Christ. Second, therefore, in each of these models, Christ is different from other human beings primarily due to his intensive degree of holiness or moral union with the divine, rather than the ontology of the hypostatic union. The union of God and man in Christ is deciphered primarily in terms of the human consciousness of Christ (his knowledge and moral action). Last of all, the transformed religious consciousness of Jesus of Nazareth is what makes of him the exemplary human being. A new evolutionary development becomes possible in human history because of Christ.

Friedrich Schleiermacher

I have noted above that Schleiermacher reinterprets the ontology of Chalcedon in light of the "God-consciousness" of the man Jesus. It is the uniqueness of Jesus's awareness of God and surrender to God that makes of him the exclusive redeemer of the human race.[57] Given our analysis of scholastic understanding of a union according to "habitual grace," we are now in a better position to understand the ontol-

---

57. Friedrich Schleiermacher, *The Christian Faith*. The idea referred to is developed thematically in 2:385–424 (§94–99).

ogy of union that is implicit in Schleiermacher's views. By Thomistic standards, his position is not entirely novel, but instead is something like a modern reiteration of the "single person—dual hypostasis" theories of the later medieval period. For Schleiermacher treats Jesus of Nazareth as a single subject, but he clearly posits a union of God and man in Christ merely by virtue of the knowledge and moral activity of Christ. This being the case, the union of God and man in Christ is merely "operative," rather than substantial.

> The Redeemer, then, is like all men in virtue of the identity of human nature, but distinguished from them all by the constant potency of His God-consciousness, which was a veritable existence of God in Him.... For this particular dignity of Christ, however, in the sense in which we have already referred back the ideality of His person to this spiritual function of the God-consciousness implanted in the self-consciousness, the terms of our proposition alone are adequate; for to ascribe to Christ an absolutely powerful God-consciousness, and to attribute to Him an existence of God in Him, are exactly the same thing.[58]

Interestingly, Schleiermacher appeals here to a "dignity" that accrues to Christ by virtue of "an existence of God in Him." As with Alexander of Hales, however, the dignity in question can only be a quality and cannot pertain to the substance of Christ as such. This is the case because Jesus's consciousness of God is an attribute or property of his human nature, and not the substantial being of his person as such. Consequently, there results something akin to what Aquinas calls a union by "indwelling." It derives from the "habitual grace" of Christ (loosely conceived, as Schleiermacher does not of course use such terminology), rather than to the "grace of union" by which God the Word subsists personally as a human being. Whatever one might wish to say in defense of Schleiermacher, the slant of his thought tends inevitably toward a "subtle" form of Nestorianism.

John Hick

We see something analogous in the work of John Hick, theorist of religious pluralism, who draws upon Schleiermacher directly but also modifies his thinking in noteworthy ways. Consider this passage

58. *The Christian Faith*, 2:385–87 (§94).

from his essay "Jesus and the World Religions," in *The Myth of God Incarnate*:

I see the Nazarene, then, as intensely and overwhelmingly conscious of the reality of God. He was a man of God, living in the unseen presence of God, and addressing God as *abba*, father. His spirit was open to God and his life a continuous response to the divine love as both utterly gracious and utterly demanding. He was so powerfully God-conscious that his life vibrated, as it were, to the divine life; and as a result his hands could heal the sick, and the poor in spirit were kindled to new life in his presence. If you or I had met him … we would have felt the absolute claim of God confronting us, summoning us to give ourselves wholly to him and to be born again as his children and as agents of his purposes on earth.[59]

For Hick, there is in Jesus of Nazareth an exemplary realization of conscious union with God (by what scholasticism would term "habitual, sanctifying grace"). Here, however, Hick will make a noteworthy claim. *If* Christ is different from others due only to his *degree* of union with the divine or the absolute, then it is in fact an illusion to claim that he is personally God or that in him God was united with humanity in a wholly exclusive way. In this case, the metaphysics of the hypostatic union are in fact, as Hick notes, a kind of dogmatic superstructure imposed on the person of Christ extrinsically, not indicative of what he really is in himself.

Thus it was natural and intelligible both that Jesus, through whom men had found a decisive encounter with God and new and better life, should come to be hailed as son of God, and that later this poetry should have hardened into prose and escalated from a metaphorical son of God to a metaphysical God the Son, of the same substance as the Father within the triune Godhead…. But we should never forget that if the Christian gospel had moved east, into India, instead of west, into the Roman empire, Jesus' religious significance would probably have been expressed by hailing him within Hindu culture as a divine Avatar and within the Mahayana Buddhism which was then developing in India as a Bodhisattva, one who has attained to oneness with Ultimate Reality but remains in the human world out of compassion for mankind and to show others the way of life. These would have been the appropriate expressions with those cultures, of the same spiritual reality.[60]

---

59. John Hick, "Jesus and the World Religions," in *The Myth of God Incarnate*, ed. John Hick (Philadelphia: Westminster Press, 1977), 172.

60. "Jesus and the World Religions," 176.

Secondly, then, *pace* Schleiermacher, the person of Christ cannot be said to be the exclusive mediator of salvation for all human beings. The great figures of other religious traditions might just as well have experiences of consciousness of the absolute similar to those of Jesus of Nazareth. Consequently, religious traditions that stem from their teaching might serve as equally adequate ways to elevate human awareness of the divine to a higher plane.[61] In Hick's thought we find, then, an original, overt form of Nestorianism, allied with a highly innovative theology of religious pluralism.

Interestingly, Hick's claims maintain a point of contact with those of Aquinas. For St. Thomas, as we have noted, the moral union with God that results from habitual grace is not something proper to Jesus alone, but is present in the saints as well. Christ is sanctified in his human nature as are other human beings, and differs in this order only by a question of degrees (albeit quasi-infinitely).[62] Aquinas thinks that this truth points toward the inadequacy or instability present in any "Nestorian Christology": such theories are unable to articulate adequately the unity of the person and existence of the Son made man. Thus, one needs to have recourse to a theology of the grace of union in order to articulate what is proper to the hypostatic union as such. Here he and Hick are of course in complete disagreement regarding the reality of the incarnation of God. Hick's thought resembles the Gnosticism condemned in 2 John 1:7 as one that denies that "Christ has come in the flesh." However, this Gnostic thought is in agreement with Thomism in noting that *if* the mediating holiness of Christ depends *only* upon the graces of his soul, then there can be no real ontological exclusivity in Christ as the God-man. Hick is quite right that a Christology based uniquely upon exemplarity of degrees of grace (and thus accidental union alone) is one that is inherently open to pluralism.

Jacques Dupuis

In the later work of Jacques Dupuis one finds Rahnerian Christological themes recast overtly in ways that resemble the proposals of

---

61. Ibid., 180–82.
62. See ST III, q. 48, a. 2.

Schleiermacher and Hick. As with Rahner and Schleiermacher, Dupuis takes the consciousness of Christ as the primary locus of God's self-revelation in Jesus.[63] Again, what Aquinas terms the "habitual grace" of the humanity of Christ has become the ground for the articulation of the hypostatic union. Furthermore, Dupuis underscores that this consciousness in Christ is distinct from God in himself; consequently, it is limited and cannot fathom God in his plenitude. It follows that the knowledge of God which Christ possesses as man is not capable of communicating to human beings all that is present in the mystery of the eternal Logos. Acceptance of this fact leaves room for knowledge of truths about God the Logos that comes not through the humanity of Christ, but by means of other mediators, particularly through non-Christian religious traditions and their founders.

Just as the human consciousness of Jesus as Son could not, by nature, exhaust the mystery of God, and therefore left this revelation of God incomplete, in like manner neither does nor can the Christ-event exhaust God's saving power. God remains beyond the man Jesus as the ultimate source of both revelation and salvation. Jesus' revelation of God is a human transposition of God's mystery; his salvific action is the channel, the efficacious sign or sacrament, of God's salvific will. The personal identity of Jesus as Son of God in his human existence notwithstanding, a distance continues to exist between God (the Father), the ultimate source, and he who is God's human icon. Jesus is no substitute for God.[64]

Note that Dupuis speaks of the "human existence" of the Son of God, implicitly committing to a duality of *esse* in Christ. Jesus is one person (the Son of God) but there are in him two distinct existences. The fashion in which this notion is deployed seems to suggest that there are in Christ even distinct existents or *supposita*: that of the eternal Logos and that of the human historical man Jesus in and through which the Logos is revealed. Here one is verging toward a more overt form of Nestorianism, even if an explicit language of two subjects is avoided. The union between the two (the Logos and the man Jesus) is located in the consciousness of Christ, and occurs through a kind

63. Jacques Dupuis, *Toward a Christian Theology of Religious Pluralism* (Maryknoll, N.Y.: Orbis, 1997), 270–71. The legacy of both Schleiermacher and Rahner present in these pages is unmistakable.

64. *Toward a Christian Theology of Religious Pluralism*, 298.

of accidental union. One might speculate, therefore, that the grace of the Logos can and should manifest itself apart from Jesus Christ in ways that are original and not derived from his humanity.

The mystery of the incarnation is unique; only the individual human existence of Jesus is assumed by the Son of God. But while he alone is thus constituted the "image of God," other "saving figures" may be … "enlightened" by the Word … to become pointers to salvation for their followers…. Admittedly, in the mystery of Jesus-the-Christ, the Word cannot be separated from the flesh it has assumed. But, inseparable as the divine Word and Jesus' human existence may be, they nevertheless remain distinct. While, then, the human action of the Logos *ensarkos* is the universal sacrament of God's saving action, it does not exhaust the action of the Logos. A distinct action of the Logos *asarkos* endures—not, to be sure, as constituting a distinct economy of salvation, parallel to that realized in the flesh of Christ, but as the expression of God's superabundant graciousness and absolute freedom.[65]

This viewpoint fails to acknowledge sufficiently that all sanctifying grace given to human beings comes to them only through the instrumental mediation of Christ's sacred humanity.[66] However, an even more serious problem emerges in the last sentence of the citation. The phrasing there is unambiguously Nestorian, simply because Dupuis overtly ascribes divine action to the Logos *asarkos* that is not ascribed to the man Jesus Christ.[67] If Dupuis had said that the Logos *ensarkos* acts in some ways uniquely by virtue of his divinity and not by virtue of his humanity (for example, in actions implying creation *ex nihilo*), then his statement would be unextraordinary. What he has said, however, necessarily implies a dual-subject Christology, because the Logos who acts in such cases must be a Logos who is not *ensarkos*. Rather, the Logos is *asarkos* when such actions occur,

65. *Toward a Christian Theology of Religious Pluralism*, 298–99.
66. See the theological concern regarding this aspect of Dupuis's teaching in the magisterial document *Dominus Jesus* (2000), para. 4. http://www.vatican.va/roman_curia/congregations/cfaith/documents/rc_con_cfaith_doc_20000806_dominus-iesus_en.html
67. Logos *asarkos* and Logos *ensarkos* are traditional theological terms, denoting "the non-incarnate Word" and the "incarnate Word," respectively. Traditionally, the former term denotes the eternal Word prior to or preexisting his incarnation as a human being. The latter term denotes the eternal Word incarnate as the man Jesus Christ, beginning from the first instant of Christ's earthly life but also continuing on in the glorified life of the resurrection.

and consequently, the humanity of Jesus must be something substantially distinct from the Logos. The Logos may inhabit the man Jesus, and we may call this the "Logos *ensarkos*" by a kind of equivocal use of language, but in truth the Logos *asarkos* is an independent subject distinct from the individual man Jesus. Otherwise Dupuis's theological claim makes no sense. But if it does make sense (which it does) then it clearly falls under the condemnation of the fourth canon of the Council of Ephesus, which underscores that all characteristics of Jesus Christ as both divine and human must be ascribed only to one subject, that of the incarnate Word.

The irony here is that Dupuis has pushed Rahner's insistence on the real historicity of Christ's human consciousness to the extreme, and has reached a theological breaking point. He does so in part by recourse to a philosophical historicism that Rahner himself might well disavow. For Dupuis, Christ's human consciousness is thoroughly historical, *but therefore* it is also inherently limited and bound by the constraints of a particular cultural situation. Jesus in his historical consciousness, then, can only mediate revelation of the eternal Logos to us in an inherently restricted way.[68] This fact makes room for complementary revelations that can speak to humanity from outside of the mystery of the incarnate Word as such. These are revelations that come from the Logos *asarkos* and through other mediating figures.

Jon Sobrino

Like Jacques Dupuis, Jon Sobrino builds upon aspects of Rahner's Christology so as to develop a reinterpretation of Chalcedonian Christology in light of the consciousness of Christ.[69] Sobrino emphasizes that the initial formulations of Chalcedon are "mythological" in the same sense claimed by Rahner: they seem to make the historical humanity of Christ unreal, like a piece of clothing worn by God from the outside.[70] Christ is thus envisaged in a static or ontic way rather than in a historical and dynamic way.[71] If we wish to understand Christ we should look not to the relation of his humanity to the Word, but to

68. Ibid., 300, 305–7.
69. Jon Sobrino, *Christology at the Crossroads: A Latin American Approach*, trans. J. Drury (Maryknoll, N.Y.: Orbis, 1978), 22–25.
70. Ibid., 329.   71. Ibid., 385–86.

the relation of Jesus of Nazareth to God, whom he experiences as his Father.[72]

In differentiation from Rahner, however, Sobrino places particular emphasis upon the faith of Christ as his mode of knowing God. It is in this faith that Christ places full trust in God as his Father and offers obedience to him on behalf of humanity whom Christ seeks to liberate. "In concrete terms the faith of Jesus can be summed up in his attitude of exclusive confidence in the Father ... and his total obedience to his mission of proclaiming and making present the kingdom.... This twofold attitude makes explicit the unique faith of Jesus."[73] This faith develops historically in and through trials, such that Jesus passes through a succession of "conversions" and comes to a deeper progressive understanding of who God is.[74]

Sobrino goes further, however: if Jesus is united with God the Father in his consciousness, and this consciousness develops in history, then Christ progressively becomes the person of the Son of God. Otherwise said, Christ becomes the Son of God in and through a development of his historical consciousness.

The model I propose here to enable us to understand [this] filiation is the model of Jesus' personal oneness with the Father.... Here I do not view the notion of person as meaning the self-assertion and self-affirmation of a spiritual subject. Here "person" represents the end of a long process of self-reconciliation in which the subject surrenders his self to another. Historically speaking, Jesus' surrender to the Father takes place through his complete incarnation in a particular situation. Through this concrete, historical surrender to the Father, Jesus becomes the Son in a real rather than an idealistic way.... To put it in more concrete terms, Jesus lives "for" the Father by living "for" human beings. These two kinds of living "for" others coincide completely in Jesus. That is why and how he becomes the Son. That is why and how he attains fulfillment both in his relationship to God and in his reality as a human being.[75]

It seems quite clear that Nestorian tendencies emerge from Sobrino's historical approach to Christ's sonship. For on the one hand, Sobrino is quite willing to speak of the man Jesus as a "creature" who is turned

72. Ibid., 331.   73. Ibid., 103.
74. Jon Sobrino, *Jesus the Liberator: A Historical-Theological Reading of Jesus of Nazareth*, trans. P. Burns and F. McDonagh (Maryknoll, N.Y.: Orbis, 1993), 147–54.
75. *Christology at the Crossroads*, 387.

toward God in personal self-surrender.[76] This kind of language necessarily implies a hypostatic autonomy of the human nature of Christ, for even if the human nature of the Word is created, the Word made flesh ought not to be referred to as a creature.[77] Meanwhile, the Son is sometimes depicted by Sobrino as a distinct person from the man Jesus, one who is made present in the personal actions of Jesus: "From a dogmatic point of view, we have to say, without any reservation, that the Son (the second person of the Trinity) took on the whole reality of Jesus.... The Son experienced Jesus' humanity, existence in history, life, destiny and death."[78]

Such formulations seem to denote not that the Son took upon himself a human *nature* and that he became the man Jesus, but that he took upon himself the experiences of the man Jesus, a subject distinct from himself. Christ is thus a kind of *homo assumptus* who is brought into accidental unity with the person of the Word. In this case the communication of idioms is reinterpreted: the human experiences of Christ are not attributed directly to the person of the Word made flesh, but instead, the experiences of the human nature of Christ are attributed to the divine nature of Christ, such that the deity itself is a subject of historical becoming.

Unsurprisingly, this is precisely what we see Sobrino affirming in his theology of the suffering of God.[79] What Jesus undergoes as a victim of persecution and political execution in history is also something God undergoes, and in such a way that we may attribute suffering to the deity of God himself.[80] Nestorius developed his own Christological reflections out of a concern that Apollinarius's "one nature" Christology might compromise the transcendence of God, thus implicating the deity in passibility and suffering.[81] Cyril was at pains to show that the sufferings of Christ had to be attributed to the very person of the Word, but could not be attributed to his divine nature as

76. *Jesus the Liberator*, 147: "Jesus' openness to God was a going out of himself toward God, and its realization was therefore something fulfilling for Jesus as a creature."

77. Aquinas, ST III, q. 16, a. 8: "Whether this is true: 'Christ is a creature'?" Aquinas explains here that the word "creature" cannot be used of Christ in an unqualified manner, due to the fact that the hypostatic *suppositum* is uncreated.

78. *Jesus the Liberator*, 242.   79. Ibid., 240–46.

80. Ibid., 244.

81. See Gavrilyuk, *The Suffering of the Impassible God*, 147–48.

such.[82] Sobrino, however, shows a contrary concern to that of Nestorius and Cyril: he wants to emphasize the historical reality of Christ's developmental consciousness so as to underscore his true solidarity with the poor and suffering in faith, ignorance, and hope. However, he also posits that the divine nature is present in this historical event, revealing a more general feature of God's relationship to all the poor and oppressed. The human history of Christ shows us that God is suffering in solidarity throughout history with all victims of political and moral injustice.[83] Consequently, Sobrino has taken Rahner's "Christianity within an Evolutionary View of the World" and reinterpreted it in liberationist terms. The grace of Christ's consciousness (exhibited in his faith amidst suffering) serves as the exemplar or template for the sonship of all who come after him and who approach God based on the praxis or moral example established by Christ. They too, like Christ in his "habitual grace," can become sanctified and united with God, who himself is present in solidarity with them even in their suffering, even into the very reaches of his deity.

With Sobrino, then, we have come full circle from the original concern of Rahner regarding historicity in Jesus: not only is the historical consciousness and its development the primary locus for our interpretation of the hypostatic union, but it is also now the case that history has been imported into God's own deity as the expression of God's own developmental history through his interaction with human beings. Through the medium of Christology, ontology has indeed been reconceived in historical terms not only "all the way down" into every aspect of human existence, but also "all the way up" into God.

The summaries given above are necessarily succinct and incomplete, but they do allow us to draw an important conclusion. Rahner was worried about a mythological-scholastic vision of the hypostatic union in which the humanity of Christ is seen as a "mere" instrument of the divine person of the Word. On this model, the historicity of Jesus of Nazareth supposedly ceases to mean very much, and is the mere cipher through which his divine identity is expressed in time. However valid this concern may be, we can conclude at the end of our

---

82. Cyril, *Ad Acacium* 7; *Ad Succensum*, II, 4; *Scholia* 5, 13, 26; *Ad monachos*, 23–24. See *The Suffering of the Impassible God*, 159–62.

83. *Jesus the Liberator*, 246.

study that there are clear dangers at the opposite end of the spectrum. Rahner's program of "historicization" of the Word based on Jesus's human consciousness eventually gave rise to profound imbalances in Christology. One should acknowledge the real historicity of the Word made flesh, but one should also find a way of underscoring the absolute uniqueness of the hypostatic union and the corresponding truth of the instrumentality of the sacred humanity of Jesus. Only the latter ideas will allow us to see how Christ in his human thoughts, words, decisions, and gestures truly reveals who he is personally as the Son of God, one in being with the Father. It is the Son of God existing as man who can truly offer a cumulative meaning to the history of human religion, one that is authentic, final, and unsurpassable. Only he can truly liberate a humanity enslaved to sins that are personal as well as social and political. As a means of thinking through the equilibrium that needs to be recovered, I will return in the last section of this chapter to briefly consider the Christology of Aquinas once again, in view of responding to Rahner's concerns with scholastic "mythology."

THOMISTIC PRINCIPLES FOR A CHALCEDONIAN UNDERSTANDING OF THE HUMAN HISTORICITY OF JESUS

Up to this point, the argument of this chapter has been concerned with the accurate diagnosis of what I have termed a tendency toward Nestorianism in modern Christology. What I mean by "Nestorianism," however, is clearly something quite complex. Given my examination of the modern authors above, one can see the utility of Aquinas's identification in "Nestorianism" of two distinct problems. One problem emerges when someone posits a real distinction of persons in Christ, human and divine. The subject Jesus is not personally the Word of God but someone very close to God in the order of grace. A second, more subtle problem arises when one attempts to conceive of a personal union of God and man in Christ, but does so through the medium of the human spiritual operations of Christ alone (Christ's consciousness of God). Such thinking fails to locate the hypostatic union in the very substance of Christ as a singular entity, in the personal subsistence of the Word made flesh. By articulating the personal union in merely accidental terms, this more mild form of Nestorianism inevitably invites us to embrace the more acute form. "Jesus is one with God/the Logos only insofar as he is remarkably conscious of God" can readily be interpreted as "Jesus is a subject distinct from God/the Logos with whom he is united in virtue of his consciousness of God/the Logos." The second idea follows logically from the first once we realistically concede that a human being is not his or her consciousness, but is an entity who possesses human consciousness.

To remedy *both* these misleading forms of thought, then, two things must be emphasized. First, the union of God and man in Christ is hypostatic, taking place in the person who is one in being, not two. Second, this union does not occur merely by means of habitual grace or operations of consciousness (both of which are merely accidental properties of the person). Rather, the latter properties flow from and are expressive of the hypostatic union, which is something substantial and more foundational. If we identify the more subtle root of the problem (present in Rahner and Schleiermacher) we will be able also to avoid its more extreme expressions (present in Hick, Dupuis, and Sobrino).

We began our consideration of Rahner's theology with his objections to the classical metaphysics of the hypostatic union. These were based on his concern that scholastic theology could not take seriously the human historicity of the Word made flesh. In this concluding section I would like to sketch out a succinct positive response to Rahner that avoids the problems of Nestorianism examined above, but which also responds to Rahner's charges against classical scholasticism. To do so I will articulate four Christological principles, each based upon a Thomistic understanding of the mystery of the incarnation. The goal is to envisage in a preliminary non-comprehensive fashion the proper balance that a Christology might seek so as to avoid the problems raised by Rahner's own Christology, while also responding adequately to his legitimate concerns.

Hypostatic Subsistence and Instrumentality Are Foundational

We should begin by thinking about a proper theological remedy both to "overt" Nestorianism (which in fact posits two subjects) and "subtle" Nestorianism (which posits a moral union via operations or acts of consciousness). Over against each of these variants, we need first to reconsider the mystery of the hypostatic union and why this union cannot be reducible merely to a union by way of habitual grace.

The first principle to be underscored, then, is the following: "hypostatic union" as a term refers to the divine person of the Word uniting a human nature to himself *in* his own person. This person is one in being and is one subsistent individual. This personal unity, as such, does not imply a confusion of natures, nor is it merely an accidental association of two beings, the man Jesus and the Word of God. Rather, the Word subsists personally as man in a human nature. Consequently, Jesus's concrete body and soul are the subsistent body and soul of the person of the Word. The person of Jesus simply is the person of the Son existing as man.

It follows from this line of thinking that the human nature of Jesus (his body and soul) is an instrument of his person, in an analogical and unique sense of the term. That is to say, because he simply is a pre-existent, divine person, *and* because the union is hypostatic, *therefore*, the humanity assumed cannot be a subsistent human person on its own (a *homo assumptus*). But if this is the case, then the humanity subsisting in the Word *is* expressive of the identity of the Word. The Word of God lives out his own personal identity as the eternal Son *in and through* his real human history among us as a human being. In this sense, then, his humanity is "instrumental." It is not an inanimate instrument (like a violin or a saw), nor is it a rational instrument that is substantially separate from the person who employs it (like the thoughtful diplomat who is an instrument of the king). Rather, the human nature of the Word is a rational instrument that is "conjoined" hypostatically to the person of the Word and is expressive of that person.[84] Jesus can reveal to us who God is precisely by being human, in and through his human actions.

If we attempt to forgo the appeal to these dual principles (hypostatic union, instrumentality), we will be forced (like Rahner) to evacuate the hypostatic union of any real *intrinsic* ontological content, and thus even if we affirm it nominally, in reality its formal

---

84. Aquinas employs the notion of "conjoined instrument" (*coniunctum*) to speak of the sacred humanity of Christ. See, for instance, ST III, q. 62, a. 5; q. 64, aa. 3–4.

meaning will be transferred entirely into the domain of the "sanctifying" or "habitual" grace of Christ as man. However, as Rahner himself notes repeatedly, in this domain as such, Christ is not radically different from every other human being. All are called to sanctification through the infusion of created grace. This grace is oriented toward the beatification of the souls of all who cooperate with it. But it is obvious that we cannot obtain in this domain as such to a form of union that is truly hypostatic or substantial, for several reasons.

Consider first that sanctifying (habitual) grace sanctifies and elevates a human nature (body and soul) that is "something" (*aliquid*) integral and substantial. But if this is the case, then such grace is necessarily "accidental" in the scholastic sense, that is to say, a property of a human being under grace, not the very human being itself.[85] Otherwise, the human being simply would be grace "essentially" in all that it is. This would be absurd, however, for then a person possessing a human nature could not gain grace as a gift, nor lose grace without ceasing to exist. The person qua human simply would be grace. Nor could this nature have any integrity of its own apart or in distinction from grace.

If sanctifying grace is a property of our human nature, however, and not the substance of that nature, then it cannot realize a substantial union of that nature with the Word of God. Personal subsistence of human nature in the Word of God cannot result from however high or exalted a degree of sanctifying, habitual grace, just because that union must be substantial in kind but such sanctifying grace is accidental in kind. By necessity, any theory which claims that such grace does effect personal union is implicitly Nestorian. It settles all the weight of the union firmly on the accidental properties of the person rather than the person himself.[86]

Second, consider that the union with God effectuated by habitual grace takes place not in the flesh of the human being, nor in the human emotions, but primarily in the spiritual faculties of the human being: the intellect and the will. However, neither of these faculties

85. Aquinas makes arguments to this effect in ST I-II, q. 110, aa. 2 and 4, regarding the accidental nature of habitual grace.

86. Aquinas makes this argument in ST III, q. 2, a. 10, corp., against Nestorian conceptions of union by habitual grace alone.

can be equated with the very substance of the human person. It is a preposterous error for a human being to claim that "I am my act of thinking," full stop, or "I am my act of obeying," as such. To begin with, the intellect and will are distinct if intimately related faculties of the human person, so that if one of them were to be equated with the human being's essence (that is, just what the person is) then the other faculty either would not exist or would be a property of the former (if it is truly essential). Consequently, we would be obliged to deny that there is any real distinction between the intellect and will. Free acts of the will would be essentially acts of knowledge, or acts of knowledge would essentially be acts of choice. But these are absurd conclusions that deny the principle of non-contradiction as applied to discrete mental acts. Likewise, if either of these two faculties were essential, then the human body would not pertain to the substance of the human person (as something essential to our very being). But the body does pertain to the very substance and essence of what it means to be human, and so consequently, the intellect and the will cannot be substantially what the human person is, but are very important properties of the human person.[87]

Again, if there is a historical development of the spiritual faculties (within a given person's life), then they must be accidental properties of the person. For if the intellect were to develop and if it were to be equated with the essence of the person, then each time the intellect reached new insights or developed new capacities, we would have to decide whether the person was substantially the same person or had essentially changed identity. After all, a new actual realization of properties in the mind would be a substantial realization and so would pertain to the essence of the person. A new being would constantly be coming into being.

Rather than flirt with such absurdities, we should say rather that the human person is essentially the same subsistent reality throughout the course of his or her embodied life, and the intellectual and moral faculties of the person develop through time as properties (or "accidents") of that person, not as the essence of the person him or herself. Therefore, *pace* Rahner, precisely in order to take seriously

87. This argument is presented in ST III, q. 2, a. 10, ad 2.

the historicity of the person as embodied and as developing the spiritual capacities of intellectual thought and freedom in and through a given history, it is necessary to understand the faculties as "accidents" of the substance.

If this is the case, however, nothing in the order of habitual, sanctifying grace can actualize a hypostatic union. For such grace is accorded to the spiritual faculties of the intellect and will so as to permit the human person to participate imperfectly and inchoately in the uncreated wisdom and love of God. Such supernatural acts of knowledge and love transpire in and through the intellect and will. We may graciously know God habitually by the gift of faith and love him above all things habitually by the gift of charity, but however noble these habits may be (and truly essential to human salvation), they are not identical with the substance of the person as such, but are properties of the person. Therefore, no such act of grace, no matter how elevated or intense, can effect a change in the subject on any other level than the level of accidental properties. It cannot somehow "effectuate" a substantial, hypostatic union. Making Christ a primary exemplar of faith, hope, and love (or religious dependence for that matter) will not permit us to make of him the Word made flesh. For the hypostatic union pertains to the substance of human nature as such: the body and soul of the man Jesus subsisting in the person of the Word. This mystery cannot be reduced merely to a property of human nature, no matter how important such a property may be.

Hypostatic Union as the Basis for
True Historicity of the Word

Our second point concerns the relationship between hypostatic identity and historicity. Rahner is rightly concerned to avoid any scholastic "mythology" that would deny the historicity of the Word existing as a human being, having an authentic human history. This is a legitimate concern and identifies rightly the dangers of an all-too-conceptual or reified vision of the person of Christ that is insufficiently sensitive to the biblical, historical life of Jesus of Nazareth as it is portrayed in the Gospels. However, the New Testament and the four Gospels are themselves complex and do indeed, when read attentively, indicate by various channels that Christ is the Wisdom of God, the

Word and image of the Father, the pre-existent Son, and the truth who is God from all eternity.[88] Seeking to understand the New Testament claims about Christ non-ontologically is in the end a non-biblical exercise.

What must we maintain minimally, then, in order to take seriously the historicity of God in Jesus Christ? Here the theology of the hypostatic union is not too abstract but is in fact the correct indication of the concrete grounding for the historicity of the Logos in human flesh. It is precisely because it is the *person* of God the Son who *exists* as a human being that the actions carried out by this person and all that he undergoes in and through history are attributed truly and realistically to God the Son. It is the second person of the Trinity who exists as a human being, from conception to natural death, so as to undergo all the stages of human development (biological, sensible, spiritual) that are proper to the human condition. Consequently, it is God who is conceived in the womb of the Virgin Mary. It is God who gestates and is born, God who develops physiologically and grows in "wisdom and stature" intellectually as a human being (Lk 2:52). It is God who begins his public ministry by being baptized and it is God who preaches, lives an itinerant life, heals and performs miracles, challenges the religious authorities, and performs signs of prophecy in the Temple. It is God who is stripped and beaten, tortured, and mocked, God who is crucified and who dies. All of this happens to God in his human nature, as man. But it happens to *One who* exists as human. Thus it happens *to* the existent Son and Word, as the hypostatic subject of this history.

Nor is this a mythology in the classical sense, in which the god would undergo an anthropomorphic alteration as a condition for becoming the consort of human beings. God is the *author* of our existence *and* our very being participates in existence due to the sheer gift of God. Therefore, God can exist as a human being without changing in any way *as* God, in his incomprehensible deity. Why is this the case? First of all, because creation is "merely" the expression of the creative goodness of God and therefore has nothing in it that is not

88. See the arguments illustrating this truth by Simon J. Gathercole, *The Preexistent Son*, and Larry Hurtado, *Lord Jesus Christ*, works both referred to above in the introduction to this volume.

received from the outpouring act of the creator. This means, however, that nothing in creation can rival God ontologically by being different from him, alien to him, or by existing alongside him as an extrinsic or complementary principle. Rather, God is present everywhere and in everything in creation not as identical with that creation, but as the cause of the entirety of that creation. He thus utterly transcends and remains distinct from this creation as its cause. For the same reason, then, God can begin to be present "anew" in a hypostatic way in a created human nature, and nothing in that existent nature will be alien to the deity of the Godhead. The humanity of Christ is not identical to his divinity, but it is not a principle that excludes the presence of divinity. It is possible that the "fullness of the deity dwells in [Christ] bodily" (Col 2:9) without any diminishment or "shadow of change" (Jam 1:7) entering into the eternal, ineffable life of God himself.

It is also precisely because our very being participates in existence, due to the sheer gift of God, that God can exist as a human being without distorting or violating the existence and essential properties of our created human nature.[89] If the human nature of Jesus is created (which of course it is) it is created in such a way as to exist in the Word without damage or violence occurring to this human nature, with its inherent limitations but also with its proportional integrity and developmental history. The human nature of Christ is more humane and perfect because it is the human nature of God, but it is also that of a genuinely historical human being. Likewise, the existence of the Son made man does not serve to enslave or limit the gradual development of his humanity through time, but causes it to flourish in an appropriate and essentially normal human way.

---

89. ST III, q. 17, a. 2. Aquinas insists in this text on the singularity of the existence of the Son incarnate as that of God himself, existing as a human being. The human essence of the Son is actuated by the *esse* of the Word himself. Aquinas does speak in passing about a human *esse* of Christ in *De Unione*, q. 4, a text that has given rise to a substantial amount of scholarly controversy. It is clear even in that text, however, that St. Thomas thinks that the human nature of Christ has a unique existential subsistence, that of the person of the Word. For a helpful treatment of the issues surrounding the interpretation of the two texts, see Corey Barnes, "Albert the Great and Thomas Aquinas on Person, Hypostasis and Hypostatic Union," *The Thomist* 72 (2008): 107–46.

Instrumentality Is Not Opposed
to Moral Autonomy

The third point to be considered is the following: the instrumentality of the sacred humanity of Jesus is not opposed to his natural, human moral autonomy. In some real sense the exact opposite must be the case. The capacity of the human nature to serve as an instrument of the person of the Word presupposes that the Word made flesh possesses an authentic human moral autonomy. Why is this the case? Here we can appeal to the traditional principle of Gregory Nazianzus, writing against Apollinarius of Laodicia when the latter denied the existence of a human intellect in Christ: "What God has not assumed he has not redeemed."[90] In his *Letter to Cledonius* Gregory makes special appeal to the redemptive importance of the human obedience of Christ, who was subject to the Father in his will such that he might redeem human beings from the disobedience that resides in us as a result of the sin of our first ancestors.[91]

Aquinas takes up this line of argument in his explanation for why there must be a true human faculty of the will in Jesus Christ.[92] He argues that there must exist real human choice-making in Christ precisely because Christ is a free human agent who thinks, decides, and obeys God.[93] So if the hypostatic union is a reality and God the Son has personally assumed human nature for our redemption, then God the Son must also personally think with a human intellect and make human choices freely in and through his historical existence and life experiences. But just because these reflective decisions are the decisions of the person (those of the Son of God), they are also therefore expressive of that person: they are instrumental for making manifest to us in and through time who that person is. Such moral autonomy is a condition for the possibility of genuine hypostatic instrumentality and consequently is not inherently opposed to it.

90. Gregory Nazianzus, Letter 101, *Ad Cledonius*. Literally: "What is not assumed is not healed."

91. See the analysis of Lionel Wickham in St. Gregory of Nazianzus, *On God and Christ: The Five Theological Orations and Two Letters to Cledonius*, trans. L. Wickham (Crestwood, N.Y.: St. Vladimir's Seminary Press, 2002), 149–52.

92. ST III, q. 18, a. 1, corp.

93. ST III, q. 18, a. 4, corp. and ad 1. This is a topic I will return to in chapter 5.

In the case of Christ, however, this process of free human self-expression is also affected intimately by the theandric character of his free human actions. Jesus decides things in a genuinely human historical way, in reflective thought and free, active decision. But he also decides humanly what to do with reference to God the Father, and God the Holy Spirit, and so with reference to the divine nature that he bears within himself and which he shares with the Father and the Spirit. So his free human actions and decisions bear the mark, so to speak, of the divine life and will that are present within him, in his person and by virtue of his divine nature. His human spontaneity, passion, desire, intention, decision, and free choice are all real, but they are also imbued "from the start" with the presence of the Father and the Spirit, acting with and in him in a divine way, to bring about the Kingdom of God. His free human autonomy is that of the Son of God made man, for the purpose of the redemption of the human race.

One might object that this characterization would seem to delimit the authentic human freedom of Christ, since his human choice-making never operates in independence from the will of God, but must always unfold in correspondence to it. Here, however, we should recall a fundamental metaphysical truth: in God freedom is expressive of sovereign goodness. When Christ as man acts freely in accord with the divine will, then, his human will is assimilated to the sovereign goodness that is proper to him by virtue of his deity. Consequently, the horizon of his human freedom is expanded and ennobled, not lessened or restricted. Because he is God, Christ makes human choices that are most excellent and most human. He is not less free than all others, therefore, but is the freest of all, and is the model of authentic moral liberation.

The human freedom of Christ depends in part upon the sanctifying grace of Christ. As I have noted above, Aquinas thinks that Christ must have possessed the highest degree of sanctifying grace of any human being because of the hypostatic union. The human nature of the Word exists in the closest proximity to the source of all grace (the deity). Consequently, it must fittingly possess the highest intensity of sanctifying grace, overflowing, as it were, from the deity of Christ into his humanity.[94] In this understanding, the hypostatic identity

94. ST III, q. 7, a. 1.

of the Son is the foundation for his habitual grace, not the product of it. Because Christ has such a plenitude of grace, however, he also has a more perfect autonomy than that of any other human being. He is capable of a human knowledge and love of God that are higher and more perfect (more freeing) than those found in any other historical person. This plenitude of grace does not inhibit, but rather allows for a more perfect progressive history in which the grace of Christ "deploys" itself in more and more perfect expressions and actions, such as in the multiple teachings, actions of forgiveness, effective words of grace and conversion, institution of the sacraments, and deliberate actions of the atonement. Furthermore, because Christ's moral autonomy in history *is* instrumental for our salvation, *therefore* it can be communicated to us—"from *his fullness* we have all received, grace upon grace" (Jn 1:16)—and this communication of grace in turn can "set us free" (Jn 8:32) for a greater moral autonomy and a new developmental history under grace. The instrumentality of the sacred humanity of Jesus, then, is not ahistorical, but something that invites humanity to a new history that only Christ can realize in and among us.

Historical Development of Consciousness Is Not Constitutive of Hypostatic Relationality, but Is Expressive of It

The fourth and final point derives organically from the previous ones discussed above. We can first state the point negatively: the human spiritual development of the man Jesus is a *property* of his person, but it is not *constitutive* of his subsistent personhood as such. Jesus as man can be rationally conscious, for instance, of the mystery of his Father and of the Holy Spirit. This conscious awareness might develop throughout his childhood, into adulthood, and throughout his adult life until death. Christ in his acts of human consciousness (reflection and moral action) can be relationally turned toward the person of the Father in prayer, obedience, decision, witness, acting, and suffering. But this set of conscious activities as such (by which he is related to the Father and the Holy Spirit) is not the very substance or hypostatic subsistence of his person per se. Rather, it is a property of his person.

This understanding is significant because, as we have seen above, Rahner argues that Jesus's relational consciousness to the Father is that which gives him his identity as the Son of God. Sobrino prolongs this idea by historicizing the developmental consciousness of Jesus, who relates more and more to the Father, becoming *progressively*, in some real sense, the Son of God. Do we need to choose, then, between a theology of the hypostatic union and a theology that takes seriously the human relationality of Jesus in his developmental consciousness?

We can avoid such a problematic juxtaposition if we first accept that the hypostasis of the Son as the second person of the Trinity cannot somehow be equated or reductively identified merely with the relationality of his human mental actions. We might be tempted by such an idea, if we consider that the Son who is eternally one in being with the Father is also rightly considered a "subsistent relation" in his very person, insofar as he is a divine person. Can we not see, then, the "unfolding" of this subsistent relationality of his personhood in the relationality of his human consciousness, in his thinking and willing? If we mean by this that the human relational actions of Christ in his consciousness simply are the hypostatic subsistence, then clearly this is an error of important proportions. For Jesus does not become or cease to be the hypostatic person (the "subsistent relation") of the Word depending on whether he engages humanly in relational consciousness of a particular reality. In that case, his divine identity would depend upon whether he was awake or asleep, thinking of this or that, willing or deciding one thing or another. Christ is always the Word made flesh, and his human thoughts and actions accrue to him or cease to accrue to him through the flux of time and history in such a way as to be properties of his person, but not in such a way as to constitute his person.

How, then, does Jesus's historical relationship to the Father reveal to us who he is as the Son of God? Through a positive restatement, we can say that the human conscious activity of Jesus (while not *constitutive*) is in fact *indicative* or *expressive* of his hypostatic identity as the Son. The human thoughts and decisions of Jesus are turned toward the Father and the Holy Spirit precisely because he is one with the Father and the Holy Spirit. When Christ, in John's Gospel states "I and the Father are one" (Jn 10:30), this mental activity does not effectuate the hypostatic union, but it is a new conscious activity and intentional action of Jesus as man that manifests what is already, always the case: that the Son is one in being with the Father. Likewise, when Christ in the garden of Gethsemane asks the Father that the cup of suffering might pass from him (Lk 22:42), he also states "not my will but thy will be done." This human decision in the heart of Christ to obey the Father does not constitute Jesus as the Son of God. The hypostatic union does not intensify in degree or come more perfectly into being as the result of a more perfect conformity of Christ's human will to the divine will. Rather, because Christ is "already" the eternal Son of God, he chooses as man to do freely what the Father wills, and what he also wills with the Father as God.[95] Christ as man possesses a natural, adverse inclination of the will away from suffering and death, but he can surmount this inclination by the "rational will" of human free decision, not unlike a soldier accepting and choosing to enter into battle, despite the fear of death.[96] In doing so, Christ is manifesting his Sonship: that he from all eternity has all he has from the Father, and that from all eternity he wills with the Father to redeem the human race.[97] The human action of obedience in Christ is not that which causes him to be one eternally with the Father as the Word, God from God, light from light, true God from true God. But it is that which expresses this unity in time, making it manifest to us in and through the human history of the Lord's passion.

Last of all, this understanding of human relationality can accommodate not only the activity of Jesus as man, but also his passivity. Jesus undergoes in the substance of his own flesh a series of alterations or sufferings, as well as exaltations: the conception, gestation, and birth, his eating and growing and sleeping, his walking and suffering, his torture and physical execution, his cadaveric burial and resurrection or exaltation. All of this is experienced in the flesh of Christ and relates him to others. In addition, there is the relational affectivity of his senses and his passions or emotions: all that Jesus feels or senses through these diverse experiences. Because Christ is the Word who undergoes all these physical, sensible, and emotional changes, they occur to him or within him. Consequently, they are not them-

95. ST III, q. 18, a. 5.   96. ST III, q. 18, a. 6.
97. *In Matt.*, XXVI, lec. V, 2232.

selves constitutive of his personal identity and of his being eternally one with the Father. But because of the hypostatic union, they can be expressive of his personal identity as the Son, and of the subsistent unity he has with the Father as the Word. The conception of Christ, or his sleeping in the boat of the disciples during the storm, his fear in Gethsemane, or his suffering blows and emotional mockery: all of this occurs to the subject of the Son made human. So it also indicates the personal relationality of the Son to others: to the Virgin Mary, to the twelve, to Pilate or the Roman soldiers, but also and before all else to the Father. In all that the Son undergoes physically and emotionally, then, he is expressing his relational dependence upon the Father, and therefore his personal subsistence toward the Father, even in his body. For it is the Word who became flesh and dwelt among us (Jn 1:14), and it is even this hypostatic presence of God *in the flesh* that "speaks" to us of who the Son is, even in his perennial relation to the Father. The passivity of the flesh of Christ crucified and glorified is "taken up" as it were into the personal relations of the Trinity, and becomes an imperfect but real icon or epiphany of the inner life of God.

CONCLUSION

The organic unity of theology is not only speculative but also historical. This was the great argument of John Henry Newman: development of doctrine occurs over time in homogeneous fashion, even if this development often takes place in what can seem like historically confusing and conceptually agitated circumstances. Notions of "orthodox" Christology are complex and have frequently been heavily contested, but we should not deny that great progress has been made through time. There are essential doctrinal acquisitions in the church that stand through the centuries and indicate to us in genuine fashion the deeper mystery of the revelation as it is offered to us in the person of Christ and in the deposit of scripture and sacred tradition. Likewise, if we can speak in lasting ways of doctrinal truths, we can and must also identify theological errors that can persist through time.

To speak of "Nestorianism," then, is not to speak of an error without content or without identity. It is also not to speak of ideas that have occurred only in antiquity. The future of Christology, on this score, remains in various ways open to further determination. At the heart of Nestorian theology remains a permanent question: in what way is Jesus Christ truly different from us? Does he differ from us only by a matter of degrees? Or is he differentiated from others fundamentally: as the eternal Son and Word of God subsisting in time and in human flesh? To ask this question is really, in its own way, to ask a simpler question: is Jesus God? Classical Christianity has a definitive answer to that question. Karl Rahner had an unambiguous desire to uphold that classical teaching. However, his Christology lacks sufficient resources to perfectly maintain the traditional teaching of the church: that the Word of God has personally become human. Theology that takes its inspiration from such figures as Cyril, Damascene, and Aquinas cannot fail to note Rahner's pertinent questions and interrogations about the historical realism of the person of Jesus of Nazareth. But this same tradition can accommodate Rahner's concerns sufficiently in thorough and profound ways, without in any way mitigating or abandoning the fundamental principles of the tradition. Newman was surely right about the organic continuity of the church's ongoing, historical development of doctrine. If we wish to seek a way forward in Christology even amidst the contemporary questions, then we would do well to seek enlightenment from the perennial principles of patristic and Thomistic theology. For within them, the central key to the future of theological progress is to be found.

2

———— : ————

The Human Nature and
Grace of Christ

The most contested affirmation regarding Jesus of Nazareth pertains to his divinity. It is the case, however, that the traditional affirmation of the perfect humanity of Jesus is also utterly controversial in modern theology. In one sense, this is simply because it is inherently controversial to affirm that there exists a real "essence" of human nature that God could assume. The subjacent question is philosophical: can we speak about perennial natures present in things in general and in human beings in particular down through time, and if so, how is it the case? In another sense, the controversial character of the affirmation is theological. Should we take our understanding of what human nature is from Christ alone (or above all) or should we take our understanding of Christ's humanity from a more general consideration of human nature as it pertains to all human beings? In seeking the "content" of human nature, what is the relationship of the revelation of the New Testament to all our other forms of knowledge of human beings? In various ways, then, we encounter difficulty in the doctrine of the humanity of God. For it is one thing to ask how God personally exists as a human being, and it is another thing to ask: how are we to understand the human nature of Christ?

It might be thought, mistakenly, that controversies surrounding the inherent content of human nature are absent from modern Catholic theology. Is it not the case, after all, that Catholic Christianity plac-idly maintains a metaphysics of perennial essences? However, the ques-tion was raised in an acute manner, particularly within debates over the relationship between grace and human nature. Henri de Lubac's thesis in *Surnaturel* was that the final end of the human person can only be one that is supernatural.[1] If this is the case, it follows that the creaturely *essence* of what it is to be human can be understood only in the light of supernatural grace, since a natural form is only intelligible in light of its inherent end. But then a philosophical identification of the content of human nature becomes inherently problematic. So, too, Karl Rahner's theological anthropology depends upon a very particular reinterpreta-tion of Kantian transcendental idealism. The human spirit is portrayed as a dynamic process oriented toward the infinite. In our concrete ex-istential history, this process can only ever be adequately brought to fulfillment through the supernatural activity of grace.[2] Hans Urs von Balthasar's important work on grace and nature in his study of Karl Barth entails the Christological recentering of a concept of human na-ture, as he attempts to coordinate philosophy and anthropology within an all encompassing Christological synthesis.[3]

While Rahner, Balthasar, and de Lubac are widely known for their writings on the issue of what human nature is, there can be no ques-tion that the most authoritative theological text on this topic formulat-ed in the twentieth century is found in the 1965 document of the Sec-ond Vatican Council, *Gaudium et Spes*. There we see at work a complex set of ideas regarding human nature. The document approaches the hu-man being simultaneously in light of Christ and in light of the natural law with direct allusions to philosophical ontology. How, then, are we to understand the humanity of Christ, and how does this relate to our understanding of all other human beings? In what follows, I will make use of the document as a venue for asking this Christological question in depth, engaging from a Thomistic point of view two important in-terpreters of *Gaudium et Spes*—Karl Rahner and Marie-Dominique Chenu.

1. Henri de Lubac, *Surnaturel: Études historiques* (Paris: Aubier, 1946).
2. Rahner, "Nature and Grace," in *Theological Investigations* IV:165–88.
3. Balthasar, *The Theology of Karl Barth*, 251–378.

A QUESTION CONCERNING THE
CHRISTOLOGICAL EVALUATION OF WHAT
IS NATURAL, AND THE PHILOSOPHICAL
(NATURAL) EVALUATION OF CHRIST

There is arguably no statement from the Second Vatican Council as well known as paragraph 22 from *Gaudium et Spes*, the Pastoral Constitution on the Church in the Modern World. The paragraph contains these memorable lines:

> In reality it is only in the mystery of the Word made flesh that the mystery of man truly becomes clear.... For since Christ died for all, and since all men are in fact *called to one and the same destiny*, which is divine, we must hold that the Holy Spirit offers to all the possibility of being made partners, in a way known to God, in the Paschal mystery.[4]

This statement in turn also alerts us to a fundamental theme in modern Catholic theology: the idea that the ultimate meaning of human existence is only unveiled in the historical mystery of Christ. It is a theme we find solemnly elaborated, again, in paragraph 41:

> The Church is entrusted with the task of opening up to man the mystery of God, who is the last end of man; in doing so it opens up to him the meaning of his own existence, the innermost truth about himself. The Church knows well that God alone, whom it serves, can satisfy the deepest cravings of the human heart, for the world and what it has to offer can never fully content it.... Whoever follows Christ the perfect man becomes himself more a man.

These passages point us toward a theological enigma that remains present at the heart of modern Catholic theology. On the one hand, theologians commonly assert that the true fulfillment of our natural human desire for happiness is made possible only in the light of Christ, by the grace of his mystery. This mystery is gracious, and is given from God as the gratuitous accomplishment of human history, in such a way that the principles and exigencies of man's natural searching would not arrive at this terminus by their own powers. (In this respect, such grace is extrinsic in origin.) On the other hand, such fulfillment is intrinsic to the human community, as it comes from within the history of man, and responds to the hidden search-

4. Emphasis added.

ing of the human heart. In other words, the search for meaning in the concrete historical life of man is undergirded by the energies of grace in such a way that the *nature* of man is illuminated in particular by the mystery of Jesus, by his life, death, and resurrection from the dead. We can recognize in him, then, the destiny of our own perfectibility.

This theological stance raises two key questions for Christology, however. First, what is human nature, and how does a theological understanding of human nature relate to Christ's humanity? Or what is the universalized understanding of human nature that is made available to human thought in light of Christ? And second, what is the universalized conception of human nature that is available to human thought apart from or at least in distinction from Christology? *Gaudium et Spes* itself raises these questions acutely but does not answer them as such. The document is, after all, replete with moral exhortations that appeal directly to the conscience of modern human beings of all backgrounds (including the non-Christian and the non-religious),[5] exhortations concerning the nature of marriage and the family,[6] the dignity and rights of human life from conception to natural death,[7] the human political and economic practices of a just society,[8] the evil of total war and the basic good of political peace,[9] the rational truth of equality among all human beings,[10] and so forth. In other words, the document is replete with appeal to principles of the natural law.[11] This appeal is not explicitly or overtly Christological, and in fact seems to presuppose in the recipients to whom it is addressed at least some genuine human capacity for rational receptivity (principles of synderesis and basic conceptions of the common good and of intrinsic evils that threaten the common good).

Likewise the document examines at various intervals, in a form of classical Augustinian *apologia*, the moral frailties or human weaknesses that are experienced in the struggle to accomplish the natural

5. *Gaudium et Spes*, nos. 2–3, 21, 41–43 [hereafter "GS"].

6. GS, no. 47.

7. GS, no. 51: "Life must be protected with the utmost care from the moment of conception: abortion and infanticide are abominable crimes."

8. GS, nos. 63–72, 73–76.   9. GS, nos. 78–82.

10. GS, no. 29.

11. Explicit appeal to the concept of "natural law" appears three times in the document, in nos. 74, 79, and 89.

good. In doing so it suggests that there are distinctly philosophical grounds for the theological claim that man finds himself in need of assistance if he is to accomplish the good that he wishes to do according to the inclinations of his better self, and not the evil that he does not wish to do.[12] Although there is a corresponding insistence on the need for the grace of God for the transformation of human action in the concrete sphere of history, this insistence simultaneously appeals to the concrete *nature* or natural aspirations of human civilization, and promises that only a Christian polity can offer any ultimate resolution even to the historical, intra-temporal aspirations of human beings to the building up of a political common good.[13] In short, the document proposes a very developed interpretation of what constitutes human nature, as intellectually distinguishable from the life of Christian grace, and yet simultaneously underscores that the healing, strengthening, and fulfillment of the former are only made possible by recourse to the latter. If nature is not *historically and existentially* separable from the mystery of God's gracious action in history, it is nevertheless distinguishable and can even be appealed to *precisely as a way toward understanding* the goodness of the mystery of life in Christ. Likewise, the mystery of Christ is seen to illumine one's understanding of the meaning of human nature.

12. GS, no. 13: "What Revelation makes known to us is confirmed by our own experience. For when man looks into his own heart he finds that he is drawn towards what is wrong and sunk in many evils which cannot come from his good Creator." See likewise GS, nos. 37–38, 41. In a not dissimilar way, Aquinas claims that such arguments are (from a strictly rational point of view) only probable signs of a fallen human nature. See SCG IV, c. 52: "Certain signs of the original sin appear with probability in the human race." Such arguments rightly underscore the experiential observation of ontological and moral disorder in human nature and civilization, but cannot demonstrate the rational necessity of prior creation in a state of grace, or demonstrate that this disorder results in great part from the prior loss of grace. The reason for this is that grace is itself a mystery that can be understood only in the light of supernatural faith, and is a principle that originates from causes necessarily transcending the natural range of human reason.

13. GS, no. 38: "The Word of God, through whom all things were made, became man and dwelt among men: a perfect man, he entered world history, taking that history into himself and recapitulating it. He reveals to us that 'God is love' (1 Jn. 4:8) and at the same time teaches that the fundamental law of human perfection, and consequently of the transformation of the world, is the new commandment of love. He assures those who trust in the charity of God that the way of love is open to all men and that the effort to establish a universal brotherhood will not be in vain."

In what follows, then, I would like to consider two areas of controversy surrounding the "harmony" of these two poles (natural aspiration to Christian life and Christological, graced fulfillment of nature) in the document. The two topics (which can be considered in the form of questions) are the following: ought we to follow what has become a standard post-conciliar trend in rejecting a theological concept of "pure nature," so as to make sense of the theology of *Gaudium et Spes*, no. 22? How does this question relate to a corresponding articulation of a natural desire for God in the historical life of man under grace? Second, what does it mean to affirm the Christological fulfillment of human nature in history? What metaphysical presuppositions are present or absent in the claim, as regards the intrinsically historical character of nature as such? In each case, I consider briefly a major interpreter of the Council's theology who wrote in the years just after the Council (Rahner and Chenu), and then offer critical reflections on their respective claims. In the last section of the chapter, I appeal to Thomistic considerations on the relations of nature, grace, and Christology, thereby suggesting some principles for interpreting the conciliar teaching in what I take to be a theologically constructive and reasonable way. The basic argument I pursue is the following: without a properly understood concept of pure nature, it is impossible to claim (1) that moral evil (which is prevalent in human nature in its actual state) is in truth unnatural; (2) that we can only become perfectly human (with a restored nature) by the grace of Christ; (3) and that what is true for human nature in general is the case in a unique way concerning Christ. To conceive of Christ as truly and perfectly human by contrast and comparison with ourselves requires a mediating concept of pure nature. Without such a concept we cannot rightly articulate why Christ is the fulfillment of what it means to be human.

PURE NATURE AND
THE GRACE-INSPIRED
DESIRE FOR GOD

In 1966, in the wake of *Gaudium et Spes*, Karl Rahner writes on the question of pure nature: "Our actual nature is *never* 'pure' nature. It is a nature installed in a supernatural order which man can never leave, even as a sinner and unbeliever. It is a nature which is continually being determined (which does not mean justified) by the supernatural grace of salvation offered to it."[14] Rahner's remark could be (and has been) interpreted as a gloss on no. 22 of that document. Of course there are other interpretations of *Gaudium et Spes* than that which takes the supernatural-existential theory of Rahner as a starting point. Yet it is clear that this central intuition of Rahner was potent, for he could employ it in a theologically consistent way to speak about a broad range of contemporary theological issues that also mirrored concerns of the Council: the possible presence of Christian grace in non-Christian persons and religious traditions,[15] the communication of Trinitarian life to the anthropological subject in the secular world[16] and amidst the mystery of death,[17] and the notion of the church's horizon as co-extensive with the mystery of grace as such and therefore as implicitly present in all the baptized, and indeed, in some latent way, as potentially co-extensive with all humanity.[18]

Within the context of this larger theological perspective, the concept of pure nature is clearly one that Rahner wishes to disavow (or significantly relativize) for theological use. Describing what he takes

14. Rahner, "Nature and Grace," 183.

15. See, for example, "Anonymous Christians," in *Theological Investigations* VI: *Concerning Vatican Council II*, trans. K.-H. Kruger and Boniface Kruger (London / New York: Darton, Longman & Todd / Seabury, 1974), 390–98. See 393–94: "Now that his thinking is illumined by the light of the revelation which has in fact been made in the historically accomplished reality of Christ, [man] can recognize this unapproachable height as that perfection of his own being which can be effected by God ... that he may more fully recognize the fact that he is ordained to this mystery.... The believer will then also grasp that this absolute eminence is not an optional adjunct to his reality; that it is not given to him as the juridical and external demand of God's will for him, but that this self-communication by God offered to all and fulfilled in the highest way in Christ rather constitutes the goal of all creation and ... that even before he freely takes up an attitude to it, it stamps and determines man's nature and lends it a character which we may call a 'supernatural existential.' A refusal of this offer would therefore not leave man in a state of pure unimpaired nature, but would bring him into contradiction with himself even in the sphere of his own being.... The expressly Christian revelation becomes the explicit statement of the revelation of grace which man always experiences implicitly in the depths of his being."

16. *Foundations of Christian Faith*, 138–53.

17. Ibid., 273–74.

18. See "Ideology and Christianity," in *Theological Investigations* 6:43–58.

to be the "average" view of scholastic theology,[19] he characterizes the scholastic theory of "pure nature" in the following terms:

Grace is [for this theory] an unsurpassable perfectioning of nature; God as the Lord of this nature can command man to submit to his *de facto* will and to be receptive to his grace, which directs man to a supernatural life and end. But of itself nature has only a *potentia obedientialis* to such an end, and this capacity is thought of as negatively as possible. It is no more than non-repugnance to such an elevation. Of itself, nature would find its perfection just as readily and harmoniously in its own proper realm, in a purely natural end, without an immediate intuition of God in the beatific vision. When it finds itself in immediate possession of itself—as part of the essence of the spirit, "*reditio completa in seipsum*"—it meets itself as though it were "pure nature." According to the well-known axiom ... it is distinguished from pure nature only "*sicut spoliatus a nudo.*" And this "state of being despoiled" is silently considered as a merely extrinsic element with regard to the absence of sanctifying grace.... We do not usually think that the lack of grace might be different in the two cases, that of pure nature and that of fallen nature.[20]

At base, one concern here is that a modern, implicitly secularized vision of man has been advanced inadvertently within baroque Catholic theology by a concept of the normative or purely natural state of man, to which grace or the Christian life is attached only accidentally or extrinsically. Thus, as we find argued at greater length in de Lubac's *Surnaturel*, the late scholastic concept of pure nature in fact introduced into theology a false complacency with the secular, and contributed to the rise of a post-Enlightenment thought-world that closes itself off within a horizon of immanence, over and against the world of grace. I will return to this claim below. However, it should also be stated here that Rahner is writing above all against the idea of a merely natural economy of concrete history, one in which *hypothetically* man might have existed in such a way that he was not—as concrete spirit-in-history—always already wounded by sin and addressed by grace, always already being moved or invited to participate in the work of redemption. This idea is countered by Rahner most especially in his own

19. "Nature and Grace," 165.

20. "Nature and Grace," 167–68. A similar claim is made in *Theological Investigations* I: *God, Christ, Mary and Grace*, "Concerning the Relationship Between Nature and Grace," 297–318, esp. 298–301.

reworking of the Lubacian theme of a natural desire for God, promoted under the auspices of a historically precise interpretation of Aquinas, to whom Rahner attributes the idea of a "*desiderium naturale in visionem beatificam*."[21] He takes up what is customarily seen to be a *via media* between the dialectic insistence of the transcendence of grace *vis-à-vis* human accomplishment in Barth's Reformed thought and what he takes to be the overly reductive integration of natural ends and graced beatitude in the early work of de Lubac.[22] Between these two ranges on a spectrum, Rahner opts for a distinction between nature considered essentially and nature considered existentially, where the latter is the only "concrete and real" formulation of nature as we encounter it in salvation history.[23] The human being exists concretely in a world in which the transcendental structure of the human spirit is open naturally (*a priori*) to a supernatural accomplishment *and* in its vital history in the world is always already addressed by the grace of Christ.[24] It is just on this point that Rahner takes issue with the notion of a historically realized pure nature:

It follows from the theological data already given that this *de facto* human nature, as it knows itself here, and in view of all its experiences (especially when this human experience is viewed in the light of the whole history of mankind, where alone its development is fully realized) cannot and need not be considered as the reflexion of that "pure" nature which is distinguished in theology from everything supernatural.... [Man] must allow for the fact that much of his concrete experience which he is almost automatically tempted to attribute to his "nature" may perhaps in fact be the effect in him of what he must recognize as an unmerited grace in the light of theology.[25]

21. "Nature and Grace," 172. Rahner summarizes Aquinas's view with this phrase, though Aquinas never uses the phrase.

22. For Rahner's implicit but clear criticism of de Lubac, see ibid., 186.

23. Ibid., 181–83.

24. Ibid., 180: "If this is so then we may say that the supernatural transcendence is always present in every man who has reached the age of moral reason. That does not mean that he is justified. He may be a sinner and an unbeliever. But where and in so far as he has the concrete possibility of a morally good act, he is in fact constantly within the open horizon of transcendence towards the God of the supernatural life, whether his free act is in accord or in conflict with this prior state of his supernaturally elevated spiritual existence."

25. Ibid., 182–83.

It is significant, however, that after disputing the worthwhile pursuit of any concept of a merely natural end for human existence[26] and even a "'pure' philosophy of the essence of natural man,"[27] Rahner does come to affirm unequivocally the utility and even necessity of a conception of pure nature as such. The concept is necessary insofar as it permits one to articulate, against the backdrop of the historical experience of grace, the possibility of human existence without grace and the simultaneous gratuity of the gift of the beatific vision as a mystery distinct from the gift of creation.[28] Therefore, there is only a tendential disposition of the natural final end of the created human spirit (which is the open-ended natural desire to know God immediately) to the final end of man under grace (the beatific vision), and not an identity of the two. The former disposition is proportioned directly to the vision of God only by the latter grace.[29] This irreducible duality must be upheld even while this vision is also understood as the only possible authentic and final accomplishment of the spiritual life of man in our concrete history.

No doubt some would wish to criticize Rahner's theories as too timid a reform of prevalent scholastic views, and would instead wish to substitute the more robust critical theories of de Lubac, or for that matter Balthasar, with a different strategy of interpretation regarding the seeming criticism of de Lubac's *Surnaturel* in *Humani Generis* (to which Rahner clearly wishes to show deference). Be that as it may, an important point to be made here is that there is something fundamentally problematic about the construal of the "average" scholastic notion of pure nature by Rahner. For what he is criticizing as the "average" position is in fact the historical position of Francisco Suarez in particular.[30] The problem with this characterization is that there were

26. Ibid., 184.   27. Ibid., 185.
28. Ibid.

29. Ibid., 186: "If it be granted, it follows that there can be no spirit without a transcendence open to the supernatural; but spirit is meaningful, without supernatural grace. Hence its fulfillment in grace cannot be demanded by its essence, though it is open for such grace."

30. See Francisco Suarez, *Opera Omnia* (Paris: Vivès Edition, 1857), Tome VII (De statibus humanae naturae), Prolegomenum IV, ch. 8: "Whether in the state of fallen nature man is intrinsically weaker for doing the good than he would be in the state of pure nature?" and ch. 9: "Whether in the state of fallen nature man is weaker in acting than

contrasting understandings of pure nature in the scholastic tradition, such that Suarez's account, far from being generally adopted, was not typical. Ironically, representative Dominican Thomistic scholastics articulated a concept of pure nature that was purposefully intended to contrast with the Suarezian account for reasons similar to those of Rahner, based upon a concrete theological realism concerning the divine economy. Rahner is in fact criticizing a traditional Jesuit position (one that in fact merits prudent theological consideration, rather than cursory dismissal) while moving only imperfectly toward a traditional Dominican one. This can be illustrated briefly by considering the teaching on pure nature of the archetypal Thomistic scholastic of Rahner's own epoch: that of the French Dominican, Reginald Garrigou-Lagrange.

Garrigou-Lagrange treats the question of pure nature in his commentary on Aquinas's *Summa theologiae* I, in a 1943 work entitled *De Deo Trino et Creatore*.[31] Here he raises the question in particular "of the various states of human nature in relation to grace" and in treating this question is indebted in particular to René Billuart, O.P. (1685–1757), from the latter's treatise *De Gratia* (d. 2, aa. 1–3), which was composed as an interpretation of Thomism in purposeful contrast to the positions of Baius and Jansenism as well as that of Suarez.[32] So the reflections here should certainly count for authentically

in pure nature, at least from extrinsic causes?" Suarez's doctrine of pure nature is rather subtle. He argues that the perfection of human operations in their natural structure, or formal perfection, is not altered by sin, so that a fallen man does not cease to be a human being, or become a different species of being than one God created originally in his image. The theological interlocutors are those who claim nature is formally corrupted by original sin, so as to be shattered in its integrity. He concludes from this, however, that there must not be said to be any intrinsically less perfect natural tendency to perfection in one who is fallen than in one who would have existed in a state of pure nature. In an attempt to respond to what he takes to be the excessive metaphysical pessimism of the Reformers, he seems to overcompensate by excess, minimizing the intrinsic wounds to human nature resultant from original sin (see, for instance, Suarez, *De gratia*, Tome VII, Prol. IV, cap. I, no. 2 [Vivès, 179]). Translations from Latin in this chapter, unless otherwise indicated, are my own.

31. Reginald Garrigou-Lagrange, *De Deo Trino et Creatore. Commentarius in Summa Theologicam S. Thomae (Ia q. xxvii–cxix)* (Turin / Paris: Marietti / Desclée de Brouwer, 1943), 418–51, esp. 421–22.

32. Reacting against the position of Suarez, the Dominican tradition tended to affirm that the essential intrinsic dignity of the human being remains after sin, but that

"Baroque Thomist," or at least "average Dominican Thomist," as distinct from other scholastic traditions or schools. Following Billuart, Garrigou-Lagrange refers to four distinct states of human nature: the state of pure nature, the state of integral nature, the state of fallen nature, and the state of nature that is being redeemed in Christ.

What is noteworthy is that the concept of the various states of human nature is employed by this tradition, as Garrigou-Lagrange points out, just so as to reject any kind of equivalency of man's actual concrete historical nature (as both fallen and subject to the conditions of grace) with the notion of a pure nature or of a rationalistic naturalism that could be considered normative independently of Christian revelation.[33] Garrigou-Lagrange goes on to show that the Dominican tradition continually opposed the notion of a pure nature created without being in a state of grace, or of a fallen nature that could be equated with a pure nature left to its own resources without grace.[34] This Dominican position was developed, as he notes, to argue (against the Reformers, Baius, and Jansenism) that human nature was created in a state of *grace*, not merely natural perfection, but that after sin, this same nature remains structurally human, so that nature is not destroyed. On the other hand, the Dominicans argued against Suarez and some other Jesuit scholastics, such as Molina, that fallen human nature is wounded *intrinsically* (in the exercise of its own powers and in the order between them) and can only be healed and fulfilled intrinsically *by grace*, in its concrete historical state. Consequently, there never has existed a state of pure nature, and the capacities of fallen human nature are more diminished (due to the historical rejection of grace and the concrete consequences of sin) than they would be had something like a state of pure nature ever existed.

The latter concept of nature in a "pure state" is necessary as a foil

---

because of the absence of an extrinsic principle (the grace of God, which is necessarily extrinsic at least insofar as it is not purely natural), an intrinsic wounding of human nature results, not from a defect in nature itself, but from the absence of grace, for which it was made. See Charles René Billuart, *Summa Sancti Thomae* (Paris: Letouzey & Ané, 1880), vol. III, Dissertatio II, Art. 3: "Whether man, in the state of fallen nature, not yet repaired, would have fewer strengths for the moral good than he would have had in the state of pure nature?" Billuart answers affirmatively.

33. *De Deo Trino et Creatore*, 422.

34. Ibid., 435–36, citing Capreolus, *II Sent.*, d. 31, a. 3 ; Cajetan, in ST I-II, q. 83, a. 2, n. IX; Ferrariensis in SCG IV, c. 52.

(an idea concerning something that did not exist but that could have existed) which one can contrast with the state of integral nature, a state pertaining to the original innocence of man's first parents. This original state of natural integrity was itself a result of the gift of grace insofar as man was truly created *in and for* the life of grace, and this original state of grace had unique positive benefits upon the nature of man considered as such. Yet in Thomistic parlance, integral nature is not simply identical with the grace of original innocence (or "original justice"). For the notion of original innocence connotes the genuinely supernatural gifts of divine life given to the first parents of man (supernatural friendship with God in faith, hope, and love, the infused virtues and the gifts of the Holy Spirit), none of which can be acquired by human powers. Integral nature, by contrast, denotes human nature in its fullness considered as nature, yet due to a development made possible by the presence of grace and under grace. In effect, for Aquinas, in distinction from many of his medieval contemporaries, human nature was created originally in a state of grace and for the life of grace and this had positive benefits for nature as such, that would not have existed except for the privileged effects conferred by the state of original justice.[35] For example:

> The *state of pure nature* means precisely nature with its own intrinsic principles and those things that follow from them or are owed to it, but apart from grace and the praeternatural gifts. Therefore, in such a state, man would have had a natural end, the natural means leading up to this end, and the helps of the natural order sufficient for all things and effective for certain things. Likewise, [man] would have had the natural law; but he would have been liable to ignorance, concupiscence, infirmity, and death.[36]

---

35. Aquinas differs from his contemporaries (including St. Albert the Great) by insisting on the creation of man in a state of grace, and he developed this notion extensively in his mature theology. This is studied carefully by Jean-Pierre Torrell, "Nature and Grace in Thomas Aquinas," in *Surnaturel: A Controversy at the Heart of Twentieth-Century Thomistic Thought*, ed. Serge-Thomas Bonino, trans. Robert Williams, trans. revised by Matthew Levering (Naples, Fla.: Sapientia Press, 2009), 155–88.

36. *De Deo Trino et Creatore*, 421. There is no developed concept of "a state of pure nature" as such in Aquinas's writings, nor one of "praeternatural gifts" given to nature in its original integral state. But as Garrigou-Lagrange rightly notes (*De Deo Trino et Creatore*, 428–29), Aquinas gives implicit credence to these notions insofar as he considers the majority position of his time (that man was created first in a state of pure nature, yet without sin) to be *metaphysically* possible, but theologically unfitting. See *II Sent.*, d. 31,

While a nature that was not created in grace would not be free from defects of ignorance, potential subjection to concupiscence, physical infirmities, and the power of death, the *status naturae integrae* was not subject to these deficits *precisely because grace was not unrelated to but intimately present and active within its original constitution.* As Jean-Pierre Torrell has recently noted (and as Garrigou-Lagrange accurately comments on ST I, q. 97, aa. 1 and 3), the notion of a nature that is "integral" is understood by Aquinas as *ontologically distinct and intellectually distinguishable* from the graces of that same nature, even as the aforementioned integrity is possible only in a state of original justice, and therefore as a reality *ontologically inseparable* from the participation in divine life.[37] Therefore Aquinas insists that one can analyze "what" human nature could do by its own natural powers (*per pura naturalia* or *in puris naturalibus*). This allows us to identify what is natural in man in the state of original innocence as distinct from what he possesses only through the inspiration and agency of grace.[38] This is not an artificial "abstraction" but rather a profound form of insight into the natural structure of the graced human being. The archetypal example concerns love: created, integral human nature was so constituted that human beings could love God above all things *nat-*

---

q. 1, a. 2, ad 3: "God was able from the beginning when he made man, to form another man from the mire of the earth, which would have remained in the condition of its nature: that is, it would be mortal and passible, experiencing the fight of concupiscence in the reason; in which nothing would be taken away from human nature, because it follows from the principles of nature" (see also SCG IV, c. 52). The idea of pure nature present here is simply identical with that of the later Thomist tradition.

37. See Torrell, "Nature and Grace in Thomas Aquinas," here at 169–71. He cites Aquinas at ST I-II, q. 114, a. 2: "Two states of *man without grace* can be considered, as was said above. One state is of integral nature as it was in Adam before his sin; the other is of corrupt nature as it is in us before the reparation of grace." It is of course essential to keep in mind that integral nature, for Aquinas, only existed when man was *in a state of grace*, prior to the fall. The point here, then, is not that integral nature exists in ontological separation from grace, but that it can attain certain goods by intrinsic natural powers, without immediate dependence upon grace for these activities.

38. Torrell, "Nature and Grace in Thomas Aquinas," 169n38. Thomas Aquinas, *Quodlibet* I, q. 4, a. 3 [8]: "If man was made in grace, as one can hold from the words of Basil and Augustine, this question does not have a place: for it is clear that someone existing in grace loves God through the charity which is above him. But, because it was possible for God to make man in pure nature [*in puris naturalibus*], it is useful to consider to what extent natural love is able to extend itself."

urally by virtue of their intrinsic rational and voluntary powers. Were this not the case, then the higher, supernatural love of God given to man in grace would be something alien and purely extrinsic to natural, human love.[39] Yet even as human beings created in a state of grace could love God above all things naturally by their own powers, they were moved existentially also to love God above all things by grace in accordance with the theological virtues of faith, hope, and charity. The natural love of God above all things (as an action of human reason and worship) and its graced exercise in subordination to the theological virtues of faith, hope, and charity remained distinguishable dimensions of a given human action (the perfected worship of God by charity) but were also inseparable, just as nature is distinguishable from grace but completed and perfected by the latter.[40]

Consequently the third state considered is the *status sanctitatis et justitiae originalis*, which is not a state of being ontologically distinct from the previous, but is the same state considered with respect to the supernatural elevation of nature by grace into the life of intimate friendship with God. This twofold consideration of the same existential reality (man in original innocence) is requisite so that one understands that the fall of man from original justice affects man intimately in two distinct ways: namely it affects *not only his possession of the life of divine grace, but also the integrity and harmony of his very nature.* Therefore the *status naturae lapsae nondum reparatae* implies not only the loss of sanctifying grace, the infused virtues, and the gifts of the Holy Spirit, but also the loss of the *gifts* of integrity, and is such that the fallen human being, far from being demoted to a state of pure nature (as Rahner rightly claims is not the case), is now affected by the mysterious wounds of original sin that characterize this state of *natura lapsae*: ignorance in the intellect, malice in the will, concupiscence

39. ST I, q. 60, a. 5: "Since God is the universal good, and under this good both man and angel and all creatures are comprised, because every creature in regard to its entire being naturally belongs to God, it follows that from natural love angel and man alike love God before themselves and with a greater love. Otherwise, if either of them loved self more than God, it would follow that natural love would be perverse, and that it would not be perfected but destroyed by charity."

40. See here, most importantly, Aquinas, ST I-II, q. 109, a. 3, a text I will return to below.

in the concupiscible sensitive appetite, and weakness in the irascible sensitive appetite.[41] The natural faculties and powers of the human person are affected internally by the absence of grace: reason is no longer subject to God supernaturally *or naturally*, the body is no longer subject to the soul (death is a punishment of sin), and the passions are no longer subject to reason.[42]

Finally, in the *status naturae reparatae*, in which the just are redeemed by Christ, there are the gifts of sanctifying grace, the infused virtues, and the gifts of the Holy Spirit, but without the original gifts of integral nature (freedom from error, concupiscence, sickness, and death). In a passage not wholly unlike *Gaudium et Spes*, no. 39, Garrigou-Lagrange states: "Nature will not be completely repaired except in glory, and further, it will have integrity with the resurrection of the dead."[43] The *return* to the integrity of nature as such is

41. Garrigou-Lagrange, *De Deo Trino et Creatore*, 422, cf. ST I-II, qq. 83, 85.

42. ST I-II, q. 85, a. 1; see Garrigou-Lagrange, *De Deo Trino et Creatore*, 449–50: "Many Thomists who hold this opinion reply: the faculties of the soul—its properties, so to speak—just as the essence of the soul itself, do not admit of more and less, especially intellect and will, which, since they are spiritual, are altogether incorruptible and unchangeable. Thus, they are not intrinsically diminished. But man in the state of fallen nature is born as *habitually and directly adverse to God, his ultimate and supernatural end*, and as *indirectly adverse to God, his final and natural end*. For every sin that is posed directly against the supernatural law is posed indirectly against the natural law which teaches that one ought to be obedient to God. In sinning, Adam thus turned away all his posterity from God, the author of nature. In pure nature, however, there would not be such an aversion, because there would be no sin, and man would be born as capable both of a positive turning to God and a turning away from God. Therefore, he would be more apt to turning himself to God than if he were born turned away from God. This aversion thus pertains to the *wound of the will*, which, as St. Thomas says in I-II, q. 85, a. 3: 'is deprived of an ordering to the good.' ... From this there follows the *wound of ignorance* in the practical intellect especially, because each person judges practically according to his inclination, and if this inclination is not right, the intellect is inclined to error. Similarly, there follows [from this] in the sensitive appetite the *wound of infirmity* and the *wound of the concupiscence*, because the higher faculties are less strong in the directing of the sensitive appetite to what it should desire. Therefore, fallen man is compared to man in pure nature not only as a denuded man to a naked one but as a wounded man to a healthy one." The last line stands in contradiction to Rahner's portrayal of the "average" scholastic position, precisely because it contrasts with the teaching of Suarez.

43. *De Deo Trino et Creatore*, 422. Compare GS, no. 39: "When we have spread on earth the fruits of our *nature* and our enterprise—human dignity, brotherly communion, and freedom—according to the command of the Lord and in his Spirit, *we will find them once again, cleansed this time from the stain of sin, illuminated and transfigured*, when Christ presents to his Father an eternal and universal kingdom.... Here on earth

possible for the concrete historical life of fallen man only through redemption in Christ, and eschatologically, through the glorification of the souls of human beings and the resurrection of their physical bodies from the dead. Interestingly, where Rahner was hesitant to speculate about the "natural" character of the resurrected body in grace (doubting whether one could claim such a thing),[44] Garrigou-Lagrange does not hesitate, particularly due to his Thomistic notion of "integral nature" under grace, and the corresponding rejection of a historically concrete "state of pure nature." It is arguably his thought which is closer to the true sense of *Gaudium et Spes*, no. 22!

Up to this point, these may seem like playful polemics, and in fact on one level they are. But I am seeking to make a deeper point. Not only is the reflection above meant to suggest that we ought to be careful to avoid historically superficial and rhetorically facile shibboleths against the banshee of pure nature and the arcane plots of baroque Thomists. More to the point, the consideration of the divine economy requires a careful thinking through of the particular theological states of human nature (1) in dependence upon grace, (2) in secession from the life of grace, (3) in the still wounded yet partially redeemed economy of Christian grace, (4) in the eschaton, and (5) in Christ himself. These states are simply not reducible to one another, and yet it is necessary to affirm the existence of a persisting human nature undergirding all of these different states.

Were this not the case, consider some inevitable theological con-

the kingdom is mysteriously present; when the Lord comes it will enter into its perfection" (emphasis added).

44. "Nature and Grace," 184: "Let us ask, for instance, whether the resurrection of the body appertains to any form of the fulfillment of man as a spirit-person, or is it something that is only a consequence of grace. Or let us ask how we are to think of the fulfillment of pure nature in the concrete. Then we find ourselves faced with questions which could only be answered if one could make experiments on pure nature and draw up a concrete teleology on this basis." As Garrigou-Lagrange's own thought suggests, however, it is in fact quite the opposite. In a state of pure nature (which never existed) the resurrection would not be possible, as it could not be procured by the intrinsic principles of man, who is a spiritual animal, naturally subject to corruption. However, in the concrete Christian economy in which a state of pure nature never existed, but only a state of integral completeness, such preservation from death was normative, through an effect of the agency of grace, and consequently there is something unnatural about human death and something profoundly "natural" about the Christian eschatological promise of resurrection.

sequences. Concerning original justice and the fall: we would be unable to consider man in the state of original innocence as truly and essentially human *or* we would be unable to consider the fallen human person as retaining his or her essentially human characteristics (as still being made in the image of God, despite the consequence of sin). Concerning redemption: we would be unable to consider the redeemed human person as essentially human in continuity with the fallen human person and yet as more perfect *qua human*, that is to say in the potencies of his or her nature. Concerning Christology: we would be unable to understand the incarnate Lord in his passion and resurrection as bringing our human nature to an eschatological fulfillment, distinct in mode, yet identical in kind to our current state of being. Any understanding of Christ's redemption thereby would appear wholly alien (that is, extrinsic) to our human historical condition—and the reason for his redemption of our human nature from "sin" would be unintelligible as well. Or contrastingly, we would be obliged to abolish all distinction of nature and grace, thus seeing our human historical condition as *necessarily bound up with Christ* such that human salvation in Christ simply would be co-extensive with our "natural" existence (a not-so-subtle version of *apokatastasis panton*). Nature in separation from Christ would be literally inconceivable.

Both of the final alternatives, however, are theologically unfeasible and deeply unrealistic. Respect for the historically configured states of human nature, shown by a complex set of theological-ontological reflections, is the precursor and condition for a right understanding of the divine economy *in distinctly Christological terms*, terms that presuppose original integrity, the fallen state of man, the remainder of wounds of sin and death even in redeemed humanity, and the possibility of eternal loss as well as of eternal salvation. A correct consideration of the divine economy entails comparisons which in turn presuppose a concept of human nature, one that applies to all human persons. Without this concept, such a consideration is impossible. But how then should we deal with the question of the historicity of our human nature and that of Christ, a reality to which *Gaudium et Spes* refers?

THE CHRISTOLOGICAL HISTORICIZATION
OF HUMAN NATURE

If we turn then to the question of the Christological fulfillment of human nature and of the historical perfection of humanity found in salvation history through Christ, a suggestive exegesis of *Gaudium et Spes* is offered by Marie-Dominique Chenu. In an essay published in 1966, shortly after the Council, Chenu claimed that the underlying question of the document was the relation of the church to the world "and therefore underlying this the relation of nature and of grace, considered not in an abstract distinction, but in their concrete situation today."[45] The subtext, then, is also profoundly ecclesiological: how ought the church to understand her mission in the modern world? Formulated positively, Chenu's claims in the essay are threefold.

First, there is no realm of nature that is not open to God's transcendent activity and that cannot be claimed "already, from above" for higher, divine ends. Consequently, there is no time or place in history that is not already open to the hidden, higher purposes of grace, working within the aspirations of nature (which are in man *potentially* intrinsically open to a higher completion in Christ).[46] Second, man is by definition a historical being, subject to configurations of place and time, and in particular, open to the construction of his own destiny *as man* through the technological processes and social progress of culture.[47] Correspondingly, the mission of Christ is one of God *in his human historicity*, and the mission of the church must be itself thoroughly centered on the needs of its historical age.

45. Marie-Dominique Chenu, "Une Constitution Pastorale de l'Église," in *Peuple de Dieu dans le Monde* (Paris: Cerf, 1966), 12. The essay published here was originally the text of a conference given in Rome to the Dutch episcopacy at the beginning of the fourth session of the Second Vatican Council, in regard to the turbulent debate surrounding Schema XIII, from which the Pastoral Constitution was to emerge.

46. In an adjoining essay in *Peuple de Dieu dans le Monde* (35–55), entitled "Les Signes des Temps," Chenu claims that there is a Thomistic basis for his interpretation of social development in *Gaudium et Spes* in the notion of "obediential potency."

47. "Une Constitution Pastorale de l'Église," 20–21: "We observe the upheavals of a scientific and technical civilization at the source of multiple and profound mutations which establish man—in both his body and spirit—in a new *condition*, by and in which the relation of man to the universe is intrinsically modified.... 'Nature becomes the humanized being of man' (K. Marx), and in humanizing nature, man becomes more

What [the Pastoral Constitution] is concerned with is not a contingent and opportune "adaptation" of "eternal truths" but in the strong sense of the word, a "presence" today in act of the Gospel, by and in the Church. "An active presence in the construction of the world" .... We are no longer dealing here with "solutions" *ex cathedra* taught from on high and from outside to the evolving problems of the world.... These are Evangelical *stances* ... insofar as grace completes nature within the [concrete] regime of the Incarnation, according to the rhythm of history.[48]

Otherwise stated, God himself took on historical flesh to bring to fulfillment the dynamic, ever-developing history of man, and so likewise, doctrine must be rearticulated according to the inner living historical spirit of a given age and in keeping with the adaptive evangelical life of the church in history. Chenu is well known to have had a life-long (perennial!) concern with the topic of the cultural-historical and intrinsically temporally-situated character of human existence, culture, and ecclesial pronouncements. In his early work he proposes ways to make this viewpoint intelligible in Thomistic terms,[49] and in his later work (especially after the Council) he criticizes vehemently what he takes to be the ahistorical dogmatic essentialism of his former teacher, Garrigou-Lagrange.[50] Clearly in this text, then, Chenu insists that humanity and the church are intrinsically historical entities subject to cultural reformulations over time, and sees this viewpoint as being vindicated or embraced by the Council in general and by *Gaudium et Spes* in particular.

Third, then, the question is raised: where within man's historical

human. Already old Aristotle noted in *techne* a human value. Today, *homo artifex* reveals himself apt as such to be fully human by the progress of this *techne*, even prior to the accomplishment in him of the *homo sapiens*."

48. "Une Constitution Pastorale de l'Église," 15.

49. See Marie-Dominique Chenu, "Raison psychologique du développement du dogme," *Revue des Sciences Philosophiques et Théologiques* 13 (1924): 44–51, where Chenu interprets Aquinas's theory of the Aristotelian agent intellect (knowledge by abstraction, in time, and by progressive synthetic judgments) as the anthropological basis for a historical evolution of dogma. He suggests that a historically situated determination of the content of faith is 'essential' to the faith as such (49).

50. Marie-Dominique Chenu, "Vérité évangélique et métaphysique wolfienne à Vatican II" in *Revue des Sciences Philosophiques et Théologiques* 57 (1973): 632–40. See on this point of Chenu's thought, Henri Donneaud in his "La constitution dialectique de la théologie et de son histoire selon M.D. Chenu," in *Revue Thomiste* 96 (1996): 41–66, and Fergus Kerr, *Twentieth-Century Catholic Theologians* (Oxford: Blackwell, 2007), 17–26.

horizon can one locate an authentic, universal measure of the value of human existence? Here Chenu practices a form of Christological "concentration" to respond to this anthropological question. It is in Christ alone that the full measure and scope of human becoming and of human possibilities are unveiled under grace. The process of transformation that is characteristic of the historical being of man finds its resolution only in Christ.

In fact, underlying the debate concerning perennial truth claims there is quite clearly an ambiguity in Chenu's own thought, one concerning the very notion of human nature as such, since he is engaged in a purposeful attempt to rethink the character of human existence in radically historical terms. What is it that serves as a common measure of the human across all times? It seems that Christology is introduced in order to resolve the question. For example, it is noteworthy that he appeals to Christological existence not only in order to justify a historically and technologically evolutive vision of human becoming, but also to indicate the place where this becoming is resolved. Christ's deity is introduced into history such that the latter (understood now as *salvation* history) is seen as a process of divine-human encounter and communion.

A new light cast upon man today supports the rediscovery of the Incarnation as the human historicization of God.... Over and against an unconscious docetism—which has for a long time nourished itself from an abstract "spirituality" that is atemporal and acosmic—[renewed] interest in the concrete and historical humanity of Christ has led to a recognition of man as partaking of God in the history of the world. God having become man, man is now the measure of all things.[51]

Chenu underscores that there exists no absolute identification of the earthly progress of civilization and of evangelization.[52] Nevertheless, ultimately the two rejoin eschatologically. "Creation and the new

---

51. Chenu, "Une Constitution Pastorale de l'Église," 19.
52. Ibid., 26. "Neither nature, nor history have the capacity to reveal the mystery of God. His Word comes 'from above' by the initiative of a gratuitous love, engaging itself in a loving communion [with humanity]. Grace is grace and profane history is not the source of salvation. Evangelization is of another order than civilization. To feed human beings is not in itself to save them, even if my salvation requires of me to feed them. The promotion of culture is not in any way equivalent to conversion to the faith."

creation are certainly distinct, but their [common] eschatological finality, already at work in time, forbids us from treating them as two juxtaposed realities in two different domains."[53] Consequently, when *Gaudium et Spes* identifies *loci* of authentically teleologically oriented *natural* human developments, these latter are themselves potential indications of the work of Christ's *grace* in history. "Wherever human intelligence engages not to the benefit of ideology but in the true service of man: in the construction of the world, of the values of socialization, in the political order of the state, of rights, of science and of morals, we can perceive there the indirect sign of the Lordship of Christ, even outside of the Church."[54]

It is evident that Chenu's reflections in these pages raise numerous theological questions. Often his critics signal the questionable character of the alliance that is envisaged between technology, social "progress" broadly defined, and the Christological concentration of grace.[55] Is the grace of Christ not being appealed to here to lend support to a modern culture of technology that all too often in practice disregards true human dignity in favor of technological prowess and power? Is the kingdom of Christ being invoked here to underwrite an intra-human (French socialism *circa* the 1960s) political vision fixated on the means of production and the freedom from class alienation that can occur through the technological progress of civilization and a more just distribution of goods? Chenu presents claims to the contrary, insisting that the presence of these latter phenomena must in fact be subordinated to the higher and more ultimate ends of the life of grace and of the Gospel.[56] Be that as it may, the query is one worthy of careful consideration.

Here, however, it seems to me more germane to focus on the

53. Ibid., 30.
54. Ibid.
55. See in this respect the very different evaluation of the moral ambivalency of technology in modern culture by Pope Benedict XVI (in *Caritas in Veritate*, chap. VI) in continuity with the appeal to the "signs of the times," in para. 18. See also, Richard Schenk, "*Officium signa temporum perscrutandi.* New Encounters of Gospel and Culture in the Context of the New Evangelisation," in *Scrutinizing the Signs of the Times in Light of the Gospel* (*Bibliotheca Ephemeridum Theologicarum Lovaniensium*, CCVIII), ed. J. Verstraeten (Leuven / Leuven: Leuven University Press / Peeters, 2007), 167–203.
56. See especially Chenu, "Une Constitution Pastorale de l'Église," 31.

question of the perennial versus intrinsically temporal character of human nature, and its relation to the mystery of Christ. For although the historical character of humanity and the redemptive mystery of Christ are deeply interrelated, the claim that Christ could be the key to understanding the meaning of human nature precisely *because he is a historically unique individual* (and one in a culturally unique, biblical setting) is one that has received important criticisms in modernity, and it is not clear from the tenor of Chenu's proposals that he is prepared to meet these objections adequately.

First, we could ask with Immanuel Kant whether the historical-cultural particularity of Christ is not the proof of an intrinsic limitation to his universal appeal, rather than a sign of the latter. In his *Critique of Pure Reason*, Kant casts this argument by appeal to an ethical form of argumentation. True universality in the ethical domain stems from natural reason, which derives precepts that are applicable to all times and places. However, the moral example of Christ is presented in the Gospels in the form of sensible-temporal narratives that are bound up with a particular historical-cultural setting. *By that very fact* this moral example of Christ is not universal in kind. Consequently, it cannot produce the kind of first principles necessary for transcendental reason, insofar as this reason touches upon practical action.[57]

We see the poignant echo of Kant's argument in the modern post-Christian theology (or gnosis) of the religious-pluralism movement, exemplified by the thought of John Hick. While historical-

---

57. See Immanuel Kant, *The Critique of Pure Reason*, "The Idea of Pure Reason," A568/B596–A570/B598: "Human reason contains not only ideas, but ideals also, which although they do not have, like the Platonic ideas, creative power, yet have *practical* power (as regulative principles), and form the basis of the possible perfection of certain *actions*.... But to attempt to realize the ideal in an example, that is, in the field of appearance, as, for instance, to depict the character of the perfectly wise man in a romance, is impracticable. There is indeed something absurd, and far from edifying, in such an attempt, inasmuch as the natural limitations, which are constantly doing violence to the completeness of the idea, make the illusion that is aimed at altogether impossible, and do cast suspicion on the good itself—the good that has its source in the idea—by giving it the air of being a mere fiction" (trans. N. K. Smith [New York and Toronto: St. Martin's and Macmillan, 1965]). That Kant seems to have the Gospel portrait of Christ in mind can be confirmed by consulting a parallel text, i.e., *Religion within the Boundaries of Mere Reason*, 6:60–6:66).

critical scripture studies demonstrate the culturally limited sphere of
the temporal consciousness of Jesus of Nazareth as a first-century Jew
(whose identity is not, Hick claims, accurately depicted by later dogmatic pronouncements of the Catholic tradition), so likewise an expanded contemporary understanding of the profundity of varied religious traditions suggests that the speculative as well as moral truth
about "Ultimate Reality" can only be found in and through a comparative theology that disavows the uniqueness of Christianity and the
uniquely saving role of Christ in history. Christocentricity is the ene-
my of true ethical universality.[58]

A theologically positive way of framing this objection is to ask
what metaphysical criteria are required for the Christological concentration that Chenu, following *Gaudium et Spes*, wishes to defend? For
it seems that we are invited to consider at least three senses in which
human nature in Christ and in human history must be discernible,
that is, under both (1) perennial aspects and (2) particular economic
states (that is, our nature as "typically'" encountered in history in fall-
en and redeemed states), and (3) as particularly perfected in Christ
and in the vision of the God-human presented in the Gospels. For if
we cannot attain knowledge of nature as such then we cannot compare the various economic states of this nature evaluatively. In fact,
we cannot even reflect on the *question* of whether behavior theology deems to be "fallen" or "redeemed" has a basis in natural human
structures and teleology. And likewise only if we can consider the
distinctive state of Christ's human nature in comparison with both
our fallen human nature and the essential and teleological exigencies of nature as such can we think out reasonably the natural perfection of Christ in terms that are universally accessible (in philosophical as well as theological refutation of Kant and Hick). Only such a
comparison of states of nature will allow us to develop both an appreciation and a critique of other forms of non-Christian religiosity
in terms that underscore the universality of Christian truth. A metaphysics of nature is needed in order to articulate the perfection of
Christ in keeping with a sufficiently universalist moral teaching and
eschatology that are applicable to all human persons.

58. Cf. John Hick, *An Interpretation of Religion: Human Responses to the Transcendent* (New Haven, Conn.: Yale University Press, 1989).

Second, and perhaps more seriously, has Chenu not naively un-
derestimated the degree to which his own theology most especially
presupposes recourse to perennial principles of wisdom from which
to evaluate the contingent circumstances of a given age? This is especially manifest in his concept of world-construction as teleologically oriented, as guided by a providential order into a supernatural
beatitude that can in intrinsic fashion assume and accomplish the legitimate aspirations (the "obediential potency") of human civilization. What sort of vision could be more explicitly metaphysical and
therefore trans-historical, in structure? And if one refuses overt recourse to such perennial principles, how then might one reply to the
post-structuralist tradition of reflection that was emerging in Chenu's
own time, and which was to render any idea of a universal social order superfluous or intrinsically problematic for many? Otherwise
said, once we admit that human nature is radically conditioned (determined?) by its cultural-historical circumstances, then what is there
to prevent us from accepting that truth constructs are historical-
critical "all the way down"[59] and that postmodern deconstructionist techniques are simply the most logically consistent outcome of
any ontology that would present man as a being subject to becoming
through history in all that he is? If this is the case, then a historicist
ontology of man is "intrinsically disharmonious" with, or radically
alien to what must be considered *purely violent and extrinsic* Christian
ends that claim for man a universal and transcendent teleology. This
was, at any rate, the thinking of Friedrich Nietzsche, who perceived
in the Christian pretext to historical universalism a *purely* historically
situational and individually interested sacerdotal exercise of the will-
to-power.[60] This supposedly universal ethic of mercy was a pretext

59. As Antonio Gramsci claimed in developing a radicalized interpretation of Marx's
anthropology. Cf. Antonio Gramsci, *Prison Notebooks* (New York: Columbia University
Press, 1992), and the analysis by Renate Holub, *Antonio Gramsci: Beyond Marxism and
Postmodernism* (London: Routledge, 1992). Something akin ought to have been familiar
to Chenu via the Frankfurt school, for example in Adorno's and Horkheimer's *Dialektik
der Aufklärung*, first published in 1947.

60. "All that has been done on earth against 'the noble,' 'the powerful,' 'the masters,'
'the rulers,' fades into nothing compared with what the *Jews* have done against them;
the Jews, that priestly people, who in opposing their enemies and conquerors were ultimately satisfied with nothing less than a radical revaluation of their enemies' values,
that is to say, an act of the *most spiritual vengeance*. For this alone was appropriate to a

stemming genealogically from the ancient Jewish experience of political impotence, intensified subsequently by the teaching of Jesus as
an inauthentic response to the problem of violence.[61] Or to formulate
the objection (if possible) in a more pointed way (because less distinctly fixated on Christianity), a simple citation from that most ingenious of twentieth-century "deconstructionists" should suffice:

[My] essential task was to *free the history of thought from its subjection to transcendence.*... My aim was to analyze this history, in the *discontinuity that
no teleology would reduce in advance*; to map it in a dispersion that no pre-
established horizon would embrace; to allow it to be deployed in an ano-
nymity on which *no transcendental constitution would impose the form of the
subject*; to open it up to a temporality that would not promise the return of
any dawn. My aim was to cleanse it of all transcendental narcissism.... It had
to be shown that the history of thought could not have this role of revealing
the transcendental moment that rational mechanics has not possessed since
Kant, mathematical idealities since Husserl, and the meanings of the perceived world since Merleau-Ponty—despite the efforts that had been made
to find it there.[62]

In other words, is Chenu's transcendental world order not simply another manifestation of the metaphysical Christian triumphalism he
elsewhere so disparages? And should we not wonder if he could be
accused himself by any logically consistent deconstructionist of "nar-

---

priestly people, the people embodying the most deeply repressed priestly vengefulness.
It was the Jews who with awe-inspiring consistency dared to invert the aristocratic value equation (good = noble = powerful = beautiful = happy = beloved of God) ... saying
'the wretched alone are the good; the poor, impotent, lowly alone are the good' ... with
the Jews there begins *the slave revolt in morality*: that revolt ... which we no longer see
because it—has been victorious" (Friedrich Nietzsche, *On the Genealogy of Morals* I, 7,
trans. W. Kaufmann and R. J. Hollingdale [New York: Vintage, 1989]), 33–34. The central issue here is not the question of Nietzsche's emotional prejudice *vis-à-vis* the Jewish
people, but his intellectually arguable claim that their morality should not carry universal import, and stems at base from a particular cultural self-interest, underscoring the
yet more universal will-to-power that inhabited them and every other ancient and modern people.
    61. "This Jesus of Nazareth, the incarnate gospel of love, this 'Redeemer' who
brought blessedness and victory to the poor, the sick, and the sinners—was he not this
seduction in its most uncanny and irresistible form, a seduction and a bypath to precisely those *Jewish* values and new ideals?" *On the Genealogy of Morals* I, 8, 35. This idea is developed at greater length as the central argument of Nietzsche's *The Antichrist*.
    62. Michel Foucault, *The Archaeology of Knowledge and The Discourse on Language*,
trans. A. M. Sheridan Smith (New York: Pantheon, 1972), 203 (emphasis added).

ratives of civilization" of attempting to subject history to the transcendental narcissism of a Christian utopianism? And in this is he not
simply the more subtle arbiter of the will to power that is less concealed in the older, triumphalistic ecclesiological dogmatism of the
epoch of the First Vatican Council (and its scholastic defenders)? Or
so the argument might run.

Again, framed positively, the argument being underscored here is
that Catholic interpreters of *Gaudium et Spes* cannot avoid a self-conscious and overtly metaphysical moment of explanation within theology that responds to the critique of the postmodern anti-metaphysician.
The latter would see *any* attempt to assign prescriptive ends to human
civilization as nothing less than an overt or covert assault on human
freedom through an ultimately arbitrary attempt at world-construal
that is purely contingent (and therefore ineffectual). But a response to
such a claim entails an articulation of the epistemic basis for a philosophical understanding of human nature. Unless some natural knowledge of essences is possible, then Christian discourse is inevitably reduced to being a mere meta-narrative among others, a tribal rhetoric
that is not subject to laws of universal verification in any respect, and
that cannot in turn make an appeal to human nature (or educate Christians or non-Christians as to what is proper to nature and to the natural
law) *even from within the domain of Christology and even in light of Christ.*
To say the very least, this would entail, for Catholic theologians, the acceptance of a seeming caesura running right down the middle of *Gaudium et Spes*, separating the Christological hermeneutic of salvation history irrevocably from the multiple appeals to the natural law, and to the
profound moral truths that can be attained by human reason. In fact,
the two might even be seen (as they perhaps are by some Barthian interpreters) as mutually exclusive. Correspondingly, the same stance
would necessarily undermine the theme in the document of a rational *apologia* which attempts to suggest that life in Christ is more perfectly human and that in fact it is only possible for a culture to be fully human if it is liberated from the denaturalizing irresolution of its
own inner tensions (that are the consequence of sin) by the grace of
Christ.

Christological fulfillment of history, then, requires the Christological accomplishment of human nature and of nature's various

cultures, and therefore establishes a perennial standard of what is human. The apprehension of such a standard must exist *at least as regards Christ*: what does it mean to say that he is especially human? To announce that God has become *human*, after all, requires in us some intrinsic natural knowledge of what humanity is, and the realization that he fulfills some of the *natural* tendencies or aspirations of the human heart that cannot find completion concretely without him or apart from him. If metaphysically perennial, essential knowledge of human nature is not possible, then the message of Christ as the historical fulfillment of human existence is a message *purely extrinsic* to human culture, a grace that is present to nature "as if from without, lacking a relation to nature and to history ... as if the Kingdom of God was set on top of the world, like the scaffolding of a future city."[63]

What about nature, then? And how ought we to understand the role of a concept of nature in the theological claim that Christ is the fulfillment of all that is human? In the next and final section of this chapter, I would like to consider these questions briefly from a Thomistic point of view.

THOMISTIC REFLECTIONS: INTEGRAL PHILOSOPHICAL ANTHROPOLOGY AS A NECESSARY DIMENSION OF CHRISTOLOGY

Karl Rahner famously asserted that the Council of Chalcedon could not be seen uniquely as a concluding point of resolution in which the church acquired a set of principles by which to discern the parameters of orthodox Christology. It must also be seen as a new starting point for ongoing and ever-developing study in theology.[64] A different analogy—and one perhaps more apt for the interpretation of *Gaudium et Spes*—could be drawn from the Council of Ephesus. For if Ephesus identified the hypostatic union as a basic first principle of Christological reflection concerning the God-man (that is, the recognition of the *unity* of the person of Christ) then Chalcedon was the

63. Chenu, "Les Signes des Temps," 46.
64. Karl Rahner, "Current Problems in Christology," in *Theological Investigations* I, 150.

proper qualification of this fundamental principle: that within the person of the incarnate Son there exists the distinction without separation of the two *natures*. The passage was made from recognizing the unity of the person of Christ to recognizing the distinction of natures in this unity. Similarly, what *Gaudium et Spes* and its early interpreters such as Rahner and Chenu rightly underscore is a principle of unity: the existence of humanity within a unique historical economy of grace, such that there exists a concrete phenomenological unity of grace and nature, in which grace precedes and can affect the diverse historical states of man (as innocent, fallen, and redeemed), his natural abilities, and his culture. Grace thus invites human beings in varied ways into the life of God, through participation in the redemptive history of Christ. There is not a pure exteriority between grace and nature *in exercitu*, or a "history before grace." Likewise, there is a uniquely graced fulfillment of the teleological aspirations of human nature made possible through the designs of God in human history that cannot be found apart from Christ, while Christ is the concrete exemplar or eschatological point of concentration of the human as such. In him the true nature of man and the teleological fulfillment of human desire and of human culture are made manifest in a determinate and final way.

Nevertheless, if this principle of the concrete unity of nature and grace is important to recognize, the distinction of nature and grace is no less important and has been significantly underemphasized in recent times. This is particularly the case when nature is deemed something unintelligible in itself (apart from Christ) or when grace is simply rendered synonymous with history, such that the distinction between the work of salvation and the existential life of human persons is all but eclipsed.[65] Either error, however, renders unintelligible the claim that Christ is the fulfillment of natural human aspirations, and ironically makes Christological truth claims something imposed upon human philosophical traditions *arbitrarily*, that is to say in a way that is purely extrinsic to them.[66] I have suggested above that

65. It seems that John Milbank wishes to take his theological interpretation of grace-nature relations in this direction. See his *The Suspended Middle: Henri de Lubac and the Debate concerning the Supernatural* (Grand Rapids, Mich.: Eerdmans, 2005). The idea is clearly stated as programmatic (11–14).

66. This would not be the judgment of Blondel, clearly, in his *l'Action*, a work that

a rational, philosophical concept of nature is requisite in order to articulate in sufficiently universal terms the distinctly theological claim that Christ is the historical fulfillment and exemplar of human existence. (That this concept of nature might at times be especially well elaborated within the context of Christian culture and even within the context of theological reflection—as in the case of St. Augustine or the high Scholastics—is of significant importance, but it is incidental to my argument.) I have also claimed that a notion of "pure nature" (of nature possibly existing as neither originally graced, nor as fallen) is the logical corollary of any claim that human nature was originally graced, is indeed in a fallen state, and that it has been redeemed by Christ, in whom human nature has attained (by grace) an acutely particular perfection, even while Christ is truly human like us. In the remainder of this chapter, then, I would like briefly to address a specific and limited but important aspect of each of these claims. The first concerns the indispensability of a notion of nature as a condition for the meaningful narrative articulation of historical change and teleological orientation. The second concerns the indispensability of a notion of pure nature for the articulation of one of the key Christological affirmations of *Gaudium et Spes,* no. 22: the claim that "it is only in the mystery of the Word made flesh that the mystery of man truly becomes clear."

Nature as the Indispensable Concept Underlying All Meaningful Narrative History

Chenu claims that a theology that bases itself on what it presumes to be perennial principles runs the risk of ignoring its cultural circumstances and of failing to construct a theological response to the signs and needs of a given time and locus. Appeals to the perennial are deemed timeless but therefore abstract as contrasted with the temporal becoming of historical and teleological change, circumstances

---

sought to argue just the opposite: to provide a rationale from within philosophical scrutiny of the ascending desires of the human will toward a uniquely supernatural vision of the final end of man. However, the risk of this perspective is that it in fact manages surreptitiously to render natural desires formally unintelligible apart from grace, or to render claims about grace wholly alien to rival philosophical accounts of the meaningfulness of human willing.

that must be taken into account for a realistic presentation of the gospel. However, it is reasonable in this context to raise the question of which form of appeal to perennial principles of theology and of human nature one might be referring to. For it was against a Platonic conception of timeless forms which Aristotle considered all too abstract that he was to conceive of progressive (historical) knowledge of *an enduring human nature* that one discovers experientially *in and through* time.[67] And it was in consideration of Parmenides's denial of the existence of multiplicity and change that he would insist on the possibility of a universal *science* of change that could discover the explanatory principles of physical beings not beyond or outside of but in and through their formal and teleological developments in time (because change occurs in an intelligible subject and in relation to intelligible ends or the non-realization of these ends).[68] Most relevant to the point at hand, Aristotle argued convincingly in *Metaphysics* IV against the sophist tradition that the condition of possibility for the logical articulation of change is in fact knowledge of unchanging ontological structural principles in realities that are being described.[69] Simply put, coherent narratives of change of any kind *simply to be logically coherent in themselves* as forms of discourse must evaluate change in terms of stable forms of identity (essences) that undergo or are the subjects of history, and in terms of teleological grammar. The

67. See, for example, the critique of the Platonic theory of the Forms as an account of natural substances in *Metaphysics* VII, 15–16, culminating in the identification of the substance in VII, 17 as the formal determination of the material individual, abiding in it, and discernible to human thought in and through its history and development. An analogous point is made in *Metaphysics* XII, 5, 1071a18–23: "The primary principles of all things are the actual primary 'this' [the concrete singular existent] and another thing that exists potentially [latent in the matter of what already exists]. The universal causes, then, of which we spoke do not *exist* [i.e., as separated forms]. For the *individual* is the source of the *individuals*. For while man is the cause of man universally, there *is* no universal man; but Peleus is the cause of Achilles, and your father of you, and this particular *b* of this particular *ba*, though *b* in general is the cause of *ba* taken without qualification."

68. This is one of the central arguments of *Physics* I, 1–8, and leads to affirmations of the formal and final causes of material change in II, 1. See especially 184b15–186a3 and 188a13–b26.

69. See *Metaphysics* IV, 5–8, especially 1010a1–36 and 1011a3–b23. He also raises this point in *Physics* I, 2, 185a1–b5 in response to Parmenides's denial of the real multiplicity of beings in the world and of contingent change within these beings.

latter ideas are an intrinsic component of the articulation not only of purposeful development (and therefore of any possible narrative *revaluation* of values). They are also necessary even for a description of efficient causality, insofar as decisive historical factors that alter the narrative circumstances of a reality point back themselves to an identifiably ordered (that is, teleological) action. Form, efficiency, teleology, and material alterability: these are basic principles of thought, and therefore are also inevitable conceptual properties of any possible discourse.

Behind the meaningful use of language, then, there is the implicit assertion of an ontological foundation expressed by the principle of identity ("each thing we experience has a given unity and essence"). An acknowledgement of this truth leads to the admission of a dependence of the science of logic upon the truths of ontology. As Aquinas points out in commenting on Aristotle, the sophist (a not-so-distant relative of the present day poststructuralist) can only avoid admitting this by making two artificial and ultimately irrational reductions: one of all ontology to mere logic, the second of the study of logic from being either theoretical or practical to being practical only (for a political use).[70] Indeed, the practical study of logic then becomes that

70. Aquinas, *In Meta.* IV, lec. 4, 570–77. More accurately, sophist theoretics studies the logical structure of argumentation in view of merely practical use of argument: a mimicry of it or an unmasking of it as a discourse about social power. Nevertheless, sophisms have less real power than philosophical discourse, Aquinas notes, in that their discourse fails to truly convict the intellect through demonstrative reasoning, in contrast to philosophical science. As he writes (574–75): "The philosopher differs from the *dialectician* in power, because the consideration of the philosopher is more efficacious than that of the dialectician. For the philosopher proceeds demonstratively in dealing with the common attributes mentioned above, and thus it is proper to him to have scientific knowledge of these attributes. And he actually knows them with certitude, for certain or scientific knowledge is the effect of demonstration. The dialectician, however, proceeds to treat all of the above-mentioned common attributes from probable premises, and thus he does not acquire scientific knowledge of them but a kind of opinion. The reason for this difference is that there are two kinds of beings: beings of reason and real beings. The expression 'being of reason' is applied properly to those notions which reason derives from the objects it considers, for example, the notions of genus, species and the like, which are not found in reality but are a natural result of the consideration of reason. And this kind of being, i.e., being of reason, constitutes the proper subject of *logic*. But intellectual conceptions of this kind are equal in extension to real beings, because all real beings fall under the consideration of reason. Hence the subject of logic extends to all things to which the expression real being is applied. His conclusion is, then, that

of dialectics *in view of* power, of the use of rhetoric as a dialectical art
to manipulate the intellectual persuasions of one's auditors and one's
culture, or to seek to analyze the political and cultural uses of dialectic by others. If ontology is merely the logical manipulation of the
culture of thought, Aristotle argues, then indeed all truth is merely
appearance, and has no ontological signification.[71] But in this case,
all propositions can be equally true or untrue (including contradictory ones).[72] If this is the case, then we must abandon the axiom of
non-contradiction, which, as Aristotle observed, is what sophists are
willing to concede (and which many deconstructionists consider inevitable).[73] This means, in turn, that there can be no meaningful articulation of narrative history or teleology, since a determination and
its contradictory are simultaneously equally true or untrue. To attempt to narrate even a history of that which one wishes to decon-
struct is already to attempt to identify at least a formally intelligible
entity with determination and ends (the narrative of a person). Language that is anti-metaphysical all the way down, then, is incapable
even of this. What is most important to grasp from Aristotle's analysis of sophism is not only that the underlying logic of the sophist is
incoherent or contradictory as soon as he begins to analyze (though

the subject of logic is equal in extension to the subject of philosophy, which is real being. Now the philosopher proceeds from the principles of this kind of being to prove
the things that have to be considered about the common accidents of this kind of being.
But the dialectician proceeds to consider them from the conceptions of reason, which
are extrinsic to reality. Hence it is said that dialectics is in search of knowledge, because
in searching it is proper to proceed from extrinsic principles. But the philosopher differs
from the *sophist* 'in the choice,' i.e., in the selection or willing, or in the desire, of a way
of life. For the philosopher and sophist direct their life and actions to different things.
The philosopher directs his to knowing the truth, whereas the sophist directs his so as
to appear to know what he does not."

71. *Metaphysics* IV, 5, 1009a6–1010a15.

72. *Metaphysics* IV, 8, 1012b14–22: "Further, all such arguments are exposed to the
often-expressed objection, that they destroy themselves. For he who says that everything is true makes the statement contrary to his own also true, so that his own is not
true (for the contrary statement denies that it is true), while he who says everything is
false makes himself also false. And if the former person excepts the contrary statement,
saying it alone is not true, while the latter excepts his own as being alone not false, none
the less they are driven to postulate the truth or falsehood of an infinite number of statements; for that which says the true statement is true, is true, and this process will go on
to infinity."

73. *Metaphysics* IV, 8, 1012a29–b31.

indeed this is the case), but even more fundamentally, that language operating without reference to natures simply ceases to mean anything at all.[74]

Aristotle's lucid argumentation implies by contrast (and in differentiation from some of Chenu's statements) that *if* one is committed to a narrative history of dynamic development, change in view of progress and of fulfillment in some overarching teleological mode, then one *is* committed to a concept of perennial nature, and indeed, we might even add, to an understanding of human nature that employs the classical four causes (formal, material, efficient, and final). For there must be at least *some concept of natural teleological ends* in human beings based upon *what* human beings are that can be identified rationally as a precondition for any narrative of human teleology, *theological or otherwise*. Were this not the case, the notion of teleological order that is presented in uniquely theological definitions with respect to the Christological and graced "fulfillment" of human nature would have to be unintelligible to one's natural understanding of man, and therefore purely extrinsic.[75] But this is to say that the claims of *Gaudium et Spes* (no. 22) concerning the Christological fulfillment of human history would appear necessarily as something purely extrinsic to natural human action.[76]

74. *Metaphysics* IV, 4, 1010a10–14; 7–8, 1011b23–1012b31.

75. This is what I take to be the note of truth in Le Guillou's appreciative critique of the early work of de Lubac on grace and nature. See Marie-Joseph Le Guillou, "Surnaturel," *Revue des sciences philosophiques et théologiques* 34 (1950): 226–43, and the helpful study of Henri Donneaud, "*Surnaturel* through the Fine-Tooth Comb of Traditional Thomism," in *Surnaturel*, especially 51–55.

76. Alternatively, one's concept of nature could be merely assimilated to the dynamic history of grace so that nature simply is always, already graced in view of a transphilosophical end that renders philosophy as a subject of study (and natural reason as such) unintelligible as notions. Thus human reason is simply a dimension of a pan-Christic immanentism, arguably a form of what Erich Przywara called theopanism (see also Garrigou-Lagrange's cotemporaneous criticisms of pantheism), in which humanity simply is always already the pure expression of God's divine life outside of himself, from which he is ontologically inseparable, so that the two are determined mutually and theoretically within a common history. On Przywara's notion of theopanism, see John R. Betz, "Erich Przywara and Karl Barth: On the *Analogia Entis* as a Formal Principle of Catholic Theology," 35–87, and David Bentley Hart, "The Destiny of Christian Metaphysics: Reflections on the *Analogia Entis*," in *The Analogy of Being: Invention of the Antichrist or Wisdom of God?*, 395–410.

One must speak therefore of natural ends, of a hierarchy of ends (for there is a diversity of natural goods), and indeed of a supreme natural end (the natural desire for God) that is open to the higher end of grace such that the latter is not understood as something violent to or exterior to the former. It is possible in this way to affirm that the grace of divine life can assume integrally (and not extrinsically) all of the former natural ends of man, and most especially his ultimate natural final end, while remaining extrinsic *in its originating causes* (from God!) precisely *as grace*. This is the classical Thomistic perspective of the twofold final end of man as imperfect (in nature) and perfect (in grace), and as a single phenomenological unity. Man is created with his rational, natural desire for God *so that* he is capable of election to the life of grace, just as one final end is created for the sake of the other. Understood in this way, the teleological dimensions of man, as natural and supernatural, stand in existential ordination to one another as intrinsically related.[77] Man is naturally open to intrinsic fulfillment from a gratuitous, supernatural source. This view has been articulated plausibly by, for example, Sylvester of Ferrara, John of St. Thomas and more recently, Jacques Maritain, Santiago Ramírez, and Marie-Joseph Le Guillou. It certainly can be argued

---

77. See on this *Expos. de Trin.*, q. 6, a. 4, ad 3; SCG I, c. 2; ST I-II, q. 3, a. 6. Santiago Ramírez explains it in this sense: "When the final natural end is subordinated to the final supernatural end, the same man is able simultaneously to intend and possess either end. When the final natural end is not subordinated to the final supernatural end, but struggles against it or is contrary to it, the same man is not able at the same time to have either end or to intend them efficaciously. . . . When the final natural end is subordinated to the final supernatural end, it is not that two final ends simply exist as each being complete and equal, but that one alone exists simply as the final end, which is the supernatural end. For the end subordinated to the other, by that very fact, ceases to exist as the ultimate final end. Nevertheless, the same man can wish or intend two or many ends when these are ordered to one ultimate end, which he intends first and in itself. . . . Therefore, the same man is able both to will and to intend the final natural end (which is final only in a qualified sense [*secundum quid*] in comparison to the final supernatural end), and the final supernatural end, which is the ultimate end simply" (*De Hominis Beatitudine*, Tome I [Salamanca: Biblioteca de Teólogos Españoles, 1942]), 8:339. This permits us to understand why human beings can will a number of normative final ends while simultaneously ordering them to one another hierarchically. It also permits us to see that only if there is a natural end open to graced supernatural completion can all of the inferior goods of human existence be effectively ordered from within (intrinsically) to the all surpassing good and final end *simpliciter* of the beatific vision.

to have the most firm textual mandate from within the writings of St. Thomas Aquinas himself.[78]

What, however, about the effects of sin? Do they not eradicate the basic capacity of the human person to be naturally oriented toward God, and in this case is it not precisely grace that is necessary in order to render human beings apt to perceive in any way a final and therefore ultimately meaningful teleological end that is characteristic of a truly fulfilled human existence? Aquinas offers a qualified interpretation of the damage rendered by the effects of the fall upon human nature.[79] The gifts of grace are destroyed in man by original sin.[80] The *natural* capacity to love God *effectively* above all things is itself also undermined (which is of central importance for the question under consideration).[81] The human being is *incurvatus in se* by virtue of a disordered and malicious will of self-love infecting even the exercise of otherwise natural loves for authentic goods.[82] Nevertheless, the natural (that is, ontological-structural) orientation of the will to God as the supreme good remains inscribed in the rational appetite of the human being as a spiritual animal,[83] and so the inclination or tenden-

78. See in recent years, Georges Cottier, *Le désir de Dieu: sur les traces de saint Thomas* (Paris: Éditions Parole et Silence, 2002); Reinhard Hütter, "Thomas on the Natural Desire for the Vision of God: A Relecture of *Summa Contra Gentiles* III, 25 *après* Henri de Lubac," *The Thomist* 73 (2009): 523–91; Lawrence Feingold, *The Natural Desire to See God according to St. Thomas Aquinas and His Interpreters* (Naples, Fla.: Sapientia Press, 2010); Steven A. Long, *Natura Pura. On the Recovery of Nature in the Doctrine of Grace* (New York: Fordham University Press, 2010).

79. See the aforementioned study by Torrell, "Nature and Grace in Thomas Aquinas," 172–79.

80. ST I-II, q. 85, a. 1.

81. ST I-II, q. 109, a. 3: "In the state of perfect nature man referred the love of himself and of all other things to the love of God as to its end; and thus he loved God more than himself and above all things. But in the state of corrupt nature man falls short of this in the appetite of his rational will, which, unless it is cured by God's grace, follows its private good, on account of the corruption of nature. And hence we must say that in the state of perfect nature man did not need the gift of grace added to his natural endowments, in order to love God above all things naturally, although he needed God's help to move him to it; but in the state of corrupt nature man needs, even for this, the help of grace to heal his nature."

82. ST I-II, q. 84, a. 2, corp. and ad 3; q. 85, aa. 1 and 3.

83. ST I-II, q. 109, a. 3: "Now to love God above all things is natural to man and to every nature, not only rational but irrational, and even to inanimate nature according to

cy of this appetite toward God, while weakened, is still present in fall-en man.[84] Likewise, certain first principles of moral perception (the principles of synderesis) are ineradicable, and under the right condi-tions could in principle lead man to the rational understanding of the primacy of the love of God and recognition of basic moral goods.[85] This rational understanding would not suffice, however, for the ex-istential *action* of virtuous religious behavior; see Romans 1:18–21.[86] In other words, even in the fallen state there remains in man enough rational and voluntary inclination toward the supreme good to en-able him to know that he should exist for God, that he is less than he

---

the manner of love which can belong to each creature. And the reason of this is that it is natural to all to seek and love things according as they are naturally fit (to be sought and loved) since 'all things act according as they are naturally fit' as stated in Phys. ii, 8." See also q. 85, a. 2.

84. ST I-II, q. 85, a. 1: "The good of human nature is threefold. First, there are the principles of which nature is constituted, and the properties that flow from them, such as the powers of the soul, and so forth. Secondly, since man has from nature an inclina-tion to virtue, as stated above, this inclination to virtue is a good of nature. Thirdly, the gift of original justice, conferred on the whole of human nature in the person of the first man, may be called a good of nature. Accordingly, the first-mentioned good of nature is neither destroyed nor diminished by sin. The third good of nature was entirely de-stroyed through the sin of our first parent. But the second good of nature, viz. the nat-ural inclination to virtue, is diminished by sin. Because human acts produce an inclina-tion to like acts, as stated above. Now from the very fact that a thing becomes inclined to one of two contraries, its inclination to the other contrary must needs be diminished. Wherefore as sin is opposed to virtue, from the very fact that a man sins, there results a diminution of that good of nature, which is the inclination to virtue."

85. Cf. ST I-II, q. 100, a. 1; ST I-II, q. 94, a. 2.

86. Commenting on Rom 1:21, "For, although they knew God, they did not glori-fy him as God or give thanks, but became vain in their thoughts, and their foolish heart was darkened," Aquinas writes (*In Rom.* I, lec. 7, 127): "That their basic guilt was not due to ignorance is shown by the fact that, although they possessed knowledge of God, they failed to use it unto good. For they knew God in two ways: first, as the super-eminent being, to Whom glory and honor were due. They are said to be without excuse, there-fore, because, *although they knew God, they did not honor him as God*; either because they failed to pay Him due worship or because they put a limit to His power and knowledge by denying certain aspects of His power and knowledge, contrary to Sir. (43:30): 'when you exalt him, put forth all your strength.' Secondly, they knew Him as the cause of all good things. Hence, in all things he was deserving of thanks, which they did not render; rather, they attributed their blessings to their own talent and power. Hence, he adds: *nor did they give thanks*, namely, to the Lord: 'Give thanks to Him in all circumstances' (1 Thess. 5:18)." Translation by Fabian Larcher, *Commentary on the Letter of Saint Paul to the Romans* (Lander, Wyo.: The Aquinas Institute, 2012).

ought to be as a religious being, that he is a noble but fault-ridden being, and that he is in unresolved contradiction with himself. It is in continuity with such a perspective that *Gaudium et Spes* addresses the human person, promising him a fulfillment and liberation of his human nature that is possible only with Christ.

Grace meanwhile can and must strengthen both the natural tendencies toward God *and* the natural knowledge of these tendencies, so that in fact a condition for the right cooperation with grace is the re-actualization or studied pursuit of a Christian *philosophical* knowledge of the constitution and qualities of human nature.[87] This is necessary not only to respond to the postmodernist dissolution of nature into a flux of pure cultural becoming and the cultural construction/ deconstruction of the self and of society by the will to power. It is also necessary in order to articulate a reasoned evaluation of authentic ends and purposes that transcends a given age and that thereby allows for the determination of the moral health and legitimate aspirations of a given culture or historical period in relation to universal standards.[88] Just such a concept of nature is therefore the *sine qua non* condition for an evaluative narrative history of culture. But this implies consequently that one can provide even from within theology an articulation of aspects of the natural order and of what nature can do (*per pura naturalia*, in Aquinas's sense)[89] by recourse to natural philosophical and scientific knowledge, and that one can distin-

87. Evidently it is not my goal here to explore how one might, by a philosophical form of investigation, rightly identify what a human person is, the nature of the human being as a soul-body composite, or reason demonstratively about the final ends of man. Nor do I intend to consider the historical and existential ways that Christian faith affects the concrete historical exercise of natural philosophical reason. On these questions, one may consult with profit the writings of Benedict Ashley, Lawrence Dewan, and Robert Sokolowski.

88. Nothing I am saying here excludes the idea that human culture might make *progress* in its understanding of what a human person is, or that it might not significantly regress as well. Consider here the paradox of our progress in understanding the physical body of the embryonic human person, and our cultural regress in failing to understand the intrinsic dignity of that same person as transcending the rights of the human freedom of others. An augmented scope of scientific understanding of the material world coexists with an expanding sense of the range of human permissions of the exercise of freedom. The two are commonly understood as mutually reinforcing processes.

89. Cf. Torrell on Aquinas's discussion of the natural capacities as such in fallen human nature in "Nature and Grace in Thomas Aquinas," 180–84, with reference to 168–70.

guish this as nature acting by its own powers from nature under the motion of grace.[90] Likewise, the same consideration must be able to determine *something* of what nature *should* be able to do due to tendencies toward natural ends, tendencies which are nevertheless hampered by sin (or human faults). Only the latter (an evaluative concept of sin as *in part* the unbecoming of nature) will allow for at least some basic evaluation of genuine human good and evil. Such a concept is also necessary in order to articulate distinctly theological notions of original sin and of the redemptive promises of grace, in order to show that these concepts touch upon something "intrinsic" to concrete historical human nature (as wounded and redeemed in its own ontological capacities and tendencies). Finally, then, to recapitulate the argument, a natural sense of teleology and of a hierarchy of goods is necessary (including recognition of a natural end that can be found in God alone as the supreme good who should be desired and loved above all else) to allow for the intelligibility of the promise of supernatural life as a supreme good that is not something violent to human nature, but capable of subsuming all lesser ends and goods into itself, just as *Gaudium et Spes* would seem to promote. In short, an ontology of human nature—and a robust philosophical project that goes with it—are indispensable conditions for a sane and viable theology of grace.

The Implicit "Pure Nature" of Christology

If the scholastic concept of pure nature became a bugbear of modern Catholic theology, this was especially due to the insistence that historical human nature never did or was never meant to exist outside the field of graced communion with God. This insistence is perfectly warranted, but as I have attempted to show succinctly above, this was the purpose of and justification for a concept of pure nature as articulated in the Dominican Thomistic tradition. In addition, one might add that if this tradition emphasized the extrinsic *origins* of grace *vis-à-vis* human nature, it was in order to underscore that grace as a gift

---

90. I am saying it is a condition *sine qua non*, but not a *sufficient* condition for an extensive moral understanding of good and evil. For a clear example of this way of thinking in Aquinas, see ST I-II, q. 85, a. 6.

of divine life offered to human persons is not something that they can procure in virtue of themselves or by reason of their own resources. It was *not* to claim (in fact the most common perspective is the logical contrary) that grace is something extrinsic to the final purposes or ends of ordinary human nature. The scholastic Thomistic tradition was quite sensitive to the claim of St. Thomas that the grace of justification is *not a miracle* (something wholly outside the order of nature) because it touches upon the intimate natural orientation of the human person toward God.[91] Nevertheless, justification and sanctifying grace *are pure gifts* (*sola gratia*) and not intrinsic dimensions of man's nature, either in the original state (contrary to the claims of Baius), or in the economy of redemption (as Augustine rightly argued, against Pelagius).

What, then, should we make of the claim of *Gaudium et Spes*, no. 22: "In reality it is only in the mystery of the Word made flesh that the mystery of man truly becomes clear .... For since Christ died for all, and since all men are in fact *called to one and the same destiny*, which is divine, we must hold that the Holy Spirit offers to all the possibility of being made partners, in a way known to God, in the Paschal mystery"? Much could be said about this dense and important passage. My goal in this concluding section of the chapter is only to make three claims in the light of what has been argued above.

First, the notion that the mystery of man only becomes clear in the mystery of the incarnate Word is of course distinct from the notion of the human nature of the Word as it illumines the human nature of all men. The former notion implies the grace of union (of the humanity of the Word to his person) and the capital graces of Christ, the illumination concerning the problem of evil, suffering, and death that his passion alone affords, and the eschatological revelation of the

---

91. See ST I-II, q. 113, a. 10. In *De Deo Trino et Creatore*, 430–37, Garrigou-Lagrange comments upon the significance of Aquinas's teaching that children born prior to the fall would have been conceived in a state of grace (ST I, q. 100, a. 1) and emphasizes (434–37) that this teaching excludes any purely extrinsicist account of the relations of grace to the constitution of human nature (434): "It cannot be said, according to the definitive teaching of St. Thomas, that sanctifying grace is radically extrinsic to [the state of] original justice." He shows that the teaching of Aquinas is mirrored by Capreolus, Cajetan, and Sylvester of Ferrara (436), and contrasts this with what he takes to be the extrinsicism of Suarez and Bellarmine (449–50).

final end of the human soul and body that is made manifest in his resurrection. None of this is intelligible without the grace of faith. Nevertheless, a studied understanding of Christ's human nature in relation to our own is an integral part of the theological reflections just alluded to. To take just one example: during the passion narrative, the Lord is struck by a servant of the high priest and responds in turn, "If I have spoken wrongly, bear witness to the wrong; but if I have spoken rightly, why do you strike me?" (Jn 18:23). The scene takes on its deepest intelligibility only in light of a perception of who has been struck, and reflection on the grace of desire in the human heart of Christ that leads him to bear witness to the truth and to embrace persecution and the cross. His charity, which is universal, is expressed in the love for his persecutors during his passion. These are all mysteries of grace. However, there is also present here a profound truth concerning the rectitude of human judgment and the dignity of human virtue in the face of moral evil. If we assign a non-stoic interpretation to this incident, then the natural integrity of Christ is truly remarkable: his sensitive passions are fully ordered to his reason, and his reason is in perfect subordination to God and to the virtue of speaking the truth out of compassion—"Ecce homo" (Jn 19:5). Like Pilate, we perceive in Christ a nobility to which we might *naturally aspire* (by our innate moral tendencies and best ethical judgments), but which is also so fragile and endangered in us as to seem almost perilously idealistic. And it is here in particular that we are able to see the correspondence of grace to the integrity of nature, and of the grace of Christ to his uniquely natural humanity, to a human way of being that instructs us more deeply—and universally—as to what it means to be human. This perfection exists only in Jesus and comes to human beings universally from him alone, *pace* Kant and Hick, as well as Nietzsche and Foucault.

Second, then, a Christological accomplishment of all human history presupposes not only the use of a universal concept of the human and its applicability to both Christ and to all other men, but also requires in turn the implicit acceptance of the real ontological possibility of a state of pure nature, even if this state has never concretely existed. Nor is this a trivial point, but is in fact something quite significant and intrinsic to all basic thinking on the Christological fulfillment of the human. For the claim of *Gaudium et Spes* (and of Chenu and Rahner) that we are rightly pursuing is the understanding that human beings cannot be fully themselves (in their deepest natural aspirations) without the life of grace within them, and that this life is made most manifest and clear (so as to illumine the whole world universally) only in the mystery of the incarnate Word. This means in turn that human beings can exist without grace (because it is a gift), but also that they cannot be fully themselves (naturally) without that gift, and that in its absence (in the wake of sin) they suffer devastating intrinsic effects to their nature, both personally and collectively. Underlying the states of integral, fallen, redeemed, and Christic (Christ's own) human nature, there is something that is collectively the same. Just as this reality that is the same did not *need* to be created in a state of original holiness (although it was) so likewise it did not *need* to be subject to sin by the faulty use of freedom (although it now is, failing redemption in Christ). Consequently, nature as it existed in original innocence and as it exists now, as fallen and offered redemption in Christ, did not *need* to exist in either state, due to its intrinsic requirements as nature. It could have existed in a state of pure nature. To think otherwise is simply either to make grace something other than a gift of God, or to make evil a normative (natural rather than unnatural) constitutive dimension of the human person.

Finally, these reflections reach their apex when we consider the case of Christ. For if Christ is without moral evil (that is, sinless) and for this reason (though not exclusively so) more perfectly human than we are, then he is a more perfect example of humanity because evil is not intrinsic to our human nature as such. And likewise, if Christ the pre-existent Son as incarnated in human form is truly a *gift* of the Father (for the Son truly became one of us because the Father so loved the world that he sent his only-begotten Son), then Jesus is not someone we merited or deserved to have as our brother, and is not ours by a kind of natural right or as the product of an merely intra-historical evolutionary history.[92] Although he is the most perfect instantiation of what it means to be authentically human, and though this can be understood to some extent in philosophically uni-

---

92. As, I take it, Schleiermacher is in danger of suggesting.

versalizable terms (for example, through a distinctly *philosophical* examination of the virtues of Christ), nevertheless he is this *only by the gift of God's grace,* the grace of union of the humanity of Christ to the Word and the gift of infused, habitual graces in the human mind and will of Christ. Ultimately what is at stake in maintaining the ontological possibility of a state of pure nature is nothing less than the capacity to hold together three claims: (1) Christ is truly human in the most preeminent and universally intelligible sense, (2) the grace of the incarnation is the ultimate source of the uniquely perfect human nature of Christ (and yet is distinguishable from the latter *as grace*), (3) there is no moral evil in the soul of Christ, and his innocence and virtue manifest a more natural form of human existence, such that we can claim analogously, that only with the grace of Christ can human beings truly overcome the power of evil in human history.

CONCLUSION

It should be clear that the arguments of this chapter are made in the attempt to challenge respectfully some prevalent presuppositions of thought surrounding what constitutes a genuine form of pre- versus post-conciliar theological anthropology. But this dialectical interplay of old and new is not meant to suggest that there is a "hermeneutic of discontinuity" between the post-conciliar reflections of Chenu and Rahner (discussed above) and the preceding tradition. There is some problematic discontinuity present, no doubt, in the rhetorical posturing of these two theologians, due in part to some of the metaphysical visions with which they associated themselves. These are points worth questioning and challenging, and sometimes, or such is my conviction, with recourse to more classical forms of thought, including that of Aquinas and his commentators. However, their insistence on the historicity of our human nature alludes to something true as well. The dialectic of Aristotle does not entail a vanquishing of the argument of the other, but the consideration of his or her legitimate concerns, insights, oversights, and errors. This is undertaken in view of a more comprehensive grasp of the fundamental principles, and a more expansive vision of the complete truth. The conversation about grace and nature that *Gaudium et Spes* invites us to is not one that is completed by judicial fiat of a "spirit of the Council" or by a dismissive disinterest in favor of pre-conciliar tradition. On the contrary, there is a great deal of reflection yet to be done.

What might we conclude, then, from the arguments elaborated above? Given the internal logic of *Gaudium et Spes*, what theological adjudications might we consider "settled matter" for Catholic theology? First, we should affirm that a theology that is Christocentric must take most seriously the fact that grace is not an essential dimension of human nature. It is something given graciously, and necessarily extrinsically, even if it addresses the intrinsic depths of the human person. Therefore, there must be a human nature that grace presupposes, and so it is meaningful to speak of our created human nature as something distinct from the order of grace derived from Christ alone.

Second, however, what is true in the ontological realm is mirrored in the epistemological realm: if we can think of our human nature in a new and a more complete way only by virtue of the mystery of Christ, we cannot do so without presupposing the natural possibility of a concept and analysis of human nature. Otherwise said, to speak theologically of the unique perfection of the humanity of Christ we must presuppose some subjacent understanding of human nature in general. Does this idea not lead to a problem? Are we not bound in this case to interpret the mystery of Christ in a rationalistic way, just as a form of philosophical reflection "extrinsic" to the gospel might alienate us from a distinctively theological understanding of the inward content of the revelation? Not if we understand the science of theology rightly. For the human nature we share with Christ is common to all human beings, and so correspondingly, Christ's human nature does "fall under" our ordinary human mode of understanding in a specific sense. Without grace we might only recognize him as a mere human being like ourselves, but even in grace we still recognize him as a genuinely human being like ourselves. In the order of specification (regarding our human essence) we are naturally identical to Christ. The theological challenge is to articulate the unique personal *state* of this human nature in Christ: the Christological perfection of the *mode* in which God is human. For Christ alone as man is "full of truth and grace" (Jn 1:14) in a way that makes him absolutely unique with regard to all others, just as he alone is also the "man of sorrows"

(Is 53:3) who bore the marks of the passion for the sake of all others. If we follow Aquinas in distinguishing the human essence from the mode in which that essence subsists, we can recognize the Christological mystery of all humanity while also maintaining the essentially unified character of all human nature. There is no opposition between these two realities, but an order of intelligibility and wisdom that is common to both. Ultimately, this wisdom points us back to the mystery of God, who is both the author of human nature, and who himself became man.

3

---:---

The Likeness of the Human
and Divine Natures

I have argued in the previous chapter that there exists a profound correspondence between our philosophical knowledge of human nature
and our theological knowledge of the humanity of Christ. This notion alludes in an indirect but real way to the controversies surrounding the *analogia entis*, the famous twentieth-century debate between
Karl Barth and Erich Przywara. Why? Because that controversy centered on the relationship between philosophical reason and theological science. Consider three acute questions at the heart of that debate.
First, what does it mean to say that our philosophical knowledge is
capable of cooperating with and of being assimilated into theological
reflection on revelation? Second, what is the philosophically discernible relationship of created being to the existence of God? Does there
exist natural, analogical knowledge of God derived from the metaphysical consideration of creatures? Third, what are the implications
of the ontological similitude that exists between the humanity and
divinity of Christ? If we affirm that there are two natures in Christ,
does it not follow that such a similitude must exist? And if so, does
this not imply that we can speak not only theologically but also philosophically of the likeness of created natural realities to the uncreated
existence of God? In other words, does Christological doctrine of the

existence of the Word in two natures (divine and human) also necessarily imply the possibility of natural theology?

Karl Barth famously rejected the possibility of a philosophical theology that could attain to natural knowledge of God, and to the use of such a form of thought within the context of Christological reflection. In the following two chapters I engage the Barthian position on natural theology and the *analogia entis* in two stages. In this chapter I consider Barth's Christological objections to the analogy of being and argue that the Barthian representation of analogy in Aquinas is misguided. In the second stage (chapter 4) I argue that the affirmation of Chalcedonian Christology in fact implies an underlying consent to the necessary possibility of natural theology. We cannot derive knowledge of the incarnation from knowledge of the *analogia entis,* or the likeness between creatures and their creator. To think otherwise would be to deny the character of divine revelation as such. But if we were constitutionally unable to think about God naturally, we would also be constitutionally unable to receive revelation that is supernatural, and likewise, if we can think theologically about the incarnation (under the effects of the supernatural grace of faith) then this presupposes at least the *possibility* of thinking philosophically about God according to the innate powers of natural reason.

The argument of this first chapter, then, seeks to do three things. First, it considers central Barthian objections to analogical knowledge of God, especially as these are reformulated by Barth's disciple Eberhard Jüngel. I argue that Barth's objections rest upon well-meaning but seriously inaccurate misrepresentations of Thomistic thought. They present what are in fact incredible caricatures of the true content of that historical doctrine. Jüngel, meanwhile, presupposes rather than demonstrates the philosophical soundness of the Kantian critique of classical metaphysics. This presupposition is itself philosophical and not theological, and consequently it is itself not Christological but extraneous to theology as such. Second, then, I argue that rightly understood, analogy theory in Aquinas not only does not betray a right understanding of the relationship between God and man that is established in the incarnation of the Word, but that on the contrary it seeks to safeguard exactly some of the key principles that Barth sought to defend in attacking what he wrongly took to be the analogy doctrine in Aquinas. Third, I develop an argument introduced in the prolegomenon to this volume, namely, that the adoption of a thorough-going Kantian critique of classical metaphysics by Barthians (such as Jüngel) is not in fact compatible with the affirmation of classical Chalcedonian orthodoxy. For the latter form of thought must affirm that Jesus Christ is truly God and man, and that we are truly capable of being elevated to the state of grace wherein we can know of this mystery. But if this is the case, then there must be some possibility in human nature for conceiving of the mystery of God as active and present in the world, by way of an analogical form of causality, not entirely equivalent to "intra-mundane" natural forms of causality. And it is exactly this form of transcendent causality that Kant's philosophy rejects as impossible and that Aquinas's analogy theory safeguards as inherently intelligible. A true Barthian affirmation of the reality of the incarnation, then, should in fact invite us to embrace the Thomistic position on the doctrine of analogy.

INTRODUCING THE
BARTHIAN OBJECTIONS: THE CASE OF
EBERHARD JÜNGEL

Let us begin our investigations by considering succinctly the influential interpretation of Barth on analogy developed by Eberhard Jüngel. Why consider Jüngel first, if he is the disciple of Barth? Jüngel's interpretation of the *analogia entis* debate is illuminating and serves as a point of entry. It can help us, therefore, to frame the debate between Thomists and Barthians.

For Jüngel, Barth's rejection of philosophical theology in his debate with Przywara is centered on a more fundamental preoccupation: how should modern theology react to the critique of classical metaphysics elaborated by Immanuel Kant? Kant, as is well known, argued that there can exist no demonstrative knowledge of God based upon the premises or conclusions of mere natural reason. If this is the case, then how might one evaluate the important role that metaphysical reflection on divine attributes has played in traditional theological discourse? In fact, Barth sought in the wake of Kant to develop a *theological* critique of the tradition of metaphysical reflection concerning God. For Jüngel, it is because of the irreversibility of the Kantian critique that Barth's theological reformulation of Christian doctrine in a post-Kantian key is of central importance for the future of Christian thought. After the Kantian critique, Barth's thought gives us the best possibility for a future form of genuine theological reflection about God.

At the heart of the debate between Barthians and Catholics, then, there is the question of the Kantian prohibition on analogical language for God as the "cause" of created reality. Like Barth, Jüngel argues that the use of traditional (patristic and scholastic) doctrines of causality and analogy are detrimental to Christian theology.[1] This is particularly the case with regard to Aquinas's notions of God's causality of creation, and the analogical names of God, which St. Thomas believes can be derived from creatures considered as God's effects.[2] More specifically, Jüngel claims that this medieval causal metaphysics cannot withstand the challenge of Kant's criticisms of classical metaphysics, and in a Barthian vein argues that Aquinas's causal metaphysics inevitably leads to an anthropomorphic, conceptual reification of God that obscures the true knowledge of God given uniquely in Christ.[3]

How can we focus in on the particular character of this critique? For the sake of brevity, let us consider three of Jüngel's principal arguments against the Thomistic tradition. First, Jüngel's critique of Aquinas's thought on creation and analogy takes aim at Aquinas's use of the neo-Platonic principle of causal resemblance ("effects resemble their cause") which was commonly discussed and defended in medieval scholasticism.[4] The axiom is particularly problematic when applied to the relationship between creation and God. This is the case because it subsumes both God and creatures under the no-

1. See Jüngel, *God as the Mystery of the World*, 226–98. Jüngel's influence can be seen in contemporary Barthian authors such as Archie J. Spencer, "Causality and the *Analogia entis*: Karl Barth's Rejection of Analogy of Being Reconsidered," *Nova et Vetera* (English edition) 6, no. 2 (2008): 329–76, and Kevin W. Hector, *Theology without Metaphysics: God, Language, and the Spirit of Recognition* (Cambridge: Cambridge University Press, 2011). I am grateful to Archie Spencer for helping me understand the views of Barth and Jüngel on this subject in greater depth.
2. *God as the Mystery of the World*, 272–81.
3. Ibid., 263–67, 281–86.
4. Ibid., 241–45.

tions of "cause" and "being" together into a proportionally analogical form of conceptual reflection (a:b::c:d) in which a latent univocity is contained.[5] This results in a conceptual anthropomorphism that understands God reductively (and problematically) in terms of creatures. God is understood as being and cause in a way that is at base reducible to the way we understand creatures as beings and causes, in which each has a respective place within a system of human making. This anthropocentric way of thinking displaces and obscures the true knowledge of God (in his genuine alterity and humanity) that comes from God's free initiative in grace, through Christ alone.[6]

Second, Jüngel argues that the structure of Aquinas's thought needs to be understood in light of Immanuel Kant's critique of causality in his *Critique of Pure Reason* and other works.[7] The idea here comes not directly from Barth, but rather from Jüngel himself as he seeks to assimilate Barth's criticism of Thomistic causality to a Heideggerian critique of western metaphysics and theism as "ontotheology."[8] *Because* Aquinas conceived of all causality in intra-worldly terms (that is, with God acting as an ontic entity rivalling other entities), *therefore* he could only conceive of God's alterity in terms entirely inconsistent with this world (that is, God as wholly outside the world).[9] The only way that Thomism could affirm a real difference between God and the world as we experience it, then, was by formulating a radically apophatic conception of the divine essence and divine causation. Kant himself accurately diagnosed the antinomy of divine and human freedom that results from such thinking.[10] If we can conceive of God's freedom in causal terms, then human freedom becomes inconceivable, and vice versa. The Kantian diagnostic at base entailed the insight that "cause-effect relations" are in fact constructions of the human mind permitting one to organize the data of em-

5. Ibid., 277. "Within the framework of analogy, the problem has confronted us up to now as the question of how human talk about God could be possible without a 'humanization' of the divine essence which is inappropriate to God, since language in all its forms of expression is bound to the form of being of speaking man."

6. Ibid., 288: "The Christian faith confesses that God's becoming man, the incarnation of the word of God in Jesus Christ, is the unique, unsurpassable instance of a still greater similarity between God and man taking place within a great dissimilarity."

7. Ibid., 263–66.   8. Ibid., 47–49, 208–10, 285–86.
9. Ibid., 279–81.   10. Ibid., 261–66, 278–79.

pirical sense impressions, but that the scholastic tradition had illegit-
imately attempted to transfer these pure constructions of reason into
the "trans-sensible" sphere. In turn, Kant made clearer something
that was latent in the Thomistic tradition: once we have recourse to
philosophical notions of causality to speak about God, God cannot
be known in terms of the forms of this world, and God is banished
from the sphere of empirical existence once and for all.[11] It was scholasticism, and Aquinas's thought in particular, that set this process in
motion.[12]

   Third, then, it is Barth's recovery of an authentic sense of theological divine "causality" that is called for, a form of analogical and
causal reflection that is exclusively Christological.[13] It is possible to
speak of a certain analogy between God and creation, but only insofar as this likeness is revealed in faith (the *analogia fidei* of Barth) and
not derived through philosophical speculation. This presumes that
we understand God's causality of creation only in light of God's self-
revelation in Jesus Christ.[14] God is made known to us in his relation
to the world as creator only through the human life of Jesus Christ,
and in the Son's relation to the Father. Creation is never conceptualized except within the context of a theological study of God's mystery
of the election of humanity in Jesus Christ.

   On one level it is odd, of course, that Jüngel should choose to challenge Catholic Christians to take seriously Karl Barth's critique of
the *analogia entis* or "natural theology" by underscoring the diagnostic truthfulness and historical irreversibility of the Kantian critique of
Aquinas's medieval understanding of divine causality and analogy. After all, in the spasms of modernity's contemporary self-questioning,
need we really affirm auto-reflexively that the age of classical metaphys-

---

   11. Ibid., 279–80: "The traditional theological usage of *analogy* as we observe it in
Kant is predominantly agnostic—for the sake of God's perfection.... The divinity of
God excludes humanity. God is not permitted to be human."
   12. Ibid., 184, 276.
   13. Ibid., 281–98.
   14. Ibid., 383–84: "In faith in the eternal Son [alone], God is asserted to be the one
through whom all things are and toward whom all things are.... In that the eternal Son
is eternally from the Father, God is aiming in him as well toward a becoming in which
God not only comes from God, but, beyond that, man with his world is made, caused,
created by God."

ics is definitively vanquished? Indeed, one of the principal concerns of Thomists in the nineteenth and twentieth centuries was to refute the basic principles, conclusions, and cultural effects of Kantianism as intellectually flawed and illusory.[15] It is significant, then, that Jüngel's narrative fails even to acknowledge the classical Thomistic responses to the Humean and Kantian doctrines of causality.[16]

Furthermore, Jüngel's basic claims are colored by some logical and historical problems. Jüngel's assimilation of Aquinas's doctrine of analogy and causality to that of Kant is called radically into question by careful historical research conducted in the last few decades on the Enlightenment origins of Kantian and Heideggerian theories of "ontotheology." This research quite convincingly differentiates the targets of the criticisms of Kant and Heidegger (and consequently their own presuppositions) from Aquinas's genuine thought.[17]

In another sense, however, Jüngel's interrogation of Aquinas is

15. One need only briefly recall in this context the historical trajectory from Vatican I and its interpretation by the Thomistic Roman school of Kleugen and others who taught Leo XIII, to the modernist crisis and the Thomistic revival conducted under Pius X, to Cardinal Mercier and the Louvain school, to Marechal's, Rahner's, and Lonergan's diverse formulations of Thomism in critical response to Kant, to French Thomism's aggressive writings in response to Kant, from such authors as Reginald Garrigou-Lagrange, Jacques Maritain, Étienne Gilson, etc. Unfortunately, Jüngel makes no references to any of the arguments in these traditions of thought.

16. A long list could be given here, but see classically, Reginald Garrigou-Lagrange, *God: His Existence and His Nature*, trans. B. Rose (London: B. Herder Press, 1939), 1:100–106, 1:205–32; Étienne Gilson, *l'Être et l'Essence* (Paris: J. Vrin, 1981), 187–207, and more recently, Denys Turner, *Faith, Reason and the Existence of God* (Cambridge: Cambridge University Press, 2004); Lawrence Dewan, "St. Thomas and the Principle of Causality," *Form and Being: Studies in Thomistic Metaphysics* (Washington, D.C.: The Catholic University of America Press, 2006), 61–80.

17. The contemporary French literature on the subject of Aquinas in relation to Kant and Heidegger is especially important. See, for example, Olivier Boulnois, *Être et représentation*, especially 457–515; "La destruction de l'analogie et l'instauration de la métaphysique," in *Duns Scot, Sur la connaissance de Dieu et l'univocité de l'étant* (Paris: Presses Universitaires de France, 1988), 11–81, and "Quand commence l'onto-théo-logie? Aristote, Thomas d'Aquin et Duns Scot," *Revue Thomiste* 95 (1995): 85–105; Jean François Courtine, *Suarez et le Système de la Métaphysique* (Paris: Presses Universitaires de France, 1990); *Inventio analogiae: Métaphysique et ontothéologie* (Paris: J. Vrin, 2005); Jean-Luc Marion, "Saint Thomas d'Aquin et l'onto-théo-logie," *Revue Thomiste* 95 (1995): 31–66; Vincent Carraud, *Causa sive ratio: La raison de la cause, de Suarez à Leibniz* (Paris: Presses Universitaires de France, 2002); Thierry-Dominique Humbrecht, *Théologie Négative et Noms Divins chez Saint Thomas d'Aquin* (Paris: J. Vrin, 2005).

more original insofar as it is distinctly theological. And from this point of view, he is posing a question that is not sufficiently considered. What is the advantage or disadvantage, *in theological and Christological terms*, of Aquinas's use of an analogical metaphysics of causality, which he employs to speak about God's causal activity of creation, as well as the divine names of God? Does this manner of thinking help or hinder (and if so, how) a more profound understanding of the divinity of Christ? And, if we may be permitted to turn the question around, what are the presuppositions of a theology that repudiates this form of thinking (one species of which is present in the thought of Karl Barth)? And what are the theological consequences of such a repudiation, including the Christological consequences? The question is not uninteresting, and yet is largely left unexamined—by Thomists, in part, but perhaps especially by Barthians.

In what follows I will not focus on the philosophical question of Thomism as it relates to the Kantian critique of metaphysics, important though this may be.[18] Instead, I will pursue the theological line

18. The question is not unimportant, but rather, too substantial to try to treat within this context. I examine this issue, with references to contemporary literature, in White, *Wisdom in the Face of Modernity: A Study in Thomistic Natural Theology*. For the sake of brevity, one can note that the basic contrast between the two thinkers does not concern their views on knowledge of God or analogy per se, but their starting points as regards epistemological realism, and knowledge of existence and causality *in beings we experience immediately*. If we understand the knowledge of the latter on Aquinas's terms, then natural knowledge of God is possible. Not only did Kant not read Aquinas, his critique of metaphysics and knowledge of God as it stands in fact does not apply to Aquinas's metaphysics in the terms in which the latter understands it, but rather to Enlightenment philosophers whose presuppositions differ vastly from those of Aquinas. Three points can be mentioned here to illustrate the contrasts between Kant and Aquinas, and the obstacles facing any critique of the latter through the prism of the thought of the former. (1) Kant affirms that all metaphysical notions are the results of *a priori* synthetic judgments and are pure concepts of understanding, pertaining immediately to the way in which the thinking subject organizes sensations internally and logically, but not immediately to the order of reality in itself (see *Critique of Pure Reason*, A84/B117–A92/B124; B407–13). Aquinas, meanwhile, understands metaphysical thought to begin from first, indemonstrable principles that are epistemologically realistic, by which we gain judicative insight into the very nature and structure of existents around us, in what they are, and by virtue of their existence. If Aquinas is correct, then Kant's critique is itself deeply flawed in its presuppositions. (2) Kant's theory of natural theology as ontotheology affirms the usefulness of the concept of God, but merely as a regulative notion of reason permitting the construction of systematic knowledge based upon experience, ordering this knowledge in reference to a needed, ideal first principle

of questioning that Jüngel proposes. This can be done in two stages. First, I will examine Barth's theological objections to Aquinas's theory of causality and show why a number of these are either inaccurate or theologically problematic. To make this claim perfectly clear, I will contrast Aquinas's theory of creative causality and non-generic analogical predication with *Barth's own* description of "Thomistic" thought, and will argue that in fact, *only if* one has a theory of analogical predication like the one Aquinas develops can one avoid the kind of *generic* assimilations of God to creatures that Barth himself (falsely) criticizes Aquinas for making. Aquinas offers clear solutions to a problem that Barth seems to have resolved only partially and imperfectly. In

---

that stimulates the deepening of human research. As is well known, then, Kant understands the ontological argument to be at the base of all theistic speculative argumentation, such as that found in the cosmological argument (taken from the contingency of creatures), or the physio-theological argument (based upon the presence of teleology in creatures). For Aquinas, by contrast, analysis of the question of God cannot begin from notions of possible beings (which pertain to mentally immanent beings of reason) nor from the idea of a possible perfect being. The premises of Kant's approach to any possible knowledge of God are therefore flawed. Instead, Thomistic arguments for the existence of God are *a posteriori* in nature, derived uniquely from the awareness of intrinsic ontological compositions and extrinsic dependencies that characterize the existence of the things around us (and ourselves). The philosophical question of the existence of God is justified by the consideration of the existence of the sensible world as we experience it, which itself suggests the necessity of a transcendent source for its existence. (3) Kant holds to the idea that God is signified by our most common notion of being and is understood by an additional difference added to this most general concept (such as the attributes of omnipotence, infinity, etc.). See, for example, *Critique of Pure Reason*, A845/B873–A846/B874. As known by our human thinking, God is a subcategory of the broader "science" of being, even as the notion of God refers to that which is the condition of possibility for all possible being (the ultimate explanation of conceivable reality). We only know God, therefore, under the rubric of an extension of human concepts as a special instance of being among others. Aquinas, by contrast, insists that God is not an object of study within the subject of metaphysics, and that the idea of God is not a logical or epistemological prerequisite for the metaphysical consideration of causality in creatures. Not only is God not a member of any genus of being. In addition, he can only be understood as the transcendent cause of the subject of metaphysics (*ens commune*), that is to say, as the cause of everything that depends for its existence on another, and who is himself uncaused. Therefore, God can be known to exist but remains incomprehensible, transcending every human science. At the heart of these three differences, there are radically different conceptions of our knowledge of being in realities that we experience, that in turn give rise to incompatible notions of metaphysics, causality and analogy. Jüngel's assimilation of Aquinas's sense of analogy to that of Kant's amounts to a very artificial and unconvincing flattening of the history of ideas.

fact, given his theoretical statements about analogy theory, it is inevitably Barth, and not Aquinas, who is in danger of assimilating God and creatures to a generically common set of features in a conceptually anthropomorphic fashion.

Second, in the final section of the chapter I will turn to the more fundamental theological question raised by Jüngel's criticisms. Why should Kant's critique of causality help advance a theological program that wishes to be genuinely Christocentric, both ontologically and epistemologically? Kant, after all, offers arguments against the intelligibility and possibility of the incarnation and the existence of grace that stem directly (and logically) from his epistemological presuppositions. Here in particular I will argue that the absence of a sense of the analogical causality of the creator endangers, rather than accentuates, a true understanding of Christ as God, particularly as concerns right reflection on the "divine nature" or "essence" of Christ as distinct from his human nature. In fact, the Thomistic sense of analogy and causality serves precisely to underscore not only the transcendence and otherness of the divine nature as that which is unlike human nature, but also the intelligibility of human nature as that which is like the divine nature. This is something Barth's critique of Aquinas does not grasp adequately but which is in fact essential for defending Chalcedonian doctrine in the face of Kant's arguments against the incarnation. Aquinas's teaching permits us to understand rightly the freedom of the divine nature to be present in a human nature without any rivalry with human freedom. This is the case not despite, but because of God's absolute transcendence of his creation. At the same time, Aquinas's theory helps us see the capacity of human nature, due to its likeness to the divine nature, to receive the divine revelation, yet without being able in any way to anticipate or procure that presence. In short, Aquinas's doctrine of analogical causality offers us crucial resources by which to respond to Kantian criticisms of Christianity in ways that Barthian thought does not.

BARTH'S CENTRAL CRITICISMS OF
ANALOGY THEORY IN AQUINAS

What, then, are the reasons that Barth rejects a Thomistic account of "analogical causality" and under what conditions would he
be willing to entertain such a notion in order to speak about the relation between the world and God? There is not sufficient space to examine all the texts of Barth that are pertinent to the discussion. I will
examine, however, a passage that is central to Barth's own arguments
on this subject. It is a list of five conditions that Barth gives in *Church
Dogmatics* (III, 3) for a right *theological* use of the analogical notion
of *causa* to speak of God's positing of creation, and the God-creature
relation.[19] We might first note these criteria and in doing so, examine closely the criticisms of St. Thomas's thought presented in this
text. We can then note several ways in which Barth seriously failed
to understand Aquinas's own doctrine of creation as "causality." Subsequently, it can be shown that Aquinas's doctrine of analogical creation is set out precisely in such a way as to avoid the very errors of
thought that Barth falsely accuses Aquinas of holding. We may begin
then with the five criteria Barth gives for a right use of the notion of
causality in a distinctly theological context. The five criteria of Barth
are the following:

First, a theological notion of causality may in no way be equated
with a mechanical (post-Newtonian) concept of causality, as such a
notion of causality would be inadequate to signify either the creative
causality of God, or creaturely causality within the order of nature derived from God's creative activity. Barth rightly notes that Aquinas
did not affirm such a notion of causality, and that the latter is distinctly modern.[20]

Second, "if the term *causa* is to be applied legitimately, care must
be taken lest the idea should creep in that in God and the creature
we have to do with two 'things.'"[21] Barth equates reification of God
through the concept of cause with the claim to be able to define
God—that is, to pretend to have quidditative knowledge of what God

19. Karl Barth, CD III, 3, 94–107.   20. CD III, 3, 101.
21. CD III, 3, 101.

is. If God and the creature are reified under the common concept of causality, as if one could "think and speak about them directly," this leads man to think that "[God and creatures] and their relationship to each other [are] somehow below him."[22] That is to say, the human mind pretends to comprehend by its own powers God and his relation to creatures. Aristotle's "dialectic of the causal concept"[23] is to be suspected of leading to this form of thinking. Barth also sometimes intimates that the Thomistic notion of causality reifies both God and creatures within a common system of *quantities* because the oneness of God and the oneness of creatures are articulated as diverse "beings" within a common system.[24]

Third, Barth writes:

> If the term *causa* is to be applied legitimately, it must be clearly understood that it is not a master-concept to which both God and creature are subject, nor is it a common denominator to which they may both be reduced. *Causa* is not a genus of which the divine and creaturely *causa* can then be described as species. When we speak about the being of God and that of the creature, we are not dealing with two species of the one genus being.[25]

If causality is to be applied to God and creatures, it must be understood that because there is no common genus, there is no similarity between causality in God and causality in creatures, nor even any comparability between the two. The idea of such a similarity—which Barth attributes to the *analogia entis* of the Catholic tradition and explicitly to Thomism[26]—would unwittingly understand God and creatures within a "common genus" of causality, and God as a being relative to creatures. It is unable to safeguard the absolute unlikeness between *both* God and creatures, *and* between creatures and God.[27] In fact, only through revelation is a similitude between *both* God and creatures *and* between creatures and God disclosed to human thought.[28] This theological similitude can be called an *analogia op-*

---

22. CD III, 3, 102.

23. CD III, 3, 102.

24. See CD III, 3, 102 and 104, where he intimates that philosophical analogies are only possible through a quantitative comparison of entities. See also the explicit claim to this effect in CD II, 1, 580.

25. CD III, 3, 102.   26. CD III, 3, 103.

27. CD III, 3, 104.   28. CD III, 3, 102.

erationis or *analogia relationis*. Evidently for Barth, such "operations" and "relations" that are common to both God and creatures are not to be conceived of within a common genus. According to this theological analogy, "the divine *causa*, as distinct from the creaturely, is self-grounded, self-positing, self-conditioning and self-causing [*causa sui*]."[29]

Fourth, the notion of causality in theology may at no point be turned into "purely philosophical thinking," as distinct from theological reflection on revelation, philosophy being understood as "projecting a kind of total scheme of things."[30]

Fifth, divine and creaturely causality can only be understood within the narrative context of a distinctly theological reflection on the divine economy, in which "God, the only true God, so loved the world in His election of grace that in fulfillment of the covenant of grace instituted at the creation He willed to become a creature, and did in fact become a creature, in order to be its savior."[31] If we abstract from this theological context to speak about God as a primary cause, we will no longer be speaking about the God of Jesus Christ, and will in fact introduce alien speculation into Christian theology that detracts from a realistic appreciation in faith of the similarity between God and the world *revealed uniquely in Christ*.

If we list the criticisms of Thomistic notions of causality from these pages that are either mentioned explicitly or intimated, we can find (at least) the following: (1) Thomistic notions of causality tend toward a conceptual reification of God. (2) They place both God and creatures within a common intellectual system of quantification, such that the divine unity of God is conceived of as a quantity among other quantities, a numeric being and cause justifying or explaining other beings and causes. (3) Thomism attempts to think of God and creatures from within a common genus of "causality" and "being." (4) Thomistic notions of analogical causality are unable to safeguard the absolute unlikeness between *both* God and creatures, *and* between creatures and God. (5) Thomistic notions of causality portray God as a being that is necessarily relative to creatures. (6) Thom-

29. CD III, 3, 103.   30. CD III, 3, 104.
31. CD III, 3, 105.

istic metaphysics aspires to a "purely philosophical form of thinking" about God, one that would attempt to understand the deity "within a total scheme of things" derived from merely human projections, rather than divine revelation. (7) Thomist notions of causality seek (in part, at least) to derive knowledge of God as a cause from non-biblical sources and thereby introduce elements of reflection into theology that ignore or abstract from the God of Jesus Christ. In this sense, they adulterate our understanding of revelation and obscure the Christocentric character of all true knowledge of God.

All of these claims are highly problematic, and despite Barth's undisputed greatness as a thinker and theologian, most are fairly clumsy and suggest that Barth did not seriously engage Aquinas's thought in any substantive way before writing about him. Here, I would like to attempt briefly to refute the first five statements by appealing to Aquinas's own teachings (in contra-distinction to Barth's portrayal of Aquinas), and I will refer briefly to the last two in the next section of this chapter.

The most important and most problematic of the characterizations of Thomism concerns the third point mentioned above: the idea that God and creatures might be understood in Thomism as species of a common genus by appeal to either the concept of being or of causality. Due to his rhetorical style, it is difficult to tell how aware Barth is of the depth of miscomprehension of classical and medieval thought that this characterization represents. Leaving aside for the moment any question of God, we can focus more immediately simply on creatures. According to both Aristotle and Aquinas, as well as other influential medievals such as Scotus and Suarez, being and causality even in realities we experience immediately are never themselves confined to realization within a single genus. To claim that they could be is in fact to have fundamentally misrepresented one of the most basic structures of classical metaphysics, such that a charge like this one renders a serious dialogue between Thomists and Barthians nearly impossible. For contrary to this account being offered of the *analogia entis*, it is precisely against such an idea (of generic predication) that Aristotle developed his analogical notion of being. How is this the case?

In his study of the categories of being (present in the *Categories*

but also in the *Metaphysics*), Aristotle seeks to identify the diverse ontologically basic determinations that one finds in reality. Each of the
"categories" represents a genus irreducible to any other genus. What
are the categorical determinations of being? Reality as we experience
it is composed of diverse substances, and these in turn possess diverse natures, qualities, quantities, relations, habits, operations, time,
place, position, and environment. These are the generic "divisions"
of reality. However, there is also something that all these determinations have in common: they all have a certain kind of existence, unity,
goodness, and truth. Consequently, being, the good, unity, and truth
are "transcendental" properties that are found in each genus of being.[32] Being is ascribed *analogically* to substances, natures, qualities,
quantities, relations, operations, and so on because it is not reducible
to any one of the generic categorical modes of being.[33] The analog-

32. See, for example, *Metaphysics* III, 4, 1001a4–29; VI, 1, 1026a24–32; XII, 4,
1070b1–3, 5–10; 5, 1071a24–36, and the helpful study of Enrico Berti, "Multiplicity and
Unity of Being in Aristotle," *The Aristotelian Society* 101, no. 2 (2001): 185–207. In *Nicomachean Ethics* I, 6, 1196a23–b29 it is particularly clear that Aristotle is reacting against
Plato's theory of Forms with the conception that being and goodness are not in a genus: "Further, since things are said to be good in as many ways as they are said to be
(for things are called good both in the category of substance, as God and reason, and in
quality, e.g. the virtues, and in quantity, e.g. that which is moderate, and in relation, e.g.
the useful, and in time, e.g. the right opportunity, and in place, e.g. the right locality and
the like), clearly the good cannot be something universally present in all cases and single; for then it would not have been predicated in all the categories but in one only.…
But of honor, wisdom, and pleasure, just in respect of their goodness, the accounts are
distinct and diverse, the good, therefore, is not something common answering to one
Idea.… Are goods one, then, by being derived from one good or by all contributing to
one good, or are they rather one by analogy?"

33. Aquinas, *In V Meta.*, lec. 9, 889–90: "Being cannot be narrowed down to some
definite thing in the way in which a genus is narrowed down to a species by means of
differences. For since a difference does not participate in a genus, it lies outside the essence of a genus. But there could be nothing outside the essence of being which could
constitute a particular species of being by adding to being, for what is outside of being is
nothing, and this cannot be a difference. Hence the Philosopher proved that being cannot be a genus. Being must then be narrowed down to diverse genera on the basis of a
different mode of predication, which flows from a different mode of being; for 'being is
signified,' i.e., something is signified to be, 'in just as many ways' (or in just as many senses) as we can make predications. And for this reason the classes into which being is first
divided are called predicaments, because they are distinguished on the basis of different ways of predicating. Therefore, since some predicates signify what (i.e., substance);
some, of what kind; some, how much, and so on; there must be a mode of being

ical and transcendental structure of being by its very nature implies the impossibility of the idea that being could be signified in a generic fashion. Furthermore, because there are four causes for Aristotle and Aquinas (formal, material, final, and efficient), causality itself is also understood without reference to one genus, and is understood only in a diversified fashion. These ideas are not proper to Aristotle alone. They are also commonly held by the entire medieval scholastic tradition. It is a simple fact of history that no one of consequence in Catholic theology has ever argued that being is in a genus.

What I have mentioned here refers, of course, only to created beings. When it comes to the question of signifying God analogically, even greater problems emerge with the Barthian portrait of St. Thomas. For, in fact, as medieval intellectual historians commonly emphasize, Aquinas is quite insistent that even the transcendental notion of being (which is non-generic) only signifies the "common being" (*ens commune*) that is found in all creatures. It does not in itself signify God in any way. Why is this? Because God is not a creature, therefore he is not a member of *ens commune*. Furthermore, Aquinas insists that God is not even an object within the science of being as such (such that he could be considered as a "being" alongside creatures). The science of being considers *ens commune* (being in things we can experience), and so God can only be approached tangentially by the human mind as the transcendent cause of all that exists.[34] This is why we must say, for Aquinas, that not only is God *not* in any genus of being whatsoever (such as substance, or quantity, or operation, or relation), but he is not even a member of the set of all beings as such. He utterly transcends all that exists, all that is common to being, all that has being (signified variously as *ens commune* or *esse commune*).

These observations also help us to understand why the charge made against Aquinas of assimilating both God and creatures to a system of quantities is intrinsically problematic. First, this would be to presume that unity as a transcendental notion was reducible to the genus of quantity, which is incompatible with what has been said

---

corresponding to each type of predication. For example, when it is said that a man is an animal, is signified substance; and when it is said that a man is white, is signified quality; and so on."

34. See, for example, Aquinas's explicit discussion of this in *In Meta.*, prologue.

above concerning transcendental notions. Quantity is a dimension of
being intrinsically related to matter, and is only one categorical mode
of being, while unity is co-extensive with all that exists. All that has
being is in some way one. We can speak, for example, of one quality, one time, or one nature. Consequently, unity is not reducible to
something in any one genus.[35] Second, however, Barth's charge presumes that when we attribute oneness or unity to God, we do so in a
way that is identical with the way that we attribute unity to creatures.
But precisely because God is not a member of *ens commune* who has
been given existence, his unity is utterly unlike that of creatures. *Because* God is utterly un-derived and uncaused, *therefore* the unity of
God is utterly unlike that of creatures, particularly in their quantitative dimensions.[36]

This leads to the refutation of the fourth and fifth points mentioned
above. What Barth does not see in Aquinas is that for St. Thomas

35. See Aquinas, *In IV Meta.*, lec. 2, 561–63. Commenting upon the idea that being
and unity are co-extensive, trans-categorial properties, Aquinas states (561): "Since being
and unity signify the same thing, and the species of things that are the same are themselves the same, there must be as many species of being as there are of unity, and they
must correspond to each other. For just as the parts of being are substance, quantity,
quality, and so on, in a similar way the parts of unity are sameness, equality and likeness."

36. In ST I, q. 11, a. 3, corp. and ad 2, Aquinas makes clear that unity in God is utterly unlike that of creatures because of the creator's simplicity: in contrast to all creatures
he is uniquely individuated by *what* he is, and his nature is transcendent and incom-
municable. "For it is manifest that the reason why any singular thing is 'this particular
thing' is because it cannot be communicated to many: since that whereby Socrates is a
man, can be communicated to many; whereas, what makes him this particular man, is
only communicable to one. Therefore, if Socrates were a man by what makes him to be
this particular man, as there cannot be many Socrates, so there could not in that way be
many men. Now this belongs to God alone; for God Himself is His own nature, as was
shown above [ST I, q. 3, a. 3]. Therefore, in the very same way God is God, and He is
this God. It is impossible therefore that many Gods should exist." Aquinas goes on to
specify why God cannot be in a common genus with material quantities: "'One' which
is the principle of number is not predicated of God, but only of material things. For
'one' the principle of number belongs to the 'genus' of mathematics, which are material in being, and abstracted from matter only in idea. But 'one' which is convertible with
being is a metaphysical entity and does not depend on matter in its being. [It signifies
the absence of multiplicity.] And although in God there is no privation, still, according
to the mode of our apprehension, He is known to us by way only of privation and remotion. Thus there is no reason why a certain kind of privation should not be predicated
of God; for instance, that He is incorporeal and infinite; and in the same way it is said of
God that He is one."

there is a *non-reciprocity* between the similitude attributed to creatures in relation to God and the non-similitude attributed to God in relation to creatures. Aquinas is quite clear about this in ST I (q. 4, a. 3, ad 3 and 4):

Likeness of creatures to God is not affirmed on account of agreement in form according to the formality of the same genus or species, but solely according to analogy, inasmuch as God is essential being, whereas other things are beings by participation.... [Therefore], although it may be admitted that creatures are in some sort like God, it must nowise be admitted that God is like creatures; because, as Dionysius says (*Div. Nom.* IX, 6): "a mutual likeness may be found between things of the same order, but not between a cause and that which is caused." For, we say that a statue is like a man, but not conversely; so also a creature can be spoken of as in some sort like God; but not that God is like a creature.

The reason for this is precisely because God is not in a common genus of creaturely existence, and cannot even be signified with creatures as "equally" participating in a transcendental characteristic.[37] Rather, because he is the unique source of all else that exists, his being and nature are signified only by recourse to analogies of "causality" that respect his non-relationality to creatures and his incomparable dissimilarity with respect to creation.

This understanding is illustrated vividly in Aquinas's discussion of creation as a form of causality in ST I, qq. 44 and 45. There he underscores the fact that creation may not be understood as a form of change, as if God were a being among beings acting upon them (and being acted upon by them) as intra-worldly created causes do. When we consider the notion of God's action of creation and the creature's reception of being, while removing from our notion of causality all that pertains to change and mutual alteration, what remains is the notion of relation: God is the source of the very substance of the creature, which is therefore really relative to him in all that it is.[38] Cre-

---

37. This is one of Aquinas's chief concerns in ST I, q. 13, a. 5 in refusing any use of the analogy of attribution in which God and creatures are understood as two instantiations of being that are both relative to a prime analogate, a more common conception of being.

38. ST I, q. 45, a. 2, ad 2: "Creation is not change.... For change means that the same something should be different now from what it was previously. Sometimes, indeed, the same actual thing is different now from what it was before, as in motion according to

ation, therefore, presupposes nothing on the side of the creature. It is not a historical process of change in a preexisting substrate that God must cooperate with.[39] Rather, creation is the very gift to the creature of existing per se, with all that in fact characterizes it.[40] However, for this very reason, *there is no real relation between God and creatures*, because God does not possess an identity that is in any way determined or perfected by his causation of creatures.[41] Rather, the contrary is the case: creatures are caused by God because of who he is in his transcendent perfection, and God alone can create.[42] Evidently, in such a form of reflection, there is no possibility of God being determined in his existence by his relation to creatures, nor of his needing to cause them to be in order to be God, nor of his causality as creator stemming from something other than his eternally free wisdom and love. In fact, only if God's causality is characterized in this radically transcendent fashion is it possible to understand creation as an entirely free gift, and God's act of creation as truly contingent, that is to say, as something that is in no way compelled but which derives uniquely from the entirely unnecessary initiative of divine goodness.[43]

---

quantity, quality and place; but sometimes it is the same being only in potentiality, as in substantial change, the subject of which is matter. But in creation, by which the whole substance of a thing is produced, the same thing can be taken as different now and before only according to our way of understanding, so that a thing is understood as first not existing at all, and afterwards as existing. But as action and passion coincide as to the substance of motion, and differ only according to diverse relations (Phys. III, 3; 202b20), it must follow that when motion is withdrawn, only diverse relations remain in the Creator and in the creature."

39. ST I, q. 45, a. 2.

40. ST I, q. 45, a. 3: "Whether creation is anything in the creature? ... Creation places something in the thing created according to relation only; because what is created, is not made by movement or change. For what is made by movement or by change is made from something pre-existing. And this ... cannot happen in the production of all being by the universal cause of all beings, which is God. Hence God by creation produces things without movement. Now when movement is removed from action and passion, only relation remains, as was said above. Hence creation in the creature is only a certain relation to the Creator as to the principle of its being; even as in passion, which implies movement, is implied a relation to the principle of motion."

41. ST I, q. 45, a. 3, ad 2: "Creation signified actively means the divine action, which is God's essence, with a relation to the creature. But in God relation to the creature is not a real relation, but only a relation of reason; whereas the relation of the creature to God is a real relation."

42. ST I, q. 45, a. 5.

43. Aquinas states things succinctly in *In Ioan.* V, lec. 3, 753: "For since the good

This leads us at last to Barth's first charge listed above: that the notions of causality and being implicitly lead theologians to reify in conceptual form a notion of "what" God is. Here again we find Aquinas contradicting Barth concerning the content of "Thomism." For Aquinas appeals to the analogical way in which we name God precisely in order to insist that there is no "quidditative" (or essentially reifying) way to characterize God. It is true that, for Aquinas, because creatures *do resemble* God as their cause, we can derive names for God from creatures, and can say in truth that God is "good" or "wise." He goes as far as to note that these names signify what God is *substantialiter*, in contradiction to the radical apophaticism of Maimonides (or Kant).[44] Analogical predication of divine names is not radically equivocal, and does denote, however indirectly, what God is. However, Aquinas (in seeming contradiction to Barth's characterization of him) also adds that God may not be signified in his perfection as a "cause of beings," but only as the one in whom the perfections of all that is preexist in a most perfect and incomprehensible fashion.[45] Ironically, then, *just because* the fashion in which we think

alone is loveable, a good can be related to love in two ways: as the cause of love, or as caused by love. Now in us, the good causes love: for the cause of our loving something is its goodness, the goodness in it. Therefore, it is not good because we love it, but rather we love it because it is good. Accordingly in us, love is caused by what is good. But it is different with God, because God's love itself is the cause of the goodness in the things that are loved. For it is because God loves us that we are good, since to love is nothing else than to will a good to someone. Thus, since God's will is the cause of things, for 'whatever he willed he made' (Ps 113:3), it is clear that God's love is the cause of the goodness in things."

44. ST I, q. 13, a. 2.

45. ST I, q. 13, a. 2: "But as regards absolute and affirmative names of God, as 'good,' 'wise,' and the like, various and many opinions have been given. For some have said that all such names, although they are applied to God affirmatively, nevertheless have been brought into use more to express some remotion from God, rather than to express anything that exists positively in Him. Hence they assert that when we say that God lives, we mean that God is not like an inanimate thing; and the same in like manner applies to other names; and this was taught by Rabbi Moses. *Others say that these names applied to God signify His relationship towards creatures: thus in the words, 'God is good,' we mean, God is the cause of goodness in things; and the same rule applies to other names.* Both of these opinions, however, seem to be untrue.... First because in neither of them can a reason be assigned why some names more than others are applied to God. For He is assuredly the cause of bodies in the same way as He is the cause of good things; therefore if the words 'God is good,' signified no more than, 'God is the cause of good things,' it

of God (employing the *modus significandi* of our concepts) takes its origin from creatures, *therefore* we cannot know God "quidditatively" as he is in himself.[46] We cannot know "what" God is.[47] The similitude between creatures and God, then, safeguards the idea that God can be signified, but also includes the idea that God cannot be known in a reified fashion because he is known as creator only *through the medium* of his causation of creatures.[48] The fact that God is named from creatures in the terms that Aquinas formulates from analogical causality is not the obstacle to a doctrine of divine transcendence, or an instigation to some form of conceptual idolatry, but is in fact the true safeguard against such idolatrous thinking, inspired by a true sense of divine transcendence.

Ironically, in the absence of such a reflection, Barth's own theological appeals to an *analogia relationis* or an *analogia operationis* run an even greater risk of understanding God in a common genus with creatures than anything Aquinas posits, precisely because, of course, "relation" and "operation" or "activity" are themselves generic modes of being and are not necessarily intrinsically analogical notions such as those of being, unity, or causality. Therefore, precisely in order to appeal to them in an analogical sense, it is necessary to underscore

---

might in like manner be said that God is a body, inasmuch as He is the cause of bodies. So also to say that He is a body implies that He is not a mere potentiality, as is primary matter. Therefore we must hold a different doctrine—viz. that these names signify the divine substance, and are predicated substantially of God, although they fall short of a full representation of Him.... So when we say, 'God is good,' the meaning is not, 'God is the cause of goodness' ... but the meaning is, 'Whatever good we attribute to creatures, pre-exists in God,' and in a more excellent and higher way. Hence it does not follow that God is good, because He causes goodness; but rather, on the contrary, He causes goodness in things because He is good" (emphasis added).

46. ST I, q. 13, a. 3: "Our knowledge of God is derived from the perfections which flow from Him to creatures, which perfections are in God in a more eminent way than in creatures. Now our intellect apprehends them as they are in creatures, and as it apprehends them it signifies them by names. Therefore as to the names applied to God—viz. the perfections which they signify, such as goodness, life and the like, and their mode of signification. As regards what is signified by these names, they belong properly to God, and more properly than they belong to creatures, and are applied primarily to Him. But as regards their mode of signification, they do not properly and strictly apply to God; for their mode of signification applies to creatures."

47. ST I, q. 3, prologue.

48. ST I, q. 13, a. 1.

the difference between relation or operation with respect to God and these genera as they are found in creatures. In practice, it is simply impossible to do this without recourse to a notion of analogical causality that designates the utter transcendence of God in his operations and relations with respect to creatures.

Whatever terms the Barthian might wish to use to talk about God—being, cause, relation, activity, or anything else—he or she is presumably going to have to clarify ways in which these significations are not to be equated with our ordinary (philosophical) uses of the terms, yet still preserve some real signification that is not wholly unintelligible. Many of Barth's disciples, and perhaps Barth himself, think that the "philosophical" meaning of these terms is completely inapplicable to God, but that the terms have a "theological" meaning, given by revelation alone, which is true only for God. But what is this meaning? If we circumvent the red herrings of Barthian rhetoric, which is constantly playing off theology against philosophy, the answer—to the extent that one is given—turns out to be some kind of extension or qualification of ordinary (often "philosophical") usage of terms. This would suggest that Barth and Barthians are just as committed to some sort of analogical naming of God from creatures as anybody else. Indeed, how could it be otherwise? And so, unsurprisingly, we find Barth appealing to what are implicitly analogical senses of ordinary terms when speaking about God in the very passages in which he condemns the thought of "Thomists" for their appeal to analogy.[49] Yet Barth's own rhetoric seems to obscure this truth, and his lack of systematic reflection on the topic leads him to do some analogical naming in a roughshod, improper way. For example, Barth's Spinozist idea of God as *causa sui* is problematic—as Augustine long ago pointed out, nothing, least of all God, can be the cause of its own existence. The irony is that the preservation of theo-

---

49. See, for example, CD III, 3, 103: "The divine *causa*, as distinct from the creaturely, is self-grounded, self-positing, self-conditioning, and self-causing.... [The] creaturely *causa* is not grounded in itself but absolutely from outside and therefore not at all without itself. It owes the fact that it is a *causa* and is capable of *causare*, not to itself but first of all to God, who created it and as the Creator still posits and conditions it, and then to the other *causae* of its own order, without whose conditioning or partial conditioning it would not exist."

logical reflection against an anthropomorphic, generic assimilation of God to creatures, and the cultivation of an adequate conceptual respect for the utter transcendence of God both rely in practice upon a seasoned reflection on analogical discourse concerning being and causality, as well as categorical notions such as substance, nature, activity, relation, and so on. It might be that a more careful study of the texts of both Barth and Aquinas would reveal that there is on several levels a fundamental alignment of perspective.

CAUSALITY AND CHRISTOCENTRISM: FROM KANT TO AQUINAS

The reflections above leave untreated, however, the last two of Barth's criticisms of Aquinas on causality that I have listed above, both of which relate to the Christological character of our knowledge of God. It is true, after all, that while Aquinas and Barth in fact seem to agree in some sense on the transcendence of God and the corresponding dissimilarity between God and creatures, they also disagree (in principle, at least, whether or not this is so in practice) on the question of the human capacity for a philosophical identification of divine names for God. For Aquinas, the human mind is able to identify perfections of created being that can be attributed to God in an analogical fashion, thereby properly signifying (however imperfectly) something of what God is in himself. This capacity does not derive from divine revelation as such, and is grounded in the natural aspirations of our human reason, even if the latter have been severely affected by the negative effects of original and personal sin.[50]

The concern of both Barth and Jüngel seems to be that Aquinas's importation of an alien metaphysical apparatus into the realm of theological reflection on Christ and revelation in fact runs the risk of undermining that reflection from within. It does so firstly with regard to our ontological speculation concerning Christ, as we might seek to

50. See the study by Reinhard Hütter, "The Directedness of Reason and the Metaphysics of Creation," in *Reason and the Reasons of Faith*, eds. P. Griffiths and R. Hütter (Edinburgh: T. & T. Clark, 2005), 160–93.

understand both the divine and human "natures" of Christ with recourse to the metaphysics of divine causality.[51] In doing so, we would
assimilate the divine nature to a human, intra-worldly concept of nature (a kind of univocity of genus) and correspondingly would be
obliged to maintain the transcendence of the divine nature of Christ
only by negating the intelligibility of this nature in any terms resem-
bling the human (a radical apophaticism). In this way, we would implicitly banish the divine from the sphere of human existence and
history, and not unlike Kant's critical philosophy, would render the
incarnation unintelligible. Secondly, by introducing into theology the
recourse to metaphysics we would initially abstract from the concrete
narrative of revelation—the mystery of God's triune identity, election in Christ, providence, incarnation, etc. This epistemological Pelagianism would seek to find God not where he is revealing himself
(in Christ alone) but in works of alien human speculation that distort
or obscure the true character of scriptural revelation. Barth's rejection
of a distinctly philosophical reflection on causality and creation stems
most profoundly, it seems, from concerns such as these.

A Thomistic response to these charges can readily be formulated
as follows: why does the Barthian *presuppose* the validity of the Kantian critique of classical metaphysics and the epistemological conditions for its warrant? Jüngel, after all, seems to take for granted the
authority of Kant's critique without a sufficient defense of his views.
This serves simply to obscure the real issue: that Barth and Barthians tend to import wholesale Kantian *philosophical presuppositions*
into their theology without sufficient justification, despite their prohibition of an "autonomous philosophy" that is distinct from revelation. But why in fact should we consider the classical metaphysical tradition something alien to the right interpretation of scripture
when there is strong evidence to suggest that divine revelation itself
(especially in the Deutero-canonical works and the New Testament)
was purposefully communicated through the medium of Hellenistic
philosophical concepts? The metaphysical arguments of the Greek fathers, Augustine, and Aquinas certainly can be understood to develop in logical continuity with the metaphysical presuppositions of the

51. See Barth, CD III, 3, 103 and 105.

New Testament itself. Meanwhile, many of the philosophical speculations of Kant and Hegel that stand in opposition to the classical philosophical tradition also distort profoundly any right understanding
of the Gospel, and yet these same speculations deeply affect the project of Barth, even as they did the theologies of his liberal Protestant
teachers (which he partially rejected). In this case, perhaps Barthians
are the ones working in insufficiently examined dependence upon
the conventional, non-Christian speculations of their age, and might
profit from a deeper engagement with the Thomist tradition. At any
rate, when it comes to making strident claims in this domain, careful
arguments are needed rather than mere assertions.

Here I would like to conclude this chapter with brief reflections
that might contribute to further discussion concerning Aquinas's
metaphysics, Barth's Christocentricism, and Chalcedonian Christology. Barth has rightly insisted that the two natures of Christ cannot be conceived in a common genus, and Barthians rightly insist
(against Kant) that we cannot conceive of divine freedom and human
freedom over against one another, such that the events of the incarnation, or of grace, would be cast as intrinsically unintelligible concepts,
incompatible with our empirical and moral realism. I would like to
suggest, then (in a necessarily abbreviated fashion), three distinctly
theological advantages of Aquinas's doctrine of analogical causality
precisely with regard to the Barthian concerns. First, it allows us to conceive of the two natures of Christ so as to understand the genuine
transcendence of God the Son with respect to every genus of created nature, while *simultaneously* underscoring the immanent presence
of the Son's divine nature in history. Second, it allows us to affirm the
genuine freedom of God to be truly present in history in the incarnation as God without in any way introducing history into his own triune identity, that is to say, without God becoming intrinsically determined by creation in what he is from all eternity. Third, it allows us
to understand why there can be no ontological rivalry between the
divine freedom of God the Son and the human freedom of the Son
made man. In each of these cases, recourse to the Thomist understanding of analogy and divine causality facilitates a speculative vindication of a Christological concern that is seemingly shared by Aquinas and Barth alike.

The first of these points can be made fairly simply by returning to one of the arguments made above. "Nature" (like "relation" and "operation," other concepts that Barth ascribes to God analogically), is itself historically associated with the classical genera of the categorical modes of being. It is, then, a "genus." To attribute it to Christ in a twofold sense, as Barth wishes to do, without reducing the human and divine natures of Christ to a common genus of being, it is necessary to ascribe "nature" to God in a wholly non-generic sense.[52] But such non-generic ascription is possible (as Aquinas shows) only because there is a merely analogical resemblance between created natures as we come to know them, and the transcendent nature of God. Precisely because God is the *cause* of all created natures to which he gives existence, his nature is as such outside of every created genus of being.[53] Likewise, his divine nature utterly transcends our knowledge; therefore he cannot be considered as a being of a determinate kind among other beings.

Does this arrangement not risk banishing the divine nature from the world altogether, precisely because of the dissimilitude between God and all intra-worldly natures? On the contrary, because God gives existence to all things as their transcendent cause, their existence is not alien to him nor something "outside" of him, even if he utterly transcends them as their divine source. God's creative causality does not effectuate a change in the creature, nor cause something in the creature, but is itself the source of the entire existence of the creature. Therefore, to paraphrase Aquinas, "God is everything as the cause of everything."[54] God is present to all things insofar as they exist.[55] Far from being banished from the world by his transcendence,

---

52. See in particular CD IV, 2, in which Barth develops notions of the divine and human "essences" of Christ in a systematic fashion.

53. ST I, q. 3, aa. 4–5.

54. ST I, q. 4, a. 2: "Since therefore God is the first effective cause of things, the perfections of all things must pre-exist in God in a more eminent way. Dionysius implies the same line of argument by saying of God (*Div. Nom.* v): 'It is not that He is this and not that, but that He is all, as the cause of all.' Secondly, from what has been already proved, God is existence itself, of itself subsistent. Consequently, He must contain within Himself the whole perfection of being." The paraphrase is taken from Te Velde, *Aquinas on God*, 65. See the excellent discussion of Aquinas's understanding of our knowledge of God (65–93).

55. ST I, q. 8, a. 1.

then, God as Aquinas understands him is uniquely immanent in all that is, without being identified with anything he has created.[56] He is more intimately present to creatures than they are to themselves because of his transcendence as creator.[57] As a consequence, we can say that if Aquinas ascribes to Christ a "divine nature" this implies that Christ's deity is not something contained under the genus of nature that is proper to all creatures, and that by the fact that the Son's nature is divine, he is present to all that exists in created history as God is present to his effects.[58] The transcendence of Christ the Word is mirrored in his radical immanence with respect to all that depends upon him for its being, for "through him all things were made" (Jn 1:3).

This leads us to the second point: only because of the uniqueness of the form of causality that is proper to God as creator is he alone free to "become" human, to adopt a created nature hypostatically without being in any way alienated from what he is eternally. The substrate of the hypostatic union *is* the existent person of God the Son.[59] Therefore, if there is a hypostatic union, the causality entailed cannot transpire in a pre-existent material subject in which change is subsequently effectuated. Rather, this union is the new presence of God in creation existing as a man, with a human soul and body. Precisely because God alone can act at the level of existence in a causal fashion, *therefore* he alone can become incarnate in the being of man (at the deepest level of created reality) without ceasing to exist as God. It is truly God the Son (the author of life, in whom we live and move and have our being) who is present in history, yet without any loss of his deity that might somehow result from the incarnation.

Aquinas, in turn, stresses quite clearly that while the union of the Word incarnate is hypostatic (taking place in the person of the Son), it in no way renders the nature of God the Son relative to the human nature of the Son. The union does, however, render the human na-

---

56. ST I, q. 8, a. 2: "God fills every place; not, indeed, like a body, for a body is said to fill place inasmuch as it excludes the co-presence of another body; whereas by God being in a place, others are not thereby excluded from it; indeed, by the very fact that He gives being to the things that fill every place, He Himself fills every place."

57. ST I, q. 8, aa. 3 and 4.

58. A point made explicitly in ST I, q. 45, a. 6, corp. and ad 2.

59. ST III, q. 2, a. 3.

ture of the Son absolutely relative to his divine nature.[60] The non-reciprocity of relationality and similitude of the divine and human that are present in Aquinas's doctrine of creation (and which Barth mis-characterizes) are carried over into his doctrine of the hypostatic union, with respect to the two natures of the God-man. The deity of Christ is in no way dependent upon what is created, while what is created is wholly relative to the deity.

This is a non-trivial matter, for if by contrast we remove the appeal to the analogy of creative causality from our understanding of the divine and human natures of Christ that are united in his person, then we must conceive of the union of God's divine and human natures not in a trans-historical fashion (aided by recourse to an analogical doctrine of creative causality), but rather by appeal to a likeness from causal becoming in a pre-existent subject. The hypostatic union of the natures will then have to be "narrated" by a movement of the Son from being God alone into being human, understood after the fashion of the change from one specific state or contrary to another within a common genus, whether this be the genus of "nature," "relation," or "operation." The non-relativity (and non-mutual reciprocity) of the divine and human natures will be lost. Instead, God will be understood in a narrative fashion, through historical becoming, as one who is eternally relative in his deity to the human nature of Christ. The divine nature and the human nature will then be mutually determined through a common interaction. As a consequence, the incarnation becomes inconceivable without ascribing history to the very life of God *in se*, and so the very notion of the "immanent Trinity" is threatened. Interestingly, this is precisely what we see in the post-Hegelian Barthian-inspired theologies of Jürgen Moltmann,

60. ST III, q. 2, a. 7: "The union of which we are speaking is a relation which we consider between the Divine and the human nature, inasmuch as they come together in one Person of the Son of God. Now, as was said above (ST I, q. 13, a. 7), every relation which we consider between God and the creature is really in the creature, by whose change the relation is brought into being; whereas it is not really in God, but only in our way of thinking, since it does not arise from any change in God. And hence we must say that the union of which we are speaking is not really in God, except only in our way of thinking; but in the human nature, which is a creature, it is really. Therefore we must say [the hypostatic union] is something created." Aquinas goes on in a. 9 to affirm that the unity of the incarnation is greater than any other created unity.

Eberhard Jüngel, and Robert Jenson, all of whom interpret Chalcedonian Christology while distancing themselves from a classical metaphysical understanding of creation.[61] It seems that something like this
is present in Barth's later thought as well, as Bruce McCormack has recently argued poignantly.[62] And at this point, speaking from a Thomistic point of view, one might argue that David Bentley Hart—in his
writings on the "analogy of being"—has rightly questioned whether
such theologies maintain in sufficient fashion a sense of the transcendence of God with respect to the history of the divine economy.[63] After all, if God is only intelligible in himself as the triune God in relation to the historical economy (which includes moral evil, suffering

61. See the particularly clear statement of Jüngel (*God as the Mystery of the World*,
346–47), in which he claims that our understanding of the incarnation as a *historical
becoming of God toward man* entails the notion of history and election as constitutive
of the very life of God: "Where the economic doctrine of the Trinity speaks of God's
history with man, the immanent doctrine of the Trinity must speak of God's *historicity*.
God's history is his coming to man. God's historicity is God's being as it comes (being
in coming). We must ponder this seriously if we want to take God's history with man
seriously as an event in which God is God. In the process, of course, the immanent doctrine of the Trinity, which considers the historicity of God, must take seriously that God
is *our* God."

62. See Bruce McCormack, "Karl Barth's Christology as a Resource for a Reformed
Version of Kenoticism," 243–51.

63. See David Bentley Hart, *The Beauty of the Infinite: The Aesthetics of Christian
Truth* (Grand Rapids, Mich.: Eerdmans, 2003), 165–66: "The God whose identity subsists in time and is achieved upon history's horizon—who is determined by his reaction
to the pathos of history—may be a being, or indeed the totality of all beings gathered in
the pure depths of ultimate consciousness, but he is not being as such, he is not life and
truth and goodness and love and beauty. God belongs to the system of causes, even if
he does so as its total rationality; he is an absolute *causa in fieri*, but not a transcendent
causa in esse. He may include us in his story, but his story will remain both good and
evil, even if it ends in an ultimate triumph over evil. After all, how can we tell the danc-
er from the dance? The collapse of the analogical interval between the immanent and
economic Trinity, between timeless eternity and the time in which eternity shows itself,
has not made God our companion in pain, but simply the truth of our pain.... Only a
truly transcendent and 'passionless' God can be the fullness of love dwelling within our
very being, nearer to us than our inmost parts, but a dialectical Trinity is not transcendent—truly infinite—in this way at all, but only sublime, a metaphysical whole that can
comprise us or change us extrinsically, but not transform our very being.... Theology
must, to remain faithful to what it knows of God's transcendence, reject any picture of
God that so threatens to become at once both thoroughly mythological and thoroughly metaphysical, and insist upon the classical definitions of impassibility, immutability,
and non-successive eternity."

and death), then these latter attributes of history are also in some real sense intrinsically necessary to the developing identity of the historical God. God stands in need of moral evil in order to be God. In this case, the results of the abandonment of a classical metaphysics of divine causality are in fact disastrous, not only for the speculative contemplation of the Trinitarian mystery itself, but also for our ethical and soteriological understanding of the agency of God.

Last of all, only a doctrine of analogical causality allows us to understand that there can be no rivalry whatsoever between the *existence* of created freedom and divine freedom, and consequently no rivalry between the divine and human freedoms of Christ. Because he alone is the cause of the existence of creatures (in Aquinas's qualified sense of the term "cause"), God alone is free to be present in and even as a creaturely reality without acting on that reality in the way a created cause would. That is to say, God alone can be freely present in the most intimate depth of the reality he has created without acting extrinsically upon the creature by violence or alienation, and without therefore causing changes in the natural structure of the reality.[64] In this sense, God in his sovereign will and freedom can be intimately present in the human nature of Christ (even through the medium of the hypostatic union) without changing the structure of Christ's created freedom. The presence of the divine will in Christ, on the contrary, liberates human freedom so that it can be fully itself.[65]

However, the incarnation touches not merely upon the question of God's freedom but also of his ordering wisdom with respect to a created nature that is "adequately proportioned" to represent him. It is essential that there exist a natural similitude between our created human nature and God in order for the incarnation to take place. For only if there is a natural similitude of the rational nature of man to God is the human nature capable of becoming a vehicle for the gratuitous revelation of God's divine life in human flesh. Only because

64. See ST I, q. 19, aa. 4 and 8; q. 103, a. 6. This point contrasts spectacularly with the thought of Kant. See the study by Brian Shanley, "Divine Causation and Human Freedom in Aquinas," *American Catholic Philosophical Quarterly* 72, no. 1 (1998): 99–122.

65. This is why Aquinas emphasizes in ST III, q. 18, a. 4 (in a subtle correction to John Damascene) that Christ made truly human choices in view of the good, and in fact, made these choices more profoundly and freely than other human beings.

the human nature of Christ is not wholly alien to his divine nature (that is, entirely dissimilar to it), but is in some sense similar to it, can the human nature of Christ become the medium for the reception of the mystery of God without doing violence to what that nature is. Concretely, this mediation of God's personal subsistence in a created human nature transpires especially through the medium of human reason.[66] Because God is not wholly alien to human thought and freedom, therefore the freedom of Christ can find its authentic fulfillment, perfection, and beauty in being utterly relative to God, that is to say, in knowing and doing the will of the Father. Through the medium of his human reason illumined by grace, Christ as man has knowledge of his own divine will that he shares with the Father, and this in turn renders him humanly free to do the divine will. Were there an absolute ontological dissimilitude between the human nature of Christ and the divine nature, there would simply be no possibility of a cooperation of the human will of Christ with the divine will, as the revelation of the will of the Father would remain wholly alien and unintelligible to Christ's human nature, even in the presence of divine grace. In point of fact, however, Christ's human knowledge of his own deity deepens his human freedom by augmenting his human potential to love and to choose what is authentically good with wisdom. In this way it is the source of the unique freedom of Christ.[67]

CONCLUSION

If what I have sketched out above is correct, then Thomists are warranted in their spirited defense of the analogical metaphysics of divine causality as understood by Aquinas. When responsibly portrayed, that metaphysical account does not fall prey to the Barthian critique of divine causality as a system of ideas that falsifies a right understanding of the divine transcendence and immanence of God by

---

66. See ST III, q. 6, aa. 1–2.

67. Aquinas points out in ST III, q. 7, a. 13, ad 2 that the habitual grace of the soul of Christ is "natural" to him in a way that is unique among all men, insofar as it stems from his hypostatic identity as Son. It acts within the depths of his human nature so as to conform his human freedom to his divine will, and yet this is only "normal" for Christ, because he is the Son himself existing as man.

introducing an alien system of philosophical speculation into divine revelation. Rather, it safeguards a true sense of the uniqueness of God with regard to any and every created reality, such that God may in no way be assimilated to the world of human creatures. But precisely for this same reason, God may be present in creation in a way that no created reality can be.

Furthermore, this notion of causality does not supplant or distort the knowledge of God that comes through Christ and the mystery of the incarnation. Rather, it allows us to understand more profoundly how it is God who is truly present in Christ historically, and who without prejudice to either his divine transcendence or his human nature, truly acts in an integral way by virtue of both his divine freedom and his human freedom. A deepened discussion between Barthians and Thomists should focus on the subject of Christ's two natures, and the ways that the Chalcedonian tradition makes implicit use of an analogical discourse concerning being and causality to reflect on the incarnation of the Word. In this conversation, perhaps it is the philosophical theology of Aquinas, and not that of Kant, that has a more constructive role to play for the right formulation of thinking about the Christological deposit of faith. It is to this subject that I turn, then, in the following chapter.

4

———— ᛭ ————

Why Christology
Presupposes Natural
Theology

In the last chapter I sought to show how a correct use of an analogical metaphysics of being could serve to uphold the doctrine of the
incarnation. In this chapter I would like to turn the argument around
and suggest that the mystery of the incarnation invites us to uphold
an analogical metaphysics of being. An ecumenical version of this
argument was developed in mid-twentieth-century Catholic theology. A string of authors such as Erich Przywara, Gottlieb Söhngen,
Hans Urs von Balthasar, and Henri Bouillard emphasized the role
that grace plays in the concrete historical formulation of all intellectual truths about God, even truths accessible to natural human reason.[1]
For each of these thinkers—in differing ways—philosophical aspi-

---

1. Erich Przywara, *Analogia entis: Metaphysik* (Münich: Josef Kösel & Friedrich Pustet, 1932) and "Reichweite der Analogie als katholischer Grundform," *Scholastik* 3 (1940): 339–62, 508–32; Gottlieb Söhngen, "Analogia fidei I: Gottähnlichkeit
allein aus Glauben?," *Catholica* 3 (1934): 113–36; "Analogia fidei II: Die Einheit in der
Glaubenswissenschaft," *Catholica* 3 (1934): 176–208; "Wunderzeichen und Glaube,"
Catholica 4 (1935): 145–64; Balthasar, *Karl Barth*; Henri Bouillard, *Karl Barth, Genèse
et évolution de la théologie dialectique,* 3 vols. (Paris: Aubier, 1957). See also the excellent
Protestant study of Henry Chavannes, *L'analogie entre Dieu et le monde selon saint Thomas d'Aquin et selon Karl Barth* (Paris: Cerf, 1969).

rations to metaphysical knowledge of God, when seen in a theological light, are understood as depending upon the stimuli of the grace
of the incarnate Word, and as being exercised in view of that grace.
Consequently, any natural orientation toward God has as its unique
condition of possibility and governing regulatory principle the divine
agency of the grace of Christ. Indeed, the First Vatican Council maintained the capacity of the human person to arrive at certain natural
knowledge of God by rational powers.[2] Nevertheless, this natural operation could never be properly exercised in man's fallen state without the agency of grace.[3] On this reading of things, we know God in
Christ truly, and the restorative effects of Christ's grace invite us to
"rediscover" our natural capacity to know God philosophically. For
the sake of argument, let us concede that basically there is a common theme present in these authors, and that their argument is theologically defensible. But let us then recast the question from another
point of view. Here we might develop a stronger argument than that
noted above.

Let us take "nature" to designate the essential determinations of
a created reality as it is constituted in existence, such that it can normally accomplish certain actions by its own intrinsic powers that
tend towards such actions, and such that it behaves according to cer-

2. "The same Holy Mother Church teaches that God, the source and end of all
things, can be known with certainty from the consideration of created things, by the
natural power of human reason (Rom. 1:20).... If anyone says that the one, true God,
our Creator and Lord, cannot be known with certainty from the things that have been
made, by the natural light of human reason, let him be anathema" (*Dei Filius*, chap. II,
and anathema 1, in Tanner, *Decrees of the Ecumenical Councils*).

3. Such an idea certainly finds echoes in Aquinas's own thought, even if the Angelic Doctor within his historical context can be seen to emphasize the distinct powers of
our philosophical knowledge of God, over and against the Augustinian illuminism of
his age. Aquinas clearly thinks that the human intellect is capable by its natural powers of attaining to some natural knowledge of God. See the helpful analysis of Aquinas's
epistemology with respect to nature and grace by Santiago Ramírez, *De Gratia Dei* (Salamanca: Editorial San Esteban, 1992), 61–107, as well as the study by Paul Synave, *La
révélation des vérités divines naturelles d'après saint Thomas*, in *Mélanges Mandonnet* (Paris:
J. Vrin, 1930), 1:327–71. Nevertheless, in *In Ioan*. XVII, lec. 6, 2265, Aquinas makes especially strong statements about the frailty of natural knowledge of God in the fallen state.
In *In Ioan*. XVII, lec. 2, 2195, Aquinas claims that Gentiles did know something of the
creator, but did not worship him properly by the worship of exclusive *latria*. See also ST
I-II, q. 109, a. 1, and *In de Div. Nom.*VII, lec. 5, 740.

tain stable, integral ways of being. Let us take "grace" to be the life of God, transmitted to our created human nature in supernatural ways, through means and channels that we cannot attain to naturally, but that can complement, heal, and elevate what we are naturally. If in the fallen state of our common human nature, grace is a great and perhaps even necessary aid for the right exercise of any natural human knowledge of God, is a human capacity for natural knowledge of God a condition for our understanding of divine revelation? If we have emphasized rightly the primacy of divine grace for a developed knowledge of God by nature, should we not also examine the question of the presuppositions of nature for a right knowledge of God by grace? In other words, in thinking out the *analogia fidei* (to use the term of Söhngen and Karl Barth), in what ways are we perhaps implicitly or explicitly committing ourselves to the *analogia entis*?

Let us again be clear from the beginning about the meaning of terms as I am using them here. By *analogia fidei*, I mean to denote ontological resemblances between creatures and God that are known to us uniquely by virtue of the supernatural revelation of God in Christ. By the term *analogia entis* I mean to denote ontological resemblances between creatures and God that can be discerned and understood by the powers of natural human reason, that is to say, by virtue of the kind of thing we are and the world we live in, and which are not given by supernatural revelation. In the case of both analogies of faith and analogies of being, I am presuming that analogous propositional language (analogy as propositional naming) is distinct from but also intrinsically related to real analogies between things. Analogical propositional naming is capable of truly signifying analogical, ontological resemblances in realities themselves. Consequently, recourse to terms such as "the analogy of the incarnate Word," or the "analogy of being between creatures and God" as I am denoting them here, entails both an ontological foundation in the things themselves, and a propositional mode of signifying this reality that is characterized by analogical terms.[4]

4. While "analogy" is sometimes meant to denote one of these two senses more precisely than another, neither sense of the word is meant to exclude the other, nor are they meant to be identical, but rather always interrelated, as the analogical mode of signifying realities as "being" is meant to signify in fact the real distinctions and likenesses

Here I will argue that the theological analogy of the incarnate Word (the Logos *ensarkos*) is not fully intelligible even as a specifically Christian and dogmatic notion without the capacity to ascribe to God analogical notions of being and unity, in comparison with creatures. Furthermore, we are only capable of ascribing such analogical notions if there is a real ontological resemblance between creatures and God that is naturally intelligible to the human intellect without formal recourse to divine revelation. Consequently, the knowledge

---

between the analogical modes of being in the things themselves. Interpreters of Aquinas such as Ralph McInerny (see especially *Aquinas and Analogy* [Washington, D.C.: The Catholic University of America Press, 1996]) have argued that analogy pertains especially to the logical structure of mental, intentional thinking, rather than to the nature of things in themselves. Bruce Marshall has presented a lucid version of this interpretation in his essay, "Christ the End of Analogy," in *The Analogy of Being: Invention of the Antichrist or the Wisdom of God?*, 280–313. While Aquinas clearly does use the term *analogia* to denote logical terms in many instances, he also quite clearly affirms that there exist ontological similitudes between realities themselves, or between accidents of substances, or between accidents and substances, as well as between creatures and God. In his *In Meta.* IV, lec. 1, 534–47 he makes quite clear that analogical naming ultimately derives from and refers back to ontological resemblances in realities, that result from causal dependencies. These realities and their similitudes are denoted by recourse to terms that are analogical, such that our discourse "by analogy" maps onto—and denotes insightfully—real resemblances and differences. See, for example, ST I, q. 4, a. 3, where Aquinas is speaking about a similitude in the order of being where there is no common *ratio* by which to denote this similitude, because the agent is not of the same genus or species as the effect. "If therefore the agent is contained in the same species as its effect, there will be a likeness in form between that which makes and that which is made, according to the same formality of the species; as man reproduces man. If, however, the agent and its effect are not contained in the same species, there will be a likeness, but not according to the formality of the same species; as things generated by the sun's heat may be in some sort spoken of as like the sun, not as though they received the form of the sun in its specific likeness, but in its generic likeness. Therefore if there is an agent not contained in any 'genus,' its effect will still more distantly reproduce the form of the agent, not, that is, so as to participate in the likeness of the agent's form according to the same specific or generic formality, but only according to some sort of analogy; as existence is common to all. In this way all created things, so far as they are beings, are like God as the first and universal principle of all being." See the helpful study of Lawrence Dewan, "St. Thomas and Analogy: the Logician and the Metaphysician," in *Form and Being: Studies in Thomistic Metaphysics* (Washington, D.C.: The Catholic University of America Press, 2006), 81–95; Reinhard Hütter, "Attending to the Wisdom of God—From Effect to Cause, from Creation to God: A *Relecture* of the Analogy of Being according to Thomas Aquinas," in *The Analogy of Being: Invention of the Antichrist or the Wisdom of God?*, 209–45; and Steven A. Long, *Analogia Entis: On the Analogy of Being, Metaphysics, and the Act of Faith* (Notre Dame, Ind.: University of Notre Dame Press, 2011).

of Christ's divinity that we are given by grace implies that we have a natural capacity for knowledge of God. Even more strikingly: if there were in our fallen condition no persisting capacity for natural knowledge of God (if we are not capable in principle of a so-called natural theology), then human beings would be radically and irremediably incapable of receiving knowledge of Christ by grace alone *under any form whatsoever*. The revelation of Christ would remain utterly extrinsic to our human manner of knowing. Consequently, if in our concrete historical state as fallen creatures, the grace of Christ is necessary in one sense in order to cultivate a right understanding of the ontological similitudes between creatures and God, then in another sense, our capacity of natural reason to attain to true analogical knowledge of God is a precondition in human beings for our capacity to receive grace.

I will make this argument in three stages. The first stage will examine the properly theological analogy of the Word incarnate that originates not from human philosophical ingenuity, but from divine revelation. What does it mean to say by analogy that the Son incarnate is truly God yet distinct from the Father *as his Word*? Here I will argue that a theological understanding of the incarnate Word *as God* necessarily implies an analogical analysis of the Word in his pre-existence, and the ways that the eternal procession of the Word is both like and unlike a human intellectual "procession" of conceptual thought. The clarification of this latter "analogy of faith" necessarily entails an understanding of the Word as the unoriginate ground or cause of existence in creatures.

The second stage will examine the metaphysical presuppositions necessary for the articulation of the transcendence and divinity of the incarnate Word in his likeness and difference with regard to creatures, illustrating how analogies of being and unity are implicit in any right understanding of the divinity of the Word as presented by scripture itself. Use of the analogy of being is logically entailed by the articulation of the analogy of the Word. Without recourse to this form of thinking (which presupposes ontological analogies between creatures and God), the *theological* analogical knowledge of the Word as God *in faith* is literally unthinkable.

The third stage argues that the affirmation of divine revelation presupposes a minimal distinction between natural and supernatural modes of knowledge, as well as the understanding that our natural manner of knowing must be intrinsically capable of transformation by the knowledge of faith in grace. Yet if we are naturally capable of receiving grace so as to think truly of God by means of theological analogies of faith, then this presupposes a natural, epistemological capacity to conceive of God in terms of our experience of creatures. If these terms are either equivocal or univocal, rather than analogical, a capacity to cooperate intellectually with revelation is intrinsically neutralized. Correspondingly, while knowledge of Christ implies a natural capacity for knowledge of God by natural reason (natural theology), the absence of an intrinsic capacity for the latter would render belief in the divinity of Christ impossible. This suggests that to the extent that there is a Christological *analogia entis* (an analogy between creation and God disclosed in Christ) this mystery presupposes a natural *analogia entis* intrinsic to creation. To believe rightly in Christological knowledge of God, then, one must affirm the possibility and necessity of natural theology.

THE ANALOGY OF THE
WORD INCARNATE

Aquinas holds to three principles for understanding the mystery of the Word incarnate that place him in essential continuity both with the patristic traditions of east and west and with certain critical affirmations of Karl Barth. First, the knowledge of the Son and Word of God as distinct from the Father is a knowledge available to us only by means of the economy of the Word's visible mission. That is to say, it is only the Word incarnate, or Logos *ensarkos*, who makes known to us the immanent life of God as Trinitarian. Commenting on the birth of Christ in the Gospel of Matthew, Aquinas appeals to Augustine's comparison of the manifestation of God in Christ with the manifestation of the mental concept in human speech through the spoken word:

For in us there is a two-fold word [*verbum*]: the word of the heart and the spoken word. The word of the heart is the intellect's concept, *which is hidden from human beings, unless it is expressed by the human voice, or by the spo-*

ken word. To the word of the heart is compared the eternal Word prior to the Incarnation, *when he was with the Father and hidden from us;* but the spoken word is compared to the incarnate Word, which has already appeared to us and has been manifested.[5]

The affirmation here is consistent with Aquinas's argument elsewhere that the mystery of God as a Trinity of persons is something radically inaccessible to natural reason. (Aquinas here differs from Richard of St. Victor and Bonaventure.) That God is triune remains for us naturally unknown and indemonstrable even after revelation, even by way of philosophical arguments from reason given in light of the incarnation.[6]

Second, however, this revelation of the Word makes present to us the very life of God in the flesh, the life of God as he is in himself, as the eternal Son, in relation to the Father and the Holy Spirit. Aquinas states quite clearly that there is no ontological similitude between the Word incarnate and the Word of the immanent Trinity, but rather a pure identity: an economic presence in Christ of God as he truly is.[7] Consequently, the Word is manifest to us in his unity with the

5. Aquinas, *In Matt.*, c. 1, lec. 4; emphasis added. Augustine employs the comparison, for example, in *De Trinitate*, IX, c. 12.

6. See ST I, q. 32, a. 1, in contrast with Richard of St. Victor, *De Trinitate* I, c. 4; III, c. 19; Bonaventure, *Itinerarium Mentis in Deum*, VI, 2. See the helpful analysis of Bruce D. Marshall, "Putting Shadows to Flight: the Trinity, Faith and Reason," in *Reason and the Reasons of Faith*, eds. Paul Griffiths and Reinhard Hütter (London: T. and T. Clark, 2005), 53–77.

7. Aquinas holds that the Word incarnate is *known by us* through analogical comparisons but is himself the personal, eternal Word of the Father. Commenting on the above-mentioned similitude of the mental and spoken word, he writes in *De Ver.*, q. 4, a. 1, ad 6: "The Incarnate Word in some respects resembles, and, in other respects, does not resemble the vocal word. They have this in common as a basis for comparison: a vocal word manifests the interior word as flesh manifested the eternal Word. They differ, however, in the following respect: the flesh assumed by the eternal Word is not said to be a word, whereas the vocal word used to manifest an interior word is said to be a word. Consequently, the vocal word is something other than the interior word, but the Incarnate Word is the same as the eternal Word, just as the word signified by the vocal word is the same as the word within the heart." This seems to me to differ from Rahner's *Grundaxiom* not because it refuses an identification of the "economic Trinity" and the "immanent Trinity," but rather, because it presupposes no "economic Trinity" at all, that could be differentiated from God's immanent and transcendent life. Otherwise said, there is only the immanent and incomprehensible Trinity who manifests himself to us imperfectly but truly in and through the economy, by means of the missions of the

Father, but also in his distinctness, divine reciprocity, and mutual immanence. In short, the Son is revealed to us as truly God, equal to the Father, yet as personally distinct from the Father.

Nevertheless, our knowledge of the triune God transpires not through immediate vision but through an analogical, propositional form of knowing, derived from the divine economy. Based upon God's revelation in the flesh and the language of scripture, the church has formulated propositions that prescribe true analogical names to the Son: he is identical in "nature" with the Father, yet "personally" or "hypostatically" distinct. Aquinas repeatedly makes this point by using Arianism and Sabellianism as a foil against which to assert that the affirmations of doctrine really designate what God is in his immanent Trinitarian life.[8] There is a real unity of nature in God (against Arianism), but also a true distinction of persons (against Sabellianism). Such notions of nature and person are analogical (theological analogies), derived from a comparison of revelation and creation, and they are also true—they delineate in an imperfect and mediate fashion what God is in himself.

Third, then, the Word who is made known in the incarnation is truly the Word through whom God upholds all things in being. Being one with the Father he is before all time (that is to say, pre-existent) and is the creator himself, in whom all things were made.[9] In his reading of scripture (Phil 2:6–7: "though he was in the form of God ... [he] emptied himself"), Aquinas is careful to exclude from

---

Son and Holy Spirit. I also think Aquinas would be unlikely to embrace the language of David Bentley Hart (*The Beauty of the Infinite*, 165) when the latter refers to "the analogical interval between the immanent and economic Trinity, between timeless eternity and the time in which eternity shows itself," only because such language could give the impression of an ontological self-differentiation that takes place in God, between God in himself and God in his self-limiting decision to exist and reveal himself in time. The latter idea is developed at painstaking length by Sergius Bulgakov, *The Lamb of God*, trans. Boris Jakim (Grand Rapids, Mich.: Eerdmans, 2008), especially chapters 1, 3 and 4.

8. See, for example, SCG IV, c. 11; *De rationibus fidei*, c. 9; ST I, q. 27, a. 1.

9. Aquinas explicitly employs the notion of pre-existence. *In Ioan.*, I, lec. 7, 176: "If Christ was not God as to his person, he would have been most presumptuous to say 'I and the Father are one,' (John 10:30) and 'Before Abraham came to be, I am,' as is said below (John 8:48). Now 'I' refers to the person of the speaker. And the one who was speaking was a man, who, as one with the Father, existed before [*praeexistebat*] Abraham."

theological understanding of the Son's *kenosis* any notion of the cessation or surrender of his divine prerogatives as God, instead attributing "humility" to God in the incarnation as an expression of the free condescension of divine love. The Word who is incarnate is also the author of creation who sustains all things in being as God, even as he experiences historical life, suffering, and death as a human being. As God he is one in essence, power, and will with the Father and the Spirit, even as he empties himself by taking on the form of human nature out of divine compassion. Consequently, Aquinas could be said anachronistically to hold to what the Lutheran tradition has sometimes named the *extra Calvinisticum*.[10] This is the position not only of Calvin, but also of Athanasius, Augustine, Gregory Nazianzus, the medievals and, arguably, Karl Barth himself (although the reading of this last figure on this topic is disputed).[11]

These three features are important because they suggest that when Aquinas reflects upon the distinctly theological mystery of the Son incarnate as Word, he will do so while being committed to two complementary truths. First, God the Son is known to us through his historical self-revelation. Second, however, because *in that revelation* he makes known to us who he is eternally, *therefore* we are permitted and invited to reflect upon the conditions of his existence as the true God and the ground of creation. We must pass from the visible mission of Christ in the flesh to the eternal procession of the Son that is truly revealed to us in that mission.[12] That is to say, we must think an-

10. In his commentary on Heb 1:3 (*In Heb.* I, lec. 2, 30–36), Aquinas notes that if the Son "upholds all things by the word of his power," then he is God and "the cause of every substance" as well as its historical "operations." Yet this same verse claims that the Son "makes purgation for sins." Indeed, Aquinas will argue (37–39), these two things are understood to be simultaneously true, since the divinity of Christ is seen as the fitting precondition for the effectuation of our redemption through the Son's historical life in the flesh. See also, I, lec. 3, 57: "He was first in the world invisibly by his power, [and subsequently] visibly by the presence of his humanity."

11. See, for example, John Calvin, *Institutes of the Christian Religion*, trans. F. Battles (Philadelphia: Westminster Press, 1960), II, c. 13, n. 4 [hereafter "ICR"]. For Barth's analysis of the Calvinist notion that the Son while incarnate upholds all things in being as God and the Lutheran reactions to this doctrine in the kenotic theories of the seventeenth-century schools of Giessen and Tübingen, see CD IV, 1, 180–83.

12. For Aquinas, the missions of the Trinitarian persons derive from the eternal processions of God, yet only insofar as these processions are made manifest to us in

alogically, by way of causality, negation, and pre-eminence (the three-fold Dionysian *viae*), of what it must be for the Word to be eternally one in nature with the Father and distinct in person, and this in real distinction from (but not separation from!) and with ontological priority to his human historical existence as Christ. Even if we only know the Son in history, we must necessarily be able to think of him analogically through the medium of revelation from before history, as eternally God. Otherwise, we will not think rightly of the mystery of him who is truly *God* in history. We will not recognize him for who he is as one who is "among us," but who, in the words of John's Gospel, "existed before us" (Jn 1:14–15) as God's Word, the Word "who was in the beginning with God," and who "was God" (1:1) "through whom all things were made" (1:3).

In his mature Trinitarian theology, Aquinas understands the notion of "Word" (*verbum*) to apply to Christ as a *proper* name.[13] Proper names here are to be distinguished from natural or essential names for God. Essential names pertain not to the Trinitarian persons in their hypostatic distinctness, but to the ineffable essence of God that is common to the Father, Son, and Holy Spirit, a mystery we designate when we speak about divine simplicity, goodness, unity, all-powerfulness, and so on. By contrast, the name "Word" is proper: it

the human history of the Son incarnate and the visible mission of the Holy Spirit. ST I, q. 43, a. 1: "The mission of a divine person [denotes] [1] the procession of origin from the sender, and [2] a new way of existing in another. Thus the Son is said to be sent by the Father into the world, inasmuch as He began to exist visibly in the world by taking our nature." Consequently, the eternal processions of the persons are truly revealed to us within the economy *by the missions*, yet the immanent life of God is not *identical* with God's manner of existing in these visible missions, insofar as the latter imply the created order of grace and nature *through* which the triune God is revealed (ST I, q. 43, a. 8). I will return to this topic in chapter 6 below.

13. On Aquinas's evolution on this point, as well as for a more general exposition of his theology of Christ as the Word of God, see Gilles Emery, *The Trinitarian Theology of Saint Thomas Aquinas*, trans. F. Murphy (Oxford: Oxford University Press, 2007), 176–218; *Trinity in Aquinas* (Naples, Fla.: Sapientia Press, 2005), 71–120; see also Harm Goris, "Theology and Theory of the Word in Aquinas," in *Aquinas the Augustinian*, eds. Michael Dauphinais, Barry David, and Matthew Levering (Washington, D.C.: The Catholic University of America Press, 2007), 62–78; L.-B. Geiger, "Les rédactions successives de *Contra Gentiles* I, 53 d'après l'autographe," in *St. Thomas d'Aquin aujourd'hui*, eds. J. Y. Jolif et al. (Paris: Desclée de Brouwer, 1963), 221–40; Henri Paissac, *Théologie du Verbe: St. Augustin et St. Thomas* (Paris: Cerf, 1951).

indicates the mystery of the person of the eternal Son alone. Further-more, Aquinas makes a point to interpret systematically other scrip-tural proper titles for Christ—such as "Son" and "Image"—*in light of the theological similitude of the Word.* This theological decision has its precedent in the thought of Athanasius, transmitted to Aquinas by his reading of both Augustine and John Damascene.[14] In essence, against Sabellianism and Arianism, Aquinas wishes to maintain that there exist eternally in the mystery of God (1) a real relation of ori-gin of the Son from the Father, who proceeds as a distinct hyposta-sis or person generated ineffably by the Father, and (2) a shared and identical, incomprehensible nature of the Father and Son. Following Athanasius and Augustine, Aquinas maintains that only the consider-ation of an analogy from human thought will allow us to understand something (albeit very imperfectly) of immaterial generation.[15] This in turn alone gives us the capacity to understand the mystery of the procession of the Son from the Father as one in which these persons of the Trinitarian God share in one nature and being without subor-dination or confusion.

To understand this revealed mystery theologically, then, Aqui-nas employs the similitude of the mental *verbum* or "word" in the hu-man person, where *verbum* denotes an intellectual concept proceed-ing from the mind rather than a spoken word proceeding through speech.[16] The mental concepts in and through which we know things are expressions of our abstracted knowledge, drawn initially from the things themselves through the operation of the agent intellect. Just as our knowledge of a thing depends upon our abstracting its intelligible species or essence from multiple sensible experiences of the thing it-self, so then the intellect, having abstracted the intelligible form, fash-ions a concept in and through which it proceeds back to the existing

---

14. Athanasius, *C. Arianos* I, para. 16: "If, then ... the Offspring of the Father's es-sence be the Son, we must be certain, that the same is the Wisdom and Word of the Fa-ther, in and through whom He creates and makes all things." See also, I, paras. 15, 24–29; II, paras. 2, 5, 36–37. For an insightful discussion of these points, see Lewis Ayres, *Nicaea and Its Legacy* (Oxford: Oxford University Press, 2004), 110–17. See also Augustine, *De Trin.* XV, 10; John Damascene, *De Fide Orth.*, I, 6, 8, 13, 17.

15. SCG IV, c. 11; *De Pot.* q. 9, a. 5; q. 10, a. 1; ST I, q. 27, a. 1; *Comp. Theo.*, c. 52; *In Ioan.*, I, lec. 1, 23–66.

16. Cf. ST I, q. 34, a. 1.

thing in order to consider the experienced reality in overtly conceptual terms. This concept is generated from the mind through an act
of the mind. It is an accident of the being of the knower, but is also
in some fundamental sense one in being with the knower. It contains
the truth whereby the knower knows the essential properties of the
reality in question. In addition, this interior word is the *terminus* of
our act of understanding. It is not therefore something that precedes
or leads to the act of understanding, but what the intellect produces
when it understands.[17]

Once we have grasped this truth about the way our own intellect
understands, we can then see why the interior word provides a helpful analogy for us in order to consider the procession of the Son in
God: the Word in God proceeds not as that by which the Father understands (the Father is the source of the Son; the Son cannot be a
principle of anything in the Father himself), but rather as the perfect
expression of what the Father understands about himself. Analogously, Aquinas argues, the Word or *Verbum* in God is the proper name
for the Son because it expresses the spiritual generation whereby the
Son comes forth from the Father's knowledge of himself as the expression of his own wisdom.[18] The Son possesses in himself the plenitude of the divine nature and wisdom—and therefore is equal to the
Father, but as one who receives eternally all that he is from the Father,
as his eternal Word, through whom the Father knows all things. The
analogy of the Word thereby helps us interpret the analogy of Sonship. Sonship entails begetting according to an identity of nature or
essence (implying equality), while Word connotes the immateriali-
ty proper to spiritual intellect. Because the Word proceeds spiritually

17. In his mature position on the subject, Aquinas distinguishes in human spiritual
cognition the intelligible species abstracted from sensible phantasms *by which* the mind
has understanding, and the expression of this same species in and through a concept *in
which* the mind turns back to reality to think about it. It is the latter that is said analogously to "proceed" from the understanding by a relation of origin, not the former. *In
Ioan.* I, lec. 1, 25: "The Philosopher says that the notion (*ratio*) which a name signifies
is a definition. Hence what is thus expressed, i.e., formed in the soul, is called an interi-
or word. Consequently it is compared to the intellect, not as that by which the intellect
understands [i.e., the intelligible species], but as that in which it understands, because it
is in what is thus expressed and formed that it sees the nature of the thing understood.
Thus we have the meaning of the name 'word.'"

18. ST I, q. 34, a. 2.

from the Father's wisdom, we can envisage a distinction of persons in God without quantity or spatio-temporal extension (without "history," if you will). Because the Son possesses in himself the plenitude of the Father's wisdom, the generation in question does not imply ontological inequality. The Father and Son are not merely one in kind, but are one in being, *homoousios*.[19]

However, in order to convey the transcendent perfection of the Word of God, we must underscore not only the likeness, but also the dissimilitude between God the Word and the created *verbum*. Only by means of the *via negationis* can we in turn arrive at the affirmation of the incomprehensibly unique perfection of the Son's generation, the *via eminentiae*.[20] These reflections are necessary in order to rightly contemplate the mystery of the filial generation of the Son, in its uniqueness and transcendence, while safeguarding our understanding against improper anthropomorphisms.

Aquinas identifies three principal *loci* of theological dissimilitude between human thought and the eternal generation of the Word.[21] First, in us the intellectual concept is merely a property or metaphysical "accident" of our being (a non-essential characteristic of our person), that qualifies our understanding in some way, through our acquired knowledge. In God, however, the Word is in no way accidental but is "of the very substance" of the Father (Heb 1:3). In his incomprehensible perfection, the Father's generation of the Son communicates to him all that the Father has and is as God. And yet in differentiation from the procession of the concept in us, the Son who is God is truly eternally distinct from the Father hypostatically or personally even as he proceeds from him as his Word.[22]

19. See the beautiful and exacting analysis of this point in SCG IV, c. 11.

20. Aquinas typically employs Dionysius's threefold *viae* in speaking about analogical names for the divine essence. See, for example, ST I, q. 13, a. 2. However, it seems to be clear that he employs a similar kind of thinking when speaking of the proper name of the Son as Word in SCG IV, c. 11 and *In Ioan.*, I, lec. 1.

21. Aquinas's treatment of this subject is most extensive in SCG IV, c. 11, and the first *lectio* of his commentary on St. John's Gospel. On these three dissimilitudes, see in particular *In Ioan.*, I, lec. 1, 26–29. I am inverting the order of exposition of Aquinas's three arguments and expressing them in a slightly different form, introducing complementary elements from SCG IV, c. 11.

22. "Consequently, the word which our intellect forms is not of the essence of our soul, but is an accident of it. But in God to understand and to be are the same; and

Second, in us, the generation of thought leads (eventually) to a greater maturity and perfection, and thus actuates a latent intellectual potentiality. In our knowledge we pass from imperfection to greater perfection. In God, however, there is no potency of operation in the generation of the Word. Rather, in his transcendent perfection, the Word *is* the very act of being that the Father is.[23] He is light from light, or act from act, containing in himself the very existence, nature, and operation of the Father, all of which is hidden from our direct gaze. As such, he is without any perfection to acquire, being in himself as God the source and summit of all lesser, created perfections, each of which participates in some way in his uncreated image.[24]

Third, our concepts are mere *intentiones* (mental intentionality, not reality) by and through which we aspire to know reality as it is, while the subjects of our thinking are (typically) realities distinct from ourselves and from our own thought. But in God, the Word himself contains the very truth of God. This truth in question is not abstract or intentional, but is God's very essence, God's very being. Nor does God formulate his knowledge through a prior encounter with beings other than himself that he comes to know intentionally, and from which he learns. Rather, God is the truth who created all things in the knowledge that he has of himself.[25] (All that exists depends upon God's self-knowledge, and not the inverse.) All that is in the Father, then, is present in the Son as the personal truth that proceeds forth from the Father, through whom he made all things.[26] In knowing himself (by means of the divine truth that he shares with the Father and the Spirit), the Son as God knows not only the Fa-

---

so the Word of the divine intellect is not an accident but belongs to its nature. Thus it must be subsistent, because whatever is in the nature of God is God. Thus Damascene says that God is a substantial Word and a hypostasis, but our words are concepts in our mind" (*In Ioan.* I, lec. 1, 28).

23. *In Ioan.* I, lec. 1, 27. See also ST I, q. 34, a. 3; q. 27, a. 1, ad 2; SCG IV, c. 11, para. 11.

24. "Since we cannot express all our conceptions in one word, we must form many imperfect words through which we separately express all that is in our knowledge. But it is not that way with God. For since he understands both himself and everything else through his essence, by one act, the single divine Word is expressive of all that is in God, not only of the Persons but also of creatures; otherwise it would be imperfect" (*In Ioan.*, I, lec. 2, 27).

25. SCG IV, c. 11, para. 9.

26. *In Ioan.* I, lec. 2, 76.

ther and the Spirit, but also all things that proceed forth from God as God's creatures.[27]

FROM THE ANALOGY

OF THE WORD TO THE

ANALOGY OF BEING

In the second section of this chapter I would like to examine some of the implicit logical consequences of the aforementioned analogy of the Word incarnate as I have briefly presented it above. Basically my argument will be that we cannot rightly conceive of the divinity of the Word without recourse to the analogy of being: the affirmation of an ontological likeness between creatures and God, specifically as applied to resemblances in the order of existence and unity. Following Aquinas, I am presuming here that unity, or oneness, is a transcendental notion co-extensive with being. All that exists *insofar as it exists* has a certain unity. To say that "something exists" is to say also that it is in some sense "one." [28]

We can take our starting point from the prologue of John's Gospel and Aquinas's interpretation of that text. The text of scripture affirms that "in the beginning was the Word, and the Word was with God, and the Word was God" (Jn 1:1), and so we may reasonably infer from this the divinity of the eternal Word who is one with the Father. The

27. ST I, q. 34, a. 3: "Word implies relation to creatures. For God by knowing himself, knows every creature. Now the word conceived in the mind is representative of everything that is actually understood. Hence there are in ourselves different words for the different things which we understand. But because God by one act understands himself and all things, his one only Word is expressive not only of the Father, but of all creatures."

28. The basic text on the transcendentals in Aquinas is *De Ver.* q. 1, a. 1, where he justifies a fivefold distinction of terms co-extensive with *ens* and *esse* (*res, unum, aliquid, bonum, verum*) through a series of modes of differentiation. Being can be considered either per se or with respect to another. If per se then either positively (as *res* or a determinate reality) or negatively (as *unum*: that which is indivisible), and if with respect to another then either in distinction from it (as *aliquid* or 'something other') or as fitted to it (*convenientia*). If the latter is the case, this can be with respect to appetite (*bonum*: all that is, is somehow good) or with respect to intellect (*verum*: all that is is somehow true). On the co-extensive character of unity and being in Aquinas, see the study of Jan Aertsen, *Medieval Philosophy and the Transcendentals* (Leiden: Brill, 1996), 201–42.

text goes on to tell us, then, that "all things were made through him, and without him was not anything made that was made" (Jn 1:3). So we see that the Logos, who is one with the Father, is also the source of all that exists in creation. However, the same prologue goes on to affirm that "the Word became flesh, and dwelt among us, full of grace and truth" (Jn 1:14). In other words, the Word became human, and existed among us as a man in our historical time.

This teaching provides explicit affirmation of the pre-existence and divinity of Christ but also suggests that Christ, as God the Logos, is the author of creation. This idea is made even more explicit in John 8 and 10, where Christ is confronted by denials of his authority. There he invokes his identity as God, and his unity with the Father, as the basis for his teaching authority. "When you have lifted up the Son of man, then you will know that I am" (8:28), "before Abraham was, I am" (8:58), and "I and the Father are one" (10:30): these phrases make an unambiguous appeal to two central themes in the Old Testament. The first is that of the divine name, revealed in Exodus 3:14–15. There God is designated by a proper name (YHWH) that is explained by a gloss (in 3:14), which can be translated: "I am he who is."[29] Read in this way, God is understood to be the unique creator

29. Aquinas follows Maimonides (*Guide for the Perplexed* I, 60–62), as well as Origen and Jerome, in distinguishing between YHWH (from Ex 3:15) and "I Am He Who Is" (Ex 3:14) as distinct but interrelated divine names. See especially Armand Maurer, "St. Thomas on the Sacred Name 'Tetragrammaton,'" *Mediaeval Studies* 34 (1972): 275–86. Nevertheless, Aquinas also interprets the names as inseparable and mutually related. In his metaphysical exegesis in ST I, q. 13, a. 9 and a. 11, ad 1, he identifies the Tetragrammaton as the divine name that signifies the incommunicability of the divine nature in its individuality, just as a singular name signifies the incommunicability of the individual man. This contrasts with the name "God," which signifies the nature (a. 8), and the name "He Who Is," which signifies the uniqueness of the perfection of God as *Ipsum esse subsistens* (a. 11). Although these signifying terms are diverse, their multiplicity is derived from our human manner of knowing God based upon terms drawn from creatures that are themselves complex. For as ST I, q. 3 (especially aa. 3–4) has already made clear, while in material creatures there is a real distinction between individuality and nature, as well as between essence and existence, there is no real distinction in God between either nature and individual or essence and existence. Therefore, while we may rightly designate God in various senses (as existence, deity, or individual) under these terms, in their ultimate ontological ground, they signify him who is absolutely simple. By consequence, the multiplicity of terms can only be seen as complementary and interrelated, within a larger biblical and metaphysical framework of apophatic and kataphatic approaches to naming God. For a modern biblical treatment of the name "He Who Is"

who possesses existence of himself and who alone can give being to all else other than himself. By appealing to the divine name ("I am") Jesus is identifying himself with the creator who has given all things being. The second text is: "Hear Oh Israel, the Lord our God is one Lord" (Deut 6:4). The divine name here is signified ("Lord"), but in addition, the verse underscores vehemently the unity of God, his oneness of being. There is one Lord and God of Israel, the creator of the heavens and the earth.

We can reasonably infer, then, that John's Gospel asserts that Christ is one with the God of Israel, and also that he bears in himself the property that is characteristic of the creator alone. Christ as God, as the Logos who is one with the Father, does not come into existence through creation by God. Rather, it is he as the one God who alone gives existence to all others. His own divine essence remains hidden and incomprehensible as the unoriginate ground of all created, participated being. Commenting on this idea, Aquinas writes:

[Christ] says, I am, and not "what I am," to recall to them what was said to Moses: "I am he who is" (Ex. 3:14), for existence itself (*ipsum esse*) is proper to God. For in any other nature but the divine nature, existence (*esse*) and what exists are not the same: because any created nature participates its existence (*esse*) from that which is being by its essence (*ens per essentiam*), that is, from God, who is his own existence (*ipsum suum esse*), so that his existence (*suum esse*) is his essence (*sua essentia*). Thus, this designates only God. And so he says, "For if you do not believe that I am," that is, that I am truly God, who has existence by his essence, "you will die in your sin" (John 8:24).[30]

It follows from this sound interpretation of the Johannine revelation that to think through the analogy of the Word as applied by scripture to the *incarnate* Lord, is also to think of Jesus Christ as the preexistent causal origin of all that is, as "He Who Is," and as the one upon whom all things depend for their existence. All that exists receives its existence from God through the eternal Word, who has taken on a human nature in Jesus Christ.

---

in the New Testament suggesting profound and necessary connections of this title with the Tetragrammaton (Lord), see Bauckham, *God Crucified*, 63–77. I am grateful to Kendall Soulen for his discussions with me on this important point.

30. *In Ioan.* VIII, lec. 3, 1179.

We can argue from this basic scriptural theology, then, that reference to the analogy of being is logically entailed by the affirmation of the divinity of the Word made flesh. Why? Basically, it is because the theology of John presses us to identify what is distinct about *this man* here, Jesus of Nazareth. This man *exists* in history as one of us, and he is *one* human being like us. We refer to his existence and unity as properties of his human nature, of his historical life as a man. Yet what makes him different from the rest of us is that *this man* here is also God, the eternal Word, who exists from all eternity and through whom all things were made. He is distinct in his unity, as a person, because he is *one with God.* In fact, he is the one God of Israel, who created the heavens and the earth. Consequently, we cannot really think about what makes *this man* different from us in his existence and ontological unity, unless we can also think of him as possessing in himself the existence of God the creator, who is one in a very different way than creatures are one. We might also say that we can only understand who Jesus is as one who exists in history, if we understand him to be the one who exists "before us" as the Word who has given us existence.[31] Therefore, to think about Jesus correctly, in the terms that John's Gospel itself designates, we must be able to compare the existence of all things visible and invisible on the one hand, and on the other hand, the God who alone is, or who alone exists in the transcendent sense in which God the creator exists. We must be able to compare temporal existence in creatures with the eternal existence of God the creator. It is only because we are able to think in these comparative terms in the first place that we are able even to understand the scandalous claim of Christ regarding his unity with God, and his eternal pre-existence. The analogy of being is present in an implicit but irreducible way whenever we think rightly about the divinity of the incarnate Word.

This point can be briefly restated negatively in a slightly more polemical way. If this relation between creatures and God on the level

---

31. *In Ioan.* VIII, lec. 8, 1290: "For eternal existence knows neither past nor future time, but embraces all time in one indivisible [instant]. Thus it could be said: 'He who is, sent me to you,' and 'I am who am' (Exod. 3:14). Jesus had being both before Abraham and after him, and he could approach him by showing himself in the present [at the time of Abraham] and be after him in the course of time."

of existence is not conceivable in terms of a real ontological analogy between creatures and their transcendent cause, then the notion of the triune God as creator is also not conceivable. Certainly God is ineffable and incomprehensible and as such cannot be captured or comprehended within any concept of being. Yet if there is such a dissimilitude between the notion of God as one who is eternally, and creatures as beings that depend upon God, that a pure equivocity is established between them, then we cannot speak in any intelligible way about what it means for God "to be" he who "is," nor even what it means for God "to be" the causal origin of the creation. Nor then could we speak intelligibly about the Word in the Father as the principle of creation because it would mean nothing for us to signify that the Word is the source of all that exists, and that the Word is "He Who Is." And so finally, we would not be able to speak about the incarnation at all, since we would not be able to say that the one who is the creator of the world (meaning what?) had become flesh.

Let me conclude this argument by employing the concrete example of the crucifixion. If we wish to affirm that Jesus Christ existed in history as a historical subject, then we must be willing to say at least minimally that he was truly crucified under Pontius Pilate. (Here I am appealing to Barth's minimal criteria for historical realism concerning the incarnation in his book on the Apostles' Creed.)[32] This means in turn that this same Jesus was truly crucified in our existent, physical world, in the common history that we share with Pontius Pilate and the lineage of historical personages that have truly existed from his time down to our own. Correspondingly, the kind of singular existence each of us now has as a human being can be attributed analogically to Pontius Pilate, who really *existed* then, and to Jesus of

32. Karl Barth, *Credo*, trans. Robert McAfee Brown (New York: Charles Scribner's, 1962). The German original was written in 1935. See 79–80: "How does Pontius Pilate get into the Credo? The simple answer can at once be given: it is a matter of date. The name of the Roman procurator in whose term of office Jesus Christ was crucified, proclaims: at such and such a point of *historical time* this happened. And the symbol intends to express just that: that what it has to say about Jesus Christ happened at a definite and definitively assignable time *within that time that is ours also*. With that a line is drawn, a polemic is directed against a Gnostic Christ-idealism. If the Word became flesh, then it became temporal, and the reality of the revelation in Jesus Christ was *what we call* the lifetime of a man" (emphasis added).

Nazareth, who was crucified under the Roman procurator. To admit this is to accept already that there are analogical predications of existence that are presupposed by the historical realism of faith in the crucifixion of God. In fact, such thinking makes use of the analogy of being absolutely unavoidable at what modern Thomists (following Fabro and Montagnes) term the "predicamental level," because such a use is simply co-extensive with rational thought.[33] Pontius Pilate exists, Jesus exists, Peter exists, and so do you and I, each in an analogically signified fashion. Unless we can think analogically about existence common to creatures, we cannot think about Jesus's existence in his shared history with us.[34] Now let us add to this the con-

33. Here we are speaking about the so-called analogy of proper proportionality, employed by Aristotle and Aquinas to speak about the diverse predicamental categories of being (quality, quantity, relation, etc.) *or* the diverse individual realizations of given substances. In this case, the latter is being employed. A is to B as C is to D; Pilate (A) exists and Peter (C) exists. The existence of these two is not identical, but each has something in common with the other. Therefore the existence of Pilate (B) is analogous to that of Peter (D). The attribution of existence to each transpires by a process of analogical thinking and is consistent with our sense of the real multiplicity of and likenesses between things. On the distinction between predicamental and transcendental analogies of being, see especially Bernard Montagnes, *The Doctrine of the Analogy of Being according to Thomas Aquinas*, trans. E. M. Macierowski (Milwaukee, Wis.: Marquette University Press, 2004), 43–112; Cornelio Fabro, *Participation et Causalité selon Thomas d'Aquin* (Louvain / Paris: Publications Universitaires de Louvain / Éditions Béatrice-Nauwelaerts, 1961), 319–412.

34. Bruce Marshall in his essay, "Christ the End of Analogy," in *The Analogy of Being: Invention of the Antichrist or the Wisdom of God?*, 280–313 has rightly emphasized that Aquinas attributes human nature to Christ univocally, as Christ partakes of the same human nature as all others. Yet when Aquinas writes that "Deus est homo" (ST III, q. 16, a. 1), I do not think this should be translated as "God is a human *being*," for being (*ens*), as we all know is precisely that which is "said in many ways," according to Aristotle, or in Aquinas's terms, "analogically." Aquinas is quite explicit about this in *In Meta.* IV, lec. 1, 534–35. At any rate, nothing could be less controversial than to affirm that for Aquinas, *ens*, like *esse*, is predicated analogically of the diverse genera of being (which is precisely why *ens* and *esse* are not contained within a genus). It is true that some Thomists would dispute whether *ens* and *esse* are attributed to individuals of the same species in an analogical or in a merely univocal fashion. So, for example, one might argue that *esse* is attributed to Peter and to Paul univocally due to the commonality of their natural form, since both are human, even though as concrete existents, they are of course truly distinct and do *resemble* one another ontologically. It seems to me, however, that this way of thinking would leave us with no way of allowing the full signification of *esse* to unfold, i.e., as signifying not only an existent natural kind, but also as signifying the irreducible existence of *this* singular reality (Peter) in its ontological uniqueness, as both

fession of faith: that in this historical Jesus, one of the Trinity was crucified. He who was crucified historically under Pontius Pilate was truly one with the Father and truly himself God, the Logos through whom all things were made. In this case, this one here, Jesus of Nazareth, is distinct from Pontius Pilate and Peter not only because he is a distinct human existent in history (the predicamental analogy mentioned above) but also because he is truly one in being with God who is the origin of all that exists and is himself God, through whom all things were made. And if this is the case, oneness and existence as they are applied to God alone must be applied to him. He is the one God. This occurs by what modern Thomists, following Aquinas, term an *ad alterum* analogy, or a "transcendental" analogy of being.[35] Since being and unity are co-extensive notions common to every genus of being (transcendentals), an analogy of being also implies an analogy of unity. Jesus is truly one person like us, but in a wholly other way

---

similar to and distinct from others (such as Paul). For a study of Aquinas's metaphysics that tends towards this sense, see Lawrence Dewan's "On Anthony Kenny's *Aquinas on Being*," *Nova et Vetera* (English edition) 3, no. 2 (2005): 335–400. However, even if we concede the point about univocal attribution of *ens* and *esse* to individuals of the same species (uniquely for the sake of argument), the larger point I am making here would in no way be undermined. One could simply refer to the more common and irrefutable example of the analogical predication of *ens* to the diverse genera of being according to proportional analogy. Insofar as one would claim that (1) the qualities, (2) the quantities, and (3) the substantial beings of Pontius Pilate, Peter, and Jesus all "existed" in historical time, these diverse dimensions of their beings (as substances with certain diverse accidents that undergo change) were in fact ontologically complex, and the accidents of their beings participated in the existence of their substances, upon which they depended aetiologically, even while themselves truly existing as properties of those substances. If Pontius passed from a state of indetermined legal judgment to a state of determined legal judgment concerning Jesus, this was only possible because he first existed; but in making his decision, he did not cease to exist substantially, nor come to be. Consequently, the judgment has to be said to "exist" (as a quality of his soul) differently from his "existence" as a substantial being in time (a subsistent person). In short, *if* we accept the premise that *esse* is not in a genus but is attributed to the genera in ways that are analogical, *and* if we accept that the genera of being (qualities, quantities, relations, etc.) truly denote features of reality, then the analogical predication of being (and the implicit acknowledgement of the analogy of being) is unavoidable. Nor can it be absent from our discourse concerning the historical humanity of Christ, especially if he has taken on a human nature univocally identical with our own.

35. ST I, q. 13, a. 5; *De Pot.*, q. 7, a. 7. See Montagnes, *The Doctrine of the Analogy of Being*, 64–91.

than us (analogical difference on the predicamental level) because he alone—as the Son eternally distinct from the Father—can say personally "I and the Father are one." Yet we can only understand that this man among us is truly one with the Father if *their* oneness in being has something in common with unity-of-being as we otherwise experience it (analogical similitude on the transcendental level). In sum, if we are to claim both that he is one who exists in time to whom we relate historically, and that *in him* the one God who is the cause of all that exists "exists" as man, then we must also posit an ontological similitude between all that exists and the existence of God present in Christ. Were this not the case, his presence in history would be for us utterly inconceivable (or indecipherable) and, therefore, ultimately meaningless.

THE CHRISTOLOGICAL INEVITABILITY OF NATURAL THEOLOGY

Up to this point, I have argued that the ascription of an ontological analogy between creatures and God is logically implied by the realism of the incarnation and by the expression of a biblical understanding of God as the Word incarnate. In the third part of this chapter, I would like to turn to the epistemological presuppositions of this viewpoint. My claim is that the natural human capacity to think analogically about God in his unity and existence as the cause of the world—with the help of concepts drawn from creation—is a necessary epistemological presupposition for any scriptural or dogmatic account of the incarnate Word. The *analogia Verbi* presupposes the possibility of an analogical ascription of *esse* to God as a necessary (but not sufficient!) condition, just as grace presupposes created nature. It follows from such a claim that if we are able to come to a true theological—and even dogmatic—understanding of what it means for God to become man, we are also able in principle to achieve a distinctly philosophical understanding of God analogically (no matter how imperfect and indirect) from the consideration of creatures. That is to say, if Christianity is true, then human beings are necessarily capable of natural theology.

My argument for this claim is fairly simple. First, I will argue that the affirmation of a supernatural revelation (given in grace) presupposes the existence of knowledge in human persons that is not derived from revelation (so-called natural knowledge). Second, I will argue that there can be no correlation between the workings of the human mind and the grace of revelation unless the human mind is *naturally* capable *under grace* of recognizing such revelation *as grace*, that is to say, as something given from outside the ordinary spectrum of truths obtained by human reasoning and intra-worldly experience. Third, however, this potentiality of the mind to receive a graced revelation is only subject to such recognition of the gratuity of the gift of revelation if it has in itself the natural or intrinsic capacity to recognize the existence of God as a reality that transcends the sphere of created existence. That is to say, only if we are intrinsically able to compare by analogy the existence of realities in our ordinary experience with the existence of God who is incomprehensible, and who utterly transcends the sphere of creaturely being, are we in turn able to recognize—in and by grace—the revelation of God's identity as a gift transcending the sphere of created being. Failing this natural openness to the mystery of God's transcendence, the recognition of God in Christ becomes epistemologically impossible.

First, let us begin with a presupposition from our earlier discussion. Aquinas rightly underscores the gratuity of the revelation of the triune God, which cannot be either predicted or derived from human rational reflection. God reveals his triune identity (the eternal generation of the Son and spiration of the Spirit) by the missions of the Son and Spirit within the divine economy. Consequently, because the missions alone truly reveal to us who God is in himself (albeit imperfectly and indirectly) they are also the condition of possibility for any such knowledge of this identity. To affirm this is to maintain with the First Vatican Council the supernatural character of revelation as something not derived from human ingenuity or deluded religious fancy.[36] At stake for Aquinas, as for this Council, is the claim

---

36. *Dei Filius*, c. IV: "The perpetual agreement of the Catholic Church has maintained and maintains this too: that there is a twofold order of knowledge [*duplicem ordinem cognitionis*], distinct not only as regards its source, but also as regards its object. With regard to the source, we know at the one level by natural reason, at the other level

that the revealed knowledge of God is a grace and as such is unmerited and gratuitous (exceeding ordinary human powers). Trinitarian truth is not to be considered some kind of unintelligible, purely equivocal discourse that is dialectically opposed to our ordinary language. Nevertheless, it is situated beyond the horizon of our ordinary conceptual and linguistic capacities as a truth to which we can never attain by our own powers.

My first argument is that there is a necessary corollary to this last claim. If the revelation is given gratuitously, it is not something that we already possess through our ordinary human powers. It is not identical with natural knowledge that we have of the world or even (presupposing the possibility of such) of God the creator based upon his effects in the creation. If this is the case, then the affirmation of the gratuity and non-derived, transcendent origin of knowledge of the Son incarnate also entails the affirmation of an intra-worldly, non-revealed form of knowledge. Even if all things that we know belong to the world of Christ, the unique creation of the Logos, they are not all known directly and immediately through the encounter with Christ by grace and in faith. Thinking about unity in calculus or in the philosophy of Plotinus is different from reflection upon the unity of the Father and the Son. The natural knowledge we have of the world through our own powers, then, does not simply co-exist along a gradient of degrees with the knowledge that comes through the light of faith in the incarnate Word. The two forms of knowledge are different in kind, or to use the phrase of the First Vatican Council, there is a *duplex ordo cognitionis* in which each form of knowledge is distinguished by its originating principles as well as its objects.[37]

This brings us to the second stage of my argument. I have claimed above that to know the man Christ as God is to know him as one with the Father and the Holy Spirit and to know him as the Son and Word through and in whom all things are given being. Consequently, to

---

by divine faith. With regard to the object, besides those things to which natural reason can attain, there are proposed for our belief mysteries hidden in God which, unless they are divinely revealed, are incapable of being known. ... If anyone shall have said that no true mysteries properly so-called are contained in divine revelation, but that all the dogmas of faith can be understood and proved from natural principles, through reason properly cultivated, let him be anathema."

37. For a Thomistic parallel, see SCG IV, c. 1, especially para. 5.

know the Trinitarian God revealed in the incarnate Son is to think analogically of God the creator in terms of his unity and being by comparison to the created order that depends upon him. How is this previous claim related to the argument that has just been made, the claim that there is knowledge of the world (in its existence and multiplicity) that does not derive epistemologically from the gift of faith in Christ? If we are able to recognize the triune God as being like the realities of our world, *even while recognizing* that the realities of this world *are known differently* (that is to say, without explicit recourse to revelation), then we are also capable of recognizing a likeness and dissimilarity between the world as we know it naturally and God as he is revealed supernaturally (something akin to what Barth calls the *analogia fidei*).[38] We come, then, to a second claim: if we receive knowledge of God through divine revelation, we must necessarily be capable of recognizing a comparison and contrast between God *as he is revealed to us in Christ*, and the world *as we know it by our ordinary powers of human reason*. We can judge, therefore, *from within the scope of our own natural reason* under grace that what we know by revelation is not the product of ordinary reflection, but is a gift. And this means that in order to think rightly of the divinity of the man Christ by recourse to theological analogies of faith (the divinity of the Word, etc.), we must have *an intrinsic natural capacity* to recognize such revelation as something exceeding the scope of our ordinary natural powers of reflection and knowledge, *even while understanding it to be knowledge of a form that is not wholly alien to the human mind*.[39]

---

38. In his commentary on Jn 10:30 ("I and the Father are one"), Aquinas illustrates this truth very eloquently by way of a response to Arianism [*In Ioan.* X, lec. 5, 1451]: "The Arians ... try to deny this [affirmation of divine unity], and say that a creature can in some sense be one with God, and in this sense the Son can be one with the Father. The falsity of this can be shown ... from our very manner of speaking. For it is clear that 'one' is asserted as 'being'; thus, just as something is not said to be a being absolutely except according to its substance, so it is not said to be one except according to its substance or nature. Now something is asserted absolutely when it is asserted with no added qualification. Therefore, because 'I and the Father are one,' is asserted absolutely, without any qualifications added, it is plain that they are one according to substance and nature. But we never find that God and a creature are one without some added qualification, as in I Cor. 6:17: 'he who is united to the Lord becomes one spirit with him.' Therefore, it is clear that the Son of God is not one with the Father as a creature can be."

39. Aquinas typically addresses this question within the context of the medieval

This leads me to the third and final part of the argument. Knowledge of Christ is not wholly alien to us because some dimension of the human mind is naturally open to knowledge of the creator. Unless we have an intrinsic, natural capacity to think about God as the transcendent causal principle of existence in creatures, the revelation of God in Christ as the origin of the being of the world will remain something intrinsically unintelligible to the human intellect. Such "epistemological extrinsicism" would in turn render knowledge of God as creator impossible, even if it were given in Christ, and by consequence would impede our capacity to affirm the divinity of Christ, even if it were unveiled to us through the medium of divine revelation.

The reason for this is that Christian revelation stipulates that God, the Trinitarian God, has given being to all that exists. He is the cause of the world's coming into being. But if God is to be intelligible by comparison with all we know naturally of the existent world (as must be the case) and yet as not identical with but utterly distinct from the world (as must also be the case), then we must be naturally capable of thinking of God in comparison with creatures as something (or someone) that *is not created, but rather which is the source of all that exists in ontological dependence upon him*. Were this idea of causal dependency upon God for existence intrinsically unintelligible to us by means of natural, ordinary powers of reflection, the revelation of God *in Christ* as the creator of the existent world *would remain inconceivable*. The "existence" of Christ *as God the creator* (the source

---

debate concerning whether the human person is naturally *capable* of receiving the grace of the beatific vision, or whether this gift (itself the final end of divine revelation) is something wholly extrinsic to the human mind, rendering Christianity philosophically untenable. At the same time, he wishes to underscore the traditional Augustinian understanding that the beatific vision is an absolute grace, one which our human powers are intrinsically incapable of procuring. He in fact resolves this seeming paradox by arguments that show that from its knowledge of creatures that are God's effects, the human mind may naturally aspire to a perfect knowledge of God as their primary cause, since knowledge of God through his effects remains intrinsically unsatisfactory. Nevertheless, this aspiration may in no way be fulfilled by that same natural desire, and this must in consequence leave the mind both naturally receptive to divine revelation and the grace of the immediate vision of God (in a way that non-rational creatures are not), even while underscoring the absolute gratuity of divine revelation and the vision as gifts that utterly transcend the powers and resources of created human nature. For examples of this argumentation, see SCG III, c. 50–54; *Comp. Theol.*, c. 104; ST I, q. 12, a. 1.

of created existence) would remain entirely alien to "existence" as we encounter it in creatures. Consequently, one of two extremes would result. Either we would be forced to understand the existence of God in terms that are purely homogenous with those derived from the world (a form of univocal thinking effectively destroying the possibility of the knowledge of the transcendent otherness of God's existence as distinct from that of his creation), and in this case God's being would only be intelligible as a being among beings, or God would not be made known to us in any way that is in continuity with what we know naturally (an equivocal form of thinking making God's existence unintelligible to human thought). In this latter case, God's existence would remain so wholly other to the world as to be entirely inconceivable and alien.[40] To conceive of God, then, as the creator of all that exists, and in terms drawn from the world as we ordinarily know it, requires that we can attain to true analogical knowledge of the existence of God, departing from existence in things that we experience and that are themselves derived from God.[41]

40. In this sense, I am arguing something that is logically contrary to Barth's claims in his criticisms of the *analogia entis* in CD II, 1, 82–85. There he suggests that the understanding of God attained from natural reason as "the first principle and final end of all things" (as stated in Vatican I) (1) introduces a mere abstraction into theology such that (2) we fail to understand God at all times uniquely as the God of salvation and reconciliation in Jesus Christ. This is to introduce an entirely "foreign god into the Church" (84). No doubt false philosophical conceptions can render obscure Christian theological truths. However, it seems to me that there is also an inverse danger that Barth does not observe. (1) The negation of any capacity to conceive of God as the transcendent origin of the world brings with it (2) a radical "alienation" of the God of Jesus Christ from the world of human understanding, rendering him a "mere abstraction" or gnostic deity, dialectically counterposed to this world, and incapable of being understood by it in any way. Evidently, such perspectives remain entirely foreign to Barth's theological intentions. But if univocal conceptuality brings with it the danger of an abstract anthropomorphism, the dangers of agnosticism promoted by a thoroughgoing equivocity are no less great.

41. Restated in linguistic terms, we could say that (1) to speak of God we have to speak of creatures, but (2) to be able to speak of God in terms derived from knowledge of creatures, it has to be the case that creatures have to resemble God as their source. If there is a "divine grammar" given in revelation that is distinct from our ordinary human grammar, it is nevertheless not a substitute for the latter, and indeed in some real sense can only be understood in comparison with and by being grafted onto our pre-existing ordinary ways of speaking. This ordinary discourse must itself be capable of deriving terms for God that are true, if the divine grammar concerning God is to be able to take root adequately in our ordinary modes of discourse.

We can further clarify the form such analogical reflection must take by considering the following. Being, as both Aristotle and Aquinas rightly note, is not itself identical with any genus or species of thing.[42] Rather, every genus of being is rightly said to "exist" or to "be" in an analogical and non-generic fashion, without prejudice to any other mode of being or concrete existent. *Ens commune* (that is, "being that is common to all creatures") transcends every genus but is also found within every genus of being.[43] However, if God is the creator of all that exists, then not only is God not located within a genus or species of being (that is, within *ens commune*), he is also the transcendent cause of *ens commune* as such, or all that exists.[44] Therefore, if the God who has been revealed in Christ is truly the creator of all that exists, he is not conceivable for our human nature in his distinctness from creatures *as creator* by recourse to univocal predication of any genus of created being, since he is not a being among beings in the created order.[45] Nor is he intelligible in his distinctness in comparison to the beings of this world merely by recourse to "proportional" analogical notions common to all that exists (transcendental notions such as being, oneness, goodness and the like). God is not intelligible from within the *ratio* of these terms that are capable of signifying all created beings for he is the transcendent source of all the realities that are designated by these common terms.[46] Rather, if God is conceivable in distinc-

---

42. Aquinas, *In Meta.* V, lec. 9, 889–90. A sign of this is that every genus of creature (whether substantial or accidental) may either actually exist or not exist. It is therefore composed of actuality and potentiality. *De Pot.*, q. 3, a. 8, ad 12: "Actuality and potentiality are not different accidental modes of being, such as go to make an alteration: they are substantial modes of being. For even substance is divided by potentiality and act, like any other genus." As I argued in the last chapter, Barth does not seem to have grasped this metaphysical point correctly.

43. ST I, q. 4, a. 3.

44. ST I-II, q. 66, a. 5, ad 4; ST I, q. 3, a. 4, ad 1.

45. ST I, q. 3, a. 5.

46. Aquinas, *In de Causis*, prop. 6: "For what the intellect first grasps is being [*ens*]. The intellect cannot apprehend that in which the character of being is not found.... But, according to the truth of the matter, the first cause is above being [*supra ens*] inasmuch as it is itself infinite *esse*. 'Being,' however, is called that which finitely participates in *esse*, and it is this which is proportioned to our intellect, whose object is the quiddity or 'that which is' [*quod quid est*].... Hence our intellect can grasp only that which has a quiddity participating in *esse*. But the quiddity of God is itself *esse*. Thus it is above intellect" (trans. V. Guagliardo, C. Hess, and R. Taylor; slightly modified).

tion to creatures *at all*, it is only as a heterogeneous cause is known analogically apart from his effects. That is to say, God is known truly from creatures as containing in himself the perfections that are present within them, in a wholly other and preeminent way.[47] Yet he is not known as one possessing these perfections through a common participation in these attributes that are shared with creatures, but rather as their ineffable and incomprehensible source.

In conclusion, we can say that if human beings can think, by grace, of Christ as the Logos *ensarkos* through whom all things were made, but are not *naturally* able to think of things *as made*—as given existence—by God who is one and who exists in a way analogous to creatures (transcending every genus of being, and even *ens commune* as such), then a contradiction results. Human beings cannot both think of things as given existence by and in the Word of the Father, who is the one God (*analogia fidei*), and understand the existence of things in this world *without any possible reference to God* (prohibition on the *analogia entis*). In this conflict something is obliged to yield.[48] Even if God were to give to a human being in grace to know God intellectu-

---

47. See ST I, q. 13, aa. 5–6. In particular, a. 6: "For the words, 'God is good,' or 'wise,' signify not only that He is the cause of wisdom and goodness [though they also signify this!], but [also] that these exist in Him in a more excellent way."

48. It seems to me that this tension is manifest in Barth's CD I, 1, in his simultaneous rejection of Emil Brunner's "point of contact [in created human nature] for the divine message" (27), and his revelatory epistemology of the Holy Spirit as principal agent in the human subject's reception of revelation. See 453: "The Spirit guarantees man what he cannot guarantee himself, his personal participation in revelation." See also 462: "Even in receiving the Holy Ghost man remains man, the sinner sinner. Similarly in the outpouring of the Holy Ghost God remains God. The statements about the operations of the Holy Spirit are statements whose subject is God and not man, and in no circumstances can they be transformed into statements about man. *They tell us about the relation of God to man, to his knowledge, will and emotion, to his experience active and passive, to his heart and conscience, to the whole of his psycho-physical existence, but they cannot be reversed and understood as statements about the existence of man*" (emphasis added). Barth seems to posit a thoroughgoing ontological and epistemological extrinsicism of revelatory grace with respect to human natural powers even while maintaining a profound insistence on the thoroughly intrinsic character of the work of the Holy Spirit in the human person. What is the relation here between the extrinsicism of all God's action with regard to creaturely actions or dispositions, on the one hand, and God's work in and for the creature on the other? How might one coherently describe the work of God in the existence of man while simultaneously maintaining a prohibition on something existing in man that is potentially open to, or which stands in relation to, the work of God?

ally as the Son and Word, and even if this gift were derived from an omnipotent freedom, this grace would necessarily be ineffective unless we were able by our natural powers to understand *something of the oneness* of God and of his transcendence as the creator of existents. *Because* we can know something of God by our ordinary, natural powers, *therefore* we can receive knowledge of him by grace that is not wholly alien to our ordinary form of knowing. Correspondingly, if we do truly know God through the revelation of Christ given in grace, then we are also necessarily capable in principle of knowing God through the medium of our natural human powers by a knowledge derived from creatures. If we are able to affirm the divinity of Christ as "eternally begotten of the Father, begotten not made ... true God from true God, through whom all things were made," then we are also necessarily capable of natural knowledge of God, or "natural theology."

CONCLUSION

I conclude the argument of this chapter by adjoining a brief theological caveat. Nothing I have said above presupposes that human nature laboring under the effects of fallen existence and *acting without grace* might realize effectively in history a well-reasoned philosophical argument for the existence of God or a lucid reflection on the analogical names for God as understood by comparison with creatures. Aquinas himself, who is not pessimistic about the human capacity to arrive at knowledge of God, notes the effects on the intellect in its concrete historical exercise by the draw of disordered passions,[49] the cupidity of the heart,[50] ignorance and laziness,[51] the difficulty of the subject matter,[52] and the weight of received opinions that are erroneous.[53] Nevertheless, Aquinas also recognizes that human beings remain essentially the same *kind* of reality even after sin, and even in redemption.[54] Otherwise, neither prelapsarian humanity nor Christ would have been "human" as we are in an unequivocal sense.[55] The

---

49. *Comp. Theol.*, c. 192.   50. ST I-II, q. 83, a. 3, corp. and ad 3.
51. ST I-II, q. 85, a. 3.   52. SCG IV, c. 1, para. 3.
53. SCG I, c. 4–5; ST I, q. 1, a. 1.   54. ST I-II, q. 109, aa. 1–2.
55. *In Sent.* II, d. 28, q. 1, a. 1; SCG IV, c. 30, para. 3. In the latter text, Aquinas argues

metaphysical consequence of this is that the natural substrate of all salvific divine agency and of all human fallenness, is something—the human essence, a distinct human nature—that is not reducible to the nothingness of sin that eats away at human being nor to the graced life of Christ that recreates the human substrate, healing and restoring a fallen human nature and turning it toward its final purpose. To claim that we have natural capacities for philosophical knowledge of God, then, implies that these capacities exist as properties intrinsic to the soul, even in its state of fallenness without grace. This does not mean, however, that we can employ them properly in our fallen state without the agency of the grace of Christ, or even flawlessly with such grace. Revelation, the illumination of faith, and the workings of hope and charity stimulate not only the human person's ascent to God in Christ, but also facilitate his or her progressive recovery of the habitual exercise of natural capacities (virtues) that have been neglected due to sin. And yet again, when the pursuit of natural knowledge of God is inspired by revelation and stimulated by grace, it remains distinct from the knowledge of God given through revelation and accepted in faith. This distinctness in no way implies a rivalry, as if the *saving* knowledge or love of God occurs through recourse to the natural knowledge of God (whether within or apart from faith).[56]

against Valentinus: "For in every single species there are determined essential principles … from which comes the essential constitution in things composed of matter and form. But just as human flesh and bone and the like are the proper matter of man … therefore, if the body of Christ was not earthly, it was not true flesh and true bone, but in appearance only. And thus, also, [Christ] was not a true, but an apparent man, whereas he himself nonetheless says: 'A spirit hath not flesh and bones, as you see me to have' (Luke 24:39)."

56. As was mentioned above, according to Aquinas, non-Christians have attained to some true knowledge of God—sometimes through philosophical reflection—yet this knowledge was frequently admixed with errors, and led to forms of religious practice that were inimical to the true Christian worship of God (*In Ioan.* XVII, lec. 2, 2195; lec. 6, 2265). In our fallen state, according to Aquinas's anti-Pelagian writing, a *natural* love of God above all things is impossible without grace (ST I-II, q. 109, aa. 1–4). This means that in the concrete historical order, in order to recognize God as one's true final end *even naturally*, some kind of *supernatural* grace of God (that itself presupposes the gift of supernatural faith) is necessary. Justification, meanwhile, occurs only through faith, informed by charity, and depends upon the revealed knowledge of God that accompanies this faith (ST I-II, q. 109, aa. 5–10). Therefore, if one were to know something true of God naturally, without authentic love for God above all things, this could potentially serve only to augment the soul's culpability before God, by removing an excuse from ignorance (cf. Rom 1:20–21).

On the contrary, the claim that there is a natural capacity for such knowledge is merely the mirror image of the claim that we are saved by grace, and justified by faith, such that this grace and this faith have a true natural substrate that is sufficiently proportioned to them so as to be susceptible to redemption. It is not the claim that the natural substrate can in any way substitute itself for the redeemed state of being in Christ. The latter state is made possible uniquely due to God's incarnation and crucifixion, and through participation in the sacramental graces of Christ's church, the ecclesial body of the crucified and risen Lord.

I have argued above that some form of analogical, metaphysical thinking about God is in fact intrinsic to Christological dogmatic theology, and unavoidably so. We must be logically committed to a metaphysics of divine names if we wish to safeguard a true sense of the transcendent divinity of the Son as the incarnate Word in and through whom all things were made. This means in turn that the analogical consideration of the Word incarnate by comparison with creatures requires of us the analogical consideration of the being of God by comparison with creatures. Lest the conclusion of the argument seem insignificant, let me briefly note three fairly important consequences that follow from this line of thinking. First, statements concerning the natural capacity of the human intellect to attain to demonstrative knowledge of God have an irreducibly philosophical character and therefore cannot be justified uniquely by recourse to the intuitive, deductive, or moral force of theological arguments to which these philosophical claims are attached. We might wish, for example, to argue that in light of the *Critique of Pure Reason*, theology must accept that it has been demonstrated that there is no possible speculative demonstration of the existence of God, nor any analogical naming of God from creatures that is other than conjectural, and that we cannot appeal to "causality" in such a way as to speak of what transcends the realm of sensation. In arguing thus, however, we are at least implicitly accepting distinctly philosophical claims that are open to dispute, or rebuttal, from philosophical premises, and which cannot be maintained simply as an outcome of an *a priori* theological dogmatism. If Barthians frequently adopt Kantian epistemological premises, they do so not because of a theological understanding derived from divine revelation, but because they have inherited a set of philosophical commitments and presuppositions from the German Enlightenment and modern liberal Protestantism. Second, Christian theology cannot unfold in a coherent explanation of itself in relation to both God and ordinary knowledge and experience without the integration into itself of a lucid philosophical form of thought that is open to the knowledge of God that comes by way of grace. To the extent that profound philosophical errors or presuppositions emerge within a theology that do not harmonize with the theocentric tasks of theology, they will in fact anthropomorphize theology in erroneous and problematic ways. Finally, if what I have suggested in this chapter is correct, then the progressive rejection of the classical analogical names of God in much of the modern philosophical tradition inexorably works to secularize Christian culture in a profound and unhealthy way. It does so because it habituates the mind to a form of thinking that constantly rejects in principle every point of contact for grace to work within the life of the human intellect, and consequently renders basic facets of Christian dogma unintelligible. To the extent that post-metaphysical philosophy and its presuppositions are introduced into theology from within—even if such decisions are conducted in the name of Christocentrism—they have the capacity to obstruct and to undermine the very basis for a reception of the grace of Christ within the human mind and within ecclesial culture. Such features of an otherwise well-intentioned theology may in turn work to undermine the Christological confession that they are meant to serve. In thinking of this phenomenon, we may recall the pertinent saying of the Lord: "For those who have not, even what they have will be taken from them" (Mk 4:25), and perhaps correspondingly, and not wholly inappropriately, the words of Karl Barth, which contemporary theology would do well to ponder anew: "Fear of scholasticism is the mark of a false-prophet."[57]

57. CD I, 1, 279.

5

———— : ————

The Necessity of
the Beatific Vision in the
Earthly Christ

Let us assume for the sake of argument that the central claim of this book hitherto is correct: Chalcedonian Christology has a permanent importance for Christian theology. The first four chapters of this book sought, then, to articulate an understanding of the mystery of the incarnation in traditional terms by appeal to the notions of the hypostatic union, the two natures of Christ, and the discussion of Jesus's being and existence as the Word made flesh. I have purposefully contrasted this approach with the modern subject-oriented Christologies of Schleiermacher and Harnack. These latter sought to circumvent the formulas of the traditional dogma of the church, displacing the locus of Christological reflection from the realm of being and nature into the realm of subject-consciousness. As is evident from the previous chapters, I hold that Christology should begin not from a reflection on the consciousness of Christ but from the revealed principles of the New Testament authors such as Paul and John concerning the identity and nature of the Son of God.

This need not mean, however, that a consideration of the knowledge and freedom of Christ is out of place in Thomistic theology. On the contrary, we would do well to say the following: the consciousness and ontology of Christ, when rightly understood, are mutually self-interpreting. Christ was certainly deeply psychologically integrated within his culture and historical epoch, but his self-awareness and discourse were also extraordinary. The consciousness of Christ manifests who he is (the Son of God), and the ontological mystery of Christ as the incarnate Word is the source and root of his action and self-awareness. Neither pole (ontology—consciousness) can be abandoned without the risk of a reductive, one-sided Christology. However, in the very structure of personal being, ontology is more fundamental than consciousness. Self-awareness is only one dimension of human being, and ultimately needs to be explained in terms of the latter. Consequently, in Christology, a hypostatic ontology is primary because it explains the principles of Jesus's filial consciousness.

How, then, should we understand the human consciousness of Jesus, if he is indeed the incarnate Lord? In this chapter I take up this question by examining first the extraordinary character of the human knowledge of Christ and, second, that of his human willing. Did Jesus know that he was God? If so, how was this the case? And likewise, did Jesus know the Father's will, not only in a conjectural way, but in an intimate and detailed way? Did Christ's human will always conform perfectly freely, but also indefectibly, to the divine will? And if so, how was this the case?

Traditional Catholic theology has an answer to these questions that takes root in a particular doctrine of Thomas Aquinas. St. Thomas holds that during his earthly life, Jesus of Nazareth possessed in the heights of his human intellect the beatific vision. That is to say, Christ as man possessed the immediate, intuitive knowledge of his own deity, the divine life that he shared with the Father and the Holy Spirit. Furthermore, this idea—that Christ in his earthly existence possessed the beatific vision or immediate knowledge of God—has been traditionally affirmed by Christian theology. The doctrine was rarely questioned from the thirteenth to the mid-twentieth century, and the teaching even today has prominent theological defenders. It has been reaffirmed in various instances by the modern Catholic magisterium.[1]

1. Medieval authors are mentioned below. For the recent Magisterium, see especially Pius XII, *Mystici Corporis* (1943) Denz. 2289; *Catechism of the Catholic Church*, no. 473; and John Paul II, *Novo Millennio Ineunte* (2001), nn. 25–27, as well as the 2006

At the same time, however, this Christological theory is frequently questioned by modern theologians who are deeply committed to the Catholic tradition, precisely on the grounds that they believe the theory in fact endangers more essential, traditional doctrines of Catholic belief. The latter include the patristic affirmations of the complete reality of Christ's historical human nature and the unity of subject in Christ's human actions.

In this chapter, I would like to present briefly two common objections against the classical theory and offer a response inspired by the Thomistic tradition. Both Jean Galot and Thomas Weinandy have argued that the doctrine of the beatific vision in the earthly life of Christ compromises the reality of the humanity of Jesus, on the one hand, and the unity of his filial personhood, on the other. Having presented these claims, I will argue (against this perspective) that the affirmation of the beatific vision of the historical Christ was and is essential for maintaining the unity of his person in and through the duality of his natures, and most particularly in safeguarding the unity of his personal agency in and through the duality of his two wills (human and divine). This is not an argument Aquinas makes explicitly.[2]

Notification on the works of Fr. Jon Sobrino, S.J., Jesus the Liberator (1991) and Christ the Liberator (1999). This last text cites Jn 6:46: "Not that anyone has seen the Father except the one who is from God; he has seen the Father," and goes on to state (n. 8) that "the filial and messianic consciousness of Jesus is the direct consequence of his ontology as Son of God made man. If Jesus were a believer like ourselves, albeit in an exemplary manner, he would not be able to be the true Revealer showing us the face of the Father.... Jesus, the Incarnate Son of God, enjoys an intimate and immediate knowledge of his Father, a 'vision' that certainly goes beyond the vision of faith. The hypostatic union and Jesus' mission of revelation and redemption require the vision of the Father and the knowledge of his plan of salvation. This is what is indicated in the Gospel [text] cited above." For recent Thomistic theological arguments in favor of the traditional teaching, see Romanus Cessario, "Incarnate Wisdom and the Immediacy of Christ's Salvific Knowledge," in Problemi teologici alla luce dell'Aquinate, Studi Tomistici 44:5 (Vatican City: Libreria Editrice Vaticana, 1991), 334–40; Jean Miguel Garrigues, "La conscience de soi telle qu'elle était exercée par le Fils de Dieu fait homme," Nova et Vetera (French edition) 79, no. 1 (2004): 39–51; Matthew Levering, Christ's Fulfillment of Torah and Temple: Salvation according to Thomas Aquinas (Notre Dame, Ind.: University of Notre Dame Press, 2002), 32–33, 39, 59–63, 73–75; Guy Mansini, "Understanding St. Thomas on Christ's Immediate Knowledge of God," The Thomist 59 (1995): 91–124. Unless otherwise stated, all references to Denzinger ("Denz.") in this book are taken from The Sources of Catholic Dogma, trans. R. J. Deferrari from the 13th ed. of Henry Denzinger's Enchiridion Symbolorum (Fitzwilliam, N.H.: Loreto Publications, 1955).

2. Aquinas's explicit arguments for the beatific vision of Christ are soteriological:

However, it is a conclusion that can be derived from his Christological principles. I will show this by referring to the studies of Herman Diepen, Jacques Maritain, and more recently Jean Miguel Garrigues. They argue that in order for the created will of Jesus to be the instrument of his transcendent person, it must have a filial mode of being: it is expressive of the person who directs the human action of Christ, the incarnate Son of God. This requires in turn that the human will of Christ conform to his divine personal will in all actions. However, so that the exercise of the human will of Christ might be specified by the directives of his transcendent (divine) personhood and will, a higher knowledge concerning the divine will of the Son of God is necessary. This ultimately requires not only an "infused science" but also immediate knowledge of God present in the soul of Christ in and through all of his human actions. Having appropriated arguments from these thinkers on these points I will conclude (with reference to Galot and Weinandy) that if the human action of Jesus is to be the personal action of the Son of God, it must be immediately subject to the activity of the divine will which it expresses. This requires that the human intellect of Jesus possess the vision of God.

Finally, I will show that only with this classical analysis of Christ's human vision of God can one understand the mystery of Christ's obedience and prayer without falling into either a confusion of the natures or a denial of the unity of his person. I will examine briefly Aquinas's treatment of both the obedience and the prayer of Christ as *human* manifestations of his *divine identity,* that is, as expressions of his intra-Trinitarian, filial relationship with the Father. Through both of these activities, which are proper to his created human nature, the man Jesus manifests *in his human acts* his personal, hypostatic mode of being as the eternal Son of God. As I will show, this is not possible without the presence in Christ of an immediate knowledge of his own filial nature and divine will. Therefore, without this traditional theological teaching one cannot make adequate sense of the obedience and prayer of Jesus as revelatory of the Trinitarian persons. This being the case, the central objections to Aquinas's theory offered by Galot and Weinandy are unfounded. On the contrary, the

---

Christ must have the vision so that he can communicate it to others. See ST III, q. 9, a. 2; *Comp. Theol.,* c. 216. I return to this argument in chapter 8 below.

classical theory of the immediate vision is necessary to safeguard the traditional Christology they wish to defend, as it is exemplified in the action of the earthly life of Christ.

Jean Galot offers foundational contemporary criticisms to the traditional theory of the beatific vision in the earthly life of Christ.[3] His argument presents the most comprehensive and forceful criticism of the tradition in question, and has since found favor with other authors.[4] More recently, Thomas Weinandy has developed criticisms that echo some of Galot's initial viewpoints.[5] In assessing the most pertinent challenges to the traditional teaching on this subject, I will briefly consider two of their criticisms, the first from Galot and the second from Weinandy. The accord between them on this subject gives a fair sense of the contemporary challenges to the tradition.

Jean Galot: Beatific Vision
as Latent Monophysitism

Galot begins his argument with the claim that the doctrine of the immediate vision of God in the earthly life of Christ stems from an *a priori*, purely deductive reflection derived from the reasoning of medieval scholastic theology without sufficient reference to the evidences of scripture or the patristic theological heritage. He traces the teaching's historical origins from Candide (ninth century) to Hugh of St. Victor, and from the latter to the *Sentences* of Lombard, from which it was developed into its classical form by Aquinas and other influential theologians of the high scholastic period.[6] What all of

3. Jean Galot, "Le Christ terrestre et la vision," *Gregorianum* 67 (1986): 429–50. Other related works include *La conscience de Jésus* (Paris: Duculot-Lethielleux, 1971) and *Vers une nouvelle christologie* (Paris: Duculot-Lethielleux, 1971).

4. See in particular Jean-Pierre Torrell, "S. Thomas d'Aquin et la science du Christ," in *Saint Thomas au XXe siècle*, ed. S.-T. Bonino (Paris: Éditions St. Paul, 1994), 394–409.

5. Thomas Weinandy, "Jesus' Filial Vision of the Father," *Pro Ecclesia* 13 (2004): 189–201.

6. Galot, "Le Christ terrestre," 429–31; cf. Candide, *Epistola* 6 (PL 106:106); *Opusculum de Passione Domini* 17 (PL 106:95AB); Hugh of St. Victor, *De sapientia animae*

these thinkers have in common is the appeal to an argument based upon the necessary perfection of the human nature of Jesus. Because of the dignity of the hypostatic union, the humanity of Christ should be accorded the perfection of all human attributes from the time of his conception, excluding those which may act in some way as a hindrance to the realization of his soteriological mission, such as not being subject to emotional and physical suffering, as well as death. The vision of God must be included among such privileges. Therefore, Christ possessed the perfection of all human knowledge, and this would include, of course, not only the vision of God, but also the infused science of prophetic *species,* by which he might know all that man could possibly come to know.[7]

Galot argues that, besides lacking sufficient reference to scriptural evidence of the earthly Christ, such a perspective in fact leads to an implicit denial of the real humanity of the earthly Christ, who was in his *created* humanity (like all intellectual creatures) subject to certain natural intellectual limitations. Among these would be the historically and culturally conditioned mode of his self-understanding as well as social interdependencies for the exercise of his learning. The affirmation of this terrestrial vision in fact divinizes the earthly man Jesus in an unrealistic way. It is tantamount to a certain kind of Monophysitism in the epistemological realm:

Christi (PL 176:853AB); *De sacramentis christianae fidei* 2.1.6 (PL 176:388D–89B); Peter Lombard, *III Sent.,* d. 14, n. 2 (PL 192:783–84); Aquinas, ST III, q. 9, a. 4; III, q. 12, aa. 1 and 3. Galot writes ("Le Christ terrestre," 429n3): "The patristic sources furnish no explicit testimony in favor of a beatific vision in the earthly life of Christ." However, he does admit that the doctrine is evidently implicit in the affirmations of St. Fulgentius (468–533), *Epist.* 14, q. 3, 25–34 (PL 65:415–24). All references in this book to the *Patrologia Latina* ["PL"] are from *Patrologiae Cursus Completus. Series Latina,* ed. J.-P. Migne, 221 vols. (Paris: Garnier and J.-P. Migne, 1844–64).

7. Aquinas, ST III, q. 9, a. 1: "Now what is in potentiality is imperfect unless reduced to act. But it was fitting that the Son of God should assume, not an imperfect, but a perfect human nature, since the whole human race was to be brought back to perfection by its means. Hence it behooved the soul of Christ to be perfected by a knowledge, which would be its proper perfection [namely, the beatific vision and the plenitude of infused science]." For further evidence of this "principle of perfection," see also ST III, q. 9, aa. 2 and 4; III, q. 11, a. 1; III, q. 12, aa. 1 and 3. I will argue below that Galot's treatment of Aquinas's thought is selective on this point and fails to take sufficiently into account the "economic" character of Christ's extraordinary knowledge as St. Thomas understands it.

First of all, instead of referring to the testimony of the Gospels in order to discover the forms of knowledge which were manifest in the words and gestures of Jesus, the theological method proceeds in this case by positing an ideal of perfection from which is deduced all of the human knowledge of Christ. This *a priori* deduction leads to a maximum of perfection which itself impedes one from accurately taking account of the concrete conditions in which the human thought of Jesus developed. This perfection attributed to Christ's knowledge is such that one no longer respects sufficiently the distinction between the divine nature and the human nature.... Human understanding is clothed with divine properties as regards the entire domain of knowledge. One can see immediately the risk of Monophysitism, and more precisely the difficulty in acknowledging the inherent limitations of human knowledge, a necessary recognition for avoiding all confusion with the perfection of divine knowledge.[8]

Furthermore, this affirmation has soteriological consequences. Galot argues: if the earthly Christ possesses the vision of God and the consequent joy that follows from it (even if confined to the "heights" of the spiritual soul as Aquinas affirms), then the true sufferings of his human life are attenuated in their salvific reality. They can no longer be true acts of human self-emptying (*kenosis*) in loving solidarity with our human condition, as portrayed by St. Paul in his letter to the Philippians.[9] The agony of the crucifixion and the cry of dereliction are not permitted their reality, and thus revelation is muted. In fact, the affirmation of such a vision of God obscures something of the epiphany of self-emptying love that God manifested through the event of the crucifixion, and which the gospel writers wished to relate to us.

A Jesus whose soul would have been continually immersed in the beatific vision would have only assumed the exterior appearances of our human life.... His resemblance to us would only have been a façade.... What would become of the sufferings of the passion? ... Not only does [the doctrine of the vision] put at risk the reality of the incarnation, but also that of the redemptive sacrifice. How can we attribute to a Savior who is filled with heavenly beatitude these words: "My God, My God, why have you abandoned me?"

8. Galot, "Le Christ terrestre," 431–32.

9. Phil 2:7–8: "He emptied himself, taking the form of a slave, coming in human likeness; and found human in appearance, he humbled himself, becoming obedient to death, even death on a cross."

... The cry of Jesus on the cross makes manifest the depths of a suffering that is incompatible with the beatitude of the vision.[10]

In place of these theological motifs, then, Galot proposes the existence in the historical Christ of a form of prophetic insight (infused science), by which he was endowed with a human awareness (albeit, extraordinary) of his divine identity and soteriological mission. Certainly, Galot concedes, Christ did not know of his own identity by the theological virtue of faith. Yet his inspired conscious awareness of his own divine, filial identity was properly human, respecting the limitations of his created nature.[11] This more "sober" recognition of an extraordinary form of knowledge in the earthly Christ can account sufficiently for his privileged knowledge of his Father and his own filial identity, as well as his prophetic insights into salvation history, scriptural meaning, and the hidden thoughts of men's hearts. No recourse to the beatific vision is necessary.

Thomas Weinandy: The
Vision of God in Jesus as a Nestorian
Division of Subjects

Thomas Weinandy has published a great deal on the consciousness of Christ, and is in part influenced by Galot. He has attempted to rethink the traditional understanding of the vision of God in Christ to emphasize the unity of the person of Christ and the Trinitarian character of Jesus's human knowledge of and relation to the Father.[12]

---

10. Galot, "Le Christ terrestre," 434.

11. Ibid., 439–40: "It is certainly true that Jesus [as portrayed in the scriptures] did not live in faith.... He knows the Father and he is conscious of being the Son. He does not believe in himself. He possesses the certitude of his own identity, by way of his personal consciousness. Others are invited to believe in him.... This consciousness implies an illumination received from above, an infused knowledge.... However, this infused knowledge that makes possible the conscious awareness of a divine 'I,' does not transform Jesus' human self-awareness into a vision. It implies neither a human vision of God, nor a heavenly beatitude. It respects the ordinary conditions of human consciousness, and accords with the historical development of the latter." See also Jean Galot, "Problèmes de la conscience du Christ," part 2, "La conscience du Christ et la foi," *Esprit et vie* 92 (1982): 145–52.

12. See especially Weinandy, "Jesus' Filial Vision of the Father," but also Thomas Weinandy, *Does God Change?* (Still River, Mass.: St. Bede's Press, 1985), and *Does God Suffer?* (Notre Dame, Ind.: University of Notre Dame Press, 2000).

Weinandy, following Galot, claims that in one respect the affirmation of the vision of God in the earthly life of Christ denies Jesus his natural, human manner of knowing, and therefore implies a kind of semi-Monophysitism as regards Christ's consciousness.[13] However, the central criticism of the Franciscan theologian is that the theory of the beatific vision falls *in a different respect* into the opposite Christological heresy of Nestorianism. Precisely in order to render Christ invulnerable to the limits of a human form of knowledge, traditional theology has claimed that he knows the divine essence immediately. But this seems to suggest that the man Jesus knows the divinity as a transcendent object, distinct from himself as subject. The soul of Christ is conceived in the same sense as the soul of any other creaturely person, but in Christ's case he knows his transcendent creator immediately by a special privilege. The latter idea of the man Jesus receiving a special knowledge of God implicitly imposes upon Christology a duality of personal subjects, or Nestorianism.[14]

Weinandy argues that if Christ is to stand personally in relation to God intellectually, it must be as the Son who is *humanly aware* of the Father. Christ's filial awareness need not imply the beatific vision as classically conceived, but could be understood instead in terms of a grace of filial insight (unique to Christ alone), unfolding in Jesus's consciousness progressively through the ordinary processes of human self-reflexivity.[15] He goes on to argue that an authentic ad-

13. Weinandy, "Jesus' Filial Vision," 189–90.

14. Ibid., 192: "The subject (the 'who') of any vision of the Father is not a subject (a 'who') different from that of the divine Son, but *the divine Son himself* since it is actually the Son who *is* man. Since it is the Son who must be the subject of any such vision of the Father, his vision of the Father cannot be a vision of the divine essence as an object ontologically distinct from and over against himself. As traditionally asked and answered, the question concerning Jesus' beatific vision, by the very nature of the question, always necessarily posited another subject (another 'who') distinct from that of the Son who possessed an objective vision of God who was other than 'himself,' and it is this positing of another subject (or 'who') which is why this question of Jesus' beatific vision was necessarily asked and answered in a Nestorian manner." For a similar consideration, see also Galot, "Le Christ terrestre," 440. Weinandy and Galot claim that Aquinas falls into precisely such a Nestorian manner of conceiving of the earthly Christ in relation to God in ST III, q. 10, aa. 2 ("Whether the soul of Christ knew all things in the Word?") and 4 ("Whether the soul of Christ sees the Word more clearly than any other creature?").

15. Weinandy, "Jesus' Filial Vision," 193: "While traditionally Jesus is said to have possessed the beatific vision, I would want to argue, in keeping with the above, that it

mission of the unity of personhood in Christ entails only one cen-
ter of consciousness in his earthly existence. This would be the self-
awareness of Christ that is proper to his human nature *alone*. The
man Jesus has a human awareness of being a divine person, and this
reality cannot be abridged or obscured by appeal to a grace such as
the beatific vision, which would make God an object of knowledge
extrinsic to his person.[16]

Summary

For the purposes of the argument of this chapter, two central criticisms can be culled from the arguments examined above. Galot and
Weinandy claim, in effect, that the affirmation of the beatific vision in
the earthly life of Christ implicitly denies the reality of the human nature of Christ in its historical mode of functioning, and instead stems
from *a priori* deductive argumentation concerning the perfection of
the humanity of Jesus. The latter idea lacks a sufficient grounding in
scripture and the most profound principles of patristic theology. Furthermore, it seemingly conceives of Christ as a creaturely subject distinct from the Trinity of persons who are the object of such beatify-

---

is more properly correct, in accordance with the hypostatic union, to speak of a human
'hypostatic vision': the person (*hypostasis*) of the Son possessed as man, a personal human vision of the Father by which he came to know the Father as the Father truly exists
… in coming to know the Father as truly Father, the Son equally became humanly conscious of himself as Son"; see also 197: "As Jesus, as a young boy, studied the Scriptures
and prayed the Spirit illumined his human consciousness and intellect with the vision
of the Father such that he became hypostatically aware of the Father's glory and love,
and within such an awareness he became conscious of his divine identity and so came
to know that he was indeed the Father's eternal and only begotten Son."

16. Weinandy, "Jesus' Filial Vision," 195–96: "The Son as divine is conscious of himself as God within his divine 'I.' However, within his incarnate state I would not want to
posit two 'I's'—one divine and one human—for within his incarnate state the one divine Son *is only conscious of himself as man,* within a human manner (as man he cannot
be conscious of himself in a divine manner), and thus there is, as man, only one 'I' and
that human. Therefore, I think it is better, for clarity's sake, to speak of a human 'I' of a
divine person or subject (a divine 'who'), rather than confuse the issue by positing a
second 'I' that is divine" (emphasis added). The question this raises (which I will return
to below) is: what correspondence exists between this human knowledge Christ has of
the Father and his own properly *divine* knowledge of himself as the Son? What rapport
exists between the Son's eternal self-knowledge and will and his human knowledge, if
any? Do they relate to each other in the human action of Jesus, and if so, in what way?

ing knowledge. In response, I would like to examine the different but related question of the cooperation of wills (human and divine) in the earthly Christ. Both scripture and the patristic tradition insist on the distinction and cooperation of the two wills in the one subject of the Son of God. I will argue that this cooperation can only take place in one unified activity due to the presence in the created soul of Christ of an immediate knowledge of his own personal, divine will and divine essence. Referring to studies of Aquinas by Diepen, Garrigues, and Maritain, I will argue that it follows from Thomistic Christological principles, then, that only this immediate vision permits the human will and intellect of Christ to take on a particular hypostatic mode: that of the Son of God. In other words, only this vision safeguards the unity of the personal actions of Christ in and through his two distinct natures and operations. It is after examining these points that I will respond to Galot's and Weinandy's respective concerns about the reality of Jesus's humanity on the one hand and the unity of his person on the other. I will show that the beatific vision of Christ, if correctly understood, is filial in *mode* and thus is essential for there to be personal unity in the voluntary acts of the man Jesus (contrary to claims of Nestorianism). However, in its *nature,* this vision is accorded to the created intellect and will of the humanity of Christ, which it respects, even in their historical and human mode of functioning (contrary to claims of Monophysitism). After this, the examples of the obedience and prayer of Christ can be studied as concrete illustrations of this doctrine.

AQUINAS ON THE
VOLUNTARY ACTION
OF CHRIST

In what follows I will make three brief points, relying in part on the insights of recent Thomistic commentators. First of all, as I have underscored in chapter 1, the human nature of Jesus must be understood first and foremost in *instrumental* terms, as subsisting in his divine person, and as expressive of the latter. Second, if Christ's humanity is the instrument of his divinity, then this intimately affects the way his human will cooperates with his divine will. As Jean Miguel Garrigues has shown, Aquinas follows Maximus the Confessor and John Damascene in distinguishing between the specifically human character of the natural will of Christ and its hypostatic mode. This distinction helps explain how the man Jesus can manifest his identity as the Son of God through his human actions from within the *unity* of his person. Christ must personally will as man what he personally wills as God, such that the two operations remain distinct, but his human will acquires a filial mode or manner of exercise. The personal unity of Christ will only be adequately expressed if there is a perfect cooperation between his human will and his divine will in all his human actions.

Finally, if Christ's human will and consciousness must act as the instruments of his divine subject, then his human will must be specified at each instant by his divine will through the medium of human knowledge. For this to take place, Christ as man must have human knowledge of his own filial divine nature and will. The virtue of faith, or a uniquely prophetic knowledge (by infused species), is not sufficient. The unity of activity of the incarnate Word requires, therefore, the beatific vision in the intellect of Christ, so that his human will and his divine will may cooperate within one subject.

The Integrity of
Christ's Human Nature and Its
Filial Mode of Subsistence

At stake in this debate is the capacity of "beatific vision theology" to make sense of the incarnation as it is presented in scripture and patristic tradition. A central concern of Galot is to recognize the human integrity of Christ's intellectual life in its historical setting. Ordinary human knowledge is subject to limitations and the conventional understandings and modes of expression of a cultural context. For Aquinas, however, the integrity of the human nature of Christ is first understood not in epistemological but in ontological terms, and is seen as guaranteed by a classical scriptural principle: revelation teaches that God assumed in Christ a true and complete human nature.[17] Herman Diepen showed in an important series of articles that in this respect Aquinas's Christology is directly inspired by the Greek patris-

17. Cf. Jn 1:14, Phil 2:7–8, Heb 4:15.

tic tradition (especially Cyril of Alexandria, the Councils of Ephesus, Chalcedon, and Constantinople III, and John Damascene) and that Aquinas purposefully appropriated this tradition in continuity with his own metaphysics of *esse*.[18] In his critique of the Scotist Christologist Paul Galtier, Diepen notes that the former argues from the autonomous human psychological consciousness of Christ to the necessity of a human subject in Christ distinct from that of the Word.[19] Galtier claimed that only the beatific vision could permit the human subject (Jesus) to be continually aware of the divine subject (the Word), so as to assure a unity of action on the part of these two component natures within the incarnation.[20] This dualistic conception in fact closely approximates the kind of position that Galot and Weinandy are criticizing, and so Diepen's Thomistic response is significant. Noting the poignantly Nestorian tendency of this thought, Diepen points out that the unity of Christ's person for Aquinas follows first and foremost from the ontological subsistence of his humanity in the existent Word, the Son of God, and not from his intellectual assent to the will of God. Aquinas affirms this unity of personal subsistence in the Word made man, and notes how it relates to the divine *esse* of the Word:

Being (*esse*) pertains to both the nature and the hypostasis; to the hypostasis as that which has being, and to the nature as that whereby it has being.... Now it must be borne in mind that if there is a form or nature which does not pertain to the personal being of the subsisting hypostasis, this being is said to belong to the person not simply but relatively.... [But] since the human nature is united to the Son of God hypostatically or personally, and not accidentally, it follows that by the human nature there accrued to Him no new personal being, but only a new relation of the pre-existing personal being to the human nature, in such a way that the person is said to subsist not merely in the divine, but also in the human nature.[21]

18. I have referred in passing to these studies in chapter 1: Herman Diepen, "La critique du baslisme selon saint Thomas d'Aquin," *Revue Thomiste* 50 (1950): 82–118 and 290–329; "La psychologie humaine du Christ selon saint Thomas d'Aquin," *Revue Thomiste* 50 (1950): 515–62. In addition to the Latin translation of Damascene's *The Orthodox Faith*, Aquinas was familiar with these other sources from various medieval *florilegia* of the Greek fathers, such as the *Collectio Casinensis*.

19. Diepen, "La psychologie humaine du Christ selon saint Thomas d'Aquin," 531.

20. See Paul Galtier, "Unité ontologique et unité psychologique dans le Christ," *Bulletin de littérature ecclésiastique* (Toulouse) 42 (1941): 161–75 and 216–32.

21. Aquinas, ST III, q. 17, a. 2. See also ST III, q. 2, aa. 2–3; a. 6, ad 3; III, q. 16, aa. 7, 10, and 12; III, q. 18, aa. 1–2.

In effect, subsistence in the ontology of Aquinas pertains to a property of *esse*. It denotes both a separateness of existence and a certain mode or manner of being. That which has its own subsistence *exists apart from others* and has its *own mode of being* different from others.[22] For our purposes here, the central point of importance is that Aquinas's theology of the incarnation (following John Damascene) distinguishes between the specific determinations of the complete human nature of Jesus and the unique hypostatic mode in which this nature subsists.[23] This human nature, by the mystery of the incarnation, has no existence apart from its hypostatic union with the Word and thereby acquires a unique mode: it has the person of the Son as its unique subject.[24] As a consequence of this fact, as Diepen notes, there is not an autonomous "personality" in the humanity of Jesus, other than that of the hypostasis of the Son:

There is certainly a human consciousness in Christ, but not the consciousness of a human self, either metaphysical or psychological.... To say that the humanity knows, acts, is aware, these are different expressions which are certainly improper, because it is always the Word to whom these acts belong. It is he who is the proper and exclusive subject of their attribution .... He alone who possesses and exercises existence, the existent properly speaking, that is to say, the subject [*suppôt*] exerts operations.... The Son of God, by his human intelligence, is conscious of his human activity ... [but these acts] are perceived *as the acts of someone who is not simply a subsistent human nature on its own....* These acts are perceived as acts that are not autonomous but dependent [on the subsistent Word].[25]

22. Thus Aquinas claims that the unique subsistence of each concrete personal subject gives his natural acts a particular manner of being proper to that subject. See ST III, q. 2, aa. 2–3.

23. See for example John Damascene, *De Fide Orth.* III, 15–17, 21. Damascene's distinction between the specifically human nature (*logos*) of Christ and its filial mode (*tropos*) was originally developed by Maximus the Confessor. See the study by Jean Miguel Garrigues, "Le dessein d'adoption du créateur dans son rapport au fils d'après S. Maxime le Confesseur," in *Maximus Confessor,* eds. F. Heinzer and C. Schönborn (Fribourg: Éditions Universitaires, 1982), 173–92.

24. ST III, q. 2. a. 3: "to the hypostasis alone are attributed the operations and the natural properties, *and whatever belongs to the nature in the concrete....* Therefore, if there is any hypostasis in Christ besides the hypostasis of the Word, it follows that whatever pertains to man is verified of some other than the Word, e.g. that He was born of a Virgin, suffered, was crucified, was buried. And this ... was condemned with the approval of the Council of Ephesus (can. 4)" (emphasis added).

25. Diepen, "La psychologie humaine," 531–32. Aquinas writes on the same subject:

Consequently, the human nature of Jesus acts as an "assumed instrument" of his divinity. Because the Word subsists in a human nature, the humanity of Christ bears the mark of his divine identity and makes it manifest in and through all of his human activities.[26]

Speaking in broader terms than those of consciousness, then, Aquinas's theory of the incarnation responds reasonably to the concerns of Galot and Weinandy. The integrity of human nature is preserved with respect to its specific determinations (vis-à-vis Galot). Yet through its manner of subsisting in the Word, this human nature assumed in Christ acquires a new mode such that nothing in it falls outside of the divine subject of the Son (as Weinandy insists must be the case).[27] Thus on this more fundamental, ontological level, we can see how the mode/nature distinction safeguards both the reality of the humanity of Christ and the unity of his person.

"Yet we must bear in mind that not every individual in the genus of substance, even in rational nature, is a person, but that alone *which exists by itself*, and not that which exists in some more perfect thing. ... Therefore, although this human nature [of Christ] is a kind of individual in the genus of substance, *it has not its own personality, because it does not exist separately, but in something more perfect, viz., in the person of the Word*" (ST III, q. 2, a. 2, ad 3; emphasis added).

26. Aquinas, ST III, q. 2, a. 6, ad 4: "Not everything that is assumed as an instrument pertains to the hypostasis of the one who assumes, as is plain in the case of a saw or a sword; yet nothing prevents what is assumed into the unity of the hypostasis from being as an instrument, even as the body of man or his members. Hence Nestorius held that the human nature was assumed by the Word merely as an instrument, and not into the unity of the hypostasis.... But Damascene held that the human nature in Christ is an instrument belonging to the unity of the hypostasis." As Theophil Tschipke and Diepen after him pointed out, Aquinas purposefully revived this Cyrillian insistence on the humanity of Christ as *organon* of the divinity, and used this to explain the way that his intellect and will, especially, could be the subservient instruments of his divinity. See Theophil Tschipke, *Heilsorgan der Gottheit: Unter Besonderer Berücksichtigung der Lehre des Heiligen Thomas von Aquin* (Freiburg im Breisgau: Herder, 1940), republished in French as *L'humanité du Christ comme instrument de salut de la divinité*, trans. P. Secrétan (Fribourg: Academic Press Fribourg, 2003); and Herman Diepen, *Théologie d'Emmanuel* (Bruges: Desclée de Brouwer, 1960), 275–93 on this point with respect to the non-autonomy of the psychological subject in Christ.

27. On this point Weinandy is in complete accord with Aquinas (i.e., it is actually the Son who *is* man), understanding the latter's metaphysics of the incarnation as a true and careful expression of Chalcedonian orthodoxy. See Weinandy, *Does God Change?*, 82–88; *Does God Suffer?*, 206–8.

The Nature/Mode
Distinction and the Two Wills
of Christ

Having begun on the ontological level, I will now consider the personal actions of Christ. These too acquire a unique mode of being
due to the fact that they subsist in the person of the Word. If the human will of Christ is the instrument of his person, it must express this
hypostatic mode in its operations. Jesus must personally will as man
what he personally wills as God. Only in this way can the singularity and unity of Christ's person be manifest in and through his human action. Furthermore, this cooperation between the human will
of Christ and his divine will must be perfect and indefectible in all his
human actions, precisely so as to express adequately his personal unity. How might we make this argument?

First, we should note that in the Christology of the *Summa*, Aquinas explicitly applies the nature/mode distinction discussed above
directly to the particular spiritual faculties of intellect and will in
the incarnate Word.[28] In doing so, Aquinas is following the understanding of the "theandric acts" of Christ developed by Maximus the
Confessor, which Aquinas assimilated through the writings of John
Damascene.[29] This theology was developed in confrontation with
Monothelitism precisely to affirm the Chalcedonian confession of
the complete and real human nature of Christ (including his human
actions of the will), while safeguarding (against the charge of Nestorianism) the Cyrillian confession of the singularity and unity of the
person of the incarnate Word. The distinction safeguards the fact that
these operations are both fully human (in their nature) and expressive of Jesus's unique filial personhood (in their mode).

28. See the arguments to this effect by Garrigues, "La conscience de soi," 39–51, and
"L'instrumentalité rédemptrice du libre arbitre du Christ chez saint Maxime le Confesseur," *Revue Thomiste* 104 (2004): 531–50. As will become clear, this section of the chapter in particular is greatly indebted to the argument and perspective of these articles.

29. The notion of "theandric acts" originated with Dionysius (*Div. Nom.* 2), and
was appropriated by Maximus and Damascene in a sense consistent with Chalcedon
against Monothelitism. Aquinas follows Damascene, denoting by the term the cooperation of the divine and human wills in Christ such that they form together the actions of
a unique person; see ST III, q. 19, a. 1, ad 1.

The nature assumed by Christ may be viewed in two ways. First, in its specific nature, and thus Damascene calls it "ignorant and enslaved" (*De Fide Orth.* III, 21)…. Secondly, it may be considered with regard to what it has from its *union with the Divine hypostasis,* from which it has the fullness of knowledge and grace.[30]

In effect, as Garrigues shows in detail, the Greek fathers developed an understanding of the personal mode of the human will of Christ by distinguishing the *logos* of this will and its *tropos.* "Logos" here signifies a distinct essence common to many who share a determinate nature, while "tropos" signifies a manner of existing particular to an individual hypostasis. In their essential specification, Christ's human will and intellect are identical with those of other men, but they acquire a unique mode because of the hypostatic union, through which they are appropriated *instrumentally* as the human expression of the person of God the Son.[31] Because they subsist in God the Son, the human will and intellect of Christ are necessarily rendered relative to his divine intellect and will as the primary source of their personal operation.[32]

30. ST III, q. 15, a. 3, ad 1. See also ST III, q. 18, a. 1, obj. 4 and ad 4.

31. Maximus, *Disputatio cum Pyrrho* (PG 91:293A): "The fact of willing and the determined mode of willing are not identical, just as the fact of seeing and the determined mode of seeing are not either. For the fact of willing, like that of seeing, concerns the nature of a thing. It is common to all those who have the same nature and belong to the same kind. The determined mode of willing, however, like that of seeing, that is to say, to will to walk or not will to walk, to see what is at the right or at the left or high or below, or to look by sensual desire or in order to understand the essential principles in beings, all this concerns a mode of exercise [*tropos*] of willing or seeing. It concerns only him who exercises [these faculties of nature] and in so doing separates him from others according to particular differences." See Garrigues's analysis of this text and others in "L'instrumentalité," 542–50. As he points out, Aquinas also uses these same examples (eyesight, voluntary action) to denote the distinction between *specification* and *exercise* in *De Malo,* q. 6. Damascene reproduced this identical doctrine in *De Fide Orth.* III, c. 14. All references to the *Patrologia Graeca* ["PG"] are from *Patrologiae Cursus Completus. Series Graeca, ed.* J.-P. Migne, 161 vols. (Paris: Gamier and J.-P. Migne, 1857–66).

32. Damascene, *De Fide Orth.* III, 14–18. See, for example, c. 17: "Wherefore the same flesh was mortal by reason of its own nature and life-giving through its union with the Word in subsistence. And we hold that it is just the same with the deification of the will; for its natural activity was not changed but united with His divine and omnipotent will, and became the will of God, made man. And so it was that, though He wished, He could not of Himself escape (Mk. 7:24), because it pleased God the Word that the weakness of the human will, which was in truth in Him, should be made manifest. But

Aquinas develops this theological motif, interpreting it in light of the metaphysics of the incarnation mentioned above. Because the personal existence of the Word gives the subsistent humanity of Christ its unique mode of being, the will of Christ also receives a unique mode of being. It is the human will of the divine person of the Son of God.

Damascene says (*De Fide Orth.* III, c. 14) that "to will this or that way be-longs not to our nature but to our intellect, i.e., our *personal* intellect." ... When we say, "to will in a certain way," we signify a *determinate mode* of willing. Now a determinate mode regards the thing of which it is the mode. Hence since the will pertains to the nature, "to will in a certain way" belongs to the nature, not indeed considered absolutely, *but as it is in the hypostasis. Hence the human will of Christ has a determinate mode from the fact of being in a Divine hypostasis,* i.e. *it was always moved in accordance with the bidding of the Divine will.*[33]

Although the divine agency must always take the initiative in the hu-man acts of Christ, Jesus is not therefore any less human than we are. On the contrary, his human nature is an "instrument" that operates in accordance with its own divine identity. Therefore, precisely be-cause he has in his human intellect an immediate knowledge of his own personal divine goodness at all times, the judgments and practi-cal choices of Christ are more and not less human than ours.

Whatever was in the human nature of Christ was moved at the bidding of the divine will; yet it does not follow that in Christ there was no movement of the will proper to human nature.... It is proper to an instrument to be moved by the principal agent, yet diversely, according to the property of its nature.... And an instrument animated with a rational soul is moved by its will, the servant being like an animate instrument. And hence it was in this manner that the human nature of Christ was the instrument of the Godhead and was moved by its own will.[34]

He was able to cause at His will the cleansing of the leper, because of the union with the divine will" (trans. S. D. F. Salmond, in *Nicene and Post-Nicene Fathers,* vol. 9 [Oxford: James Parker, 1899]).

33. ST III, q. 18, a. 1, obj. 4 and ad 4 (emphasis added).

34. ST III, q. 18, a. 1, ad 1 and 2. As Garrigues notes ("L'instrumentalité," 545–47), Aquinas differs from Maximus and Damascene insofar as these Greek fathers denied the existence of an autonomous human moral deliberation and judgment in Christ, due to his superior knowledge of the good. Aquinas argues that moral deliberation and

This line of argument leads, then, to a second point. The singularity and unity of the person of Christ can only be sufficiently manifest in his human actions if his divine and human wills cooperate concretely in all of his personal actions. The human intentions and choices that Christ makes as a man are indicative of his divine personal will, intentions, and choices. It is this cooperation of the two wills that permits the human willing of Christ to take on its filial mode of expression.

We should note that it is not the case that the hypostatic unity of the person of Christ is *constituted* by the cooperation of his human and divine wills. However, this personal unity must be manifested adequately through the human actions of Jesus. This follows from the principles of the incarnation. For the human actions of Jesus are actions of one person who is divine, and what the Son wills humanly is expressive of his personal identity. However, this person, the Son of God, possesses a divine will, and it is impossible for the Son of God to act personally in such a way that his divine will should be absent from his personal action. The Word incarnate, then, must be humanly conscious of his own divine will in all of his actions, so that his human actions are indicative of his personal, divine willing as God.[35]

---

judgment are necessary to any human nature and therefore existed in Christ, but were always inspired by a sense of the higher good of the divine will, which made the human choices of Christ freer and more pure. Colman O'Neill comments: "Christ was unique in that he had no choice [concerning the possible final end of man]; for with his human mind he saw God and his will was necessarily held by this Supreme Good (cf. ST III, q. 9, a. 2; q. 10). But anything less than God was powerless to compel his will. With respect to all created things he was supremely free for he could measure their value against his vision and possession of the divine good (III, q. 18, a. 4)…. His obedience dedicated him to the will of his Father; far from restricting his liberty, it set him free from attachment to any created thing so that he could rise to the summit of human liberty and renounce his life for the sake of what his will held dearest." See "The Problem of Christ's Human Autonomy," appendix 3 in *Summa Theologiae*, Blackfriars edition, vol. 50, trans. C. O'Neill (London: Eyre and Spottiswoode, 1965), 233–34.

35. Garrigues, "La conscience," 40, writes: "Certainly, in becoming man, [Christ] assumes in his human nature the same rational desire for the Good that is proper to spiritual creatures. But since his human soul exists within the very person of Him who, as God, is the Good as such, the rational desire of Christ need not search in and through a deliberation how to attain the ultimate Good by a moral progression transpiring through the choice of particular goods. The human will of Christ, while endowed naturally with the same free-will as us, nevertheless does not have an autonomous deliberation (*gnome*) characteristic of the mode of exercise found in created persons…. Fixed forever from the first instant of the Incarnation, by the hypostatic union, upon

This affirmation has a basis in sound Trinitarian doctrine as well. We might affirm, for example, that the Son incarnate must be humanly conscious of the divine will that he shares with the Father and the Holy Spirit. Why is this the case? Because all through his human life, the Son of God reveals in and through his human actions the will of the Father and the activity of the Holy Spirit. If the Son is going to adequately manifest the mystery of the Holy Trinity in his human decisions and choices, then he must be humanly aware of what the Father who sent him wills and of what he wills with the Holy Spirit, so that he can express this in his human actions and choices. He can only do this because he is conscious in his human decisions of the divine will that he shares with the Father and the Holy Spirit.

It follows from this line of reasoning that the conformity of the human will of Christ to the divine will of Christ cannot occur only in some of his human choices, but must be something perfect and indefectible. This must be the case because the cooperation of the two wills stems from the hypostatic identity of Christ and is indicative of the unity of his person. This cooperation cannot, therefore, exist only at certain times in Christ's life. The man Jesus Christ is always the Son of God, and so his human consciousness and free decision-making must always develop in active conformity with the operations of his divine will, expressing thereby who he is personally as the Son. This conformity has to be perfect and without defect, because Jesus's human actions are actions of his person, and the divine will of Christ is something intrinsic to his filial person. If Christ as man were able to make some choices in seeming oblivion of his own divine will, it would follow that he would be able to make choices in seeming oblivion of his own hypostatic identity. He would then make decisions in reference to what he (mistakenly) took to be an alternative personal identity: that of a created personal subject who is not one in will with the Father. On this model, Christ would be the Word incarnate, but he might act as if he were a subject distinct from the Word, because he would not be aware of sharing in one will with the Father. This is,

---

the supreme Good which is One of the Trinity, and by the plenitude of habitual grace which follows from this, the rational desire of the humanity assumed by the Son exists and is exercised in a unique mode, of perfect docility with respect to the divine will of the Trinitarian person who exercises this will as its subject."

of course, entirely unfitting, and so it is reasonable to affirm that there existed at all times a perfect conformity of the human, free actions of Jesus as man, with his divine activity as God.

The conclusion to be drawn from all this is that in at least one very important respect (that is, with regard to the divine will), Christ's human actions *must not* be characterized by ignorance or defectibility. What is at stake is not a principle of ideal humanity, but the very unity of the operations of Christ in his practical actions. In order for Christ to be fully human, his psychological choices must be rational and natural (against Monophysitism), but for them to be the choices of his divine person, they must be unified with his divine will on the level of his personal action (against Nestorianism). The nature/mode distinction as applied by Aquinas to the will of Christ makes it possible to negotiate this theological challenge. The nature is respected but takes on a hypostatic mode, by which it accords always (instrumentally) with the divine, filial will of the Son. Thus a perfect and continual correlation between the divine and human wills is essential for surmounting the dual Christological errors that Galot and Weinandy wish to combat. But how can this occur?

The Necessity of the Son's Immediate Human Knowledge of the Divine Will

The conclusion of the previous section is significant: in at least one important way, the absence of ignorance in the mind of Christ is not immediately related, for Aquinas, to the extra-scriptural "principle of perfection" that Galot refers to, but rather, must exist for reasons *essential to the divine economy*. If Jesus is truly the Son of God, and therefore a divine person, then his divine will is present in his person as the primary agent of his personal choices. This means that, necessarily, his human will, in its rational deliberation and choice making, must be continually subordinated to, informed by, and indefectibly expressive of his personal divine will. But of course movements of human choice follow upon knowledge (apprehension of the good as well as deliberative judgments) informing the human intellect.[36]

36. *De Malo*, q. 6; ST I-II, q. 8, a. 1; q. 9, a. 1; q. 11, a. 1; q. 12, a. 1; q. 13, a. 1; q. 14, a. 1. On the intellect's role with respect to the exercise of the will as regards practical

Here, then, I will introduce an argument that moves beyond Aquinas's explicit statements to one which is homogeneous with his principles as they have been presented above. I will show that it is only if Christ's human intellect is continuously and immediately aware of his own divine will (by the beatific vision, and not merely by infused knowledge and by faith), that his human will can act in immediate subordination to his divine will as the "assumed instrument" of his divine subject. Only such knowledge will assure the operative unity (in and through two distinct natures) of Christ's personal actions, because this knowledge alone gives the mind of the man Jesus an evidential certitude of the will he shares eternally with the Father.

In order to present this argument, it is first necessary to make an important clarification. I have suggested above that only the immediate knowledge of God in the soul of Christ permits him to exert his divine will in a human way through the activities of his human consciousness. However, the vision of God is not conceptual or notional, but immediate and intuitive.[37] Consequently, it cannot be "assimilated" by Christ's habitual, conceptual manner of knowing and willing in any direct fashion. As Aquinas and many Thomists after him have rightly insisted, then, the knowledge of Christ's vision is "communicated" to his ordinary human consciousness through the medium of a so-called infused prophetic science.[38] The judgments and choices that inform the will of Jesus depend above all upon this "habitual" prophetic consciousness (which is in some sense abstract knowledge), rather than his immediate vision. Because of this, his knowing and obeying the Father "in a human way" (that is, in his human consciousness) would seem to depend *essentially* upon his prophetic science (or infused *species*). Why, then, might such a "prophetic light" in Christ not suffice *alone* without recourse to the vision of God? The latter does not add anything *necessary* to the human way of thinking and

---

action, see the excellent study of Michael Sherwin, *By Knowledge and by Love: Charity and Knowledge in the Moral Theology of St. Thomas Aquinas* (Washington, D.C.: The Catholic University of America Press, 2005), especially 18–62.

37. ST I, q. 12, aa. 4–5 and 9.

38. The basis for this position is found in ST III, q. 11, a. 5, ad 1. See its development by John of St. Thomas, *Cursus Theologicus*, vol. 8 (Paris: Vivès, 1886), d. 11, a. 2, especially n. 15, where he argues cogently that Christ had to possess infused science in order to receive the knowledge of the vision into his consciousness in a way that was connatural with his human nature.

willing that characterizes the activity of the *earthly* Christ, and therefore seems unnecessary for the purposes of his economic mission.[39]

In order to answer this objection, two things need to be kept in mind. First of all, in the absence of the immediate knowledge of vision, Christ would necessarily have to exercise the theological virtue of faith. The presence of a prophetic, infused knowledge cannot act as a substitute for faith in the way Galot proposes. Galot claims that there is no faith in Christ, nor vision, but only a higher knowledge attained by prophecy. Yet as Jean-Pierre Torrell has shown, prophetic or infused knowledge alone is only a mediate *indirect* knowledge of God attained through the *effects* of God.[40] Necessarily, outside of the vision, all knowledge of God is through effects, and *only faith* permits a quasi-immediate contact with God, through love. Therefore even infused knowledge requires faith in order to orient it toward God. This contact of faith, however, is obscure (non-evidential) and is therefore supported by a voluntary act of the will that believes in God by a free act of love. Without the vision, then, the intellect of Christ would not have "direct access to God," but would believe in his divinity and divine will through faith and in a free adherence of love.

Second, as Jacques Maritain has argued convincingly, the pre-

39. The above paragraph contains an approximation of the argument presented by Torrell in "S. Thomas d'Aquin et la science du Christ," 394–409, influenced by Galot's perspective.

40. Ibid., 403–4: "If one renounces the beatific vision and if one follows the logic of the Thomistic perspective, it must be said that Christ had faith.... The [bearer of prophecy] does not attain God in his experience [of infused science] but only expressive signs of the divine. He knows *that* God speaks to him, but *what* God says he can only believe.... The grace of faith is another kind of supernatural gift ... a created participation in the life of God, it conforms the believer ... to the mystery itself (II-II, q. a. 2, ad 2). In other words, with faith we are in the order of the supernatural *quoad essentiam*, while with prophetic knowledge we remain in the order of the supernatural *quoad modum* (*acquisitionis*). The two orders do not exclude one another, certainly, but the second is ordered to the first, and because the two are different kinds of realities, they must not be confused or made to play the role of one another. Concerning Jesus, then ... if we accord to him infused illuminations characteristic of the charismatic knowledge of revelation, he will be enabled for his role as a divine messenger, but he will still not have direct access to God, since these illuminations do not suffice as a replacement of faith." Aquinas makes related claims, denying that Christ is a prophet in the usual theological sense of the word, since he does not *believe* through an "obscure knowledge" the things he is given to reveal, but *knows* them in a more perfect, immediate way. See *In Ioan.* IV, lect. 6, 667.

sumed presence or absence of this vision must alter profoundly the character of this infused knowledge in the consciousness of Christ.[41] Only if the vision is present in Christ's soul can such infused knowledge participate in the evidence of Christ's divine identity and will which are immediately known by the vision.

Insofar as *viator*, [Christ] knew himself God through his infused science, — finite and increasing under the state of way, but which under this state (in the here-below of the soul of Christ) *participated in the evidence of the beatific vision.* . . . And it is this participated evidence of the vision which gave to the infused science of the Son of God *viator* a *divinely* sovereign *certitude* with regard to all that which it knew, and especially with regard to the very divinity of Jesus.[42]

In other words, because of the vision of God in the heights of Christ's soul, his intellect adheres immediately to his divine identity and his human will is "informed" immediately by the knowledge of his divine will. The prophetic knowledge that informs his consciousness then acts in subordination to the immediate knowledge he has as man of his own identity and will as God, expressing this in and through his ordinary human consciousness.[43] By contrast, in the absence of the vision, the infused science of Christ would lack such immediate evidence and would need to be accompanied by faith. In this case, the prophetic awareness Christ had of his own divinity and will would have to be continuously accompanied by an autonomous decision of faith in the human heart of Christ and a repeated choice to welcome in trust this revelation *from his own divine self.* This would create, in effect, a kind of psychological autonomy in the man Jesus distinct from the willing of his divine subject, resulting in a schism between the two operations of the incarnate Word. Jesus as man would have to will to believe in his divine activity as God. He would not perceive it directly. If we return to the theandric activity of Christ, then, we can see that this point has significant consequences. Only due to the *immediate* knowledge of the vision can the human will of Christ be

41. See Maritain, *On the Grace and Humanity of Jesus*, 107.

42. See the developed argument of Maritain in ibid., 54–61, 98–125, especially 101–2, 107.

43. For reflections on the relationship between this "supra-conscious" character of the vision, and its manifestation in consciousness, see ibid., 114–20.

directly moved (or specified) by his divine will so as irremediably to correspond to its inclinations.[44] *Because of* the beatific vision, the prophetic knowledge in Christ's consciousness is suffused by the evidence Christ has of the will he shares eternally with the Father. Thus, the human will of Christ acts "instrumentally," that is to say, through an immediate subordination to his divine will.[45] The infused science of Christ permits his ordinary consciousness to cooperate with this knowledge which the vision alone provides. By it Christ always knows immediately and with certitude who he is and what he wills in unity with the Father. His human will cooperates indefectibly with his divine will in the unity of one personal subject.

In the absence of the vision, by contrast, the infused knowledge of Christ would still be the medium by which the man Jesus would be conscious of his own divine will, but it would no longer participate in any evidential certitude of that will. Consequently, the human mind of Christ could no longer be immediately influenced by the will of his divine person. Instead the man Christ would continually need to make acts of faith in what he believed obscurely to be the divine will he shared (as God) with his Father. He would have to hope (as a man) that he was doing what his own transcendent identity (which he also believed in) willed for him. Christ would not know with evidential certitude, therefore, who he was and what he willed (as God) in each instant. Thus his human operations of willing might subsist in the person of the Word, but in their operative exercise they would work on a separate "parallel track" to the operations of the Word without immediate influence in their mode of exercise. Both operations could subsist in one person, but they would not be immediately related to each other as the operations of one person. In this case, no

44. In ST I-II, q. 4, a. 4, Aquinas shows that the *permanent and necessary* rectitude of the creaturely will in relation to the eternal goodness of God is dependent for man upon the *immediate* knowledge of the final end (the vision of the essence of God). John Damascene in *De Fide Orth.* III, c. 14 suggests that the movement of the human will of the Word occurs by a direct specification of it by the divine will.

45. I am employing the notion of "instrumentality" differently from Maritain here so as to emphasize not only the instrumentality of the vision with regard to his infused knowledge, but the instrumentality of his entire human consciousness (with all of its forms of knowledge) as an expression of his divine personhood and will. Yet I follow him in holding that such a state of affairs depends upon the vision as a mediating principle.

true unity of subject is manifest in the actions of Jesus, and a kind of "operational dualism" results that has a semi-Nestorian quality.

Christ is one person having two natures and operations (as is maintained by Constantinople III). However, in the model we are considering, the actions of Christ as man do not reveal the will of God the Son, but only what Jesus as man hopes to be the will he shares in eternally with the Father. In fact, Christ would need to believe that God exists, that God is his Father, and that God has a concrete will regarding history for him to believe in. Such an idea is clearly dualistic since it prohibits the earthly Christ from being epistemologically proportioned so as to know immediately his own identity and will. It also does not permit him an adequate knowledge of the Father's will in each concrete circumstance, such that he can reveal this will to us in each of his human choices and desires. Theologians who wish to affirm uniquely an indirect knowledge of God (and therefore, also the existence of faith) in the historical Christ *and* the *real existence in him of a divine will and identity* must consider the question: how are these two phenomena capable of producing *a unity of personal action* that belongs to the Son of God as its principal source? How can such a theology maintain a unity of cooperation between the divine and human wills of the one Christ? How might it permit us to maintain that Jesus, in each of his concrete human actions, can manifest to us directly the revelation of the Father's will?[46]

Contrary to Weinandy's claim, then, Aquinas's discussion of the grace of the beatific vision in the soul of Christ—which has the Word (and the "divine essence") as its object—is important for a Chalce-

---

46. I do not believe that this dilemma is capable of positive resolution. One option I can see for avoiding a semi-Nestorian dilemma is to assert that the Son of God, *in his incarnate state,* does not know or will in his divine nature, but *only* in his human nature. See, for example, the proposals of Bernard Sesboüé in *Pédagogie du Christ* (Paris: Cerf, 1994), 160–61, following the ideas of Joseph Moingt. Such a kenotic theory of the person of Christ does surely safeguard the unity of his personhood (since he is aware of himself uniquely in a human way, without recourse to his own divine will), but this is attained at the expense of the duality of his natures and wills. Christ seemingly cedes the privileges of his divine nature and will for the interim of his temporal mission, and regains these at the resurrection. Such a kenotic theory implicitly breaks with the confession of faith of Chalcedon concerning the two natures of Christ, and with Constantinople III on the duality of wills. Moreover, it requires the direct negation of the divine aseity and therefore renders itself metaphysically irrational or "nontheistic."

donian theology of the hypostatic union. Aquinas recognizes that the human intellect of Christ is created and as such is infinitely removed from his divine essence. Due to this natural limitation, the humanity of Christ must be subject to an extraordinary grace so that his human spiritual operations adequately attain to his divine life, and consequently bear its impressions in their own activity. So in fact it is the immediate vision that safeguards the unity of activity in the person of Jesus. This particular grace is the condition of possibility of an authentically unified filial consciousness, through which Christ expresses his intra-Trinitarian relationship with the Father, and his true identity, in his human actions.

Weinandy, however, is no doubt correct to insist on the unique character of this vision: it is indeed "filial." As Garrigues points out, not only the human nature but also the *graces* of the humanity of Christ *subsist* in the Word, and thus have a filial *mode* as well. This grace of the vision of Christ, then, while analogous to that grace received in a human person or angel who sees God, is different insofar as it does not give the soul of Christ an awareness of the Trinity as a subject ontologically distinct from himself, but rather permits the Son to know *himself* "objectively" and to understand his own filial personhood in a certain and evidential way.[47]

THE OBEDIENCE AND PRAYER LIFE OF THE SON OF GOD AS EXPRESSIONS OF HIS FILIAL CONSCIOUSNESS

The Intra-Trinitarian Mode of the Human Acts of Christ

Having considered above the principles of theandric cooperation in the action of Jesus, I will now reflect on concrete examples. The analysis can now be applied to actions characteristic of the human nature of the incarnate Word in order to illustrate how these actions reveal

---

47. Garrigues, "La conscience," 43–46. By "objectively" I do not mean "notionally" (since the vision is an intuitive, *immediate* knowledge), but "pertaining to true knowledge of reality."

his divine person. This is particularly evident with respect to Jesus's obedience and his prayer, two activities that do not occur between the uncreated persons of the Trinity per se, and that are proper to created nature, yet that in Christ express something of his filial identity through distinctly human acts.[48] This is only possible due to the correspondence between the human and divine wills of Christ within his *unified* personal action, effectuated by means of the beatific vision. Because the human will of Christ participates in the evidential certitude that he has of his own divine will, shared with the Father, his human acts of obedience and prayer express this certitude in gestures and words. The classical theory of the immediate vision, then, can be seen to be necessary in order to safeguard the personal unity of Christ's obedience and prayer as instrumental, *filial* actions, even while respecting the distinctly human character of these actions. By way of contrast, without this traditional theological teaching, one cannot make adequate sense of the obedience and prayer of Jesus as revelatory of the Trinitarian persons. This being the case, the central objections offered by Galot and Weinandy to the presence of the vision in Christ are unfounded. The Chalcedonian Christology they wish to defend is exemplified in the life and action of the historical Jesus who obeys the Father and prays to the Father, *because he knows immediately* the Father, and acts, even in his human nature, as the Son who proceeds from the Father.

The Obedience of Christ

To refer briefly to this dimension of the incarnation, I will first mention certain aspects of Aquinas's treatment of the *divine* will of Christ in relation to the Father. As can be shown, obedience in Christ, for Aquinas, is the human expression of the divine will that he receives eternally from the Father. Consequently, his prayer life is also a tangible manifestation of the same relation of origination from the Father, expressed in a specifically human way. On the one hand, as has been noted, Christ's human nature (including his intellect and will) takes

---

48. ST III, q. 20, preface. Aquinas notes here that the obedience, prayer, and priesthood of Christ, while being activities of his human nature, express his filial relation with respect to the Father.

on a particular mode because it is the human nature in which the incarnate Word *personally subsists*. However, this nature/mode distinction is also applied by Aquinas in a different but related way to the subsistent hypostasis of God the Son *regarding the divine nature*.[49] In a wholly different and higher way, the divine nature that God the Son receives eternally from the Father through the procession of begetting takes on a particular mode of being (of subsistence) in the person of the Son. Therefore, the divine attributes that the Father and Son share in common (such as wisdom, goodness, eternity, etc.) are present in a unique way in each of the persons of the Trinity. In Jesus this mode of being of the divine nature is that of the subsistent hypostasis of the Son and consequently is the same filial subsistence that informs the human nature of Christ assumed in the incarnation. In other words, the mode of being of Christ's humanity is the very same as the mode of being of his divine nature (even though these two natures are utterly distinct).[50] So for example, the Son subsists in divine eternity as God in a distinctly filial way (as eternally begotten of the Father), even as the Son subsists in his human historical development as man in a filial way (due to the incarnation).[51] But if this is the case with respect to attributes such as the divine eternity, then it is also the case for the divine will, which is an attribute of God's nature common to the three persons of the Trinity. The will of God is

49. ST I, q. 29, aa. 2 and 4. Aquinas's treatment of subsistence in the Trinity is complex and exceeds the scope of this study. Gilles Emery in *Trinity in Aquinas*, 142–44 and 198–206 has examined this aspect of Aquinas's thought in detail. In "Essentialism or Personalism in the Treatise on God in St. Thomas Aquinas?," *The Thomist* 64 (2000): 534, he comments: "One cannot conceive of the person without the substance or without the nature belonging to the very *ratio* of the divine person, this latter being defined as 'distinct subsisting in the divine nature.'"

50. ST I, q. 39, aa. 1–3; ST III, q. 2, a. 2, obj. 1 and 3, ad 1 and 3; III, q. 3, a. 3. This doctrine is also found in Damascene and originates with Maximus the Confessor. See the study of Garrigues, "Le dessein d'adoption du créateur dans son rapport au fils d'après S. Maxime le Confesseur," and the remarks of Christoph von Schönborn, *The Human Face of God* (San Francisco: Ignatius Press, 1994), 113–16.

51. See ST I, q. 42, a. 4, ad 2, concerning the divine attribute of dignity that the Son receives from the Father: "The same essence which in the Father is paternity, in the Son is filiation, so the same dignity which in the Father is paternity, in the Son is filiation. It is thus true to say that the Son possesses whatever dignity the Father has." Similarly, ST I, q. 39, a. 5, ad 1 (wisdom); q. 42, aa. 1–2 and 6 (power, perfection, greatness, and eternity).

present in the person of the Son in a unique way. The Son subsists eternally, having in himself the unique divine will. However, he also has this divine will in a filial mode, since all that he has (even as God) is received eternally through the begetting of the Father and stands in relation to the Father as its principle and source. Commenting on John 5:30 ("I am not seeking my own will, but the will of him who sent me"), Aquinas applies the saying to Christ's divinity:

But do not the Father and the Son have the same will? I answer that the Father and the Son do have the same will, but the Father does not have his will from another whereas the Son does have his will from another, i.e., from the Father. Thus the Son accomplishes his own will as from another, i.e., as having it from another; but the Father accomplishes his own will as his own, i.e., not having it from another.[52]

Because Christ's human nature is united hypostatically to this divine will in its filial mode, the latter must exact upon this nature the expression of its own hypostatic identity: that of God the Son. Because of the union in one subsistent person, the created desires, intentions, and choices of Christ's human will must express the filial character of the divine will that is present in him *personally*.[53] Certainly, his obedience is proper to his created nature, and does not reflect the uncreated relations of the Trinity *per se*.[54] Nevertheless, due to the hypostatic mode in which this obedience is exercised in the person of Christ, it can express through his specifically human acts his filial relativity toward the Father. This is only the case due to the fact that an absolute correspondence exists between the human and divine wills of Christ, a point Aquinas makes implicitly in his commentary on John 5:30:

---

52. *In Ioan.*, V, lect. 5, 798.

53. ST III, q. 18, a. 1, ad 1 and 2.

54. Aquinas insists on the irreducible distinction of natures in Christ. This is why, following Augustine (*De Trin.* I, 7), he claims that in a sense it is necessary to say that Christ "is subject to himself," i.e., subordinates his created will to his divine will (ST III, q. 20, a. 2). He does so, however, in invoking Cyril of Alexandria as a witness to the non-subordination of the hypostasis of Christ with respect to the Father. In ST III, q. 20, a. 1, ad 1 and 2 he notes that obedience as such pertains to Christ's human nature, but is not in him the act of a *creature*. Rather, it is an act of the hypostasis of the Son *in* his human nature. I will return to this topic in some detail below in chapter 6, where I will argue that one can rightly ascribe obedience to the divine *person* of Christ, but not to his divine *nature*.

For there are two wills in our Lord Jesus Christ: one is a divine will, which is the same as the will of the Father; the other is a human will which is proper to himself, just as it is proper to him to be a man. A human will is borne to its own good; but in Christ it was ruled and regulated by right reason, so that it would always be conformed in all things to the divine will. Accordingly he says: "I am not seeking my own will," which as such is inclined to its own good, "but the will of him who sent me," that is, the Father.... If this is carefully considered, the Lord is assigning the true nature of a just judgment, saying: "because I am not seeking my own will." For one's judgment is just when it is passed according to the norm of law. But the divine will is the norm and the law of the created will. And so, the created will and the reason, *which is regulated according to the norm of the divine will,* is just, and its judgment is just. Secondly, this saying is explained as referring it to the Son of God.... Christ as the Divine Word showing the origin of his power. And because judgment in any intellectual nature comes from knowledge, he says significantly, "I judge only as I hear it," i.e., as I have acquired knowledge together with being from the Father, so I judge: "Everything I have heard from my Father I have made known to you" (John 15:5).[55]

The judgments of Christ's ordinary decisions are specified by his prophetic knowledge, such that he is mentally conscious of the will of God for him in a conceptual way. Yet as I have discussed above, the judgment of Christ concerning the will he shares with the Father acquires its *evidential certitude* only through the beatific vision. This knowledge is an essential component, then, of the filial mode of the acts of Christ, because it alone permits the Lord as man to know immediately his own divine will, being moved by it and cooperating with it at each instant. This in turn permits his human will to function *instrumentally* with his divine, personal will as two wills of one subject. By the vision, the man Jesus knows immediately that he receives his divine will from the Father, and his human acts of obedience bear the imprint of this unique filial certitude. Nor can the human obedience of Christ have this same "instrumental mode" without recourse to this knowledge. Without the vision, the man Jesus—moved by faith—could only obey what he *believed and hoped* was *his own* divine will, but his acts would not stem from an evidential knowledge of this will. Consequently, the human obedience of Christ would func-

---

55. *In Ioan.,* V, lect. 5, 796–97 (emphasis added).

tion with a kind of independence, moved by the decision of faith. It
would not manifest Christ's certitude of his own divine will received
eternally from the Father but would instead reflect an autonomous
human desire to act in accordance with the unknown operative will
of God (perceived obscurely and indirectly through the medium of
prophecy). The human obedience and the divine will of Christ would
therefore run on parallel tracks but never touch directly. His human
operations could not be immediately moved by his divine operations
in the unified cooperation of one subject. It follows that even though
Christ as man would subsist in the Word, in his acts of obedience he
would seek in faith to obey himself in his divine nature.

We must conclude, then, that a Chalcedonian Christology, which
wishes (following Cyril, Maximus, and John Damascene) to affirm
the instrumental unity of Christ's human actions with those of his divine will, should affirm the presence in his humanity of the beatific
vision as well. The actions of his distinct, created nature are subordinate to and expressive of his divine personhood through the medium of his immediate knowledge of his divine filial will. In this way his
identity as the Son of God who is doing the work of the Father at all
times (Jn 5:18–19) can be expressed in a filial mode through human
voluntary submission to the paternal will.

The Prayer of Jesus to the Father

Analogous things can be said about the prayer life of Christ. Why
does Christ pray if he already has the vision of God and knows that
he and the Father will be "victorious over the world"?[56] First, as Aquinas makes clear, Christ's prayer is an expression of his created, dependent nature, and does not pertain to his divine nature.[57] Consequently, it does not imply an eternal subordination or obedience within the
uncreated Trinity. Yet this prayer is expressive of an intra-Trinitarian

---

56. Cf. Jn 16:33.
57. ST III, q. 21, a. 1: "Prayer is the unfolding of our will to God, that He may fulfill
it. If, therefore, there had been but one will in Christ, viz. the Divine, it would nowise
belong to Him to pray, since the Divine will of itself is effective of whatever He wishes
by it.... But because the Divine and the human wills are distinct in Christ, and the human will of itself is not efficacious enough to do what it wishes, except by Divine power,
hence to pray belongs to Christ as man and as having a human will."

relation. It reveals to us the relation that the person of the Son has with respect to the Father: Jesus receives all that he is and has, both as God and man, from the Father as his origin.

Being both God and man [Christ] wished to offer prayers to the Father, not as though He were incompetent, but for our instruction ... *that He might show Himself to be from the Father,* hence he says (John 11:42: "Because of the people who stand about I have said it [i.e., the words of the prayer], that they may believe that Thou has sent Me").... Christ wished to pray to His Father in order to give us an example of praying; and also to show that His Father is the author [*auctor*] *both of His eternal procession in the Divine nature, and of all the good that He possesses in the human nature.*[58]

Significant in this respect is the fact that, in praying, Christ does not regard himself (the Word) as an object to whom he offers petitions. He does not adore the Trinity.[59] Rather, the scriptural evidence suggests that his prayer is directed to the Father: it is primarily, therefore, a human mode of expression of his intra-Trinitarian filial identity. It can only be this because of the perfection of the prayer of Christ: it mirrors the will of the Father, due to the fact that Christ's heart is always "in the Father."[60] For Aquinas, then, Christ's exemplarity in prayer is not a kind of docetic play-acting, but a human expression and enactment of his eternal relation to the Father, meant to reveal to

58. ST III, q. 21, a. 1 and a. 3, respectively (emphasis added).

59. I differ on this point from those who would attribute to Aquinas the idea that Jesus adores the three persons of the Trinity in his human soul. To the best of my knowledge there are not texts to support this view (which resembles Scotus's doctrine) in Aquinas's writings. Aquinas never ascribes either *adoratio* or *latria* to Christ as a subject in relation to the Father as object or to himself as object. It seems, rather, that devotion in Christ receives a peculiar mode that is hypostatic. It is a recognition by the Son *in his human nature* of having the Father as the origin of his divine and human natures. As with obedience and prayer, therefore, it designates the procession of the Son from the Father in human terms, and demonstrates that Christ receives the impetus of all his actions from the Father. Diepen ("La psychologie humaine du Christ selon saint Thomas d'Aquin," 540) envisages the prayer of Christ as directed to all of the three persons as objects, citing as his authority Thomassin, *De Verbo Incarnato,* lec. 9, c. 11. Diepen's inconsistency on this point, with regard to his own teaching that there is no "psychological autonomy" (535–56) of a unique *human* subject in Christ, is evident. In my opinion the position of Diepen on this point would justly incur the objections of Weinandy concerning an implicit Nestorianism by attributing to the human Christ an adoration of the Word.

60. Jn 14:8–11.

us that all things are received from the Father. His prayer initiates us into an analogous "Trinitarian" relationship as sons of the Father adopted by grace.

In light of what has been said above, however, it is clear that Christ as man could not prayerfully recognize his origin from the Father *with evidential certitude* without the beatific vision. Even though his prayer is conceptual, this conceptuality participates in the immediate knowledge of the Father's will imparted by the vision. This in turn permits his human intellect and will to cooperate instrumentally with his divine, personal will as the two wills of one subject. By the vision, the man Jesus knows who he is and what he wills as God, and his human acts of prayer bear the immediate imprint of this knowledge. As such the prayer of Christ attains a unique, filial mode. It reflects through specifically human acts his personal recognition as the Son of God that he receives all things from the Father. This is why, even in praying for those things that his intercession would merit, Christ was acting in accordance with the plan he foresaw in light of the Father's will, a will he shared in his divine nature.[61]

Could this form of "instrumental" revelatory prayer be possible uniquely by means of prophetic knowledge in the soul of Christ, lived out in faith? In this case the man Jesus would lack evidential knowledge of the will he receives eternally from the Father. His prayer would therefore not be moved immediately by his filial will as the Son of God, but would express instead the desire in his human heart to do the will of God which he only believed that he shared eternally with

61. ST III, q. 21, a. 1, ad 3. Aquinas cites Damascene's *De Fide Orth.*, III, c. 24, agreeing with the latter that Christ did not "raise his mind to God" in the sense of progressively acquiring knowledge of God through prayer because he possessed the "blessed vision" of God. However, because of this grace, Christ's mind was always raised up to the contemplation of the divine nature and was moved in accordance with the divine will. Christ therefore prayed for things that he knew would be merited by his prayer (ST III, q. 21, a. 1, ad 2). This does not mean, however, that his natural will and his human psychology (i.e., sensuality) were not revolted by the imminence of torture and death. On the contrary, Christ could overcome these natural reactions only by his "deliberate will," under the movement of the divine initiative in the heights of his soul (ST III, q. 21, a. 2; a. 4, ad 1). The fact that his rational will was naturally repulsed by the prospect of death at Gethsemane does not imply a struggle of faith concerning the divine will, but a rational desire to overcome the natural fears of death that are proper to being human in order to obey the divine will (see ST III, q. 18, a. 5, especially corp. and ad 3).

the Father. Therefore, his prayer would operate on a parallel track to his divine will, without direct contact. It could no longer manifest to us an immediate awareness that he receives all things from the Father as Son. Instead of taking on this "Trinitarian form," then, the prayer of Christ would seemingly acquire a kind of human autonomy of operation, imploring in faith the divine activity of the Trinity that transcended the scope of its knowledge. It is difficult to resist the conclusion that Christ in his divine nature and activity would become an object of petition for Christ in his human nature and activity. Here again, then, the need for the vision of the divine will in the human soul of the Son is manifest: only this can bring into perfect accord the cooperation of the human and divine wills of Christ in his concrete agency as the Son of God. The unity of the person of Jesus is manifest in his prayer because this action reveals his immediate awareness that "all things come from the Father" (cf. Jn 13:3).

This leads to a final objection. True prayer implies desire, but could Christ really have desired anything in his earthly state if he possessed the vision of God? Desire suggests an incompleteness, an absence, and therefore also broaches upon the problem of Jesus's true suffering and the privations imposed by his historical condition. As Galot poignantly objects, could a Jesus who possessed the immediate vision of God have suffered in reality in the ways that the Gospels themselves suggest? Could he truly have desired some state of affairs other than that to which he was immediately subject? Could a Jesus with the vision of God have implored the Father during his crucifixion?

As Jean-Pierre Torrell has demonstrated, Aquinas was innovative in rendering a theological account of the fully human character of the experiential knowledge of Christ even against the tendencies of his theological age and environment.[62] This perspective was present in a particular way in his understanding of the existence of the beatific vision of the historical Christ. This vision, according to Aquinas, was a grace accorded to the humanity of Christ for the purposes of his soteriological mission. Consequently, it was regulated by a particular economy of grace, or *dispensatio*, proper to the earthly life of the

---

62. Jean-Pierre Torrell, "Le savoir acquis du Christ selon les théologiens médiévaux," *Revue Thomiste* 101 (2001): 355–408.

incarnate Son of God.[63] As Torrell shows, Aquinas explicitly applies this notion to *the way in which* the vision of God existed in the soul of Christ *in his earthly life*:[64]

From the natural relationship which flows between the soul and the body, glory flows into the body from the soul's glory. Yet the natural relationship in Christ was subject to the will of His Godhead, and thereby it came to pass that the beatitude remained in the soul, and did not flow into the body; but the flesh suffered what belongs to a passible nature.[65]

Far from deriving uniquely from a non-scriptural principle of perfection, then, this dimension of Aquinas's thought takes into consideration precisely the spiritual needs of the human Christ for the purposes of his saving mission. Among these is the need of the Son to know indefectibly in his human nature the will of the Father (which the Son receives eternally from him) so as to express it in a human way.[66] Yet this grace also coexists simultaneously with the natural

63. Aquinas uses the term *dispensatio* as a Latin expression of the Greek concept of *oikonomia* (divine government). As is well known, Aquinas understands the redemption of fallen man as the teleological purpose of the incarnation (see ST III, q. 1, a. 1). This "redemptive" logic of divine government therefore affects not only *why* the incarnation took place, but also *how*. For example, so that he could merit salvation for humanity through the crucifixion, Christ assumed a human nature without sin but simultaneously capable of physical, emotional, and spiritual suffering as well as corporeal death (see ST III, qq. 14–15).

64. Cf. Torrell, "St. Thomas d'Aquin et la science du Christ," 400–401. Cf. ST III, q. 14, a. 1, ad 2; q. 15, a. 5, ad 3; q. 45, a. 2; q. 46, a. 8.

65. ST III, q. 14, a. 1, ad 2.

66. Throughout this chapter I have emphasized the teachings of the Johannine theology of Christ. However, a number of texts from the Synoptic tradition also describe Christ referring (implicitly but evidently) to his divine will in his concrete human actions. See, for example, Mt 11:25–27 ("Yes Father such has been your gracious will. All things have been handed over to me by my Father"); Lk 10:18–20 ("I have given you the power to tread on scorpions"); and Lk 13:34–35 ("Jerusalem, I yearned to gather your children together"). In all of these cases Jesus expresses in his human desires his divine identity and will. He does not have to ponder the nature of this will through a consideration of prophetic revelation. This can only be the case because, in the unity of his subjective action, he knows in an immediate human way his own divine power, identity, and will. The Synoptic miracle tradition is particularly eloquent in this regard. Mt 8:2–3: "And then a leper approached, did him homage, and said, 'Lord, if you wish, you can make me clean.' He stretched out his hand, touched him, and said, '*I will do it*. Be made clean.' His leprosy was cleansed immediately." See also Mt 9:27–29, Mk 2:5–12, and Lk 8:22–24.

possibility of experiential learning as well as terrible physical and mental suffering.[67] This means that for Aquinas, what is denoted in contemporary parlance by the "psychology of Christ" (his imagination, emotions, ideas, etc.) is not structurally changed by Christ's extraordinary knowledge of his own divine identity, will, and mission. Once again, the human faculties of Christ are not affected in their natural *specification*, but only in their *mode of exercise*.[68] They are fully natural but in their concrete exercise they are organized from within by a higher spiritual awareness that Christ has of his transcendent identity, will, and mission. This means that they retain all of their natural vulnerability.

Consequently, for Aquinas, the prayer of Christ in a very real sense is a genuine expression of the historical character of his consciousness and of his real submission to the contingent circumstances of providence. Christ could and did hope for his own deliverance (through resurrection) from the terrible spiritual and sensible experiences of suffering and death. He also hoped for the future establishment of the church among his followers, and for their eventual earthly mission and heavenly glorification.[69] The fact that he foresaw these realities in the heights of his soul was not a substitute for his more or-

67. ST III, q. 19, a. 1. In ST III, q. 46, aa. 7–8, Aquinas follows Damascene (*De Fide Orth.*, III, c. 19) in underscoring the economic mode of Christ's experience of the passion. Spiritual and physical agony were permitted to coexist with the pacifying beatitude of immediate knowledge of the Father and of the divine will. In counter-distinction from the beatific vision in the life of the glorified Christ and of the blessed, the *mode* of the beatific vision in the earthly life of Christ is such that it affects only the "heights of the soul," that is to say, uniquely the operations of intellect and will in their direct relation to the divine nature. This extraordinary knowledge presupposes, respects, and integrates the natural order of Christ's human thinking, feeling, and sensing without changing its essential structure. An excellent analysis of this point is made by Colman O'Neill ("The Problem of Christ's Human Autonomy," 234–37). See also Édouard-Henri Weber, *Le Christ selon saint Thomas d'Aquin* (Paris: Desclée, 1988), 179–98. Garrigues has extended this principle, showing how it applies for Aquinas to the "infused science" of Christ, which is "habitual" and in potency to know all that can be known (ST III, q. 9, a. 3), but in act uniquely with respect to those things Christ must know for the sake of his mission (ST III, q. 11, a. 5, obj. 2, corp. and ad 2). See Garrigues, "La conscience," 47–51. As Garrigues points out, this teaching is mirrored in the recent *Catechism of the Catholic Church*, paras. 473–74, with reference to Mk 13:32 and Acts 1:7.

68. ST III, q. 19, a. 1, ad 3.

69. A point Aquinas makes clearly in analyzing the desires of Christ: ST III, q. 21, a. 3, corp., ad 2 and 3; see also q. 7, a. 4.

dinary human way of thinking and feeling about them: the latter co-existed with this higher knowledge.[70] Thus his vision was not a consolation for the absence of the human experience of these specific objects of desire. In fact, it could be the source of an existential dissatisfaction: the desire for something known to be in the future but as yet unattained. This was particularly acute with respect to Christ's hope for the reconciliation of human persons with God.[71]

What conclusion is to be drawn from these reflections concerning the claims of Galot and Weinandy? On the one hand, we see that St. Thomas's treatment of the human will of Christ permits us to take seriously the specifically human character of the willing of Jesus manifest in his obedience and prayer. On the other hand, it also accounts for the filial mode of this same voluntary activity in the human Christ. Therefore, it allows us to take seriously the historical contingency of the man Jesus in the limitations of his human historical state even while simultaneously insisting on the way in which his human nature reveals intra-Trinitarian relations between the Son and the Father. Only because of Aquinas's key distinction between the nature and mode of Christ's human activity is this insight available. At the same time, this operational correlation in Jesus between his human will and the will of the Father with whom he is in relation in his personal acts can itself only occur through the medium of an immediate knowledge of his own identity and divine will. Because this is the case, the Trinitarian intelligibility of the obedience and prayer of Christ requires that the immediate vision of God be present in Christ. Only this grace can effectuate the personal unity of the action of Jesus in and through a differentiation of natures so that the di-

---

70. This is Aquinas's point in insisting on the simultaneous existence in Christ of both an immediate knowledge of God and an "experiential, acquired knowledge" of his human surroundings. Cf. ST III, q. 12, a. 2, where he notes his change of mind on this issue with respect to the earlier position of *III Sent.*, d. 14, a. 3.

71. Cf. Lk 13:34, 23:34; Jn 17:1, 5, 15–24. This principle is illustrated most acutely in Jn 17:24: "Father, I desire that they also, whom thou hast given me, may be with me where I am, to behold my glory which thou hast given me in thy love for me before the foundation of the world." The clear indication is that Christ actually beholds in his human nature the glory he has eternally from the Father and that he simultaneously desires this glory to be shared in by his disciples. This prayer therefore both expresses a filial awareness of an identity received from the Father and an unfulfilled desire on behalf of the disciples, which motivates Christ to suffer the forthcoming passion.

vine will of the Son of God is revealed to us instrumentally, through Christ's human action. Only because of this grace do these activities in the consciousness of Christ appear in all of their "Chalcedonian" integrity. If we deny the existence of this grace, in light of what has been said above, then we make the filial and instrumental character of the obedience and prayer of Christ unintelligible.

CONCLUSION

In these brief observations I have argued (following a host of recent commentators) that Aquinas's theology of Christ bears within it significant resources for treating the contemporary challenge of a theological reflection on "the consciousness of Christ." Contrary to the claims of Galot and Weinandy, I do not believe that a Thomistic account of the presence of the beatific vision in Christ falls into the extremes of either Monophysitism or Nestorianism. On the contrary, the Thomistic understanding of this grace is central to an integral Christology that avoids either of these errors. The inner life of Jesus, as this chapter has suggested following Herman Diepen, is to some extent irreducibly different from our own. There is no pure similitude between his self-awareness and ours due to the fact that his human self-awareness is that of the incarnate Word. However, all that is human in Christ flourishes under the influence of grace, and his human actions are more perfect than our own precisely because of the presence in this humanity of the transcendent personhood of God. The immediate knowledge of God (or the beatific vision) is a necessary element of his humanity due to the duality of natures that are present in the life of the Son of God and their simultaneous cooperation in one personal subject. Only through this vision can the human actions of Jesus acquire their particular filial character as "instrumental" actions of the Son of God. Theologians who wish to reconsider this classical teaching of the church must face the real challenge of explaining how, in the absence of this vision, the unity of the theandric acts of Christ may properly be maintained.

Part Two

The Mystery of the
Redemption

6

The Obedience
of the Son

The first half of this book examined the mystery of the incarnation. What does it mean to say that Jesus of Nazareth is the incarnate Lord? The second half examines the mystery of the redemption. What does it mean to say that Jesus of Nazareth is the crucified Lord? The considerations of this part of the book proceed in two main parts. Chapters 6–8 examine Aquinas's understanding of the obedience, passion, and death of Christ, each in conversation with modern kenotic Christology. The modern kenotic tradition has focused upon the Paschal mystery as the primary locus of Trinitarian revelation. It is at the cross that the inner life of God is revealed to humanity. This tradition has done so, however, while simultaneously emphasizing that the suffering and dereliction of Christ are not only indicative of his personal identity but also of the inner nature of the Godhead (the divine nature of Christ). In these chapters I seek to sketch out a plausible Thomistic alternative to the modern tradition. This Thomistic account, while respectful of the strengths of modern kenoticism, is ultimately rooted in the traditional Chalcedonian account of Christ that was articulated in the first half of this book.

The second section below (chapters 9 and 10) considers the descent into hell and resurrection of Christ, engaging the modern theological perspectives of Balthasar and Ratzinger, respectively. The goal here is to examine in some depth the eschatological and anthropological issues raised by modern Catholic Christology. What does it mean to say that Christ experienced the separation of body and soul at death? What happened to the soul of Christ in the period of time between his death and resurrection? What does it mean to say that the spiritual soul and physical body of Christ were reunited in the mystery of the resurrection and glorification of the physical body of Jesus? In the first half of this book, close attention was paid to classical notions of divine and human nature, in the service of a Chalcedonian Christology. In this second half, close attention is paid to the divine and human natures in the mystery of the passion. What does it mean for the divinity of Christ to say that Christ obeyed, suffered, and died? What does it mean for the humanity of Christ (and our humanity by extension) to say that Christ descended into hell and rose from the dead?

It makes sense to begin with the obedience of Christ as a way into the consideration of his passion, death, and resurrection. Theological attention to the theme of Christ's obedience is of course traditional, and is found in the earliest of Pauline motifs: the hymn of the Epistle to the Philippians (2:6–11). There the obedience of Christ is seen as the inner essence of the human redemptive act of Christ. "Being found in human form, he became obedient, even unto death." It is also the formal motive for the resurrection of Christ from the dead. "Therefore, God has highly exalted him, and given him the name above every other name." The study of the obedience of Christ is certainly therefore of central importance in classical eastern and western Christian theology.[1] As I have noted in chapter 5, Aquinas studies this question in *Summa theologiae* III, q. 20, a text I will return to below.

All of this being said, however, the treatment of the obedience of Christ in modern theology has been qualified by a different accent. This accent almost inevitably can be traced back, in its sources, to a major theme developed by Karl Barth in his mature Christol-

---

1. See in this respect the study of Guy Mansini, "Can Humility and Obedience be Trinitarian Realities?" in *Aquinas and Barth: An Unofficial Catholic-Protestant Dialogue*, eds. Bruce L. McCormack and Thomas Joseph White (Grand Rapids, Mich.: Eerdmans, 2013), 71–98.

ogy. In *Church Dogmatics* IV, 1, section 59, Karl Barth seeks to found a theology of redemption upon the crucifixion of Christ as an intra-Trinitarian event. In doing so he posits a "divine obedience" of God the Son in relation to God the Father, expressed in human form through the obedience and humility of Christ.[2] The idea has become a *locus classicus* for modern Trinitarian theology, as subsequent thinkers like Balthasar, Moltmann, and Jüngel have all drawn inspiration from this text in their own writing.[3] I will examine in chapter 9, for example, Balthasar's interpretation of the descent of Christ into hell. Balthasar sees in Christ's obedience even unto damnation the expression of an outpoured love that is proper to the inner life of the Trinity. The influence of Barth's theology is, therefore, vivid, even in modern Catholic theology. Yet Barth's claim that the obedience of God the Son is the "inner side of the mystery of the divine nature of Christ"[4] also raises important questions. How consistent is Barth's notion with the classical perspectives of Nicene-Chalcedonian Christology? Does his theological vision in fact import distinctly creaturely characteristics into the life of God? Does it adequately respect the unity of the Trinitarian God?

As a way of responding to these questions, I will examine in this chapter two basic ideas in Barth's treatment of divine obedience in CD IV, 1, section 59. The first is his affirmation that God is able to exist in the man Jesus Christ as one who is humble and obedient and that he does this without ceding his immutability, eternity, and omnipotence. In other words, God can take on the attributes of lowliness and service without ceasing to be the sovereign Lord of his cre-

2. See Barth, CD IV, 1, 157–357.

3. For Jürgen Moltmann's dependence upon this text, see *The Crucified God*, 200–278, especially 202–4 which leads off Moltmann's core reflection in the book. Balthasar's work is deeply influenced by Barth's theology of divine obedience. See *Mysterium Paschale: The Mystery of Easter*, trans. A. Nichols (San Francisco: Ignatius Press, 1990), 79–83; *The Glory of the Lord: A Theological Aesthetics* Vol. I: *Seeing the Form*, trans. E. Leiva-Merikakis (San Francisco: Ignatius, 1982), 478–80; *Theodrama: Theological Dramatic Theory* Vol. V: *The Last Act*, trans. G. Harrison (San Francisco: Ignatius, 1998), 236–39. Eberhard Jüngel's *God's Being Is in Becoming; The Trinitarian Being of God in the Theology of Karl Barth*, trans. J. Webster (Grand Rapids, Mich.: Eerdmans, 2001) adopts the perspective of this text systematically.

4. CD IV, 1, 193.

ation. The second idea is that obedience, found in the man Jesus, in fact has its condition of possibility in a transcendent "pre-temporal" obedience in the immanent life of the Trinity. God the Son is in some sense eternally obedient to God the Father, and this is the ontological presupposition for the incarnation.

I will argue that the first of these ideas can be understood as profoundly consistent with a classical understanding of Chalcedonian Christology (represented here by Aquinas). I will argue that the second idea, however, is problematic for two reasons. As it is stated by Barth, the theory seems to suggest that obedience characterizes the *procession* of the Son from the Father.[5] If this is the case, then the positing of such obedience in God renders obscure the confession of the unity of the divine will and power of God. Consequently, it would also make problematic the affirmation of a divine immutable omnipotence present in the incarnate Son. If this is the case, then, the second idea of Barth is in some real tension with the first one mentioned above, resulting in a kind of Trinitarian antinomy. There is an inevitable discord between the affirmation that the eternal, wise, and omnipotent God became human, and the affirmation that there is obedience within the very life of God that characterizes the person of the Son as distinct from the Father.

A more benign (re)interpretation of Barth's pre-temporal obedience is possible, however. If we understand the Son's "pre-temporal obedience" as pertaining to his *mission* to become incarnate, received from the Father, then continuity between Barth's two ideas is possible. According to classical Nicene orthodoxy, God the Word receives and possesses from the Father the unique divine nature, power, and will of God from all eternity. This personal relationality of the Word implies a receptivity of the divine nature without any ontological subordination or dependence. Extrapolating from this view one can affirm that the Son's divine receptivity is the transcendent ontological foundation for his temporal mission among human beings. It is the

---

5. In this chapter I employ the term "procession" in the broader Latin sense of *processio,* applicable to both the generation of the Word and the spiration of the Holy Spirit. However, this is without prejudice to the legitimate eastern Orthodox concern to interpret the biblical and patristic Greek notion of *ekporeusis* (procession) as pertaining uniquely to the spiration of the Holy Spirit from the Father.

Son as God who wills to become incarnate, yet he wills this mission not only with but also *from* the Father. Because this receptivity (as proceeding from the Father) characterizes his very person, he can be obedient *in and through his human actions* in a characteristically filial way, that is to say, as the *Son* made man. His human obedience thus reveals his eternal, personal relativity to the Father.

This latter perspective does not imply any real multiplicity of wills in God, nor an obedience in God according to his divine nature. It certainly does not imply ontological dependency of the creator with regard to the creature. Rather, it predicates obedience to the pre-incarnate Word uniquely in a figurative or metaphorical sense, as denoting improperly what is in fact the transcendent divine receptivity proper to eternal generation. Despite the fact that this Thomistic interpretation contradicts some of Barth's explicit statements, it nevertheless renders some of Barth's influential intuitions more internally coherent, and permits an interpretation of his theology more consistent with the classical Christological tradition.

OBEDIENCE IN
GOD WITHOUT DIVINE
SELF-ALIENATION

God in Christ has revealed himself as one who is obedient. Therefore, divine obedience exists in God. These are affirmations which Barth establishes in CD IV, 1, section 59 by recourse to an epistemological principle and a principle of the divine economy. The epistemological principle is his insistence that the obedience of Christ is a unique locus of revelation which must in turn critically regulate any other concepts of God. The God of the New Testament alone has revealed himself as one who chose in his freedom to become obedient and humble in the man Jesus. Correspondingly, then, there can be no epistemological warrant in "alien" speculation as to whether God is *able* to exist in this "lowly" way *in himself.* He is free to do it because he has done it.[6] The second principle is related: what God has done in Christ, through the temporal economy of the servant Jesus, reveals

---

6. See these points in CD IV, 1, 159, 163–64, 176–77, 186–87.

who God is in his very being. Consequently, the humility and obedience of the Son of God as man manifest to us that a divine lowliness exists in God, in his mode of being as Son.[7]

Second, however, God is also able to do this without relinquishing in any way the prerogative of his divine sovereignty. The latter implies a divine transcendence, constancy (or immutability), and omnipotence, all of which characterize God's dynamic relationship to creation as its Lord. His obedience made manifest in Christ, therefore, entails no contradiction with respect to such attributes. On the contrary, God can humble himself without ceding his sovereign freedom and without ceasing to be God.[8] It is important to note that Barth frequently restates this point in soteriological terms: God is revealed in Jesus as one who is free to be God-with-us, who can truly enter our sphere of life as a servant and in humility. Yet precisely in order to reconcile us with himself (in his Lordship), God can and must do this while remaining truly himself. More to the point, it is because he is not alienated from his divine prerogatives (of eternity, omnipotence, etc.) that he can act dynamically and authoritatively in

7. CD IV, 1, 177: "Who the true God is, and what He is, i.e., what is His being as God ... [including] His divine nature ... all this we have to discover from the fact that as such he is very man and a partaker of human nature, from His becoming man.... For— to put it more pointedly, the mirror in which it can be known (and is known) that He is God, and of the divine nature, is His becoming flesh and His existence in the flesh.... From the point of view of the obedience of Jesus Christ as such, fulfilled in that astonishing form [i.e., his human obedience unto death], it is a matter of the mystery of the inner being of God as the being of the Son in relation to the Father." Although Aquinas would certainly disagree with Barth's prohibitions on any natural, philosophical knowledge of God, these two principles can be reformulated succinctly in Thomistic terms: (1) An agent is known by its effects, and consequently God as an unknowable transcendent agent is known in a unique way by his actions and effects of grace. (2) The revelatory agency of God *ad extra* reveals (imperfectly but truly) who he is *ad intra*. For more on this latter principle in Barth, see Paul Molnar, *Divine Freedom and the Doctrine of the Immanent Trinity* (Edinburgh: T. & T. Clark, 2002), 128–34.

8. CD IV, 1, 186–87: "As God was in Christ, far from being against Himself, or at disunity with Himself, He has put into effect the freedom of His divine love, the love in which He is divinely free. He has therefore done and revealed that which corresponds to his divine nature. His immutability does not stand in the way of this. It must not be denied, but this possibility is included in His unalterable being. He is absolute, infinite, exalted, active, impassible, transcendent, but in all this He is the One who loves in freedom ... and therefore not His own prisoner." On the same page Barth also mentions the eternity of the deity of Christ.

Christ in order to save human beings effectively. And in choosing in particular to assume suffering and obedience as a way to save humanity, God has in fact offered the distinctively Christian evidence of his authentic power and dynamic freedom as savior and creator.[9]

There is no doubt that this first idea concerning a divine obedience takes on a paradoxical form of expression in Barth's writing. Yet the prescribed view of the *Church Dogmatics* in IV, 1 on this point is also in substantive continuity with the classical Christological tradition of Chalcedon. To show this, we can make a brief comparison between Barth and Aquinas. Here I will note three relevant parallels between the two theologians.

First, Aquinas follows the Chalcedonian tradition in ascribing all properties and actions of both the divine and human natures of Christ to their one and only concrete subject, who is the incarnate Son of God.[10] This logical pattern of ascription follows upon an ontological foundation: it is the hypostasis of Christ who is the principle of unity in the incarnation. Because the Son exists as both God and man, his subsistent, personal being is the ground of attribution of all predications, both human and divine. The concrete subject is that one who is truly God, who is this obedient man, etc., because the subject is the Son, the God-man who operates dynamically in and through two natures.[11]

9. CD IV, 1, 185 and 187: "Of what value would His deity be to us, if it came to be outside of Him as He became ours? What would be the value to us of His way into the far country [of our humanity] if in the course of it He lost Himself? ... His omnipotence is that of a divine plenitude of power in the fact that ... it can assume the form of weakness and impotence *and do so as omnipotence, triumphing in this form*" (emphasis added).

10. ST III, q. 16, a. 1: "Now of every suppositum of any nature we may truly and properly predicate a word signifying that nature in the concrete, as *man* may properly and truly be predicated of Socrates and Plato. Hence, since the Person of the Son of God for whom this word *God* stands, is a suppositum of human nature, this word *man* may be truly and properly predicated of this word *God*, as it stands for the Person of the Son of God" (translation slightly modified; emphasis added).

11. ST III, q. 16, a. 4: "[The Nestorians] granted that Christ was born of a Virgin, and that He was from eternity; but they did not say that God was born of a virgin, or that the Man was from eternity. Catholics on the other hand maintained that words which are said of Christ either in His Divine or in His human nature may be said either of God or of man.... The reason of this is that, since there is one hypostasis of both natures, the same hypostasis is signified by the name of either nature. Thus whether we say *man* or *God*, the hypostasis of Divine and human nature is signified. And therefore ... of God may be said what belongs to the human nature, as of a hypostasis of human nature."

Second, for Aquinas this dynamic activity of God in the man Jesus cannot entail any loss or curtailment of the prerogatives of the divine nature. The reason for this is that the union is hypostatic rather than natural, such that the "essential characteristics" of the divine and human natures of God remain distinguishable. It also follows for the same reason that for Aquinas there is no *contradiction* implied by paradoxical phrases such as "the impassible One suffers" or "the sovereign Lord obeys and is humbled." This is the case because such seemingly contrary attributes are not attributed directly to one another. (To be so they would have to be predicated of each other abstractly!) Nor, however, are they predicated of the unique subject of Christ *under the same aspect*, but rather to the same subject *under different aspects*, by virtue of the two natures in which the Son of God *exists*.[12] The contraries of obedience and omnipotence both exist in the unique being of God the Son made man (as do, for St. Thomas, impassibility and suffering). Yet they subsist in a unique subject without existing under the same natural aspect. To say, therefore, that there is obedience in the very being of God the Son is entirely warranted, according to this form of Chalcedonian predication of attributes.

Thirdly, one might even admit the phrase, "the divine nature has assumed a human nature into itself," so long as the claim is rightly qualified. This qualification would need to be twofold, pertaining to efficient and final causality respectively. To say that the divine nature is *able* to unite itself with human obedience and suffering is true for Aquinas first insofar as this refers to God's *capacity* (by virtue of his omnipotence) to take a human nature into God's very *existence*. However, since this union does not entail any alteration of God's transcendent and ineffable nature, one must inquire into the mode of this assumption. Here, a teleological qualification is required. The deity is able to assume human obedience into itself in a hypostatic mode of being, or "enhypostatically," to use Barth's terminology. That is to say, "the divine nature can assume human obedience into itself *personally*" in God's mode of being as Son.[13] It does so without in any way

12. ST III, q. 16, a. 4, ad 1: "It is impossible for contraries to be predicated of the same in the same respects, but nothing prevents their being predicated *of the same in different aspects*. And thus contraries are predicated of Christ, not in the same but in different natures" (emphasis added).

13. This conceptual interpretation can be found in ST III, q. 3, aa. 3–4. The idea has

diminishing itself in its divine prerogatives of immutability, omnipotence, eternity, etc.

Does this perspective correlate profoundly with Barth's own affirmations, or is such an attempt at conciliation artificially irenic? It is true
that Barth's work contains no distinct development of a "Christian philosophy" of existence as the basis for his enhypostatic explanations of
the incarnation, nor does he present an explicit study of logical regula-
tions governing the communication of idioms. Nevertheless, his densely ontological Christology does clearly parallel Aquinas's Chalcedonian
reflections on each of the above-mentioned points.

The first parallel is evident in Barth's affirmation of an irreducible diversity of "essences" in Christ, united enhypostatically in the
Son incarnate (or in Barth's language, in God's mode of being as Son).
Barth insists that God the Son in Christ is a unique agent always acting in and through two distinguishable natures.[14] Even in the dynamic unity of the being of Christ, a transcendence of the divine essence

---

recently been studied by Gilles Emery in his "The Personal Mode of Trinitarian Action
in Saint Thomas Aquinas," *The Thomist* 69 (2005): 31–77, especially 47–48.

14. It is true that Barth also seems to posit one unique subject in God, who is present as Father, Son, and Holy Spirit in three modes. Yet he also clearly wishes to maintain
the Cyrillian insistence on the unity of Christ as a personal agent. This point of view is
thematic in CD IV, 2, section 64. Clear indications of it are found in CD IV, 1, 183. Correspondingly, Barth distances himself at points from classical Lutheran orthodoxy's use
of the communication of idioms. The seventeenth-century Lutheran schools of Giessen
and Tübingen, for example, presupposed a certain communication of properties of the
divine nature to the human nature due to the grace of the hypostatic union. They then
disputed whether one might affirm that the historical Jesus during his earthly life was in
fact omnipresent and omnipotent in creation *as man* and whether these attributes were
ceded during this time or merely veiled. See CD IV, 1, 180–82 for Barth's description of
this controversy, where he ultimately refuses any such perspective by refusing the principle upon which both sides of the controversy are predicated. This is more readily apparent in CD IV, 2, 76–80, where he goes on to discuss what he terms the Lutheran
theory of a *genus majestaticum* in which divine attributes such as impassibility and omnipotence are communicated to the human nature of Jesus in glory by virtue of the incarnation, and again reaches the same conclusions. In CD IV, 2, 73–76, Barth appeals to
a Reformed doctrine of the communication of idioms very similar to that of Aquinas,
and distinguishes this from what he takes to be the above-mentioned perspectives. He
cites the pithy formula of Polanus, the seventeenth-century Reformed thinker: "Propri-
etates utriusque naturae Christi personae ipsi communicantur. Quae enim naturis sin-
gulis sunt propria, ea personae Christi sunt communia." Bruce McCormack has recently explained very clearly aspects of Barth's thought on these matters in his "Karl Barth's
Christology as a Resource for a Reformed Version of Kenoticism," 243–47.

and subordination of the human essence remain. While on earth, God acts historically through his humanity as the "instrument" or "organ" of salvation. Even when the man Jesus is exalted and glorified at the ascension, his human characteristics cannot partake of or be identified with some of the characteristics he possesses uniquely by virtue of his divine essence (as omnipotent, omnipresent, etc.).[15] Correspondingly, the operations of the divine nature of Christ remain distinct from those of his human essence during the time of his earthly life. Arguably, therefore, according to Barth the Word of God continues to operate in all creation even while being historically present in the limited human agency of Jesus.[16]

Second, Barth refuses what he deems a Hegelian theory of the incarnation whereby the human attributes of the man Jesus exist in God in some form of contradiction with the prerogatives of the divine nature. He explicitly refuses the idea that there can be any contradiction in the life and being of God.[17] Yet if obedience can exist in

15. For Aquinas's doctrine of theandric actions of the Son, which transpire in and through two co-operative natures, see ST III, qq. 18–19. He specifies in q. 16, a. 5, ad 3 that the human nature, as an instrument of the Son's person, does participate in the divine nature by the derivation of the effects of the latter. However, because certain attributes of God can in no way be transmitted to created reality they are not participated in by the human essence of Christ. Here he specifically refers to omnipotence as such an unparticipated characteristic. Barth alludes to what is at least in certain ways an analogous doctrine with regard to the humanity of Christ as the organ of the divine nature in CD IV, 2, 70 and 97. And he develops an explicit doctrine of non-reciprocal mutual participation between the divine and human natures in Christ (70): "The participation of His divine in His human essence is not the same as that of His human in His divine .... The determination of His divine essence is *to* His human, and the determination of His human essence *from* His divine. He gives the human essence a part in His divine, and the human essence receives this part in the divine from Him." He makes clear that this participation entails no admixture. Even in the exalted glory of Christ his human essence remains utterly distinct from his transcendent divine essence and is determined to cooperation with it by the grace of the latter: see CD IV, 2, 63 and 88–92. Clearly, while there are important differences between the two thinkers on these points, there are also significant similarities.

16. I am referring here to Barth's qualified acceptance of the so-called *extra-Calvinisticum*: the Word continues to sustain the world in being even during the incarnation. See CD IV, 1, 180–83.

17. Stating a view which he rejects categorically, Barth writes: "It pleased Him [in His activity and work as the Reconciler of the world created by Him] not to alter Himself, but to deny the immutability of His being, His divine nature, to be in discontinuity

God the Son without being in contradiction with his immutable omnipotence as God, then this is only because (as with Aquinas) there
is not an attribution of contraries to the same subject under the same
aspect. This unity of divine and human properties seemingly transpires without contradiction because it occurs in the being and the
person of Christ, and not in a confusion of natures.[18] This seems to
be what is implied, at any rate, by the claim that God's becoming man
does not require any self-alienation on God's part. God can enter history without introducing any new alterity or contrary into himself,
and without any dialectic in his being.

Third, for Barth, the assumption of obedience "into the being of
God" does not entail any evacuation, or substantial alteration of God's
divine nature per se. This affirmation is evident above all in Barth's
rejection of the nineteenth-century kenotic theories of Gottfried
Thomasius. The latter claimed that God the Son *as God* ceded his
omnipresence and omnipotence during the time that he was dynamically present and active as the historical man Jesus. (These were supposedly attributes of God that were somehow proper to him only by
virtue of his relation to creation, and not characteristic of God per
se. They could therefore be ceded freely by the deity.) In contradistinction to such an idea, Barth insists that God the Son does not and
cannot cede or alter his divine characteristics when he becomes man.
Nor does he relinquish his omnipotence and omnipresence with re-

with Himself, to be against Himself, to set Himself in self-contradiction. In Himself He
was still the omnipresent, almighty, eternal and glorious One.... But at the same time
among us and for us He was quite different ... limited and open to radical and total at-
tack ... His identity with Himself [across these two states] consisted strictly in His determination to be God ... the Reconciler of the world, in this inner and outer antithesis
to Himself." He goes on to state explicitly (184–88) that God entered into our state of
contradiction with God (through sin and death) and reconciled us with himself without
incurring contradiction within himself. See also CD IV, 2, 146–47 for similar views. Paul
Molnar (*Divine Freedom and the Doctrine of the Immanent Trinity*, 264) has contrasted
this understanding of Barth's with Jüngel's idea of a dialectic of being and non-being
which occurs in the essence of God. For examples of this latter view, see Jüngel, *God as
the Mystery of the World*, 219, 346–47.

18. This point could be contested if in fact Barth wishes to maintain that there is
only one subject in God, who is omnipotent in "his" mode of being as Father and impotent in "his" mode of being as Son. Yet whatever we make of such language, we cannot
ignore Barth's important insistence (especially in CD IV, 2) on the unicity of the subject
of Christ in whom there are the irreducibly distinct divine and human essences.

spect to creation. The divine life does not undergo a process of self-ab-dication or self-transformation in the incarnation.[19] God is *free* in his being to assume a human obedience into himself. Yet he is free to do so without altering what he is *from all eternity*.[20] If our concept of the divine being and nature of God is to be guided by what he has done in Christ, then it must hold firmly to *both* the principles initially elaborat-ed above: the action of God in history reveals who God truly is. It re-veals who he is precisely in his non-created, and transcendent identity, that is to say in his sovereignty as Lord.

It is this last point, however, which leads to the next *aporia* in our consideration of Barthian thought. If God *can* assume a temporal obedience into himself without self-alteration, and if he has this ca-pacity in his being from all eternity, then what does the event of the incarnation reveal about the immanent, eternal life of God? What is the eternal "capacity" in the life of God which makes his existence in humility and obedience possible? It is in answering this question that Barth develops his second idea of divine obedience: as something pre-temporal, existing in the eternal life of the Trinity. It is to this idea which I will turn next.

PRE-TEMPORAL
OBEDIENCE OF THE SON
AS PROCESSION

According to Barth, there must exist a condition of possibility in the life of God such that God can become obedient in history in the

19. CD IV, 1, 183: "God for His part is God in His unity with this creature, this man, in His human and creaturely nature—and this without ceasing to be God, without any alteration or diminution of his divine nature."

20. CD IV, 1, 193: "It is His sovereign grace that He wills to be and is amongst us in humility, our God, God for us. But He shows us this grace, he is amongst us in humili-ty, our God, God for us, as that which He is in Himself, in the most inward depth of His Godhead. He does not become another God. In the condescension in which he gives Himself to us in Jesus Christ He exists and speaks and acts as the One He was from eter-nity and will be to all eternity. The truth and actuality of the atonement depend on this being the case. The one who reconciles the world with God is necessarily the one God Himself in His true Godhead. Otherwise the world would not be reconciled with God. Otherwise it is still the world which is not reconciled with God."

incarnate Son.[21] Therefore, the transcendent corollary for the economic manifestation of God in Christ is a "pre-temporal" obedience
which exists in God from all eternity.[22] It is the latter which serves
as the ontological foundation for the event of the passion and cross
of Christ. Based upon a successive exclusion of modalism and subordinationism, Barth determines dialectically that this reality of divine
obedience must concern God in himself, as the "posited and self-positing God" in his modes of being as Son and Father, respectively. In
other words, this reality has to be understood in Trinitarian terms. It
is something that characterizes the eternal relation between the Father and the Son, in their distinctness and reciprocity. This relationship is prior to creation, and serves as the basis for both the election
and creation of humanity, as well as for the incarnation of the Son in
history.[23]

Two important observations need to be made concerning the description of this intra-Trinitarian obedience. Firstly, this eternal divine obedience clearly seems to concern the *deity* or *divine nature* of
Jesus Christ.

In this happening we have to do with a divine commission and its divine execution, with a divine order and *divine obedience*. What takes place is the divine fulfillment of a divine decree.... But it is clear that once again, and this
time in all seriousness, we are confronted with the mystery of *the deity of
Christ*.[24]

Secondly, this relationship of obedience is a characteristic through
which one can and must understand and interpret the eternal *generation* of the Son by the Father.

21. CD IV, 1, 194: Obedience in Christ reveals an eternal "possibility grounded in
the being of God."
22. CD IV, 1, 201: "It belongs to the inner life of God that there should take place
within it obedience.... God is both One and also Another, His own counterpart, co-
existent with Himself.... He exists as a first and a second, above and below."
23. CD IV, 1, 201: "We have to reckon with such an event even in the being and life
of God Himself. It cannot be explained away either as an event in some higher or supreme creaturely sphere or as a mere appearance of God. Therefore we have to state
firmly that, far from preventing this possibility, His divine unity consists in the fact that
in Himself he is both one who is obeyed and Another who obeys."
24. CD IV, 1, 195 (emphasis added).

The One who in this obedience is the perfect image of the ruling God is Himself—as distinct from every human and creaturely kind—God by nature, God in His relationship to Himself, i.e., God in His mode of being as the Son in relation to God in His mode of being as the Father, One with the Father and of one essence. *In His mode of being as the Son He fulfils the divine subordination,* just as the Father in His mode of being as the Father fulfils the divine superiority. *In humility as the Son who complies, He is the same as is the Father in majesty as the Father who disposes. He is the same in consequence (and obedience) as the Son as is the Father in origin.* He is the same as the Son, i.e., as the self-posited God ... as is the Father as the self-positing God.... The Father as the origin is never apart from Him as the consequence, *the obedient One.* The self-positing of God is never apart from Him as the One who is posited as God by God. The One *who eternally begets is never apart from the One who is eternally begotten.*[25]

We can conclude from these two points that the divine obedience thus characterized somehow pertains for Barth to what is classically termed the eternal *procession* of the Son from the Father. The reasons for concluding this should be, I think, uncontroversial. In classical Trinitarian monotheism, the divine nature of God is considered an ineffable and transcendent mystery, but it is also confessed to be unique: there is only one God. Because this divine nature is common to the three persons of God, the latter can only be distinguished hypostatically by their relations of origin.[26] The Son possesses the fullness of the divine nature in a relative way, as one proceeding eternally from the Father as his Word. Being generated constitutes the Son as Son, because he receives all that he is (the ineffable, transcendent being and nature of God) from the Father. And indeed, as Aquinas points out, these same subsistent relations of the persons of God themselves constitute the inner life of God.[27] Ultimately, then, they *are* the divine nature itself.[28] This nature subsists *hypostatically* in three Trinitarian modes of being: it is communicated from the Father

25. CD IV, 1, 209 (emphasis added).
26. This theological formulation has its origins in the Cappadocians as well as Augustine. The simple, ineffable nature of God subsists in three persons distinguished uniquely by their "relations of origin." Aquinas discusses the point in ST I, q. 29, a. 4; q. 30, a. 4; q. 31, a. 2. On the historical origins and structure of this way of thinking, see Emery, "Essentialism or Personalism in the Treatise on God in St. Thomas Aquinas?"
27. ST I, q. 29, a. 4.
28. ST I, q. 39, a. 1.

to the Son by way of generation, and to the Holy Spirit from the Father and the Son by way of spiration.[29]

It follows from such perspectives that whatever "founds" the relations of origin *in* God serves as the principle for the distinction of persons in the life of God, permitting us to interpret the persons in light of such relations. In turn, this distinction of persons (through their relations of origin) constitutes the very nature of God, insofar as that nature itself only exists in distinctly personal ways. For Barth obedience characterizes the relations of origin of the Son from the Father, and therefore characterizes the distinction of persons (or "modes" of God's being) in God eternally. This relationship of commanding and subordinate obedience is, therefore, also constitutive of the divine nature and "deity" of God as triune, as Barth affirms repeatedly. This obedience as described in CD IV, 1, then, may reasonably be interpreted as characterizing the eternal procession of the Son from the Father.[30] It is the foundation for their distinction from one another.

Here I would like to note what I think are two interrelated problems with such a view. First, positing such obedience in God jeopardizes the confession of the unity of the divine nature, power, and will of God. Second, it risks undermining the intelligibility of Barth's own soteriological affirmation that God, in order to save us, must in no way be alienated from his own prerogatives of omnipotence in the incarnation. To argue for these points, I will briefly consider some elements of classical Trinitarian thought as elaborated by Athanasius. In turn, Barth's views can be contrasted profitably with these. As is well known, fourth-century Arian or anti-Nicene theologians appealed to New Testament examples of the obedience of Christ in order to argue for a pre-existent, ontological subordination of the Logos to the Father. In countering this claim, Athanasius develops three interrelated principles which relate in certain ways to our considerations.

Athanasius notes in the *Contra Arianos* that the Nicene affirmation of a unique being of God (the *homoousios* formula) required the

---

29. ST I, q. 42, a. 4.

30. Paraphrasing this idea in Barth, Bruce McCormack writes ("Karl Barth's Christology," 249): "The eternal relation in which the Father 'commands' and the Son 'obeys' is the very relation by means of which the one God freely constitutes his own being in eternity."

elaboration of an understanding of a *shared nature* common to the Father and Son. One of his central contributions in this text is to discuss meaningfully how this nature could be understood to *proceed* from the Father in the Son, and how such a filial generation could be constitutive of the very life of God. For this he appeals to the analogy of the Word of the Johannine prologue. St. John's doctrine of the Logos *asarkos* (according to Athanasius's reading) provides a revealed, theological analogy that allows one to perceive how God could exist in and as a procession of persons even while being unique in nature and being. If this being is spiritual, then it can be transmitted (or engendered) after the analogy of spiritual processions in the human soul: the Logos is the Son eternally begotten of the Father as his *wisdom*, in and through whom he knows all things.[31] This begotten wisdom contains in himself all that is proper to the divine essence. Consequently, if the Father gives the Son to possess in himself the plenitude of divine attributes (ineffable power, goodness, divine willing, etc.), this is not because the divine substance is divided. Rather, the Father communicates to the Son his very being as God, and he does so by virtue of his own identity, since he is himself eternally relative to the Son. This is why Athanasius emphasizes, against Arianism, that the Father does not choose to beget the Son by an act of will. Rather, the Father and the Son share in two different ways in the unique will of God, just as they share in the unique nature and being of God.[32]

Second, it follows from the biblical affirmations of God's spiritual (non-physical) manner of being that his unique nature is "wisdom"

---

31. *C. Arianos* I, para. 16: "If, then … the Offspring of the Father's essence be the Son, we must be certain, that the same is the Wisdom and Word of the Father, in and through whom He creates and makes all things" See also: I, paras. 15, 24–29; II, paras. 2, 5, 36. For an insightful discussion of these points, see Lewis Ayres, *Nicaea and Its Legacy*, 110–17. It is worth emphasizing that this Athanasian understanding of the Logos *asarkos* could in principle be held without in any way denying the Barthian principle that this same Logos is only known by means of the incarnation. Neither the Gospel of John nor Athanasius deny that the pre-existence or ontological priority of the Logos *asarkos* to the economy of the incarnation was made known *in and through* that economy. See, for example, Jn 3:13.

32. *C. Arianos* II, para. 2: "God's creating is second to His begetting, for 'Son' implies something proper to Him [as God] and truly from that blessed and everlasting Essence, but what is from His will [i.e., created], comes into consistence from without, and is framed through His proper Offspring who is from It [the divine essence]."

(that is to say, that God is personal: intelligent and freely loving), and God's wisdom directs the decisions of his will. Consequently, because the Son is the only begotten Word of the Father, he is the principle through whom the Father wills all that he wills.[33] Because the Son receives from the Father's begetting the very nature of God, he possesses in himself the plenitude of divinely ordered potency with regard to creatures. Consequently, the Son cannot obey the Father precisely because he enjoys in himself the same plenitude of divine life from all eternity. The Son could only be subordinate in some way to the Father were he to *not* fully share in the power and willing of the Father. Yet this would contradict the confession of a *unique spiritual will* in God, as suggested by the Johannine analogy of the Word (through whom all things were freely made), and would in turn be inconsistent with the Nicene affirmation of *a unique spiritual nature or essence* which exists in the one God.[34] In other words, for Athanasius such subordination would undermine the confession of a Trinitarian *monotheism*.

Finally, Athanasius saw that a soteriological concern of major proportions lay at the heart of his debate with the anti-Nicene theologians. If the Son of God is to save human beings by uniting God's own divine nature with the human flesh he has to save, then the Arian denial of the divine nature of the Son will undermine the confession of the saving character of the incarnation of the Logos.[35] In other words, if we deny the divinity of Christ and the presence in him of the divine nature, then we irremediably render obscure the confession of Christ as an effective savior of human beings.

One can see immediately a logical connection between the three

33. *C. Arianos* II, para. 31: "For the Word of God is Framer and Maker and He is the will of God."

34. *C. Arianos* II, para. 2: "If He has the power of will, and His will is effective, and suffices for the consistence of the things that come to be, and His Word is effective, and a Framer, that Word must surely be the living Will of the Father, and an essential (*enousios*) energy, and a real word, in whom all things both consist and are excellently governed."

35. *C. Arianos* II, para. 70: "For man had not been deified if joined to a creature, or unless the Son were very God; nor had man been brought into the Father's presence, unless He had been His natural and true Word who had put on the body." See also I, para. 15; III, para. 11, and Ayres's comments on this theme in Athanasius (*Nicaea and Its Legacy*, 113–15).

ideas: the Logos is the wisdom of God, the Logos possesses the plenitude of the divine nature, power and will of God, and the Logos became flesh to save us by uniting us with him in his divine nature, power, and will. It follows that any attempt to attribute obedience to the Logos in his personal relation to the Father will undermine the second affirmation. Yet the denial or questioning of the second principle will in turn undermine the intelligibility of the first and the logical necessity of the third.

Barth's reflections on the errors of "semi-Arian" perspectives are both extensive and subtle, and he clearly eschews any form of subordinationism which would jeopardize the confession of the divinity of the Son. However, I would like to suggest that the doctrine of divine obedience in God contradicts the second principle established by Athanasius. It therefore creates potential problems with the other two theses which Barth does wish in some way to maintain. The affirmation of a divine obedience between the persons makes it unclear how there can be a unique divine nature and will in God consistent with the Johannine psychological analogy. It therefore renders problematic the confession of a divine agency (divinely ordered power, omnipotence) present in the person of the Son. This in turn affects the soteriological claim that the transcendent freedom of God is truly present in Christ as a necessary condition for our effective redemption.

The first problem can be considered by contrasting Barth's views with those of Aquinas. As noted above, St. Thomas will affirm that there is a unique nature and will in God, differentiated hypostatically in three distinct modes of being, as the Father, Son, and Holy Spirit. "The same essence is paternity in the Father, and filiation in the Son: so by the same power the Father begets, and the Son is begotten."[36] There is, in other words, a uniquely paternal mode of being of the power and will of God, as well as a filial mode of being of this same power and will. The former is eternally begetting while the latter is eternally begotten, such that the Son receives all that he is and wills from the Father. Yet the two persons both possess in plenitude the same divine nature, power, and will of God. So while the Son is entirely relative to the Father, he is also the omnipotent God.[37]

36. ST I, q. 42, a. 6, ad 3.
37. ST I, q. 42, a. 4: "It belongs to the very nature of paternity and filiation that the

This classical Trinitarian perspective rests upon a crucial axiom: any notion of the one God as a multiplicity of divine persons can only be intelligibly construed by taking account of *both* the generation of the Word and the procession of the Spirit which "found" the relations of origin *and* the common nature which they share. To speak about the Father and Son as subsisting relations one must refer *both* to subsistence (the divine essence) *and* relations (the relationship to another that distinguishes). The uniqueness of the divine essence, therefore, enters into the very "definition" of the Son as a person distinct from the Father.[38] By a process of notional "reduplication" the person must be thought of both in terms of relations and in terms of nature. Otherwise, the monotheistic character of the Trinitarian faith literally becomes inconceivable.

How does this differ from Barth's presentation? In CD IV, 1 and 2, Barth clearly affirms a doctrine of "two natures" in Christ. It might seem from this that the Son partakes as Son of the divine attributes we have spoken about previously (omnipresence, omnipotence, immutability, etc.). He possesses these attributes in his person as a "mode of being" eternally distinct from the Father. (In much earlier

---

Son by generation should attain to the possession of the perfection of the nature which is in the Father, in the same way as it is in the Father himself.... Therefore we must say that the Son was eternally equal to the Father in greatness." See also q. 42, a. 6, corp.: "The Son is necessarily equal to the Father in power. Power of action is a consequence of perfection of nature. Now it was shown above (a. 4) that *the very notion of the divine paternity and filiation requires that the Son should be the Father's equal in greatness*—that is, in perfection of nature. Therefore, it follows that the Son is equal to the Father in power; and the same applies to the Holy Spirit in relation to both" (emphasis added). See the discussion of this point by Emery in *Trinity in Aquinas*, 132–34, 139–44.

38. Emery (*Trinity in Aquinas*, 144) comments: "The capacity of subsistence [implying reference to the divine essence] does not belong to the relation under the aspect of the relationship to another (*ratio*), but it belongs to the relation in so much as this relationship is divine (*esse*). St. Thomas explains, in similar terms, that the person designates 'the distinct subsistent in the divine nature,' by specifying that this 'distinct subsistent' is the relation taken in the integrality of its constitution in God, in its *esse* (divine substance) and in its *ratio* (relationship *ad aliud* that distinguishes). It is therefore in the 'subsisting relation,' which guarantees a strict Trinitarian monotheism, that St. Thomas effects the synthesis of his doctrine on God the Trinity." The passage makes reference to *De Potentia Dei*, q. 10, a. 3 and q. 9, a. 4. It is interesting to note that in CD I, 1, 355–66 Barth expresses reservations about such notional reduplication precisely with regards to Aquinas's notion of subsistent relations (see 366). He intimates that the persons of the triune God should be understood by their relations of origin *without* reference to a commonly shared intellectual and voluntary "*res* et *natura*."

writings—such as CD I, 1—Barth affirmed as much explicitly.) Yet according to CD IV, 1, this same Son also only exists eternally *as one who obeys* the Father. Obedience here characterizes the procession of the Son from the Father in his eternal generation. Because it determines the character of his eternal relation to the Father, obedience is *entirely constitutive of his person*. There is nothing in him that is not consent of will to another. But in this case, how should we understand Barth's opinion that the Son is characterized in all that he is by obedience, *and that he simultaneously possesses in himself eternally the unique omnipotent will of God*? Or, inversely, if God the Son is eternally omnipotent (possessing the plenitude of the divine nature, power, and will), how, then, is his eternal generation characterized hypostatically by consent to the will of another? It would seem that one must forfeit either the notion of a unity of will in the persons, or reinterpret Barth's notion of a distinction of persons in God derived through obedience.

One might object that there is no substantial dilemma here. After all, it is true that for a thinker like Aquinas, the Son receives his being and omnipotence from the Father eternally. Therefore the Son must also eternally receive the Father's will through generation, even while being eternally omnipotent.[39] But Aquinas also qualifies this affirmation by simultaneously insisting that the Son possesses the very will of the Father, which he receives from the Father. There is a strict *identity* of will, communicated from the Father to the Son and shared by them in two hypostatic modes.[40] In Barth's view, by contrast, the generation of the Son simply cannot result in the Son's plenary pos-

---

39. In ST I, q. 42, a. 6, ad 2, Aquinas interprets Jn 5:30 ("As I hear, so I judge") as follows: "The Father's *showing* and the Son's *hearing* are to be taken in the sense that the Father communicates knowledge to the Son, as He communicates His essence. The command of the Father can be explained in the same sense, as giving Him from eternity knowledge and will to act, by begetting Him. Or better still, this may be referred to Christ in his human nature."

40. *In Ioan.* V, lect. 5, 798: Aquinas here comments on Jn 5:30 ("I am not seeking my own will, but the will of him who sent me"). "But do not the Father and the Son have the same will? I answer that the Father and the Son do have the same will, but the Father does not have his will from another whereas the Son does have his will from another, i.e., from the Father. Thus the Son accomplishes his own will as from another, i.e. as having it from another; but the Father accomplishes his own will as his own, i.e., not having it from another." Evidently, the idea expressed in this citation ties in with the themes examined in the previous chapter.

session of the *Father's* essence and will. Instead, the Son can only exist eternally as distinct from the Father and therefore be Son in and through his act of consent *to* the will of the Father. Reciprocity of will enters into the very notion of both the distinction of persons and the nature of the Godhead.[41] Taken literally, then, the language of divine obedience excludes an identity of will between the Father and Son. So while for Athanasius and Aquinas, the procession of the Son from the Father as his Logos allows one to see how the Son can both receive and have the one will of the Father, in Barth the viewpoint is inverted. The will to be receptive in the Son is the foundation for his procession and differentiation from the Father as Son and Word.[42]

Here the potential difficulties become clearer. If God the Son proceeds from the Father *in and through* his act of obedience to the divine will of the Father, then whatever he receives from the Father (that is, omnipotence), he receives through an act of consent to the Father's will. May we say, then, that the Son proceeds from the Father through the Son's consent in obedience to his being good, wise, immutable, and omnipotent? If this is the case, he must consent eternally to his being invested with attributes of the divine nature. Yet this implies that the Son could somehow act freely in all eternity "prior" to possessing the divine nature received from the Father, and so constitute himself as God through an elective act of choice, which is patently nonsensical.

Perhaps instead we might ask if God who is omnipotent as Father is obedient in his mode of being as Son, such that the Son is eternally "void" of such attributes. Barth's language in CD IV, 1 at times certainly leans more in this direction when he speaks about the Son's obedience.[43] In this case, however, it would seem that God would emp-

41. CD IV, 1, 209: "In His mode of being as the Son He fulfills the divine subordination, just as the Father in His mode of being as the Father fulfills the divine superiority. In humility as the Son who complies, He is the same as is the Father in majesty as the Father who disposes."

42. Again, to cite McCormack's paraphrasing of this idea ("Karl Barth's Christology," 249): "If the relation in which God 'commands' and 'obeys' is identical with the relation which constitutes the very being of God as triune, then it is very clear that what the Son does and therefore is in time finds its ground in what he does and therefore is in eternity. [This suggests] that 'humility' is not something added to God in his second mode of being at the point at which he assumes flesh; it *is* his second mode of being already in eternity."

43. See the suggestive comments of CD IV, 1, 203: "In the work of the reconciliation

ty himself of his omnipotence as a condition for being in his mode
as the Son. His omnipotence would somehow have to be ceded by a
kind of voluntary kenosis, occurring through all eternity. How, then,
is there a unique will and power of God present in the two persons?
And how is the transcendent freedom of the Son with respect to creation assured? Even more fundamentally, how can we affirm the identity of the Son as the eternal creator if he is not omnipotent with respect to creation?[44]

While Barth's explicit proposals concerning divine obedience
certainly rest far afield from our considerations here, a certain inward
logic nested within them seems to push us toward either the affirmation of a filial consent to the possession of a divine nature or the
idea of a kenosis of divine prerogatives *within* the life of God. Both
are Trinitarian antinomies of a sort, and neither is consistent with the
confession of a unity of will and power in the life of the Trinity. One
can therefore plausibly suggest that either we must rethink the claim
to eternal obedience in the Son, or else qualify in important ways any
affirmation of his omnipotence.[45]

---

of the world with God the inward divine relationship between the One who rules and
commands in majesty and the One who obeys in humility is identical with the very different relationship between God and one of His creatures, a man.... To do this he empties Himself ... but as the strangely logical final continuation of, the history in which He
is God."

44. McCormack ("Karl Barth's Christology," 249n6) suggests that these problems
can be resolved by (1) understanding that it is Jesus Christ and not "merely" the Logos
asarkos who is the active *subject* (not object!) of divine election *from all eternity*, and
that (2) "the Spirit is, first and foremost, the mode of being in which the self-positing
God empowers the self-posited God, Jesus Christ, to live a human life and to live it *humanly*." I agree with Paul Molnar ("The Trinity, Election and God's Ontological Freedom: A Response to Kevin W. Hector" *International Journal of Systematic Theology* 8,
no. 3 [2006]: 294–300) that this interpretation results in a problematic identification of
the triune God and the act of election in such a way that God and creation are ontologically distinct but eternally indissociable. Inevitably election and creation (as well as incarnation and dereliction) thus become necessities for God, and in turn *must* constitute
a dimension of his identity. Barth himself clearly advocates against any idea that election
is a 'necessity' for God in his CD II, 2, 309, 313, and elsewhere. It is possible, however, as
McCormack suggests, that the later work of Barth stands in fundamental tension with
his earlier affirmations on this point. See the relevant remarks (and theological defense
of his own position on these matters) by McCormack in "Seek God where he may be
found: a response to Edwin Chr. Van Driel."

45. I am in sympathy with Bruce McCormack on this point: there exists a potential

A second issue this raises concerns the coherence of Barth's claim that the incarnate Son does not cede his divine attributes in the incarnation. As stated above, this insistence on Barth's part is of fundamental importance soteriologically, and in this respect his thought parallels the view of Athanasius. God cannot save us if he is in fact alienated from himself in the act of living among us as a man in history. A dimension of this soteriological principle concerns divine freedom: because of who he is, God is free to become man and act in obedience without ceding or altering his divine being. It is because he is not alienated from his omnipotence that he remains free to redeem us with authority in Christ, and to exalt our humanity into the life of God through the incarnate Son.[46]

Yet it is unclear how this affirmation is itself entirely consistent with the concept of a divine obedience, if that obedience characterizes the procession of the Son from the Father. Is it in fact the case that the Son himself as Son retains the freedom of divine transcendence in his person even during his historical life as man? Presumably, God the Son was eternally free in his unity of will shared with God the Father to choose (contingently) whether or not to create us, to become incarnate for our salvation, etc. But if the Son receives *in obedience* the entirety of his being as Son, does this not include his reception of his eventual mission and existence as the Son incarnate? In other words, does the Son of God eternally will our salvation with the Father by a

tension or antinomy between the affirmation of classical divine attributes such as immutability, omnipresence, and omnipotence (which Barth here and elsewhere ascribes in unqualified fashion to the Son incarnate), and Barth's relativization of the classical "psychological analogy" in his rendering of divine obedience. However, I do not think (contrary to what McCormack suggests in "Karl Barth's Christology," 250) that the idea of an eternal, intra-divine kenosis of omnipotence by the Son in view of his human mission is compatible with the continued possession by the Son of the subsistent omnipotence of God. McCormack suggests that this is possible due to the agency of the omnipotent Spirit in the historical existence of the man Jesus. Against this, one can argue that to be very God, the Son incarnate must partake of the very being of the Father and the Spirit, and yet this implies in turn the hidden presence in Christ of the Father's and the Spirit's unique will and power as *his own filial* will and power. Jesus Christ, therefore, must be understood as omnipotent God in the proper sense of the term, even when he is obedient in his historical existence.

46. For clear evidence of this view in Barth's writings as least as late as in CD II, 2, see Molnar, "The Trinity, Election and God's Ontological Freedom," 296–301.

free decision of the Trinitarian God, or does he eternally consent to the Father in everything he is, including his consent to the commandment to save us? If the latter is the case (and it seems it must be), then the Father is free to choose to save us but the Son is not (since he can only exist as one who receives this command from the Father). Or, the Father is only Father in generating the Son as obedient to him, and since this obedience includes our election in Christ, the election of Jesus Christ as the God-man enters into the very differentiation of the eternal persons. The Father can only be the Father by commanding the Son to suffer and die for us.[47]

In either of these cases, however, does Christ still have the power and freedom to choose as God to redeem us? It would seem not. Presumably, he must depend for these attributes on the interventions of the Father and the Holy Spirit. Consequently, if obedience characterizes the eternal procession of the Son from the Father, have we really avoided the problems of "traditional" nineteenth-century kenosis theory (as Barth says he wishes to do), or have we merely displaced them from time into eternity? God no longer empties himself of his divine prerogatives while he is incarnate, but does so, rather, from all eternity in his mode of being as Son, in view of the incarnation in time. In addition to the problem of its metaphysical incoherence, any inversion of the Son's mission into the life of God poses serious soteriological risks. A God who is eternally on mission to save humanity through suffering and death seems to be himself immersed inextricably in the problem of moral and natural evil as a constitutive dimension of his identity. God can only ever be God from all eternity if he is engaged with the problem of evil and suffering. Consequently, he seems to require exposure to evil and suffering for the achievement of his own inner history as God. It follows from this that suffering is in some way essential to the identity of God. Can such a God truly be expected to save us?

47. One can find an interpretation of Barth which resembles this description in Bruce McCormack's "Grace and Being: The Role of God's Gracious Election in Karl Barth's Theological Ontology," in *The Cambridge Companion to Karl Barth*, ed. J. Webster (Cambridge: Cambridge University Press, 2000), 92–110.

THE PRE-TEMPORAL
"OBEDIENCE" OF THE SON
RECONSIDERED

Barth's central intuition is that there needs to be an eternal foundation in the life of God for all that transpires between the persons of
God in the economic missions of Christ and the Holy Spirit. Were
there not such a transcendent corollary in the life of God, the temporal obedience of the incarnate Son would not effectively reveal his
eternal relation to the Father. Therefore, while the direct application
of obedience to the life of the persons of the immanent Trinity raises
difficulties, a more benign interpretation of this "eternal foundation"
seems necessary.

One possibility is to consider the Son's origination from the Father *alone* as *a sufficient condition* for the filial character of his economic mission.[48] In this case, God the Son receives and possesses from
the Father the unique divine nature, power, and will of God from all
eternity. This divine receptivity in turn acts as the transcendent ontological foundation for the temporal mission of Christ. The Son wills
with the Father that he become incarnate while simultaneously receiving this will from the Father. This filial receptivity in turn is reflected in all the actions of the incarnate Son in his temporal history as man. Because the Son becomes the obedient servant Jesus, his
voluntary human obedience reveals his personal relativity toward the
Father, as well as the receptive character of his divine mode of being.

In this second interpretation of divine obedience, the person of
the Son is revealed in and through the obedience of God in history.
Yet this obedience pertains to his human nature and does not characterize the eternal life of the Son in virtue of his deity. It does not stand
at the origin of his procession from the Father. Rather, the inverse is
true. The procession of the Son from the Father is the eternal "basis"
for his relation to the Father in his temporal mission.[49] The latter in

---

48. In framing the issue in these terms, I am influenced by various insightful sug-
gestions of Bruce Marshall.

49. ST I, q. 43, a. 2, ad 3: "Mission signifies not only procession from the principle,
but also determines the temporal term of the procession. Hence mission is only temporal. Or we may say that it includes the eternal procession, with the addition of a tem-

turn is the basis for his filial way of being a man, that is to say, as the Word made flesh who proceeds from the Father. In this case, then, the eternal Son is also omnipotent throughout his history as an obedient man. This viewpoint can be examined through a threefold series of interrelated claims, each of which helps us further clarify this position.

As we have noted above, the eternal *relativity* of the Son to the Father has its fundamental basis in his *procession* from the Father. The Son proceeds eternally from the Father as his Word, and receives in this generation the totality of the divine life, power, and will. The same is true of the Holy Spirit through eternal spiration. Therefore, while the nature of God is one, this ineffable nature exists in the three hypostases of the Trinitarian God in irreducibly distinct ways. "The same essence, which in the Father is paternity, in the Son is filiation."[50] Likewise, for the power and will of God: "The Son has the same omnipotence as the Father, but with another relation; the Father possessing power as *giving* signified when we say that he is able to beget, while the Son possesses the power of *receiving*, signified by saying that He can be begotten."[51] This means that the hypostatic character of the person utterly characterizes the *way in which* the divine essence subsists in that person.[52] Because this relationality is absolutely fundamental within the very life of God, it characterizes in some way not only God's immanent activity of knowledge and love, but also all action of God *ad extra* in creating and redeeming.[53]

---

poral effect. For the relation of a divine person to His principle must be eternal. Hence the procession may be called a twin procession, eternal and temporal, not that there is a double relation to the principle, but a double term, temporal and eternal."

50. ST I, q. 42, a. 4, ad 2.

51. ST I, q. 42, a. 6, ad 3.

52. As noted in chapter 5, Aquinas is influenced in making this distinction between the essence and its personal mode by the Greek Christological and Trinitarian distinction between the *logos* (nature) and the *tropos* (mode) found in Maximus the Confessor and John Damascene. Barth advances compatible views, no doubt informed indirectly by this tradition, throughout his reflection on the essence and threefold modes of God's being in CD I, 1, section 9.

53. Emery has studied this concept in Aquinas at length in his "The Personal Mode of Trinitarian Action in Saint Thomas Aquinas": "The Son exists from the Father and, accordingly, acts by receiving his being and his power of action from the Father: the Son acts as the 'principle from the principle.' This means no subordination but only the relation of origin by which the Son is referred to the Father. This distinction does not

Second, then, God is in no way compelled to create or redeem the world and human beings, but rather acts freely in creation *by his omnipotence* with respect to a radically dependent creation. Nevertheless, based upon the first point discussed above, this *same divine freedom* exists *within* the immanent life of God in three subsistent modes.[54] Thus while the contingent economic decisions of the Father and Son occur through the unique act of both persons with respect to creatures, such action is possessed within the Trinitarian life in two distinct ways. The eternal decree that the Son assume flesh and die for us exists in the Father as in its unoriginate source, and in the Son as the begotten wisdom through whom this action is willed. The Son wills as omnipotent God to become incarnate as man, but he also necessarily receives this will eternally from the Father.[55] In all that occurs in his temporal mission, therefore, the incarnate Son "naturally" expresses through human actions *both* his divine being and willing, *and* the fact that this being and willing are received from the Father.

Finally, the voluntary human obedience of the Son in temporal history implies a dynamic subordination of his human will to the agency of his transcendent will which he shares with the Father. It

---

divide the action of the Trinity, or its power, or the principle of action, which are common to the three persons by reason of their one nature. It also does not concern the effects of the action: these effects come forth from the three persons in virtue of their one action. One could also, indeed, show this by the doctrine of perichoresis: the Father is in the Son, the Son is in the Father, the Holy Spirit is in the Father and in the Son, and reciprocally. For this reason, the action of the three persons is inseparable. Thomas Aquinas explains, for example: 'The Son acts by reason of the Father who dwells in him by a unity of nature.' (*In Ioan.* 14, lec. 12, 1898) The profundity of the perichoresis is such that, in the act of the Son, the Father himself acts, and the Holy Spirit acts in them, inseparably. The action of the Son and of the Holy Spirit is not therefore different from that of the Father, since the persons act in indwelling the one in the other, according to their mutual immanence and thus by one and the same operation" (52).

54. See on this ST I, q. 43, a. 2, ad 3, and the remarks of Emery, "The Personal Mode of Trinitarian Action in Saint Thomas Aquinas," 67. Barth himself emphasizes both these points together in CD, I, 1, 371–74.

55. Commenting on Jn 3:16 ("For God so loved the world that he gave his only begotten Son"), Aquinas writes (*In Ioan.* III, lec. 3, 478): "But did God give his Son with the intention that he should die on the cross? He did indeed give him for the death of the cross inasmuch as he gave him the will to suffer on it. And he did this in two ways. First, because as the Son of God he willed from eternity to assume flesh and to suffer for us; and this will he had from the Father. Secondly, because the will to suffer was infused into the soul of Christ by God."

thus implies a duality of wills (and natures), human and divine, in the God-man who is Christ. Yet this subordination also transpires in a unique historical person, in accordance with his aforementioned filial mode of being. Thus while the operations of the two natures and wills of Christ are distinct, they have an *identical* mode of being. This mode of being in turn informs all the operations of divine and human life in Christ. Both operations subsist in him and cooperate in such a way as to express Jesus's *unique filial relation* to the Father. Consequently, the human thoughts, desires, emotions, words, and gestures of Jesus manifest and conceal the hidden presence of an ineffable divine nature working in him, *and* show this same divine nature to be received from the Father. God's actions of obedient subordination to the Father's will transpire historically in the incarnate Son, and can only occur because of his human agency. Yet these human actions are always and everywhere theandric: they manifest and conceal his *filial* relation to the Father, *and* the presence in Jesus of a divine *will* received from the Father. This is true on the one hand when Christ performs miracles by the power he shares with the Father, and receives from him. But it is also true when he accepts as man to submit himself to passive torment and physical execution in obedience to the Father, for our sake. Both his passive historical submission and his self-determined human actions find their perfect, transcendent exemplar in his filial manner of being as the Son, at once eternally receptive of the divine life he receives from the Father, and active (in this same divine life) in all things.

Evidently, obedience, suffering, and death are ways in which the human being inevitably experiences a greater dependence or relativity with regard to others, and particularly toward God. Such events *in human nature* speak more profoundly of relativity than any other conceivable kinds of human activity or passivity, since they connote for each person a unique and last recourse to God alone as regards the destiny of his or her own being. It was only fitting (and very beautiful) that these human forms *of extreme dependency* should be assumed by the incarnate God as ways to denote to us in and through our contingent state of being his *own* inner life of fundamental receptivity constituted by the "subsistent relations." God the Son reveals himself through his obedience, humiliation, and suffering as one who

is utterly relative to another in his very existence. This can occur because the historical human actions of Jesus exist and subsist in his
personal mode of being as the Son of God, in his dynamic relation
to the Father. Yet this also occurs without the Son ceding in any way
the omnipotence and omnipresence which he possesses as God, by
virtue of his deity received from the Father. Rather, the deity is hidden in Christ, even as he is mocked, scourged, beaten, and killed for
our sake.

In this sense, the obedience of Christ is to be understood in light
of three distinct but interrelated "levels" of reflection. It implicates
the processions of the persons in one respect, their common will to
undertake the mission of our salvation in another respect, and the
human actions and words of Christ in a third respect. The latter reveals the first two (procession and mission) without collapsing these
three dimensions of the "divine obedience" into one another. Clearly,
this perspective does not allow us to attribute obedience to God the
Son in his eternal procession as God. Therefore, it is improper to say
(as Barth does at times) that this obedience characterizes Christ in
his deity and divine nature. But this perspective does safeguard the
reality of the transcendent freedom of the persons *vis-à-vis* the creation and temporal mission of Christ, and distinguishes clearly the
two natures of Christ as human and divine. It does so while still in-
dicating something about *how* the human, temporal obedience of
Christ could reveal the eternal relativity of the Son to the Father. This
revelation occurs by virtue of the hypostatic union: the obedience of
the Son made man not only exists in God, but also subsists *hypostatically* so as to reveal that Jesus is *personally* relative to the Father.

CONCLUSION

It is clear that Karl Barth's theory of "divine obedience" contains a
multitude of rich intuitions. His understanding of the way God exists
in Christ as one who is both omnipotent and obedient is profound,
and can be profitably compared with the principles of Christology
that are characteristic of classical Chalcedonian thought. Nevertheless, Barth's claim that the generation of the Son from the Father is
itself characterized essentially by obedience is an affirmation laden

with difficulties. One central question Barth's theory raises concerns the unity of God's will. If obedience characterizes the very procession of the Son from the Father, how are we to avoid the conclusion of a kenotic dimension in the life of God which ruptures his unique nature? In this case, can the will of the Father in fact be possessed in plenary fashion by the person of the Son? And if the Son is omnipotent, how is it that his procession from the Father, and therefore his entire person, is characterized by consent to another's will?

There is also a problem concerning the presence of the effective saving will of God in the person of Christ. Christ is the savior because he bears within himself the action of God who reconciles us with himself effectively, through the event of Jesus's passion, death, and resurrection. Does the Son, however, possess the plenitude of the divine action in himself if his person is characterized hypostatically by obedience? It would seem that he cannot, and that he would therefore depend upon the Father and the Holy Spirit in order to act in himself to save us. And if the latter is the case, then the soteriological principle enunciated above cannot continue to hold true.

A fruitful counter-proposal is to consider the "obedience" of the Son as a figurative expression of his eternal reception of the divine will from the Father. In this case, however, three "levels" of reflection need to be carefully distinguished, that pertaining to procession, mission, and human obedience respectively. The Son proceeds eternally from the Father and therefore possesses his divine will from the Father. This eternal relativity of being permits him to receive from the Father his temporal mission to become man for our salvation. The existence of the Son as a human being in temporal history in turn reflects his personal relativity toward the Father in all that the incarnate Logos does as man. In this way the obedience of God the Son in his human nature reveals the essence of his temporal mission, the truth that he is sent from the Father. It also reveals, however, something of his relation to the Father in his divine nature: that the Son is eternally relative to the person of the Father from whom he proceeds. It does not, however, teach us that there is an obedience in the divine nature itself. Nor does it oblige us to posit a relation of commandment and obedience as constitutive of the immanent life of the Trinitarian persons.

It is all the more important to maintain these distinctions as we approach the mystery of the cross in a theological perspective. For the crucifixion and death of Jesus do reveal to us the mystery of the Holy Trinity, but this revelation occurs only in and through the distinct natures of Jesus, as one who is both divine and human. In the dereliction of Christ, the divinity of the Lord is not equated with his humanity. Rather, the transcendent majesty and power of Christ as Lord is manifest in and through his human abasement. It is to this subject that I will turn in the next two chapters.

7

———:———

Did God Abandon Jesus?

The Dereliction on the Cross

Modern theology has focused upon the last words of Christ in Mark 15:34—"My God, my God, why have you abandoned me?"—as a key locus of Christological dispute and interpretation.[1] Revisionist Enlightenment historians such as Reimarus have perceived in this verse an "authentic saying" of Jesus that predates the redaction of the Gospels. For him it is the indication of the Nazarene's disillusioned apocalypticism.[2] Protestant theologians, meanwhile, have found warrant in this Scriptural text for a theology of Christ's "god-forsakenness" experienced for us as a dimension of redemption. For Calvin it indicates Christ's state of abandonment as an "experience of the dread of damnation" incurred for us.[3] For Barth it shows that "our sin is no longer our own. It is His sin, the sin of Jesus Christ. God—He Himself as the obedient Son of the Father—has made it his own. And in this way He has judged it and judged us as those who committed it."[4] This has

---

1. Biblical citations in this chapter are all taken from the Revised Standard Version, which I have occasionally slightly modified.

2. The theory originates with Samuel Reimarus in his "On the Intentions of Jesus and His Disciples," published by Lessing in 1778, and was reappropriated by theorists such as Johannes Weiss and Albert Schweitzer.

3. ICR II, c. 16, nn. 10–12, with explicit reference to Mk 15:34.

4. CD IV, 1, 238. This explanation of the death cry is used to interpret Mk 15:34 (on

led others to reflect on the agony of Christ as a mode of separation in
the Trinity itself, or as an indication of suffering transpiring within the
divine nature itself.[5] It is sometimes seen (in kenosis Christologies)
as incompatible with the "omnipotent" presence of his divine nature.[6]
At the very least, the cry of dereliction is often interpreted as an indication of spiritual darkness in the soul of Christ that is incompatible
with any notion of a "beatific vision" in the heights of his soul. I quoted above in chapter 5 the poignant words of Jean Galot: "how can we
attribute to a Savior who is filled with heavenly beatitude these words:
'My God, My God, why have you abandoned me?' ... The cry of Jesus
on the cross makes manifest the depths of a suffering that is incompatible with the beatitude of the vision."[7] Versions of these views, meanwhile, have become ensconced in exegetical research as now standard
elements of Christological commentary.[8]

All of this stands in potential contrast to the traditional Catholic affirmation that Christ possessed the "immediate vision" of God
(or "beatific vision") in the heights of his soul during his earthly life.
I have of course argued in favor of this affirmation in chapter 5. According to this theory, far from knowing himself and the Father

215 and 239). In the text cited above, Barth appeals to Luther's expression of this idea in
On Gal. 3:13; see *Martin Luthers Werke: kritische Gesammtausgabe. Weimarer Ausgabe,* 121
vols. (Weimar: H. Böhlaus Nachfolger, 1883–2009), 40, 435, 17. It is noteworthy that he
also refuses to see in this cry any form of "separation" in the Godhead itself (185).

5. For evidence of the former idea in the thought of Balthasar, see *Mysterium Paschale,* 34, 101, 209; *Theodrama,* 3:237 and 4:334, and the analysis of John Yocum in his "A
Cry of Dereliction? Reconsidering a Recent Theological Commonplace," *International
Journal of Systematic Theology* 7, no. 1 (2005): 72–80. Versions of the latter idea can be
found in thinkers such as Moltmann, Bulgakov, and Jüngel.

6. See Moltmann, *The Crucified God,* 205; Moltmann also finds a basis for his interpretation in the above-mentioned text of Barth (202–3).

7. "Le Christ terrestre et la vision," 434.

8. See, for example, Ulrich Luz, *Matthew: A Commentary,* 3 vols., trans. J. Crouch
(Minneapolis, Minn.: Fortress, 2007), 3:541–59, and Ben Witherington III, *John's Wisdom* (Louisville, Ky.: Westminster John Knox, 1995), 315–16, both of whom appeal to
Moltmann's *The Crucified God* to interpret the cry of dereliction as an expression of suffering in the divine nature itself. According to Luz, the Chalcedonian doctrine should
be put in question: "Jesus is depicted [in Mt 27:46–50] in the colors of a biblical righteous man who suffers, who struggles with his God, and who even accuses him. In this
sense, the two-natures doctrine [of Chalcedon], to the degree that in its classical orthodox form it tended to assume for Jesus a divine self incapable of suffering, is a poor
guide for interpreting this text" (*Matthew: A Commentary,* 3:554).

uniquely by faith, Christ in his human intellect possessed direct, intuitive knowledge of his own divine identity and will at all times, even during the most agonizing moments of the passion. It would follow from this that Jesus could not undergo any human alienation from the divine wisdom and will he shared in as God. Rather, his temporal obedience to the Father was the purposeful expression (in human intellectual and voluntary terms) of the unity of will he shared with the Father from all eternity. Such an idea is reinforced by the argument made in chapter 6: Christ does not obey the Father by virtue of his divine nature, and yet, in his human knowledge and the obedience that springs from it, his human actions are expressive of the divine life that he shares with the Father.

It would seem from all this that Thomistic Christology holds together with a great deal of internal coherence. There is a profoundly intelligible relation between Christ's extraordinary knowledge, his unity of wills, and his human obedience as expressive of his divine personal identity. And yet, in light of the modern theological tendency alluded to above, we rightfully can pose here a significant objection: could Jesus utter the so-called cry of dereliction from the cross and simultaneously possess the knowledge that is central to all these Thomistic theological claims? Could the agonizing Christ have had the beatific vision in the heights of his soul?

In this chapter I would like to draw some theological and biblical parameters for thinking rightly about the death cry of Christ and its theological significance. In the first part, I will draw upon theological reflections from Aquinas to argue that the final cry of Christ on the cross cannot be interpreted as a cry of either despair or of spiritual separation from God. By contrast, it must be understood theologically as a prayer of desire related to Christ's abandonment to the Father and his hope to introduce humanity into the eschatological gift of redemption. In the second part of the chapter (drawing on the exegetical work of Marie-Joseph Lagrange, Rudolf Schnackenburg, and Raymond Brown, among others) I will compare the final words of Christ in Mark with the "cry of thirst" that is their equivalent in John's Gospel (19:28). In doing so, I will explore three theological parallels that exist in both traditions, and will argue that these reveal a common theological core present in the very different perspectives of the two evangelists. I will argue that the cry of Christ as portrayed in each of these traditions implies the presence of both expectation and agony, and has explicitly eschatological overtones. It is seen to usher in a new age of redemption that has already begun at Calvary. In the third part of the chapter I will return to Aquinas, and his theory of the "economic mode" of the beatific vision of the earthly Christ. Here I will argue that the "mixed state" of expectation and suffering previously discussed is entirely compatible with (and in fact complementary to) the teaching of St. Thomas concerning Christ's knowledge of both the Father and sinful humanity. In his crucifixion, Jesus experiences in his intellect and will both the peace of union with the Father and the acute agony that derives from knowledge of our sins.

THE EXCLUSION OF
DESPAIR AND DAMNATION FROM
THE SOUL OF CHRIST

In the first section of this chapter, I will argue that (1) despair and separation from God, if strictly defined, entail sin. They cannot be attributed to Christ because of the biblical affirmation of his sinlessness. They are also counter-factual to the reports present in all four Gospels of his praying at the cross. If this is the case, however, (2) a broader "analogical" understanding of "damnation" and "despair" cannot be attributed to Christ either, because these terms can only be predicated of his loving obedience equivocally rather than analogically. Therefore, (3) the "cause" of Christ's agonizing death cry in Mark 15:34 must be sought elsewhere. This cause must be understood in some way which respects the plenitude of love that informs his acts. Following Aquinas, the best recourse is to a theory of "eschatological desire." The cry of Jesus on the cross stems from the hope and expectation of the end times which reside in his will in and through his suffering.[9]

9. Aquinas affirms in ST III, q. 7, a. 4 that Christ in his historical life *did not* possess the *theological virtue* of hope because he enjoyed the plenary possession of God in the heights of his soul, due to the beatific vision. He does add, however, that Christ possessed a unique form of hope or desire for the fulfillment of the eschaton. This includes the desire for the resurrection of his own body and the plenary salvation of the church.

Hope and Desire in Christ's
Death Cry

There can be no question that for the Gospel writer, the cry of Mark 15:34 denotes the existence of tremendous suffering and agony within the soul of Christ at the moment of his death. What can this mean, theologically? Here much depends upon one's definition of terms. Some commentators seem to suggest that Christ who was without sin experienced pains of spiritual agony and deprivation of the presence and consolations of God analogous to those of persons in a state of sinful (permanent) separation from God.[10] The suggestion is important and I will return to it below.

In the meantime, however, it must be admitted that strictly speaking, theological terms such as "despair" and "damnation" refer to spiritual states which result from terrible voluntary choices that human beings must be enjoined to avoid. The modest presupposition here is that there exist in the human soul temptations to actions which entail serious privations of grace and can lead to permanent separation from God. As Aquinas notes, "despair" understood in this theologically pejorative sense signifies the voluntary refusal to hope in God's promises and the means God provides to obtain the ends which are promised.[11] Such despair is a real temptation for the human person precisely because it contrasts with the hope of perseverance. The person who despairs no longer counts upon God to provide him or her with a concrete way toward salvation.[12]

10. See in particular, John Calvin, ICR II, c. 16, n. 10: "It was expedient for him to undergo the severity of God's vengeance, to appease his wrath and satisfy his just judgment. For this reason, he must also grapple with the dread of everlasting death.... Christ was put in place of evildoers as surety and pledge—submitting himself even as the accused—to bear and suffer *all the punishments that they ought to have sustained*.... He suffered the death that God in his wrath inflicted upon the wicked....He paid a greater and more excellent price in suffering in his soul *the terrible torments of a condemned and forsaken man*" (emphasis added). Calvin argues rightly (n. 12) that Luke's depiction of Jesus sweating blood (Lk 22:44) suggests something more than the natural fear of death. But is Calvin's explanation of this mysterious agony appropriate?

11. See ST II-II, q. 20, a. 3: "Despair consists in a man ceasing to hope for a share in God's goodness."

12. In *In II Cor.* IV, lec. 3, 135, Aquinas comments on 2 Cor 4:8 ("We are afflicted in every way ... but not driven to despair") interpreting hope and despair as opposing

Damnation, meanwhile, presupposes the absence of hope in and love for God, but also entails (1) the pain of *definitive* privation of the grace, knowledge and vision of God (2) *by a personal aversion to the will of God*.[13] The latter point is most important. Damnation as a form of suffering stems from malice toward the divine will. It is brought on by a voluntary desire to privilege the egotistical desires of one's own will to the goodness and will of God in a definitive and all-encompassing way. The greatest "punishment" incurred by this disposition, therefore, is self-inflicted. It is the deprivation of the vision of God, and knowledge that this self-inflicted loss is eternal.[14]

Defined in these terms, it is evident that from a biblical perspective, one must say that there was neither despair nor the experience of damnation in the soul of Christ on Calvary due to the fact that Christ is sinless.[15] On the contrary, the perfect human obedience of the Son in his human acts is the eloquent testimony of a love for the will of the Father, and is the necessary condition of possibility for human salvation.[16] Yet this still leaves open the possibility that the non-biblical perspective of Reimarus is essentially correct, and that the historical Jesus of Nazareth in fact died in an act of disillusioned despair. Could it be said, for example, that the cry of Mark 15:34 denotes

---

responses to temporal misfortune: *"But we are not abandoned by God.... Persons who are without hope and [therefore] without the help of God ... are left destitute. Yet those who trust and hope in God alone, however much they lack, are not abandoned"* (emphasis added).

13. ST II-II, q. 34, aa. 1–2: "God may be the object of hatred for some, in so far as they look upon Him as forbidding sin, and inflicting punishment.... But hatred of God is contrary to the love of God, wherein man's best consists.... The defect in sin consists in its aversion from God and this aversion would not have the character of guilt, were it not voluntary.... Now this voluntary aversion from God is directly implied in the hatred of God."

14. Aquinas teaches these ideas in ST I, q. 63, a. 1; q. 64, a. 2 and a. 3, corp. and ad 3. In ST I-II, q. 87, a. 4 he notes that the infinite punishment of sin is the self-inflicted pain of loss of the vision of God, whereas the punishments inflicted by God as a result of sin are finite.

15. On the sinlessness of Christ, see 2 Cor 5:21, Heb 4:15, 1 Pet 2:21–22, 1 Jn 3:5. There is no indication that Mark thought differently from the rest of the early Christian community on this matter.

16. This perspective is already found in the pre-New Testament Christology of Phil 2:8–9. Presumably an analogous doctrine is expressed by Mk 10:45 and 14:36. See the argument to this effect by Ben Witherington III, *The Many Faces of the Christ* (New York: Crossroad, 1998), 78–90, 128–38.

a bewildered accusation rendered against God due to a conviction about the absence of divine intervention?

In response to this suggestion, two ideas must be kept in mind. First of all, it is impossible to prove by historical reason alone what Christ said on the cross prior to the New Testament presentation of this event. However, if we employ the "criterion of dissimilarity" it seems probable that Mark has transmitted an accurate historical memory.[17] As Douglas Hare points out, in Mark's narrative the cry is misunderstood by onlookers due to a linguistic resemblance in the Aramaic language. They interpret it as a call to Elijah. Both the linguistic and theological interpretations of the cry given by its hearers make no sense from within an early Christian (Greek-speaking) theological perspective. Furthermore, the statement "why have you forsaken me" clearly raised theological difficulties for some members of the earliest Christian community, as denoted by Luke's purposeful omission of it from his Gospel. Therefore one can reasonably posit the cry as a pre-New Testament event correctly reported by a community which did not fully understand it.[18]

Second, however, the death cry of Mark 15:34 is also a citation of Psalm 22:1. As Justin Martyr first noted, therefore, it definitely suggests on Christ's part the *purposeful* invocation of a psalm, denoting an act of prayer and implying a claim to prophetic fulfillment.[19] This line of thinking raises the question of whether the invocation of the psalm by the historical Jesus implied that he was expressing a messi-

17. As interpreted by Ernst Käsemann and others, the criterion of dissimilarity can be employed as a principle for discerning the likelihood that a saying in the Gospel should be attributed to Christ when it helps one discern a simultaneous dissimilarity between a saying attributed to Christ and (1) aspects of the Judaism of the time of Jesus as well as (2) the later ideas of the early church. However, for N. T. Wright, the principle should be qualified by the theory of a double similarity between the sayings of Christ and the Judaism of first century Palestine, as well as between the words of the historical Jesus and the teachings of the early church. In this sense, the principle points toward both the Judaic origins of Christ's teachings as well as its originality in the context of Second Temple Judaism. It also points toward the way this teaching is the origin of (but not strictly identical with) the teaching of the later Christian movement. For this interpretation of the principle, see N. T. Wright, *Jesus and the Victory of God*, 131–33.

18. See Douglas Hare, *Matthew* (Louisville, Ky.: Westminster John Knox, 1993), 322.

19. *Dialogue with Trypho*, 97–99. This exegesis was to become widespread in the ancient church. See for example, Irenaeus, *Against Heresies*, III, 19, 2; IV, 20, 8; IV, 33, 12; V, 7, 1; Athanasius, *Contra Arian*. II, para. 66; IV, para. 28; Hilary, *De Trinitate*, XI, 15.

anic hope even during his crucifixion. Indeed, the Psalter was classically associated with the prophecies of David. In this case, the hope
of vindication by God (such as that which occurs at the end of the
psalm) could well be intended even in citing its opening line.[20] What
is certain is that the references to the psalms present in Christ's last
words in all four Gospels were interpreted in messianic fashion in
the earliest church. The entire early Christian community seems to
have believed that Christ in fact died in prayer and that his citation
of the psalms had prophetic overtones.[21] If this is the case, however, it becomes absurd to presume the existence of an experience of
radical disillusionment, despair, or accusation underlying Christ's last
words. On the contrary, the early Christian interpretation of Christ's
last words may simply be the best historical understanding of what
Jesus intended them to signify.[22] Therefore, even from the perspec-

20. For extensive argumentation concerning the messianic significance of Psalm 22
in the New Testament, see Gregory Vall, "Psalm 22: Vox Christi or Israelite Temple Liturgy?", *The Thomist* 66 (2002): 175–200. On the question of the messianic use of the
psalm at Qumran and in early Rabbinic literature, see Gilles Dorival, "L'Interpretation
Ancienne du Psaume 21 (TM 22)," in *David, Jésus et la Reine Esther*, ed. G. Dorival (Louvain: Peeters, 2002), 225–314. N. T. Wright (*Jesus and the Victory of God*, 600–601) situ-
ates the citation of Psalm 22 by Jesus within the larger context of his prophetic appropriation of the Davidic Psalter, and his messianic intention to act out the drama of Israel so
as to initiate through the events of his life the eschatological coming of God's kingdom.
In this sense, Wright speculates that Jesus's citation of the first line of the psalm may well
have indicated a messianic interpretation of the victory of the afflicted one discussed at
the end of the psalm.

21. In Mt 27:46, Jesus appeals to the same verse. In Lk 23:46 he cites Ps 31:5 (cf. Acts
7:59 and 1 Pet 4:19). Jn 19:28 ("I thirst") seems to refer to Ps 69:21, although some scholars point to a possible parallel with Ps 22:15. All of these uses imply messianic claims by
the New Testament authors: Christ's death fulfilled prophecy. On the development of
this exegesis in the earliest post-New Testament Christian writers, see the study of Jean
Danielou, *Etudes d'exégèse judéo-chrétienne* (Paris: Beauchesne, 1966), 28–41.

22. This is essentially the apologetical argumentation of Raymond Brown in his *The
Death of the Messiah* (New York: Doubleday, 1993), 2:1085–88. While he is sympathetic
to the claim that Mk 15:34 represents an authentic historical memory, he notes that it
is also recounted within an entirely theological context (2:1044–48). To claim, as Reimarus did, that the cry necessarily denotes a historical event of despair that Christian
theology cannot account for is absurd, since Mark shows us in a following verse (v. 39)
that precisely the way in which Christ died was (according to Mark) the cause for the
recognition by the gentile centurion that he was the Son of God. Brown speculates that
the historical Christ probably died with *both* a desire expressed through prayer *as well as*
the *feeling* of forsakenness which he offered to God (2:1048–51), and that this was accurately reported by the early Christian community.

tive of "historical reason alone," the interpretation of biblical faith remains an open possibility. Yet, theologically speaking, if it *need not* be
seen as an act of abandoning God through hopelessness, Christ's cry
to God *must* be considered as a cry of hope to God for deliverance.
More precisely, it is a cry of desire.

Christ's Love and Our Alienation

These statements do not exclude the above-mentioned theological
hypothesis: that Christ experienced something analogous to damnation and despair in the sufferings and agony he underwent in the
passion, and that he did so due to his identification with our state of
alienation from God out of love for us. And there is no doubt that
the biblical teaching of St. Paul on Christ's passion suggests some
kind of theology of a "reversal of roles" in which Christ takes upon
himself effects of our sinfulness precisely in order to liberate us from
them.[23] But two unavoidable qualifications need to be kept in mind
in this regard. The first is that (as all Christian theologians agree)
Christ did this out of love for us and out of loving obedience to God
the Father.[24] Therefore, theologically speaking, the spiritual agony he
underwent was an effect of his love for human beings, an agony he
endured precisely to manifest more radically that love. It in no way
stemmed, then, from the same root cause as the spiritual sufferings of
the despairing and the damned (these causes being the refusal of the
demands of divine love and the aversion to God's will).

Second, as I have noted above, the pains of damnation are *principally* the regret of the loss of God through *one's own refusal* of divine
life. They come from within the personal agent due to an aversion for
God. Therefore, there is a radical difference of causality in acts stemming from love versus those associated with the refusal of love. Because of this radical difference of causalities, the two states that derive
from them can rightfully be said to be essentially dissimilar. If this is
the case, then they cannot be compared analogically, and the attribution of a state of damnation to the sufferings of Christ implies a pure
equivocation. True, the respective *effects* of sin and love in the two

---

23. See especially 2 Cor 5:14–15, 21.
24. See the emphasis on this idea by Calvin in ICR II, c. 16, n. 12.

cases under consideration may resemble each other. However, it only follows from this that the two states may be predicated of one another in a *merely* metaphorical fashion, and need not entail any kind of real analogy.

To clarify this perspective, one may consider that for Aquinas metaphorical expressions ("he is as strong as an ox") depend upon a similitude of effects derived from two realities which share no common ratio or common essence, and are in no way the cause of one another.[25] By contrast, strictly analogical predication requires something that is essentially common to the two terms that are compared. To take an example from metaphysics, diverse facets of reality are said to be in diverse ways—as substances, qualities, quantities, etc. Despite their real differences, all of these categorical modes of being can be said to be in some common sense, albeit analogically. This analogical attribution of being must be contrasted, however, with the attribution of damnation to the terms we are considering. The reason for this is that the absence of love for God and the presence of love, unlike the categories of being, are not diverse modes of participation in a wider spectrum of analogical realizations of existence or goodness. On the contrary, sin is the absence of goodness in the appetitive will. It entails a voluntary privation of love. Therefore, sin is also the negative contrary of love, which it necessarily excludes. If we employ the so-called analogy of proper proportionality (A is to C_1 as B is to C_2) which Thomists characteristically apply to creatures to compare them, goodness can be said to reside analogically (as C_1 and C_2) in both the qualities (A) and the quantity (B) of a human person because they have existence in common, and all existence is good. It does not reside analogically in both the love for God and the refusal to love God, because one is the privation of the other.[26] True, Christ's passion is *like* an experience of damnation or despair in certain respects, because the agony he undergoes bears certain resemblances to the agony of the despairing. He

25. On metaphorical as opposed to properly analogical predication, see ST I, q. 13, a. 6. I am using "essence" here broadly to denote what Thomists mean by the *ratio entis*, the intelligibility common to diverse members of an analogically united set.

26. On the analogy of proportionality and the use of metaphorical similitudes, especially as applied to Christ, see M. T.-L. Penido, *Le rôle d'analogie en théologie dogmatique* (Paris: J. Vrin, 1931), 42–46, 397–404.

can be said to suffer the pains of deprivation of the psychologically felt presence of God in a way that is *metaphorically* similar to that of the damned (through the absence of the *effects* of joy, consolation, etc.). Yet this similarity contains *nothing* that is *essentially* the same as the latter state, because Christ's suffering does not stem from an absence of or resistance to divine love. These latter faults, by contrast, contribute to the *essence* of despair and damnation.

Calvin suggests that the pains of hell experienced by Christ consist *principally* in his dread, sorrow and fear of being forsaken by God as well as his experience of the wrath of God against human sin. Here what defines the state is the judgment and wrath of God.[27] I am suggesting, by contrast, that the pains of damnation stem, instead, from the voluntary refusal to embrace God's loving will, and the deprivation of the vision of God which results. The pain comes first and foremost from the subject who is averse to God and himself forsakes God, and only secondarily from God's punishment, which follows as a consequence.[28] The *essence* of Christ's agony, therefore, stems from something entirely different from such aversion to God (divine love) and therefore, strictly speaking, is not analogous to the state of the damned. In fact, at heart it is entirely dis-analogous.

27. On Mt 27:46, Calvin writes: "There is *nothing more dreadful* than to feel God as Judge, *whose wrath is worse than all deaths*" (*Calvin's Commentaries*, eds. David Torrance and Thomas F. Torrance [Grand Rapids: Eerdmans, 1971], 3:207; emphasis added).

28. For John Damascene and for Aquinas, God "antecedently" wills to save each person, but he *permits* the refusal of his grace and *consequently* sentences by his justice a person who perseveres in sin (see *De Fide Orth.* II, c. 29 as cited by Aquinas in ST I, q. 19, a. 6, ad 1). Calvin explicitly refuses the theological validity of the distinction between the antecedent and consequent will of God (ICR III, c. 23, n. 8). Consequently, damnation for him stems primarily from a positive will of God, rather than a divine permission. It follows logically that Christ's experience of damnation stems also from the positive will of God, which substitutes Christ as a subject of wrath for us in order that we might be justified (II, c. 16, nn. 5 and 10). Calvin does stipulate that this substitution occurs in and through the Father's love for us, and not as a condition for the latter (II, c. 16, nn. 3–4). Aquinas, meanwhile, holds that Christ did subject himself to our fallen state for our sake, and in this sense took our punishments upon himself for our redemption. But he also notes that it is impossible for an innocent man to submit to a penal substitution for the guilt due to another, as if he were to assume the sins of the other (ST I-II, q. 87, aa. 7–8). Instead, Christ substitutes his obedience for our disobedience so as to repair in our human nature the injustice done to God's loving wisdom by human sin. For a helpful Thomistic critique of Calvin's penal substitution theory, see Philippe de La Trinité, *What Is Redemption?*, trans. A. Armstrong (New York: Hawthorn Books, 1961).

Christ's Suffering Hope

Based on the testimony of scripture, it must be said that Christ in his crucifixion experienced terrible agony, both spiritual and physical. Yet he did not despair of the promises of God, nor experience the moral separation from God that is characteristic of the damned. This is impossible because a plenitude of love and obedience informs all of the human actions of Christ, and is incompatible with human sin. Yet, if we exclude such despair and separation as causes, then how might we explain his cry of want, denoted by Mark 15:34?

It must be borne in mind that this cry denotes not only love but also privation. The state of Christ on the cross is a mixed state, simultaneously implying both expectation and suffering, presence and absence. What I would propose is that Aquinas's understanding of the theological virtue of hope in the heart of Christ helps us take account precisely of such a mixed state. The latter theological virtue, according to Aquinas, is both a source of expectation (and therefore desire implying non-possession) as well as of dissatisfaction.[29] It is an expression of the tension of a personal love seeking a good as yet possessed only imperfectly. In Christ, a deeper knowledge of his own final end, as well as that of those he came to save, would certainly have meant that such a love existed in an especially radical way. Could it also have meant that he experienced a deeper desire and dissatisfaction than others, precisely because of this same love? For Aquinas, loving hope in the heart of Christ was a source of intense desire which could no doubt have coexisted with torment and even profound spiritual and emotional sadness. Aquinas claims that during his passion Christ hoped both for his own bodily resurrection by the Father and for the salvation of all human beings.[30] Yet, hope is a complex virtue, according to Aquinas, precisely because within it expectation and desire can and do coexist with the non-possession of that which is hoped for. This means that in hope, the states of desire, sadness, deprivation, and agony can and often do coexist.[31] Pushing the

29. ST II-II, q. 17, a. 1: "The object of hope is a future good, difficult but possible to obtain."

30. ST III, q. 21, a. 3, corp., ad 2 and 3. See also III, q. 7, a. 4.

31. In ST III, q. 46, aa. 7–8, Aquinas insists on this fact. This is a point I will return to below.

question one step further we can ask if this desire *was itself* the cause of an increased suffering and agony? If so, then this inner tension of desire (as both hope and suffering) is a possible explanation for the inner meaning of the death cry of the crucified Christ. To explore this possibility further, I will now turn to a comparison of the thinking of Mark and John on this subject.

MARK AND JOHN
ON THE ESCHATOLOGICAL
CRY OF CHRIST

In the second part of this chapter I would like to note briefly three parallels which exist between the theology of Christ's crucifixion in Mark and that of John. In particular I will be concerned to compare Mark 15:34 with John 19:28 as they exist within the larger context of the two respective theological visions of the Evangelists. My central claim will be this: despite (and notwithstanding) the reality of the differences in perspective between the two Gospel writers, the death cry which precedes the offering of vinegar in either narration is a cry contextualized by both desire and agony which has immediate eschatological overtones.

Christ's Expectation of Exaltation

In both Mark and John, the death cry of Christ is contextualized by desire. We are given to understand by a previously stated expectation that the death of Christ will be redemptive and the occasion for the exaltation of the Son of Man. In John's Gospel this theme is evident: the narrative informs us from the beginning of the public ministry of Jesus that his death is an event foreseen and willed by God for our salvation. It is precisely because the suffering of Christ in love is the chosen means for our salvation that this event is itself the exaltation of the Son of Man.[32] This perspective is a "precondition," then, for the

---

32. Cf. Jn 3:14: "So must the Son of Man be *lifted up*"; 8:28: "When you *lift up* the Son of Man then you will know that I am"; and 12:32: "When I am *lifted up* from the earth, then I will draw all men to myself." As Dodd, Brown, Schnackenburg, Barrett, and others have shown, the author of the fourth Gospel systematically transfers the characteristics and functions assigned by the Synoptic authors to the glorified Son of Man

right interpretation of the cross as a saving event. Consequently, the final words of Christ ("I thirst"; "It is accomplished") must be understood in light of his earlier foretelling of his suffering and death on behalf of all.[33] For John these words manifest something of the profound peace that underlies the act of self-offering which characterizes the soul of Christ in his passion.

Of course, at first this may seem simply at odds with the cry of dereliction according to Mark. In fact, as scholars commonly note, there are some signs that John wished precisely to counteract the impression that Jesus was somehow abandoned by God in his experience of death.[34] Yet if we place the cry of Mark 15:34 in its broader narrative context, we may note two important facts which moderate this sense of discontinuity. First, it is evident that the cry in Mark comes after a theological narrative in which there are three prophetic announcements of the crucifixion *and* resurrection of the Son of Man.[35] This means that the expectation of both the crucifixion as a mode of dying and a subsequent exaltation by God through resurrection must be seen as central theological motifs that structure the Markan narrative. This same theological expectation of both death and subsequent vindication seems to be borne out in the words of Jesus before the high priest in 14:62, just prior to the crucifixion, where he explicitly foretells of his exaltation as the Son of Man.[36] Second, as Rudolf Schnackenburg has noted, many of the Son of Man sayings in Mark denote the reality of an eschatological figure *already* rendered present in Jesus's ministry (in ways analogous to the perspective of

---

from the exalted state of the resurrection to the crucifixion event itself. See in particular, C. H. Dodd, *The Fourth Gospel* (Cambridge: Cambridge University Press, 1963), 432–43.

33. A point made by Schnackenburg, *The Gospel according to St. John*, 3:283.

34. See Brown, *The Death of the Messiah*, 2:1073. In Mk 14:35 Jesus asks the Father that "if it be possible, this hour might pass from him." As if to contradict the impression that Jesus is abandoned, Jn 12:27–28 has Jesus stating: "And what should I say? Father, save me from this hour? But for this purpose have I come to this hour. Father, glorify your name." In contrast to Mk 15:34, Brown notes that in Jn 16:32 we read: "I am not alone, for the Father is with me."

35. Mk 8:31: "The Son of Man must suffer many things ... and be killed, and after three days rise again" (see also 9:22 and 10:33–34).

36. On this eschatological narrative in Mark, especially as it underlies the use of Psalm 22, see Joel Marcus, *The Way of the Lord: Christological Exegesis of the Old Testament in the Gospel of Mark* (Louisville, Ky.: Westminster John Knox, 1992), 177–82.

John). Consequently, this presence must be presumed as actual and active *on the cross*.[37]

If we keep these two ideas in mind, then we must see the death cry of Mark's Gospel as a moment theologically contextualized by the reader's expectation of the cross, foreseen and embraced by Jesus "as a ransom for many" (10:45; cf. 14:24), and in view of his exaltation "to the right hand of Power" (14:62). The Gospel taken on its own, then, *as a theological interpretation of the life of Christ*, should be seen as positing an *expectant* (if agonizing) prayer present within the cry of Christ on the cross. The Jesus of Mark knew he was suffering for us, and had in view his own exaltation by the Father. Whether or not the cry of Christ in Mark should be seen to denote not only agony, but also dereliction (that is to say, an inner experience of abandonment) can therefore be disputed. M. J. Lagrange argues that Jesus's citation of Psalm 22:1 in Mark 15:34 must be seen in light of contemporary Jewish tradition. Understood in this way, it refers for Mark to the rest of the psalm and thus looks forward to the triumph of the subject in verse 25. In this case the citation of it by Christ is meant to denote an expectation of vindication by God.[38] In any case, what is certain is that it is seen by Mark as the expression of a desire that is immediately efficacious. Shortly after his cry of Psalm 22:1, and a final wordless exclamation (Mk 15:37), Christ dies and the eschatological world of God begins to unfold. This is a point I will return to below.

---

37. See Schnackenburg, *The Gospel according to St. John*, 1:535–38 on Mk 1:7, 2:10, 2:28, 8:38, 10:37, 14:62.

38. *L'Evangile Selon Saint Marc* (Paris: J. Gabalda, 1921), 433–34. For complementary reflections, see George Beasley-Murray, *John* (Waco, Tx.: Word Books, 1989), 350–52. If one were to consider Christ subject to despair *from Mark's perspective*, this would contrast notably with the portrayal of the hope of the martyrs found in texts such as 2 Mc 6 and 7, where faithful Jews are seen to have died under persecution with firm confidence in God's resurrection of the just from the dead. The ideal expressed in such texts indicates an eschatological view common to the Jews of Jesus's time, which finds numerous echoes in Mark's Gospel (6:14–16, 9:9, 10:29–31, 12:18–27, 14:58). Are we to attribute, then, to the dying Christ of Mark's Gospel a less resolute hope in the resurrection than to these others whose hopes characterized the Jewish beliefs of that period? Especially when Mark portrays Jesus as sharing in such beliefs? See on this topic N. T. Wright, *The Resurrection of the Son of God* (Minneapolis, Minn.: Fortress, 2003), 150–53, 401–29.

The Reality of Christ's Suffering

The second parallel concerns the dimension of agony that surrounds the death of Christ in both Gospels. In the Gospel of John, this is to be seen particularly in the cry of thirst which precedes the offer of the sponge with vinegar, and therefore takes the place of what would be the cry of agony in Mark. I have noted above that it communicates a sense of the desire of Christ in a solemn way, in view of a portrait of the suffering Christ as sovereignly free and victorious in love. Certainly this observation is consistent with the work of modern exegesis which has drawn attention to the eschatological character of Christ's work already effectively realized at the cross.

At the same time, the narrative structure of John conveys to us not only that Christ can suffer sadness and emotional distress, but also that he has begun to experience an inner agony precisely because of his "hour."[39] Something is radically incomplete in the experience of Christ leading up to the passion. As Beasley-Murray has noted, Jesus's citation of Psalm 69:21 in John 19:28 ("for my thirst they gave me vinegar to drink") is seen by John as the fulfillment of scripture. But it is simultaneously a reference to a psalm which in its broader context denotes both suffering and inner desolation: "This saying is part of the lengthy description of the desolation, isolation, and scorn experienced by the Righteous Sufferer, and in the psalm the giving of the drink appears to be part of the torment inflicted upon the sufferer."[40]

39. John's Christology emphasizes at various points the real human fatigue, sadness and suffering of Jesus (Jn 4:6, 11:35–38). Jn 12:27 clearly denotes the actual presence of agony in the soul of Christ: "Now is my soul troubled." Yet Jesus lives out this agony freely, with the recognition that "for this purpose [He] has come to this hour." John makes it clear, then, that Christ both suffers and that his suffering does not cause him to forfeit the prerogatives of the wisdom of God present in his person. Contrast this with the apocryphal Gospel of Peter, in which Christ is said on the one hand to be "as having no pain" during his crucifixion (4:10), but simultaneously cries out in 5:19: "My power, O power, you have forsaken me." The former quotation seems to confuse the humanity and divinity of Christ, whereas the latter separates them. Brown (*Messiah*, 1337–38) does not think the text is docetic. But one can rightfully say that the interplay of Christ's humanity and his divinity is distorted in this text, whereas John's Gospel holds them in perfect accord.

40. Beasley-Murray, *John*, 351. He goes on to add: "One may no more assume that John's emphasis on the cross as the exaltation of Jesus excludes his desolation of spirit

This fact can be coupled with the observation that throughout the Gospel we are given successive indications that Christian redemption more generally is not yet fully complete even after the occurrence of the Paschal mystery. Although Christ is the presence of eternal life already made manifest (11:25), the effect of that presence is not yet fully realized (5:28–29).[41] Given these elements in the background theological context, what difference do they make for our interpretation of the cry of thirst? The particular point we should make here is that John 19:28 is illustrative of a self-conscious tension which exists in John's theology between what is actually being accomplished on the cross and what is as yet desired. In a sense it is the most paradoxical manifestation of this tension: by it we are told that Christ fulfills scripture, thus accomplishing everything. At the same time, this fulfillment itself is expressed *as a thirst*, an incomplete desire, and one which, as we have seen, clearly includes dimensions of agony.

Given this context of suffering, what does Christ's thirst of unfulfillment cry out for? Some commentators detect a note of Johannine irony reflected by the cry.[42] Christ is thirsting for our human salvation (4:7–9), even while it is he himself (we have already been told) who gives the living water and it is we who "had [we] known, should have asked him to drink" (4:10). In fact, "from his heart will flow rivers of living water" (7:38), from which believers may live. However, this living water will only come forth *once the Spirit is given*, that is to say, *once Christ is glorified* (7:39). If this reading is correct, then the

---

than his emphasis on the deity of the Son excludes the Son's true humanity. That Jesus hung on the cross as King was not in spite of his agony, epitomized in the thirst of crucifixion, but through his agony endured in obedience and love to the glory of God."

41. C. K. Barrett, *The Gospel according to St. John* (Philadelphia: Westminster Press, 1978), 67–69 notes that on the one hand according to John, the eschaton is present already in the apostolic life of Jesus (4:23, 5:25), and the church lives in quasi-eschatological terms (cf. 14:23 on *parousia*). On the other hand, some statements (5:29; 6:39, 40, 44, 54) clearly refer to the last day, the final judgment, and the general resurrection which have yet to be realized. It cannot be claimed, then, that the Gospel of John departs essentially from the broader eschatological viewpoint that is common to the New Testament writings.

42. See in particular Barnabas Lindars, *The Gospel of John* (London: Oliphants Press, 1957), 582; R. H. Lightfoot, *St. John's Gospel* (Oxford: Clarendon Press, 1956), 318, and more recently, Gail O'Day, *John Commentary* in The New Interpreter's Bible (Nashville, Tenn.: Abingdon Press, 1995), 9:832–33.

thirst of Christ, placed in a broader Johannine context, denotes his desire for the sending of the Holy Spirit, the Paraclete, who can only be given once Jesus has "gone to the Father" (14:2; 16:7; 17:11). This result is in fact obtained in John 20:22 where the risen Christ communicates the Holy Spirit to his disciples on the evening of Easter. Consequently, the cry of thirst at the time it is uttered denotes a state of as yet unachieved suffering, even as it claims to be the fulfillment of the Hebrew Scriptures, that is, the condition of the possibility for the sending of the Spirit.[43]

What conclusion should be derived from these observations? My claim at this point is that both Mark and John presuppose a soteriological expectation or desire that informs the suffering of Christ in his crucifixion. Both of them see this desire as tending toward a later, post-resurrection state of fulfillment, and both of them see this desire as accompanied (to a greater and lesser degree respectively) by agony and suffering. In other words, both of them attribute to Christ characteristics of what we have denoted as theological hope: the expectation of salvation from God and the actual non-possession of that salvation (accompanied by actual suffering). In my final argument in this section, I would like to insist on the equally *eschatological* dimension of the death cry of Christ in both Gospels.

The Final Redemption of the World

My final claim is that for both authors, the theological results of the cry of Christ are eschatological. Yet, for both Mark and John respec-

---

43. In contrast to Lindars and Lightfoot, Brown (*Death of the Messiah*, 1074) thinks that the "I thirst" of Jn 19:28 refers directly to the words of Jesus in 18:11: "Shall I not drink the cup which the Father has given me?" This thirst, therefore, refers to the cup of suffering which Christ wishes to drink in order to accomplish the Father's will. (cf. 4:34, 5:36, 17:4). Such an interpretation must still affirm that Jesus thirsts to accomplish the Father's will, and bears the suffering of the cross in order to eventually give the Spirit to humanity. See on this point, Francis Moloney, *The Gospel of John* (Collegeville, Minn.: The Liturgical Press, 1998), 504–5. In the end, however, the discernment is literary. It seems to me that the symbols of water, thirst and rebirth in the Spirit are too important in the main body of the text to be entirely separated from the reference to thirst in 19:28. This is all the more clear when we consider the symbolic paradox that water (which we know is associated with life in the Spirit) flows forth from Christ's side almost immediately after his cry.

tively, how did the suffering and agonizing exclamation of Christ effectuate a change in the soteriological order of reality? John's Gospel offers us a clear answer in the shape of the aforementioned realized eschatology of the sending of the Spirit. The activity of the post-Paschal Spirit of Christ is articulated clearly in John 16:8 in overtly eschatological terms. Because Christ has died, the Holy Spirit can now demonstrate to the world God's eschatological judgment.[44] As Yves Congar has noted, there are multiple parallels in Johannine thought between Christ and the Spirit in their promised roles of mediating judgment from God *now* (prior to the final resurrection).[45] Consequently, we can say that the thirst of Christ (his suffering and agony) lived out in expectation of the sending of the Spirit *has for its immediate effect* the offer of eschatological (eternal) life for us in the present in the Spirit. This offer is seemingly already manifest in the blood and water poured out at the cross, which foreshadow the new birth of baptism in the Holy Spirit (cf. 19:34 in relation to 3:5). By the Spirit we enter into an eschatological continuum with the event of the Paschal mystery itself.[46] The cry of thirst finds its response, therefore, in our acceptation of the living water: the Spirit and the saving *agape* of Christ. By remaining in the latter (15:4), we receive the capacity Jesus offers in the Paraclete to accomplish the Father's will (15:10, 26), and therefore to grow in the vocation of filial adoption (1:12–13).

Is Mark's death cry equally eschatological, even if in a somewhat dissimilar way? We must answer affirmatively if we consider the key evidence of the biblical symbolism of the cry itself. As Raymond Brown has noted, an important motif in the New Testament sees the cry generally as a symbol of the initiation of the eschaton.

---

44. See Jn 16:8–15.

45. Yves Congar, *Je Crois en l'Esprit Saint* (Paris: Cerf, 1979), 1:82–86. For example, both Jesus and the Spirit are given by the Father (Jn 3:16 / 14:16) and will remain with the disciples from now on (14:20 / 14:16, 26). Both will be known to them alone (14:19 / 14:17), and will lead them into the fullness of truth (1:17, 18:37 / 16:13).

46. As Barrett notes (*The Gospel according to St. John*, 90): "The Spirit places the world in the position it will occupy at the last judgment.... The Spirit's work is to bear witness (15:26) to Christ, to make operative what Christ had already effected. The Spirit is thus the eschatological *continuum* in which the work of Christ, initiated in his ministry and awaiting its termination at his return, is wrought out."

In John 5:28 the *cry* of the Son of Man causes all those who are in the tombs to hear; and in 11:43 the *clamor* and *loud cry* of Jesus help to call forth Lazarus from the tomb. In I Thess. 4:16 the *cry* of the archangel accompanies the coming of the Lord to raise the dead, while in IV Ezra 13:12–13 the Man from the Sea *calls* the multitude to him. In judgment the Lord *speaks, roars,* and *cries out,* at times producing earthquakes, in Amos 1:2; Joel 4:16 (3:16); Jer. 25:30; and Ps. 46:7, even as in Rev. 10:3 the angel *shouts* with a loud voice as he reveals the seven thunders.[47]

In the Gospel of Matthew the cry of agony from the cross (27:46) is immediately accompanied by such eschatological signs: the sun darkens, the temple rock is split open and its curtain is torn, the earth trembles, the dead are raised, and the gentiles begin to recognize Christ (27:45, 51–54). In Mark's Gospel, the eschatological effects are more discreet but are still present. Darkness covers the earth, the temple veil is rent, and (most importantly) the centurion is converted to a recognition of Jesus as the Son of God. As Rudolf Schnackenburg has noted, this last event shows us that the death of Christ (and particularly his cry of agony) are seen by Mark as the first occasion for a fully lucid recognition of who Christ has been all along (Mark 1:1, 11, 24; 4:41; 9:7–8; 10:45), the Son of God who came to serve and to offer his life for our sake:

If we look over the picture of Jesus emerging [in Mark's Gospel] from the predication as the Son of God, we see majestic traits, namely, in the overcoming of Satan and in the power over demons, but also other assertions that reflect his path of suffering and death. He is the servant of God who obediently goes his way as the beloved Son of God. He is the Son of God who becomes apparent in death and who in the deepest distress of his humanity reveals his hidden majesty and divinity. The prayer of godforsakenness turns into the certainty that he is accepted by God. The dominant impression of the Son of God conveyed by the Gospel of Mark is the nearness of Jesus to God, which is not suspended even in death.[48]

Consequently, the narrative leaves us to conclude that the immediate result of Christ's death in agony, and his abandonment to the Father, is the redemption of the world. A new era has begun in which

---

47. *The Death of the Messiah,* 2:1045.

48. See Rudolf Schnackenburg, *Jesus in the Gospels: A Biblical Christology* (Louisville, Ky.: Westminster John Knox, 1995), 50–51.

Christ's kingdom is made available to those who believe in his mysterious identity and soteriological action.

THE VISION OF GOD AND
THE AGONY OF CHRIST

I have argued above that the cry of Christ from the cross should be interpreted theologically as a prayer of desire related to his hope to introduce humanity into the eschatological gift of redemption. Hope implies an incomplete state in which both loving desire and painful deprivation can be simultaneously present. In examining the last words of Christ according to John and Mark, I have claimed that the cry from the cross is presented by each as a desire-in-agony (with more emphasis on agony in Mark and more on desire in John). Therefore, both Gospel writers affirm the existence of such a mixed state in the soul of Christ during his crucifixion. Furthermore, this cry has explicitly eschatological overtones for both, since it is seen to usher in a new age of redemption that begins at Calvary.

In the final section of this chapter I would like to reflect theologically upon the relation of this desire-in-agony in Christ to the Thomistic affirmation of the beatific vision in the heights of Christ's soul. Are the two compatible? Might they even be complementary? I will seek to answer this question in three parts. First, I will discuss Aquinas's theory of how the immediate vision of God and intense agony could coexist in the soul of Christ during his passion. Second, I will note what I think are three dimensions of this agony. Third, I will examine the effects of the vision on both Christ's desire and his agony for each of these dimensions. I will claim that for two of these, the vision would intensify the desire of Christ and mitigate but not alleviate his suffering. For the third, however, it would intensify both his desire and his agony simultaneously. It is this last form of agony above all which should be seen to characterize the suffering expressed by his death cry.

The Beatific Vision and
Agony of Christ

Is the beatific vision in the heights of Christ's soul compatible with
any form of agony in the soul of Christ during his crucifixion? After
all, one might reasonably object that the bliss of the vision excludes
any real capacity for suffering. To respond to this difficulty we must
first recall a point made in chapter 5, that according to Aquinas, the
economic mode or dispensation of Christ's vision during his earthly life is understood to be very different from that of his vision in the
exalted state of glory.[49] In the latter state, his body and emotional psychology participate—each in its own way—directly in the glory of
his resurrected life. As a dimension of this glory, the joy and consolation of the spiritual presence of God in the heights of the soul of
Christ overflow into the whole of his humanity. His "lower faculties"
and in particular his psychological life participate intensively in the
contemplative bliss of his spiritual soul.[50]

In the former state, however, this vision is not the source of any
such experience. It *does* assure his soul of a continual knowledge of
his own divine identity and will as the Son of God, but it *in no way* al-
leviates his "ordinary" states of human consciousness and sensation.[51]
This means that Christ, for Aquinas, can experience suffering in a
typically human way in both its corporeal and psychological-spiritual
dimensions. Consequently, the vision is entirely compatible with the
intense human suffering that accompanies the kind of death that Jesus endured.

This having been said, Aquinas does not think the suffering of
Christ and his knowledge of God simply coexist on separate but un-

49. On the economic mode of Christ's immediate knowledge of God in his earthly
life, see ST III, q. 14, a. 1, ad 2; q. 15, a. 5, ad 3; q. 45, a. 2; q. 46, a. 8.

50. See on these ideas, ST III, q. 54, a. 2.

51. ST III, q. 14, a. 1, ad 2: "From the natural relationship which is between the soul
and the body, glory flows into the body from the soul's glory. Yet this natural relationship in Christ was subject to the will of His Godhead, and thereby it came to pass that
the beatitude remained in the soul, and did not flow into the body; but the flesh suffered what belongs to a passible nature." ST III, q. 15, aa. 4–6 make clear that Aquinas
understands "the body" or "the flesh" of Christ to include the passions, and human psychology of the man Jesus.

related "levels" of his soul. Rather, he distinguishes between the objects and subject of the various faculties of Christ's soul so as to make clear in what way the suffering and spiritual consolation of Christ occur simultaneously in the same human experience. On the one hand, he notes that the faculties of the human soul of Jesus experience irreducibly diverse objects during the crucifixion as either consolations or pains. Just as Christ could suffer terrible pain in his physical body or sorrow in his sensible feelings (stemming from the "objects" of his bodily sensation and inner emotional life, respectively), so he could also enjoy the immediate knowledge of God stemming from the object of his intellectual activity.[52] The objects experienced remain entirely distinct, yet the same subject (the man Jesus) is the one in whom these various experiences occur simultaneously, and in this way, Christ could suffer in the "entirety of his soul," since the entire humanity of Jesus was subject to suffering. Likewise, he could experience the consolation of the Father's presence in the "entirety of his soul," since his entire humanity was subject to consolation.[53] In this way, the happiness of being united in will with the Father could coexist with extreme agony in Christ, such that the two experiences were objectively distinct but subjectively (and therefore experientially) inseparable. While one was a source of extreme trial and distress, the other could be a source of consolation and moral stability.[54] This contrast (without contradiction) in the life of Jesus would necessarily result in a complex spiritual experience: of confident expectation of deliverance on the one hand, and the presence of intense agony, on the other. The inevitable result in the soul of Christ would be a unique

52. ST III, q. 46, aa. 7–8.

53. ST III, q. 46, a. 7: "It is evident that Christ's whole soul suffered ... Christ's 'higher reason' did not suffer thereby *on the part of its object*, which is God, who was the cause, not of grief but rather of delight and joy, to the soul of Christ. Nevertheless, all the powers of Christ's soul did suffer according as any faculty is said to be affected *as regards its subject*, because all the faculties of Christ's soul were rooted in its *essence, to which suffering extended* while the body, whose act it is, suffered" (emphasis added).

54. In ST III, q. 14, a. 2, q. 15, aa. 4–7, and q. 46, a. 2, ad 2, Aquinas argues that the sensible pain, sorrow, and fear of Christ were not *directly* affected by the vision, but only *indirectly* through the mediation of his reason. The vision stabilized the moral activity of Jesus, in and through his intense suffering, such that these passions were not permitted to overturn the rational desires of the mind of Christ. By a distant but real analogy, one could compare this to someone suffering in a hospital bed who is genuinely consoled by the presence and conversation of a friend.

form of intense soteriological desire or hope for the resurrection of his body and the salvation of others.

Three Dimensions of

Christ's Agony

Having clarified the above points, we can clearly distinguish (but not separate) three distinct dimensions of the agony of Christ. The first of these concerns his human nature as related to the form of his execution: public crucifixion. This is the physical and spiritual suffering of the human being who is betrayed, abandoned, judged unfairly, humiliated, rejected, beaten, and crucified. It would be common to any innocent person sentenced to such a death. Yet, as Aquinas points out, Jesus must also have felt physical and psychological pain with a greater acuity than other persons, due to the perfection of his human nature, the nobility of his soul, and the sensitivity of what we might call his cognitive psychology.[55] Indeed, because of the refinement of his sensibility and the purity of his moral innocence, Christ must have experienced such suffering in an especially poignant way.

Second, there is the mysterious agony more particular to Christ in his role as redeemer, which is a dimension of his "exchange" with a sinful humanity. This role entails an acceptance upon himself of some of the *consequences* of sin in our fallen humanity (including the fear of mortality, deep sadness, and a loss of the sense of the consoling presence of God) without an experience of that sin itself.[56] While one may discuss this state in varying terms, I have insisted that theologically speaking, it should not be equated with an experience of separation from God (the pain of damnation), nor be equated with an

55. ST III, q. 46, a. 6: "The magnitude of His suffering may be considered from the susceptibility of the sufferer as to both soul and body. For His body was endowed with the most perfect constitution.... And consequently, Christ's sense of touch, the sensitiveness of which is the reason for our feeling pain, was most acute. His soul, likewise, from its interior powers, apprehended most vehemently all the causes of sadness."

56. On this state of profound sadness which was permitted to occur in the soul of Christ despite the presence of the vision, see ST III, q. 46, a. 3 and a. 6, corp. and ad 2. Following Damascene (*De Fide Orth.* III, 19), Aquinas insists that the divine will suspended some of the experiences of consolation in the soul of Christ which would normally be present even in the suffering of a virtuous man. The point of such unique suffering is to manifest more profoundly the gravity of human sin as well as the unique love of Christ for human beings.

experience of the "wrath of God."[57] Such experiences are despair-ridden and derive essentially from a refusal of God as one's own final good. From the point of view of Pauline and Johannine theology, by contrast, it is necessary to affirm that Christ freely embraced some of the states of our fallen human nature precisely because of his more fundamental embrace of the Father's will. He did this so as to infuse them with loving obedience on our behalf. In this way, he demonstrates to us a greater love for and unity with the Father than might be manifest otherwise.[58]

Third, there is the agony of Christ that results from his love for us. This form of anguish stems above all from his extraordinary awareness of our human sinfulness, distance from God, and refusal of God. The object of his suffering in this case is not found in himself, but in us.[59] Therefore, it depends upon and stems from Christ's possession of an extraordinary knowledge of the real spiritual state of human beings before God, and a corresponding desire to save them from eternal separation from God. This is the agony due to which "Christ loved [us] and gave his life for [us]" (Gal 2:20) throughout the duration of his passion, desiring to communicate a new life in God to human beings by means of the gift of the Holy Spirit (Gal 4:6; 5:25). Precisely in order to save human beings, Jesus is obliged to confront consciously and vanquish willingly the reality of their complicity with evil.[60]

57. In discussing Paul's claim that "For our sake [God] made him to be sin who knew no sin, so that in him we might become the righteousness of God." (II Cor. 5:21), Aquinas (*In II Cor.* V, lec. 5, 201) purposefully excludes any idea of a penal substitution (in which Christ would be himself representative of the sinner and suffer a vicarious punishment for guilt on our behalf). Instead, he refers this verse to Christ's assumption out of love for us of a human nature capable of death and suffering (states which are consequences of sin). One sees consistent evidence of this exegetical tendency in his interpretations of Rom 3:25–6 (*In Rom.* III, lec. 3, 310–12); Rom 8:3 (*In Rom.* VIII, lec. 1, 608); Gal 3:13 (*In Gal.* III, lec. 5, 148–49); Col 2:13–14 (*In Col.* II, lec. 3, 115) and Heb 2:17 (*In Heb.* II, lec. 4, 139).

58. Aquinas makes these points in ST III, q. 46, aa. 1 and 4, commenting upon Jn 3:14 and Phil 2:8.

59. ST III, q. 46, a. 6, corp. and ad 2: "The cause of the interior pain [of the passion] was, first of all, all the sins of the human race.... In truth some sadness is praiseworthy ... namely, when it flows from holy love, as, for instance, when a man is saddened over his own or other's sins.... And so to atone for the sins of all men, Christ accepted sadness, the greatest in absolute quantity, yet not exceeding the rule of reason."

60. It is here that I would locate the origins of extra-ordinary suffering such as that

The Inauguration of the
Kingdom of God

We have established above that there is a theoretical possibility of the simultaneous coexistence of profound illumination and great suffering in the soul of Christ during his passion. Furthermore, as I have already noted, Aquinas thinks the state of vision in the earthly Christ is compatible with the existence of desire and hope within his soul. It is precisely because he knows of his mission as the Son sent from the Father, that Jesus can intensely desire to see it accomplished, both in himself (psychologically and corporeally) as well as in his spiritual members, the body of the church. Therefore, the question can be raised of *how* the extraordinary knowledge of Christ relates to the *desires* he has for the realization of redemption. More particularly, how does it relate to the desires he would have as regards each of the three above-mentioned sources of agony?

As regards the first dimension of agony (the natural experience of the terrible sufferings of Roman crucifixion), the Gospels tell us that Christ experienced a desire for deliverance *for himself.* In fact, it is reasonable to see this as an essential component of the cry/prayer of Mark 15:34 and Psalm 22:1: "Why have you abandoned *me?*" Here the vision of God in the heights of Christ's soul as an object of knowledge would in no way alleviate the reality of his physical and spiritual agony, experienced violently in both his body and psyche. Indeed, it may have intensified his desire for release from this state uniquely in and through an extreme abandonment to the Father's will. However, it would also simultaneously have mitigated the effects of this experience of suffering by permitting Christ in his human consciousness to know that he was accomplishing the Father's will which he shared in as Son.[61] It would have given him (in the heights of his soul) certain knowledge of his future exaltation as the Son of Man and a corre-

---

related by Lk 22:44 (the sweating of blood), and not in Christ's awareness of "the Father's wrath" and "the dread of hell," where Calvin places them. See ICR II, c. 16, n. 12.

61. The will of the Father is that same will which Christ as God the Son receives eternally from the Father in his divine nature. As I have argued above in chapter 5, Jesus's human acceptance of the Father's will in the crucifixion need not entail an alienation from the divine will he shares in as God. On the contrary, it is the temporal, finite expression of this shared, divine love, expressed in and through his human acts.

sponding prayerful expectation, lived out in hope despite his terrible suffering, of this vindication received from the Father.[62] In this case, the suffering of Christ was mitigated by his certainty of the Father's will and his unshakable hope for final deliverance in the resurrection.

Similar comments can be made regarding the second dimension of Christ's agony: his mysterious experience of certain spiritual and moral consequences of our fallen state. Christ's crucifixion seen in this light may have entailed the *sentiment* of divine abandonment and a subjection to the deep sadness that results from the non-experience of God. His corresponding desire would then have been for the eschatological presence of God fully experienced in both body and soul. If such a state is compatible with the beatific vision (as Aquinas's theology would, I think, allow), then two points must be made. On the one hand, in his earthly life Christ must have possessed the vision in such a way that his ordinary psychological consciousness could effectively function without being overcome by the felt consolations from his extraordinary knowledge of God. On the other hand, despite suffering this agony, Christ's vision played an essential role in permitting him as man to adhere to the will of the Father at all times, precisely so as to save us.[63] Agony in Christ without transcendent wisdom and salvific obedience would be of little use to others. In this sense, we must again affirm that the vision of God in the soul of Christ increased his desire for deliverance but it also mitigated his anguish.

What about the third form of agony? Here (unlike in the previous two examples) we are not speaking of suffering in Christ stemming from sensible experience and objective knowledge of his own deprivations, but due to an extraordinary awareness of the spiritual ills of

---

62. On the consoling effects of such knowledge during the passion of Christ, see ST III, q. 46, a. 8, corp. and ad 1: the consolation occurs in Jesus as a human subject through the medium of his extra-ordinary knowledge, despite the ongoing reality of his pain and inhuman treatment.

63. Perhaps interpreting Thomas Aquinas in his own way, John of the Cross, in his *Ascent of Mount Carmel* II, c. 7 discusses the idea that throughout the passion Christ experienced desolation with respect to the internal and external senses, as well as intense spiritual aridity in the lower part of his nature (that is to say, his human psychology). Yet, simultaneously he gave his life for humanity in a knowing, affective union of will with the Father.

others. In this case, as Aquinas points out, knowledge can be a cause
of suffering rather than a source of consolation.

> Christ grieved not only over the loss of His own bodily life, but also over
> the sins of all others. And this grief in Christ surpassed all grief of every con-
> trite heart, both *because it flowed from a greater wisdom and charity, by which
> the pang of contrition is intensified, and because He grieved at the one time for all
> sins,* according to Is. 53:4: "Surely He has borne our sorrows."[64]

From the above-cited passage, it is manifest that Aquinas thinks Jesus suffered not only in his sensate faculties and in his body, but in
his spiritual powers of reason and will. Furthermore, this suffering
stems from the knowledge Christ possesses of human sin, and from
his charity on behalf of sinful human beings, a love that is derivative
from Christ's plenitude of grace.

How should we understand, then, this unique knowledge of sin
to which Aquinas alludes? In his *Theological Compendium*, St. Thomas discusses the matter further by distinguishing between the "higher reason" of Christ and his "lower reason." This is a distinction based
not on differing faculties of reason, but on different objects of consideration. Higher reason looks to the eternal mystery of God and takes
consolation from the perspective of seeing all things in light of God's
providence and ultimate designs. Lower reason looks to temporal
and mutable realities themselves. The former knowledge can only be
a source of consolation, while the latter knowledge can be a source of
intense suffering. It is in this latter form of knowledge that Christ was
subject to spiritual agony.

> Christ [in his lower reason] suffered sadness from His awareness of the per-
> ils of sin or of punishment threatening other men whom He loved with the
> love of charity. And so He grieved for others as well as for Himself.... How-
> ever, although the love of our fellow men pertains in a certain way to the
> higher reason, inasmuch as our neighbor is loved out of charity for God's
> sake, the higher reason in Christ could not experience sorrow.... For, since

---

64. ST III, q. 46, a. 6, ad 4 (emphasis added). This idea has been insightfully dis-
cussed by Charles Journet, *Les Septs Paroles du Christ au Croix* (Paris: Editions du Seuil,
1954), 88–90, and more recently by Matthew Lamb in "The Eschatology of St Thomas
Aquinas," in *Aquinas on Doctrine*, eds. T. Weinandy, D. Keating, and J. Yocum (London:
T. & T. Clark, 2004), 225–40, and Matthew Levering, *Sacrifice and Community* (Oxford:
Blackwell Publishing, 2005), 80–81.

Christ's higher reason enjoyed the full vision of God, it apprehended all that pertains to the defects of others as contained in the divine wisdom ... with becoming order.[65]

What should we say about the vision of God, then? Was it the source of greater suffering for Christ in his agony? In one respect, this cannot be the case. It is the vision that gives him consolation even in the face of the reality of human sin. We might compare the soul of Christ to a mountain peak that rises up into the light above the clouds. The summit of the soul of Christ is bathed in light and is in peace, even as the lower reaches of his soul are submitted to a terrible storm.[66]

In another sense, however, the vision is the proximate cause of intense grief in the heart of Christ. Why should this be? This is the case for two reasons: first, because the knowledge of God in the heart of Christ is also the source of intense love. The perfect charity of Christ crucified fills his human heart and causes him to grieve over sin through an acute inner agony of love. Second, because the beatific vision is accompanied by a high degree of prophetic, infused insight. According to the Gospel, Christ is given the capacity to understand the thoughts of hearts and to foresee in advance certain key events of the divine economy. This prophetic knowledge has a great deal of intensity precisely because of the beatific vision, as it must permit Christ to communicate or "translate" his higher intuitive awareness of the Godhead into conceptual and linguistic idioms.[67] This prophetic knowledge is the source, then, of his understanding of human hearts, but it is also the immediate cause of suffering in the mind and heart of Christ.

Due to the beatific vision as their proximate cause, then, there are forms of knowledge and love present in the rational faculties of Christ which are themselves the source of intense inner suffering. In this way we can say that during the passion and crucifixion, Christ knew our human hearts better than we do, and in human actions he was able to perceive sin not only as a direct refusal of love, but also in all its subsequent consequences. The immediate vision in the soul

65. *Comp. Theol.* I, c. 232.

66. This is the image of Reginald Garrigou-Lagrange, *The Saviour and His Love for Us*, trans. A. Bouchard (London: B. Herder, 1951), 276.

67. ST III, q. 9, a. 3, ad 2.

of Christ gave him a profound spiritual and psychological awareness of the acute gravity of moral evil. In the words of Matthew Levering:

> Christ's suffering has the intensity, then, of a "dark night," in which the horror of the *darkness* of sin is finally and perfectly exposed in Christ's soul by contrast to the glorious light of the divine Goodness, which Christ also knows. It is only by contrast to this light that "darkness" is intelligible. Christ bears interiorly the darkness in his anguish over the sins of each one of us, but it is crucial to note that he can only bear this darkness fully because of his simultaneous "light" by which he knows God.[68]

The conclusion we can draw from these reflections is as significant as it is clear. In some real respect, Christ's extraordinary knowledge present throughout his passion necessarily *augmented* his desire for our salvation *even as it simultaneously augmented his agony*. The two are inseparable, and both result from the presence in the soul of Christ of the beatific vision. In fact, in a certain sense we may even say that the desire for the salvation of human beings was itself the cause of suffering. Consequently, the real potential "despair" and "separation from God" that Christ perceived at Calvary were *not in himself, but in us*. These attributes of humanity as known in the clarity of his extraordinary knowledge and the intensity of his love became, for him, the source of terrible agony.

Is it this agonizing, soteriological desire *on our behalf* which characterizes above all the cry of Christ from the cross? This would seem a likely interpretation for the cry of thirst in John 19:28, especially if we understand it as a plea for the gift of the Spirit. Christ thirsts for the salvation of all human persons and consequently implores the Father for the coming of the Paraclete (Jn 16:7–11). But could this kind of desire rightly be said to inform the cry of Mark 15:34? If we understand Christ's dereliction as a confrontation with *our sin* by which he is humanly overwhelmed, and understand the eschatological importance of that cry in Mark's Gospel, then the answer is yes.[69] This cry

---

68. Levering, *Sacrifice and Community*, 80.

69. A patristic parallel to this idea is found in Origen's *In Matt.*, n. 135. There he understands Christ's cry of agony in Mt 27:46 to be the result of his comprehension of human sin, simultaneously compared with his knowledge of the glory of the Father from which human beings had alienated themselves. Although he attributes faith to Christ, Vincent Taylor (*The Gospel according to St. Mark* [London: Macmillan, 1966], 594) offers similar views as to the origins of Christ's sufferings.

is an exclamation of suffering due to the presence of evil, but it simultaneously marks an end to the reign of that evil. Through his cry of agony and desire, Jesus intends (through his consciousness of himself as the eschatological Son of Man) to inaugurate the kingdom of God (Mk 14:62). This being the case, we may speak (at least on one level) of Christ's last words as an act of abandonment to God lived out in trust not only for himself individually, but also for us. Yet we might also add that the eschaton can be said to begin by his own divine prerogative precisely with the final cry which follows the cry of dereliction and immediately precedes his death (Mk 15:37; Mt 27:50). By this visceral but efficacious protest against the powers of sin, Jesus signals an accomplishment of the mission the Father has given him, and divinely initiates the end times.

In light of these reflections, we might conclude that the beatific vision in the soul of Christ as Aquinas presents it is certainly compatible with a spiritual realism concerning the agony of Christ on the cross. This is particularly the case if we conceive of this agony as an expression of desire. Just as the Gospels of Mark and John can be seen to harmonize theologically in their respective forms of emphasis on agony and desire, so the account of Christ's passion that we give theologically may do the same in terms of suffering and knowledge. Both these poles of his experience must be respected in some integral fashion, no matter how much a particular account may wish to emphasize one aspect with respect to the other.

CONCLUSION

I have argued above that the death cry of Christ is a cry of both desire and agony, and that this cry is compatible with the simultaneous presence in Christ's soul of both extraordinary knowledge and intense suffering. Fundamentally, the desire that informs this exclamation should be interpreted as a beseeching by Jesus for both his own deliverance/exaltation and our salvation in one inseparable act. In praying for both these objects, Christ's words on the cross are eschatological in nature. His cry tends toward the final possession of a gift of redemption for humanity that is not yet fully possessed. Furthermore, the theological affirmation of such a mixed state of expec-

tation and suffering in the soul of Christ is entirely compatible with
(and in fact complementary to) the teaching of St. Thomas concerning Christ's knowledge of both the Father and sinful humanity in and
through his crucifixion. The knowledge of the Father's will afforded
by the beatific vision is not the cause of suffering in itself, but of confidence and consolation. Yet because this same vision is accompanied
necessarily by intense knowledge of human evil in the world, it is also
the source of both profound redemptive desire and intense agony. Jesus experiences in his ordinary consciousness as man a deeper suffering on our behalf because of this grace.

8

---:---

The Death
of Christ and the Mystery
of the Cross

In the Prolegomenon to this book, I argued that modern Christology
has been characterized by two important challenges: how should we
respond to the Kantian critique of classical metaphysics? How might
theologians employ modern historical-critical studies of the person
of Jesus of Nazareth? Both topics impact the theology of the incarnation, but they affect the theology of the redemption as well. How
should we understand the saving character of the death of Christ?

In the nineteenth and twentieth centuries, a kenotic turn transpired in Christian theology that sought to respond to these two modern concerns, and which did so in view of specifically soteriological
ends. According to this modern "tradition," God has chosen to identify himself—even in his very deity—with us in our suffering, death,
and separation from God. In doing so, he has shown an ultimate form
of solidarity with the human race and has reconciled us to his divine
life, even amidst the greatest of antithetical circumstances. This idea
reaches its epitome when we consider the death of the Lord. How do
human death and even "non-being" attain to the very deity of God?
How is Christ's own human limitation in the face of death an indication of God's ontological solidarity with humanity?

In this chapter I set out to examine briefly the chief intellectual concerns of modern kenoticism, and argue that there are soteriological difficulties inherent in its treatment of the death of Christ. I also argue that there are contrasting advantages to the classical Christological understanding of the redemption. The first part of the chapter examines succinctly how modern kenotic Christology tends to treat the soteriological work of the passion of Christ. I argue that there are inherent difficulties to which this way of thinking inevitably gives rise. The second part of the chapter seeks to confirm and deepen this thesis by examining Aquinas's theology of the divinity of Christ crucified. Here I am taking Aquinas as a representative of the soteriology of the classical tradition, both patristic and scholastic. How, for this tradition, is the divinity of Christ manifest in the Paschal mystery? First, in that Christ as man knew of his own divine identity and therefore delivered himself over freely to suffering and death for our sake; second, through the manifestation of the divine power of Christ during the crucifixion (the divinity of Christ is operative in and through his passion); third, in the teaching that the one who was crucified raised himself from the dead.

After exploring each of these ideas, I briefly compare them in the third part of the chapter with representations of the mystery of Christ present in the modern kenotic tradition. The last part of the chapter reflects on particular differences and notes their repercussions with a view to thinking about the contemporary relevance of scholastic Christology. I argue that Aquinas's thought helps us see why the deity of Christ crucified has an essential soteriological importance. His theology of the passion thereby helps us understand how the modern kenotic turn in Christology merits to be challenged or rethought in light of the classical patristic and medieval tradition.

TWO FACETS OF MODERN KENOTIC CHRISTOLOGY AND THEIR SOTERIOLOGICAL CHARACTERISTICS

Two Facets of Modern Kenotic Christology

Modern Christology has been marked by a kenotic turn in a twofold way. The first stems from a response on the part of theologians to the

Kantian critique of classical ontology. Modern German Protestant theology has tended to concede as a premise of dogmatic theology that human beings are naturally incapable of attaining to metaphysical knowledge of the divine essence or nature, at least in the ways that pre-Kantian thinkers often presumed. New questions emerge from this theoretical stance: how—epistemologically—might we even conceive of the divine nature and what characteristics might be prescribed to God in light of his historical incarnation? How, specifically, might we speak of the two natures in Christ, and particularly of the divine nature of the incarnate Son, if the very idea of the divine nature remains ultimately alien to natural human thought?

One very influential answer to these questions was developed in the nineteenth century in the kenoticism of Gottfried Thomasius, who was himself influenced by the speculative thought of G. W. F. Hegel regarding divine becoming.[1] Thomasius argued that God the Son divested himself of various divine attributes (relational attributes such as omnipotence or omniscience) for the duration of his earthly sojourn.[2] God could thus be known in our limited spatiotemporal domain as one who lived an authentically human life among us (the condition for the latter being the disinvestment of certain divine attributes). Yet this self-emptying does not deepen the gulf between the world and God, for God in his eternal wisdom and love is revealed to us precisely in his act of self-limitation.[3] This view was criticized and reformulated in the twentieth century by thinkers like Karl Barth and Sergius Bulgakov.[4] These thinkers insist that it is not

1. On Hegel's Christology see James Yerkes, *The Christology of Hegel* (Albany, N.Y.: State University of New York Press, 1983).

2. Gottfried Thomasius, *Christi Person und Werk*, 3rd ed., 2 vols. (Erlangen: A. Deichert, 1886–88). On the self-emptying of relational divine attributes, see 1:608. Thomasius's views are presented in the English translation of his work by Claude Welch, *God and Incarnation in Mid-Nineteenth Century German Theology* (Oxford: Oxford University Press, 1965), 64–74. An excellent analysis of the initial development of modern kenotic Christology is given by Wolfhart Pannenberg in his *Jesus God and Man*, 2nd ed., trans. L. L. Wilkins, D. A. Priebe (Philadelphia: Westminster Press, 1968), 307–23.

3. *Person und Werk*, 1:412.

4. For Barth's treatment of Thomasius, see CD IV, 1, 180–82. I have examined Barth's particular version of kenoticism above in chapter 6. For Bulgakov's interpretations of kenosis in light of Thomasius, see *The Lamb of God*, 219–47, and the analysis by Paul Gavrilyuk, "The Kenotic Theology of Sergius Bulgakov," *Scottish Journal of Theology* 58 (2005): 251–69.

the case that God divests himself of his deity in becoming man, but it is the case that the human vulnerability of God in Christ is an expression of the divine essence. God in his personal being as Son is free to identify with us in our suffering and lowliness as an expression of his very deity as love. This view in turn influenced (in complex, historically varied ways) the thinking of Pannenberg, Balthasar, Jüngel, Kasper, and others.[5] All of these thinkers affirm the presence of the divine nature in the historical Son incarnate. Yet God the Son in his human life need not reveal his divinity as something transcendent of or in distinction from his human characteristics in order for us to know that he is truly God. Rather the human characteristics of finitude, obedience, suffering, etc., are indicative of what God is in his personal mode of being as the Son, and the Son's incarnation has itself revealed to us in new ways the latent capacity of the divine nature for historicization.[6] Human thought, to find God, then, need not surmount the horizon of human sensible and historical experiences. Rather, the transcendent God who evades our natural knowledge has made known to us who he really is (in his very deity) precisely in and through his sensible and historical forms of being. The continuity between the heights of the divine identity of God and his human lowliness is guaranteed by a kenosis originating from the divine freedom and love that constitute the divine essence. Free self-emptying on the part of God is the condition that allows us the possibility of discovering who God is within our creaturely sphere. In his love, God is free to be both supreme and lowly, both impassible and suffering, both eternal and temporal, and so on.[7] The wedding between these

5. Pannenberg pursues a variant of this idea in *Jesus God and Man*, 307–23, and develops a later position in his *Systematic Theology*, trans. G. W. Bromiley (Grand Rapids, Mich.: Eerdmans, 1994), 2:375–79. I have given references to Balthasar and Jüngel in chapter 6. Walter Kasper adopts a qualified version of kenotic theology in *Jesus the Christ*, trans. V. Green (London: Burns & Oates, 1976), 181–85, and *The God of Jesus Christ*, trans. M. J. O'Connell (New York: Crossroad, 1989), 189–97.

6. Pannenberg, *Systematic Theology* 2:377: "By distinguishing the Father from himself as the one God, the Son certainly moved out of the unity of the deity and became man. But in so doing he actively expressed his divine essence as the Son. The self-emptying of the Preexistent is not a surrender or negation of his deity as the Son. It is its activation. Hence the end of his earthly path in obedience to the Father is the revelation of his deity." Pannenberg here references Barth, CD IV, 1, 129; 177; 179.

7. Kasper, *The God of Jesus Christ*, 194–95. The view is expressed more radically by Bulgakov, *The Lamb of God*, 221–23, 231–32.

seeming contraries is guaranteed by God's freedom to diversify his attributes.[8] The free self-emptying of God incarnate in Christ takes place because of love, and reveals that love to man in human historical terms, particularly in and through the Paschal mystery.

The second feature of modern Christology is its assimilation of historical-critical study of the Gospels. Here too, kenotic Christology has a distinctly modern genealogy. The nineteenth century post-Enlightenment critique of the Gospels as historical sources led to prevalent acceptance of two ideas. First, the four Gospels cannot be presumed to be accurate portrayals of the sayings and aims of the historical Jesus free from any post-Paschal theological reconstruction of the early Christian community. Therefore Jesus's explicit claims in the Gospels to a high knowledge of himself as Son need not be considered historical. Second, the aims and intentions of the historical Jesus of Nazareth must be understood in some sense by attempting to situate him within the limited horizon of his particular cultural-historical context. Initial history-of-Jesus portraits thus gave way eventually (particularly in the work of Johannes Weiss and Albert Schweitzer) to the idea of the historical Jesus as an early first century self-designated eschatological prophet.[9] Under the pressures of this twofold tendency of thought modern kenoticism sought a middle way between classical orthodoxy and modern skepticism. One need not presume (in the face of modern historical-critical thought) that God became man in such a way as to maintain an extraordinary human historical consciousness of his divinity (such as that which is presented in the Gospel of John). The historical Jesus need not have had a prophetic knowledge of his own identity and of his impending death. On the contrary, consistent with the metaphysics of kenosis, the Son could cede any such supernatural awareness of his unique dignity, and precisely in doing so could reveal ever more deeply the mystery of his

8. See the analysis of this "di-polar" idea of God in modern kenotic Christology by Gilles Emery in "The Immutability of the God of Love and the Problem of Language Concerning the 'Suffering of God'" in *Divine Impassibility and the Mystery of Human Suffering*, eds. J. F. Keating and Thomas Joseph White (Grand Rapids, Mich.: Eerdmans, 2009), 27–76.

9. Johannes Weiss, *Die Predigt Jesu vom Reiche Gottes* (Göttingen: Vandenhoeck & Ruprecht, 1892); Albert Schweitzer, *Geschichte der leben-Jesu-forschung* (Tübingen: J. C. B. Mohr, 1913).

identity as God. For God has shown his solidarity with us precisely in adopting a typically human experience of historical life and consciousness.

This is a view we find, again, clearly expressed in Thomasius, but taken up subsequently by thinkers such as Bulgakov, Pannenberg, Jüngel, and Kasper.[10] The historical Jesus could be understood within his historical context as a Jewish prophetic figure animated by the hope of an imminent apocalypse. His relative nescience and even his disappointed cry of dereliction all indicate here not a disjuncture between the claims of the church and the claims of modern history, but rather a discovery of the continuity between the two.[11] Theological study of the Gospel informed by the concerns of modern historiography leads us to a deeper understanding of the unique revelation of the love of God who freely unveils himself in the historical limitations and lowliness of man. Even more, such limitations reveal the inner life of God, who can "come to be" and thus manifest his very self (deity) in the event of human suffering, obedience, and death.[12] The limitations of the historical consciousness of Christ as man are the occasion for God to be in his very essence "God with us."

Two Points of Contrast with
Classical Christology

Any student of the history of doctrine regarding the person of Jesus Christ cannot fail to be struck by a singular contrast between this modern development and the classical patristic and scholastic patrimony of Catholic theology. What can we identify as the fundamental differences between the two traditions? Certainly there are the out-

10. Thomasius, *Christi Person und Werk*, 1:465; Bulgakov, *The Lamb of God*, 232–37; Pannenberg, *Systematic Theology* 2:375–77; Jüngel, *God as the Mystery of the World*, 343–47; Kasper, *Jesus the Christ*, 115–19, 163–68.

11. Pannenberg, *Systematic Theology* 2:375: "This obedience [of Christ] led him into the situation of extreme separation from God and his immortality, in the dereliction of the cross. The remoteness from God on the cross was the climax of his self-distinction from the Father."

12. Bulgakov, *The Lamb of God*, 232: "The *historical* Golgotha was only a *consequence* of the metaphysical one. The metaphysical Golgotha made the historical one possible and real." The idea is discussed thematically in a different way by Balthasar in his concept of Trinitarian inversion. See *Theo-Drama*, 3:515–23.

standing issues raised by the classical treatments of the attributes of the divine nature of Christ (divine simplicity, eternity, immutability, etc.). There is also the question of the classical treatment of the qualities of Christ's human knowledge. Against Arius, for example, the fourth-century patristic tradition formulated an understanding of the incarnation that was to remain fundamentally normative in the subsequent tradition up until modern times. Christ is God the eternal Word and as God he is eternally begotten of the Father before all creation in an ineffable, transcendent way that excludes all ontological subordination.[13] Being one with the Father, he cedes none of his divine prerogatives in becoming man, yet is truly begotten of the Virgin Mary as a human being born in time. The incarnate Word therefore truly lives, suffers, and dies in his human nature, even while he remains eternal and impassible as God.[14] Consequently the kenosis of Philippians 2:6–11 refers not to a surrender of the divine prerogatives or attributes, nor to a diremption of God's being into what God formerly was not, or into what he was eternally intended to become.[15] Rather, as I have argued above in chapter 4, it refers to the condescension and love with which God—without ceasing to be the transcendent Lord—assumes a human nature and suffers as man to redeem us.[16]

This view carries over into a treatment of the human knowledge of Christ. Against Apollinarius, the tradition insisted that Christ

13. Athanasius, *Contra Arian.* I, paras. 15–16, 28; Gregory of Nyssa, *Contra Eunomius* II, 7; IV, 1; Gregory of Nazianzus, *Theological Orations* 29 and 30.

14. See, for instance, Cyril of Alexandria, *De Symbolo*, 24; *Ad Acacium*, 7; *Ad Succensum* II, 4. A helpful study of Cyril on this point is offered by Paul L. Gavrilyuk, *The Suffering of the Impassible God*, 135–71.

15. Athanasius, *C. Arian.* I, paras. 39–40: "For he is offspring of the Father's essence, so that one cannot doubt that after the resemblance of the unalterable Father, the Word also is unalterable.... He was not from a lower state promoted; but rather, existing as God, he took the form of a servant, and in taking it, was not promoted but humbled himself."

16. Friedrich Loofs noted that the modern concept of a kenotic self-emptying of the deity is absent from patristic readings of Phil 2. Rather, the kenosis of the Son is based upon his divine assumption of human nature, as an act of free divine goodness. See *"Kenosis"* in *Realencyklopädie für protestantische Theologie und Kirche*, eds. J. J. Herzog and A. Hauck, 3rd ed. (Leipzig: J. C. Hinrichs, 1901), 10:246–63, especially 248. Aquinas follows this view in his *In Phil.* II, lec. 2.

The Death of Christ

347

as man has a true human soul (implying knowledge and will), and against Arius, it was insisted that this knowledge can be limited (humanly) without there being any compromise of the divine nature of Christ as God.[17] This means, however, that the distinction of natures implies a distinction of forms of knowledge. The Lord's knowledge is limited as man because he is truly human. In his Sonship, however, he remains immutably the divine Wisdom of the Father, creating and upholding all things in being.

From within this tradition of thought, the modern kenotic turn is problematic for at least two reasons. First, such a view surrenders artificially a true sense of the transcendent deity of Christ and his unity with the Father, instead ushering into God a problematic conception of divine becoming and temporal historicization. If the Son is distinguished from the Father precisely in and through the economy, does God in the distinction of Son and Father then depend upon the economy to be triune? Here, as I have suggested above in chapter 3, we might question the underlying philosophical presuppositions. Instead of reconceiving Trinitarian ontology in light of the Kantian critique, one might take issue with several of its prohibitions as premature and artificial. Contemporary theology must promote once again an ontology of the divine names (of classical attributes of the divinity) and apply this form of thought to the consideration of the divine nature of Christ. This, at least, is the claim of the First Vatican Council (*Dei Filius*) and papal encyclicals such as *Aeterni Patris* and *Fides et Ratio*, even if how best to proceed in such an endeavor continues to be a subject of controversy in modern Catholic theology.[18]

Second, regarding the human knowledge of Christ, the unmitigated adoption of the Enlightenment presuppositions is questionable as well. The argument seems to be: *if* the Gospel portraits of the historical Jesus are subsequent theological reconstructions of the early Church (which they are) *then* the historical Christ could not have had

---

17. Athanasius, *Contra Arian.* III, para. 45, and *Tom. ad Antioch.*, 7; Gregory of Nazianzus, *Letter* 51 (to Cledonius). Irenaeus had already expressed the idea of a real but limited human knowledge in Christ in *Against Heresies.* II, 28, 6–8.

18. See the contemporary presentations of Aquinas on the classical divine names by Rudi Te Velde, *Aquinas on God*; Edward Feser, *Aquinas: A Beginner's Guide* (Oxford: Oneworld, 2009), 62–130.

both a first-century Jewish historical consciousness *and* an extraordinary prophetic and supernatural awareness of his own filial identity. Why does this follow? The claim is neither metaphysically nor historically compelling. Could the early church not have constructed a theological account of the historical Jesus's extraordinary self-awareness and portrayed his aims and intentions in ways that corresponded to the supernatural inspiration that he himself possessed? Such a view, as Romano Guardini pointed out long ago, is at least as historically compelling simply to pure reason as anything that affirms the contrary, if not more so.[19] Simply as a principle of rational causal explanation: someone of extraordinary character seems to have been the inspiration behind the movement that led to the composition of the Gospels. Why could the historical Jesus not have had an extraordinary, prophetically informed self-understanding?

Soteriological Characteristics:
Classical Christology Rearticulated
by Kenoticism

In addition to the speculative and historical issues that have been alluded to above, however, there is another important context for determining what is at stake in the theology of Christ's self-emptying and death, one which presupposes the contrasting positions briefly described above, and which raises related but logically distinct issues. This is the issue of soteriology. Classically, Christological doctrines of salvation presuppose that the divinity of Christ plays an integral role in the salvation he effectuates on our behalf, by means of the incarnation and Paschal mystery. For Athanasius, this occurs principally by way of the union of human and divine that transpires in and because of the incarnation. After the image of God had fallen into the slavery of sin, death, and non-being, God took upon himself human life so as to restore the human race to life and reunite it with God.[20] The deity of Christ is essential to the mystery of salvation precisely because it

19. Romano Guardini, *The Humanity of Christ: Contributions to a Psychology of Jesus*, trans. R. Walls (New York: Random House, 1964).

20. Athanasius, *De Incarn.*, 3–10; *Contra Arian.* II, para. 70. Aquinas takes up this argument in ST III, q. 1, a. 2; SCG IV, c. 54, para. 2.

bears in itself the power and authority to elevate our frail humanity to a state that transcends death, suffering, and hell.[21]

Without contesting this more typically eastern account, western soteriology, especially after Anselm's *Cur Deus Homo*, understands the divinity of Christ as integral to the power of the atonement (*satisfactio*) offered by Christ as man. In and through his suffering and death, Christ substitutes his obedience and love for our injustice, lovelessness, and disobedience, so as to render us just. Only because he is a man like us in all things but sin are Christ's human obedience and love redemptive and just (in substitution for our injustice). Only because Christ is God are his human actions of a uniquely infinite dignity by virtue of the Godhead united to his human action.[22]

Modern kenotic theories of atonement typically do not seek to deny the validity of these classical theories at base, but rather to modify them (albeit radically) in light of the kenotic Trinitarian metaphysics mentioned above. Typically the traditional theories are reread in two innovative and interrelated ways. First, the free kenotic movement of the divinity into history is appealed to in order to understand that God takes suffering, death, non-being, and separation from God (hell) into his own deity in order to save us.[23] The journey of the Son into the far country of our human condition is the result of a free decision by God to take up *into himself* our condition in its most abject state of distance from God in order that ultimate-

---

21. Athanasius, *De Incarn.*, 18: "We have, then, now stated ... the reason for his bodily appearing: it was in the power of none other to turn the corruptible to incorruption, except the Savior himself, that had at the beginning also made all things out of nought: and that none other could create anew the likeness of God's image for men, save the Image of the Father; and that none other could render the mortal immortal, save our Lord Jesus Christ, who is the very Life."

22. Aquinas offers his own interpretations of Anselm on this point in ST III, q. 1, a. 2; q. 48, a. 2 corp. and ad 3. In the latter article he notes especially the irreducible role of the divinity of Christ in granting the merit of the atonement an infinite value. Responding to the objection that the human bodily suffering of Christ was of finite value, he responds (ad 3): "The dignity of Christ's flesh is not to be estimated solely from the nature of flesh, but also from the Person assuming it—namely, inasmuch as it was God's flesh, the result of which was that it was of infinite worth."

23. The most extreme examples are found in Jüngel, *God as the Mystery of the World*, 343–47, 361–65; see also Bulgakov, *The Lamb of God*, 257–61, 344–79, and Balthasar, *Theo-Drama*, 4:332–38. I will return to this topic below.

ly we might be reconciled with God in the life of the resurrection.[24] The theme of "solidarity" with us in our human state hereby is given a metaphysical tone of a decidedly unique kind, and this movement within the life of God becomes the condition not only for our knowledge of God (who reveals his Trinitarian life to us through this kenosis) but also for our "divinization" or union with God in something like the classical Athanasian sense of the term.[25]

Second, then, the kenosis of Christ's human understanding plays a key role in this event. The descent of Christ's understanding into the night of hell on the cross becomes the key juncture where he shows his solidarity with us in our separation from God. This is the place where the innocent Son of Man in his obedience to the Father takes upon himself the consequences of the sin of the world. Anselm's atonement theory is, therefore, reinterpreted by appeal to Calvin's penal substitution theory (which I introduced in the previous chapter). Christ represents us as sinners, becoming a subject of divine punishment or dereliction in our stead. In truth Calvin's idea is alien to and even explicitly contradicts Anselm and Aquinas on the subject of Christ's atoning justice.[26] Nevertheless, it has typically been reinterpreted within the context of a kenotic theology to suggest how or where in particular God identifies with us historically in his very deity, and thereby not only reconciles us with God but also makes restitution for all human sin. God himself takes upon himself the burden

24. Karl Barth gave this theme a famous prominence in CD IV, 1, section 59 (215): "In this event God allows the world and humanity to take part in the history of the inner life of His Godhead, in the movement in which from and to all eternity He is Father, Son and Holy Spirit, and therefore the one true God. But this participation of the world in the being of God implies necessarily His participating in the being of the world, and therefore that His being, His history, is played out as world-history.... The self-humiliation of God in His Son would not really lead Him to us, the activity in which we see His true deity and the divine Sonship of Jesus Christ would not be genuine and actual, ... the way into the far country would not be followed, if there were any reservation in respect of His solidarity with us, of His entry into world-history."

25. See, for example, Balthasar, *Theo-Drama*, 4:361–67.

26. See the arguments to this effect by Philippe de la Trinité, *What Is Redemption?* Also, Anselm's *Cur Deus Homo* I, 8 contains an explicit repudiation of the notion of penal substitution. Aquinas follows this line of thinking in ST III, q. 47, a. 3, corp. and ad 1; SCG IV, c. 55, para. 23. On the late medieval origins of penal substitution theory, see Léopold Sabourin, "Le bouc émissaire, figure du Christ,"? *Sciences Ecclésiastiques* 11 (1959): 45–79.

of guilt on our behalf. In his kenosis, God alone is reprobated on the cross, so that we might be deemed righteous and reconciled to God in grace.[27]

Here, however, we can raise two trenchant questions. The first of these is something I have suggested above in chapter 6. Is it reasonable to assume that God can save us truly and effectively if he "freely" introduces into his own deity the historical states of suffering, death, non-being, and separation from God? Besides the metaphysical absurdities that these views suggest, there is the question of the justice and soteriological purpose of such proposals. For if God saves us only at the cost of introducing into his own being the very grave ills that threaten us, then our union with God is of a questionable soteriological value, for our ills have now been introduced into the very life of God. There is ultimately, in a kenotic world, nothing that itself necessarily transcends the world of ills, insofar as these have now become a constitutive part of the being of God, or so it would seem.[28]

Second, we can raise the issue of the knowledge of Christ and the meaning of the atonement. Originally the atonement theory of Anselm was meant to articulate how it is that Christ as man can be authentically just before God in such a way as to repair the intrinsically disordered state of the human race as it stands before God. Christ as man brings authentic love, obedience, and justice where it was lacking in the human race. In at least some versions of kenotic theory, however, the atonement is conceived of primarily in terms of substitution in the realms of suffering, where the substitution is forensic. Christ is deemed sin or separated from God for us, while for his sake we are deemed reconciled with God. Irrespective of how we understand the latter of these concepts (our reconciliation through "extrinsic justification" versus the doctrine of justification of the Council of Trent, etc.) the former idea is somewhat odd. If Christ as man is in-

27. In CD IV, 1, section 59, Barth reinterpreted Calvin's theology of penal substitution, affirming the descent of Christ into hell on the cross as the reprobation unique to Christ so that all might be elect. The idea is central to Balthasar's theology; see *Theo-Drama*, 4:338–51. See also Jüngel, *God as the Mystery of the World*, 361–65; Pannenberg, *Systematic Theology*, 2:375–79.

28. See, on this point, the insightful reflections of Bruce D. Marshall, "The Dereliction of Christ and the Impassibility of God," in *Divine Impassibility and the Mystery of Human Suffering*, 246–98.

nocent and Christ as God is one with the Father, then his assumption of separation from God for our sake has no *intrinsic* meaning in the order of justice and no real metaphysical intelligibility. Therefore an arbitrary extrinsic imposition of a declaration of Christ as sin for our sake by God is not only unjust but also intrinsically ontologically absurd. One can argue that in Christ God was reconciling the world to himself by himself becoming sin for our sake, thus introducing into *his* very deity the wedding of contradictories that has been mentioned above. God is free as Father to transcend suffering, while as Son he is free to take upon himself in his very deity the lowliness and obscurity of the cross event. But even if this ontology is conceded, it makes little sense in the order of justice as such because it obfuscates or even removes the key Anselmian notion: that Christ substituted his human moral innocence for our moral guilt, and in this way made restitution or satisfaction for our sins by restoring the human race to intrinsic righteousness and friendship with God.[29]

On both of these points then, we can question whether modern kenotic Christologies truly stand in continuity with and maintain the truths of classical soteriology as elaborated by Athanasius and Anselm, respectively. In what follows I would like to explore a sense of the contrast further by examining a key set of ideas about redemption in the scholastic tradition. St. Thomas presents us with a profoundly different portrait of Jesus than virtually any twentieth-century Christology. Precisely one of the most acute points of difference lies in Aquinas's classical understanding of Christ's divinity as it is present in the event of his crucifixion and as it is manifest though his death and resurrection. In addition, this presence has profound soteriological implications.

In the second part of this chapter, then, I would like to consider three examples of Aquinas's thinking on a precise subject: How is the divinity of Christ manifest in the Paschal mystery? First, in that Christ as man knew of his own divine identity and therefore *delivered himself over freely* to suffering and death for our sake; second, through the manifestation of the *divine power of Christ* during the crucifixion (the divinity of Christ is operative in and through his pas-

29. See Anselm, *Cur Deus Homo* I, cc. 11–25; II, cc. 6–7, especially as interpreted by Aquinas, ST III, q. 48, aa. 1–4, SCG IV, c. 55.

sion); third, in the teaching that the one who was crucified *raised himself* from the dead. How for Aquinas is the divinity of Christ crucified present, how is it active and manifest, in and through these different moments of Christ's human death and resurrection? After exploring each of these ideas, in the third part of the chapter I will consider alternative interpretations of the mystery of Christ as represented in the modern kenotic tradition and reflect on particular differences between the two approaches.

AQUINAS ON THE DIVINITY OF CHRIST IN HIS PASSION

Christ Delivered Himself Over to Death Freely

Let us consider first, then, the teaching of Aquinas that Christ as man knew of his own identity in his passion, and correspondingly freely embraced the mystery of the cross, delivering himself over freely to suffering and death for our sake. This theological perspective weds two distinct ideas: that Christ knew who he himself was, and that he could freely choose whether or not to give his life. Each notion should be considered distinctly and in sequence.

In speaking about Jesus's self-understanding, it is significant to begin by noting that St. Thomas does not ignore the idea of a progressive development of understanding in the faith of believers, leading to a gradual enlightenment and doctrinal clarification through time.[30] On the contrary, his treatise on faith shows marked sensitivity to this phenomenon at multiple points by its use of the distinction between implicit faith and explicit faith.[31] The ancient Israelites knew certain things implicitly within faith that were subsequently rendered explicit to human knowledge after Christ.[32] Likewise, the Apostles pos-

---

30. See Serge-Thomas Bonino, "The Role of the Apostles in the Communication of the Divine Revelation according to the *Lectura super Ioannem* of St. Thomas Aquinas," in *Reading John with St. Thomas Aquinas*, eds. M. Dauphinais and M. Levering (Washington, D.C.: The Catholic University of America Press, 2005), 318–46.

31. ST II-II, q. 1, a. 7; *In Heb.* XI, lec. 2.

32. ST II-II, q. 2, aa. 7–8.

sessed an imperfect form of faith during the earthly life of Jesus, and only at Pentecost was the understanding of the disciples perfected.[33] Church teachings develop as what lies implicit within the original apostolic deposit of faith is rendered more explicit to us who come after the apostolic age, and thus is defined solemnly by councils and by the Pope.[34] Individuals, likewise, can be held more or less responsible for rendering an account of what is to be believed (as *minores* or *maiores* in the faith), depending on the teaching they have received and how explicit their understanding of Christian truths has become.[35]

Yet if Aquinas is more than aware of the developmental character of human understanding of divine mysteries in general, he refrains from applying this doctrine of development to the mystery of Christ's self-awareness in particular. It is the case that Aquinas in his mature works (very originally, in comparison with his medieval contemporaries) posits the notion of a natural acquired knowledge that is proper to the human mind of Christ.[36] Evidently, in this sense Christ is understood to have undergone a progressive natural development in his self-understanding throughout his life. Jesus as a human being has an active intellect that progresses in understanding through time, from childhood to maturity, in keeping with the ordinary developmental traits of our human nature.[37]

Nevertheless, in his knowledge of supernatural mysteries (including that of his own identity as the Son of God), Christ is not receptive of a revelation communicated by another as we are. Rather, Jesus as man is aware of divine truth in an extraordinary way because he must in turn communicate this saving truth to us. Here, Aquinas explicitly invokes a soteriological principle.[38] Salvation consists of knowledge of God by way of authentic revelation in this life and of the reception of the beatific vision in the next. Christ is not saved by another, but is, rather, himself the unique savior. Consequently, as the redeemer of human beings, the Son made man must in some sense already

33. And not after the Resurrection, where modern theologians tend to place the transformation. See ST II-II, q. 174, a. 6; q. 176, a. 1, ad 1; *In Eph.* I, lec. 3; Aquinas's *Emitte spiritum* (Sermon for the Feast of Pentecost).

34. ST II-II, q. 1, aa. 7 and 10.   35. ST II-II, q. 2, a. 6.

36. ST III, q. 9, a. 4; q. 12, aa. 1–4.

37. See Aquinas's comments, therefore, on Lk 2:52 in ST III, q. 12, a. 2.

38. ST III, q. 9, a. 2.

"see" the term of our process of salvation and himself have a prophetic knowledge sufficient to enlighten us as to who he is and as to the meaning of the divine economy.[39] As I have argued above, St. Thomas does qualify these affirmations carefully: Christ does not believe in the Father but sees the Father in an immediate filial vision. However, during his earthly life this immediate knowledge of the Father exists in such a way that Christ can still be humanly subject to ordinary natural learning and even intense intellectual and psychological suffering.[40] Likewise, Christ has infused prophetic knowledge of the mystery of God, but his infused prophetic knowledge is exercised in a *habitual* fashion, meaning he need not know *all things actively* in an extraordinary fashion. Rather, while he has the *capacity* to know all that is necessary for his mission, he is given to know *actively in a punctual fashion* only those things that it is fitting for him to reveal to us, in order to facilitate our salvation.[41] This knowledge exists in and amidst his ordinary natural knowledge procured through human experience, and in the midst of a particular cultural-historical milieu that informs his mode of self-expression.

In consistency with these principles, Aquinas is insistent that the earthly Christ prior to the time of his crucifixion understood and taught explicitly of his own identity as the Son of the Father, as he who is one with the Father (that is to say as God).[42] Jesus as man knew that he "came into the world," in the sense that he preexisted the world.[43] Simply put, Aquinas takes it as a theological given that Christ knew as man of his own divine origins.

39. Ibid.: "Men are brought to this end of beatitude by the humanity of Christ ... 'the author of their salvation' (Heb. 2:10).... And hence it was necessary that the beatific knowledge, which consists in the vision of God, should belong to Christ pre-eminently, since the cause ought always to be more efficacious than the effect."

40. See ST III, q. 14, a. 1, ad 2; q. 15, a. 5, ad 3; q. 45, a. 2; q. 46, a. 8.

41. ST III, q. 11, a. 5. I am purposefully choosing here to underscore selective elements of Aquinas's thought, in a sense that I take to accord best with the evidences of scripture. Aquinas does speculate, for instance, in q. 12, a. 1 that Christ as man knew all things by his acquired knowledge that man can know naturally (including presumably mathematics, natural science, etc.). As Torrell has pointed out (*Le Verbe Incarné*, 2:362–63) we would do best to consider that Christ as man, in his infused and acquired knowledge, knew all that he needed to know for the accomplishment of his mission as savior.

42. *In Ioan.* XVII, lec. 1.

43. *In Ioan.* I, lec. 7, 176.

How is this relevant to the question of the free gift of his life in the event of the passion? Love follows upon knowledge, because we can only love what we already in some way know.[44] Nowhere are the repercussions of this doctrine so important as when we consider the relation between Christ's human freedom and his free embrace of the event of the passion in obedience to the Father for the sake of our salvation. Following Anselm, Aquinas holds that Jesus gave his life freely in loving obedience as an all-sufficient atonement (*satisfactio*) for human sin.[45] If we consider this idea in light of that explored in the previous paragraph (extraordinary self-knowledge as well as a self-offering originating from love), then we can unite the two principles safely to derive a third: Christ can choose to redeem the world freely in love only because he knows of the value of his sacrifice, and its meaning. His act of free self-offering requires that he know that he has been sent by the Father for our salvation, but it also requires that he know who he himself is who is making the offering.

This idea is advanced implicitly in St. Thomas's discussion of sacrifice.[46] Following Augustine, he thinks that to know the value of a sacrifice, knowledge of four things is required: what is being offered, who is making the offer, for whom it is made, and why it is offered. But who makes the offer of this sacrifice, if not the Son incarnate, and is it not he himself who is offered, for us? It follows from Aquinas's reasoning that if Jesus does not know who he is as the Son, he cannot truly offer his life for the salvation of the world.[47] From within this purview, Christ's knowledge of who he is conditions all of his free actions, precisely those actions of Jesus crucified that reveal his personal identity as the Son who is one with the Father—"Father, forgive them for they know not what they do," in Luke 23:34—and the presence in him of a divine life that is saving the world. It is necessary, therefore, that Christ understand in some real sense the significance of his own *self*-offering going into his passion. For only in doing so does he thereby merit our salvation through love.

44. ST I-II, q. 9, a. 1.

45. ST III, q. 48, a. 2.

46. ST III, q. 48, a. 3. Aquinas refers here to Augustine, *De Trin.* IV, 14, as well as *De Civ. Dei* X, 20.

47. See ST III, q. 22, a. 4, *sed contra*, where Aquinas affirms that the denial that Christ intended explicitly to give his life for others is contrary to the orthodox faith.

The argument that Christ knew humanly who he was, however, is only a prerequisite for the second idea mentioned above. Christ not only knew who he was, but also gave himself over to the passion *freely*. This does not mean uniquely that he accepted a situation that was cast upon him, but also that he chose freely to allow this event to occur, and did this not only as God (because he is one with the Father and is Lord of all things) but also as man.[48] This is not a notion foreign to the Gospels but is in fact advanced forcefully in manifold ways. Christ is able to avoid stoning or physical violence prior to the appropriate time of his foreseen death (Lk 4:29–30; Jn 10:30–39), and he is able to avoid suffering even in the Garden of Gethsemane should he wish (Mt 26:53–54; Jn 18:4–11). The event of his physical death itself is in fact ultimately the result of a choice (Lk 23:46; Jn 19:30, 32–34). Are these passages simply to be read as post-Paschal theologoumena? Here St. Thomas appeals to the unity of the personal acts of Christ as the Son made man, who wills simultaneously as the Wisdom of the Father (in his divine will) and freely as man (in his human will). "Christ delivered Himself up to death by the same will and action as that by which the Father delivered Him up [as God]; but as man He gave Himself up by a will inspired of the Father. Consequently there is no contradiction in the Father delivering Him up and in Christ delivering himself up."[49]

In effect, as we have seen, Christ's human will—the kind of human freedom that he shares with us as true man—is lived out in concord with his divine will, the will that he shares in perfectly with the Father, as true God. This is a necessary repercussion of the incarnation, but it also has profound soteriological consequences. Christ continually acts in his human operations of willing in coordination with his saving divine actions and operations. He can freely reach out his human hand to the man who is blind, and by the divine power of charity inhabiting in him he can heal the man through his human touch.[50] This is simultaneously a divine and human act of salvation.[51]

---

48. ST III, q. 47, a. 1.
49. ST III, q. 47, a. 3, ad 2 (translation slightly modified).
50. ST III, q. 19, a. 1, corp. and ad 5.
51. ST III, q. 19, a. 11: the notion of "theandric action" stems from Dionysius (*Ep. IV Ad Caium; Div. Nom.* II, 6).

Due to the same harmony Christ can also will freely as man what
he can accomplish or prohibit as God, only by virtue of his deity.
Among such objects of the divine will there is included God's willing that the Son suffer at the hands of sinful humanity. Christ *as man*,
therefore, because he is God, can choose whether or not to give his
life freely for the salvation of the world. Otherwise stated, for Aquinas, the Gospels reveal something historical that is of noteworthy realism: *just* because this man is God and only because he is, he can
also *as man* decide freely whether he wishes to be subject to the vicissitudes of human suffering and embrace the passion. It is in this sense
that Christ, as the God-man, gives himself freely over to death in a
way no one else could. This is due to the power of the deity of Christ
crucified. So Aquinas comments upon John 10:18 ("No one takes [my
life] from me, but I lay it down of my own accord. I have power to lay
it down, and I have power to take it again"):

> He adds something about his power when he says, "I have power to lay it
> down." Apropos of this it should be noted that since the union of the soul
> and body is natural, their separation is natural. And although the cause of
> this separation and death can be voluntary, yet among human beings death
> is always natural. Now nature is not subject to the will of any mere human,
> since nature, as well as the will, are from God. Therefore, the death of any
> mere human person must be natural. But in Christ, his own nature and every
> other nature are subject to his will, just like artifacts are subject to the will of
> the artisan. Thus, according to the pleasure of his will, he could lay down his
> life when he willed, and he could take it up again; no mere human being can
> do this, although he could voluntarily use some instrument to kill himself.
> This explains why the centurion, seeing that Christ did not die by a natural
> necessity, but by his own [will]—since "Jesus cried again with a loud voice
> and yielded up his spirit" (Matt. 27:50)—recognized a divine power in him,
> and said: "Truly, this was the Son of God" (Matt. 27:54). Again, the Apostle
> says in 1 Corinthians (1:18): "For the word of the cross is folly to those who
> are perishing, but to us who are being saved it is the power of God," that is,
> his great power was revealed in the very death of Christ.[52]

The soteriological consequences of this idea are weighty. If Christ
is to give his life for us freely as the means of our salvation, this requires that Christ as man not be entirely unaware of his divine identi-

---

52. *In Ioan.* X, lec. 4, 1425. See also the clear comments of ST III, q. 47, a. 1, corp.
and ad 1–3.

ty. In this case, however, he necessarily must be able as man to freely give his life in a way others cannot. The ideas are interrelated. Thus, if we claim that Christ does not have this unique privilege as man, then we should also be committed logically to the conclusion that either he does not know of his identity as the Son made man, or that he does not intend to offer his suffering to God as a means of atoning for human sin. But in either case, the classical Anselmian idea that Christ knowingly gave his life out of love in reparation for human sinfulness is undermined.

The Power of Christ as
God Is Operative in and Through
His Passion

Secondly, then, according to Aquinas, the power of the Son as God is not only present at the origins of his free acceptance of the passion, but is also active in Christ crucified even during the time of his human suffering and mortal expiration. It is significant to note in this respect that in his analysis of the Paschal mystery in the *Summa theologiae*, Aquinas in numerous instances makes a fundamental distinction between Christ's meritorious acts of will and his activities as man that are "effective" of our salvation.[53] The former category pertains to the atoning work of Christ in his acts of human righteousness before God on our behalf, while the latter concept denotes the way Christ *as man* through his human actions causes our salvation effectively. Subsequent interpreters have sometimes alluded to this distinction in terms of an ascending (impetrative) and descending (instrumental) mediation: Christ can intercede for us or can act upon us.[54] The latter transpires in the crucifixion as well as the former: God the Son acts as man with divine power even as he also endures physical and mental agony, as well as death.

How does the power of God operate in one who is crucified? Aquinas does not diminish the reality of Christ's human suffering and weakness. Rather, in the tradition of western medieval Catholic

<hr>

53. ST III, q. 48, a. 6, corp. and ad 1–3; q. 49, a. 1, corp. and ad 1–5; q. 50, a. 6, corp. and ad 1–3; 56, a. 1, ad 3–4; q. 57, a. 6, ad 1; q. 64, a. 3.

54. See, for example, Charles Journet, *L'Église du Verbe Incarné: La structure interne de l'Église: Le Christ, la Vierge, l'Esprit Saint* (Paris: Saint Augustin, 1999), 2:359–62.

piety, he describes it vividly.[55] Simultaneously, however, he invokes a
principle that follows from his theology of the hypostatic union: that
of the instrumentality of the human nature of Christ. The human acts
of Christ from the cross are the acts of the Word made flesh. Even
amidst weakness and suffering, then, they can communicate effects
of divine power, as Aquinas argues in ST III, q. 48, a. 6 (corpus and
ad 1). Quoting St. Paul, he writes:

The word of the cross to them that are saved ... is the power of God." (1 Cor.
1:18) But God's power brings about our salvation efficiently. Therefore
Christ's Passion on the cross accomplished our salvation efficiently. [Now]
there is a twofold efficient agency, namely, principal and instrumental. The
principal efficient cause of man's salvation is God. But since Christ's humanity is the instrument of the Godhead, therefore *all Christ's actions and sufferings operated instrumentally* in virtue of His Godhead for the salvation of
men. Consequently, then, Christ's passion accomplishes man's salvation efficiently.

Responding here to the objection that Christ was crucified in human
weakness and therefore could not act on the cross by divine power,
Aquinas responds:

Christ's passion in relation to His flesh is consistent with the infirmity which
he took upon himself [as man], but in relation to the Godhead it draws infinite might from it, according to 1 Cor. 1:25: "The weakness of God is stronger than men"; because Christ's weakness, inasmuch as He is God, has a
might exceeding all human power.

It is because of this unity of the divinity and humanity of Christ
crucified, that he is able at Golgotha to effectively rule over the powers of the world and vanquish the power of sin. Commenting on
1 Corinthians 1:18, Aquinas writes the following:

He says, therefore: The reason I have said that the cross of Christ is made
void, if the teachings of the faith are presented in eloquent wisdom is that
the word of the cross ... appears foolish, to them that are perishing, i.e., to
unbelievers, who consider themselves wise according to the world, for the
preaching of the cross of Christ contains something which to worldly wisdom seems impossible; for example, that God should die or that Omnipotence should suffer at the hands of violent men. Furthermore, that a per-

son not avoid shame when he can, and other things of this sort, are matters which seem contrary to the prudence of this world. Consequently, when Paul was preaching such things, Festus said: "Paul, you are beside yourself: much learning makes you mad" (Acts 26:24). And Paul himself says below that the word of the cross actually does contain foolishness, [for] he adds: but to us that are being saved, (namely, Christ's faithful who are saved by Him: "He will save his people from their sins" (Matt 1:21)), it is the power of God, because they [the faithful] recognize in the cross of Christ God's power, by which He overcame the devil and the world: "The Lion of the tribe of Judah, has conquered" (Rev. 5:5).[56]

This idea is also underscored briefly by Aquinas in an original way when he comments upon the "kingship" of Christ in his commentary on the fourth Gospel. There he notes that for St. John, Christ is the "king" of humanity on the cross, vanquishing by the power of the Godhead within him the angelic and worldly powers of sin that rule over man, so as to reestablish the kingship of God.

Although this seems extremely bizarre to the irreligious and to unbelievers, it is a great mystery for believers and the devout: "For the word of the cross is folly to those who are perishing, but to us who are being saved it is the power of God" (1 Cor. 1:18). Christ bore his cross as a king does his scepter; his cross is the sign of his glory, which is his universal dominion over all things: "The Lord will reign from the wood" (Ps. 95:9); "The government will be upon his shoulder, and his name will be called 'Wonderful, Counselor, Mighty God, Everlasting Father, Prince of Peace.'" (Isa. 9:6). He carried his cross as a victor carries the trophy of his victory: "He disarmed the principalities and powers and made a public example of them, triumphing over them in himself" (Col. 2:15). Again, he carried his cross as a teacher his candelabrum, as a support for the light of his teaching, because for believers the message of the cross is the power of God: "No one after lighting a lamp puts it in a cellar or under a bushel but on a stand, that those who enter may see the light" (Luke 11:33).[57]

This leads us to a second idea: because of the power of the deity of Christ (what Aquinas calls the *virtus divinitatis* or *virtus spiritualis*) the humanly contingent, historically situated acts of Jesus in the Paschal event can have contact with human beings at all times and

---

56. *In I Cor.* I, lec. 3, 47. [Translation by Fabian Larcher, unpublished manuscript.]
57. *In Ioan.* XIX, lec. 3, 2414.

places.[58] Christ's passion can affect all of human history as an efficient cause of salvation, and this is by virtue of his deity. In accord with this notion, Aquinas will posit that the past event of the crucifixion, while no longer a contemporary reality, is still acting instrumentally upon human beings who come after Christ to effectuate their salvation.[59] He says the same even about the dead cadaver of Christ (!), the historical event of his resurrection (two days after the crucifixion), and the time of his ascension (forty days after the resurrection).[60] While no longer in existence, these past mysteries were the instrumental causes of the grace we now receive. Consequently they continue to effectuate change in our lives.[61] "For God was in Christ reconciling the world to himself" (2 Cor 5:19).

Can this really be the case? In what sense? In ST III, q. 56, a. 1, obj. 3 Aquinas considers an objection to this idea: the past events of the life of Christ no longer exist and therefore cannot come into physical contact with us now (*contactum corporalem*). It follows that there is no possibility of the events of the Paschal mystery affecting our lives now as *instrumental efficient* causes. One might hold that the *merits* of Christ's passion still affect us, and that the living, resurrected humanity of Christ is a *living* instrument of our salvation, but not that the past mysteries are present causes of grace.

Aquinas responds to this objection in turn: the causality we are speaking of is not by way of physical contact (by way of an extension of now terminated events somehow preserved in the life of God, as Odo Casel problematically posited). Rather, Aquinas specifies that it is a spiritual contact (*contactum spiritualem*) that is facilitated by the divinity of Christ itself.[62] In other words, because he is God, the hu-

58. ST III, q. 49, a. 1, ad 2: "Passio Christi, licet sit corporalis, sortitur tamen quandam spiritualem virtutem ex divinitate, cuius caro ei unita est instrumentum. Secundum quam quidem virtutem passio Christi est causa remissionis peccatorum." See also ST III, q. 48, a. 6, ad 2; q. 56, a. 1, ad 3.

59. ST III, q. 49, a. 1, ad 1–5; q. 79, a. 1.

60. ST III, q. 50, a. 6; q. 56, a. 1, esp. ad 3; q. 57, a. 6, ad 1. Regarding the resurrection of Christ, it is clear from obj. 3 of q. 56, a. 1 that Aquinas is referring principally to the historical "Christus resurgens" and not to the now living glorified humanity of Christ.

61. This idea has been explored by modern Thomistic commentators such as Charles Journet, Jean-Hervé Nicolas, and Jean-Pierre Torrell. See on this Jean-Pierre Torrell, *Le Christ en ses mysteres: la vie et l'oeuvre de Jesus selon saint Thomas d'Aquin* (Paris: Desclée, 1999), 2:637–43.

62. ST III, q. 56, a. 1, obj. 3: "Manifestum est autem quod resurrectio Christi non

man acts of Jesus Christ in history (all the *acta et passa* of his life, but particularly the events of his redemption) can have an instrumental effect subordinate to the work of his divinity. In this way, the event of the redemption acts as a true efficient cause upon all subsequent human beings. The medium by which the past events of the passion now act upon us is *the deity of God* working both then and now, through and in light of the passion. By the power of the Godhead, the Paschal mystery is the source of our grace, such that our supernatural faith, hope, and charity, our sacramental graces and so on, come to us by virtue of what Christ did and underwent for us in and through his crucifixion and resurrection.

Evidently, this soteriology ties in with the Athanasian theme of divinization which is also prevalent in Aquinas's work: God became man so that man might become God, or be united to the divine life.[63] The effective salvation realized in and through the power of the cross, therefore, also has an exemplary dimension.[64] God has united himself to us amidst death so that we might be united to God in life. Aquinas notes here how Christ patterns himself after the "First Adam" so that we in turn might be patterned after him as the "New Adam."[65] On the one hand, suffering results from Adam's fall into sin, and Christ who was himself fully human endured suffering not as a punishment from God, but virtuously out of love.[66] He did so while maintaining an internal harmony of sense and reason that was truly Adamic, like that originally intended in paradise. In him the human passions were subordinate to reason and reason was perfectly subordinate to God.[67] This is something like the "integral humanity" of Adam we considered in chapter 2. Yet here it is present in a person subject to suffering,

---

agit per contactum corporalem ad mortuos qui resurgent, propter distantiam temporis et loci. Similiter etiam nec per *contactum spiritualem*, qui est per fidem et caritatem, quia etiam infideles et peccatores resurgent." See also ST III, q. 48, a. 6, ad 2: "Passio Christi, licet sit corporalis, habet tamen spiritualem virtutem ex divinitate unita. Et ideo per *spiritualem contactum* efficaciam sortitur, scilicet per fidem et fidei sacramenta" (emphasis added).

63. ST III, q. 1, a. 2.   64. ST III, q. 56, a. 1, corp. and ad 3.
65. ST III, q. 14, a. 1; q. 15, a. 1.
66. ST III, q. 14, aa. 2–3. See the study by Rik van Nieuwenhove, "'Bearing the Marks of Christ's Death': Aquinas' Soteriology," in *The Theology of Thomas Aquinas*, eds. R. Van Nieuwenhove and J. Wawrykow (Notre Dame, Ind.: University of Notre Dame Press, 2005), 277–302.
67. ST III, q. 15, aa. 2–4.

who has been crucified. The cross, then, is a new tree of life in which the harmony of man in paradise is reestablished, albeit in a crucified form, endured even unto death. The death of Adam is adopted, as it were, by the Son made man, in view of the redemption from death that is the resurrection.[68] Believers can follow Christ by virtue of his grace, being conformed to this re-creation that his passion effectuates in us by the power of God. In this life internal graces received by virtue of the mysteries of Christ permit the soul to be subordinate to God in love.[69] Perfect submission of the passions to reason (and of the body to the soul) is promised only eschatologically, as believers are called to undergo physical death and resurrection in dependence upon the grace of Christ.[70] Otherwise stated, the events which save us effectively also conform us to themselves in order to save us: we are invited to pass through death in solidarity with Christ as a way into the mystery of the resurrection.

The Son of God Raised Himself
from the Dead

Lastly we can speak briefly about the cause of the resurrection. If Christ is God who suffers out of love in his free will as man, and if God is present in Christ actively triumphing over the powers of the world, restoring order to a fallen world, then for St. Thomas, Christ as God is also the origin of his own resurrection. By resurrection we are speaking according to St. Thomas about the glorification of the body and soul of Christ that took place after his death. The body that lay in the tomb was restored to life and reunited to the soul, but it was also radically transformed so as to acquire new properties of physical matter more proximate to the divine nature.[71] The glorified body of Christ—which is physical—is now spiritually agile and dynamic, transparent to the radiance and glory of God in a way that it was not in its historical, pre-Paschal state.

In his article in the *Summa theologiae* treating of this question (ST III, q. 53, a. 4: Whether Christ was the cause of his own resurrection?), Aquinas first notes that Christ claims explicitly in John 10:18 to be able to raise himself up from the dead by the power of God:

68. ST III, q. 50, a. 1.   69. ST III, q. 56, a. 2.
70. ST III, q. 69, aa. 3–4.   71. ST III, q. 54, aa. 1–4.

"No one takes [my life] from me, but I lay it down, and I have the power to take it again." In the corpus of the article he then correlates this Johannine text with a Pauline verse that speaks of Christ being raised from the dead by the power of God, citing 2 Corinthians 13:4: "For although he was crucified through our weakness, yet He lives by the power of God." He then draws a logical conclusion: the divine power of God that raised Jesus from the dead truly resides in the Word made flesh, throughout his life, death, and resurrection. This is the case, then, even on Holy Saturday, the day on which the soul and body of Christ are separated due to physical death.

> Therefore, *according to the virtue of the Godhead united to it*, the body took back again the soul which it had laid aside, and the soul took back again the body which it had abandoned: and thus Christ rose by His own power … but if we consider the body and soul of the dead Christ according to the power of created nature, they could not thus be reunited, but it was necessary for Christ to be raised up by God.[72]

Aquinas is saying that if we consider Christ as man, we may say that God raised Christ from the dead, as 2 Corinthians 13:4 attests, but that if we consider Christ as God, we must also say that Christ raised himself from the dead, as is said in John. There is no incongruity here (ad 1): "The Divine power is the same thing as the operation of the Father and the Son [which both possess identically]; accordingly these two things are mutually consequent, that Christ was raised up by the Divine power of the Father, and by His own power."

It is worth bearing in mind that the deeper point here for Aquinas is Trinitarian: the event of the resurrection reveals the unity of the Father and the Son amidst their personal distinction as well as their personal distinction amidst unity. It reveals the divine unity precisely because what the Father does, the Son does as well, but this undivided operation also manifests the personal distinction of the Son from the Father, for what the Son does with the Father, he also does precisely as Son, that is to say, as one who proceeds eternally from the Father. Commenting upon John 5:21 ("For just as the Father raises the dead and grants life, so the Son grants life to those to whom he wishes") Aquinas underscores this point:

72. Emphasis added.

Hilary calls our attention to the remarkable relationship of the passages so that the errors concerning eternal generation can be refuted. Two heresies have arisen concerning this eternal generation. One was that of Arius, who said that the Son is less than the Father; and this is contrary to their equality and unity. The other was that of Sabellius, who said that that there is no distinction of persons in the divinity; and this is contrary to their origin. So, whenever he mentions the unity and equality [of the Father and Son], he immediately also adds their distinction as persons according to origin, and conversely. Thus, because he mentions the origin of the persons when he says, "the Son cannot do anything of himself, but only what he sees the Father doing" (5:19), then, so we do not think this involves inequality, he at once adds: "for whatever the Father does, the Son does likewise." Conversely, when he states their equality by saying: "For just as the Father raises the dead and grants life, so the Son grants life to those to whom he wishes," then, so that we do not deny that the Son has an origin and is begotten, he adds, "the Father himself judges no one, but he has given all judgment to the Son."[73]

If the Son is with the Father, then, he is so as one who receives from the Father all that he has and is. As noted in chapter 5, Aquinas speaks here of a filial mode of the Son's being God. This mode of being God as one who is eternally begotten affects as well the mode in which the Son is "the Resurrection and the Life" (Jn 11:25). We must say that the Father raised Christ and that Christ as God raised up his own human life, but we must also qualify this: the Son acted in the resurrection in a distinctly filial mode, as one who receives all that he has from the Father. The raising of the Son as man, therefore, also reveals the divinity of the Son, but shows forth the primacy of the Father as he who gives to the Son all that he receives, not only as man, but also as God. The Father gives us to know, through the death and resurrection of the Son, the reality of the Son's identity. He does this also in giving the Son as God to be the source of resurrected life not only on the day of Easter, but also eschatologically for all mankind. Commenting again on the fifth chapter of John, Aquinas notes:

Although Christ had the complete fullness of power from eternity (because "whatever the Father does, the Son does likewise"), he still speaks of this power as being given to him after the resurrection, not because he was then receiving it for the first time, but because it was through the glory of the res-

73. *In Ioan.* V, lec. 4, 769.

urrection that it became most known. In this interpretation, then, he says that power is given to him insofar as he exercises it in some work. As if to say: "he will show him even greater works than these," i.e., he will show by his works what has been given to him. And this will come about when you are amazed, i.e., when the one who seems to you to be a mere man is revealed to be a person of divine power and as God.[74]

CLASSICAL VERSUS KENOTIC
SOTERIOLOGY

Clearly the three above-mentioned points differ from the views encountered in modern kenotic Christology as the latter is typically articulated. How is this the case? In the last section of this chapter I would like to allude to three characteristic kenotic views encountered among Catholic and Protestant thinkers alike, each of which contrasts in important ways with what has just been described. In discussing the viewpoints mentioned below, I do not intend to give an extensive representation of them, but only to note important points of contrast with Aquinas. The goal thereby is to identify what is at stake soteriologically in the classical versus the kenotic representations of redemption.

Jesus's Free Acceptance
of His Own Death

Consider first a typical modern understanding of Christ's free acceptance of his own death. Nineteenth- and twentieth-century historical-critical scholars since Johannes Weiss and Albert Schweitzer have often attempted to argue that the Jesus of history understood himself primarily as an apocalyptic preacher or teacher, standing on the cusp of and possibly inaugurating the end times. Their hypothetical portraits have suggested that the real Jesus of history did not intend his death to have a universal significance or enduring salvific import, but rather that his death came as a disappointment in the face of a failed apocalypticism.[75] This point of interpretation has moved Chris-

---

74. *In Ioan.* V, lec. 4, 760.
75. This was, for example, the view of Willi Marxsen, "Erwägungen zum Problem

tian scholars in turn to make use of the historical-critical study of the scriptures "apologetically" as it were, to ward off such interpretations. Pannenberg, for example, is careful to defend a number of valid theological points in the face of historical-critical studies: that the New Testament provides rational warrant for the affirmation that the historical Jesus truly intended to inaugurate the kingdom of God, that he correspondingly believed himself to have the unique authority to do so, and that he expressed this conviction in the language and theological idioms of the thought-world of his times. Ultimately, he foresaw his death and accepted it in light of his eschatological expectation. Due to Jesus's fidelity to God, his death implicitly had a salvific value for all human beings, one that was made perfectly manifest, however, only in the resurrection.[76]

This approach has many advantages. It takes historical reasoning seriously, defends the rationality of Christian faith in the face of modern historical studies, and attempts to think realistically about the humanity of God the Son in his life among us. What is distinct about it, however, in comparison with the classical views considered above, is that it emphasizes virtually exclusively the human character of the event of Christ's suffering and death (understood primarily by reference to its historical context), *disinvesting from this event any apparent activity of the divinity of the Son* in and through the passion. Given the self-awareness of Jesus that is presumed, the Son made man must attempt to discern the divine will amidst the contingent circumstances of history, and to be faithful to it in ways analogous to those of other believers, as a person of his age.[77] In this view, prophetic graces need

---

des verkündigten Kreuzes," in *Der Exeget als Theologe. Vorträge zum Neuen Testament* (Gütersloh: Mohn, 1968), 160–70. This line of thought runs back through Schweitzer and Weiss, present already as far back as Reimarus.

76. Pannenberg, *Jesus: God and Man*, 225–58; *Systematic Theology*, 2:325–63. A similar approach is found in Kasper, *Jesus the Christ*, 65–123.

77. On the faith of Christ, see *Systematic Theology*, 2:337–79. Pannenberg appeals here to Ritschl as the historical forebear of the soteriological interpretation he is offering. On Jesus's historical consciousness, see *Jesus: God and Man*, 325–34, especially 332–34: "Jesus knew himself to be related to the God whose future, consummated with the coming Son of Man, would have to decide the rightness or wrongness of his own activity.... As an awareness of the not yet decided future, the knowledge of one's own ignorance is a condition of human openness and freedom. It is to be understood in the sense that Jesus' lack of knowledge was apparently not only related to the Day of Judgment,

not be invoked as the cause of Christ's self-awareness and intentions. Rather, Christ's foreknowledge and free acceptance of his passion can be seen merely as the result of his natural capacities of historical estimation in the face of persecution and the threat of execution, events that he interpreted eschatologically as a first-century Jew.[78] To this epistemology there corresponds an ontology. What is absent is not only the notion of prophetic light, but also that of divine willing present in the Son made man himself. We are no longer given to think that Jesus acted in two wills as both God and man; classical dyothe-letism is problematic. Rather, as we have seen with Barth, the personal Sonship of Christ is revealed through his human obedience.[79] Of course, this point of view is deliberately related to a reconsideration of the notion of God as such. Invoking the heritage of kenotic theology, Pannenberg suggests that Jesus's human cognitive limitations tell us theologically something about *what God is*, and invite us to revise our classical conceptions of God in accord with the nature of the deity made known in the New Testament.[80] The kenosis of the Son's knowledge as man is an expression of the divine solidarity with us, in which God empties himself of divine prerogatives (or expresses himself at a distance from himself) out of concern for solidarity with us in a life of faith and obedience lived in love.[81]

---

but thereby to his own person as well. Precisely this fact of Jesus' perfection in dedication to the God of the eschatological future reaches its consummation. This lack of knowledge is actually the condition of Jesus' unity with this God."

78. *Systematic Theology* 2:334–35, 337; *Jesus: God and Man*, 239–43, especially 242: "The mere process of historical time makes every attitude that can be assumed today different from Jesus' imminent expectation [of the kingdom]. Thus we can no longer share Jesus' imminent expectation. We can, however, live and think in continuity with it and thus with Jesus' activity if we recognize Jesus' imminent expectation ... as having been previously fulfilled in Jesus' own resurrection."

79. *Jesus: God and Man*, 294: "The tendency of the two-natures doctrine to destroy the unity of Jesus Christ became especially clear in the condemnations of Monothe-letism, because the basis for affirming Jesus' divinity lies precisely in his unity of will with the Father in the execution of his mission .... The decision about Jesus' own divinity as the Son can be made only indirectly, through his unity of obedience and mission with the Father."

80. *Systematic Theology* 2:375.

81. *Systematic Theology* 2:377: "In his form of life as Jesus, on the path of his obedience to God, the eternal Son appeared as a human being. The relation of the Son to the Father is characterized in eternity by the subordination to the Father, by the self-distinction

What has been eclipsed in such a viewpoint, if we compare it with that of Aquinas, is the presence of the divinity of Christ in Christ's decision to give his life for our sake. For Pannenberg, the Son *as man* confides himself to the Father in faith and in trust. But we no longer can say that Jesus—knowing who he is—*freely lays down his life as the God-man*, for us, for the salvation of human beings. The theology of theandric activity is obscured. More specifically, we can no longer speak of a freedom to accept death that is unique to Christ as man because he is God. These differences raise important Christological and soteriological questions. Most notably: is the act of Jesus's meritorious sacrifice specifically the same in either case, or do the two conceptions in fact implicitly lead us to attribute two distinct objects or intentions to Christ in his historical death? For it is one thing to intend to be faithful to the God of Israel in order to bring in the eschatological kingdom of God, while it is quite another to intend to give one's life as Son of God on behalf of sinful humanity. We can now see the soteriological consequences of our arguments from chapter 5 regarding the unity of Christ's personal actions. According to tradition, Christ has both a human will and a divine will. But how can the divine-human agency still be the action of one agent, if our Christology gives no account of the divine will of Christ operative in his human activity? Is the unity of the person sufficiently maintained by Pannenberg? One might ask if such a view (for all its genuine historical value) tends in fact toward a kind of soteriological Nestorianism, where a man dies trusting God the Father will save him, even as in another, parallel way, his being is one with the Father who raises him up. He is both God and man, but the personal unity of the two in the event of the passion is inadequately expressed. For based on this view, it seems that Christ as man hopes to be delivered and saved by God in his passion, thereby inaugurating the eschatological kingdom of God. Yet he does this in accord with a transcendent divine will for his and for our salvation that is *extrinsic to his own personal, human act.*

---

from the majesty of the Father, which took historical form in the human relation of Jesus to God. This self-distinction of the eternal Son from the Father may be understood as the basis of all creaturely existence in its distinction from God, and therefore as the basis of the human existence of Jesus, which gave adequate embodiment in its course to the self-emptying of the Son in service to the rule of the Father."

What we see emerge, then, is a consistency in Pannenberg between his understanding of Christ's epistemological kenosis and his
penal substitution theory. Christ's dereliction is the expression not
primarily of his intrinsic righteousness (though his human innocence
is of course maintained) but of his solidarity with us as one coming
under the judgment of God. He is condemned in our stead so that
we can be forgiven.[82] Whereas Anselm and Aquinas underscore the
intrinsic righteousness of the human Christ in his passion, this account of the redemption turns to the extrinsic attribution of the guilt
of humanity onto the Son. What happens, then, to the saving merit of Christ's human acts of obedience accomplished in charity? Can
Christ as man truly intend to give his life for our sake if he is not explicitly aware of the value of his life as the God-man and of the soteriological efficacy of his death? Aquinas's affirmation of the divinity of
Christ at work in Jesus's saving knowledge and human choices in the
face of death clearly has crucial soteriological repercussions. Correspondingly, the obscuring of the presence of the deity of the Son in
Jesus's personal act of decision to embrace the cross threatens to render unintelligible Anselm's atonement theology of the passion. This
is to render theologically inaccessible (or conceptually unintelligible)
the very love or charity with which Christ as man willingly laid down
his earthly life for us.[83]

Behind all this stands a question of methodology. There is a certain kind of approach to soteriology that wants to unite the Catholic
creed and historical-critical research but which does not want to speak
about the divine action of Christ prior to or during the crucifixion,
because we do not have any historical-critical access to it. If historical-critical methodology is allowed to construe things thus, the classical instrumentality of Christ's humanity is necessarily ignored. It is

82. *Systematic Theology* 2:421–29.

83. Although this is my claim, it should be noted that this is anything other than
the intention of Pannenberg, who sees the incarnation as a kenotic expression of divine
love (*Systematic Theology*, 2:379) and who defends his understanding of penal substitution theory as compatible in some sense with Anselm's views (429–37). However, the
obedient love of God in the passion is thus transferred from the humanity of Christ as
mediator between God and men into the deity of God in his mode of being as Son, and
the righteousness of the Son is found not in his human love and obedience per se, but in
his divine ontological identification with us in our distance from God.

as if we were to say: "Before the resurrection, all hail the historical-critical method which considers the humanity of Christ alone. After the resurrection, all hail the Nicene Creed—for his divinity is retrieved." By contrast, then, if Aquinas is saying something essential to the faith, the methodological use of the historical-critical method on a point like this, however valid, has to be carefully reconsidered in its extension and purposes. We know as a matter of revealed faith that before the death of Christ he acts as man instrumentally in the service of the divine will and this instrumentality is reflected in his human knowledge and willing. Historical-critical reflection on the Gospels might be able to defend rationally the historicity of this mystery or discuss its cultural context and circumstances. It cannot procure, however, the basis itself for belief in the mystery, because this is given to us only supernaturally—through faith in the portrayal of Christ given by the New Testament, which we know *by faith* to correspond to the historical Jesus himself.

The Kenosis of God Crucified

These reflections lead organically to the second point discussed above, pertaining to the power of Christ that is present in his passion, working even through his human weakness and suffering to restore order to a fallen world. Here the contrast with classic soteriology is more vivid. For we find in a host of modern theologians—we can take Eberhard Jüngel as a typical example—a doctrine of divine kenosis in the passion, in which there comes to be within God the embrace of a seeming contrary to the power of God.[84] The powerlessness or self-emptying of God the Son on the cross even unto death pertains not only to the human nature of Christ, but in fact to God's own deity. This idea is common to other kenotic thinkers. In the death of Christ, there enters into the very being of God as God,

---

84. Jüngel, *God as the Mystery of the World*, 363–64: "In this sense, God's identification with the dead Jesus implies self-differentiation on God's part. The being of this dead man defines God's own being in such a way that one must speak of a differentiation between God and God. But it must immediately be added that it is an act of God himself who effects his identity with the dead Jesus and as its precondition the differentiation of God and God.... And for that reason it must be said that *God defines himself* when he identifies himself with the dead Jesus. At the same time he defines the man Jesus as the Son of God."

either ontological separation (of the Son from the Father), or suffering (an intrinsic alteration in the being of God due to a wound of love that God is subject to) or death and nothingness (the negation of God's very being).[85]

This theme of diremptive becoming within the life of God is expressed in various ways. The common idea, however, is that God assumes into his divine life something seemingly contradictory to omnipotence (be it alienation, suffering, or death) in order to be in solidarity with human beings, and in order to overcome that which he assumes.[86] This is accomplished however at the expense of a doctrine of divine simplicity, power, and transcendence, since historical change and passion, or ontological separation, are introduced into the very life of God. The larger point for our purposes is that this represents a very different soteriological conception of the divinity of Christ as it is present in his passion from the one we have been considering. For Aquinas underscores not the kenosis of the divine attributes of the Son in his passion, but rather the importance of their inalienable presence. *If God the Son were to forfeit his divine unity with the Father in the crucifixion, his capacity to save us would not only be compromised, but in fact forfeited.* His oneness with his Father in their unity of operation from the cross is the basis for the victory of God's wisdom and goodness even through the event of the passion.

For Aquinas, God can make use of any evil, even the worst, in order to manifest the power of divine goodness. Even intense human suffering can contribute to the triumph of Christ over the powers of sin and death precisely because of the union of human suffering with the divine nature in the person of the Son (who does not cease to be one with the Father). Jesus's human crucifixion and death operate effectively (by a *contactum spiritualem*) to touch the lives of human beings in all times and places. But this is only possible because of the

85. See Emery, "The Immutability of the God of Love and the Problem of Language Concerning the 'Suffering of God,'" for his analysis of this theme in Balthasar, Bulgakov, and Moltmann.

86. Jüngel, *God as the Mystery of the World*, 344: "In that the living God in his deity bears the death of Jesus, in that he burdens the eternity of his being with the crucifixion of Jesus, he demonstrates his divine being as a *living* unity of life and death.... The faith ... proclaims and tells the tension which defines the being of God itself, the tension between eternal life and temporal death, as the story of Jesus Christ."

virtus divinitatis of the Godhead of Christ that works instrumentally in and through Christ's humanity. If, instead, God overcomes suffering by adopting it into his own deity so as to forfeit his power (for instance, in his mode of being as Son), then this whole order of salvation collapses. The cross loses its universal instrumental power. What is more, has God then truly overcome the power of evil, or has he rather united himself with it for eternity? Are his goodness and wisdom vindicated by this exercise of power, or is the expression of his goodness and wisdom now inherently and necessarily related to a history of evil, a history that has entered into God himself?

The Resurrection of the Son
by the Father

Last, and most briefly, let us consider the resurrection. Who raised Jesus from the dead? Following Karl Barth, Hans Urs von Balthasar has articulated a modern kenotic theology that stresses the obedience of Christ in his dereliction on the cross. This obedience is seen as expressive not only of his human submission to the Father's will, but also of his divine identity as the Son.[87] In other words, there is an obedience in God that is characteristic of the person of the Son as God, who is eternally responsive or obedient to the Father. In Balthasar's theology a central motif is the descent of the Son into hell on Holy Saturday, experienced as a separation from the Father.[88] This

---

87. *Theo-Drama*, 4:325–26, 329–30: "The Father, in uttering and surrendering himself without reserve, does not lose himself.... For in this self-surrender, he *is* the whole divine essence. Here we see both God's infinite power and his powerlessness; he cannot be God in any other way but in this 'kenosis' within the Godhead itself.... It follows that the Son, for his part, cannot *be* and *possess* the absolute nature of God except in the mode of receptivity: he receives the unity of omnipotence and powerlessness from the Father. This receptivity simultaneously includes the Son's self-givenness.... For the Son, following truth to the end means making a fitting response to the Father's total gift of himself by freely and thankfully allowing himself to be poured forth by the Father, a response that is made in absolute spontaneity and in absolute 'obedience' to the Father."

88. *Theo-Drama*, 4:335: "Here the God-man drama reaches its acme: perverse finite freedom casts all its guilt onto God, making him the sole accused, the scapegoat, while God allows himself to be thoroughly affected by this, not only in the humanity of Christ but also in Christ's trinitarian mission. The omnipotent powerlessness of God's love shines forth in the mystery of darkness and alienation between God and the sin-bearing Son."

occurs prior to his being raised by the Father.[89] Such moments in the life of Christ are subsequent expressions of the Son's obedience. They are also expressions, then, of the mystery of the inner life of God: of obedience as separation and reunion that is characteristic of the very generation of the Son from the Father, and of his unity with the Father in love, by virtue of the Holy Spirit.[90] On this account, evidently, the Son in his divinity cannot raise himself from the dead, because his human receptivity on Holy Saturday is expressive of an ever-deeper divine receptivity of the Son in his eternal obedience to the Father.

What is clear even from a brief comparison of this form of thought with that of Aquinas is that St. Thomas's Christology offers a distinctly different conception of the unity of will of the Father and the Son from that of Balthasar, and this particularly in his treatment of Holy Saturday and even in the resurrection of Christ. According to Aquinas, the Son raises himself up even as he is also raised by the Father, and this is due to the unity of will, the identity of operation, shared eternally by the Father and the Son, with the Holy Spirit as the one God. Each undertakes this unique action in a way that is distinctive to him, yet the action is single. What would happen, then, if we were to posit a distinction of commandment and obedience within the very divine life of the Father and the Son, a distinction that also distinguishes them as persons in their reciprocal relationship? How would this affect the unity of the will of the Father and Son, and therefore their ontological unity, as the one God? I have argued above that the idea of obedience in God in fact compromises the right understanding of the divine unity and simplicity, thus risking implicitly to undermine the monotheistic character of Trinitarian faith.

Yet whatever we say about the speculative question, there are

89. Like Bulgakov, Balthasar places the pre-existent condition for the historical God-forsakenness of Christ in the eternal processions of the persons. See *Theo-Drama*, 4:333: "If Jesus can be forsaken by the Father, the conditions for this 'forsaking' must lie within the Trinity, in the absolute distance/distinction between the Hypostasis who surrenders the Godhead and the Hypostasis who receives it."

90. *Theo-Drama*, 4:361–67, especially 362: "Within the Son's absolute, loving obedience (which persists in the realm of the immanent Trinity), according to which he walks into an utter forsakenness that surpasses the sinner's isolation, we find the most radical change from eternal death to eternal life, from the absolute night of the Spirit to the Spirit's absolute light, from total alienation and remoteness to an unimaginable closeness."

clearly also soteriological consequences to the Balthasarian proposals. The Athanasian soteriological tenet is that God can save us
in Christ because he unites our humanity to his divinity. However,
this presupposes that even in the incarnation he retains within himself the power and life of God.[91] Christ who is "the Resurrection and
the Life" (Jn 11:25) can only overcome the power of death actively
as God because he is fully one with the Father in will and operation,
as well as in substance and divine power. His unity with the Father,
even in death, is what saves us from death, just as his unity with the
Father in the activity of the resurrection allows him to be the source
of resurrection for other human beings. If the Son is understood by
kenosis to forfeit this active power to give eternal life—even in his
human death, and especially in his resurrection—then how can the
Son be understood as the active source of divine life by whom human beings are eternally united to God? For the Son would then be
dependent upon another (the Father) to effectuate the reconciliation
with God that is characteristic of the resurrection. He would not possess the unity of the divine life with the Father in an absolutely simple way, such as is in fact characteristic of the divine nature. It would
seem that the modern kenotic tradition renders obscure the unity of
the Son with the Father in the act of the resurrection of the humanity of Christ. It thereby risks, however unwittingly, undermining the
intelligibility of a central tenet of classical soteriology: God became
man so that he could save us by uniting us with divine life.

CONCLUSION: THE
SOTERIOLOGICAL PROMISE OF
CLASSICAL CHRISTOLOGY

Let me conclude this chapter with some irenic considerations. The
modern kenotic tradition has sought to solve modern Christological
conundrums, but it has thereby also introduced soteriological problems into modern Christology that would seem to require correction.

---

91. Aquinas follows Athanasius in arguing against Arius that this implies necessarily that there is no obedience or subordination of the Son to the Father. See SCG IV, c.
8, paras. 9–10.

A return to the classical tradition seems advisable, then, at least under certain aspects. Nevertheless, we might also say that there are positive concerns of the kenotic tradition that need to be taken into consideration, or at least rearticulated in continuity with the classical tradition. For instance, it is fitting to underscore the truth of faith that the historical Christ did possess some extraordinary knowledge of his own identity and could foresee his death prophetically. He was able to lay down his life knowingly and freely, with a freedom that was both human and divine. At the same time, however, Jesus of Nazareth was a first-century Jew of the Second Temple period. He did articulate his saving knowledge and intentions within the idioms and cultural-linguistic context of the Judaism of his time. This is consistent with his having an acquired knowledge similar to that of all the other human beings of his age. Theology can rightly aspire, then, to see in an integrated fashion the simultaneously prophetic and historically situated character of Christ's self-understanding. It was both naturally and supernaturally that the incarnate Word communicated his identity as the Son of God.

It must also be underscored that Christ as God retained the power to save effectively human beings even in and through the mystery of the cross, and that the Paschal mystery itself is applied to our lives by the power of God in order to save us. At the same time, however, one can underscore the radical solidarity of the divine freedom with our human condition of suffering. This is done not by arguing that the deity of God is free to divest itself of its own inalienable perfection, or mode of being in sovereignty, to embrace uniquely in Christ a mode of being in lowliness. Rather, it is highlighted by noting that God, because he is the immutable author of all that is, is also free to be present in all that exists in dependence upon him, even in love for and out of solidarity with suffering human beings. Consequently, God without ceasing to be God can *show forth for us* the depths of his love and mercy more powerfully by personally suffering crucifixion and by being active even in his very deity in and through his own human suffering and death. The contrary conditions not of God but of human nature are the diverse "places" in which God expresses himself: in human lowliness and in human exaltation, in suffering and in glorification, in passivity and in instrumental activity. There is no dialectical movement in God, but rather a mystery of the wisdom of God's mercy, as he employs even his own human agony and death as a means to restore us to life.

Finally, it is the case that all works of the triune God *ad extra* are works of the three distinct persons acting in their identical unity of being. Thus, the Father, Son, and Holy Spirit equally raised up the sacred humanity of Christ (body and soul) to a new, glorified life. We can also say, however, that the Paschal mystery does manifest for us, in and through the human agony, death, and resurrection of Christ, the relations of the persons and the processions of the Son and Holy Spirit from the Father. The human obedience of the Son in his passion is proper to his created nature alone, but it is also expressive of his personal intentions and willing. Therefore even Jesus's human acts of obedience do reveal to us something of his personal relation to the Father, a relation that is constitutive of his divine identity. The Son as God is given to us to save us, judge us, and raise us from the dead, insofar as he proceeds from the Father and receives all that he has from the Father. Consequently, even in his own divine action of saving us from the cross, or of glorifying his body and soul as God in the resurrection, he is personally manifest as the Son who is relative to the Father, who receives all he is from the Father. The transposition from the Paschal mystery to the consideration of the immanent life of the triune God is legitimate and necessary. It has to be done in a twofold respect. One must avoid the extreme of reducing the immanent life of the Trinity to that of a historical life among us (based upon an anthropomorphism derived from the human character of the cross event), and one must avoid severing all connection between the cross and the revelation of the inner life of the triune God, so as to fall into a kind of practical Sabellianism. Kenotic theology tends toward the first extreme, but it also serves as a warning to classical Trinitarian thought to avoid the danger of the latter.

By the very shape of the arguments offered above, I have sketched out a set of evident tensions or interesting contrasts between the thought of Aquinas and themes found in a number of modern Christological thinkers. In presenting the ideas of the latter I have indicated only very succinctly some ways that I think Aquinas's approach to the mystery of the cross is advantageous. An underlying theme is the following: whether we adopt St. Thomas's views or not has significant soteriological consequences. How we understand the presence of Christ's divinity in his Paschal mystery will in turn greatly affect how we think that Jesus Christ saves us through his passion, death, and resurrection. All this is based upon a more fundamental point: something simpler and more profound. Aquinas's theology of the cross is utterly accepting of the most fundamental teaching of the New Testament: that this man Jesus—who was crucified, died and was buried—is truly God. His thought, then, as a prototypical expression of the classical Christological tradition, can help us today to recover a sense of the divinity of Christ, even in his Paschal mystery—or especially in his Paschal mystery.

9

Did Christ Descend into Hell?

The Mystery of Holy Saturday

Is it an irony of modern theology that in the age in which Rudolph Bultmann should raise the question of the fundamentally mythological character of many New Testament ideas, Hans Urs von Balthasar should seek to reinvigorate the theological meaning of the descent of Christ into hell on Holy Saturday? Perhaps not. By offering a distinctive and in many ways innovative reading of this teaching of the Apostles' Creed, Balthasar sought to challenge an age of overly reductive scientist rationality, underscoring in Catholic theology the permanently valid interplay of literary symbolism, metaphysics, dramatic beauty, and Trinitarian mystery. In the words of Aidan Nichols, the event of the death of Christ is for Balthasar "no bloodless myth," but it is a reality that can be denoted through the richness of a rationality that aspires to be simultaneously poetic and rigorously theological.[1]

This being said, Balthasar's theology of the descent of Christ into hell is quite original by any theological standard of measure, and it has

1. Aidan Nichols, *No Bloodless Myth: A Guide through Balthasar's Dramatics* (Washington, D.C.: The Catholic University of America Press, 2000).

produced a flurry of stern critics and avid defenders.[2] I would like in this chapter, then, to compare key aspects of the teaching of Balthasar and Aquinas on the descent into hell. The goal here is not to give a comprehensive account of the teaching of either (a potentially vast project). Rather, the purpose is to note core concerns that lie behind the treatment of this mystery by Balthasar and to consider the way these same concerns are treated alternatively by Aquinas from within the parameters of a very different account of the mystery. At the same time, we should wish to consider the potential theological advantages and disadvantages, strengths, and weaknesses of the two accounts in comparison with one another. The goal of this reflection is not to definitively vanquish one form of thinking from the conversation, but to evaluate more comprehensively all that is entailed in the options taken by either thinker. As I will make clear eventually, I believe the account of Balthasar is conceptually rich and theologically provocative, but that Aquinas's account ultimately harmonizes more profoundly with the broader commitments and deeper constants of the Catholic faith.

BALTHASAR ON THE DESCENT OF CHRIST INTO HELL

A comprehensive examination of Balthasar's teaching regarding the descent of the Lord into hell on Holy Saturday lies beyond the scope of this chapter. In fact, what I would like to offer by way of introduction to the discussion is not an analysis of the intricate features of his doctrine. Rather, I will underscore three interrelated concerns that animate Balthasar's work on this point. Each of these helps to signal, even in the face of his critics, some of the valid concerns that traverse his thinking on this issue. The first of these pertains to the universal

2. Most notably Alyssa Lyra Pitstick, *Light in Darkness: Hans Urs von Balthasar and The Catholic Doctrine of Christ's Descent into Hell* (Grand Rapids, Mich.: Eerdmans, 2007). And for a response, see Edward Oakes, *Infinity Dwindled to Infancy: A Catholic and Evangelical Christology* (Grand Rapids, Mich.: Eerdmans, 2011), 382–93. Other responses to the work of Pitstick are to be found in Paul Griffiths, "Is There a Doctrine of the Descent into Hell?" and Thomas Joseph White, "On the Universal Possibility of Salvation," in *Pro Ecclesia* 17, no. 3 (2008): 257–68, 269–80.

possibility for salvation offered to all. The second pertains to the ecumenical treatment of the soteriology of the cross and Holy Saturday. The third pertains to the revelation of the Trinity in and through the kenotic life of the Son of God in the Paschal mystery. In treating each of these features of Balthasar's thought briefly, I will attempt to identify the chief concern of this theology of Holy Saturday as it touches upon more fundamental and central features of the Catholic faith. How does his understanding of this mystery seek to promote and advance our understanding of other equally or even more primordial dimensions of the mystery of Christ, salvation, and the church?

At the Heart of
Holy Saturday: The Universal
Possibility of Salvation

Balthasar's doctrine of Holy Saturday is related in many ways to his basic concern for the possibility of salvation for all human beings. This interpretive starting point should not be controversial, for the Swiss theologian emphasizes the idea himself in the final volume of his *Theo-Drama*.[3] It is commonly claimed that Balthasar's theology of the descent is deeply indebted to the mystical experiences of Adrienne von Speyr, and this claim has been employed both by Balthasar's detractors and defenders as a core component for evaluating the worth of his theology.[4] It is also true that Balthasar insisted on the inseparability of his own writing from the thought of Von Speyr, and she did indeed claim to have had vivid experiences of the abandonment of Christ by the Father.[5] However, we should still be very wary of overinflating the appeal to Von Speyr's influence for the fundamental reason (ignored by almost all Balthasar's Catholic commentators, *pro et contra*) that the doctrine of the descent into hell of Balthasar is deeply dependent especially upon the precedent thought

3. Hans Urs von Balthasar, *Theo-Drama*, 5:269–90: "The Question of Universal Salvation." This section follows after the preceding one: "The Descent of the Son" (247–68).

4. See in this regard the important study of Michele Schumacher, *A Trinitarian Anthropology: Adrienne von Speyr and Hans Urs von Balthasar in Dialogue with St. Thomas Aquinas* (Washington, D.C.: The Catholic University of America Press, 2014).

5. Hans Urs von Balthasar, *First Glance at Adrienne von Speyr*, trans. A. Lawry and S. Englund (San Francisco: Ignatius Press, 1981).

of Karl Barth on this same subject. What is more, Balthasar not only does not ignore this point, but emphasizes it quite expressly when he takes up the subject of Christ's descent into hell precisely as it relates to the universal possibility of salvation.[6]

What Balthasar notes in his own study of Barth's doctrine in the *Theo-Drama* is that the Swiss Reformed thinker provided a blueprint for rethinking traditional doctrines of election (both Catholic and Protestant), one which was to have wide influence in twentieth-century German-speaking theology.[7] How is this the case? As Balthasar was well aware, Barth sought to reinterpret the significance of John Calvin's doctrine of election in ways that were profoundly innovative, particularly with regard to the meaning and scope of the election and reprobation of Jesus Christ.[8] On the one hand, Barth believed that Calvin had made a crucial contribution to theology by his decision to place the theology of election and covenant at the heart of Christian doctrine: election is the fore-determining ground or the structural backbone of the creation. Consequently, *Church Dogmatics* II, 2 is a volume of central importance for understanding Barth's thought as a whole, and as Balthasar rightly understood, it has profound consequences upon Barth's interpretation of creation in *Church Dogmatics* III. The covenant with God in Christ is that which determines the inner dynamic meaning of created human existence.

On the other hand, however, Barth wished to radically reconceive the restrictive scope of election and predestination as understood in the classical Reformed tradition. Influenced by Pierre Maury, he reformulated the content of the doctrine: it is Jesus Christ alone who is the eternal object of election, and this in view of all those elected or predestined in him.[9] The latter however are not a minority of the human

6. *Theo-Drama*, 5:270: "Whatever one may think of Karl Barth's great 'doctrine of election,' it represents the breakthrough that brought the discussion into being." See the study of David Lauber, *Barth on the Descent into Hell: God, Atonement and Christian Life* (London: Ashgate, 2004), which considers Barth's influence on Balthasar.

7. *Theo-Drama*, 5:277.

8. See Hans Urs von Balthasar, *The Theology of Karl Barth*, 174–88. This work was of course initially published in 1951, years before the composition of the *Theo-Drama*. "Innovation" is a word Barth himself employs, with some ambivalence, regarding his own doctrine of election in CD II, 2, 156.

9. See the treatment of election particularly in CD II, 2, sections 32 and 33. In sec-

race, but rather, in Christ, God predetermines to elect all human beings. As Balthasar notes, Barth thus turns away from Calvin's doctrine
of restrictive election of a minority of the human race, in the direction of soteriological universalism. All will be saved in Christ, or so we
might rightfully hope. Simultaneously, for Barth it is Jesus Christ alone
who is reprobated for us in the cross event, such that he alone suffers
the abandonment by God that is hell. Because of this substitutionary
form of atonement, the human race is collectively spared the possibility of damnation by the grace of Christ.[10] This is a form of penal substitutionary atonement doctrine with roots in the Protestant Reformation, but clearly reformulated in a distinctive and novel form.[11]

Balthasar does not follow this form of thinking in all of its de-
tails. He is critical of the notion of a covenant with God in Christ that
would obscure or forbid the possibility of a strong concept of created nature as something distinct from the mystery of grace and from
the mystery of the incarnation. Philosophical reflection on the nature of man, the world, creation, and God is all made possible by the
metaphysical range of thinking that characterizes natural human intelligence (the so-called doctrine of the *analogia entis*).[12] He also is
wary of a doctrine of irresistible grace which would remove from the
human will any possibility of refusal of salvation and so make universal salvation a foreknown inevitability.[13] Last, he is critical of any
concept of penal substitution that would make the Son the objective
bearer of divine wrath *if* by this we mean to suggest that there occurs
an exteriority of divine love in the event of the descent into hell, such
that the Father's wrath for the Son should *not* be exercised within or
as the expression of an ever greater love that they share. Wrath in this
problematic case would be extrinsic to love.[14]

---

tion 33.2 (154–55), Barth mentions the influence of Pierre Maury's essay, "Election et
Foi," at the Congrès international de théologie calviniste in Geneva in 1936.

10. On universal election and singular reprobation, see for example, CD II, 2, 317–
18. This viewpoint is programmatic in CD IV, 1, section 59.

11. Pitstick's study, despite its many accurate depictions of Balthasar, does not examine this influence of Barth and his reinterpretation of Calvin.

12. *The Theology of Karl Barth*, 161–67, 267–325. This is not to ignore Balthasar's assertion of the necessity of *gratia sanans* for a right exercise of this native natural power.

13. *Theo-Drama*, 5:285. Though here again analogies exist with Barth on the divine
will for universal salvation, and its eschatological inexorability (see 295).

14. *Theo-Drama*, 4:284–316.

All of this being said, there are important parallels at work. The first thing to be noted is that Balthasar perceives a parallel between Barth's reaction to Calvin's doctrine of election and his own critical reflections on the Augustinian heritage of western Catholicism.[15] The later Augustine in his anti-Pelagian reflections speculated upon the idea that God predestines to eternal salvation a minority of the human race.[16] Councils of the Catholic Church such as Orange II (529), Quiersy (853), and Valence III (855) upheld the idea of God's selective predestination of the elect. God in his freely given grace takes the primary initiative in every act of salvation. At the same time, these same Councils refused the notion of a reprobation of the damned from all eternity, antecedent to any foreseen demerits.[17] In other words, the Catholic church insisted from early on that human beings may be offered graces of salvation that they refuse or resist. Consequently, if they are not saved and are subsequently reprobated, this is due to their fault and not to an eternally willed intention on the part of God, "prior" to all creation. Salvation comes from the primacy of God's activity. Eternal loss comes from the primacy of culpable defect in the creature. "[The] omnipotent God wishes all men without exception to be saved (I Tim. 2:4) although not all will be saved. However, that certain ones are saved, is the gift of the one who saves; that certain ones perish, however, is the deserved punishment of those who perish."[18]

Such a strategy of interpretation of the scriptural deposit of faith seems to differ markedly from the thinking of Calvin on the subject of reprobation, and this difference would be underscored vividly in the teachings of the Council of Trent.[19] And yet, Balthasar, without

---

15. *Theo-Drama*, 5:316–17.

16. Augustine, *Cor. et grat.*, 12–13, 16, 28.

17. Orange II, sec. III (Denz., 200); Quiersy, can. 3 (Denz., 318); Valence III, can. 2 (Denz., 321).

18. Quiersy, can. 3 (Denz., 318).

19. Council of Trent, Decree on Justification, canon 17 (Denz., 827): "If anyone shall say that the grace of justification is attained by those only who are predestined unto life, but that all others, who are called, are called indeed, but do not receive grace, as if they are by divine power predestined to evil; let him be anathema." Note three different affirmations that seem to be implied: God offers grace even to those who are not predestined. Even among those justified by grace some may culpably fall from grace. God is not the cause of moral evil and predestines no one to eternal damnation.

denying the perennial truth of conciliar thinking, is not at rest with this seemingly settled doctrine. What are the reasons he finds himself theologically ill at ease? One reason concerns the mystery of the divine will. The classical interpretation of, say, the Third Council of Valence, seems to place the final reason for the reality of hell in the power of the human will culpably to resist or ignore the initiatives of God, whether in the realm of natural or supernatural aid.[20] This vision presupposes that man's finite human freedom is a gift that participates imperfectly in the uncreated freedom of God, yet that same human freedom can be misused. Man can refuse the aid of God and turn away from him in definitive fashion. Balthasar, however, seems unsatisfied with the classical theological idea that God does accept or permit the loss of some due to their own free decision. To accept such an idea, for Balthasar, is tantamount to the concession that God might not really and truly will the salvation of all, as if God's saving will is in fact restricted.[21]

It is significant in this respect that like Calvin and Barth before him (and in distinct contrast to the Council of Trent), Balthasar rejects the distinction between the antecedent and the consequent will of God: between what God wills from all eternity (the salvation of all) and what God permits but does not will (the culpable refusal of the good and of salvation by the reprobate).[22] Aquinas, following

20. Council of Valence III, can. 2 (Denz., 321): "Nor do we believe that the wicked thus perish because they were not able to be good; but because they were unwilling to be good." This view is reiterated in the *Catechism of the Catholic Church*, para. 1033: hell is precipitated by an act of *self-exclusion* from communion with God on the part of the creature.

21. *Theo-Drama*, 5:295: "Human freedom is not self-constituted: it is appointed by God to operate in its limited area; ultimately it depends on *absolute* freedom and must necessarily transcend itself in that direction.... While infinite freedom will respect the decisions of finite freedom, it will not allow itself to be compelled, or restricted in its own freedom, by the latter." See also Balthasar's *Dare We Hope "That All Men Be Saved"?*, trans. D. Kipp and L. Krauth (San Francisco: Ignatius Press, 1988), 15: "Man is under judgment and must choose. The question is whether God, with respect to his plan of salvation, ultimately depends, and wants to depend, upon man's choice; or whether his freedom, which wills only salvation and is absolute, might not remain above things human, created, and therefore relative."

22. On the distinction between the divine will for the good alone and the divine permission of sin, see the Decree on Justification of the Council of Trent, can. 6 (Denz., 816). Both Luther (*The Bondage of the Will*, in WA 18, 614–20, 630–39) and Calvin

Damascene, had employed this distinction in order to underscore the reality of God's divine innocence in the face of human damnation.[23] The Council of Trent rearticulated the distinction in a dogmatic formula, in the face of the Lutheran and Calvinist refusal of the distinction of divine will and divine permission. For Luther and Calvin, all grace from God is irresistible and converts the predestined incontrovertibly, while the reprobate are designated from all eternity antecedent to any foreseen demerits ("double predestination"). Barth and Balthasar refuse the restrictive scope of divine predestination inherited from Augustine, Luther, and Calvin, but they retain the nondistinction of the divine permissions and of the divine will. God does not "permit" anything, but wills all outcomes effectively. Balthasar also seems, in some passages at least, to follow Barth in insisting on the intrinsically irresistible character of all grace.[24] Consequently, if God truly elects all persons in Jesus Christ, and if there is no conditional divine will for the salvation of all that *might be* refused culpably when God permits the creature to disobey, then ultimately we must expect that all will be reconciled to God infallibly, by virtue of the incontrovertible prerogatives of the divine will. Eventually God's desire

---

(ICR III, c. 23, n. 8, and c. 24) expressly refused the distinction between God's will and his permissions. God's will and his grace are always irresistible. Barth refuses the distinction in his discussion of Judas in CD II, 2, 502: "In what he himself wills and carries out, Judas does what God wills to be done.... In one sense Judas is the most important figure in the New Testament apart from Jesus. For he, and he alone of the apostles, was actively at work in this decisive situation, in the accomplishment of what was God's will and what became the content of the Gospel. Yet he is the very one who is most explicitly condemned by the Law of God. He is the very one who might cause us to stray completely from the insight that in the New Testament no one is merely rejected." The will of God working through all things is ultimately a will of universal reconciliation. Without ceding to the extreme of Barth's language, Balthasar articulates a convergent position rather forcefully in *Dare We Hope*, 183–84, 187.

23. See ST I, q. 19, a. 6, ad 1, where Aquinas invokes Damascene's idea of God's antecedent universal will for the salvation of all, as distinct from his conditional will for the salvation of those who do not refuse God's help. The distinction is found in Damascene, *De Fide Orth.* II, 29 and has its proximate origins in the work of Maximus the Confessor, where it was formulated as a response to the problems of Origenist universalism. See *Ambigua* 7, 1069A11–1102C4, and particularly 1085C9–1089D3. In this latter section of the text Maximus clearly affirms that God truly wills the salvation of all but also truly permits the eternal loss of those who refuse his grace.

24. Compare CD II, 2, 417–18 and IV, 1, 86–88 with Balthasar, *Dare We Hope*, 80 and 208–10.

for the salvation of all should be triumphant over all contingent and temporal efforts to persist in disobedient sinfulness.[25]

As an alternative to the classical view he is uneasy with, Balthasar proposes instead that our knowledge of the divine will for universal salvation is merely proleptic and must look ahead to an unresolved eschaton. In other words, it is always premature to claim that there exist souls who are lost irrevocably. The warnings of damnation given by Christ in the Gospels are given prior to his own crucifixion and descent into hell. They are salutary warnings but have to be reread in light of the descent not as prophecies or teachings of realities that exist, but as cautionary heuristic tales made in view of the passion.[26] The descent into hell of the Lord reconfigures back upon Christ himself every other definition of death, judgment, and hell.[27] He himself undergoes alienation and separation from God *for us*, so that our own separation from God is no longer our own, but has been united in some mysterious way to the grace of God in Christ. Consequently, we should remain epistemically humble regarding the future possibility of damnation for anyone. The last word must belong to God, who has spoken in a most definitive way in the alienation of Christ experienced on Holy Saturday, and in the reconciliation of the resurrection.

Ecumenical Concerns

In his writings on Holy Saturday, Balthasar wishes to underscore the universality of the possibility of salvation, and yet this idea itself is deeply interrelated to a significant ecumenical concern. He wishes to make the eschatological dimension of Christ's experience in the passion a central focus of theological reflection, one which can serve as a basis for theological discussion between Christians of Protestant, Catholic, and Orthodox backgrounds.

The idea that Christ suffered the pains of damnation on the cross for the sake of sinners is not an idea unique to Protestant thinkers, such as Luther and Calvin. It was taught by many Catholic thinkers of the late medieval period and was a theme in popular preaching in

25. *Dare We Hope*, 26, 178.
26. *Theo-Drama*, 5:269; *Dare We Hope*, 20–22, 29–46, 177, 183–84.
27. *Theo-Drama*, 5:311–12.

Catholic Europe throughout the seventeenth, eighteenth, and nineteenth centuries—for example, in the writings of Louis Chardon, OP (1595–1651), and Jacques-Benigne Bossuet (1627–1704). If this idea never became the preferred theory for church doctrine, nevertheless it was never officially banned from use in theological speculation or from public expression in the pulpit. John Calvin, therefore, is not unique (or exclusively "Protestant") in holding to a form of penal substitution theory that posits Christ's experience of hell on the cross.

Yet in the *Institutes of the Christian Religion*, Calvin did famously seek to articulate this doctrine in an original way, such as to radically reinterpret the traditional teaching that Christ descended into hell on Holy Saturday. Partially in order to dissipate any appeal to the notion of a purgation after death for the saints of the Old Testament, Calvin understood the "descent" of Christ in the Apostles' Creed as a merely symbolic expression of Jesus's subjection to the agony of damnation *during the time* of his earthly experience on the cross.[28] This dimension of the crucifixion was effectively a kind of substitution in which Christ accepted the punishment of sin (the anguish and spiritual pain of separation from God) for the sake of the elect so that these latter might receive the gift of justifying grace. Christ descended into hell on the cross to save us from experiencing hell. This suffering on the part of Christ was a glorious yet kenotic expression of his love.

In at least two important ways, Barth's subsequent reinterpretation of this theology in *Church Dogmatics* posed the basis for a reconciliation of the classical Calvinist doctrine with that of contemporary Catholic and Orthodox theology. As discussed above, Barth reinterpreted the election of the predestined in Christ not in exclusive terms (over and against the eternally reprobated) as Calvin had, but instead as a mystery of universality. In doing so he approached in his own way (but by a logically distinct position, of course) the traditional Catholic idea of the universal offer of the grace of salvation. The doctrine of a restricted offer was never an unequivocal majority position in classical Catholic theology, and in fact it was prohibited definitively in the seventeenth-century condemnations of the theses of

---

28. See ICR II, c. 16, nos. 10–12, with explicit reference to Mk 15:34. Calvin is entirely aware that his interpretation of the Apostles' Creed concerning the "descent into hell" on Good Friday is quite original.

Cornelius Jansen. Pope Innocent X, in his 1658 document *Cum occasione,* demarcated as "impious ... dishonoring to divine piety, and heretical" the proposition of the *Augustinus:* "It is semi-Pelagian to say that Christ died or shed His blood for all men without exception."[29] But if Christ died for all human beings, then he offers to each human being the possibility of embracing the grace of salvation. Nearer to Barth's own epoch, the idea would be reiterated overtly by the document *Gaudium et Spes* of the Second Vatican Council: "For, since Christ died for all men (Rom. 8:32), and since the ultimate vocation of man is in fact one, and divine, *we ought to believe that the Holy Spirit in a manner known to God offers to every man the possibility of being associated with this paschal mystery.*"[30]

Second, Barth held that to accomplish this election, Christ *alone* accepted to be reprobated in the stead of all others.[31] The "descent" of Christ into the state of godforsakenness on the cross is the divinely sanctioned condition for the universal reconciliation of all persons with God, no matter how great the chasm opened between themselves and God by human sin. Despite its distinctively Calvinist features, this second idea finds echoes with certain variants of eastern Christian theology regarding the "harrowing of hell." Ancient eastern fathers held a variety of opinions regarding the event of Holy Saturday. Some, like Irenaeus and John Chrysostom, maintained that Jesus's soul "descended to" or illumined only those who had died in a state of righteousness (the just Jews and Gentiles who lived prior to the time of the New Covenant).[32] Others, particularly Origen and Gregory of Nyssa, held that Christ also descended into the hell of the damned to preach to the unconverted, suggesting that these latter received yet another opportunity for conversion even after their death, subsequent to the separation of body and soul.[33] The latter doctrine

29. Denz., 1096. This was the fifth of the five condemned propositions of the *Augustinus.*

30. *Gaudium et Spes,* no. 22 (emphasis added).

31. As I have noted in chapter 7, Barth follows Calvin in affirming that Christ experienced reprobation and hell on the cross. See, for example, CD II, 2, 164.

32. Irenaeus, *Contra Haer.* IV, 22, 1–2; John Chrysostom, *Homil. XXXVI in Matt.*

33. Origen, *Contra Celsus* II, 43; Gregory of Nyssa, *Orat. Catech.,* 23. For a helpful treatment of the early patristic material, see Jared Wicks, "Christ's Saving Descent to the Dead: Early Witnesses from Ignatius of Antioch to Origen," *Pro Ecclesia* 17, no. 3 (2008): 281–309.

which has been cultivated by many theologians of the modern Orthodox church would seem to suggest the impossibility of a separation from God by sin so great that it cannot be overcome by the agency of God's persistent grace, whether in this life *or in the next*. It is the
victorious descent of Christ into hell that is the occasion of this over-
whelming exertion of the power of redemption, even in the souls of
those who have culpably refused the truth prior to this time.[34]

Balthasar's doctrine of the descent is no doubt influenced deeply by the experiences of Adrienne von Speyr. Yet Balthasar also clearly rearticulates themes found in Barth in his own innovative fashion.
First of all, like Calvin and Barth, Balthasar envisages the mystery
of Christ's descent into hell beginning in the passion, and especially in the crucifixion. On the cross, the Lord suffers the pains of a
separation from God even greater than that experienced by any sinner.[35] Unlike Calvin and Barth, however, Balthasar maintains at least
some aspect of the reality of Holy Saturday itself as a historical event.
Christ descends into the state of death, and after death into an *atemporal state* of separation from God, in order to unite himself to all
human beings who undergo this same experience of death and potential separation from God.[36] In fact, Balthasar is quite ambivalent
about the theological possibility of an interim state of the immaterial
soul separated from the body.[37] Rather, the whole person undergoes
in death a kind of annihilation and entry into the world of the final
judgment.[38] In the passage between the two, there is the possibility of
separation from God, insofar as the person experiences the distance
from God created by sin and death. Like Origen and Gregory of Nyssa, then, Balthasar portrays Christ as descending into the hell of the

34. See most notably, the argument of Hilarion Alfeyev, *Christ the Conqueror of
Hell: The Descent into Hades from an Orthodox Perspective* (Crestwood, N.Y.: St. Vladimir's Seminary Press, 2009).

35. *Theo-Drama*, 5:256–68, 311–12.

36. This state of atemporal separation from God begins on the Cross, but continues
in and after death: *Theo-Drama*, 5:305–12, 341, 357, 361, 364.

37. The ambivalence is clear: *Theo-Drama*, 5:356: "The man who has died in faith already lives in the risen Lord, and whether there will be an 'intermediate state' between
his death and his resurrection 'on the last day' is an open question, and not one of great
moment." See also 5:359, which seems to posit a resurrection of the faithful immediately
after death. I return to this idea at some length in the following chapter.

38. *Theo-Drama*, 5:323–51.

damned. But unlike them, he sees this descent not primarily as a victory, but as a mystery of solidarity with those most bereaved of the presence of God.[39] It is this presence that makes it possible even for those who are furthest from God to have the opportunity to choose or reject union with God by grace in a final and definitive way.[40]

Last, then, this theory is connected with the first point underscored above: Balthasar thinks that what occurs historically on Holy Saturday is exemplary of a larger pattern of the grace of Christ extended throughout the whole range of human history. All human beings, even in the time in which they come to die, *and even after the time of death in the body*, are invited into a new possibility of choice for the grace of Christ. Christ's story of salvation, then, embraces all human beings both in life and in death, and extends beyond embodied history into a new possibility of spiritual encounter with Christ after death.[41] This ecumenical theology contains a blend of elements from Calvin, Barth, Origen, and Gregory of Nyssa, but it is also extremely novel. A persistent theme that ties the whole together is that of the insistence on hope in the possibility of *apokatastasis panton*, the salvation of all.

Holy Saturday as
Kenosis and Trinitarian
Revelation

A third fundamental concern present in Balthasar's theology of the descent is based upon his understanding of Trinitarian theology. It is in the descent into hell that we perceive one of the deepest truths regarding the identity of God: that there is within the very life of God an eternal mystery of divine obedience and receptivity that is characteristic of the person of the Son.[42] I have underscored above (in chapter 6 and chapter 8) that this doctrine first comes to prominence in modern theology in the thought of Karl Barth. Without returning to

---

39. *Theo-Drama*, 5:277: "The Crucified Son does not simply suffer the hell deserved by sinners; he suffers something below and beyond this, namely, being forsaken by God in the pure obedience of love. Only he, as Son, is capable of this, and it is qualitatively deeper than any possible hell."

40. *Theo-Drama*, 5:288–89.   41. *Theo-Drama*, 5:313–15.

42. *Theo-Drama*, 4:325–26, 356.

the topics of divine obedience or divine kenosis, we can simply underscore here the relation that the descent of Christ into hell bears to
these two ideas. As has already been mentioned, for Barth, the dereliction of Christ is indicative of his unique reprobation: Christ descends into hell alone so as to be the sole human being that travels
into the far country of separation from the Father, in exclusion of and
substitution for sinful humanity.[43] This idea is wed, however, to one
that is even more radical. Barth holds to the very original doctrine of
the communication of idioms that he characterizes by the title *genus
tapeinoticum*.[44] According to this understanding, it is not the case that
the divine attributes of Christ are attributed to his human nature (as
if, for example, the humanity of Christ were now eternal or omnipresent). That idea of a *genus majestaticum* was developed by Lutherans
such as Martin Chemnitz but eschewed by the Reformed theological tradition. Barth, however, inverts the direction of the attributions
between the two essences of Christ: by virtue of the incarnation, the
human attributes of Christ can be attributed to the divine essence of
the Son. If the Son is humanly obedient in the descent into hell, this
is indicative of something pertaining to the very being and life of God
itself. That is to say, the kenosis of Good Friday has its eternal precondition in this eternal kenosis of the Son which takes place always already in the life of God. Consequently, the divine dereliction of the
Son on the cross does not change who God is from all eternity, but
it does manifest who the Son is or wills to be eternally, as God in his
mode of being-in-lowliness, as the Son always sent from the Father or
subject to the Father.[45] The distinction or "separation" of wills made
manifest in the cross event and particularly in the obedience of the
Son pertains to the ultimate revelation of who God is.

Balthasar adopts from Barth this theme of Trinitarian revelation
in the descent, but also joins it with two other ideas. First, he takes

43. CD IV, 1, 772: "The publican in the temple in Luke 18:9f. and the prodigal son of
Luke 15:11f. are a likeness of the One who as the Lamb of God took away the sin of the
world: no more, but no less. And the man who believes in this One and knows himself
in Him can and must and will unreservedly place himself at least alongside the publican
and the prodigal—we have in them the minimum—and with them be the likeness, the
analogatum, of what Jesus Christ has been and done, and is and does, for him."

44. CD IV, 2, 84–85, 108–15.

45. CD IV, 1, 215, 239, 264, 306, 308, 458, 566, 590.

from Bulgakov and Von Speyr the notion of a pure passivity in the life of the Son who is abandoned by the Father, and in some real sense separated from God the Father in the event of the descent into hell. "God the Father can give his divinity away in such a manner that it is not merely 'lent' to the Son: The Son's possession of it is 'equally substantial.' This implies such an incomprehensible and unique 'separation' of God from himself that it *includes* and grounds every other separation—be it never so dark and bitter."[46] The notions here of "separation," "self-surrender," and "passivity" mostly clearly do not pertain to the humanity of Christ alone, but to his Godhead as such. In that sense, they come to characterize the very relations of the Father and the Son from all eternity. This builds upon Barth, but it goes further by introducing overtly the notions of sundering and passivity into the very life of God in a way that Barth did not.

Second, Balthasar introduces his notion of a "Trinitarian inversion," the idea of a world in which the mystery of Holy Saturday is in some real sense ongoing. That is to say, the relations of the Son and the Holy Spirit are inverted for the sake of the economy, where the kenotic Son does not spirate the Holy Spirit but is passive and subordinate to the inspiring mission that comes from the Spirit.[47] This inversion occurs for our sake and continues in the larger mystical body of the church. It connotes something concerning the inner life of God as it is present to each historical person: the Son's mystery of obedience to the Father and to the Holy Spirit in his descent into suffering and estrangement from the divine presence is itself indicative of the shared love of the Trinitarian persons *as it comes to us*. The transcendent "precondition" for God's expression of solidarity with fallen men in the passion, therefore, is the kenotic love of the Son for the Father, as the Son undertakes this ultimate form of passivity at the instigation of the Holy Spirit.[48]

Ultimately, then, Balthasar thinks that the temporal kenosis of the Son has a foundation in the eternal self-emptying of the Trinity. He therefore posits some real form of eternal "separation" between the

46. *Theo-Drama*, 4:325. For the direct influence of Bulgakov for this kind of language, see 313–14, 323–28. For a good example of the influence of Von Speyr for this kind of language, see *Theo-Drama*, 5:256–65.

47. See *Theo-Drama*, 3:515–23.

48. *Theo-Drama*, 4:327–32.

persons in the Godhead as the precondition for the mystery of Holy Saturday. This raises acutely the question of whether (along with a thinker like Bulgakov) Balthasar has inserted Trinitarian life into history in a problematic way, projecting a temporalized portrait of God torn asunder from God onto the backdrop of eternal life in God. If this is the case, then, theologians may rightly take issue with the mythological dimensions of Balthasar's mode of self-expression. This being said, it is clear that the classical patristic tradition does perceive the Paschal mystery as an event pregnant with the revelation of the intra-Trinitarian life. The mystery of the agony of Christ must in some way be a manifestation of the interpersonal communion of the Trinitarian God. In this respect, then, Balthasar's theology seeks to ground the soteriological mystery of the crucifixion and descent of Christ's soul into hell in the highest of the hierarchy of truths. The sentiment is estimable and might itself be considered without reproach, even if one has reservations regarding how well the motif is employed.

THOMAS AQUINAS ON THE DESCENT OF CHRIST INTO HELL

We can compare Aquinas to Balthasar by considering in this section parallel themes to those discussed above as they appear in the work of St. Thomas. First, how does Aquinas conceive of the universal possibility of salvation? Second, what is his treatment of the descent of Christ into hell in the *Summa theologiae*? Last, how is the mystery of the Holy Trinity revealed on Holy Saturday according to St. Thomas? Examination of Aquinas's alternative set of proposals will provide grounds for a treatment of the advantages of his theological vision in comparison with Balthasar's in the final section of the chapter.

The Possibility of Salvation Offered to All

There can be little question that Aquinas affirms that the possibility of salvation is offered to all human beings who attain to the age of reason. (I will return to the question of Limbo below.) His most explicit affirmation of this idea is found in his biblical commentary on 1

Timothy 2:4, where he speaks unambiguously of the antecedent will of God that all men be saved and of the permission of God that some human persons reject this offer by their own fault.[49] A similar doctrine is found in *Summa theologiae* III, q. 8, a. 3 ("Whether Christ is the head of all men?"), on the subject of the headship of Christ in the order of grace. God wills that all human beings participate in the grace of Christ. Aquinas there distinguishes between the potential membership in Christ that is open to all persons as distinct from the membership of the predestined.[50] The implication is that all are offered the possibility of salvation even if God wills from all eternity to permit that some might be lost due to their own culpable refusal of grace.[51] This teaching coheres with St. Thomas's explicit avowal that Christ died for all human beings and that the merits of the passion are sufficient to procure effectively the salvation of everyone.[52]

At the same time we might ask how it is that this salvation is effectively realized in the lives of human persons before the time of the Old Testament, or subsequent to the revelation of the Old and New Law, but outside of the scope of the knowledge of these covenants? Here Aquinas invokes several interrelated principles. First, all salvation comes about only by way of grace, and particularly through the

---

49. *In I Tim.* II, lec. 1. See also *In Heb.* XII, lec. 3 and SCG III, c. 159 for unambiguous affirmations that God offers the grace of salvation to all human persons.

50. Domingo Bañez offers this reading of the article in question in his *Scholastica Commentaria in Primam Partem Summae Theologiae S. Thomae Aquinatis* (Madrid: F.E.D.A., 1934), in commenting on ST I, q. 23, a. 3, ad 3 (495). His understanding of Aquinas on this point is indicative of the subsequent teaching of the "Thomist school."

51. One finds this doctrine also in ST I, q. 23, corp. and ad 3. Commenting on this passage, Bañez emphasizes rightly that for St. Thomas those who are lost to eternal life are reprobated only in light of their own culpable sin and that they *could have and should have* done otherwise. See *Scholastica Commentaria in Primam Partem*, 491: "Indeed, as St. Thomas indicates in the third solution to this article, reprobation does not remove anything from the power of willing in the reprobate, nor diminish his freedom, just as we have said that the permission, by which God permits someone to sin, removes nothing from the power and freedom [of that person]. Therefore, he freely sins, he who could have not sinned, had he wished."

52. ST III, q. 48, a. 2. See also q. 46, a. 6, ad 4. As a seventeenth-century representative of the Thomist school, Jean-Baptiste Gonet offers a thorough defense of Aquinas's teaching against the charge of restrictive atonement (as found in Jansenism) by appealing to a range of such texts. See his *Clypeus Theologiae Thomisticae* (Paris: Vivès, 1875), "Depulso Jansenismi," art. X, sect. CXL–CXLIV, 1:583–84.

grace of the theological virtues: faith, hope, and love.[53] Therefore, if all human persons are offered some form of membership in Christ, they are offered this only by way of participation in the grace of God, and in and through the mystery of supernatural faith. Such faith is in some real sense specifically identical in every human person, from the dawn of time until the end of the ages.[54] In this respect, Aquinas commonly refers to Hebrews 11:6: "Without faith it is impossible to please God. For he who approaches God must believe that he exists and that he rewards those who seek him."

Second, however, this specifically identical supernatural faith can know a gradation of degrees of perfection or explicit elicitation in various ages. Aquinas does not hesitate to speak of ages of faith: according to the time of the natural law, the Old Law, and the New Law.[55] In each age, there are distinct degrees of explicit as opposed to implicit supernatural faith. For instance, St. Thomas fathoms that even prior to the age of biblical revelation there is the possibility of some kind of imperfect knowledge of God and of divine providence. Such knowledge is natural and not meritorious for salvation, but supernatural faith can make use of such knowledge, assimilating it into a higher, grace-inspired form of explicit supernatural belief in God.[56] Religious humanity seeking the knowledge of God in the night of human history is often subject to superstition and idolatry, but is also susceptible to hidden influences of grace. Human beings may receive these graces in their religious and moral consciences so as to be elevated into a hidden but real relationship with God. In reading the eleventh chapter of Hebrews, which speaks of "holy gentiles" from the past who had faith, Aquinas notes that such faith is implicitly Christian. Why? Because those who believe explicitly in God and his providence (by supernatural faith) adhere implicitly to Christ insofar as they believe in a providence that rewards those who seek to know God and to obey him.[57] Analogous if more explicit ideas are ascribed to the Old

53. ST II-II, q. 2, a. 7.   54. ST II-II, q. 1, a. 7.
55. ST II-II, q. 2, a. 7, corp. and ad 3; a. 8; ST I-II, q. 98, aa. 5–6; q. 103, a. 1.
56. ST II-II, q. 2, a. 5.
57. *In Heb.* XI, lec. 2. See the discussions of the faith of holy pagans such as Abel and Noah, who are archetypes of salvation by faith found outside of the visible covenants of the Old Testament and New Testament.

Law, where the God of Israel can be known and loved by grace in explicit fashion, and wherein the mystery of Christ, the unique savior, is indicated obliquely in a symbolic and hidden way.[58]

It is noteworthy that Aquinas goes so far in this line of thinking regarding implicit faith as to affirm that every human being is offered supernatural faith when he or she reaches the age of reason, on the occasion of the awakening of the moral conscience to authentic responsibility. In the first activities of the moral reflection of every spiritual person, there is an implicit invitation to order his or her life toward integral moral rectitude and this offer is accompanied by the grace of sanctification in faith, hope, and love, a grace analogous to that procured by the sacrament of baptism.

> It is impossible for venial sin to be in anyone with original sin alone, and without mortal sin. The reason for this is because before a man comes to the age of discretion, the lack of years hinders the use of reason and excuses him from mortal sin, wherefore, much more does it excuse him from venial sin, if he does anything which is such generically. But when he begins to have the use of reason, he is not entirely excused from the guilt of venial or mortal sin. Now the first thing that occurs to a man to think about then, is to deliberate about himself. And if he then direct himself to the due end, he will, by means of grace, receive the remission of original sin: whereas if he does not then direct himself to the due end, and as far as he is capable of discretion at that particular age, he will sin mortally, for through not doing that which is in his power to do. Accordingly thenceforward there cannot be venial sin in him without mortal, until afterwards all sin shall have been remitted to him through grace.[59]

What this form of thinking presumes is that the moral order of human rational decision making can become the forum wherein God freely offers grace, amidst the decisions human beings make in view of various significant moral goods. The choice of the true final moral good, God, is that which must ultimately determine the concrete moral decisions of the human agent. However, it is reasonable to read Aquinas as suggesting that intermediate moral goods that are chosen

---

58. ST I-II, q. 101, a. 2.

59. ST I-II, q. 89, a. 6. See the helpful commentary on this passage by Bañez, *Scholastica Commentaria in Primam Partem*, 492, who argues from it to the universal possibility of salvation by grace.

in honest fashion—under grace—can be formal means that orient the soul implicitly toward God.

Likewise, the choice directly to act against intermediate moral goods implicitly turns the soul away from the grace of a relation to God as the sovereign good.[60] On this reading of Aquinas, there is no "fundamental option" theory of determination for the absolute good of God that could somehow fail to take note of lesser but real goods such as the respect of innocent human life or the respect of the human institution of marriage. (There is no reading of Aquinas upon which one could love God above all things yet sin gravely in the moral realm.) But it is the case, by contrast, that the respect of these lesser goods *could* be the "places" in which an implicit cooperation with grace transpires in each human being. In this way, human beings may be subject to the grace of God and implicitly oriented toward God when they make basic discernments and choices about objective moral goods. Salvation comes by way of grace, not the natural law. And yet within the encounter with decisions of good and evil that are grounded in the natural law, there is the possibility of the presence of grace at work in each human life.

Consequently, Aquinas has a doctrine of the universal offer of salvation by grace to each human being. As distinct from Origen, however, and in keeping with the normative doctrinal discernments of the eastern and western church of antiquity, this offer of salvation occurs in time. That is to say, the possibility of salvation occurs for human beings not after nor before the time of corporeal, embodied existence, but only during the time of one's corporeal life in the body. Aquinas offers philosophical reasons for this that touch directly upon the structure of spiritual creatures and which affect also his doctrine of the innocence of God.

Structurally, Aquinas thinks that angels and human beings are quite different when it comes to moral decisions. Unlike human beings, the angel does not abstract knowledge from sensible forms through the medium of phantasms. Consequently it has infused natural knowledge from the first instant of its creation, and this knowl-

---

60. Consider in this respect the argument of Thomas de Vio Cajetan regarding ST I-II, q. 109, a. 4, Leon. VII, 297–98.

edge is given in plenitude.[61] The angel is "born in light," produced thus *ex nihilo*. The consequence of this is not that the angel exists outside of all becoming: angels are imperfect at their inception in their stance *vis-à-vis* God's grace, and must make significant moral choices. There is the possibility of movement from potency to act within their immanent spiritual life, and so they have something *analogous* to temporal duration within their spiritual actions: the angelic *aevum*.[62]

But in differentiation from human beings, this "duration" of angelic decision is utterly succinct precisely because of the luminous clarity of the angelic intellect. Because of the perfection of its intellect, an angel can and *must* deploy all of its spiritual decision-making capacity in one simple act because the angel "sees at once" intellectually the whole content and consequence of its spiritual action.[63] Grace is not entirely intellectually transparent to the angel and so it can sin against the grace of faith, preferring natural intelligence to the realm of the supernatural. However, in making a decision in response to the order of grace, the angel chooses at once for or against God in a way that is holistic as to its own nature, with a complete perception of all consequences of the act for its own nature in relation to God.[64]

Thus angelic evil is literally of another species than human evil and has depth and intensity that are unimaginable for our human psychology. Likewise the angel is capable of an extraordinary merit in cooperating with grace by way of one single act of faith. There is an intensity, simplicity, and depth in angelic subjectivity that human beings are not capable of reproducing in the same specific form.[65] The conclusion to be drawn from all this is that the angelic "history" of decision for or against God occurs in a singular event and has immediate, irrevocable consequences. To exist as an angelic creature is to make a decision once and for all. In creating such creatures, then, God makes beings that simply do choose for or against God in a radical and irreversible way from the beginning.

61. ST I, q. 55, aa. 2–3; q. 56, aa. 2–3; q. 58, aa. 1–5. For a comprehensive study of Aquinas's angelology, see Serge-Thomas Bonino, *Les Anges et Les Démons: Quatorze leçons de théologie catholique* (Paris: Parole et Silence, 2007).

62. ST I, q. 62, aa. 1, 3–4; ST I, q. 10, aa. 5–6.

63. ST I, q. 62, a. 5; q. 63, aa. 1, 5–6; *De Malo*, q. 16, a. 3.

64. ST I, q. 64, a. 2.

65. ST I, q. 64, a. 3.

The comparison to human beings, for Aquinas, is analogical. Human beings do not and structurally cannot fulfill all of their spiritual potency in one act. Instead, as spiritual *animals* that are corporeal and sensate, they learn and choose progressively, developing habits that can be exerted and strengthened for the duration of their human lives.[66] And these habits are to some extent subject to revision and reformation, or conversion. This means that human beings can and must decide what they are ultimately to live for and how they are to live over the course of their whole lives, and they can in principle choose for or defect from the supernatural good even up to the last moment of their earthly existence.[67] However, like the angel in its supreme, vertical act of decision, the human being must choose in relation to the supernatural prior to death. The reason is structural or metaphysical: the human soul learns and reasons in dependence upon sensible phantasms received from the bodily senses and is made for this manner of learning.[68] Once the spiritual soul is separated from the body, it does not cease to exist, but it is incapable of further free self-determination.[69] Were it not for new graces proper to the soul in its separated state, the human soul would remain "frozen" or fixed irremediably in the choices it has made for or against the grace of God in the course of its human existence.[70]

The consequence of this is that human salvation is offered to the human person only in the historical time of the soul's embodiment. Were this not the case, the new choices made by the person after death would occur not in keeping with the natural structure of the human subject under grace, but outside the ordinary moral order of free human self-determination by rational deliberation. For each human being in this world, then, the time of salvation is now: it occurs in the time of history, and not in an ahistorical time concocted artificially by Origen and his neo-Platonic spiritual heirs.[71] In insisting upon this point, the ancient church was incarnational, biblical, and metaphysically realist. Aquinas's philosophy of the human person is consistent with this Catholic realism.

66. ST I, q. 75, a. 7; q. 76, a. 1; q. 77, aa. 2–3; q. 83, a. 2.
67. ST I-II, q. 114, a. 9.   68. ST I, q. 84, aa. 6–7.
69. ST I, q. 84, a. 8; q. 89, a. 1.   70. ST I, q. 84, aa. 1–4.
71. See Aquinas's extensive argument against the notion of a pre-existent human soul, developed in particular in response to the theories of Origen (SCG II, cc. 83–84).

The idea touches also upon the divine innocence of God. For if the natural history of angels and men is in fact intrinsically, metaphysically open-ended, then the ultimate reason they are determined for or against God has nothing to do with their own natures and falls back only onto the inscrutable decisions of God. This is the case in the vision of Duns Scotus, who believes that the possibility of eternal damnation arises for angels and men ultimately not from the decisions of creatures (because their uses of freedom remain always intrinsically revisable), but from the voluntary decision of God who at some point in the process determines to cease offering the possibility of salvation.[72] The magisterium of the Catholic church, however, has followed Aquinas in underscoring the natural structure of angelic and human free choices, which occur within a dynamic but determinate *aevum*, or historical time.[73] God did not have to create finite, free spiritual creatures, but once he does, these have from the very nature of their creaturely character a potency in being, and a potency of the will in particular. This means necessarily that they can choose contingently for or against the immutable good and may prefer the mutable good. In other words, free spiritual creatures are naturally capable of choosing moral evil, and this is the inbuilt ontological consequence of their creation as such.[74] Furthermore, such creatures are necessarily capable of doing good or evil freely within the aforementioned circumscribed bounds. In the case of human beings, they are capable of choosing freely for good or for evil, for the supernatural or against it, within the scope and reality of their temporal historical existence.

Aquinas underscores also, of course, that there is a mystery of predestination in which the free spiritual creature is saved only by way of the initiatives of God's grace, that not only invite but also move the creature effectively to salvation.[75] "What do you have that you have

72. See the analysis of Scotus's angelology on this point by A. Vacant, "Angé. D'Après Les Scholastiques," *Dictionnaire de Théologie Catholique*, Tome I, pt. 2 (Paris: Letouzey et Ané, 1903), col. 1228–39, esp. 1236 and 1239. Key passages in Scotus include *II Sent.*, d. 6, q. 2; d. 7, q. unica.

73. *Catechism of the Catholic Church*, para. 393 (regarding the definitive character of angelic sin) and 1021–22 (regarding the definitive character of human self-determination at death and immediate divine judgment after death).

74. ST I, q. 63, a. 1.

75. ST I, q. 23, aa. 1–2 and 4.

not received?" (1 Cor 4:6); "Without me you can do nothing" (Jn 15:5). The human being cannot elevate itself into the state of grace, nor positively incline itself naturally to the mystery of the supernatural, absent a new initiative from God that is transcendent to created human nature as such.[76] However, according to Aquinas, the possibility of eternal loss does not work in precise parallel to the mystery of predestination. The predestined are elected to eternal life antecedent to all foreseen merits, and their meritorious cooperation with grace is itself a sheer gift of grace.[77] By contrast, the reprobate are not rejected by God, nor are they punished for sins antecedent to their foreseen demerits.[78] Rather, God punishes human beings only because they have culpably rejected the first gifts, powers, and instigations of grace and of nature that are themselves truly sufficient for the accomplishment of the good.[79] God knows from all eternity that he will *permit* certain angels and human beings to resist and reject the gifts of grace and supernatural life.[80] But this permissive will is in no way causal: the permission to allow some creatures to resist culpably or refuse the grace of God is in no way the cause of the intrinsic defect of the sin itself. This defect does not come from God, but originates from the creature.

Reprobation differs in its causality from predestination. This latter is the cause both of what is expected in the future life by the predestined—namely, glory—and of what is received in this life—namely, grace. Reprobation, however, is not the cause of what is in the present—namely, sin; but it is the cause of abandonment by God. It is the cause, however, of what is assigned in the future—namely, eternal punishment. But guilt proceeds from the free-will of the person who is reprobated and deserted by grace. In this way, the word of the prophet is true—namely, "Destruction is thy own, O Israel" (Hos. 13:9).[81]

From the multiple points that have been underscored above in succinct fashion, we can return to our first idea regarding the divine

76. ST I, q. 62, a. 2; ST I-II, q. 62, a. 3. 77. ST I, q. 23, a. 5.
78. ST I, q. 23, a. 3, corp. 79. ST I, q. 19, a. 6, ad 1; q. 23, a. 3, ad 2.
80. ST I, q. 19. a. 9, ad 3.
81. ST I, q. 23, a. 3, ad 2. See the helpful commentary by Bañez, *Scholastica Commentaria in Primam Partem*, 501–2, who reads this article in tandem with ST I-II, q. 112, a. 3. There Aquinas insists in the corpus on the initiatives of God with regard to any creature's salvation in grace but also stresses (in ad 2) the culpability of the creature who freely refuses the offer of grace.

economy and the possibility of implicit faith, drawing a significant conclusion. According to Aquinas, the life of supernatural grace is offered in some way to all human beings. It is offered, however, within the historical scope of their life in this world and not before or afterward. It can also be refused or rejected culpably, and this without the least prejudice to the infinite perfection, goodness, and justice of God. But we have also underscored that this grace of salvation could have been and was offered under the regime of the natural law and the Old Law, prior to the time of Christ. What is the conclusion that these reflections tend toward? Aquinas, like virtually all the fathers and scholastics before him, holds that all who came before Christ were offered salvation by grace in a hidden but real way, by way of a supernatural faith that was implicitly Christocentric. There where humanity, moved inwardly by the Holy Spirit, cooperated with this grace, it entered into the supernatural life that would be brought to perfect fruition eventually in the mystery of Christ by his incarnation, death, and resurrection.

But there where human beings—in the hidden decisions and manifest actions of their hearts—culpably rejected this grace, they implicitly but truly incurred the punishment of separation from God and eternal damnation.[82] When this occurred prior to the time of Christ, it occurred by a clear, culpable decision of the human subject. This need not have entailed a cognitively explicit rejection of the mystery of Christ itself (as presented by revelation). It could occur through a grave violation of the natural law or by a refusal of the graces of prayer or penance, wherein faith and hope in divine providence were implicitly rejected, and so the mystery of Christ was implicitly refused. The scriptures are equally clear: it is possible for non-Christians to be saved, but it also possible for them to be damned. The time of salvation occurs in this life, and so it also transpired in

82. See the interpretation of Aquinas by Bañez, *Scholastica Commentaria in Primam Partem*, 492–97 where he argues at length from Thomistic principles that God offers hidden *auxilia* of supernatural grace to all human persons (492): "It can devoutly be believed that for all human beings coming to the age of reason, God will act in some way by the instigation of a supernatural aid, so that they might do the good. And correspondingly ... [if] God enlightens from a supernatural object all who come to the use of reason ... they sin against the precept of supernatural faith, hope and love, who do not convert to God as their supernatural end."

the time prior to the coming of Christ, even if it needed to be wholly recapitulated and illumined anew in light of the incarnation and the Paschal mystery.

The Descent of Christ into Hell

Aquinas's only mature and sustained treatment of the descent of Christ into hell is found in the *Summa theologiae* III, q. 52. There he considers the mystery in eight distinct articles. In the first of these ("Was it fitting for Christ to descend into hell?") he explains why the teaching is a doctrine of the Catholic faith: the idea is both affirmed by the Apostles' Creed and referenced in various passages of the New Testament.[83] In what, then, does the descent into hell on Holy Saturday consist?

We should begin by considering Aquinas's metaphysical views on the nature of human death. As is well known, Aquinas rejects the idea that the body and the soul are distinct substances. Rather, the spiritual soul is the form of the living, material body, and they are together one composite substance.[84] (I will return to this subject in the following chapter.) However, the soul is also immaterial and incorruptible and is not destroyed by death, even though the body undergoes corruption through death.[85] Therefore, death for each human being consists in the separation of the corruptible body and incorruptible, spiritual soul. Christ truly died. Therefore, between the time of the death of Christ and his physical resurrection, Christ's human, immaterial soul was separated from his body.

Why, however, should Christ have suffered the separation of body and spiritual soul? Basically, the reason is that Christ took upon himself freely the experience of death that is a consequence of original sin, and this includes the experience of the sundering of body and soul.[86] Furthermore, all those who lived prior to the age of the

83. ST III, q. 52, a. 1. Aquinas cites in particular Eph 4:9 and Col 2:15.
84. ST I, q. 76, a. 1.
85. ST I, q. 75, aa. 2 and 6.
86. ST III, q. 52, a. 1, corp. and ad 1: "It was fitting for Christ to descend into hell. First of all, because He came to bear our penalty in order to free us from penalty.... But through sin man had incurred not only the death of the body, but also descent into hell. Consequently since it was fitting for Christ to die in order to deliver us from death, so it

redemption, according to Aquinas, *even if they died in a state of grace*, stood in need of the final accomplishment of that redemption. In other words, Christ on Holy Saturday brought about the fulfillment of redemption for all those who had died in a state of grace prior to his coming.[87] He did so through the embrace in solidarity of a state similar to their own.[88]

It is the ontological reality of human death as the separation of body and soul then, that serves as the basis for the historical setting of the descent of Christ into hell. It is not an event that occurs in some ahistorical, timeless sphere, but is something Christ undergoes in his spiritual soul, *during the time* that he is dead (between death and resurrection). As such, then, the harrowing of hell itself transpires by means of the immaterial soul of Christ and not his body. It is not a sensible or physical event and does not pertain to the human body buried in the tomb. Aquinas is sensitive to the "mythology" objection: he underscores that there is no physical displacement of the soul nor any spatio-temporal forum as such for the occurrences of Holy Saturday.[89]

It is for this reason that Aquinas states (in ST III, q. 52, a. 1, ad 3) that the descent takes place not by a physical change of place, but by the soul of Christ enlightening the souls of all who died prior to the time of his death. This occurs in a fashion analogous to the way that the angelic spirits can illumine souls separated from the body.[90] Human souls separated from the body are not substances of a free-standing kind. The human soul is the subsistent form and actuating principle of a living body. Consequently, without the body, the human soul is radically incomplete. Yet it does subsist, and there re-

---

was fitting for Him to descend into hell in order to deliver us also from going down into hell. . . . The name of hell stands for an evil of penalty, and not for an evil of guilt. Hence it was becoming that Christ should descend into hell, not as liable to punishment Himself, but to deliver them who were." Aquinas is not saying that Christ substituted himself for us as the object of God's divine wrath against sinners (penal substitution theory). Rather, he is saying that Christ, while innocent, took upon himself the consequences of our sin (suffering, death, and separation of body and soul) to manifest therein his obedience to the Father and his love for human beings.

87. ST III, q. 52, a. 1, ad 2.
88. ST III, q. 52, a. 4.
89. ST III, q. 52, a. 1, ad 3; a. 4, ad 1 and ad 3.
90. ST I, q. 53, a. 1; ST I, q. 56, a. 2; q. 89, aa. 1–2, ad 2; q. 111, a. 1.

main within the soul the innate powers of human intellect and free will, even if the normal, ordinary exercise of these powers is hindered by the lack of corporeal life and human sensations.[91] The soul in this subsistent, separated state is still a spiritual principle potentially subject to divine illumination. Insofar as it is separated from the body, it is *more readily* subject to intellectual influences from superior spiritual forms than it would be in the corporeal state.[92] By a new life of grace and a new natural gift of God, human souls may in the separated state receive illuminating communications of truth from the community of angelic spirits. Analogously, during the time of his death (on Holy Saturday), Christ communicated divine truth to all separated souls, but particularly to the souls of all those who had died in a state of grace or friendship with God.[93]

This presence on the part of Christ to human souls, however, is unique and very different from that pertaining to angelic communications. This is the case firstly because Christ's soul itself is subject to a state similar to that of other human souls that have undergone separation from the body. Christ illumines all human beings not at a distance from their state of being, but through a kind of metaphysical solidarity with the souls of those who have died.[94]

Second, unlike the angels, Christ can communicate the life of grace, even in and through his human nature and through the enlightening activity of his human soul. Thus, in being present in some way to all those who have died, the soul of Christ renders *God* present to those souls in a new and unique way. He does this, Aquinas says, in a twofold way: by a presence of "effects" and a presence of "essence." The descent implies a presence of "effects" through the communication to human souls of new and higher graces and through the communication of new truths. The descent implies a presence of "essence" because in Christ, God himself is manifest in a new way to all the dead:

A thing is said to be in a place in two ways. First of all, through its effect, and in this way Christ descended into each of the hells, but in different manner. For going down into the hell of the lost He wrought this effect, that by

---

91. ST I, q. 89, aa. 1, 5–6.   92. ST I, q. 89, a. 2, ad 1.
93. ST III, q. 52, a. 2, ad 1; a. 4, ad 1.   94. ST III, q. 52, a. 5.

descending thither He put them to shame for their unbelief and wickedness: but to them who were detained in Purgatory He gave hope of attaining to glory: while upon the holy Fathers detained in hell solely on account of original sin, He shed the light of glory everlasting. In another way a thing is said to be in a place through its essence: and in this way Christ's soul descended only into that part of hell wherein the just were detained. So that He visited them "in place," according to His soul, whom He visited "interiorly by grace," according to His Godhead. Accordingly, while remaining in one part of hell, He wrought this effect in a measure in every part of hell, just as while suffering in one part of the earth He delivered the whole world by His Passion.[95]

This is the case because the person of the Son of God himself is the subject whose human soul descends, even while the soul is separated from the body, a soul which subsists in his person.[96] In this way, the person of the Word is in some real sense present in hell, and illumines in various ways the entire community of human souls who have died previous to the time of the crucifixion of Jesus.

How might we understand further, then, the idea that Christ enlightened all souls in hell, yet in different ways? Here we must return to our previous discussion regarding the universal possibility of salvation in the historical time preceding Christ and introduce necessary ontological distinctions.[97] Let us begin from the dual premises that God did indeed offer salvation to each human person prior to the time of Christ, and that a process of effective cooperation with—or truly culpable rejection of—grace took place within each human's historical existence. Let us add to these presuppositions a third: all grace offered to human beings prior to the time of Christ is given by God the Father in the Logos of God and by the Holy Spirit.[98] It is offered in view of the merits of Christ, in such a way that the subsequent encounter with Christ's soul in hell acts as a kind of confirmation of a process that has

95. ST III, q. 52, a. 2.

96. ST III, q. 52, a. 3: "Now in the death of Christ, although the soul was separated from the body, yet neither was separated from the Person of the Son of God.... Consequently, it must be affirmed that during the three days of Christ's death the whole Christ was in the tomb, because the whole Person was there through the body united with Him, and likewise He was entirely in hell, because the whole Person of Christ was there by reason of the soul united with Him."

97. In what follows I will not treat the question of Limbo as such, though I will return to that topic shortly below.

98. ST II-II, q. 2, a. 8.

already been initiated in the spiritual life of each person, and which has either been accepted or rejected prior to the time of death.[99]

Given these premises, there are three distinct results to consider with regard to those who died prior to the time of Christ. One regards persons who rejected or resisted the grace of the Logos in a truly culpable fashion, persevering in their disobedience or indifference, and who did, as a consequence, damn themselves to the state of eternal loss. Aquinas states that the soul of Christ did not descend into the state of the hell of the damned.[100] This is a state of willful ignorance of God and of culpable malice toward significant moral truths regarding God and neighbor. It is also a state of perpetual and definitive loss of the grace and charity of God.[101] Consequently, it is not a state Christ can personally undergo, but it is one he can illumine in some limited way. To the damned, Christ's presence makes clearer the reality of their willful rejection of the truth and goodness of the mystery of God, and of the rightly ordered love of one's neighbor. This presence does not change their desires or choices and might even aggravate them. But Christ's descent to the damned acts not so much as a punishment as it does a message of the victory of God and of his love, and as a confirmation of the truth regarding God and his love, over and against the "city of man" that revolves in disordered fashion around human egoism and pride.[102]

A second category pertains to the souls of those who have died in friendship with God, in a state of grace, but who are still undergoing purgation for sins. Aquinas thinks, in other words, that on Holy Saturday Christ also descended to the souls in purgatory. Again this does not mean that Christ himself suffered the "hell" of purgatory, since he is incapable of this due to his perfection in the order of grace. But he can act by way of grace to comfort these souls with the expectation of heaven.[103]

Last of all are those who rest in the "bosom of Abraham" (Lk 16:22–23). These souls who died in friendship with God are at the time of Christ free from the effects of all previous personal sin.[104]

---

99. ST III, q. 46, a. 6, ad 4; q. 49, a. 3; q. 52, a. 2, ad 3 and a. 5.
100. ST III, q. 52, aa. 2 and 6.   101. *Comp. Theol.* I, c. 174.
102. ST III, q. 52, a. 2, corp.; a. 6, ad 1.   103. ST III, q. 52, a. 8.
104. ST III, q. 52, a. 2, ad 4; a. 5, corp.

However, they still labor under the common effects of original sin that deprived the whole human race of beatitude. Consequently, in the time of Christ they are still awaiting the completion of redemption that only takes place in and through the Paschal mystery. In a sense, then, one can say that Christ comes to be present in hell in the very same "place" or state as these souls.[105] Like theirs, his soul is without sin and is separated from the body, awaiting the event of the resurrection. Yet he also assumes the state of these souls not as one awaiting the beatific vision, but as one bringing that grace to these souls. He communicates to them the fullness of grace that is an effect of the victory of the cross.[106] In this mystery of Holy Saturday, Christ illumines all of these just souls who have preceded him with the grace of the beatific vision. "When Christ descended into hell He delivered the saints who were there, not by leading them out at once from the confines of hell, but by enlightening them with the light of glory in hell itself."[107]

As a way of concluding these reflections, we might consider a slightly more precise or technical question. How does Aquinas read 1 Peter 3:18–20 and 4:6, both passages which refer to Christ preaching to the souls in hell? Let us consider the passages in question:

> For Christ also died for sins once for all, the righteous for the unrighteous, that he might bring us to God, being put to death in the flesh but made alive in the spirit; in which he went and preached to the spirits in prison, who formerly did not obey, when God's patience waited in the days of Noah, during the building of the ark, in which a few, that is, eight persons, were saved through water.

> For this is why the gospel was preached even to the dead, that though judged in the flesh like men, they might live in the spirit like God.

In these passages it could seem to be asserted that Christ descended into the hell of the damned in order to preach to the souls of the previously unconverted. This is a reading found in eastern fathers such as Gregory of Nyssa, and it is one expressly reasserted by some contemporary eastern Orthodox theologians.[108] What is more, the idea can

---

105. ST III, q. 52, a. 5, ad 3.   106. ST III, q. 52, a. 1.

107. ST III, q. 52, a. 4, ad 1.

108. See in particular the work of Alfeyev, *Christ the Conqueror of Hell*, who attempts to develop this perspective systematically.

be employed with an eschatological orientation in order to claim that
the state designated as hell or damnation is not permanent or eternal,
but temporary, such that we might affirm the existence of hell even
now, and yet hold out hope for a universal restoration (*apokatastasis
panton*) that will occur in the end of time.[109]

This idea is impermissible in the Catholic tradition which has regularly reaffirmed the scriptural teaching of divine origin that the state
of damnation in hell exists as a consequence of human sin, and that
it is a permanent state.[110] The pain of loss that characterizes the state
of damnation is unique as a specific form of suffering in part due to
the fact that the loss is permanent. Eternal damnation then remains
a real possibility for human beings, including those who existed pri-
or to the time of Christ. If this is the case, then, how ought we to read
the statements of 1 Peter?

Aquinas follows Augustine's interpretation of 1 Peter as proposed
in his famous letter to Evodius.[111] In fact, Augustine interprets the
passage in such a way that it has something in common with what
Calvin, Barth, and Balthasar wish to convey in speaking of a descent
into hell. That is to say, they do not wish to speak of Christ experiencing a state of malice or lovelessness, nor of an experience of eternal
loss of the vision of God as such. They do wish to underscore, however, a kind of solidarity established in Christ between God and all
human beings in the night of this world, including those who experience the deepest sense of spiritual suffering, alienation from God, or
ignorance of divine things. On this precise point, it is interesting to
read Aquinas's Augustinian interpretation of the passage from 1 Peter,
which does offer some limited similarity to the thinking of Balthasar:

109. This seems to be the direction taken by David Bentley Hart in "Providence and
Causality: On Divine Innocence," *Providence of God: Deus habet consilium*, eds. F. Murphy and P. Ziegler (London: Continuum, 2009), 37–56.

110. *Catechism of the Catholic Church*, para. 1035: "The teaching of the Church affirms the existence of hell and its eternity. Immediately after death the souls of those
who die in a state of mortal sin descend into hell, where they suffer the punishments of
hell, 'eternal fire.' The chief punishment of hell is eternal separation from God, in whom
alone man can possess the life and happiness for which he was created and for which
he longs."

111. ST III, q. 52, a. 2, ad 3, citing Augustine, *Ep.* 164, to Evodius.

Augustine, however, furnishes a better exposition of the text in his Epistle to Evodius quoted above, namely, that the preaching is not to be referred to Christ's descent into hell, but to the operation of His Godhead, to which He gave effect from the beginning of the world. Consequently, the sense is, that "to those (spirits) that were in prison"—that is, living in the mortal body, which is, as it were, the soul's prison-house—"by the spirit" of His Godhead "He came and preached" by internal inspirations, and from without by the admonitions spoken by the righteous: to those, I say, He preached "which had been some time incredulous," i.e., not believing in the preaching of Noah, "when they waited for the patience of God," whereby the chastisement of the Deluge was put off: accordingly (Peter) adds: "In the days of Noah, when the Ark was being built."[112]

Aquinas does not relate the preaching of Christ to the act of the descent into hell as such. Rather, the work of preaching is said to occur in history. Aquinas, like Augustine, is conscious of the dangers of an Origenist reading of the text by which the cycles of sin and salvation might extend out into the acorporeal realm, prior to or subsequent to the time of human life in this world. One effect of such a form of thinking is to subtly devalue the real importance and irreplaceable worth of human physical and animal life in the body. The genuine significance of moral responsibility for real historical decisions made in this life evaporates. Human history becomes a shadowy façade behind which the real dramas of salvation occur invisibly and unfathomably. Such neo-Platonic rumination is acorporealist and Gnostic, having little to do with the New Testament revelation of salvation in Christ.

Importantly, then, Augustine and Aquinas see the preaching of Christ to all as occurring in history first and foremost by the inward inspiration of the Logos of God. The graces received inwardly by all human beings living prior to the time of Christ are capable of orienting them mysteriously toward salvation in his incarnate person.[113] What is more, these graces can be given to human persons in a particular way amidst the experiences of solitude, suffering and even physical death. Descent into the night of death in the life of each person,

---

112. ST III, q. 52, a. 2, ad 3.

113. This of course contrasts notably with Jacques Dupuis's doctrine of the Logos *asarkos* studied in chapter 1.

then, is a "place" where the grace of the Word approaches human beings and offers them the possibility of an implicit conformity to the
mystery of Christ. This mystery is signified by the floodwaters of death
and the symbolism of the Ark as a prefiguration of the baptismal wa-
ters and of incorporation into Christ.

Here in Aquinas, then, we find something akin to the statement
of *Gaudium et Spes,* no. 22: "The Holy Spirit in a manner known only
to God offers to every man the possibility of being associated with
this Paschal mystery." Prior to the time of Christ, human beings were
offered an implicit faith and living participation in the grace of the
Word, in view of the merits of the passion of Christ. If this is the case,
then, the historical descent of Christ into hell serves to confirm and
complete the work of grace among those who heard or received the
Word even in the darkness of the world prior to the time of revelation. Christ goes down into hell to bring to perfection what was partially accomplished in history. He "preaches" to the imperfectly converted: those who in death were subject *in part* to the saving work
of grace are led by Christ into a completeness of understanding that
takes place in the course of the descent into hell.

Can this teaching be in some way universalized? The grace of
Christ continues to work in hidden ways outside of the sacraments. Is
there in death the offer of a new and final grace of salvation? Is it un-
reasonable to extend this idea forward into the life of each human being coming after Christ, including the non-baptized? This idea is suggested in the 1994 *Catechism of the Catholic Church:*

"The Gospel was preached even to the dead" (I Pet. 4:6). The descent into
hell brings the Gospel message of salvation to complete fulfillment. This is
the last phase of Jesus' messianic mission, a phase which is condensed in time
but vast in its real significance: the spread of Christ's redemptive work to all
men of all times and all places, for all who are saved have been made shar-
ers in the redemption .... Death is the end of man's earthly pilgrimage, of the
time of grace and mercy which God offers him so as to work out his earthly
life in keeping with the divine plan, and to decide his ultimate destiny.[114]

If this mystery is universal, then we may hope that all human beings who approach the mystery of death are offered a special grace

---

114. *Catechism of the Catholic Church,* paras. 634 and 1013.

of union with Christ in a new and final way. The church continually prays for the dying, therefore, that they may be moved to consent to the secret invitations of the life of God within them. These graces, if they are received, are brought to perfection after death by the illuminations of Christ (the perfection of his "preaching"), he who has himself descended into death and who enlightens all human beings through the power of his resurrection.

We might summarize the idea by way of three fundamental points. First, the Word made flesh illumines all human beings, both before and after the time of Christ, to invite them to conversion. Second, this happens particularly in the hour of death (that is to say, still in this life) and human beings can be subject to a partial conversion in which they are imperfectly but truly open to the activity of grace. Third, Christ descended into hell to further illumine and thus bring to completion the conversion of those only partially converted at death. So the "preaching" occurs formally as such in this life, but can be brought to completion through our conformity to the mystery of Christ in his descent into hell. This articulation of the matter is, it seems to me, very close to the position of the *Catechism*.

A final issue pertains to the question of Limbo. At the time of Aquinas, theologians commonly affirmed the existence of Limbo, and the idea was considered doctrinally normative. However, the exact content of the notion was also widely discussed. The theology of Limbo has its roots in the church's doctrine of original sin, and specifically in the ancient condemnations of Pelagianism, stemming from the Council of Carthage (418): it is not possible for children who die without baptism to be saved simply on the basis of their natural innocence.[115] As a consequence of original sin, all human beings are deprived of salvation unless they are redeemed in the grace of Christ, and this is given ordinarily through baptism. Therefore, children who die before the age of reason and who are not baptized have never received the opportunity to accept the grace of Christ personally. They are marked by the disordering effects of original sin and most notably by the intrinsic deprivation of saving grace.[116] However, they have not committed any personal sins. If they cannot be saved by grace,

---

115. Denz., 102.
116. *De Malo*, q. 5, a. 1.

they should not be damned to the eternal pains of hell (which follow upon personal sin).[117] Medieval theologians commonly speculated, therefore, that the souls of such children who die before the age of reason and without baptism are deprived of the life of divine grace, but that they are not subject to the pains of hell. Rather, they are in a state of natural perfection, of the contemplation and love of God that are possible by our natural powers alone. They do not suffer and they do experience a real and profound, if limited, happiness. However, they do not know the superior happiness of eternal life in the beatific vision.

As we have seen, Aquinas holds that all children who reach the age of reason are offered the grace of salvation in some form.[118] However, like his contemporaries he considers the existence of Limbo to be a sound conclusion of theological speculation. And so accordingly, he holds that Christ on Holy Saturday did not alter the situation of the souls in Limbo: of those many souls of human beings who died in infancy before the time of Christ.[119] As a consequence of original sin, they remain forever marked by the deprivation of the beatific vision. As a consequence of their lack of personal, actual sin, they exist in a state of imperfect but real natural beatitude.

What should we say about this theory? First, one must observe that the idea remained a commonplace speculation in Catholic theology well into the early twentieth century. Therefore it should not be dismissed out of hand as a theologically impermissible position.[120] The thesis originated with Augustine as a way of understanding the reality of original sin, the need for the salvation that grace alone provides, the significance of a personal acceptance or rejection of grace, and the justice and mercy of God in light of both original and personal sin.[121] These principles are all permanently applicable and should be maintained, even if one is free to speculate about an eschatology that does not give preference to the theory of Limbo.

117. *De Malo*, q. 5, a. 3.   118. ST I-II, q. 89, a. 6.
119. ST III, q. 52, a. 7.

120. This is one of the opening presuppositions of the 2007 document of the International Theological Commission, "The Hope of Salvation for Infants Who Die without Being Baptized." http://www.vatican.va/roman_curia/congregations/cfaith/cti_documents/rc_con_cfaith_doc_20070419_un-baptised-infants_en.html

121. Augustine, *Enchiridion*, 93.

Second, then, we need simply to ask whether there is the possibility to hope for the salvation of unborn children who die without baptism and of children who die without baptism before the age of reason. How could this be? Only because God acting in Christ should choose that children in this state should receive grace at some time prior to death, in which case there must be something analogous to the grace of baptism given to non-baptized children. Just as a baptized child is not saved through a personal act, but is designated for salvation through an act of the church and the child's parents, so also the church and the communion of saints could pray for the salvation in grace of all children who die without baptism.[122] Would this make baptism a mere empty symbol that adds nothing to human existence? This hypothesis is impossible, since the grace of baptism does sacramentally regenerate the soul of a child in objective, ontological ways. Consequently, there must be a difference between death in baptism and death without it. Perhaps, then, we might assimilate the teaching on the salvation of children who die without baptism to the teaching on 1 Peter 3:19 considered above. We are not positing the idea of a "general grace" given to children simply because they exist. Even less are we denying the reality of original sin, by which human beings are universally deprived of the grace of eternal life. Rather, what we are positing is the possibility of an eschatological grace given to children *in and through* the mystery of human death, prior to the time of the separation of body and soul. In dying, they are united to the grace of Christ, who descended into hell to gather to himself all who were previously imperfectly united to him in this life.

Just so, we may hope that children who die before the age of reason without baptism may be united in a mysterious way in and through death with the grace of Christ who himself died and descended into hell. In that mystery, Christ reveals his universal solidarity with all those who experience the separation of body and soul, and he elevates to eternal life all those who die in a state of grace. Christians are permitted to hope that children who die without baptism, prior to the age of reason, are included in that state through a mysterious providence of God. If so, their souls are saved by grace and not by a natural right, nor through a denial of the universal consequences of

122. ST III, q. 73, a. 3.

the mystery of original sin. Of course, what is being proposed here is only a theological theory. It is one that reposes upon the church's permission to pray for and hope for the salvation of the souls of children (both unborn and born) who die without baptism.[123]

Revelation of the Trinitarian God

It is perhaps on the issue of the revelation of the Trinity in the descent of Christ into hell that the teachings of Aquinas and Balthasar vary most profoundly. As I have underscored in the previous chapter, Aquinas has no real doctrine of divine kenosis, if by this we mean to designate there taking place in the divine nature itself any form of progressive passivity, suffering, subordinate obedience, or self-enrichment. Aquinas understands the divine nature of the Godhead to be an incomprehensible mystery for human beings. It is known and signified by us only indirectly, through God's effects of grace and nature, and under the veil of analogically formed names.[124] Nevertheless, we may speak truly about God in himself both from biblical revelation and from sound metaphysical speculation. The Catholic tradition has on both grounds insisted dogmatically on the simplicity of the divine nature, and consequently on the divine perfection, immutability, and eternity of God.[125] Another way of stating this idea is to claim that the simplicity, perfection, immutability, and eternity of the divine nature exclude certain *inherently* creaturely ways of being. These are ways of being that imply created dependence: the complexity, imperfection, mutability, and temporality that are proper to creatures. God does not possess the potencies for progressive perfection that are proper to creatures. If he did, he would be made perfect by another and therefore receive his very being (or some aspect of it) from another.[126] Therefore he would not be the unique, universal giver of being for all others, as the creator of all that exists.

Establishing the truth of the divine attributes such as divine sim-

---

123. "The Hope of Salvation for Infants Who Die without Being Baptized," para. 5.

124. ST I, q. 12, aa. 12–13; q. 13, aa. 5–6.

125. The Fourth Lateran Council (1215) makes dogmatic pronouncements on the eternity, incomprehensibility, immutability, immensity, and omnipotence of God. (Denz., 428) Divine simplicity is affirmed dogmatically by the First Vatican Council in the document *Dei Filius* (1870) (Denz., 1782).

126. ST I, q. 3, a. 4.

plicity, perfection, immutability, and eternity lies beyond the scope of this chapter.[127] For our purposes it is important simply to note that for Aquinas there can be on Holy Saturday no possibility of a separation that occurs between the Father and the Son, whether in and through a temporal medium, or as indicative of an already ever-greater separation or infinite distance that is present in the Holy Trinity by virtue of the eternal generation of the Word. There is an eternal generation of the Son as one who is utterly distinct personally from the Father, but there is not a distance between the two, whether real (by way of a spatio-temporal extension in God) or metaphorical (by way of a moral distance or disjunction of wills). By definition of the Catholic faith, the Father, Son, and Holy Spirit are one in being, nature, power, and will.[128] The doctrine of the *perichoresis* (mutual indwelling) of divine persons requires that the Father, Son, and Holy Spirit be eternally present to and within one another precisely by virtue of their shared essence—they are each the one God.[129]

Therefore, it is only to the extent that they differ by way of relations of origin (through the eternal processions) that they may be distinguished, and in no way in terms of a formal, essential, or qualitative difference of ontological "content."[130] The Father is not more powerful than the Son such that the Son should receive a progressive development in power from the Father.[131] Timelessly, from all eternity, the Son is omnipotent by virtue of the very divine omnipotence of the Godhead, even as he receives this power from the Father from all eternity.[132] He is "pure act from pure act," and consequently there is not a "time before" his enrichment with divine life in and through which he becomes enriched with the divine prerogatives of the Godhead.[133] The Son is always God and cannot be alienated from his divine identity and his immutable union with the Father and the Holy Spirit, even during his filial act of (human) obedience and self-emptying in and through the passion. "I am in the Father and the Father is in me" (Jn 14:11).

127. See the above-cited study, *Wisdom in the Face of Modernity*.

128. *Catechism of the Catholic Church*, para. 253; Lateran Council IV (Denz., 428, 431–32); Profession of Faith of Michael Palaeologus (Denz., 461).

129. ST I, q. 42, a. 5.   130. ST I, q. 28, a. 3; q. 29, a. 4; q. 40, a. 1.

131. SCG IV, c. 8.   132. ST I, q. 42, a. 6.

133. *In Ioan.* I, lec. 1, 27. See also ST I, q. 34, a. 3; q. 27, a. 1, ad 2; SCG IV, c. 11, para. 11.

Even as we emphasize the immutability of the divine perfection, is it also possible to speak with Balthasar about a revelation of the Trinity in the mystery of Holy Saturday, yet from a distinctively Thomist perspective? Here it seems that we might say two things. First, all that befalls Jesus Christ is rightly attributed only to the person of the Word, who is the personal subject of all the human actions and sufferings of Christ. This practice of the communication of idioms is itself indicative of the fundamental mystery of the hypostatic union: Jesus is the Son of God subsisting in a human nature. He is truly God, even while having a complete human nature of body and soul, like that of all other human beings. Therefore, all divine and human properties are attributed to his person.[134]

According to Aquinas, however, this is the case also on Holy Saturday, *when the body and soul of Christ are separated by death.* The human body of Christ undergoes death in the crucifixion, and the animating principle of the body is sundered from the body. His cadaver is then buried in the tomb. Here, however, the person of the Word continues to subsist personally in his cadaver.[135] The body of Christ remains hypostatically united to the Word even after death. Those who touch the dead body of Christ, then, do indeed touch the Word of life and hold in their hands the flesh of God, who is substantially and personally present in the dead cadaver of Christ. Meanwhile, the Word also continues to subsist in his spiritual soul separated from his body. This human soul is the soul of the Word.[136] And in this immaterial soul, the Word illumines the whole cosmos of human souls who have died prior to the time of Christ (enlightening them in various ways, as we have seen). It follows from all this that the Word is luminous *personally* in and through his death, both in his cadaveric body and in his separated soul. In both he teaches us about the personal identity of God the Son and Word who has come into the world to illumine our human condition. In these mysteries we perceive his solidarity with the human race, since God freely adopted our human nature for our sake and in the service of our salvation.[137] In that sense, God the Son's personal solidarity with us even in human death is in-

---

134. ST III, q. 16, a. 1.
136. ST III, q. 50, a. 3.

135. ST III, q. 50, a. 2.
137. *Comp. Theol.*, cc. 228–29.

dicative of a deeper divine will that he shares with the Father and the Holy Spirit and in which he is utterly one with them.[138] God the Trinity willed that the Son should take flesh and die for our salvation, advancing even into the experience of death and hell, as a means to demonstrate the power of God to make use of death in his own human life in order to undo the power of death over the human race as a collective whole.[139]

This brings us to the second and final point. The divine goodness and love of God are perfect and are therefore not subject to the possibility of any form of internal theological drama.[140] They cannot develop or become more perfectly enriched, as if God could grow in goodness or love as an effect of his dramatic struggle with creaturely evil, suffering, death, or hell. Nevertheless, God can reveal to us in particularly intensive ways his own goodness and intrinsically immutable love through the drama of his own *human* suffering, death, and descent into hell. It is through these mysteries not that God changes, but that the unchanging love of God is made most manifest to us precisely *in* God's all-powerful victory over the powers of death, moral evil, and hell. It is the *victory* of Christ, his triumphant, luminous entry into hell on Holy Saturday, that manifests most to us his love for the human race. He has the capacity *as God* in his goodness and love to make use even of the worst that angelic and human evil can do, to draw forth a yet greater and infinitely superior good: the good of our participation in his divine life, in the world of the resurrection. It is not, then, the passivity, misery, or spiritual loss of Christ alone that indicates his true solidarity with us out of love. Rather, as the universal tradition of the ancient fathers underscores in both west and east: Christ's true solidarity with us on Holy Saturday is most deeply expressed by the use of his genuine divine authority in the service of his victory over evil. This is an authority borne in love, but also one that originates from Christ's legitimate power as God. On Holy Saturday, Christ shows us his true solidarity with us not only as man but also as God, by conquering death, hell, and the devil with the power of love.

138. ST III, q. 47, a. 3, corp. and ad 2; q. 20, a. 2.
139. ST III, q. 1, a. 2.
140. ST I, q. 4, a. 1; q. 6, aa. 2–4.

IN VIEW OF
A THEOLOGICAL
DISCERNMENT

Clearly there are significant points of overlap as well as significant points of tension in the respective accounts of Balthasar and Aquinas on the topic of Holy Saturday. By way of conclusion, I would like to suggest why Aquinas's theology of Christ's descent into hell is more theologically satisfying. This is stated with full understanding of the indisputable spiritual, theological, and human depth of Balthasar's thought. It seems, however, that Aquinas is able to meet many of Balthasar's own concerns while also preserving and intelligibly manifesting a greater number of classical Catholic theological principles. How is this the case?

The first thing to be said is that there are many noble and intellectually appealing elements found in the theology of Balthasar on this subject. He wishes to treat seriously the question of the universal possibility of salvation by grace that is offered to all human beings. He is concerned to defend the innocence of God in the face of eternal loss, and wishes to avoid a theology of reprobation that would appear excessively callous and therefore anthropomorphic. His theology has ecumenical prospects and appeals to a broad readership across confessional lines, inspiring many to study and adopt various classical positions of Catholic theology. He is concerned to show how God responds in compassion and mercy to the solitude of human beings in the face of death and suffering. He wishes to argue that the deepest mystery of God as Trinity is revealed in a unique and preeminent way in and through the Paschal mystery. All of these intentions are laudable and in various ways the unmistakable marks of someone working in a profound and beautiful way out of the heart of the Catholic theological tradition.

Nevertheless, we have the genuine responsibility to ask whether there are other perhaps preferable ways to conceive of the mystery of Holy Saturday, and whether these might also meet many or all of Balthasar's chief theological concerns adequately while also retaining principles of Catholic theology that Balthasar's own thinking seems to represent inadequately in some regards. Below I would like succinctly to note six ways in which Aquinas's theology treats the mystery in terms that respond adequately and profoundly *either* to Balthasar's very legitimate theological concerns *or* to what seem like objective deficits in his approach to the mystery of redemption. In listing these six ideas, I am not seeking to give any kind of comprehensive assessment of either thinker, but only to indicate important ways they might be compared in view of coming to a theological discernment of the issue.

Was There a Descent into Hell?

The first comparison we should observe concerns the very existence of the mystery, or its parameters as an event. As we have observed above, Balthasar and Aquinas differ in fundamental ways regarding the existence of the human immaterial soul separated from the body after death and prior to resurrection. Balthasar is ambivalent about the very idea of such an interim state of the human soul separated from the body, either for Christ or for all the other members of the human race. I will discuss the relation between belief in the resurrection and affirmation of the immaterial soul in the following chapter. There I will argue that the two ideas, far from being incompatible, in fact evoke one another theologically in very integral ways. For our purposes here, it is important simply to note that it is in no way clear *how there can be an integral mystery of Holy Saturday for Balthasar*, at least as it is understood in the traditional sense.

Why? Because one of the necessary conditions for the possibility of this mystery is that human immaterial souls *exist in the interim state* between death and bodily resurrection. Otherwise, there is no one to be redeemed on Holy Saturday as such, and that mystery merely becomes the symbol of something else (the Lord's solidarity with us in death and life after death). In some real sense, the descent for Balthasar does entail an "atemporal" sphere of existence that comes in or after physical death. But it does not entail the life of the subsistent immaterial soul separated from the body. Consequently, it has more in common with the doctrine of Calvin and Barth, ultimately, than it does with either the classical eastern or western patristic and medieval accounts of the descent into hell as a real event that transpired on Holy Saturday. Furthermore, in the absence of a doctrine of the immaterial soul, it would seem that Christ himself must enter in some way into the resurrected state *immediately* after his human anni-hilation in death. And yet such an idea stands in contradiction to the teaching of the scriptures and the Apostles' Creed.[141]

Meanwhile, for Aquinas this mystery can exist due to the reality of the intermediate state of the soul separated from the body. In a real sense, it must exist just because Christ himself suffered a true human death, such that his soul was subject to the interim state of separation from the body. The title of this chapter is: "Did Christ descend into hell"? Ironically as it might seem, in some real sense, the only true Balthasarian answer to this question is negative, while the Thomist answer is indeed affirmative. Aquinas affirms the existence of a de-cent of Christ into hell while Balthasar's theology seems to deny im-plicitly the core reality of this mystery.

Real Grace
Universalism with the Possibility
of Eternal Loss

Arguably, the heart of Balthasar's theology of Holy Saturday is to be found in his rearticulation of penal substitution theory. Christ under-goes the most extreme form of separation from God for us out of sol-idarity with us. Through his loving obedience, he brings the mystery of divine love even into the spiritual darkness and hell of any possible

---

141. Commenting on the Creed ("He descended into hell") the *Catechism of the Catholic Church* states (paras. 632–33): "The frequent New Testament affirmations that Jesus was 'raised from the dead' presuppose that the crucified one sojourned in the realm of the dead prior to his resurrection (Acts 3:15; Rom 8:11; I Cor. 15:20; cf. Heb 13:20). This was the first meaning given in the apostolic preaching to Christ's descent into hell: that Jesus, like all men, experienced death and in his soul joined the others in the realm of the dead. But he descended there as Saviour, proclaiming the Good News to the spirits imprisoned there. Scripture calls the abode of the dead, to which the dead Christ went down, 'hell'—*Sheol* in Hebrew or Hades in Greek—because those who are there are de-prived of the vision of God. Such is the case for all the dead, whether evil or righteous, while they await the Redeemer: which does not mean that their lot is identical, as Jesus shows through the parable of the poor man Lazarus who was received into 'Abraham's bosom': It is precisely these holy souls, who awaited their Saviour in Abraham's bosom, whom Christ the Lord delivered when he descended into hell. Jesus did not descend into hell to deliver the damned, nor to destroy the hell of damnation, but to free the just who had gone before him."

human rupture with God, no matter how great. Related intimately to this soteriology is Balthasar's insistence on the Catholic belief that the grace of reconciliation is offered to all, that is to say, that there is a universal possibility of salvation.[142]

As we have seen above, Aquinas and the Thomist tradition affirm unequivocally that grace truly sufficient for salvation is offered to all human persons in the course of their lives. This is in keeping with a common affirmation of the Catholic tradition, one which stems from Prosper of Aquitaine to the Second Council of Orange and the Council of Valencia, through Aquinas and other medieval scholastics up into the modern age in the condemnations of Jansenism, Pius IX's concept of invincible ignorance, and the declarations of Vatican II. A principle of doctrinal continuity, therefore, already exists. What is distinct about Balthasar's position, however, is that he seems ill at ease with a different but accompanying traditional notion: the idea that a soul can definitively reject grace and be lost to eternal life through its own culpable actions of serious personal sin.

The classical tradition insists on the offer of salvation, but also on the possibility of culpable non-consent to grace, and of the consequences of a spiritual creature's personal decision for or against God. On one level, Balthasar upholds such an idea unambiguously insofar as he affirms the speculative possibility of eternal loss.[143] On another level, however, he is clearly ill at ease with the possibility that any final decision of God in the face of creaturely evil *could already have taken place*. This is the case with regard to those who lived prior to the time of Christ (already in the supposed hell of the damned on Holy Saturday). It is also the case with regard to all others who have come after Christ even until the final judgment.[144] It follows that such

142. This is something quite different from the possibility of universal salvation (*apokatastasis panton*). It is beyond the scope of these considerations to resolve the question of whether Balthasar holds that position as well, and why there are problems associated with it. On this subject, see Thomas Joseph White, "Von Balthasar and Journet on the Universal Possibility of Salvation and the Twofold Will of God," *Nova et Vetera* (English edition) 4, no. 3 (2006): 633–66.

143. See in this regard, *Theo-Drama*, 3:33–40, 4:350, and especially 5:285–90, where he cites Von Speyr (288) in claiming that "it is possible for [man] to become so hardened in his freedom that he must pursue to the end the path he has chosen in opposition to God."

144. Balthasar, *Dare We Hope*, 26, 178, 183–84, 187; *Theo-Drama*, 5:283–84.

"definitive" refusal may yet turn out to be impossible. God may overcome it.

Seen from an epistemological point of view, there is something
licit in this affirmation. Divine revelation does not give human beings
knowledge of the particular judgment of God with regard to any individual human soul. We may, therefore, pray for and hope for the
salvation of any and every human being. One might argue, however,
that the New Testament also reveals to us that there are those who refuse the grace of God and who are definitively lost.[145] Hope for the
offer of salvation of each one is not identical with the hope that all
are ultimately saved. Are there grounds for the latter idea in scripture?
The burden of proof is on those who claim that it is the case, since
historically speaking, such an affirmation constitutes what appears to
be a clear doctrinal innovation.[146]

More fundamentally, however, there is a moral issue at stake in
our understanding of the goodness of God. Balthasar's theology implicitly raises the question: can God allow the finite spiritual revolt
of even one spiritual creature to have a permanent, everlasting effect? If this were the case, could we still affirm and trust in the sovereign goodness, love, and mercy of God? The traditional answer
to this question is "yes." It is impossible to understand this mystery
as God does, but we can and must affirm the goodness and justice
of God's particular judgments of every angel and every human soul.
These stem from his justice, but they are also utterly compatible with
his goodness and mercy. Hell is not something that exists in spite of
the authentic goodness and mercy of God. It does exist because that
goodness and mercy are rejected in some significant way on the part
of creatures.

The problem with Balthasar's theology is not that he denies this
in an overt fashion, but that due to his theology of Holy Saturday, he
does not confront the question, and consequently does not affirm the
teaching of the tradition overtly on this point. In this sense, his theology seems to ignore or obscure an affirmation of the New Testament
itself regarding the mystery of God's just judgment. It is an explicit

145. 2 Thess 2:10: "They refused to love the truth and so be saved." See 2 Pet 2:4;
Mt 5:22, 29; 10:28; 13:42, 50; 24:31–46; Mk 9:43–48.

146. Denz., 40, 321, 410, 429, 457, 493a, 531, 693.

teaching of the scriptures and conciliar dogmatic tradition that the devil is irremediably lost to eternal separation from God.[147] If that is the case even for one spiritual being, then it can be the case for others without prejudice to the mercy, love, and goodness of God. How this is the case is a very trying question for any human being to grapple with. But that it is the case is the teaching of divine revelation. Balthasar's theology of Holy Saturday seems on this point to exhibit a potentially insufficient docility to the classical deposit of faith. It may even contain within it a hidden temptation of doubt concerning the goodness of the God of the New Testament. On this difficult topic, then, Aquinas's theological understanding seems preferable.

Salvation Is in Time:

Against Neo-Gnosticism

Balthasar's seeming decision to place the decision of the soul for or against God *after* human history in the eschatological life of the atemporal sphere and even in the hell of the damned (on Holy Saturday) suggests a necessarily impermanent effect to the actions of human freedom as they transpire in this world. This point is intimately related to the previous one. For Balthasar, the story of human salvation cannot be over yet, because God could not already have permitted the definitive loss of any human being. Therefore, there must be a continuation of the story of salvation and the choices of human freedom beyond the boundaries of the temporal, bodily realm. This may seem to contradict Balthasar's ambivalence about the interim state of the soul separated from the body, but it does not. The presumption is, rather, that the atemporal sphere that the person enters after death is a Christological domain. The death of Christ has created a new ontological space for the death and reconciliation of all human beings, and so we die in Christ and in a certain sense can be called to a final act of freedom "in Christ" beyond the temporal constraints of this world. "Being after death" seems to be something that pertains *formally* and *essentially* to the order of Christological grace rather than to the order

147. Consider the unambiguous affirmation of Rev 20:10. See Canon 9 of Vigilius (543) (Denz., 211): "If anyone says or holds that the punishment of the demons and of impious men is temporary, and that it will have an end at some time, that is to say, there will be a complete restoration of the demons or of impious men, let him be anathema."

of human immaterial nature. In this view, the grace of Christ does not merely save and heal human nature. Rather, in some real sense this grace *replaces* human nature *altogether* in the world to come.

There are three problems with such an idea. First, it stands in tension with the traditional Christian belief that human beings are saved or lose their salvation based upon the lives they live in this world. The soteriological significance of life in the body is undermined by this decision to revisit the "time" of salvation, placing it (as Origen did) outside of the parameters of bodily existence. Second, in order for the idea of a new, final choice *after death* for or against Christ really to make sense, it would be necessary to affirm that each human being has an immaterial soul that subsists after death. Some natural substrate must persist for there to be a subject who receives salvation. Human beings who die do not become Christ himself, for in that case they would be identified with God and would cease to be creatures. (God the Son would be united to every human being hypostatically in death.) They cannot be completely annihilated in death, since in that case a choice after death would be senseless. Consequently, for such a choice to transpire there must remain after death something proper to human nature that is capable of moral transformation. Salvation in Christ *after death* can only transpire if grace is given to a *naturally* incorruptible human soul.

But if there is a new choice for Christ that is made *after death*, this also implies that the person can act in a natural, intellectual and free way without the body. Consequently, human freedom is in a sense fully operative independently of the body. For Aquinas this is not the case unless there is already the presence and activity of a particular form of infused knowledge. Why? Because the human intellect normally depends upon cognition through sense experiences in order to move forward in the process of thinking and choosing. The soul without the body would be unable to make revised choices, unless by a special new favor of infused knowledge. If we affirm that the separated soul is given such new, infused knowledge in order finally to consent freely to God's grace, then we are claiming implicitly that the act of salvation becomes more natural or more likely *without the body* than it is with and in the body. The dualism of such a position undermines the value of the body for the human soul and for human existence more generally. The body becomes an obstacle to salvation. As in the case of Origen, such thinking tends toward an overt form of Gnosticism.

Third, if the soul is in fact given repeated new chances in the post-physical state, then the decision for or against God can go on indeterminately forever. In this case, resolution of the question of our relationship to God's grace does not take place in the course of our physical life in the body (as the church teaches that it in fact does). Rather, it goes on so long as God would wish, indefinitely or until such time as he resolves to move the soul effectively to salvation. In other words, Balthasar's scenario pushes us back to the question of divine innocence once again. Why would God not at some point simply choose to reconcile the indeterminate soul that has never made a final choice for or against him? The capacity to choose definitively against God seems to be taken from human nature, but then God is left as the unique agent of responsibility in giving resolution to the narrative drama. Given his goodness, is it not inevitable that we should expect some form of *apokatastasis panton* to triumph in the end? This outcome seems inevitably built into the theological scenario as Balthasar has construed it. The advantage of Aquinas's position is that it maintains the reality of a universal offer of salvation *in this life* and so avoids the neo-Gnostic problems or speculations that can arise from Origen's anthropology and various forms of eastern patristic theology that affirmed the descent of Christ into the hell of the damned.

Christ as Savior in the
Descent and as Victorious

The ancient patristic authorities of both the eastern and western church concur on the fact that the descent of Christ into hell was a descent made in triumph over the powers of evil and not a descent made in suffering. By extending the mystery of Good Friday (as promoted particularly in the modern Reformed tradition) into the event of Holy Saturday, Balthasar obscures a portion of the traditional content of the ecclesial doctrinal tradition. If that traditional content is not an arbitrary given but something denoting a mystery distinct from that of the cross, then this mystery of Holy Saturday deserves to be explored for its own sake. In this respect, Aquinas offers us an alternative, non-mythological, but also quite poetical venue for exploration. His is attuned to the patristic tradition which preserves elegantly the contours of its specificity and which allows the mystery to shine through in its proper integrity.

In a related way, we might underscore a point in continuity with the argument of the previous chapter. If Christ descends into hell not as a victor but as a passive, obedient subject of suffering, then what is the meaning of his identity as *savior* of the human race on Holy Saturday? The traditional position of the church understands Christ to be the active agent of salvation, with the power of God working through the instrumental medium of the human soul of Christ. By virtue of the inversion introduced in Balthasar's theory, Christ is himself passive before the Father and becomes himself the recipient of divine intervention. He is now in the position of needing to be saved by the Father. Here there is a parallel to the point made in the previous chapter regarding the resurrection. Just as Christ, for Balthasar, does not raise himself from the dead, but is raised by the Father, so Christ descends into hell not so much to illumine those in hell with the victory of redemption, as to become one with them in solidarity out of love, even in the midst of their distance from God. In that sense, the person of Christ lies in wait for the moment of reconciliation that can only be brought about by God the Father on Easter Sunday.

While this innovative rereading of the Holy Saturday tradition is beautiful or alluring in various ways, it does introduce profound innovations into Catholic theology. It even constitutes, in fact, a kind of break with sacred tradition. Aquinas's theology makes clear in what way the power of God and the victorious goodness of God's love are present in hell on Holy Saturday. They are present because Christ is God. With Balthasar's theory, it is not clear how we might uphold the soteriological victory of the *divine power* of Christ in his descent into hell. This problem is related in turn to the next issue: the unity of the Godhead even in the midst of the Paschal mystery.

The Unity and Immutability of the
Trinitarian God

The Council of Ephesus affirms that all the actions and sufferings of Christ are to be attributed to his person, the person of the Word, as their concrete ontological subject. Consequently they may be attributed to a person who is God: it is God who was born of the Virgin Mary, God who was crucified on Golgotha, God who died a human death, and God whose body was buried in the tomb.[148] It is also true to say, then, that God "descended" into hell, in his human soul, in the mystery of Holy Saturday. Correspondingly, the events of the Son of God in his Paschal mystery reveal who he is, as the eternal Word of God, and in doing so, reveal the Father and the Holy Spirit. It is not the Father or the Holy Spirit who suffered, died, and was buried, descended into hell, and rose on the third day. These mysteries are attributed only to the person of the Son because only the Son took upon himself a human nature for our sake, and the Son is personally distinct from the Father and the Holy Spirit. However, the Son who did experience these events is also inseparably united *as God* to the Father and the Holy Spirit, even in all that he does and all that he undergoes humanly. The human actions and sufferings of Christ are not to be confused with his divine actions, but they must not be separated from them either. Similarly, the divine actions of the Father and the Holy Spirit are inseparably present in all that the Word incarnate does and suffers, insofar as he does and suffers these things not only as one who is human, but also as one who is God.

According to Aquinas's account, there are repercussions to this point of view. All that the Son undergoes as man must also respect all that he is as God. As a human being, Jesus is capable of suffering, death, and the separation of body and soul (the "descent into hell"). As God he is subject *personally* as the Son to these events. It is God who suffers and dies, etc., but in his divine nature, the Son remains simple, immutable, and eternal. He also remains one with the Father and the Holy Spirit in that divine nature. So as where it is only the Son who dies humanly, the Father and Son are immutably one by virtue of the divine nature, even in and through that event. "I am in the Father and the Father is in me" (Jn 14:11); "I and the Father are one" (Jn 10:30).

Furthermore, if the divine agency is at work in the event of the passion, death, and descent into hell, then it is also the case that all activity of the Trinity *ad extra* (in all God's works of creation and redemption) is the work of the three persons acting in virtue of their

148. Council of Ephesus, can. 4 (Denz., 115).

unique deity.[149] If the Son of God illumines the souls of the just on Holy Saturday, then he does so in simple unity of divine agency with the Father and the Holy Spirit. It is only the Son who descends into hell in his human soul, because only the Son is human and can undergo death. But it is the Son with the Father and the Holy Spirit who illumines all the souls in question by grace, because it is the Trinity that is the cause of all grace.[150] This event may transpire by the power of God working *through* the instrumentality of the human soul of Christ (which is in some way active in the process), but it occurs by the power of God and consequently stems from the activity of the three persons.

If all this is true then it is certainly fair to consider that the mystery of the Trinitarian life of God is revealed in and through the event of Holy Saturday. However, this revelation is only possible because the Son is one in being, essence, will, and power with the Father and the Holy Spirit. *Just because* of the divine agency, power, and will that are *identical* in the three persons, this monotheistic unity can be manifest in their unified agency. And for the same reason, there is no separation or alienation *possible* between the persons of the Trinity in the events of the Paschal mystery. The condition for the revelation of the Trinity in and through the event of Holy Saturday is the absolute unity and divine simplicity of the Godhead by virtue of which the Son is absolutely inseparable from the Father and the Holy Spirit.

For this reason it is undoubtedly correct for Balthasar to wish to illustrate the presence and revelation of the Trinitarian God even in the midst of the Son's Paschal mystery. Furthermore, it cannot be said that Balthasar treated the question of the patristic and scholastic metaphysical tradition lightly in his approach to theology.[151] He is sensitive to and has his own interpretation of the teachings of Vatican I regarding the place of natural reason concerning God, even within the activity of theological science.[152] In his own unique way,

149. ST I, q. 32, a. 1; q. 39, aa. 7–8; q. 45, a. 6; ST III, q. 3, a. 4.

150. ST I-II, q. 112, a. 1.

151. To cite only one significant example, see the analysis of Hans Urs von Balthasar, *The Glory of the Lord. A Theological Aesthetics* IV: *The Realm of Metaphysics in Antiquity*, trans. Brian McNeil (San Francisco: Ignatius, 1989).

152. See *The Theology of Karl Barth*, 302–25.

he proposes a very ambitious attempt at an integral recovery and rearticulation of the classical metaphysical tradition, recast in a Christological light.

Yet Balthasar also follows Barth unambiguously in ascribing to the Son of God a capacity for obedience even in his divine essence. In fact, Balthasar goes further than Barth does explicitly, in speaking of a divine self-emptying, passivity, or receptivity within the Godhead.[153] This is something distinct from the receptivity of the person of the Son (who receives his personal being from the Father through eternal generation). A notion of receptivity of this kind is traditional and proper to any coherent Trinitarian theology. By contrast, self-emptying or passivity in the essence of the Godhead itself is something else.[154] Such a receptivity would suggest diverse modes of being (as gift on the one hand and receptivity on the other) *within* the simple, immutable, eternal essence of God. Because there is a kind of divine passivity and obedience of the Son that is ascribed to his divine nature, the unity of the persons is jeopardized. As mentioned above, the divine persons are distinguished only by their relations of origin, while they are considered to be absolutely identical in essence and in "qualities." (In fact, the essence of God is simply identical with his divine qualities or characteristics, since God just is his wisdom, goodness, love, and so forth). If the Son is distinct from the Father due not only to his eternal generation (relation of origin) but also due to a quality of passive receptivity that is not present in the Father (or that is present in the Father differently), then the Father possesses qualities of being that are not present in the Son, and vice versa. Trinitarian monotheism is implicitly compromised in this case, however, since there now exists not only a *personal* but also a *natural* ontological plurality within God. Each person has essential or natural attributes that the others do not. Correspondingly, there is the absence of a pure unity of essence and identity of being common to the Father and the Son.

Second, in this case, there is also the question of the potential for enrichment of the Trinitarian persons in and through the economy.

153. *Theo-Drama*, 3:250–58, 4:323–28, 5:506–21.

154. As we find, I would argue, in *Theo-Drama*, 4:324–25, which echoes acutely but also intensifies what we find in Barth's CD IV, 1, section 59.

For if the Son is passive and obedient *in and for his mission* (because obedience has a content: the Son accepts his mission) and if that mission is temporal, then it would seem to follow that the person of the Son undergoes a progressive actuation or certification of his ontological identity *in and through* his temporal obedience. In this case the mystery of Holy Saturday is not only *expressive* of the divine identity of the Son, but is in some way *perfective* of that identity. The temporal economy is seen in some way to contribute to or to enrich the Trinitarian identity of God. And indeed, this is just what we find Balthasar asserting in an unambiguous if qualified fashion:

"The fact that the Son returns to the Father richer than when he departed, the fact that the Trinity is more perfected in love after the Incarnation than before, has its meaning and its foundation in God himself, who is not a rigid unity but a unity that comes together ever anew in love, an eternal intensification in eternal rest."... We need not be shocked at the suggestion that there can be "economic" events in God's eternal life. When the Father hands over all judgment to the Son, "something happens in God." When the risen Son returns to the Father, "a new joy arises after the renunciation involved in the separation. This new joy ... perfects the Trinity in the sense that the grace that is to be bestowed becomes ever richer, both in the world into which it pours forth and in God himself."[155]

It is not clear, however, exactly how such notions are to be accorded with the traditional monotheistic assertions of divine aseity, simplicity, and transcendence that are proper to the Trinitarian theological tradition.

Despite their critical character, the objections posed above are not intended to serve as final arbitrations of discernment regarding the evaluation of Balthasarian theology. His project is insightful, rich, important, and innovative. But it is fair to question its potential com-

---

155. *Theo-Drama*, 5:514–15. The citations in the passage are from the mystical notebooks of Adrienne von Speyr, with which Balthasar is obviously in accord. It is striking that Von Speyr affirms here that God himself grew in grace as a result of Christ's mission. How are we to understand this, since all grace originates from God alone as its primary author? Are we to conclude that God freely self-actuated a latent perfection that came into being in and through the mission of the Son? In that case, due to an ontological composition of act and potency that pertains to the very deity of God itself, it would seem that there is some higher source of actuation that transcends even God himself. Is that higher source not the actual history that God shares with human beings? In that case, God and history seem to be one on some deeper level. We are standing in the shadow of Hegel.

patibility with classical Christian thought on multiple levels. Raising probing questions about the notion of divine unity in the Trinitarian theology of Balthasar is not meant as a form of disrespect, but as a service to the church, in the hope of further debate and clarification regarding the work of this influential theologian on a point of sensitive concern.

Ecumenical Promise of the Traditional
Western Position

A last point of comparison pertains to the ecumenical advantages of the distinct theologies of Holy Saturday that are under consideration. At the risk of being overly schematic, one might say that the traditional Catholic understanding of the mystery of redemption places great emphasis on the Anselmian theory of *satisfactio:* the atonement for sin that takes place through Christ's obedience and love in and through the passion. The human obedience of Christ is of an infinite worth due to the dignity of the subject who undertakes the action of reparation: the Son of God. The descent into hell is an application or expression of the victory of love that has taken place in the cross event. Meanwhile, without excluding this view, a prominent strand of traditional eastern thought has placed emphasis on the mystery of divinization: the Son became man in order that the human race might be united to God. The descent into hell is an expression of the Son's elevation of human beings into deifying union of life with God. Influential strands of Protestantism, meanwhile, have placed great stress on the punishment for human sin that was accepted by the Son of God in his human life. Christ takes upon himself the burden of suffering that sinful humanity has incurred in order to deliver human beings from the judgment of divine justice and to introduce human beings into a life of righteousness with God. The descent into hell, then, takes place in the soul of Christ even on Good Friday, as he bears within his human spirit the burden of spiritual separation from God in order to deliver us from that burden in a definitive way.

Aquinas holds unambiguously to the first two of these interpretations of our redemption.[156] He maintains select aspects of the third

---

156. ST III, q. 1, a. 2.

view, albeit in ways very different from the perspectives of either Luther or Calvin.[157] Likewise, Balthasar seeks unquestionably to interact with these distinct traditions in profound ways. The theology of each thinker has a great ecumenical horizon and can serve as a focal point for discussions regarding the redemption among separated Christians. There is a significant difference between the two thinkers on this front, however. As has been shown above, Balthasar rereads the diverse strands of tradition in innovative ways. Christ experiences the night of hell on Good Friday, as we see also in Calvin and Barth, but in differentiation from this, he also experiences this night on the day of Holy Saturday in the mystery of the descent among the dead. Like some of the eastern fathers, Balthasar insists on a descent of Christ even into the hell of the damned but unlike them he sees this not as a descent of triumph, but of passivity in suffering and solidarity.

We might question the ecumenical advantage of such a novel and original theology. Doctrinal unity among Christians is built up in and through time by virtue of a shared theological consensus regarding the ontological content of the divine mystery that is believed and confessed. If this content is revisited in a decisively novel and dramatic way, even in the name of ecclesial unity, there results an inevitable spark of discontinuity with the past. Traditional resources are no longer considered sufficiently valid to yield an open perspective into the mystery. As a result, the ecumenical process itself is deeply endangered or hindered. Why? Because based on such a procedure, ecumenism can only move forward on the condition that we renegotiate incessantly the shared consensus of the past. Alternatively stated, a theory that seemingly abandons or reinterprets large swaths of the traditional account of a mystery will leave us handicapped to revisit that tradition and to treat it as the *normative referent* for any substantive ecumenical adjudication.

We should not seek to conceal the important differences or points of emphasis that exist among separated Christians regarding the mode in which the redemption took place. But one way to revisit those potential tensions or differences constructively is to preserve

157. See the study of Aquinas's doctrine of the assumption of human punishments for sin by Nieuwenhove, "'Bearing the Marks of Christ's Passion': Aquinas' Soteriology," 277–302.

the original teaching that lies behind them accurately and to present this anew in search of the points of genuine unity, convergence
and contact that they contain. Aquinas's theology of divinization, for
example, contains profound points of contact with the core eastern
Christian tradition on this same subject. Analogously, Aquinas's notion of the penalties of sin, or the pains of sin that Christ took upon
himself for our sake, without any compromise of his own moral innocence, provides some point of real contact with the substitutionary atonement theories that are favored within the Lutheran and
Reformed traditions. We have no real reason, then, to abandon for
ecumenical purposes the classical western account of the descent of
Christ into hell as it is portrayed within medieval scholastic theology.
On the contrary, a hearty recovery of the clear and profound thinking
on this subject *within the tradition* can be itself a great resource for the
cause of unity among Christians even in our own age.

CONCLUSION

Despite the length of this chapter, the remarks contained herein
are clearly only cursory. The theology of Hans Urs von Balthasar is
of importance and his dense and subtle treatment of philosophical
and theological topics deserves to be considered carefully. We understand great thinkers, however, also always in conversation with other great thinkers. The presentation of the descent of Christ into hell
in the thinking of Thomas Aquinas should continue to play a normative role of reference in Catholic theology as a way of discerning the common teaching of the Catholic tradition. The overarching
claim I have presented in the reflections above concerns the value of
this tradition. It is something worth defending and promoting. Can
Balthasar's theology of Holy Saturday be seen as an organic development of traditional Catholic thinking with regard to the redemption
and to eschatology? It is my sense that it cannot. Aquinas provides
an alternative account to that of Balthasar that is preferable for many
theological reasons and which accords better with the classical Catholic theological tradition on multiple fronts. In saying this, however,
one must recognize that the conversation inevitably needs to be pursued further. Catholic theology is never the work of one person but

of a communion, and it is conducted over time and not in one particular age alone. Monolithic theological projects have to undergo revision, critique, and reconsideration so that the genuine insights of a given theological or literary genius might be integrated rightly and in true fashion into the catholicity—the universality—of the common communion of the whole church. At the same time, it should be remembered that authentic critical engagement in theology is only truly Catholic if it is open to the life of the whole church and if it is conducted in genuine charity. Here, indeed, we can rightly insist that all Catholic theology, including Thomistic theology, ascribe to the beautiful motto that Balthasar made famous: only love is worthy of belief. It is that love of Christ who was crucified, lived out in communion, that calls theological conversation to a higher plane.

10

------------- : -------------

The Ontology of the
Resurrection

Our study of the being of Christ would be incomplete without a consideration of his resurrection. What can we say about the glorification of his human nature that took place after his death? This depends in part upon what we take human nature to be. I have argued in the prolegomenon to this book that modern theology is often bifurcated. On the one side there is the tendency to reduce Christology to a form of idealized anthropology. Schleiermacher and Rahner provide models of this form of reflection. On the other side there is the theological assimilation of all natural forms of knowledge into Christology. We can only know, for example, what a human being is, or what creation is, by looking at Christ. Barth's theology remains a standard example of this form of Christological concentration, one that leaves little room for an autonomous development of a metaphysics of creation or a philosophical anthropology. His approach has distinct echoes in the theology of Balthasar.

Against such juxtaposed theologies, I have argued, particularly in chapters 2 and 4, for a kind of harmony or balance between Christology and the study of the natural structure of reality. Christ tells us what it is to be human, but our understanding of the humanity of Christ also requires that we develop some philosophical concep-

tion of the nature of the human being. Christ gives us knowledge of
the Trinity, but this knowledge also elicits an appeal to metaphysical
knowledge of God as creator. A similar balance needs to be found regarding the mystery of the resurrection of Jesus. Christ is the "New
Adam" (Rom 5:12–21) in whom alone we come to understand fully
our own human nature and its destiny. However, because Christ is
a "Son of Man," his nature is taken from the original Adam, for he is
like us in all things but sin. In Christ resurrected, then, we find someone who possesses our own nature and can only be understood in
light of that nature, but also someone who in his humanity is alive
forever in God, such that his life teaches us what it means to be authentically human.

In what follows I would like to explore the equilibrium that should
exist between philosophical anthropology and theological realism regarding the resurrection of Jesus Christ. First, I will note briefly some
influential themes in modern theological accounts of the resurrection,
arguing that problematic philosophical presuppositions have deeply affected modern theology on this topic. This gives us good reason to reconsider Thomistic theories of human nature. Second, I will
examine Aquinas's philosophical principles of hylomorphism. How
do these relate to his general theology of resurrection? Having considered this question, I will turn to the resurrection of Christ in particular.

In this last section of the chapter I wish to make two claims. First,
Christ in his glorified humanity is the exemplary cause of our resurrection from the dead. The perfection of his humanity is the eschatological measure of the perfection of ours. Second, Christ's glorified
humanity is the instrumental efficient cause of our salvation because
Christ is not only man, but also God. Only in his resurrection from
the dead is Christ fully manifest as divine. There the perfection of his
divinity shines forth most resplendently through the divine-human
actions of Christ. These actions reveal his divine power and therefore
his preexistent unity with the Father and the Holy Spirit. The risen
Lord reveals to us simultaneously, then, both perfect God and perfect man. Right consideration of the resurrection of the Son of God
helps to establish a profound equilibrium within Catholic theology.
We need not choose between theological anthropology and Christo-

centricism, for it is precisely in the New Adam, Christ crucified and glorified, that we perceive who God is.

OBJECTIONS TO THE
TRADITIONAL DOCTRINE OF
THE RESURRECTION FROM
MODERN THEOLOGY

Mainstream Catholic and Protestant theology in the twentieth century sought to reexamine thoroughly, in a variety of ways, the traditional claims of Christianity regarding the resurrection of Christ.[1] Let us begin by noting briefly, then, two dominant trends that have emerged. One tendency is to call into question the existence of the physical body of Christ after his historical death. The other tendency is to call into question the existence of the immaterial, incorruptible souls of human beings after death. This, in turn, can be applied to Christ's human death as well. Here we can note that these two developments are intrinsically opposed theologically. However, as I wish to show below, they share a common premise.

Consider, then, the position of Rudolph Bultmann, who gives clear voice to the first tendency indicated. Bultmann is famously skeptical about the historical physicality of the resurrection of Christ. In an age of electronic light bulbs, it is not possible to believe in a physical resurrection from the dead.[2] His reasons for this critical stance are based on two distinct but interrelated premises. The first prem-

---

1. See on this subject the helpful study of Bryan Kromholtz, *On the Last Day: The Time of the Resurrection of the Dead according to Thomas Aquinas* (Fribourg: Academic Press Fribourg, 2010), especially chapter 1. I am greatly indebted to Fr. Kromholtz for help and inspiration in thinking about the subject matter of this chapter.

2. See the 1941 essay by Rudolph Bultmann, "New Testament and Mythology," in *New Testament and Theology and Other Basic Writings*, ed. and trans. S. Ogden (Philadelphia: Fortress, 1984), 4: "We cannot use electric lights and radios and, in the event of illness, avail ourselves of modern medical and clinical means and at the same time believe in the spirit and wonder world of the New Testament." The retort of René Girard is pertinent: "Bultmann found it impossible to believe in the resurrection in the age of the automobile and electricity. He gives the impression of conforming to the contemporary mob that believes only in technology, the real visible power in our world. I do not. I find electricity very useful and impressive, but I do not worship it" (*The Girard Reader*, ed. J. G. Williams [New York: Herder and Herder, 2004], 280).

ise is that reasonable people who have taken account of the intellectual consequences of the scientific revolution can recognize clearly the non-intelligibility and seeming irrationality of belief in miracles. In modernity such beliefs must be left behind. Bultmann was trained in the neo-Kantianism of Marburg and in consistency with this philosophical tradition, he was theoretically disposed to the exclusion of appeal to the miraculous on the *a priori* grounds of philosophical reason alone. Transcendental reason can perceive clearly that in our construal of categorical experience in "causal" terms, there is never sufficient warrant for belief in divine interventions that would interrupt the ordinary order of nature as we regularly experience it. In fact, appeals to the miraculous are inherently unintelligible.[3]

In addition, however, Bultmann also maintained his presupposition based on a theological premise. What is important in the New Testament is not the resurrection of the body but the existential stance of faith that is given to the believer who follows Christ. Bultmann's modern skepticism, then, is not meant to render the New Testament proclamation of the resurrection irrelevant, but quite the opposite. For based on his philosophical premise we can now approach the New Testament in modernity with a clearer vision, seeking to rediscover the deeper meaning of the text underneath the mythology in which it is encoded.

Here Bultmann introduces a modernized version of Luther's core theological principle: justification occurs by way of faith alone. The idea is now reinterpreted, however, in a contemporary existentialist context. What inspired the early Christian movement was the existential faith of Christ in the face of death. The apostles then "encoded" this idea in the Semitic language of resurrection, a mythological form of symbolism. We must demythologize the claim: it is an expression in sensible representational terms of the idea of religious authenticity in the face of death. This authenticity is made possible through faith alone.[4]

What remains of the "history" of the resurrection, then? The event of Jesus's death makes available to the human race a distinctly Christian form of existential faith that transcends the domain of pure rea-

3. So Kant argues in *Religion within the Boundaries of Mere Reason*, 6:84–89, 129.
4. See, for example, the argument in *Jesus Christ and Mythology* (London: Prentice Hall, 1997), first published in German in 1927.

son.[5] Immanuel Kant was right to interiorize Christian mysteries and to see them as outward symbols of inward ethical stances. The working of pure reason alone, however, does not offer us comprehensive solutions for how we are to live meaningfully in the face of realities like guilt, death, finitude, and human suffering. Christian faith, therefore, invites us into a radical confidence in God that extends beyond the domain of natural reason as such. Such saving faith is oriented toward belief in the love of God and his mercy, even in the face of our being-unto-death.[6] Bultmann's theology assimilates many anthropological themes from Kant and Heidegger, then, but at base the theological pattern of reflection resembles that of Schleiermacher. The moral example of Jesus in the face of death and human suffering provides the modern person with an ethically significant religious understanding of reality. This is the heart of the Gospel "underneath" the symbolic apparatus of resurrection-dogma.

Bultmann's theology of the resurrection of Christ clearly reinterprets that event in view of a uniquely inward turn, and away from any sense of a physical supernatural occurrence. However, the theologians who react against his position generally have moved toward the opposite extreme: they emphasize physicality to the exclusion of the spiritual soul. Consider in this respect the positions of Wolfhart Pannenberg, Jürgen Moltmann, Karl Rahner, and Hans Urs von Balthasar. All of these figures affirm unambiguously the historical and physical event of the resurrection of Christ over against Bultmann.[7] For each of them, however, the mystery of human death and resurrection con-

5. See the suggestive analysis of the structure of faith in Paul's theology in Bultmann's *The Theology of the New Testament*, trans. K. Grobel, 2 vols. (New York: Charles Scribner's Sons, 1955), 1:314–24.

6. For Bultmann, Martin Heidegger's anthropology offers us a helpful theoretical content for what Christian theology should seek to preach in an age of anxiety: that human beings have a capacity for faith in God and love for others even in the face of the facticity of our death and finitude. On the likeness of Heidegger and Bultmann, see S. J. McGrath, *The Early Heidegger and Medieval Philosophy: Phenomenology for the Godforsaken* (Washington, D.C.: The Catholic University of America, 2006), chapter 7.

7. On the resurrection in the work of each of these thinkers, see in particular Karl Rahner, "The Intermediate State," in *Theological Investigations*, trans. M. Kohl (New York: Crossroad, 1981), 17:114–24, and *Foundations of Christian Faith*, 431–47; Balthasar, *Theo-Drama*, 5:323–69; Wolfhart Pannenberg, *Systematic Theology*, trans. G. Bromiley (Grand Rapids, Mich.: Eerdmans, 1998), 3:555–80; Jürgen Moltmann, *The Coming of God: Christian Eschatology*, trans. M. Kohl (Philadelphia: Fortress, 1996), 47–128.

cerns the whole being of man, both in Jesus and in us. In death, there is the substantial corruption of body and soul. In resurrection, there is a substantial re-creation of the whole. Consequently, the problem in traditional Christian teaching does not concern the physical resurrection of the body. Rather, it is located in the doctrine of the immaterial soul and the "interim state" between death and resurrection. As I have noted in the previous chapter, classical theology insists that Christ has an immaterial soul that persists in being after death, as do we. Why should these thinkers take issue with this teaching?

The primary reason is theological. Twentieth-century theologians have typically questioned the existence of an immaterial soul in the human person based upon the historical premise that the idea is of uniquely Greco-Roman derivation. Consequently, it is a teaching wholly alien to the biblical revelation as such.[8] A renewed modern sensitivity to this fact requires of us, then, a de-Hellenization of the classical theological position. We must challenge on biblical grounds this questionable pagan philosophical premise.[9] While Greek conceptions of the human person typically divide the human being in an artificially dualistic fashion, the Old and New Testaments stress the unity of the whole person. In death, the whole person dies. The mystery of the resurrection is concerned with the subsistence of the entire personal subject, and so the mystery of Christ's resurrection must be understood without recourse to a strong ontologically dualistic conception of the body and the soul. In the words of Rahner, "From the perspective of a genuine anthropology of the concrete person, in this question we are neither justified nor obliged to split man into two 'components' and to affirm this definitive validity only for one of them. Our question about man's definitive validity is completely identical with [i.e., reducible to] the question of his resurrection, whether the Greek and platonic tradition in church teaching sees this clearly or not."[10]

8. Particularly influential in modern theological conversation was Oscar Cullmann, *Immortality of the Soul or Resurrection from the Dead? The Witness of the New Testament* (London: Epworth, 1958). Correspondingly we see an attempt at a thoroughgoing Christological reinterpretation of the possibility of immortality. See Balthasar, *Theo-Drama*, 5:339–46; Moltmann, *The Coming of God*, 58–77.

9. See, for example, Rahner, *Foundations of Christian Faith*, 435–36; Pannenberg, *Systematic Theology*, 3:571–73.

10. Rahner, *Foundations of Christian Faith*, 273. Compare Moltmann, *The Coming*

Second, then, there is a tendency in this line of thought to see the interim state of the soul separated from the body as mythological or symbolic in meaning. In modernity, the idea should be subject to radical theological revision. This is the case whether one speaks of the sojourn of Christ unto the realm of the dead on Holy Saturday or the characteristics of the separated souls of human beings in the state of purgatory, hell, or heaven. What happens to the human being happens to him or her as a totality, and thus there is no story of the separated soul after death, prior to resurrection, that is distinct from the story of the body.[11]

Last, then, and most importantly: there is a prevalent trend among both modern Protestant and Catholic thinkers to consider the time of the resurrection as occurring just after one's own human death. The time classically accorded to the "particular judgment" of the soul is thus reinterpreted as the moment in which the human being *in death* rejoins divine eternity and experiences the life of personal resurrection in the presence of God. Rahner, for example, sees the transcendental subject who dies in grace rejoining eternity in Christ through a human act of freedom that transpires in death.

In reality eternity comes to be in time as time's own mature fruit, an eternity which does not really continue on beyond experienced time. Rather eternity subsumes time by being liberated from the time which came to be temporarily so that freedom and something of final and definitive validity can be achieved. Eternity is not an infinitely long mode of pure time, but rather it is a mode of the spiritual freedom which has been exercised in time, and therefore it can be understood only from a correct understanding of spiritual freedom.[12]

---

of God, 75: "The human being lives *wholly*, the *whole* human being dies, God will *wholly* raise the human being."

11. Rahner, *Foundations of Christian Faith*, 266–76, especially 271: "Death marks an end for the whole person. Anyone who simply allows time to 'continue' for man's soul beyond his death so that new time arises gets into insuperable difficulties both in the understanding and in the existentiell actualization of the true finality of man which takes place in death." See also Rahner, "The Intermediate State," 115; Balthasar, *Theo-Drama*, 5:31–32, 250–51, 353. See the helpful study of Balthasar's eschatology on this particular issue by Andrew Hofer, "Balthasar's Eschatology on the Intermediate State. The Question of Knowability," *Logos* 12, no. 3 (Summer 2009): 148–72.

12. Rahner, *Foundations of Christian Faith*, 437; Balthasar, *Theo-Drama*, 5:31–32, 47–48, 352–59; Pannenberg, *Systematic Theology*, 3:573–80, 595–607; Moltmann is more evasive and vague. See *The Coming of God*, 104–10.

This idea of a "death-in-resurrection" seems to presuppose the re-creation of the whole human subject *in grace*, a re-creation that begins in this world through the inward moral determinations of the transcendental subject. We are naturally subject to total corruption, but if we die in grace, the fundamental inclinations of our entire composite person will be sublimated into the new order of the resurrection life. Evidently, this supposes that there can be a fundamental discontinuity between the body that dies in this world and the body that lives anew in the next. In an extreme form, this theory permits logically that Christ himself need not have risen physically from the dead in the same body as the one laid in the tomb, for he could well have been raised in a wholly other spiritual body in the life of the resurrection to come.[13] Whether this way of thinking should be applied to the resurrection of Christ or not, it is indeed applied to the particular deaths of Christians. They are invited even in physical death in this life to enter into the new holistic resurrection of their entire person in the eternal life of the world to come. Evidently, in this case, the duration between the particular judgment and the general judgment is evacuated, and the resurrection of human persons transferred from a stage in this world at the end of time to a new spiritual creation outside the boundaries of our physical and temporal sphere.[14]

The thinkers mentioned above insist that their views are primarily biblical rather than philosophical in origin, but can this be affirmed without difficulty? After all, the New Testament does clearly assert

13. Karl Rahner famously posited that the assumption of the Virgin Mary might be considered in light of resurrection-in-death theory as archetypal of that which transpires for *all* Christians at death (Rahner, "The Intermediate State," 122). Pannenberg, meanwhile, welcomes the ecumenical possibilities that this "assimilation" of the assumption of the Virgin Mary to all other believers would entail (*Systematic Theology*, 3:577n169). However, he also sees that logically such thinking opens the door to an indifference regarding the physical resurrection of Christ, who might in turn also be "assimilated" to such thinking (579n174).

14. Balthasar, *Theo-Drama*, 5:357: "The final Judgment occurs after the death of the individual, which means that, as Karl Rahner puts it so well, it takes place 'along the temporal history of the world' and so coincides 'with the sum of particular judgments undergone by individuals.' Insofar as the individual has to step forth into his particular judgment, which is part of the judgment of the world, acts of faith are required of him, namely hope and fear. These would not arise in the case of a final judgment that was separate from the particular judgment." The essay of Rahner's that is cited approvingly here is "The Intermediate State."

that Christ rose physically from the dead (against Bultmann), but it also clearly alludes to the existence in each human being of an immaterial soul that can exist separated from the body.[15] Therefore there can and must exist an interim state after death, both for Christ and for us (against Rahner, Balthasar, Pannenberg, and Moltmann). The classical tradition is right to consider, then, that the particular judgment of the soul that takes place just after death is distinct from the general resurrection in the eschaton.

If the premise of these thinkers is not really biblical, then where does it come from? One possible answer is that it originates from the same place as Bultmann's philosophical skepticism. That is to say, perhaps the subjacent influence in Rahner and others is the philosophical anthropology of Immanuel Kant. Why should this be the case? Because in Kant we find the strict distinction between the categorical world of empirical experience that is the pure domain of modern "causal" explanations in the modern sciences, and the world of the transcendental subject who is undetermined by the realm of strictly empirical experiences. This methodological dualism, when assimilated into modern German theology, gives rise to a form of ontological dualism. There is the external world of the modern empirical sciences and natural reason, and the internal world of the self which develops in the light of grace. Based on this methodology, what is evacuated is any *philosophical* recognition of spiritual personhood *in the world of empirical appearances.* Nor can one affirm unambiguously *the presence of the miraculous* in the external, physical world. It is difficult to articulate, then, any profound continuity between the physical world as we experience it scientifically in the modern age, and a human spiritual soul that is the form of the body. It is also difficult to articulate any profound continuity between the world as we experience it scientifically, and the physicality of the resurrection.

15. In the New Testament, Lk 16:22, 23:43; Mt 16:26; 2 Cor 5:8; Phil 1:23; Heb 9:27, 12:23. See the study of Fritz Heidler, *Die biblische Lehre von der Unsterblichkeit der Seele: Sterben, Tod, ewiges Leben im Aspekt lutherischer Anthropologie* (Göttingen: Vandenhoeck & Ruprecht, 1983). Wright argues for the (problematic) idea that immortality in the interim state need not repose upon anything innate in the soul that is incorruptible, but he does show both the presence of the doctrine of the interim state in inter-testamental literature and the way that the book of Wisdom transformed Greek conceptions of immortality to accord with a biblical doctrine of particular judgment and universal resurrection. See *The Resurrection of the Son of God,* 140–46, 166–75.

We might state the matter more simply in this way: when things are seen in a Kantian light, there is no philosophical access to the soul, nor is there a way to affirm miracles in the physical world. On that basis, if there is a resurrection at all, it is going to be something radically discontinuous with life in this world. The body will not be a glorified version of this body, but a completely distinct and spiritual one. The soul, likewise, will not be the same soul that we had in this life (a soul about which the Kantian thinker remains agnostic), but rather a completely new creation, about which we know very little.[16]

Consequently, if we wish to assign a transcendent meaning to human existence in light of the resurrection, we have two choices that remain. Either we can abandon ourselves to God in death with the metaphysically agnostic trust that there may be some form of "soul-life" after death. (This is the stance of existential faith we find in Bultmann, and arguably in the late Heidegger.) Or we must posit the enduring reality of human subjectivity after death *only on the precondition of grace*. A re-creation of the human subject takes place by the immediate power of God immediately after death: total death and total resurrection. This can occur through a kind of "death in resurrection" (as we find in Rahner) or through immediate conformity in the eternity of God to the future life of Christ resurrected (as we find in Balthasar, Moltmann, and Pannenberg). In either of these cases, however, there is a problem of discontinuity that emerges between the physical life we lead in this world (known in the order of empirical experiences) and the physical world of the resurrection.

Furthermore, if we adopt the line of thinking undertaken by thinkers like Rahner and Balthasar, problems begin to emerge. First, is there any continuity between subjects who are saved in the economy of salvation? For if death entails substantial corruption of the whole person (body and soul), then if we really do die (which we do), death entails a kind of total cessation of the whole being. In this case, what is the ontological continuity that obtains between the person who dies and the person who is resurrected? There is not a continuity of the soul (because this is corrupted at death). So the new creation of the resurrected person must be a person wholly and substantially distinct from the first person. In order to avoid this prob-

16. I am grateful to Michael Gorman for help in the expression of this argument.

lem, there must be some *intrinsic* principle of human *nature* that remains across the diverse states, before death, in the interim state after
death, until after the resurrection. Otherwise, there is no subject present across the diverse states. Failing the affirmation of a spiritual soul,
it is difficult to see what this intrinsic principle might be.

Second, as Joseph Ratzinger has noted, such theologies raise the
problem of there being any continuity between historical life of the
body in this world, and the redemption of the body in the eschaton.
The body that dies in this world is incidental to the body that is immediately created in Christ in the state of the life to come. The theory under consideration, then, seems to advance a kind of Gnostic
vision of the human body. For if we are each resurrected in and after death in a wholly other spiritual sphere separated from the concrete physical history of our lives in this world, then indeed resurrection is something ultimately alien to our historical physical bodies in
this world and to their historical destiny.[17] In short, our bodies in this
world are not redeemed, and the physical matter of this world is incidental to redemption. How different is this, really, from the teaching
of Bultmann?

Last, by advancing a theory of immediate resurrection, theology
runs the risk of making death something theologically unreal or ontologically ephemeral. This has several consequences. It can trivialize
the tragic character of death, and make the personal, final judgment
of human souls seem unreal or morally empty. By this very measure it
can diminish a sense of personal responsibility for one's salvation and
that of others in the face of death. Meanwhile, such a view of immediate resurrection can discredit Christianity insofar as it may be taken
for a form of wish fulfillment that implicitly seeks to deny the reality
and seeming irrevocability of death.[18]

17. See Joseph Ratzinger, *Eschatology: Death and Eternal Life*, trans. M. Waldstein and A. Nichols (Washington, D.C.: The Catholic University of America Press,
1988), 192–93. The German original was first published in 1977. On the development of
Ratzinger's ideas on this topic see the excellent study by Patrick James Fletcher, "Resurrection and Platonic Dualism: Joseph Ratzinger's Augustinianism" (PhD Diss., 2011,
The Catholic University of America.)

18. *Eschatology*, 107–12, 192, 267. Ratzinger notes that this theology of death is also
excessively individualist, excluding particular human beings from a destiny united to
those now living and to the physical world we abide in now, and the culmination of the
history of that world. In that sense it is insufficiently ecclesial (see 172–76).

What we can conclude thus far, then, is that Christology and theological anthropology are closely bound up with one another. If our Christological reflections on the resurrection are excessively docetic, then this will affect intimately our reflections in theological anthropology and eschatology. The inverse is also the case. What we take a human being to be now and in the eschaton affects our reasoning about Christ raised from the dead. When we begin to examine modern theologies of the resurrection, then, we must pay attention to the philosophical ideas that they presuppose. Problematic philosophical premises can lead to a kind of Christological "extrinsicism" in theology. Why is this the case? If we adopt into our theology a philosophical anthropology that makes *the immaterial dimension of reality impossible to understand rationally*, the supernatural character of Christ's physical resurrection appears as something *wholly extrinsic and unintelligible* to the natural world as we ordinarily encounter it.

This occurs in one way if we deny the capacity of God to act supernaturally in the material world and so relegate the mystery of the resurrection to a purely inward, private sphere. Jesus's physical resurrection has no place in our uniquely modern scientific understanding of the physical world. His mystery is entirely alien to modern rationality. Such extrinsicism arises in another way when our philosophy admits no intelligible notion of an immaterial soul separated from the body. In this case, we cannot conceive of any intermediate state of the soul prior to resurrection. Consequently, if we are to affirm the mystery of the resurrection, we must posit the immediate re-creation of human beings who die (including perhaps Christ himself) in a wholly other physical state that has only the most ambiguous continuity with our own physicality and history in this world. Christian theology has good reason to avoid both these forms of extrinsicism. How, then, might we rightly align Christology and theological anthropology, philosophical realism, and Christology? In search of answers to these questions I will now turn to the thought of Aquinas.

AQUINAS ON
HYLOMORPHISM, HUMAN DEATH,
AND RESURRECTION

Up to this point I have made two basic methodological claims: (1) Christology and human anthropology are deeply interconnected in any rightly articulated theology of the resurrection, and (2) theological anthropology must make some overt use of philosophical study of the human person. In the twentieth century it was Joseph Ratzinger in particular who underscored these points in his aforementioned treatment of eschatology. In particular, Ratzinger saw that it is Aquinas who, historically, was able to draw the necessary *philosophical* conclusions about human anthropology from a consideration of the physical resurrection of Jesus Christ. That is to say, Aquinas purposefully interpreted the hylomorphic account of the human person he received from Aristotle in order to correlate this philosophical vision of human nature with the mystery of the resurrection from the dead. His is an example not only of faith seeking understanding, but also of metaphysical understanding that is inherently open to the truth of the Catholic faith.

Where does this method of correlation occur in particular? As Ratzinger saw, it is by means of two interrelated notions. The first is that of the spiritual soul of man as the form of the body.[19] This is an idea that Aquinas inherited from Aristotle and employed against some of the dualistic leanings of the Augustinian theology of his age.[20] Aristotle's idea that the soul is the determinate form of the organic body is itself philosophically defensible and sound, but it is also theologically advantageous.[21] Aquinas saw rightly that it helps to safe-

---

19. Ratzinger, *Eschatology*, 148–50, 178–80.

20. *In de Anima* II, lec. 1; ST I, q. 75, a. 1; SCG II, c. 65.

21. Ratzinger, *Eschatology*, 178–79: "The decisive step was the new understanding of the soul which Thomas Aquinas achieved through his daring transformation of the Aristotelian anthropology.... In Thomas' interpretation of the formula *anima forma corporis*, both soul and body are realities only thanks to each other and as oriented toward each other. Though they are not identical, they are nevertheless one; and as one, they constitute the single human being.... This insight carries with it a two-fold consequence of a remarkable sort. First, the soul can never completely leave behind its relationship with matter.... If it belongs to the very essence of the soul to be the form of the body then its ordination to matter is inescapable.... What thus emerges is an anthropological logic

guard biblical realism regarding the inherent goodness of the body. The human person was created for embodied, physical life such that the soul is not meant to exist apart from the body. Man as a soul-body composite is a holistic, singular entity.[22] The soul-body composite is one concrete substance, not two. In short, then, the body is integral to our plenary human identity.

The second idea is that the soul as form of the body is intrinsically spiritual and incorruptible, not naturally subject to annihilation at death. Aquinas develops this idea through a series of Aristotelian-inspired arguments. He begins by demonstrating that human operations of intellect and will are inherently immaterial in character.[23] These operations are accidents of a human rational animal, but in the powers of the soul, they stem from the soul itself as the form giving determination to human life in the body.[24] Therefore, these operations show us that the soul must be at root immaterial in kind. If this is the case, then the spiritual soul of the human being is not subject to material corruption but must be "subsistent" in a way that the souls of other animals are not.[25] The spiritual soul of the human being subsists after death. The reason that this anthropology is significant is that it invites us through the channel of a realistic philosophical anthropology to a particular form of Christian realism concerning the eschatological destiny of the human being. This is true for a number of reasons.

First, Aquinas's notion that the body is integral to the substantial identity of the human person underscores that the human person is made for life in the body. If this is the case, then death is in some sense natural, for it is natural that a physical body should even-

which shows the resurrection to be a postulate of human existence. Secondly, the material elements from out of which human physiology is constructed received their character of being 'body' only in virtue of being organized and formed by the expressive power of soul…. The individual atoms and molecules do not as such add up to the human being…. Just as the soul is defined in terms of matter, so the living body is wholly defined by reference to the soul."

22. *In de Anima* II, lec. 2–3; ST I, q. 75, a. 4; q. 76, a. 1. See on Aquinas's doctrine of the hylomorphic character of the person, Gilles Emery, "The Unity of Man, Body and Soul, in St. Thomas Aquinas," in *Trinity, Church and the Human Person* (Naples, Fla.: Sapientia Press, 2007), 209–35.

23. ST I, q. 75, a. 2.   24. ST I, q. 75, a. 3.

25. ST I, q. 75, a. 6.

tually be subject to the powers of material disaggregation and should undergo substantial corruption.[26] Nevertheless, *insofar as* the body of man is informed by a spiritual soul that persists in being after death, death is something profoundly unnatural for a human being, as it is deeply unnatural that a human being should suffer the separation of the organic body and the spiritual soul.[27] Philosophically speaking, then, death remains profoundly enigmatic for the human person, and stands before him or her as an insolvable ontological predicament.[28]

Second, then, if the human soul exists after death, this postmortem form of existence cannot constitute a kind of liberation from the human body such that the soul should be more complete without the body.[29] On the contrary, a "mere" soul is not a complete human person. Philosophically speaking, one might be open to the Christian idea of a judgment and/or purification of the soul that transpires after death.[30] However, even if this is the case, the soul remains incomplete without the body. In this sense, Aquinas's realism regarding the hylomorphic unity in man allows us to see, at the very least, the rational fittingness of the resurrection.[31] The biblical claim that there is a resurrection from the dead does not address the human being with an empty or meaningless claim. On the contrary, it addresses a problem at the heart of human existence that remains naturally unresolvable.

26. *De Malo*, q. 5, a. 5. See on this topic of the "natural" and "unnatural" character of death in Aquinas, Bernard Mulcahy, *Aquinas's Notion of Pure Nature and the Christian Integralism of Henri de Lubac: Not Everything is Grace* (New York: Peter Lang, 2011), 50–56.

27. *Comp. Theol.* I, c. 152.

28. Aquinas notes how easy it is for human beings without revelation to be confused by this topic. *In I Cor. XV*, lec. 2, 924: "If the resurrection of the body is denied, it is not easy, indeed it is difficult, to sustain the immortality of the soul. For it is clear that the soul is naturally united to the body and is departed from it, contrary to its nature and *per accidens*. Hence the soul devoid of its body is imperfect, as long as it is without the body. But it is impossible that what is natural and per se be finite and, as it were, nothing; and that which is against nature and *per accidens* be infinite, if the soul endures without the body. And so, the Platonists positing immortality, posited re-incorporation, although this is heretical. Therefore, if the dead do not rise, we will be confident only in this life. In another way, because it is clear that man naturally desires his own salvation; but the soul, since it is part of man's body, is not an entire man, and my soul is not I; hence, although the soul obtains salvation in another life, nevertheless, not I or any man. Furthermore, since man naturally desires salvation even of the body, a natural desire would be frustrated."

29. *Comp. Theol.* I, c. 151.   30. As one finds in Plato's *Phaedo*.

31. SCG IV, c. 81.

Third, Aquinas's vision of the human person allows us to avoid completely the problems associated with the "death-in-resurrection" accounts of eschatology that were examined above. We noted above that these views implicitly raise three questions. First, if there is substantial corruption of the whole person at death and substantial re-creation of the whole person in the life of the resurrection that follows afterward, how is there a true ontological continuity of the one personal subject in both these states? Second, how is it that there is continuity between our physical life in the body *in this world* and the resurrected life of the body in the next? Is it the same body? Third, what about the interim state of the human soul? Is it not central to the mystery of the Christian faith that we should prepare for personal judgment and that we should pray for the souls of those who die before us?

In Aquinas's account, however, these problems do not arise. Rather, the continuity of the human subject is maintained even in and through death by the continued existence of the subsistent soul of the human person. Certainly the soul is not to be identified with the whole composite human person. However, the soul of the human person is the same, ontologically, before death, afterward, and in the life of the resurrection. Given that the soul is the form of the human body *both before death and after the resurrection from the dead*, it is *formally* the same personal being who exists in both states. The same hylomorphic person is an embodied spirit both prior to death and in the resurrection from the dead, albeit in two very different states.

In Aquinas's reading of biblical anthropology, then, the enduring reality of the spiritual soul is not an obstacle to the biblically-based belief in the physical resurrection from the dead. On the contrary, it is in its own way the foundation for and presupposition of this teaching. Precisely because the soul of the human being does subsist after death, there is a hypostatic substrate who remains in need of embodied life. This is the soul of a human person in whom the "history" of life, death, and resurrection can occur. The resurrection of the body occurs for "someone" who first existed as a complete human being, and then suffered the separation of body and soul (continuing to exist as a "mere" soul), and who is finally resurrected from the dead as a complete human being with a glorified body and soul.

This account allows us, in turn, to maintain a realism about the continuity between embodied life in this world and in the physical life of the resurrection. Because the soul subsists in the interim state, we are not required to posit an immediate resurrection apart from the physical body of this world. Rather, the souls of those who die undergo immediate personal judgment, and either damnation or purification and beatitude, in view of the eventual eschatological re-creation of *this same physical world* that we now inhabit.[32] The story of the resurrection is a story of the redemption of our physical world and not the story of the creation of a wholly other, alternative world. By this same measure, it is opportune to prepare for death in view of the judgment of one's individual soul, just as it is appropriate to pray for the dead and to invoke the definitive coming of Christ (Rev 2:20) in view of the general resurrection from the dead. Aquinas's account offers metaphysical warrant for the traditional practices and beliefs of the Christian liturgy.

THE ONTOLOGY OF CHRIST RESURRECTED: THE NEW ADAM AND THE SON OF GOD

In the first section of this chapter I have argued that Kantian philosophical anthropology has had a problematic influence on modern theological discussion of Christ's resurrection from the dead. By way of contrast, then, I have presented the hylomorphism of Aquinas as a particularly helpful form of Christian philosophical reflection on the human person. Aquinas argues that the rational soul continues to exist after death, but that the human body is a constitutive principle of our human identity. His account of human nature allows us to make a great deal of sense, then, of both man's religious expectation of an afterlife (due to his immaterial soul) as well as the specifically Christian hope in the resurrection from the dead. The revelation of the resurrection speaks in a profound way to the reality of our human condition.

In this last section I would like to bring the argument full circle. If it is possible to elaborate a philosophy of the human person that benefits our *theological anthropology*, then it is also possible to employ

---

32. Aquinas maintains that the "new heavens and the new earth" will include human beings and non-living elements, but not plants or brute animals. See SCG IV, c. 97.

that same philosophy to rightly articulate a theology of the resurrection of *Christ*. If a problematic philosophy can lead to a theological extrinsicism where the mystery of Christ appears wholly alien to our modern human anthropology, then a healthy philosophy can allow us to identify a profound harmony that might exist between Christology and authentic human rationality. Christ's resurrection is not identical with ours as he is not a human person, but is the Son of God made man. However, the resurrection of the Son of God reveals to us the perfection of our human nature. It also reveals the perfection of the divine nature of Christ, who is manifest on Easter as being one with the Father and the Holy Spirit. If we take into account Aquinas's hylomorphic vision of human nature we can better understand both these ideas. I will consider in turn, then, these two aspects of the mystery of Christ resurrected from the dead: that of his perfect humanity and that of his perfect divinity. How does a hylomorphic account of the body-soul composition of Christ's *glorified humanity* allow us to understand each of these aspects of his mystery?

The Human Exemplarity of Christ

When Aquinas considers the resurrected human nature of Jesus Christ in the *Summa theologiae*, he does so under the conceptual category of "perfection."[33] The Son of God became a human being who was naturally subject, in his human life, to *imperfections* of both body and soul. He assumed a normal human body likes ours, one which was capable of suffering physical pain and death.[34] He assumed a human soul like ours, capable of experiencing sadness or anger, and subject to emotional grief stemming from experiences of moral evil, public rejection, and betrayal by his disciples.[35] In the life of the resurrection, however, Christ's human nature is now freed from subjection to such imperfections.[36] He is raised from the dead, then, no longer to live simply as one who is like us in all things but sin, but as one who is the perfect exemplar of our human nature transfigured by grace. Christ is most fully alive in the glory of the resurrection.[37]

---

33. ST III, q. 49, a. 6, ad 1; q. 54, aa. 1–2; q. 56, a. 1, ad 3.
34. ST III, q. 14.   35. ST III, q. 15.
36. *In I Cor.* XV, lec. 7, 992–94.
37. ST III, q. 54, a. 2: "Christ's was a glorified body in his resurrection ... because

In what, then, does the perfection of Christ's glorified humanity consist? Here we should not be surprised to see that hylomorphic theory plays an important role in Aquinas's understanding of the ontology of Christ's resurrected state. I have noted above that St. Thomas maintains two important ideas in this regard: (1) the soul is the formal cause of the body, such that man is one substance who is body and soul; and (2) the rational soul of man is immaterial and subsistent. The spiritual powers of the soul (the intellect and will) are expressive, then, of the inward spiritual character of the soul which is the form of the body.

According to Aquinas, the glorification of Christ's body and soul is intelligible in the light of each of these ideas. First, by the power of God, the matter of Christ's body is transformed so as to exist in profound accord with his soul. In the resurrection, the soul remains the form of the body and the body does not cease to be material. The human nature of Christ is preserved, then, and not destroyed. However, the matter of the body is "proportioned" most perfectly to the spiritual life of the soul.[38] That is to say, the glorified human body of Christ is transformed or "spiritualized" in its very materiality, so as to be most ontologically receptive to the soul's spiritual powers and activities.

Aquinas interprets this transformation of the material body by using a standard medieval notation of four characteristics of the resurrected body.[39] We can begin apophatically with an attribute that is defined negatively. In its *impassibility* Christ's resurrected body is no longer subject to physical suffering or to the corruption of death. The hylomorphic unity of the soul-body composite is more perfect, therefore, in the glorified state. Human nature enjoys an ontological stability in Christ that can no longer be diminished by death or pain. To this negatively defined freedom from suffering there corresponds a positive attribute. In its *subtlety* the body of Christ is perfected in its

---

his resurrection was the exemplar and cause of ours, as is stated in 1 Cor. 15:43.... But in the resurrection, the saints will have glorified bodies.... Hence, since the cause is mightier than the effect, and the exemplar than the exemplate; much more glorious, then, was the body of Christ in his resurrection."

38. SCG IV, c. 86, para. 4.

39. SCG IV, c. 86, para. 5; ST III, q. 45, a. 2.

status as the body of a human being who has a spiritual soul. That is to say, the material body of Christ in the resurrection is transformed so as to be most perfectly disposed to the soul as the informing principle. The physical body of Christ is utterly determined from within by the spiritual life so that ontological oppositions or tensions between the body and soul can no longer exist. A profound harmony results, one in which matter provides no resistance to the plenary realization of the spiritual activity of the soul.

This formal perfection in turn has effects. In its *agility*, the body of Christ has no difficulty or labor in movement. In the New Testament accounts of the resurrection, there is something mysterious about the way Christ is able to make himself present physically to other human beings. The spiritual presence of his person is communicated in diverse times and places, adroitly or seemingly effortlessly, always through the medium of his physical presence. Also, in its *clarity* the body of Christ is spiritually luminous. That is to say, the body of Christ by its mere presence communicates, in a mysterious way, the spiritualized quality of his body, as well as the divine identity of Christ as a person. Where the resurrected Christ is physically, people come to recognize his deity.[40]

The second point I noted above was that the soul for Aquinas is immaterial and subsistent. It is endowed with spiritual faculties of intellect and will. Evidently, these faculties are normally exercised in and through the sensate life and actions in the body by way of reasoning and choice-making. We express our spiritual dignity as persons in and through our bodily emotions and actions. The glorification of the human body of Christ, then, is not only affected by the transformation of his material body but also by the ecstatic transformation of his spiritual powers. The glorification of the soul of Christ occurs by way of the beatitude or happiness that is communicated to his human intellect and will, and through them to all the powers of his soul. This spiritual happiness beatifies or enlivens the sensate powers of the body of Christ and gives to his physical life in the body an inward physical peacefulness or repose.

What is the medium through which this beatification of the hu-

40. This is a point I will return to below.

man operations of Christ occurs? I have noted in chapter 5 that Aquinas argues that Christ possesses the beatific vision in the heights of his human intellect even in the midst of his earthly human life. In chapter 7 I argued that this vision is present even throughout the passion and dereliction of Christ. However, as I also noted, Aquinas thinks that Christ possessed the beatific vision in his earthly life only in accordance with a particular dispensation, or in a distinctly economic mode. In this way he did possess a perfect knowledge of the Father's identity and of the divine will, but this knowledge did not necessarily give him any direct consolation in his sensate life or his sensible psychology. Christ could experience simultaneously the peace of his union with the Father, and the aridity and trial of his acute human suffering in the crucifixion.

In the glorified life of Christ, this is no longer the case. Because he is the Word incarnate, Christ as man always possesses the grace of the vision of God, and so his capacity to know and love the Father and the Holy Spirit has a maximal intensity in comparison with all other human beings. In the resurrection, however, this grace takes on a new extension that it did not have in Christ's earthly life. Christ is now transformed in all of his human subjectivity by the influx of beatitude he receives from his spiritual powers. His emotional affectivity, sensate life, and body all experience the transforming effects of a profound spiritual peace and joy that descend from his intellectual vision. Not only does he know and love the Father and the Holy Spirit in the maximal intensity of holiness afforded to his intellect and will, but he also feels and senses the repose of this beatitude in the whole of his composite psychology as man.

Here again, then, we see that the exemplarity of the glory of Christ's humanity is related to the hylomorphic character of human nature. Not only is the matter of the body appropriately proportioned to the spiritual life of the soul, but the ecstatic life of the spiritual soul is felt and expressed in and through the psychological and sensible life of the human body. Aquinas's philosophical realism regarding the unity of the composite human being deeply affects, then, his articulation of the mystery of the resurrection of Christ. It allows him to demonstrate effectively why, if Christ is truly raised from the dead, he is the ontological exemplar of the human race.

The Divinity of Christ and the
Instrumental Causality of His
Resurrected Humanity

Christ in glory is not only the "New Adam," or the exemplar of human redemption. He is also "the Resurrection and the Life" (Jn 11:25). What does it mean that Christ should denote himself as *the* resurrection? When Aquinas comments on this verse from John's Gospel, he notes that Jesus's claim implies an appeal to causality. Christ is claiming to have the power to raise the dead.[41] How is it that the Son as man should have the power to raise others from the dead? Here we encounter the mystery of Christ's instrumental-efficient causality.

For the purposes of our argument, there are three important aspects to this mystery that should be noted. The first concerns the divinity of Christ. Jesus is himself perfect man and so in him we see the initial promise of the re-creation of the human race that is initiated in the historical resurrection of the flesh of Christ. However, his resurrection is not different from our own simply because he was raised first in the order of historical events. Christ is different from other resurrected human beings not only because he is the "first-born from the dead" (Col 1:18) but also because he alone, this particular man raised from the dead, is God. It is the eternal Son who subsists personally in a human nature that has been resurrected and glorified.

Second, then, we should consider what we have noted above regarding the instrumentality of the sacred humanity of Jesus. In Chapters 1 and 5 I have underscored that the human nature of Jesus is the instrument of his person, in and through which he reveals his identity as the Son of God. This is no less true, however, in the resurrection. In his resurrected state, it is the glorified soul-body composite that we have been considering that is the *instrument of the person of the Son.* Consequently, when Christ is said to be "the Resurrection and the Life," this denotes his capacity *as God* to be the cause of the resurrection of the dead. However, it also denotes his activity *as man* in the resurrection as well. The activity by which the resurrected Christ gives life to the world is "theandric": it is the simultaneously coor-

---

41. *In Ioan.* XI, lec. 4, 1516.

dinated action of Christ both in his divinity and his humanity, such that the human action of Christ as man is subordinated instrumentally to his divine action. Christ as man wishes to raise the dead and his prayer or efficacious desire for the resurrection of the dead has an effect in the world because it is conjoined to the activity of his divinity, in the unity of his person. As Aquinas states:

[Christ's resurrection] is the efficient cause [of our resurrection], inasmuch as Christ's humanity, according to which He rose again, is as it were the instrument of His Godhead, and works by Its power. And therefore, just as all other things which Christ did and endured in His humanity are profitable to our salvation through the power of the Godhead, so also is Christ's Resurrection the efficient cause of ours, through the Divine power whose office it is to quicken the dead.... But just as the Resurrection of Christ's body, through its personal union with the Word, is first in point of time, so also is it first in dignity and perfection; as the gloss says on 1 Cor. 15:20, 23. But whatever is most perfect is always the exemplar, which the less perfect copies according to its mode; consequently Christ's Resurrection is the exemplar of ours. And this is necessary, not on the part of Him who rose again, who needs no exemplar, but on the part of them who are raised up, who must be likened to that Resurrection, according to Phil. 3:21: "He will reform the body of our lowness, made like to the body of His glory."[42]

Christ is the "New Adam," then, not only in an exemplary sense (as the perfect man), but also insofar as he is a universal progenitor of the human race in the order of grace. *Christ as man alone can cause the dead to rise, because Christ alone is a man who is God.*

Last, then, the human actions of Christ in the resurrected life are indicative not only of the perfection of his humanity, but also of the perfection of his divinity. They reveal to us that Christ is God. This is the case because the human actions of Christ in glory manifest the power of God that is in him, a power he possesses personally as God. Consider here, for example, the miracles that are worked by Peter and Paul, reported in Acts 3:1–11 and 20:9–12. As Luke depicts them, these actions are accomplished by the power of the glorified Christ, working through the apostles. Let us presuppose the reality of the mystery that Luke indicates. If the resurrected Son works miracles or raises the dead in and through the ministry of Peter or Paul, then these ac-

42. ST I, q. 56, a. 1, ad 3.

tions are expressive of his identity as the Son and of the perfection
of his divinity. The man Jesus, who is raised from the dead, can work
in the world to heal the crippled or raise up the dead, because he has
within himself the power of God.

Simultaneously, we can say that these actions also manifest the
mystery of the Holy Trinity. Why is this the case? It is because the actions of Christ in glory are actions of the Son who is eternally from
the Father, and who with the Father breathes forth the Holy Spirit.
The risen Christ as man can act with the power of God because *as
the Son* he possesses this perfection of the deity *from the Father*, and
with the Holy Spirit. It is not the Father or the Holy Spirit who act *humanly* to raise the dead. This is particular to the Son of God, by virtue
of the hypostatic union. But when the incarnate Son does so, he also
acts *divinely as God*, and his actions as God are always one with those
of the Father and the Holy Spirit. Therefore, the human actions of the
glorified Christ reveal to us not only that Christ is the Son of God.
They also reveal to us the activity of the Father and the Holy Spirit. Through them, we come to know the Father and the Holy Spirit personally. In the instrumental activity of the sacred humanity of
Christ risen from the dead, the work of the Trinity is revealed to the
world. In the agency of the resurrected Christ, then, we come to perceive that he has always been one with the Father and the Holy Spirit
from before the foundation of the world. His divinity is most perfectly manifest.

Why is all of this of significance in relation to the hylomorphic
anthropology that has been discussed above? Here there is a twofold
reason that is quite simple. First, as we noted at length in chapter 1,
the humanity of Christ is united to his person substantially. The Word
subsists in his human nature, both body and soul. Second, the body
and soul of Christ are united in being such that the soul is the form
of the body. The human spiritual powers of Christ's rational soul (his
intellect and will) express themselves in and through his bodily actions and words. This expression flows forth from the composite unity of the body and the soul. If we put these two ideas together we can
conclude that the bodily actions of Christ are expressive of his hypostatic identity. Through the gestures and words of Christ, his personal identity as the Son is made manifest through the instrumentality of

his rational powers. The human flesh of Christ manifests not only the presence in him of human spiritual operations, but also the presence of God who is acting humanly. Consider now what this means for the resurrection of Christ: the flesh of the risen Christ, and his gestures and words in the bodily life of the resurrection, have the power to reveal who he is as God and to reveal his unity with the Father and the Holy Spirit.

Is it not precisely this theological motif that we discover in the resurrection narratives of the Gospels? In John 20:14–17, Mary Magdalene receives a revelation of the presence of the Son of God through his human voice and then attempts to grasp his risen body. His response to her is that she should not touch him, for "I am ascending to my Father and your Father, to my God and your God." The passage of Christ "toward" the Father *in his resurrected flesh* is indicative of his *personal* relation to the Father, and reveals this relation to the church. His actions and gestures in his resurrected flesh reveal that he is the Son. Likewise, he can "breathe" the Holy Spirit upon the apostles (Jn 20:22), revealing in a human gesture of his glorified body that the Spirit proceeds from him personally. When the apostle Thomas touches his hands and his side, he is given the revelation of the divinity of Christ—"My Lord and my God!" (Jn 20:28)—present in the glorified flesh.

Matthew portrays this idea in a similar fashion. After the resurrection, the apostles encounter the glorified Christ on a mountain in the Galilee region. It is when they "see" him alive as man that they fully recognize and worship him as God (Mt 28:16–20). In the resurrection narratives of Luke, Christ can make himself known in conversation with the apostles on the road to Emmaus and in the breaking of the bread (Lk 24:13–32). It is in his physical gestures and words, then, that Christ personally manifests himself as the Son of God in the life of the resurrection.

What we see in all these examples is a common theme. Christ has a human nature like ours, albeit in a transformed state. But he also reveals to us in and through that human nature who he is as God. Our human nature does not take on its essential structure from Christ. Each of us possesses the human nature of "Adam," that which we have inherited from our first human parents in keeping with the original creation of God. This human nature is a composite substance in which the spiritual soul is the form of a material body. Christ did not alter the essential structure of what it means to be human. On the contrary, he assumed a complete human nature identical with ours. However, Christ risen from the dead does manifest in and through his perfect human nature who he is as God, and he does so *in accord with the natural integrity of the human nature he assumed.* His nature is in a more perfect state than ours because of the very profound unity that exists between his risen body and his fully beatified soul, and because his human body is most perfectly expressive of the spiritual operations of his beatified soul. It is precisely *from within* these notes of hylomorphic *human* perfection, however, that the glorified Christ manifests to us his *divine* perfection. The incarnate Word subsists in a glorified human body, and the encounter with him in his risen human flesh is revelatory of his identity as God. He who is risen from the dead is he who is one with the Father and the Holy Spirit from before the foundation of the world. The human body of Christ, then, is not something alien that hinders in us a true spiritual knowledge of God. Rather, it is by faith in the risen flesh of Christ especially that we come to know the true identity of God, as he who has taken on a human nature like ours and revealed himself as the crucified and risen Lord.

CONCLUSION

In a certain respect, the physical resurrection of Jesus Christ is the "Alpha and Omega" of Christian theology. Christian theology takes its origin from reflection on him as a person who is physically alive to die no more. That same reflection occurs in the church *in via* or on pilgrimage toward the eschatological term of Christian existence, a pilgrimage animated by hope in the mystery of the resurrection. Theology is composed, then, "between" two resurrections from the dead—that of Christ and that of ourselves.

The argument of this chapter is that a balanced theology of the resurrection of Christ need not cultivate any dialectical opposition between a Christological account of human nature versus an anthropological construal of the existential significance of the example of

Christ. Following Aquinas, we can agree with Bultmann that Christ is an ontological exemplar, one who illumines uniquely our human condition in the face of death. We must say against him, however, that Jesus is this exemplar precisely due to his glorified life in the resurrection. This includes the fact that Jesus has physically risen from the dead. Following the proponents of "death-in-resurrection" theologies, we might be tempted to see this glorified life as something existing in substantial discontinuity with our physical existence in this world. But the body of Christ that is risen is the same body that died. And so likewise there must be substantial continuity between the bodies of those who die in this world and the life of the resurrection that is to come.

If we follow this view of things, then Christ who is alive in glory speaks to us profoundly in our actual human condition. His redemption is not something wholly alien or extrinsic to us in our current historical existence and our physical need for salvation. On the contrary, Christ is our unique savior because he can raise us physically from the dead. At the same time, the revelation of the resurrection of the Son of God is not something reducible to an "anthropology" or to an idealized portrait of perfect humanity. Christ is alive first and foremost because he is God, and he can raise us from the dead as man because of the divine power that resides in him. His revelation does not turn us toward ourselves or restrict us to life within an immanent horizon of human history. On the contrary, the resurrection of Jesus opens up our temporal history and turns it outward toward the new life of God breaking into the world. This is a divine life that is making all things new. Grace lifts up our gaze to behold the face of the risen Son and to perceive in him the presence of the Father and the Holy Spirit. In Christ risen from the dead we perceive the eternal life of God the Trinity, and we are invited to make it our true and lasting home.

CONCLUSION

The Promise of Thomism

CONCLUSION

———— : ————

The Promise of Thomism

Why Christology Is Not Primarily
a Historical Science

In the wake of the Second Vatican Council, Catholic theology embraced a primarily historical model of theological exploration. Topics such as Christology, the eucharist, and grace were treated by way of a chronological investigation: from the New Testament to the fathers, from the scholastic age to the early modern debates, terminating in a consideration of the *status quaestionis* of the subject within modern and contemporary theology. This approach represents the still standard model one encounters in virtually any theology textbook in our time. Chronology determines content.

Yet this is an inherently ambiguous approach, for at least two reasons. The first is that the method of inquiry itself provides no inherent standard by which to judge the worth of the peregrinations of historical developments. By what perduring standard is one to identify the criteria of theological truth accumulated over time? Certainly if one has a confidence in the necessarily progressive character of human thought, then it is impossible for the essential to be forgotten. Rather, the journey of theological development, no matter how winding or even dialectical and conflictual, is always marked in the end by the inevitable triumph of insight and homogeneous progress.

However, even if this were the case (and it is not) then we would still have to decide by what perduring standard we identify the marks of continuity in doctrinal truth over time. That is to say, we would have to "narrate a story" in which some essential truth becomes manifest and develops. Yet the identification of such essential truths and the study of their content are not procured for us by the historical method alone. We cannot say by studying the history of Christological opinions, for example, whether Athanasius is more in keeping with the truth on a given point than Barth, Schleiermacher, or Arius.

This ambiguity leads to a second problem—the problem of the historical narrator. The truth, indeed, may be sought in and through a developmental history of opinions. But the arrangement of these opinions, their order and the *evaluation* come from the writer or narrator, who is in turn informed by a set of principles that (while perhaps true) are not simply "read off the page" of history. Why is the patristic Christological account of Aloys Grillmeier superior to that of Maurice Wiles (who defended neo-Arian theology as the "minority report" in ancient Christology)?[1] Is it because Grillmeier presupposes the truth of the ancient conciliar definitions (Chalcedon above all) and their conformity with New Testament thought? Is it because he seeks to demonstrate the developmental homogeneity of the ancient Christian faith in the divinity of Christ throughout the course of seven centuries? Surely it is for these reasons. But just because this is the case, we can see that his intellectual effort in the systematic study of texts, coordinating them to one another plausibly in historical terms alone, is also an effort made in subordination to a superior science, a *sacra doctrina*.[2] And this science is informed by supernatural faith in the teachings of scripture and the Catholic church. It is a science of Christ.

The concluding thesis of this book is the following: the study of Christology is not first and foremost historical (even if it habitually makes use of detailed historical knowledge and argumentation).

1. See Grillmeier, *Christ in Christian Tradition. Volume One. From the Apostolic Age to Chalcedon (451)*, as compared with Maurice Wiles, *The Remaking of Christian Doctrine* (Philadelphia: Westminster Press, 1978) and *Archetypal Heresy: Arianism through the Centuries* (Oxford: Oxford University Press, 2001).

2. Aquinas, ST I, q. 1.

Rather, the study of theology in general and Christology in particular, is structural or essential. Christology studies the structure of a mystery: the mystery of the incarnation, the birth, life, death and resurrection of Christ, his grace and its effects, and the eschatological hope arising from his person and activity. Is this itself not a "historical mystery"? Of course. But it is above all a mystery by which one interprets the meaning of history in light of what unifies and transcends historical existence. Christology, in other words, is meant to communicate to us the identity of God, the author of history, and the identity of what it means to be human not only within time, but also in view of eternal life. Outside of this scientific norm, Christology as a true theological science ceases to be. Similarly, wherever true Christological claims are made within historical studies this science is implicitly present.

I would like to make this argument in three stages. The first is by recourse to the example of Eduard Schillebeeckx and his postmetaphysical hermeneutical Christology. Examination of his project helps to underscore the problems that frequently afflict Christological thinking today. The second stage is by consideration of the implicitly ontological foundations of hermeneutics, even on a philosophical level, as presented by Thomas Aquinas. Third, I will consider Christology as a science (in what sense?) and as a contemplative wisdom, with a teleological horizon that opens to union with God by grace. The goal of this concluding chapter is meant to be commensurate with the goal of this book at large: to show that there exist resources in the Thomistic and scholastic tradition that invite us to treat theological thinking "otherwise" than in the models that currently predominate. Like Wittgenstein's proverbial ladder, our dialogue with modern Christology might end with the suggestion that we kick away from the historical starting points that led us here, not so as to reject the centrality of historical learning, but so as to embrace ultimately a different kind of systematic reflection on the mystery of Christ as God and man. Theology, if it would recover its own inherent internal identity as a science, needs to rethink the possibility of a scholastic approach, one not disinterested in the most subtle indications of historical learning but above all marked (in and through such considerations) by the study of the intrinsic essence and content of the mystery of Christ.

THE ARCHEOLOGICAL
VULNERABILITY OF POST-METAPHYSICAL
CHRISTOLOGY

Principles of Hermeneutics in
Schillebeeckx's Theology

The mature Christology of Eduard Schillebeeckx (1914–2009) is represented by his well-known twofold work, *Jesus* and *Christ*.[3] These large tomes today are considered methodologically anachronistic volumes, marked by the tenor of a past epoch. Nevertheless, there are orientations in Schillebeeckx's thought that open up into contemporary theological vistas in important ways.

As a means of understanding Schillebeeckx's methodology in Christology, let us consider briefly four key hermeneutical principles that he employs. Three of these principles were developed in the earlier theological work of Schillebeeckx. These can be noted by way of a series of brief historical considerations. The fourth principle can be illustrated by examination of the works *Jesus* and *Christ* themselves.

The Truth of Doctrine is Historically Situated

As a student in the early twentieth century, Schillebeeckx received training in traditional Dominican interpretations of Aquinas. However, he was not initially a neo-Thomist, if by that we mean someone particularly indebted to Aristotelian philosophical interpretations of Aquinas. Rather, from his earliest student days, Schillebeeckx was initiated into the study of phenomenology by Dominicus De Petter in the Dominican house in Ghent. De Petter placed significant emphasis on the importance of descriptive accounts of experience and the contemporary theme of personalism. His philosophy therefore highlighted the importance of the development of human beings in and through historical time.[4]

In 1946, Schillebeeckx moved to the Saulchoir, outside of Paris,

---

3. Eduard Schillebeeckx, *Jesus: An Experiment in Christology*, trans. H. Hoskins (New York: Seabury, 1979); *Christ: The Experience of Jesus as Lord*, trans. J. Bowden (New York: Seabury, 1980).

4. See the analysis of Fergus Kerr, *Twentieth-Century Catholic Theologians*, 52–55.

and remained there until 1952, when he defended his doctoral thesis. During this period, he was immersed in the practices of *la nouvelle théologie*, and was deeply inspired by the theological examples of
Yves Congar and Marie-Dominique Chenu. Schillebeeckx successful-
ly mastered the practice of the creative retrieval of historical theological texts, which he learned under their tutelage. Through inspiration
from Chenu in particular, Schillebeeckx saw that there were ways to
integrate or interrelate the historical reconstitution of Aquinas's work
with the historically actual resituating of Catholic thought. In other
words, as a historian one may return to hitherto under-studied elements of Aquinas's own thought, casting them in a new light, while
seeking to appropriate them for today in ways that speak to contemporary philosophical, political, and cultural concerns. Historical theology acts, then, as a resource for thematic changes in contemporary
theology and in the ongoing life of the church.

In keeping with this methodological approach, there were a set
of epistemological and ontological claims that Schillebeeckx inherited from Chenu as well. From his earliest writings, Chenu had maintained that the dogmas of faith are cast within the context of a giv-
en historical milieu, and so can only be considered and interpreted
within that history. He also affirmed that the dynamic mystery of supernatural faith itself is historical in some real sense.[5] On one level, it
is our understanding of the essential mystery of faith that is open to
a diversity of forms of expression through time. On another level, it
is *the mystery itself* that is historical, transcending all fixed or essential
determinations.

Chenu was to make this idea quite clear in an essay written after Vatican II. In it he took special exception to the early twentieth-
century scholastic theology that he was taught by Garrigou-Lagrange
and others of the "Roman school":

The Word of God both creates history and is interpreted within history.…
Understanding of the unity of Word and event, in which the truth occurs, is

5. See Marie-Dominique Chenu, "Raison psychologique du développement du
dogme," 44–51. Eventually, this idea brought Chenu's work under scrutiny from the
Holy Office in the 1940s. He was required to affirm under oath the "immutable truth of
Catholic dogmas." See Kerr, *Twentieth-Century Catholic Theologians*, 19.

a fundamental point of departure for theology.... Biblical truth ... in keeping with the Hebraic mentality, does not directly confront that which is, but that which happens, that which one experiences.... Greek thought develops through a reflection on the substance of beings, and terminates in a philosophy of immutability and permanence. It ignores that which is proper to biblical thought: the dimension of time.... One must not establish a division between the act of the divine Word and the formulas in which it takes shape and which give it its intellectual content. But one also must not cede to a facile concordism in which the historical and existential character of the truth of salvation dissolves, and where the Word of God is absorbed into and neutralized by a theological "science." ... The truth is a radically Christological concept. It should not be treated as the manifestation of the eternal essence of things.[6]

The expressions employed here are admittedly somewhat ambiguous. On the one hand, Chenu seems to be suggesting that there is no form of perennial expression of Christian thought that endures down through time. On the other hand, he seems to be suggesting that nothing that exists can be perceived to exist except in and through a process of historicity and developmental becoming. In this case, temporality and change would extend not only into the farthest reaches of the being of man but also into the plenary structure of supernatural mystery, as well as the identity of God himself. Hermeneutics in this sense entails a kind of metaphysical study of history, or a historicization of metaphysics. As we shall see, such ideas are articulated forcefully by the later Schillebeeckx.

The Church Mediates the Discernment of Human Truth through Historical Process

A second related idea is that the church is the central mediating presence of humanity's ongoing temporal conversation about the truth. We can see an initial venue for this hermeneutical principle in Schillebeeckx's early work, his thesis, *De sacramentele Heilseconomie*, published in the year 1952.[7] It is a lengthy treatise (some seven hun-

6. Marie-Dominique Chenu, in the above-cited "Vérité évangélique et métaphysique wolfienne à Vatican II" (637–38).

7. Eduard Schilllebeeckx, *De sacramentele Heilseconomie* (Antwerp: H. Nelissen, 1952). French translation by Y. van der Have, *L'économie sacramentelle du salut* (Fribourg: Academic Press Fribourg, 2004).

dred pages) of analysis of the concept of sacramentality from the fathers to Aquinas, with a view toward contemporary theological applicability. The book is concerned in particular to show three things: first, that the ancient notion of sacramentality is broader than the narrow definition adopted by the Council of Trent.[8] Prior to Trent, one finds in western theology a richer conception of sacramentality that can apply to the mystery of the church and the unfolding of the divine economy through time, as well as to the sacramental gestures of the church as such. Second, then, a sacramental theology construed in this broader sense can portray all of human life and historical existence as the locus of sacramental encounter with God.[9] There is a divine-human reconciliation that is unfolding throughout human history. Third, this process becomes most visibly manifest in the work of Christ and in his visible sacramental agency. Consequently, the spiritual history of humanity finds its focal point of development within the visible life of the church.[10] To state things in a Hegelian form: the church is the cultural mediator of the dialectic of spirit within history. God makes most manifest in the church what he is doing already, always *sacramentally* in his general work of grace, both in the cosmos and in human history.

What we have in this work, then, is a complex rereading of Aquinas and the fathers in view of a modern theology of history, one in which ecclesiological and modern humanist themes blend together under the aegis of a historical and semantic treatment of "sacramentality." It is difficult to overstate the ambition and scope of this creative reinterpretation of the ancient and medieval theological tradition.

Hermeneutics in a Post-Metaphysical Key

This third point is especially significant. Never an official *Peritus* at the Second Vatican Council, Schillebeeckx was influential in discussions outside the conclaves and contributed to the schema that would become *Gaudium et Spes*, a document seeking to provide a theologically contextualized vision of historical existence, humanism,

8. *L'économie sacramentelle du salut*, 21–154.
9. Ibid., 451–531.
10. Ibid., 533–43 (see especially 533–34, 542–43).

and the church, one seemingly suited to our own age. He was a strident proponent of decentralization of Roman authority, even at the time of the Council.[11] Nevertheless, it is clear that even as late as 1966, the year after the Council concluded, Schillebeeckx remained deeply indebted to theological principles he inherited from his Thomistic formation. His two-volume collection of essays in fundamental theology, *Openbaring en Theologie* (Revelation and Theology), which was published in that year, upholds the idea that dogmatic enunciations communicate perennial truths, even while the book also engages with hermeneutical theory and phenomenology.[12] In 1968, however, we begin to see something new emerge in Schillebeeckx's thought, an inflection that developed just on the cusp of the Council's conclusion.

In 1967 Schillebeeckx's thought began to change, largely in dialogue with hermeneutical and post-metaphysical theory. He was reading the work of Heidegger avidly, but also Bultmann, Gadamer, Dilthey, and Ricoeur. It was at this time that he composed his famously controversial work *The Eucharist*, in which he more or less overtly proposed the necessity of a post-metaphysical, semantic, and phenomenological interpretation of the real presence of Christ in the eucharist.[13] In this same year, Schillebeeckx also prepared a series of conferences for a lecture tour in North America, which he later published in 1968 under the title *God the Future of Man*. The first essay in this volume, "Towards a Catholic Use of Hermeneutics," is especially helpful for understanding the methodological underpinnings of what was to unfold, not only in the book on the eucharist, but also in the subsequent volumes on Christology and in his later work on the church.[14]

11. See *The Council Notes of Edward Schillebeeckx 1962–1963*, ed. K. Schelkens (Leuven: Peeters, 2011), 36.

12. Edward Schillebeeckx, *Revelation and Theology*, 2 vols., trans. N. Smith (New York: Sheed and Ward, 1968).

13. Eduard Schillebeeckx, *The Eucharist*, trans. N. Smith (New York: Sheed and Ward, 1968); see especially 149–50. The Dutch original of the book was published one year before in 1967. This theology of "trans-signification" rather than transubstantiation had already come under overt criticism by Pope Paul VI in the 1965 encyclical *Mysterium Fidei*. Interestingly, the Roman pontiff had underscored that the key issue at stake was the preservation of an ontological interpretation of the change of bread and wine into the body and blood of Christ (see especially para. 46).

14. This work is found in English in Edward Schillebeeckx, *God and the Future of*

The essay essentially seeks to walk a line between structuralism, which would affirm that all truth claims are historically contingent constructs without enduring value, and a "pre-Heideggerian" essentialism, that would argue that there are perennial truth claims that endure down through time.[15] Catholic tradition seems to offer the perfectly balanced dynamic that advances between the two extremes, and so again, the church comes to the rescue of an intellectually disoriented humanity, offering in the form of her own practice the resolution of an as yet unsolved spiritual dilemma. For the Catholic intellectual tradition claims that we only know reality in the running course of history and may not "rise above" it to peer at immutable, non-historical truths. At the same time, we can glean authentic truths from past texts and traditions. We can only do so, however, by reappropriating what we grasp as true *within our own context* with its own new, previously unforeseen circumstances.[16] Truth is identified, then, uniquely within an ongoing hermeneutical process and lived context of praxis.

The issue this argument raises, however, is that of the real possibility of truth claims that continue down through time. Can we simply know the same truth as those who come before us? Can we transmit it perennially from age to age? Here Schillebeeckx, in the end of his presentation, falters to one side in a seemingly decisive sense:

The objective *perspective* of faith, which is not in itself thematic and cannot be conceptualized, is thus to some extent brought to light and expressed *in* reinterpretation as it were by a circuitous route (via the interpretative aspect of the act of faith), with the consequence that it becomes a power for action which is directed towards the future.... There are no formulae of faith which are, as formulae, enduringly valid, capable of transmitting the living faith to men of all ages. Is this relativism? Not at all. It is what is meant by the identity of the faith with itself *in history*. For we do not possess the absolute which acts as an inner norm to our faith in an absolute way; we possess it only within our historical situation.[17]

Man, trans. N. Smith (New York: Sheed and Ward, 1968), 1–50. See the study by Leo Scheffczyk, "Christology in the Context of Experience," *The Thomist* 48 (1984): 383–408, on this change in Schillebeeckx's theological method. For Schillebeeckx's later ecclesiology, see *Church: The Human Story of God*, translated by J. Bowden (New York: Crossroad, 1990).

15. *God and the Future of Man*, 24–28.   16. Ibid., 38–42.

17. Ibid., 39–40.

The quest to speak of truths of Christian doctrine down through time can only be accomplished by the substantial or formal re-adaptation of those truths, so that the significations of bygone ages are now re-read in the categories and forms of expression of a more recent epoch.

Ethical Praxis and Historical Experience Lead to
Temporal Speculative Schematics

Schillebeeckx develops the signal illustration of his post-metaphysical theological project in his Christological volumes, *Jesus* and *Christ*, both of which followed on the heels of the important essay mentioned above. Commentators on the first of these works typically seek to evaluate to what extent the author succeeds in appropriating the German exegetical analysis of his epoch, an analysis informed by the Bultmannian penchant for form-criticism.[18] In this respect, Schillebeeckx's diligent intellectual effort in re-specialization in a domain in which he originally was not trained was bold. But it was also untimely. For modern biblical exegesis has achieved enduring insights based upon highly probable "scientific" historical argumentations. But it also depends to a great degree on conjecture, the philosophical and theological "pre-understanding" of the cultures in which it is elaborated, and to be more blunt, upon the purely conventional scholarly trends of academics. These latter live in perpetual tension politically: they must seek mutual approbation in a university system that rewards conformity by way of peer evaluation, but at the same time, scholars in the humanities must also produce incessantly "creative" or original material in order to reinvent their disciplines by a process that mimics artificially the idea of progress found in the positive sciences. What results is a collective culture of convention that is perpetually shifting and inherently unstable. Schillebeeckx sought to enter into the full fray of the exegetical age of modern university theology, but remained academically naïve when it came to the realization that this culture is intrinsically unstable, and that the "conclusions" of his massive exegetical effort would be practically irrelevant within ten years of their publication.

18. See the cursory but helpful remarks on Schillebeeckx by Wright in *Jesus and the Victory of God*, 21–27.

All this, however, is less important than the Dominican theologian's contribution to a more general methodology in the interpretation of the ontological truths of Christology. For here we find a fourth, interrelated principle, and on this front, his pattern of reflection *has* been transmitted to a subsequent age. In keeping with what we have outlined above, the procedure of these volumes is to think about Christology as an intrinsically *historical* form of study. This is true methodologically, *but also in terms of all possible content*. For on Schillebeeckx's account, as we have seen, there is no access to trans-historical truths of Christology that are simply available to every age. The meaning of a given subject matter (in this case, the person of Jesus Christ) is itself perpetually historically evolving, depending upon the setting, language, and phenomenal conceptuality in which it is elaborated.[19] Consequently, there are mandated references for the study of Christ (we must study the monuments of the tradition, such as the New Testament Christologies considered in their original setting and the ancient Councils, particularly the Council of Chalcedon), but there are no perennial principles to Christology as such.[20] Rather, the "science" of Christology consists in the transference of meaning from one set of principles to another, across a spectrum of ages.[21] The inevitable question is, what should the person of Christ mean for us today? Our culturally-situated and temporally located stance of interpretation in turn *determines* in some real sense the "essential" content of the message of the Gospel *for us*, and *in our age*.

At this juncture, then, we can incorporate a final hermeneutical

19. A very clear expression of this viewpoint is given in *Christ*, 71–79.

20. *Jesus*, 50–51: "Still less is it permissible to absolutize in a quite unhistorical way the (biblical) articulation of what Jesus said and did in those concrete circumstances by detaching it from the historically coloured speech categories of that time, in which this Jesus event was verbalized: we cannot elevate this linguistic process into 'timeless categories.' Indeed, we are warned against that—in the New Testament itself—by the multiplicity of Christological dogmas and diverse formulae for indicating the kingdom of God, redemption and salvation in Christ. For on their side too the earliest congregations reacting to Jesus found themselves in a quite specific cultural and religious context. Not only does the language of the original creeds ... share therefore in the historical ambiguity, but the diversity of these creeds itself is likewise conditioned in the first instance by what to human understanding are the historical ambiguity ... and opaque character of this very 'phenomenon of Jesus'" (see 44–62).

21. Ibid., 576–82.

principle: every epoch constructs a speculative paradigm for Christological thought around a basic evangelical experience of God. This experience has a primarily *practical* content that is enduring, but that content is elaborated in speculative terms that can change for any given age. The prime example is found in Jesus's own "experience," ethical practice, and "speculative" teaching. According to Schillebeeckx, Jesus's own ministry was inspired by a basic "Abba experience" of God. Jesus possessed a sense of filial dependency that gave him radical confidence in God, even in the face of the oppressive forces that would mitigate against a belief in the power of God to overcome evil.[22] It is Christ's trusting experience of the Father that leads to the distinctive practice of his ethics: forgiveness of sins, eating with those considered outcasts, challenging the contemporary legal and cultic practices of the Judaism of the age, confrontation with Roman authority.[23] To this set of experience-based practices, Jesus gave an accompanying speculative teaching concerning the "Kingdom of God." He cast his experience and practice within the speculative terms of eschatology.[24] Thus Schillebeeckx perceives in Jesus's theological praxis a quasi-socialist, politically liberationist form of ministry grounded in a prior religious experience, but he also thinks it was articulated theoretically through the medium of the Judaic, eschatological idioms of his era.[25]

Analogous things take place in the post-Paschal apostolic age. Jesus's own aims and teachings were different from those of the subsequent early Christian era, with its New Testament "ontological" Christology.[26] However, the historical tension between Jesus and the New Testament portrait of Christ is alleviated when we realize that the latter teachings merely decipher the meaning of Jesus *for the ear-*

22. Ibid., 256–71.   23. Ibid., 179–249.
24. Ibid., 140–78.
25. Ibid., 172–78, 306–12; *Christ*, 499–511, especially 567–86, 661–69, 706–15.
26. *Jesus*, 545–50; 650–52. See 549: "If we should affirm our belief that in Jesus God saves human beings ('first-order assertion'), how then are we to understand Jesus himself, in whom God's definitive saving action has become a reality ('second-order assertion')? ... A primary and fundamental Christian orthodoxy is to be gauged from 'first-order' assertions above all. The history of Christological dogmas, therefore, would seem to lie in the plane of 'second-order' affirmations, albeit with the purpose of, and real concern for, bearing out the 'first-order' affirmations."

ly Christian movement in terms that were applicable to *their historical epoch.* The ontological Christology of the New Testament was in fact derived in large part through "experiences of forgiveness, grace, and liberation" that occurred *after* the crucifixion.[27] The latter experiences are accessible to us even if the ontological terminology in which they were originally articulated is problematic and no longer sustainable today.[28] Similarly, the great councils of the church might be seen as subsequent articulations of the soteriological significance of Christ for inhabitants of the Byzantine epoch, cast in ontological categories of that time period which are themselves quite different from those of the New Testament. Here again, a Christian experience of salvation occurs that is of perennial *practical* importance, but it also gives rise to a *speculative* construction that is historically contingent and bound within the contours of a given age.[29]

Ultimately, Schillebeeckx is committed to two deeper theological notions that undergird his practice of hermeneutics. One is in fact speculative, and in its own way, utterly ontological: behind the solidarity of Jesus with the socially marginal, we may perceive a more fundamental metaphysical truth of the radically kenotic historicization of God himself.[30] God in his historical being as Son and Word is united in a radical way to those who suffer political oppression in history. Consequently, the story of the church in history is the story of the constantly renewed recognition of God's solidarity with the outcast, marginalized, and socially abandoned.[31] When the hermeneutical theologian identifies the core practices of the Gospel, he or she is seeking to disclose the presence of God in history. Second, then, the task of Christology today is to find ways to articulate the meaning of

27. Ibid., 390–97.
28. Ibid., 626–36.
29. *Christ,* 62–64. See 63: "The crisis lies in the fact that Jesus is still regularly explained to us as salvation and grace in terms which are no longer valid for our world of experience, i.e., in terms of *earlier* experiences.... What the Christian community will be concerned to say in constantly changing situations, through constantly new forms of expression, even in philosophical concepts of a very complicated kind, is ultimately no more than that in Jesus Christ it experiences decisive salvation from God. When the old concepts ... no longer relate to new situations, ... interpretive concepts also change. But the original experience persists through these changes."
30. See in particular the kenotic ontology of God in *Jesus,* 652–69.
31. *Christ,* 724–30, 770–89.

Christ in a decidedly post-metaphysical age. These ways are, unsurprisingly, primarily practical and political, but also ecclesial and sacramental.[32] It is when the church's own life is lived with those who are oppressed, particularly in a corporate, political and sacramental life, that the mission of Christ is brought to bear upon our contemporary world.

In this last idea, we can see the recapitulation of the themes noted above. The hermeneuticist recovers the truth of the past by "going forward" into new horizons of political praxis, in the name of the Gospel. The truth in question is a radically historicized one. Now unusable doctrinal concepts of a past historical age are studied in view of the elaboration of new theological concepts of the future. God is himself in some sense the subject at the heart of the church's historical life who safeguards the inner workings of this process. The church mediates the ongoing sacramental expression of a perpetual divine-human encounter by taking up into herself the ongoing dialectic of human conversation regarding truth. She must do so today in decidedly post-metaphysical terms. But how can the church mediate for humanity the encounter with God in a post-metaphysical age? She can do so by being the community that follows Christ politically and sacramentally into the life of solidarity with the most outcast and politically marginalized. The church must offer the solace of religious and political hope to modern human beings bewildered in the face of the existential problems of suffering and evil.

Archeological Vulnerability

One might object that Schillebeeckx's theology is now culturally passé, except in select Catholic circles (mostly academic theology departments) in which the politics of identity still predominate. However, Schillebeeckx's "post-metaphysical" method does raise acute questions about the future of theology. It does so not primarily because of its accomplishments, but because of its methodological oversights. For the project is profoundly vulnerable to critique from a quarter that Schillebeeckx himself failed to engage seriously: that of archeological structuralism and deconstructionist theory.

32. Ibid., 804–21.

I am referring here to the thought of figures such as Michel Foucault and Jacques Derrida.[33] Foucault and Derrida each presume, in different ways, the empirical givens of structural patterns of language that endure in society, and which inform interpretation of "facts" by linguistic "subjects."[34] At the same time, they raise profound questions about how "post-metaphysical" modernity really is. After all, modern thinkers such as Schillebeeckx still presuppose that there are historical thinkers who are themselves interpreters, and that texts have some intrinsic signification that can be measured by external realities. This is a speculative commitment that remains unchallenged. But it is precisely such hidden ontological presuppositions and narrative goals of the hermeneutical process that the deconstructionists sought to question.[35] In doing so, they simply explicated the basic principles already articulated by Friedrich Nietzsche.[36]

For if, following Nietzsche, we challenge the ontological presupposition of the existence of the interpreting subject himself, or that of the metaphysical objects under consideration, or that of the values that are privileged in any given written form or intellectual tradition, then a number of new possibilities present themselves. Would it not follow that textual narratives lack a truly objective extrinsic referent, or that "we as readers," at least, cannot truly identify one? Of course it would. In this case texts are important principally because they are

33. Michel Foucault, *The Archaeology of Knowledge and The Discourse on Language*; Jacques Derrida, *Of Grammatology*, trans. G. C. Spivak (Baltimore, Md.: Johns Hopkins University Press, 1976).

34. Foucault, *The Archaeology of Knowledge*, 21–76; Derrida, *Of Grammatology*, 74–94.

35. Consider Derrida, *Of Grammatology*, 73: "This reference to the meaning of a signified thinkable and possible outside all signifiers remains dependent upon the onto-theo-teleology that I have just evoked. It is thus the idea of the sign that must be deconstructed through a meditation upon writing which would merge, as it must, with the undoing of onto-theology, faithfully repeating it in its *totality* and *making* it *insecure* in its most assured evidences."

36. Friedrich Nietzsche, *Writings from the Late Notebooks*, ed. R. Bittner, trans. K. Sturge (Cambridge: Cambridge University Press, 2003), 124–25: "The last thing in metaphysics we'll rid ourselves of is the oldest stock, assuming we *can* rid ourselves of it—that stock which has embodied itself in language and the grammatical categories and made itself so indispensable that it almost seems we would cease being able to think if we relinquished it. Philosophers in particular, have the greatest difficulty in freeing themselves from the belief that the basic concepts and categories of reason belong without further ado to the world of metaphysical certainties."

socio-cultural linguistic constructions, discourses seeking to manifest or promote some form of internally consistent (self-referential)
meaning. But then is their constitution motivated by nothing more
than a more or less blind, more or less concealed will to power? Is
this will to power emergent in the author as the expression of a col-
lectivist mentality? It must be, for the author represents a structure of
consciousness that emerges from the culture at large.[37]

What Foucault and Derrida rightly note, then, is that in a thorough-going "post-metaphysical age," the moral dimension of interpretation must go, along with the ontological interpretation. Hermeneutical projects and the moral narratives they seek to tell must
themselves be subject to radical re-evaluation from a standpoint that
seeks to set itself "beyond good and evil," for the appeal to any moral norm already implies a metaphysical commitment. In speaking of
the concept "salvation," for example, Derrida asks if the very word is
intelligible today, given that we cannot necessarily agree in our postmodern culture on a definition of the word "evil," or even whether
this word has a meaning. "Where is evil today, at present?"[38] Ironically, this is a metaphysical question. Derrida is right to note that if we
cannot answer it metaphysically, then our agnosticism undermines
all pretense to a "post-metaphysical" soteriology. Without metaphysics, there is no salvation.

How is this line of criticism applicable to Schillebeeckx's hermeneutical principles? Schillebeeckx claims that doctrine is essentially
constituted not only within a historical experience of salvation but

37. Foucault, *The Archaeology of Knowledge*, 125: "To describe a group of statements
not as the closed, plethoric totality of a meaning, but as an incomplete fragmented figure; to describe a group of statements not with reference to the interiority of an intention, a thought, or a subject, but in accordance with the dispersion of an exteriority; to
describe a group of statements, in order to rediscover not the moment of the trace of
their origin, but the specific forms of an accumulation, is certainly not to uncover an
interpretation, to discover a foundation, or to free constituent acts; nor is it to decide
on a rationality, or to embrace a teleology. It is to establish what I am quite willing to
call a *positivity*.... If, by substituting ... the description of relations of exteriority for the
theme of the transcendental foundation ... one is a positivist, then I am quite happy to
be one."

38. Jacques Derrida, "Faith and Knowledge: the Two Sources of 'Religion' at the
Limits of Reason Alone," trans. S. Weber in *Religion*, eds. J. Derrida and G. Vattimo
(Stanford, Calif.: Stanford University Press, 1998), 1–78; see 2.

also *by* that experience. There is no clear trans-historical content to dogma. But does it not follow from this that any doctrine is "merely" the expression of the religious sensibilities of a given era? Of course it must, if we seek to be consistent in our post-metaphysical thinking. In that case, are theologies anything more than the enunciation of the religious perspectives of various cultures, bound by the limitations of their respective historical horizons? No, they are not. Are all dogmas epistemically perspectivalist and spatio-temporally relative? It would seem that they are.

Let us add to this first set of questions a second set. Do the individuals that appeal to theological doctrines really act as personal agents, or are what we call "persons" and "authors" mere semiotic placeholders in a larger, deontologized field of empirical facts? If our consciousness is a product of culture "all the way down," then it is constituted uniquely by a tissue of semiotic symbols, held together by the structural features of a given discourse in a given age. Stated more critically, then, are the "values" expressed theologically by any particular sub-group anything other than the arbitrary expression of the will to power, whether this group be officially magisterial or not? Which form of post-metaphysical thought should we embrace in order to answer these questions? If our hermeneutics are those of Nietzsche, then the theological guilds that seek to challenge received doctrinal tradition through a series of "progressive" and "empowering" discourses are themselves adopting a morally arbitrary stance. They too give voice to a will to power, expressed through rhetorically manipulative practices. "Liberating" theology is no better than "magisterial" theology. Without ontological foundations, Schillebeeckx's political theology lacks the epistemological warrant to uphold the moral norms he wishes to promote. In short, without ontology, what is really left of "moral praxis" or of a progressivist "re-evaluation" of the Gospel spanning across the ages? Not much. In truth, without ontology, everything descends into night.

Despite the above-mentioned objections, however, we find that the historicist theological viewpoint is still present in academic theology today, in a form of thought we might characterize as partially Nietzschean. Consider in this respect the doctrinal perspectivalism of Chenu's theological disciple, Claude Geffré (also deeply influenced by Schillebeeckx) in his 1987 *Le Christianisme au risque de l'interpretation:*

The earlier onto-theology which provided theology with its conceptual basis was dismantled by the new ontology of Heidegger.... The claim of theology to be a perfect and universal systemization of the Christian message has come into direct confrontation with the contemporary criticism of ideology and especially with the latter's vow of non-dialectical totalization, its rejection of all historical complexity, and its stubborn resistance to what is real. All of us are, after all, marked by a Nietzschean suspicion of truth. Truth is not "perspectivalist," but we have to admit that it can only be reached within a certain perspective. All discourse is therefore provisional and relative. There is no knowledge—only a language of interpretation that is relative to the perspective of the one who speaks it.... This sharpened consciousness does not necessarily lead to the destruction of a dogmatic faith in the Christian sense of the word, but it does make us view more cautiously a certain kind of dogmatic theology that is offered to us as the only authentic way of interpreting the Christian message.... Autonomy of consciousness is an inescapable datum of modern life, and it goes together with a rejection of the claim, made in the name of the authority of God or of the Church's Magisterium, that theological knowledge is infallible.... "Authoritarian" theologies such as those of the Word of God in the Barthian sense or Catholic theologies like those of the Roman school are no longer in accordance with the contemporary order of the Spirit.[39]

These conclusions are interesting due to their seeming radicality. According to the argument I am making, however, they are not radical enough. We can restate the argument critically: on what grounds may one rule out a priori the epistemological *possibility* of infallible revelation? Whose perspective determines the identification of the "norms of the contemporary order" by which classical dogma is judged? What is the "Spirit" that the author identifies as governing the existing order of our world, what are its characteristics and how are they identified? And perhaps more fundamentally, if all discourse is provisional, are universal claims to the provisionality of discourse still philosophically advisable, or are they not inevitably subject to the ac-

39. Claude Geffré, *The Risk of Interpretation: On Being Faithful to the Christian Tradition in a Non-Christian Age,* translated by D. Smith (New York: Paulist Press, 1987), 14–15. This is the English translation of *Le Christianisme au risque de l'interpretation* (Paris: Cerf, 1983).

cusation of a hidden will to power? In this case, should we not have recourse to the more logically consistent logical inconsistency and self-consciously self-contradicting perspectives of post-structuralists such as Derrida? In such a context, however, the project of a dogmatic theology would evidently be futile. In any event, it is clear that once we adopt a post-metaphysical, hermeneutical methodology, the claims of a perennial Christian truth seem deeply compromised, and the aspirations to *any form* of perennial theological tradition are irrevocably undermined.

What might we conclude, then, from these reflections on perspectivalism? Tentatively, we could suggest the following conclusions. First, without an explicit recognition of the human mind's orientation toward the transcendent wisdom of God, and a corresponding ontologically informed dogmatic approach to the mysteries of the Trinity, Jesus Christ, the church, and human personhood, theology becomes a discourse disconnected from veridical necessities. It can then be accused (perhaps even rightly) of being primarily concerned with the uses and abuses of power, and the rhetorical discourse required to achieve cultural relevance for marginalized groups. However, even this vision of theology—with both its postmodern proponents and its theoretically nihilist critics—relies implicitly upon an unstated intellectual commitment to an ontology. This is an ontology that emphasizes either the normativity of the inclusive political good or the celebration of the will to power. Ironically, in either case, appeal to a certain form of metaphysical teleology becomes theoretically inevitable, even if the presupposition is not explicitly acknowledged. *Appeal to veridical necessities is not abolished, but only concealed.*

Second, then, we cannot in fact avoid making consistent ontological claims about reality, even if we do so from within the purview of a doctrine that is critical of what has come before. Any *possible* narrative of the development of theological themes depends implicitly upon some presupposed account of the *enduring character* of human nature, political justice, grammar, language, human volition, and so forth. Consequently, any hermeneutical methodology employed in theology works by use of implicitly ontological principles, and a transparent theory should require that this be acknowledged overtly. Understood in this light, theology may consider opinions about

Christ across a spectrum of viewpoints manifested down through time, but it does so primarily in order to understand the person, natures, and historical mysteries of Christ. This presupposes that there are things that are true about Christ perennially for all ages. It is inevitable that the human intellect seeks to move from what Aristotle terms "dialectic" (the consideration of diverse historical opinions) to the study of principles (consideration of the structure of reality that is the basis for an enduring science). Theology becomes fully itself when it advances beyond the consideration of historical opinions to the speculative practice of scholastic analysis. Only then is theology not mere rhetoric without structure or purpose, but a science that seeks the essence and meaning of the mystery of God.

INEVITABLE SCHOLASTICISM

In the second section of this concluding chapter, I should like to consider briefly the implicitly ontological foundations of hermeneutics, even on a philosophical level, as presented by Thomas Aquinas. Here I will seek only to indicate the metaphysical foundations for a realist hermeneutics. I will do so by discussing three congruent principles. First, as Aquinas notes, the human intellect is capable of a genuinely metaphysical range of knowledge. In fact, the first thing known by the human intellect is being. Consequently, the right use of language and the intelligent study of texts require that we seek the foundation for what is said by a given author (rightly or wrongly) in the natures of the things themselves of which the texts speak. Second, the reality of historical change and development that takes place in the world occurs in realities that exist and that have essences and properties. Historical study is thus always couched within the context of the study of being and has an unavoidable metaphysical context. It is metaphysical realism that makes historical study possible and not the inverse. Third, the narrator of any historical analysis inevitably pursues some kind of goal or final end in formulating his narration. This end conditions the shape of his moral evaluations and purposes in writing. Teleologically oriented activity, however, constitutes an inalienable dimension of the *being* of the human person, and it unfolds in accord with an objective scale of final ends that are inscribed in human nature. The teleological aims of an author, then, can be evaluated by a universal measure, in light of a hierarchical scale of final ends that are inherent within the being of the human person.

Primo cadit in intellectu ens

What comes first, language or reality? Which determines the content of which? When Aquinas considers this question, he claims that rhetoric is an art rather than a science, and that this art depends implicitly upon the science of being. As I have noted above in chapter 2, this viewpoint is articulated within the context of the *Commentary on Aristotle's Metaphysics*, Book IV. Here Aristotle is refuting the views of the sophists of his own time. By his account, these philosophers affirmed that there is a sense in which one might argue that every truth claim can be defended or rejected with equal validity, even those that are simultaneously incompatible. Consequently, there is a sense in which it is fair to say that all things are simultaneously true, even those truths which are contradictory.[40]

Against this early form of relativism or perspectivalism, Aristotle notes that all argumentation stems from previous principles of knowledge. In order to argue with another person about anything, one must already know something. Rational argumentation, therefore, can never be something first in the order of knowing. There must be forms of pre-rational insight available to human beings that make it possible, in turn, for us to reason to subsequent forms of knowledge.[41] Can we agree universally on what they might be? As Aristotle points out, we cannot rationally prove that such starting points exist: if they are pre-rational, their existence cannot be demonstrated! Instead, it can only be affirmed that they exist, and if someone refused to believe in them, we could then refute him dialectically (by elenchic argumentations).[42] That is to say, we could only show that no one fails to make use of such forms of such pre-rational knowledge and that rhetorical efforts to deny their existence (by use of rational demonstrations) implicitly depend themselves upon the use of such forms of knowledge.

40. *Metaphysics* IV, 4–5, 1006a1–1011a2; *In Meta.*, lec. 6–14.
41. *Metaphysics* IV, 4, 1006a1–11. See likewise *Posterior Analytics* I, 2, 72a30 and 3, 72b5–24.
42. *Metaphysics* IV, 4, 1006a12–15.

What, then, are these first forms of knowledge? It is in asking this question that Aristotle enunciates the principle of non-contradiction. The mind cannot fail to note that some existents are distinct from others (all our language bears witness to this fact), and that the natures and characteristics of diverse realities cannot be attributed to them in simultaneously contrary senses under the same aspects at the same time.[43] Otherwise, the very act of speech itself (which constantly seeks to indicate distinct realities) becomes intrinsically meaningless.[44] Our implicit use of the principle of non-contradiction denotes that we perceive a world of formally determined realities that have various properties. Were one to deny the principle in a consistent fashion, it would be necessary to be silent like a plant or like the sophist Cratylus, who indicated the consistency of his position by never speaking and by only moving his little finger.[45]

Aquinas follows Aristotle in this form of argumentation. However, he also examines more overtly the positive feature of human cognition that must be present in the apprehension of this first principle of non-contradiction. For to affirm that one thing is *not* another thing or that this characteristic is *not* identical with that characteristic, one must apprehend more fundamentally this being or that, this charac-

43. *Metaphysics* IV, 3, 1005b17–20: "Evidently then such a principle is the most certain of all, which principle this is, we proceed to say. It is, that the same attribute cannot at the same time belong and not belong to the same subject in the same respect."

44. In *Metaphysics* IV, 1006a1–1007a20 Aristotle offers a series of arguments to show that every verbal, signifying judgment implicitly makes recourse to the principle of non-contradiction: we affirm things to be or not to be under various aspects. In 1007a21–b18 he offers a further argument: In every affirmation whatsoever we attribute properties (accidents) to a subject having an essence (a substance). But if we deny the principle of non-contradiction, it follows that we will do away with substances, essences and subjects themselves. Sentences, however, are constructed around attributes predicated to subjects. If there are no subjects of attribution, there are no subjects of grammar. Realistic linguistic use breaks down entirely.

45. *Metaphysics* IV, 5, 1010a6–14: "They held these views because they saw that all the world of nature is in movement, and that about that which changes no true statement can be made; at least, regarding that which everywhere in every respect is changing nothing could truly be affirmed. It was this belief that blossomed into the most extreme of the views above mentioned, that of the professed Heracliteans, such as was held by Cratylus, who finally did not think it right to say anything but only moved his finger, and criticized Heraclitus for saying that it is impossible to step twice into the same river; for *he* thought one could not do it even once."

teristic or that. What is the first thing apprehended, then, prior to all rational argumentation? Aquinas gives his answer in the form of a famous phrase: *Primo cadit in intellectu ens.*[46] The first thing that "falls into" the intellect is being. It is important to recognize here that "ens" is a term signifying a composite reality: every *ens*, for Aquinas, is itself composed of *essentia* and *esse.*[47] That is to say, every concrete being we might encounter has a given essence or natural kind (with various properties that ensue) and it has a given existence that is unique. The one-year-old child who perceives intellectually her parents (however vaguely) perceives that they are each singular realities that really exist, and that they are realities of a given kind, different than the physical, inanimate objects around the house. Here the principle of non-contradiction is already at work. Simply put: she perceives that one is not the other and that each is unique. As her understanding advances, her initial grasp of reality will be enriched, but not overturned.

Not only does the mind have an innate capacity to grasp the reality of distinct kinds of beings in their ontological singularity, it also has the capacity to grasp them as good, as unified, and as true or real. In fact, St. Thomas thinks that these "transcendental" notions (good, unity, truth, reality) are co-extensive with being and essence. This need not mean, of course, that all human persons are overtly interested in metaphysics, but only that all human persons make use of metaphysically realistic knowledge in their day to day lives, all the

---

46. Aquinas, *In IV Meta.*, lec. 5, 605: "Now for the purpose of making this evident it must be noted that, since the intellect has two operations [i.e., apprehension and judgment], one by which it knows quiddities, which is called the understanding of indivisibles [by apprehension], and another by which it combines and separates [by judgment, in affirmations or negations], there is something first in both operations. In the first operation the first thing that the intellect conceives is *being* [primum quod cadit in conceptione intellectus ... [est] ens], and in this operation nothing else can be conceived unless being is understood. And because this principle—it is impossible for a thing both to be and not be at the same time—depends on the understanding of being ... then this principle is by nature also the first in the second operation of the intellect, i.e., in the act of combining and separating. And no one can understand anything by this intellectual operation [of judgment] unless this principle is understood." See likewise ST I, q. 5, a. 2; q. 11, a. 2, ad 4.

47. *De ente*, c. 1: "Essentia dicitur secundum quod per eam et in ea ens habet esse." *In Peri Hermeneias* I, lec. 5, 19: "Ipsum ens est fons et origo esse." SCG III, c. 66: "Nihil enim dat esse nisi inquantum est ens actu."

time. As Aristotle says, even the sophist who denies that bread exists will instinctively pick it up and eat it when he is hungry.[48] While the speculative intellect might try for a time to ward off any commitment to common-sense realism, the practical intellect indirectly reveals speculative knowledge of a realist sort, and so gives lie to the games of evasion created by sophist forms of argumentation.

What does this mean for our understanding of the practice of hermeneutics? First of all, it is important to see that Aquinas distinguishes textual interpretation from the art of rhetoric. They are two different things entirely. Rhetoric is a practical art oriented toward the swaying of one's auditor or reader to a given point of view.[49] As such it is a practical art concerned with the pursuit of persuasion, the captivation of the intellect and invitation of the will, by way of the use of language addressed to the imagination and the passions, as well as to reason. Such a practice is subject to right or wrong use depending upon the speculative convictions and moral virtues of its practitioners. It can be used for good or for ill, then, but because it is just an art, it has no intrinsic speculative content or moral color.

By contrast, hermeneutics seeks primarily to interpret the words of others, and so it must seek to pass through the narrative form of discourse, or the argumentations employed, *back to the things in themselves*, to measure the truth of the discourse against the structure of reality itself.[50] When he comments on Aristotle's *Peri Hermeneias*, Aquinas emphasizes the importance of the grammatical copula: this *is* such and such, or this *is not* such and such.[51] At the heart of every affirmation or negation that we find in a text there is an implicit semiotic referent to that which exists or does not exist. The language of affirmations and negations is one that is composed of *intellectual judgments regarding the existence of things*. Consequently, to interpret a text rightly one has to see what the judgments of the author denote concerning reality and what the structure of the reality is in itself.[52] Only then can one really evaluate the truth or falsehood of a set of claims about the nature and characteristics of that which is said to exist.

48. *Metaphysics* XI, 6, 1063a28–35.   49. Aristotle, *Rhetoric*, 2, 1355b27.
50. Aristotle, *On Interpretation*, 1, 16a1–9.   51. *In Peri Hermeneias* I, lec. 5, 19–22.
52. *In Peri Hermeneias* I, lec. 5, 20, and 22.

The conclusion we can draw from this very simple point is that the hermeneutical project of interpretation of texts sends us back to a reflection about the nature of what exists. Even literary fiction is deemed fiction because what it relates "does not really exist," and at the same time it might convey in literary motifs, extremely profound ideas about the nature of human existence. There is a broad array of literary genera, but all forms of human writing do in some way denote human judgments about what exists and what does not. In that sense, they all send us back, however circuitously, to a consideration of the structure of reality.

History and Essence

Our second point concerns the inevitably metaphysical character of historical study. Why should we believe that historical change is intelligible? After all, one might argue that history is a purely unintelligible flux. Prior to Plato, Parmenides and Heraclitus each made this claim in two opposite ways. Parmenides simply denied the existence of change, while Heraclitus affirmed the reality of change in all things and correspondingly denied the possibility of stable essences. Neither of them permitted that there could be a true science of change. As Aristotle noted, however, against these two extremes, change is neither illusory (such that being is only static) nor is it a pure becoming devoid of intelligible content (such that there is a non-causal flux).[53] What both Parmenides and Heraclitus failed to grasp is that there is a distinction in all the realities we experience between ontological potency and being-in-act. There is in every physical reality, for example, a latent potency to undergo material corruption and transformation so as to become another reality (through substantial alteration). There is also the potency in every physical substance to be transformed only under some aspect (that is, in its properties or characteristics, like the change from cold to hot or dark to light).[54] Physical realities in history, then, are constituted by distinct, essential determinations and accidental properties, but they are also subject to change. Through their internal development and mutual in-

---

53. *Physics* I, 2–3, 184b15–187a12; *Metaphysics* IV, 5, 1009a6–1010a14.
54. *Physics* I, 8–9, especially 191a23–191b13, 192a25–34.

teraction, a complex history results. Because there are stable formal determinations in things that have predictable actions and properties, we can seek scientific explanations for historical changes.[55] One can denote the patterns of behavior and causes of inanimate physical beings or living beings, or human agents and institutions down through time. Consequently there is the possibility of studying the order and causation of change in the physical cosmos: in physical processes, biological developments, and human history.

The presupposition of this realist vision is that the human mind is capable of attaining true insight into the essences of changing realities even amidst the flux of history. When Aquinas reflects on this idea, he notes that time is not something that constitutes the essence of a physical reality. Rather, what we call "time" is a measure of ontological change that occurs in or to a physical reality. How do different realities change in simultaneous and rhythmically related ways? If we are to compare two realities (for example by "age": the development of the human body in relation to the number of rotations of the earth around the sun), we must first grasp that these realities exist and have a given nature (human beings, the sun, the earth). Therefore, Aquinas notes, knowledge of an essence which in some sense "transcends" time is the precondition for a measurement of temporal change in that essence. The intellectual part of the soul that can apprehend essences or natures is situated "above" temporal change in some sense, with respect to its formal object.[56]

What all of this means is that metaphysically realistic knowing takes place in time, but that the objects of reason are not determined uniquely by the processes of temporal change. The intellect attains to "that which exists," and that which exists possesses an essential form.[57] The realism of the mind is rooted in the contact with existent forms of an essential constitution. Even if a natural form has its own history of development (the evolution of the *homo sapiens*, for example) it is a determinate form all the same, and we cannot chart out its history (from earlier bipedal primates to *homo sapiens*) unless we admit the existence of such distinct forms in the first place.

---

55. *Physics* II, 3, 194b16–195b30.
56. See for example ST I-II, q. 53, a. 3, ad 3; I, q. 85, a. 5, ad 2.
57. Aquinas, *De ente*, c. 1.

What is said here with respect to the modern sciences also applies to the study of the history of ideas. What is required in order to denote the changes that transpire in an intellectual genealogy? One must presuppose the possibility of identifying diversified forms of thought. For example, how might we characterize the ideas of Christian Wolff, and how do these differ from those of David Hume? How did the thought of Immanuel Kant come to be in reaction to both Wolff and Hume? To be able to situate ideas within the context of their historical development, mutation or substantial alteration we must be able to identify what is *essential* or *determinate* in the ideas under consideration. What characteristic properties do they possess? The fabrication of an intellectual genealogy, then, requires a noetic grasp of essential kinds. But this returns us to the point made above: When we know that things *exist* and *what* things are *essentially*, we are in some sense situated on a level "beyond" that of mere flux and becoming; and it is this "transcendental range" of knowing that makes the scientific study of historical development possible at all.

Derrida is insistent that all attempts to explain reality philosophically entail implicit and illicit appeals to ontotheological thinking (which he takes to be a bad thing). But he himself appeals habitually to genealogies of human thought, from Descartes to Leibniz to Heidegger. In doing so, he clearly presupposes some shared consensus about the structure of European intellectual history. His narration of this history is meant to be quite original (which it is), but it still presupposes a set of *intelligible forms* (diverse ideas present in distinct texts down through the ages). There is no attempt to question the existence of a set of ideas that has transpired in human culture in and through a real temporal sequence. Derrida wants to explain that sequence of ideas differently than others have done before him. But why do we presuppose the existence of the sequence and its intelligible content? Once the author is slain, is genealogy not dead as well? Is it not the case that some form of metaphysically realist thinking is the condition of possibility for any temporal genealogy? Derrida insists on the inaccessibility of such a form of thought, but from a Thomist point of view, we might ask if his post-metaphysical thinking is really that consistent? After all, his chronologically enumerated studies of human texts seem to betray his implicit commitment to the ontological dimensions of reality. The hermeneutical realism of Aristotle and Aquinas is more profound and more comprehensive. They do not oppose the study of being and the study of history. Rather, they see clearly that metaphysical realism regarding existent realities and their essences necessarily forms the basis for any sound hermeneutics of history.

Teleology and the Ethical
Context of Narration

A final and related idea concerns the inevitability of the presence of teleology in the very practice of narration. This point can be made succinctly. In one sense, it is a claim about the natures of the things themselves. If a text describes the action of a person who is motivated by a given aim, this description itself presupposes that there are persons who act in view of particular aims. If there is an orientation toward final ends inscribed in realities that we write about, then textual composition presupposes the existence of teleology in the cosmos. On a second level, however, this is a claim about the narrating subject. The act of construing meaning (or even contesting it at no matter how radical a level) is itself a teleologically ordered act, and therefore reveals the presence of a teleologically-oriented subject who construes meaning.

Alasdair MacIntyre has underscored this point in his consideration of the narrative thought of Michel Foucault.[58] Foucault consistently denied the existence of any teleological aims present in the human person who composes writing. However, when Foucault himself gave interviews about his own philosophical project, he could not explain it without the consistent use of subject pronouns and the grammar of aims, intentions, choices, and purposes.[59] What might we

58. Alasdair MacIntyre, *Three Rival Versions of Moral Inquiry: Encyclopedia, Genealogy, and Tradition* (Notre Dame, Ind.: University of Notre Dame, 1990), 196–215.

59. Notice the simultaneous affirmation and negation of authorial intent in this passage (*The Archaeology of Knowledge*, 210–11): "This book was written simply in order to overcome certain preliminary difficulties. I know as well as anyone how 'thankless' is the task that I undertook some ten years ago. I know how irritating it can be to treat discourses in terms not of the gentle, silent, intimate consciousness that is expressed in them, but of an obscure set of anonymous rules.... [The reader might ask]: 'Must

infer from this? We might suggest that there is no possibility of intellectual narration that does not depend (on some level) upon a teleological account of acting subjects. If our grammar is indicative of teleologically oriented subjects, this is because every possible form of language must at some point acknowledge implicitly an ontology of subjects that language presupposes. The use of language itself reveals what we think is the case, what we desire, and what we seek to do or become. The aims of language are reflections of the aims of subjects.

Is it really possible to purge our speech of every reference to the final cause? In the late notebooks of Nietzsche one can observe an interesting tension in this respect.[60] On the one hand, he excoriates Christianity for its emphasis on teleological purpose in human existence and decries this feature of thought as an inauthentic response to the dangers of nihilism.[61] We must learn to live life heroically in the face of the cycle of the eternal recurrence, in the absence of any metaphysical purpose or overarching designs.[62] On the other hand, Nietzsche sets out to explain the origin of Christianity genealogically *by his own* appeal to the theory of the will to power. The human being is capable of choosing a form of life-affirmation even in the face of his or her own ultimate meaninglessness. The reason we should suspect all normative Christian accounts of morality is that they are motivated at base by an undisclosed will to power that resents (and therefore fails to accept) our fundamental human contingency and meaninglessness.[63] Nietzsche does underscore, however, that Christianity had

---

I suppose that in my discourse I can have no survival? And that in speaking I am not banishing my death, but actually establishing it; or rather that I am abolishing all interiority in that exteriority that is so indifferent to my life and so *neutral*, that It makes no distinction between my life and my death?' I understand the unease of all such people.... They cannot bear (and one cannot but sympathize) to hear someone saying: 'Discourse is not life: its time is not your time; in it, you will not be reconciled to death; you may have killed God beneath the weight of all you have said; but don't imagine that, with all that you are saying, you will make a man that will live longer than he.'"

60. Nietzsche, *Writings from the Late Notebooks*, 116–26.

61. Ibid., 116: "Among the forces that morality cultivated was *truthfulness*: this, in the end, turns against morality, discovers its *teleology*, the *partiality* of its viewpoint—and now the *insight* into this long-ingrained mendacity, which one despairs of ever shedding from oneself, is what acts as a stimulus: a stimulus to nihilism."

62. Ibid., 118.

63. Ibid., 116.

the effect of granting human beings a belief in the greatness and destiny of human existence, seemingly a positive goal![64] A demythologized, realist version of this "Christian" reaction to nihilism should be sought in atheism, which may attain a stance of free existence beyond the bounds of morality, beyond good and evil.[65]

Notice how this genealogical account of intellectual history itself implies recourse to final causality as a means of normative description, diagnosis, and explanation: why are we capable of slave-morality? Why did Christianity happen historically? Why should it now be revoked? The Aristotelian must blush to point out the obvious: Nietzsche wants us purposefully to transcend the bourgeois morality of nineteenth-century European Christianity. One can even *aspire* to transcend every metaphysical construal of reality philosophers have ever fashioned. But one can only seek to do all this through teleologically ordered acts. To compose a book advocating that human beings imitate one's self is an act ordered by a final cause. To compose an explanatory narration of the history of ethics, it is necessary to appeal to some notion of final causes. And to argue for one's post-moral vision to others is to articulate a goal that one considers normative. The goal of seeking sensible pleasure in order to express one's freedom from all ontological constraints might not be an end consonant with Christian morality, but it is an identifiable end all the same. When it comes to an implicit appeal to the final cause, Nietzsche is as much a metaphysician as anyone else, and in fact, due to his attempts at consistency in this regard, he is even a kind of moral puritan in his own genus.

If the epistemological and ontological claims being made above are correct, then the attempt to demonstrate the archeological origins of the narrative of the self without any "transcendental subject" can never be a truly "self-less" act. On the contrary, the composition of an archeological genealogy or a deconstructive analysis is a planned event construed around a precise goal. One can of course deny this,

64. Ibid., 117.
65. Ibid., 124: "If there is no goal in the whole history of man's lot, then we must put one in: assuming, on the one hand, that we have *need* of a goal, and on the other that we've come to see through the illusion of an immanent goal and purpose. And the reason we have need of a goal is that we have need of a will—which is the spine of us. 'Will' as the compensation for lost 'belief,' i.e., for the idea that there is a *divine* will, one which has plans for us."

but to do so one must make a concerted effort through unified acts carried out by a personal subject. Here, then, we can invoke an argument from retorsion: the active denial of the claim that narration entails the act of a teleologically motivated subject itself seems to demonstrate the truth of the claim being contested.

From this conclusion we can move to a final idea. If the narrating subject is characterized by a teleological inclination (in his or her very being), then the end being pursued by the narrator can be situated within a greater hierarchy of goods. One can evaluate the efforts of any author or interpreter ethically, then, by reflecting on the metaphysical structure of the good. How does the narrator's action in view of a particular good take on meaning in relation to a set of more ultimate goods? Which human purpose is most ultimate?

One might argue, for example, that the purposefulness of human narration has to be inscribed within a larger cosmic order in which there is no ostensible, intellectually willed purpose to human existence. Some form of biological materialism characterizes the *ultimate* horizon of explanation for our very being and all our inclinations. Atheist scientists who believe this may write books for a reason, but they do so while claiming that the human community hovers over a cosmic void. Human sociability and public rational argument are portrayed as true goods, then, but they have to be measured against the more ultimate metaphysical backdrop of an atheistic universe. Be that as it may, such a claim inevitably entails that we are making a very clear affirmation about the structure of reality and the hierarchy of goods. If we exist primarily to promote our political animal life and to survive against the backdrop of an otherwise unplanned, non-living physical cosmos, we still have to plan our narratives and explanations of human actions (with their accompanying moral prerogatives: "study more science") against the backdrop of that larger or more ultimate truth ("the cosmos has no ultimate purpose"). The point is not that such a claim is true, but rather the point is that every narration—including that of the materialist—makes an implicit appeal not only to human ontology and teleology but also to a deeper or more primal concern with the metaphysics of the real and the hierarchy of goods.

The interpretive project of understanding and explanation is also

inevitably teleological, then, in this higher or more ultimate sense. It
is rooted fundamentally in the deeper human quest for meaning and
metaphysical explanation. The very act of articulating purposes in reality presupposes at least implicitly that we can turn to the question
of the ultimate origins and causes of reality as we know it. Our act of
narration and purposeful engagement in argument about the truth always has as its necessary context at least an implicit reference to the
ultimate meaning of reality.

THE SCIENCE OF
CHRISTOLOGY

In the final section of this chapter I would like to conclude with a reflection on Christology as a science. Having stressed the metaphysical trajectory of human thinking in general, I will now transpose this
pattern of thinking into a Christological key. If human thought inevitably touches upon that which exists (being) and considers the essential structure and causes of things as well as their final ends, then
Christology as a form of human thought can undertake speculative reflection on the being of Christ and the intrinsic structure or
"essence" of his mystery. It can consider the ultimate purpose or final end of the science of Christ, in which case it becomes a practical
and ethical form of reflection as well. The integral unity of these two
forms of reflection (speculative science and ethics) constitutes a wisdom, and so it is fitting to conclude these reflections by consideration
of Christology as a highest and ultimate form of theological wisdom.

Christology as a Science

Science as conceived in the classical Aristotelian sense entails the
derivation of necessary and universal conclusions from initial starting
points that are certain.[66] Take the example of hylomorphic theory.
Aristotle thinks (quite rightly) that it is certain that there are material beings subject to physical change through time. Under further consideration, however, we can discover a deeper universal truth: that

66. *Posterior Analytics* I, 3, 72b5–24; Aquinas, *In Post.* I, lec. 8; *Nicomachean Ethics* IV, 3, 1139b14–36.

each physical being is constituted by dual principles of form and matter. That is to say, in each physical reality there is a formal principle of organization and unification, as well as material parts, of which the reality consists. There is also a deeper material principle of potentiality present within these material parts that makes the reality subject to further alteration or change.[67] All of this is true for a hylomorphic reality considered at any level, and of any quality or physical characteristic, be it subatomic or atomic, organic or non-organic, animate or inanimate. What is more, if we deny that there is a hylomorphic constitution to physical realities we will inevitably be obliged to affirm one of two things: either that there are not discrete unified entities composed of parts (just mere relational aggregates) or that all unified physical realities are in no way subject to physical change.[68] Both of these conclusions are absurd and contradict the intellectual evidence of beings as we encounter them through ordinary sense experiences.

The example of a scientific principle that I have just given is taken from Thomistic philosophy of nature. We could just as well take examples from the modern experimental sciences. For the sake of our argument here, however, that issue is immaterial. Based upon whichever such example we might choose, it would seem that Christology ought not to be considered a form of scientific thought. Why is this the case? The problem is not that theology depends upon divine revelation rather than philosophical and empirical knowledge of the order of nature. For God can surely reveal things that are universally true, and such truths can give rise to a universal science (*sacra doctrina*, theology) founded in the knowledge that comes from faith.[69] The first principles of such a science (its initial certitudes) are derived not from natural reason but from divine revelation.[70] Even if we accept such a premise, however, the problem lies in this: science itself is concerned with the universal and necessary, but Christ is a particular person and his existence is historically contingent and absolutely unique or individual. How, then, could his historical existence and

---

67. *Physics* I, 9, 192a25–34, and II, 1, 192b9–193b21.
68. See the arguments by Aquinas, *In Meta.* VII, lec. 2, 1285–89; lec. 17, 1676.
69. ST I, q. 1, a. 2.
70. ST I, q. 1, a. 5.

person be the subject of a consideration of universal and necessary importance? This objection is not novel, of course. We find an early modern version of it in the criticism of New Testament Christology offered by Gotthold Lessing, in the problem of the "ugly ditch." Science, Lessing argues, pertains to the universal but the New Testament bears witness to a knowledge of Christ that is historically contingent. Consequently, it fails to offer us true knowledge according to the canons of modern, scientific rationality.[71]

Based upon his own hermeneutical principles, Schillebeeckx has a considered response to this objection.[72] He does not seek to define Christology as a universal science according to the eighteenth-century canons of universal knowledge. Instead, Schillebeeckx seeks to undermine the presuppositions of Lessing's Enlightenment conception of reason. If we are historical beings "all the way down" and even our rationality and reflection on the truth are utterly conditioned by the context of time and place, then the hermeneutical problem of perennial truth affects Enlightenment reason as much as Christian dogma. Why should we prefer Lessing's understanding of normative reason to that of a subsequent or previous historical age, or to that of a non-European culture? Unlike the modern rationalist, the New Testament takes seriously that the human being is a historically contextualized being of flesh, seeking political justice and religious deliverance in a given incarnate circumstance of time and place. The power of Christ's message lies precisely in the fact that it can be

71. Gotthold Lessing, "On the Proof of the Spirit and of Power," in Lessing's Theological Writings, trans. and ed. H. Chadwick (Stanford, Calif.: Stanford University Press, 1957), 53–54: "If no historical truth can be demonstrated, then nothing can be demonstrated by means of historical truths. That is: accidental [i.e., contingent] truths of history can never become the proof of necessary truths of reason.... It is said: 'The Christ of whom on historical grounds you must allow that he raised the dead, that he himself rose from the dead, said himself that God has a Son of the same essence as himself and that he is this Son.' This would be excellent! if only it were not the case that it is not more than historically certain that Christ said this. If you press me still further and say: 'Oh yes! this is more than historically certain. For it is asserted by inspired historians who cannot make a mistake.' But, unfortunately, that also is only historically certain, that these historians were inspired and could not err. That, then, is the ugly, broad ditch which I cannot get across, however often and however earnestly I have tried to make the leap."

72. In Jesus, 583–94, Schillebeeckx takes up the problematic inherited from Lessing and attempts to respond in the following section (595–625).

transmitted analogically from age to age, to all possible times and places, albeit always in a newly contextualized, liberationist mode. This might even entail that the Gospel deliver post-colonial reason from undue preoccupation with European, Enlightenment canons of "universal reason," and permit the Christian life of postmodern historical communities to challenge the received canons of what is "necessary and universal" in light of their own appropriation of the practices of Jesus of Nazareth.

In the end, however, neither of these opposed extremes is very helpful. Over against Lessing, we must insist that the human being is a composite being having an individualized body that enroots him or her in time, place, and culture. So it is of the "universal essence" of the human being to be immersed in history. Essence and individuality should not be played off against one another by undue emphasis on the abstract knowledge of essences. Every concrete essence is individuated.[73] Over against Schillebeeckx, the search for an analogous interpretation of the message of the Gospel across the ages logically presupposes the affirmation of a common core of human nature that remains identical over time, albeit realized in differing modes and in analogously similar conditions. So it is not feasible to seek to attain to a scientific universality of the meaning of human existence devoid of reference to man's concrete historicity. But it is also impossible to undertake a historical-hermeneutical study of the development of culture without grounding this study in the knowledge of the *essential form* of human nature. Lessing and Schillebeeckx on this point are two sides of the same modern coin. They each oppose in some unrealistic way essence and individuation.

Still, this leaves unresolved the question of in just what way the historical man Jesus Christ is the subject of theological science. Why ought we to think that his historical mystery necessarily affects the universal horizon of human existence? We should affirm as much for three reasons. First, Jesus Christ is both God and man, and God is himself the subject of the science of theology. He is also the universal cause of common being, the creator and the redeemer of the entire human race. The humanization of God, then, is a truth that has

---

73. As Aquinas underscores vividly in *De ente*, c. 2.

universal and necessary consequences for all. It grants us knowledge of who God is: he is revealed to us definitively in the historical subject Jesus Christ. Second, Jesus is, by his life, passion, and death, the figure who has atoned for human sin and guilt on behalf of the entire human race. This is directly related to the fact that he is the God-man, and so to the first reason noted above. But it is distinct as such. "For there is one God, and there is one mediator between God and men, the man Christ Jesus" (1 Tim 2:5). In his human nature and by his righteousness, Christ has irrevocably altered the relationship between fallen humankind and God the Trinity. Third, the human nature of Christ is unlike that of any other human, historical figure, for this figure has risen from the dead and *in his resurrection* is the cause of salvation for all others.[74] Jesus raised from the dead is the prefiguration and proleptic exemplar of the life of glory that is to come. Consequently, what has happened to him, historically, affects the entirety of the human race. "He is the beginning, the first-born from the dead, that in everything he might be pre-eminent" (Col 1:18).

These three reasons correspond in their own way, by a kind of analogical transposition, to the three principles of metaphysical thinking noted earlier. We come to know that things exist, and that these things have in themselves an essential identity. They also possess inherent teleological purposes (in various degrees of perfection and in different ways). Likewise, the science of Christ takes its foundation from the fact that in him God exists as a human being. This mystery of the incarnation has an intrinsic (or broadly speaking "essential") content: the mystery of the hypostatic union and the dual natures of Christ. These are the basis for his unique life of redemptive, atoning action and love. There is a final end of the mystery of the incarnation: to lead Christians into the life of beatitude, the world of the resurrection. This occurs most perfectly in the mystery of the glorification of the body and soul of Christ.

In these three principles, then, we have the basis for a science of Christ: in his hypostatic identity, composition of natures, and teleological orientation of life. To these three principles there correspond

---

74. We should not overlook the case of the Virgin Mary, but should simply recall that Christ in his resurrection is the cause of her bodily assumption into glory.

three mysteries: the incarnation, the atonement (which is grounded in the dual natures of the composite person of Christ), and the eschatological resurrection.[75] Through the consideration of these mysteries, Christology acquires a horizon of universality that is far greater than that of any other science. For in the study of Christ, we are given to consider the first origins of the order of being (the mystery of the Trinity), and the final end of the creation (the last judgment and the resurrection). His mystery, then, offers us a depth of explanation regarding the meaning of reality that is far more profound than that of any other science. His mystery illumines all else that exists from an ultimate point of view. This is the case because, and not although, theology is a science that depends upon revealed premises, albeit premises known in this life only by means of supernatural faith.

The Assimilative Power of This Science

Christology is not only a science based upon revealed truths or principles. It is also an assimilative science. That is to say, what we come to know in Jesus Christ regarding God and the human person attains to and assimilates all of our "lesser" or "lower" forms of knowledge. It does so without destroying or disregarding their intrinsic integrity. So, for example, our theological reflection on Christ as a human being need not do violence to philosophical reflection on the nature of the human person as a spiritual animal (consisting of body and immaterial soul). Rather, Christology can take account of such knowledge while understanding it now from within the deeper context of a theological *relecture*. One understands the body and soul of the human person differently in light of the incarnation, life, death, and resurrection of the Son of God. And yet such understanding respects the genuine insights of the philosophical patrimony of human culture, completing it from within and transposing it to a higher plane, so to speak.

---

75. I am presuming that the atonement is grounded in the very being of Christ, his dual natures as God and man, and his theandric activity. This approach points to the incarnation itself as the ground of the atonement, culminating in but not reduced to the act of the cross. Thus Alexandrian themes and Anselmian themes are both respected. God became man that we might be united to God, and Christ obeyed the Father in love even unto death in order to restore the human race to a state of justice and friendship with God.

This observation has consequences when we consider the historical forms of study that are pervasive in determining meaning for the human race, and which touch directly upon Christology in some fashion or another. Let us consider three pertinent examples. First, cosmology: the development of modern positive sciences has led to an explosion of learning regarding the history of the cosmos and the evolution of living forms, from the Big Bang to the diversification of species through the processes of natural selection.[76] This history, to be sure, cannot be interpreted comprehensively uniquely from within the purview of the modern sciences themselves, for these presuppose a deeper metaphysical realism. The discoveries of the structure of natural realities call forth a deeper philosophical reflection on the character of matter, natural form, numbers, time, place, change, movement, and so forth.[77] But even if this is the case, the reflection of a more complete rationality of this type is *itself incomplete*, considered in relation to Christ. For nothing we say of the cosmos or living beings by way of physics, biology, or even philosophy can procure for us knowledge of the incarnation, atonement, and resurrection. But knowledge of these latter mysteries does give an ultimate explicative value to the former disciplines. The mystery of Christ unveils the inner purpose of the physical cosmos, the world of living things, and the unity of the body and spiritual soul in the human person. The teleological purpose of cosmic history comes into view only in him.

Second, and analogously, we might seek to study the New Testament avidly by recourse to the best practices of historical-critical science. In doing so, one might fashion a more or less probable string of hypotheses about the historical aims of Jesus of Nazareth, how he interacted with his historical environment, and the political and sociological context of his expressions and gestures within the culture of Second Temple Judaism. We might also consider how a likely de-

76. Consider the recent articulation of this history offered by Robert Bellah, *Religion in Human Evolution: From the Paleolithic to the Axial Age* (Cambridge, Mass.: Belknap Press, 2011), 44–116.

77. See the arguments to this effect by William A. Wallace, *The Modeling of Nature. Philosophy of Science and Philosophy of Nature in Synthesis* (Washington, D.C.: The Catholic University of America Press, 1996), and Benedict M. Ashley, *The Way toward Wisdom: An Interdisciplinary and Intercultural Introduction to Metaphysics* (Notre Dame, Ind.: University of Notre Dame Press, 2006).

velopment of thought took place in the early Christian community from the time of the passion and resurrection until the composition of the earliest theological writings. All of this, however, will not allow us to substantiate as such the necessary truth of the basic givens of scripture: that Jesus of Nazareth is himself both God and man, and one with God the Father and with the Holy Spirit, that he died for the sins of the human race, and that he is risen from the dead physically and glorified in a new and higher life. If we do understand these higher principles to be true, we can assimilate and interpret accordingly the reasonable and probable arguments of historical investigation of the layers of New Testament sayings, texts, and narrations, putting them into a plausible chronological order and cultural contextualization. But failing the admission of these initial higher principles and structural features, Christology as a historical science will be unable to explain in depth the aims, words, and actions of the historical Christ. The meaning of the history of Jesus is in the end a theological one. His deepest aims and purposes are those accomplished in and through the incarnation, atonement, and resurrection. "For this I have come into the world, to bear witness to the truth" (Jn 18:37). There is no other ultimately realist horizon of historical interpretation than that provided by the principles of Christological science.

As a last example, consider the problem of the teleology of the human person that we touched upon in the second section above. The human being inevitably acts in view of purposes, and the narration of purposes presupposes a more fundamental metaphysical hierarchy of goods in which actions can be evaluated in light of what is most ultimately real and morally best. That being said, there is nevertheless a great deal of archeological history layered within the structures of human action that is not immediately subject to teleological explanation or assimilation to the life of virtue and nobly-ordered freedom. Freud, Nietzsche, and Foucault, in different ways, attempt to alert us to the ways in which human rationality and choice making are always already moved and conditioned (and even in the erroneous accounts of these authors, sometimes "determined") by the inner workings of the *id*, the will to power, *ressentiment*, or the pre-existent linguistic structures of culture that affect our own self-understanding. Let us concede for the sake of argument that these authors have struck upon real phenomena in human comportment which they analyze primarily in a descriptive fashion. Here again, analogous to the previous examples, we encounter a kind of "material causality" embedded in human existence that needs to be taken into account. Human beings are, for example, subject in various subtle ways to Nietzsche's *ressentiment* as a subconscious force influencing their less than lucid intellectual discernments and moral stances. But the self that is subject to the above-mentioned influences is also teleologically ordered both by nature and by grace toward fulfillment in God through life in Christ. There is the possibility, therefore, of a Christological *relecture* of the fallen self under grace in light of the final end of beatitude promised in Christ to the human person. Narrating the meaning of the self in this light, we can move from archeology to an architectonic vision of the human being. The human being, even while deeply internally divided and wounded, is made for the life of the infused theological virtues and for union with Christ in faith, hope, and love. "I live by faith in the Son of God" (Gal 2:20). Teleology casts the most profound interpretive light upon the substructures of human existence and shows the ultimate terminal point of their resolution. However dense and complex the archeological substructures of the human self may be, these are all only fully accounted for in their truth and "resolved" therapeutically by way of the life of virtue ordered toward God.

In each of these cases, then, the mystery of Christ offers scientific principles by which to interpret the world. The cosmos, New Testament history, and the development of the human person: these all must be understood ultimately in light of the incarnation of Christ, his atonement, and his resurrection.

Christology as Wisdom

Jesus himself is the term of our study of theology not only because he is the archetypal human but also because he is divine. The science of theology is not only a science of the ultimate purpose of human existence. It is also above all a *scientia Dei*: a science of the Trinitarian God who discloses himself in revelation.[78] And this revelation is given in view of the vision of God: the beatific vision, wherein the

---

78. ST I, q. 1, a. 7.

Trinitarian God is known intuitively and immediately, "face to face"[79] (1 Cor 13:12); "When he appears we shall be like him, for we shall see him as he is." (1 Jn 3:2). If Christology is an assimilative science, then, it is also ultimately a science oriented toward beatitude.[80] Beatitude, or happiness, is understood here as the joy and fulfillment that come about uniquely by way of the most perfect possession of God. It is only in seeing God face to face that human persons find ultimate fulfillment, and so the final end of theological knowledge is the perfect possession of God.

In one sense, this claim about the final end of theological knowledge is utterly speculative in character. The study of God is directed toward perfect knowledge of God just for the sake of God and of that knowledge.[81] Christological reflection, then, is ordered toward the perfect vision of God. "I am the way, the truth and the life. No one comes to the Father, except by me" (Jn 14:6). At the same time, however, this knowledge procures the ultimate happiness of the human person, and so it is concerned with the ultimate ethical good. The final end of man is the vision of God. This final end, then, should be taken into consideration in any practical deliberation on human action. Consequently, Christology is also the ultimate practical science because it is concerned with the highest end to be found (God himself) and the best and only means to attain to that end: union with Christ by faith, hope, and charity.[82] Christological science is thus simultaneously speculative and practical.[83] In both respects it is theocentric, and in both respects it considers the humanity of Jesus as a locus of revelation of the identity of God. In him we come to know the Father, the Son, and the Holy Spirit. The historical life and example of Christ introduce us into a concrete way of life by which we can return to the Father, in the Son, by the power of the Holy Spirit. It is due to this Trinitarian grounding that the study of Jesus has its ultimate teleological term. It is the orientation toward knowledge and enjoyment of the Trinity that stands as the first principle and final end of the science of Christ.

St. Thomas Aquinas, like his medieval colleagues St. Albert the

79. ST I, q. 12, aa. 4–5.   80. ST I, q. 1, a. 4.
81. ST I, q. 1, a. 7; I-II, q. 3, aa. 5 and 8.   82. ST III, prologue.
83. ST I, q. 1, a. 6.

Great and St. Bonaventure, considered theology to be a form of *sapientia*, and indeed, the highest such form. For Aquinas, we call the highest science "wisdom" because it alone is that form of thought which considers the first principles and highest explanatory principles of all things.[84] It is also, however, that form of thought which examines the final end of man, and so it is not only the most speculative form of reflection but also the most eminently practical.[85] Wisdom teaches us how to live concretely in light of what is most ultimately lasting and true. And so, with St. Albert and St. Bonaventure, St. Thomas considered the ultimate form of speculative wisdom to consist in the contemplative knowledge of the Trinitarian God.

This concluding chapter began with a meditation on a typical hermeneutical approach to Christology, one based upon modern historical study of Jesus of Nazareth and ordered toward political praxis within the context of contemporary sociological settings. I have argued that this sort of historicization of the object of theology ignores the inevitably metaphysical basis for true human thought about the structure and meaning of reality. At the same time, I have also suggested that a Christological reflection that is more overtly metaphysical in kind can also take full and realistic account of the historical characteristics of cosmic, historical, and human reality. In other words, in recovering (or in moving forward into) a more robustly ontological account of the mystery of Christ, we are not leaving behind the possibility of deep historical realism. We are, however, moving beyond temporal history into God. For only in God can the human being find the fullness of the truth and lasting fulfillment. "And this is eternal life, that they know thee the only true God, and Jesus Christ whom thou hast sent" (Jn 17:3).

The classical vision of Christology as wisdom may seem outdated to some, but in fact it offers a profound perspective on the intellectual problems of our own age. For in the modern era, university education is frequently a fragmented affair. Diverse disciplines have few real ways to speak to each other and lack the adequate grounds in themselves by which to achieve mutual integration and unity. To

---

84. Aquinas, *In Meta.*, prologue. See *Metaphysics* I, 2, 982a3–983a11.
85. Aquinas, ST II-II, q. 45, a. 3. See in this respect *Nicomachean Ethics* X, 7, 1177a11–1178a8.

that extent, they often leave their modern purveyors intellectually un-fulfilled and devoid of a much desired ultimate perspective. The wisdom of Christ gives that ultimate perspective in ways that are integral and unified but also gentle and magnanimous. Christ preserves every lesser truth because he is the truth itself. The arguments in this book have sought to show the interpretive depth of the thought of Thomas Aquinas in the domain of Christological reflection, even in the face of modernity and in discussion with the contours of modern theology. We should seek the wisdom of God according to this classical understanding, whether it initially makes perfect sense to our contemporaries or not. For they themselves are very often thoroughly disorientated, and stand in need of the wisdom of Christ. It is when theology takes on a true orientation toward the Trinity that it becomes the source of stability for the church, amidst the vicissitudes of this world. In studying Jesus after the example of Thomas Aquinas we come to find rest in a wisdom that surpasses ourselves, and which redeems our human history and our personal lives in time, but which also orients us toward the world to come. For it is only there, in the vision of God, that we will find perfect spiritual repose, and the peace of God that surpasses all finite comprehension.

Selected Bibliography

WORKS BY THOMAS AQUINAS

Collationes super Credo in Deum. Paris: Nouvelles Editions Latines, 1969.

Compendium theologiae ad fratrem Reginaldum socium suum carissimum. Vol. 42 of *Sancti Thomae de Aquino opera omnia.* Leonine Edition. Rome: Editori di San Tommaso, 1979.

De ente et essentia. In *Opuscula Philosophica,* vol. 1. Edited by R. Spiazzi. Turin and Rome: Marietti, 1950.

De malo. In *Sancti Thomae de Aquino opera omnia,* vol. 23. Leonine Edition. Rome: Editori di San Tommaso, 1979.

De potentia Dei. Edited by P. M. Pession. In *Quaestiones disputatae,* vol. 2. Edited by R. Spiazzi. Turin and Rome: Marietti, 1965.

De veritate. In *Sancti Thomae de Aquino opera omnia,* vol. 22. Leonine Edition. Rome: Editori di San Tommaso, 1975–76.

Expositio libri Peryermenias. In *Sancti Thomae de Aquino opera omnia,* vol. 1. Leonine Edition. Rome: Editori di San Tommaso, 1882.

Expositio libri Posteriorum. In *Sancti Thomae de Aquino opera omnia,* vol. 1. Leonine Edition. Rome: Editori di San Tommaso, 1882.

Expositio super librum Boethii de Trinitate. In *Sancti Thomae de Aquino opera omnia,* vol. 50. Leonine Edition. Rome: Editori di San Tommaso, 1992.

In duodecim libros Metaphysicorum Aristotelis expositio. Edited by M. R. Cathala and R. M. Spiazzi. Turin and Rome: Marietti, 1964.

In librum beati Dionysii de divinis nominibus expositio. Edited by C. Pera. Turin and Rome: Marietti, 1950.

In librum de causis expositio. In *Opuscula Omnia,* vol. 1. Edited by P. Mandonnet. Paris: P. Lethielleux, 1927.

Scriptum super libros Sententiarum magistri Petri Lombardi episcopi Parisiensis. Vols. 1–2, edited by P. Mandonnet. Paris: P. Lethielleux, 1929. Vols. 3–4, edited by M. Moos. Paris: P. Lethielleux, 1933–47.

Summa contra Gentiles. In *Sancti Thomae Aquinatis opera omnia,* vols. 13–15. Leonine Edition. Rome: R. Garroni, 1918–30.

Super Epistolas S. Pauli. Edited by R. Cai. Turin and Rome: Marietti, 1953.

Super Evangelium S. Joannis Lectura. Edited by R. Cai. Turin and Rome: Marietti, 1952.

Super Evangelium S. Matthaei Lectura. Edited by R. Cai. Turin and Rome: Marietti, 1951.

Summa theologiae. In *Sancti Thomae Aquinatis opera omnia,* vols. 4–12. Leonine edition. Rome: 1888–1906.

TRANSLATIONS OF
WORKS BY THOMAS AQUINAS

Aristotle: On Interpretation. Commentary by St. Thomas and Cajetan. Translated by J. Oesterle. Milwaukee, Wis.: Marquette University Press, 1962.

Commentary on Aristotle's De Anima. Translated by K. Foster and S. Humphries. Notre Dame, Ind.: Dumb Ox Books, 1994.

Commentary on Aristotle's Metaphysics. Translated by J. P. Rowan. Notre Dame, Ind.: Dumb Ox Books, 1995.

Commentary on the Book of Causes. Translated by V. Guagliardo, C. Hess, and R. Taylor. Washington, D.C.: The Catholic University of America Press, 1996.

Commentary on the Epistle to the Hebrews. Translated by C. Baer. South Bend, Ind.: St. Augustine's Press, 2006.

Commentary on the Letter of St. Paul to the Romans. Translated by F. Larcher. Lander, Wyo.: The Aquinas Institute, 2012.

Commentary on the Gospel of St. John. Translated by J. Weisheipl. Vol. 1; Albany, N.Y.: Magi Press, 1980. Vol. 2; Petersham, Mass.: St. Bede's Publications, 2000.

Compendium of Theology. Translated by C. Vollert. London: B. Herder, 1955.

The Disputed Questions on Truth. 3 vols. Translated by R. Schmidt. Chicago: Henry Regnery, 1954.

The Division and Methods of the Sciences: Questions V and VI of his Commentary on the De Trinitate of Boethius. Translated by A. Maurer. Toronto: PIMS, 1986.

Faith, Reason and Theology. Translated by A. Maurer. Toronto: PIMS, 1987.

On the Power of God. Translated by the English Dominican Fathers. Westminster, Md.: The Newman Press, 1952.

Summa contra Gentiles I. Translated by A. Pegis. Garden City, N.Y.: Doubleday, 1955.

Summa contra Gentiles II. Translated by J. Anderson. Garden City, N.Y.: Doubleday, 1956.

Summa contra Gentiles III. 2 vols. Translated by V. J. Burke. Garden City, N.Y.: Doubleday, 1956.

Summa contra Gentiles IV. Translated by C. J. O'Neil. Garden City, N.Y.: Doubleday, 1956.

Summa theologica. Translated by English Dominican Province. New York: Benziger Brothers, 1947.

Thomas Aquinas: Selected Writings. Translated by R. McInerny. London: Penguin Books, 1998.

CLASSICAL AND MODERN WORKS

Aertsen, Jan. *Medieval Philosophy and the Transcendentals*. Leiden: Brill, 1996.

Alfeyev, Hilarion. *Christ the Conqueror of Hell. The Descent into Hades from an Orthodox Perspective*. Crestwood, N.Y.: St. Vladimir's Seminary Press, 2009.

Aristotle. *The Complete Works of Aristotle*. Translated by W. D. Ross. Edited by J. Barnes. 2 vols. Princeton: Princeton University Press, 1984.

Ashley, Benedict M. *The Way toward Wisdom. An Interdisciplinary and Intercultural Introduction to Metaphysics*. Notre Dame, Ind.: University of Notre Dame Press, 2006.

Ayres, Lewis. *Nicaea and Its Legacy*. Oxford: Oxford University Press, 2004.

Balthasar, Hans Urs von. *Dare We Hope "That All Men Be Saved"?* Translated by D. Kipp and L. Krauth. San Francisco: Ignatius Press, 1988.

——. *First Glance at Adrienne von Speyr*. Translated by A. Lawry and S. Englund. San Francisco: Ignatius Press, 1981.

——. *The Glory of the Lord. A Theological Aesthetics*. Vol. I: *Seeing the Form*. Translated by E. Leiva-Merikakis. San Francisco: Ignatius, 1982.

——. *The Glory of the Lord. A Theological Aesthetics*. Vol. IV: *The Realm of Metaphysics in Antiquity*. Translated by Brian McNeil. San Francisco: Ignatius, 1989.

——. *Mysterium Paschale. The Mystery of Easter*. Translated by A. Nichols. San Francisco: Ignatius Press, 1990.

——. *Theodrama: Theological Dramatic Theory*. 5 vols. Translated by G. Harrison. San Francisco: Ignatius, 1988–98.

——. *Karl Barth: Darstellung und Deutung Seiner Theologie*. Köln: Verlag Jakob Hegner, 1951. Translated by E. Oakes. *The Theology of Karl Barth: Exposition and Interpretation*. San Francisco: Ignatius Press, 1992.

Bañez, Domingo. *Scholastica Commentaria in Primam Partem Summae Theologiae S. Thomae Aquinatis*. Madrid: F.E.D.A., 1934.

Barnes, Corey. "Albert the Great and Thomas Aquinas on Person, Hypostasis and Hypostatic Union." *The Thomist* 72 (2008): 107–46.

Barrett, C. K. *The Gospel According to St. John*. Philadelphia: The Westminster Press, 1978.

Barth, Karl. *Church Dogmatics*. Edited by G. W. Bromiley and T. F. Torrance. 4 vols. Edinburgh: T. & T. Clark, 1936–75.

——. *Credo*. Translated by R. M. Brown. New York: Scribner's, 1962.

Bathrellos, Demetrios. *The Byzantine Christ: Person, Nature and Will in the Christology of Saint Maximus the Confessor*. Oxford: Oxford University Press, 2004.

Bauckham, Richard. *God Crucified: Monotheism and Christology in the New Testament*. Grand Rapids, Mich.: Eerdmans, 1998.

——. *Jesus and the Eyewitnesses. The Gospels as Eyewitness Testimony*. Grand Rapids, Mich.: Eerdmans, 2006.

Beasley-Murray, George. *John*. Waco, Tex.: Word Books, 1989.

Bellah, Robert. *Religion in Human Evolution: From the Paleolithic to the Axial Age*. Cambridge, Mass.: Belknap Press, 2011.

Berti, Enrico. "Multiplicity and Unity of Being in Aristotle." *The Aristotelian Society* 101, no. 2 (2001): 185–207.

Betz, John R. "Erich Przywara and Karl Barth: On the *Analogia Entis* as a Formal Principle of Catholic Theology." In *The Analogy of Being: Invention of the Antichrist or the Wisdom of God?*, edited by Thomas Joseph White, 35–87. Grand Rapids, Mich.: Eerdmans, 2011.

Billuart, Charles René. *Summa Sancti Thomae.* Paris: Letouzey & Ané, 1880.

Bonino, Serge-Thomas. *Les Anges et Les Démons. Quatorze leçons de théologie catholique.* Paris: Parole et Silence, 2007.

———. "The Role of the Apostles in the Communication of the Divine Revelation according to the *Lectura super Ioannem* of St. Thomas Aquinas." In *Reading John with St. Thomas Aquinas*, edited by M. Dauphinais and M. Levering, 318–46. Washington, D.C.: The Catholic University of America Press, 2005.

Bouillard, Henri. *Karl Barth, Genèse et évolution de la theologie dialectique.* 3 vols. Paris: Aubier, 1957.

Boulnois, Olivier. *Être et representation: Une généologie de la métaphysique moderne à l'époque de Duns Scot (XIIIe-XIVe Siècle).* Paris: Presses Universitaires de France, 1999.

———. "La destruction de l'analogie et l'instauration de la métaphysique." In *Duns Scot, Sur la connaissance de Dieu et l'univocité de l'étant*, 11–81. Paris: Presses Universitaires de France, 1988.

———. "Quand commence l'onto-théo-logie? Aristote, Thomas d'Aquin et Duns Scot." *Revue Thomiste* 95 (1995): 85–105.

Bousset, Wilhelm. *Kyrios Christos: Geschichte des Christusglaubens von den Anfängen des Christentums bis Irenaeus.* Göttingen: Vandenhoeck & Ruprecht, 1913.

Boyle, John F. "The Twofold Division of St. Thomas's Christology in the *Tertia pars*." *The Thomist* 60 (1996): 439–47.

Brown, Raymond. *The Death of the Messiah.* 2 vols. New York: Doubleday, 1993.

Bulgakov, Sergius. *The Lamb of God.* Translated by Boris Jakim. Grand Rapids, Mich.: Eerdmans, 2008.

Bultmann, Rudolph. *Jesus Christ and Mythology.* London: Prentice Hall, 1997.

———. *New Testament and Theology and Other Basic Writings.* Edited and translated by S. Ogden. Philadelphia: Fortress, 1984.

———. *Theology of the New Testament.* 2 vols. Translated by K. Grobel. New York: Scribner's, 1955.

Cabrol, Jean (Capreolus). *Defensiones theologiae divi Thomae Aquinatis.* 7 vols. Edited by C. Paban and T. Pègues. Tours: Alfred Cattier, 1900–1908.

Caird, C. B. and L. D. Hurst. *New Testament Theology.* Oxford: Oxford University Press, 1994.

Calvin, John. *Institutes of the Christian Religion.* 2 vols. Translated by F. Battles. Philadelphia: Westminster Press, 1960.

Carraud, Vincent. *Causa sive ratio. La raison de la cause, de Suarez à Leibniz.* Paris: Presses Universitaires de France, 2002.

Cessario, Romanus. "Incarnate Wisdom and the Immediacy of Christ's Salvific Knowledge." *Problemi teologici alla luce dell'Aquinate*, in *Studi Tomistici* 44, no. 5, 334–40. Vatican City: Libreria Editrice Vaticana, 1991.

Chadwick, Henry. "Eucharist and Christology in the Nestorian Controversy." *Journal of Theological Studies* 2 (1951): 145–64.

Chavannes, Henry. *L'Analogie entre Dieu et le monde selon saint Thomas d'Aquin et selon Karl Barth*. Paris: Cerf, 1969.

Chenu, Marie-Dominique. *Peuple de Dieu dans le Monde*. Paris: Cerf, 1966.

———. "Raison psychologique du développement du dogme." *Revue des Sciences Philosophiques et Théologiques* 13 (1924): 44–51.

———. *Le Saulchoir: Une école de théologie*. Paris: Cerf, 1937.

———. "Vérité évangélique et métaphysique wolfienne à Vatican II." *Revue des Sciences Philosophiques et Théologiques* 57 (1973): 632–40.

Chesnut, Roberta. *Three Monophysite Christologies: Severus of Antioch, Philoxenus of Mabbug, and Jacob of Sarug*. Oxford: Oxford University Press, 1976.

Colish, Marcia L. "Christological Nihilianism in the Second Half of the Twelfth Century." *Recherches de Théologie et Philosophie Médiévales* 63 (1996): 146–55.

Congar, Yves. *Je Crois en l'Esprit Saint*. 3 vols. Paris: Cerf, 1979–80.

———. *La tradition et les traditions*. 2 vols. Paris: A. Fayard, 1960–63.

Cottier, Georges. *Le désir de Dieu: sur les traces de saint Thomas*. Paris: Éditions Parole et Silence, 2002.

———. "Thomisme et Modernité." In *Saint Thomas au XXe Siècle*, edited by S.-T. Bonino, 355–56. Paris: Éditions St.-Paul, 1994.

Courtine, Jean François. *Inventio analogiae: Métaphysique et ontothéologie*. Paris: J. Vrin, 2005.

———. *Suarez et le Système de la Métaphysique*. Paris: Presses Universitaires de France, 1990.

Cullmann, Oscar. *Immortality of the Soul or Resurrection from the Dead? The Witness of the New Testament*. London: Epworth, 1958.

Danielou, Jean. *Etudes d'exégèse judéo-chrétienne*. Paris: Beauchesne, 1966.

De Lubac, Henri. *Surnaturel: Études historiques*. Paris: Aubier, 1946.

Derrida, Jacques. "Faith and Knowledge: The Two Sources of 'Religion' at the Limits of Reason Alone." Translated by S. Weber in *Religion*, edited by J. Derrida and G. Vattimo, 1–78. Stanford, Calif.: Stanford University Press, 1998.

———. *Of Grammatology*. Translated by G. C. Spivak. Baltimore, Md.: The Johns Hopkins University Press, 1976.

Dewan, Lawrence. *Form and Being: Studies in Thomistic Metaphysics*. Washington, D.C.: The Catholic University of America Press, 2006.

———. "On Anthony Kenny's *Aquinas on Being*." *Nova et Vetera* (English edition) 3, no. 2 (2005): 335–400.

Diepen, Herman. "La critique du baslisme selon saint Thomas d'Aquin." *Revue Thomiste* 50 (1950): 82–118 and 290–329.

———. "La psychologie humaine du Christ selon saint Thomas d'Aquin." *Revue Thomiste* 50 (1950): 515–62.

———. *Théologie d'Emmanuel*. Bruges: Desclée de Brouwer, 1960.

Dodd, C. H. *The Fourth Gospel*. Cambridge: Cambridge University Press, 1963.

Donneaud, Henri. "La constitution dialectique de la théologie et de son histoire selon M.D. Chenu." *Revue Thomiste* 96 (1996): 41–66.

———. "*Surnaturel* through the Fine-Tooth Comb of Traditional Thomism." In *Surnaturel: A Controversy at the Heart of Twentieth-Century Thomistic Thought*, edited by Serge-Thomas Bonino, translated by Robert Williams, translation revised by Matthew Levering, 41–57. Naples, Fla.: Sapientia Press, 2009.

Dorival, Gilles. "L'Interpretation Ancienne du Psaume 21 (TM 22)." In *David, Jésus et la Reine Esther*, edited by G. Dorival, 225–314. Louvain: Peeters, 2002.

Dunn, James D. G. *The Theology of Paul the Apostle*. Grand Rapids, Mich.: Eerdmans, 1998.

Dupuis, Jacques. *Toward a Christian Theology of Religious Pluralism*. Maryknoll, N.Y.: Orbis, 1997.

Emery, Gilles. "Essentialism or Personalism in the Treatise on God in St. Thomas Aquinas?" *The Thomist* 64 (2000): 521–63.

———. "The Immutability of the God of Love and the Problem of Language Concerning the 'Suffering of God.'" In *Divine Impassibility and the Mystery of Human Suffering*, edited by J. F. Keating and Thomas Joseph White, 27–76. Grand Rapids, Mich.: Eerdmans, 2009.

———. "The Personal Mode of Trinitarian Action in Saint Thomas Aquinas." *The Thomist* 69 (2005): 31–77.

———. *The Trinitarian Theology of Saint Thomas Aquinas*. Translated by F. Murphy. Oxford: Oxford University Press, 2007.

———. *Trinity, Church and the Human Person*. Naples, Fla.: Sapientia Press, 2007.

———. *Trinity in Aquinas*. Naples, Fla: Sapientia Press, 2005.

Fabro, Cornelio. *Participation et Causalité selon Thomas d'Aquin*. Louvain / Paris: Publications Universitaires de Louvain / Éditions Béatrice-Nauwelaerts, 1961.

Fee, Gordon D. *Pauline Christology: An Exegetical-Theological Study*. Peabody, Mass.: Hendrickson Publishers, 2007.

Feingold, Lawrence. *The Natural Desire to See God according to St. Thomas Aquinas and His Interpreters*. Naples, Fla.: Sapientia Press, 2010.

Feser, Edward. *Aquinas: A Beginner's Guide*. Oxford: Oneworld, 2009.

Feuillet, André. "Jésus et la Sagesse divine d'après les Évangiles Synoptiques; Le 'Logion johannique' et l'Ancien Testament." *Revue Biblique* 62 (1955): 161–96.

Fischer, Simon. *Revelatory Positivism: Barth's Earliest Theology and the Marburg School*. Oxford: Oxford University Press, 1988.

Fletcher, Patrick James. *Resurrection and Platonic Dualism: Joseph Ratzinger's Augustinianism*. PhD diss., The Catholic University of America, 2011.

Foucault, Michel. *The Archaeology of Knowledge and The Discourse on Language*. Translated by A. M. Sheridan Smith. New York: Pantheon, 1972.

Fouilloux, Etienne. "Dialogue théologique? (1946–1948)." In *Saint Thomas au XXe siècle: Actes du colloque centenaire de la "Revue Thomiste,"* edited by S.-T. Bonino, 153–98. Paris: Editions Saint-Paul, 1994.

Frei, Hans. *Types of Christian Theology*. Edited by G. Hunsinger and W. C. Placher. New Haven, Conn.: Yale University Press, 1992.

Galot, Jean. "La conscience du Christ et la foi." *Esprit et vie* 92 (1982): 145–52.

———. "Le Christ terrestre et la vision." *Gregorianum* 67 (1986): 429–50.

Galtier, Paul. *L'Unité du Christ: être, personne, conscience*. Paris: Beauchesne, 1939.

———. "Unité ontologique et unité psychologique dans le Christ." *Bulletin de littérature ecclésiastique* (Toulouse) 42 (1941): 161–75 and 216–32.

Gardeil, Ambroise. *La crédibilité et l'apologétique*. Paris: J. Gabalda et Fils, 1928.

————. *Le donné révélé et la théologie.* Second edition. Paris: Cerf, 1932.

Garrigou-Lagrange, Reginald. *De Deo Trino et Creatore. Commentarius in Summa Theologicam S. Thomae (Ia q. xxvii–cxix).* Turin / Paris: Marietti / Desclée de Brouwer, 1943.

————. *God: His Existence and His Nature.* Vol. 1. Translated by B. Rose. London: B. Herder Press, 1939.

————. *The Saviour and His Love for Us.* Translated by A. Bouchard. London: B. Herder, 1951.

Garrigues, Jean Miguel. "La conscience de soi telle qu'elle était exercée par le Fils de Dieu fait homme." *Nova et Vetera* (French Edition) 79, no. 1 (2004): 39–51.

————. "Le dessein d'adoption du créateur dans son rapport au fils d'après S. Maxime le Confesseur." In *Maximus Confessor,* edited by F. Heinzer and C. Schönborn, 173–92. Fribourg: Éditions Universitaires, 1982.

————. "L'instrumentalité rédemptrice du libre arbitre du Christ chez saint Maxime le Confesseur." *Revue Thomiste* 104 (2004): 531–50.

Gathercole, Simon J. *The Pre-existent Son: Recovering the Christologies of Matthew, Mark and Luke.* Grand Rapids, Mich.: Eerdmans, 2006.

Gavrilyuk, Paul L. "The Kenotic Theology of Sergius Bulgakov." *Scottish Journal of Theology* 58 (2005): 251–69.

————. *The Suffering of the Impassible God. The Dialectics of Patristic Thought.* Oxford: Oxford University Press, 2004.

Geffré, Claude. *Le Christianisme au risque de l'interpretation.* Paris: Cerf, 1983. English translation by D. Smith. *The Risk of Interpretation: On Being Faithful to the Christian Tradition in a Non-Christian Age.* New York: Paulist Press, 1987.

Geiger, L.-B. "Les rédactions successives de *Contra Gentiles* I, 53 d'après l'autographe." In *St. Thomas d'Aquin aujourd'hui,* edited by J. Y. Jolif, 221–40. Paris: Desclée de Brouwer, 1963.

Gilson, Étienne. *l'Être et l'Essence.* Paris: J. Vrin, 1981.

Girard, René. *The Girard Reader.* Edited by J. G. Williams. New York: Herder and Herder, 2004.

Gockel, Matthias. *Barth and Schleiermacher on the Doctrine of Election.* Oxford: Oxford University Press, 2006.

Gonet, Jean-Baptiste. *Clypeus Theologiae Thomisticae.* Vol. 1. Paris: Vivès, 1875.

Goris, Harm. "Theology and Theory of the Word in Aquinas." In *Aquinas the Augustinian,* edited by Michael Dauphinais, Barry David, and Matthew Levering, 62–78. Washington, D.C.: The Catholic University of America Press, 2007.

Gramsci, Antonio. *Prison Notebooks.* New York: Columbia University Press, 1992.

Griffiths, Paul. "Is There a Doctrine of the Descent into Hell?" *Pro Ecclesia* 17, no. 3 (2008): 257–68.

Grillmeier, Aloys. *Christ in Christian Tradition: From the Apostolic Age to Chalcedon (451).* Translated by J. S. Bowden. New York: Sheed and Ward, 1965.

————. *Christ in Christian Tradition. Volume One. From the Apostolic Age to Chalcedon (451).* Second revised edition. Translated by J. Bowden. Atlanta: John Knox Press, 1975.

————. *Christ in Christian Tradition. Volume One, Part Two. From the Council of Chalcedon (451) to Gregory the Great (509–604). The Church of Constantino-*

ple in the Sixth Century, with Theresia Hainthaler. Translated by J. Cawte and P. Allen. London / Louisville, Ky.: Mowbray / Westminster John Knox, 1995.

———. "Zum Christusbild der heutigen katholischen Theologie." In *Fragen der Theologie heute*, edited by J. Feiner, J. Trütsch, and F. Böckle, 265–99. Einsiedeln: Benziger, 1957.

Guardini, Romano. *The Humanity of Christ: Contributions to a Psychology of Jesus*. Translated by R. Walls. New York: Random House, 1964.

Hare, Douglas. *Matthew*. Louisville, Ky.: Westminster John Knox Press, 1993.

Harnack, Adolf von. *Das Wesen des Christentums*. Leipzig: J.C. Hinrichs, 1900.

———. *Lehrbuch der Dogmengeschichte*. 3 vols. Freiburg: J. C. B. Mohr, 1886–89. English translation by N. Buchanan made from the 1909 third edition in 7 vols., *History of Dogma*, reprinted in 4 vols. New York: Dover Publications, 1961.

Hart, David Bentley. *The Beauty of the Infinite: The Aesthetics of Christian Truth*. Grand Rapids, Mich.: Eerdmans, 2003.

———. "The Destiny of Christian Metaphysics: Reflections on the *Analogia Entis*." In *The Analogy of Being: Invention of the Antichrist or the Wisdom of God?*, edited by Thomas Joseph White, 395–410. Grand Rapids, Mich.: Eerdmans, 2011.

———. "No Shadow of Turning: On Divine Impassibility." *Pro Ecclesia* 11 (Spring 2002): 184–206.

———. "Providence and Causality: On Divine Innocence." In *Providence of God: Deus habet consilium*, edited by F. Murphy and P. Ziegler, 37–56. London: Continuum, 2009.

Hector, Kevin W. "Actualism and Incarnation: The High Christology of Friedrich Schleiermacher." *International Journal of Systematic Theology* 8, no. 3 (2006): 307–22.

———. "God's Trinunity and Self-Determination: A Conversation with Karl Barth, Bruce McCormack, and Paul Molnar." *International Journal of Systematic Theology* 7, no. 3 (2005): 246–61.

———. *Theology without Metaphysics: God, Language, and the Spirit of Recognition*. Cambridge: Cambridge University Press, 2011.

Heidegger, Martin. *Identity and Difference*. Translated by J. Stambaugh. New York: Harper and Row, 1969.

Heidler, Fritz. *Die biblische Lehre von der Unsterblichkeit der Seele: Sterben, Tod, ewiges Leben im Aspekt lutherischer Anthropologie*. Göttingen: Vandenhoeck & Ruprecht, 1983.

Hengel, Martin. *The Atonement: The Origins of the Doctrine in the New Testament*. Translated by J. Bowden. Philadelphia: Fortress Press, 1981.

———. *The Son of God: The Origin of Christology and the History of Jewish-Hellenistic Religion*. Translated by J. Bowden. Philadelphia: Fortress Press, 1976.

Herrmann, Wilhelm. *Die Religion im Verhältniss zum Welterkennen und zur Sittlichkeit: eine Grundlegung der systematischen Theologie*. Halle: M. Niemeyer, 1879.

Hick, John. *An Interpretation of Religion: Human Responses to the Transcendent*. New Haven, Conn.: Yale University Press, 1989.

————. "Jesus and the World Religions." In *The Myth of God Incarnate*, edited by J. Hick, 167–85. Philadelphia: The Westminster Press, 1977.

Hofer, Andrew. "Balthasar's Eschatology on the Intermediate State. The Question of Knowability." *Logos* 12, no. 3 (Summer 2009): 148–72.

Holub, Renate. *Antonio Gramsci: Beyond Marxism and Postmodernism*. London: Routledge, 1992.

Humbrecht, Thierry-Dominique. *Théologie Négative et Noms Divins chez Saint Thomas d'Aquin*. Paris: J. Vrin, 2005.

Hume, David. *Dialogues Concerning Natural Religion*. London: Penguin, 1990.

Hunsinger, George. "Karl Barth's Christology: Its Basic Chalcedonian Character." *The Cambridge Companion to Karl Barth*. Edited by John Webster. Cambridge: Cambridge University Press, 2000.

Hurtado, Larry W. *Lord Jesus Christ: Devotion to Jesus in Earliest Christianity*. Grand Rapids, Mich.: Eerdmans, 2003.

Hütter, Reinhard. "The Directedness of Reason and the Metaphysics of Creation." In *Reason and the Reasons of Faith*, edited by P. Griffiths and R. Hütter, 160–93. Edinburgh: T. & T. Clark, 2005.

————. "Thomas on the Natural Desire for the Vision of God: A Relecture of *Summa Contra Gentiles* III, 25 après Henri de Lubac." *The Thomist* 73 (2009): 523–91.

Israel, Jonathan. *Radical Enlightenment: Philosophy in the Making of Modernity 1650–1750*. Oxford: Oxford University Press, 2001.

Jenson, Robert. *Systematic Theology I*. Oxford: Oxford University Press, 1997.

Journet, Charles. *L'Église du Verbe Incarné*. Vol. II. *La structure interne de l'Église: Le Christ, la Vierge, l'Esprit Saint*. Paris: Saint Augustin, 1999.

————. *Introduction à la Théologie*. *Oeuvres Complétes*, Vol. IX. Paris: Éditions St. Augustin, 2007.

————. *Les Septs Paroles du Christ au Croix*. Paris: Éditions du Seuil, 1954.

————. *The Mass: The Presence of the Sacrifice of the Cross*. Translated by Victor Szczurek. South Bend, Ind.: St. Augustine's Press, 2008.

Jüngel, Eberhard. *God as the Mystery of the World: On the Foundation of the Theology of the Crucified One in the Dispute between Theism and Atheism*. Translated by D. L. Guder. Grand Rapids, Mich.: Eerdmans, 1983.

————. *God's Being Is in Becoming; The Trinitarian Being of God in the Theology of Karl Barth*. Translated by J. Webster. Grand Rapids, Mich.: Eerdmans, 2001.

Kähler, Martin. *Der sogenannte historische Jesus und der geschichtliche, biblische Christus*. Leipzig: A. Deichert, 1892. English translation by Carl E. Braaten. *The So-Called Historical Jesus and the Historical Biblical Christ*. Philadelphia: Fortress Press, 1964.

Kant, Immanuel. *The Critique of Pure Reason*. Translated by N. K. Smith. New York: Macmillan, 1965.

————. *Prolegomena to Any Future Metaphysics*. Translated by P. Carus. Indianapolis: Bobbs-Merrill, 1950.

————. *Religion within the Boundaries of Mere Reason*. Translated and edited by Allen Wood and George di Giovanni. Cambridge: Cambridge University Press, 1998.

Kasper, Walter. *The God of Jesus Christ*. Translated by M. J. O'Connell. New York: Crossroad, 1989.

———. *Jesus the Christ*. Translated by V. Green. London: Burns & Oates, 1976.

Kelly, J. N. D. *Early Christian Doctrines*. Fifth Edition. London: A. & C. Black, 1977.

Kerr, Fergus. *Theology after Wittgenstein*. Oxford: Blackwell, 1986.

———. *Twentieth-Century Catholic Theologians*. Oxford: Blackwell, 2007.

Kromholtz, Bryan. *On the Last Day: The Time of the Resurrection of the Dead according to Thomas Aquinas*. Fribourg: Academic Press Fribourg, 2010.

Lamb, Matthew. "The Eschatology of St. Thomas Aquinas." In *Aquinas on Doctrine*, edited by T. Weinandy, D. Keating, and J. Yocum, 225–40. London: T. and T. Clark, 2004.

Lagrange, Marie-Joseph. *L'Evangile Selon Saint Marc*. Paris: J. Gabalda, 1921.

Lauber, David. *Barth on the Descent into Hell: God, Atonement and Christian Life*. London: Ashgate, 2004.

Le Guillou, Marie-Joseph. "Surnaturel." *Revue des sciences philosophiques et théologiques* 34 (1950): 226–43.

Leinsle, Ulrich G. *Introduction to Scholastic Theology*. Translated by M. J. Miller. Washington, D.C.: The Catholic University of America Press, 2010.

Lessing, Gotthold Ephraim. *Lessing: Philosophical and Theological Writings*. Edited by H. B. Nisbet. Cambridge: Cambridge University Press, 2005.

———. *Lessing's Theological Writings*. Translated by H. Chadwick. Stanford, Calif.: Stanford University Press, 1957.

Levering, Matthew. *Christ's Fulfillment of Torah and Temple: Salvation according to Thomas Aquinas*. Notre Dame, Ind.: University of Notre Dame Press, 2002.

———. *Sacrifice and Community*. Oxford: Blackwell, 2005.

Lightfoot, R. H. *St. John's Gospel*. Oxford: Clarendon Press, 1956.

Lindars, Barnabas. *The Gospel of John*. London: Oliphants Press, 1957.

Lindbeck, George. *The Nature of Doctrine: Religion and Theology in a Post-Liberal Age*. Louisville, Ky.: Westminster John Knox, 1984.

Lonergan, Bernard. *The Ontological and Psychological Constitution of Christ*. In *Collected Works*, vol. 7. Translated by Michael G. Shields. Toronto: University of Toronto Press, 2002.

———. *The Triune God: Systematics*. In *Collected Works*, vol. 12. Toronto: University of Toronto Press, 2007.

Long, Steven A. *Analogia Entis: On the Analogy of Being, Metaphysics, and the Act of Faith*. Notre Dame, Ind.: University of Notre Dame Press, 2011.

———. *Natura Pura. On the Recovery of Nature in the Doctrine of Grace*. New York: Fordham University Press, 2010.

Loofs, Friedrich. "Kenosis." In *Realencyklopädie für protestantische Theologie und Kirche*, edited by J. J. Herzog and A. Hauck, 10:246–63. Leipzig: J. C. Hinrichs, 1901.

Louth, Andrew. *St John Damascene: Tradition and Originality in Byzantine Theology*. Oxford: Oxford University Press, 2002.

Luz, Ulrich. *Matthew: A Commentary*. 3 vols. Translated by J. Crouch. Minneapolis, Minn.: Fortress, 2007.

McCormack, Bruce. "Divine Impassibility or Simple Divine Constancy? Implications of Karl Barth's Later Christology for Debates over Impassibility." In *Divine Impassibility and the Mystery of Human Suffering*, edited by James F. Keating and Thomas Joseph White, 150–86. Grand Rapids, Mich.: Eerdmans, 2009.

———. "Grace and Being: The Role of God's Gracious Election in Karl Barth's Theological Ontology." In *The Cambridge Companion to Karl Barth*, edited by J. Webster, 92–110. Cambridge: Cambridge University Press, 2000.

———. "Karl Barth's Christology as a Resource for a Reformed Version of Kenoticism." *International Journal of Systematic Theology* 8, no. 3 (2006): 243–51.

———. *Karl Barth's Critically Realistic Dialectical Theology: Its Genesis and Development, 1909–1936*. Oxford: Clarendon Press, 1995.

———. "Karl Barth's Version of an 'Analogy of Being': A Dialectical No and Yes to Roman Catholicism." In *The Analogy of Being: Invention of the Antichrist or the Wisdom of God?*, edited by Thomas Joseph White, 88–144. Grand Rapids, Mich.: Eerdmans, 2010.

———. "Seek God Where He May Be Found: A Response to Edwin Chr. van Driel." *Scottish Journal of Theology* 60 (February 2007): 62–79.

McGrath, S. J. *The Early Heidegger and Medieval Philosophy. Phenomenology for the Godforsaken*. Washington, D.C.: The Catholic University of America Press, 2006.

MacIntyre, Alasdair. *Three Rival Versions of Moral Inquiry: Encyclopedia, Genealogy, and Tradition*. Notre Dame, Ind.: University of Notre Dame Press, 1990.

Mansini, Guy. "Can Humility and Obedience Be Trinitarian Realities?" In *Aquinas and Barth: An Unofficial Catholic-Protestant Dialogue*, edited by Bruce L. McCormack and Thomas Joseph White, 71–98. Grand Rapids, Mich.: Eerdmans, 2013.

———. "Understanding St. Thomas on Christ's Immediate Knowledge of God." *The Thomist* 59 (1995): 91–124.

Marcus, Joel. *The Way of the Lord: Christological Exegesis of the Old Testament in the Gospel of Mark*. Louisville, Ky.: Westminster John Knox, 1992.

Margelidon, Philippe-Marie. *Les Christologies de l'Assumptus Homo et Les Christologies du Verbe Incarné au XXe Siècle. Les enjeux d'un débat christologique (1927–1960)*. Bibliothèque de la Revue Thomiste. Paris: Parole et Silence, 2011.

Marion, Jean-Luc. "Saint Thomas d'Aquin et l'onto-théo-logie." *Revue Thomiste* 95 (1995): 31–66.

Maritain, Jacques. *On the Grace and Humanity of Jesus*. New York: Herder and Herder, 1969.

———. *Pour une philosophie de l'histoire. Oeuvres Complètes*. Vol. X. Fribourg / Paris: Éditions Universitaires / Éditions St. Paul, 1985.

Marshall, Bruce D. "Christ the End of Analogy." In *The Analogy of Being: Invention of the Antichrist or the Wisdom of God?*, edited by Thomas Joseph White, 280–313. Grand Rapids, Mich.: Eerdmans: 2010.

———. "The Dereliction of Christ and the Impassibility of God." In *Divine Impassibility and the Mystery of Human Suffering*, edited by J. F. Keating and Thomas Joseph White, 246–98. Grand Rapids, Mich.: Eerdmans, 2009.

————. *Trinity and Truth.* Cambridge: Cambridge University Press, 2000.

Marxsen, Willi. *Der Exeget als Theologe. Vorträge zum Neuen Testament.* Gütersloh: Mohn, 1968.

Matera, Frank J. *New Testament Christology.* Louisville, Ky.: Westminster John Knox, 1999.

Maurer, Armand. "St Thomas on the Sacred Name 'Tetragrammaton.'" *Mediaeval Studies* 34 (1972): 275–86.

Menke, Karl-Heinz. *Jesus Ist Gott Der Sohn.* Regensburg: Friedrich Pustet, 2008.

Milbank, John. *The Suspended Middle: Henri de Lubac and the Debate concerning the Supernatural.* Grand Rapids, Mich.: Eerdmans, 2005.

Molnar, Paul. *Divine Freedom and the Doctrine of the Immanent Trinity.* Edinburgh: T. & T. Clark, 2002.

————. "The Trinity, Election and God's Ontological Freedom: A Response to Kevin W. Hector." *International Journal of Systematic Theology* 8, no. 3 (2006): 294–300.

Moloney, Francis. *The Gospel of John.* Collegeville, Minn.: The Liturgical Press, 1998.

Moltmann, Jürgen. *The Coming of God: Christian Eschatology.* Translated by M. Kohl. Philadelphia: Fortress, 1996.

————. *The Crucified God: The Cross of Christ as the Foundation and Criticism of Christian Theology.* Translated by R. A. Wilson. San Francisco: Harper and Row, 1974.

Montagnes, Bernard. *The Doctrine of the Analogy of Being according to Thomas Aquinas.* Translated by E. M. Macierowski. Milwaukee, Wis.: Marquette University Press, 2004.

Morard, Martin. "Une source de saint Thomas d'Aquin: le deuxième concile de Constantinople (553)." *Revue des Sciences Philosophiques et Théologiques* 81 (1997): 21–56.

————. "Thomas d'Aquin lecteur des conciles," *Archivum Franciscanum Historicum* 98 (2005): 211–365.

Moule, C. F. D. *The Origin of Christology.* Cambridge: Cambridge University Press, 1977.

Mulcahy, Bernard. *Aquinas's Notion of Pure Nature and the Christian Integralism of Henri de Lubac. Not Everything Is Grace.* New York: Peter Lang, 2011.

Müller, Gerhard Ludwig. *Katholische Dogmatik: Für Studium und Praxis der Theologie.* Freiburg: Herder, 2005.

Nichols, Aidan. *No Bloodless Myth: A Guide through Balthasar's Dramatics.* Washington, D.C.: The Catholic University of America Press, 2000.

————. "Thomism and the Nouvelle Théologie." *The Thomist* 64 (2000): 1–19.

Nicolas, Jean-Hervé. *Synthèse dogmatique: De la Trinité à la Trinité.* Fribourg: Éditions Universitaires, 1985.

Nietzsche, Friedrich. *On the Genealogy of Morals.* Translated by W. Kaufmann and R. J. Hollingdale. New York: Vintage, 1989.

————. *Writings from the Late Notebooks.* Edited by R. Bittner. Translated by K. Sturge. Cambridge: Cambridge University Press, 2003.

Nieuwenhove, Rik van. "'Bearing the Marks of Christ's Death': Aquinas' Soteriology." In *The Theology of Thomas Aquinas*, edited by R. Van Nieuwenhove and J. Wawrykow, 277–302. Notre Dame, Ind.: University of Notre Dame Press, 2005.

Oakes, Edward. *Infinity Dwindled to Infancy: A Catholic and Evangelical Christology*. Grand Rapids, Mich.: Eerdmans, 2011.

O'Day, Gail. *John: Commentary*. The New Interpreter's Bible, vol. 9. Nashville, Tenn.: Abingdon Press, 1995.

Paissac, Henri. *Théologie du Verbe: St. Augustin et St. Thomas*. Paris: Cerf, 1951.

Pannenberg, Wolfhart. *Jesus: God and Man*. Second edition. Translated by L. L. Wilkins and D. A. Priebe. Philadelphia: Westminster, 1968.

———. *Systematic Theology*. Vol. II. Translated by G. W. Bromiley. Grand Rapids, Mich.: Eerdmans, 1994.

———. *Systematic Theology*. Vol. III. Translated by G. Bromiley. Grand Rapids, Mich.: Eerdmans, 1998.

Penido, M. T.-L. *Le rôle d'analogie en théologie dogmatique*. Paris: J. Vrin, 1931.

Perego, Angelo. "Il 'lumen gloriae' et l'unità psicologica di Cristo." *Divus Thomas* 58 (1955): 90–110 and 296–310.

Philippe de La Trinité. *What Is Redemption?* Translated by A. Armstrong. New York: Hawthorn Books, 1961.

Pitstick, Alyssa Lyra. *Light in Darkness: Hans Urs von Balthasar and the Catholic Doctrine of Christ's Descent into Hell*. Grand Rapids, Mich: Eerdmans, 2007.

Politis, Vasilis. *Aristotle and the Metaphysics*. London: Routledge, 2004.

Principe, Walter H. *Alexander of Hales' Theology of the Hypostatic Union*. Toronto: Pontifical Institute of Medieval Studies, 1967.

———. *Philip the Chancellor's Theology of the Hypostatic Union*. Toronto: Pontifical Institute of Medieval Studies, 1975.

Przywara, Erich. *Analogia entis: Metaphysik*. Münich: Josef Kösel & Friedrich Pustet, 1932.

———. "Reichweite der Analogie als katholischer Grundform." *Scholastik* 3 (1940): 339–62 and 508–32.

Rahner, Karl. "Chalkedon—Ende oder Anfang?" In *Das Konzil von Chalkedon. Geschichte und Gegenwart*, edited by A. Grillmeier and H. Bacht, 3–49. Würzburg: Echter, 1954.

———. *Grundkurs des Glaubens: Einführung in den Begriff des Christentums*. Freiburg im Breisgau: Herder, 1976. Translated by W. V. Dych. *Foundations of Christian Faith: An Introduction to the Idea of Christianity*. New York: Seabury, 1978.

———. *Karl Rahner in Dialogue*. Edited by P. Imhof and H. Biallowons. Translated by H. D. Egan. New York: Crossroad, 1986.

———. *Theological Investigations* I. Translated by C. Ernst. Baltimore, Md.: Helicon Press, 1963.

———. *Theological Investigations* IV. Translated by K. Smith. London: Darton, Longman & Todd, 1966.

———. *Theological Investigations* V. Translated by K.-H. Kruger. London: Darton, Longman & Todd, 1966.

———. *Theological Investigations* VI: *Concerning Vatican Council II*. Translated by

K.-H. Kruger and Boniface Kruger. London / New York: Darton, Longman & Todd / Seabury, 1974.

———. *Theological Investigations* XIII: *Theology, Anthropology, Christology.* Translated by D. Bourke. New York: Seabury, 1979.

———. *Theological Investigations* XVII. Translated by M. Kohl. New York: Crossroad, 1981.

———. *The Trinity.* Translated by J. Donceel. London: Burns & Oates, 1970.

———. "Zur Theologie der Menschwerdung." *Catholica* 12 (1958): 1–16.

Ramírez, Santiago. *De Gratia Dei.* Salamanca: Editorial San Esteban, 1992.

———. *De Hominis Beatitudine,* Tome I. Salamanca: Biblioteca de Teólogos Españoles, 1942.

Ratzinger, Joseph. *Eschatology: Death and Eternal Life.* Translated by M. Waldstein and A. Nichols. Washington, D.C.: The Catholic University of America Press, 1988.

———. *Introduction to Christianity.* Translated by J. R. Foster. San Francisco: Ignatius, 2004.

———. *Principles of Catholic Theology.* Translated by M. F. McCarthy. San Francisco: Ignatius, 1987.

———. *Truth and Tolerance.* Translated by H. Taylor. San Francisco, Ignatius, 2004.

Reimarus, Samuel. *Apologie oder Schutzschrift für die vernünftigen Verehrer Gottes.* Edited by Gerhard Alexander. Frankfurt-am-Main: Insel, 1972.

Ritschl, Albert. *Die christliche Lehre von der Rechtfertigung und Versöhnung.* 3 vols. Bonn: A. Marcus, 1870–74.

———. *Theologie und Metaphysik: zur Verständigung und Abwehr.* Bonn: A. Marcus, 1887.

Sabourin, Léopold. "Le bouc émissaire, figure du Christ?" *Sciences Ecclésiastiques* 11 (1959): 45–79.

Sanders, E. P. *The Historical Figure of Jesus.* London: Penguin, 1993.

———. *Jesus and Judaism.* Philadelphia: Fortress, 1985.

Scheffczyk, Leo. "Christology in the Context of Experience." *The Thomist* 48 (1984): 383–408.

Schenk, Richard. "*Officium signa temporum perscrutandi.* New Encounters of Gospel and Culture in the Context of the New Evangelisation." In *Scrutinizing the Signs of the Times in Light of the Gospel. Bibliotheca Ephemeridum Theologicarum Lovaniensium* 208, edited by J. Verstraeten, 167–203. Leuven: Leuven University Press, 2007.

Schillebeeckx, Eduard. *Christ: The Experience of Jesus as Lord.* Translated by J. Bowden. New York: Seabury, 1980.

———. *Church. The Human Story of God.* Translated by J. Bowden. New York: Crossroad, 1990.

———. *The Council Notes of Edward Schillebeeckx 1962–1963.* Edited by K. Schelkens. Leuven: Peeters, 2011.

———. *De sacramentele Heilseconomie.* Antwerp: H. Nelissen, 1952. French translation by Y. van der Have. *L'économie sacramentelle du salut.* Fribourg: Academic Press Fribourg, 2004.

———. *The Eucharist.* Translated by N. Smith. New York: Sheed and Ward, 1968.

———. *God and the Future of Man.* Translated by N. Smith. New York: Sheed and Ward, 1968.

———. *Jesus: An Experiment in Christology.* Translated by H. Hoskins. New York: Seabury, 1979.

———. *Revelation and Theology.* 2 vols. Translated by N. Smith. New York: Sheed and Ward, 1968.

Schleiermacher, Friedrich. *Der christliche Glaube.* Berlin: G. Reimer, 1821–22. *The Christian Faith.* 2 vols. Edited by H. R. Mackintosh and J. S. Stewart. New York: Harper and Row, 1963.

Schnackenburg, Rudolf. *The Gospel according to St. John.* 3 vols. Translated by C. Hastings. New York: Seabury, 1980–82.

———. *Jesus in the Gospels. A Biblical Christology.* Louisville, Ky.: Westminster John Knox, 1995.

Schönborn, Christophe. *The Human Face of God.* San Francisco: Ignatius Press, 1994.

———. *Sophrone de Jerusalem: vie monastique et confession dogmatique.* Théologie historique 20. Paris: Beauchesne, 1972.

Schumacher, Michele. *A Trinitarian Anthropology: Adrienne von Speyr and Hans Urs von Balthasar in Dialogue with St. Thomas Aquinas.* Washington, D.C.: The Catholic University of America Press, 2014.

Schweitzer, Albert. *Geschichte der leben-Jesu-forschung.* Tübingen: J. C. B. Mohr, 1913.

Sesboüé, Bernard. *Pédagogie du Christ.* Paris: Cerf, 1994.

Shanley, Brian. "Divine Causation and Human Freedom in Aquinas." *American Catholic Philosophical Quarterly* 72, no. 1 (1998): 99–122.

Sherwin, Michael. *By Knowledge and by Love: Charity and Knowledge in the Moral Theology of St. Thomas Aquinas.* Washington, D.C.: The Catholic University of America Press, 2005.

Sobrino, Jon. *Christology at the Crossroads: A Latin American Approach.* Translated by J. Drury. Maryknoll, N.Y.: Orbis, 1978.

———. *Jesus the Liberator: A Historical-Theological Reading of Jesus of Nazareth.* Translated by P. Burns and F. McDonagh. Maryknoll, N.Y.: Orbis, 1993.

Söhngen, Gottlieb. "Analogia fidei I: Gottähnlichkeit allein aus Glauben?" *Catholica* 3 (1934): 113–36.

———. "Analogia fidei II: Die Einheit in der Glaubenswissenschaft." *Catholica* 3 (1934): 176–208.

———. "Wunderzeichen und Glaube." *Catholica* 4 (1935): 145–64.

Spencer, Archie J. "Causality and the *Analogia entis*: Karl Barth's Rejection of the Analogy of Being Reconsidered." *Nova et Vetera* (English edition) 6, no. 2 (2008): 329–76.

Suarez, Francisco. *Opera Omnia.* Tome VII. Paris: Vivès Edition, 1857.

Swinburne, Richard. *Revelation.* Second edition. Oxford: Oxford University Press, 2007.

Synave, Paul. *La révélation des vérités divines naturelles d'après saint Thomas.* In *Mélanges Mandonnet*, 1:327–71. Paris: J. Vrin, 1930.

Taylor, Vincent. *The Gospel According to St. Mark.* London: Macmillan, 1966.

Te Velde, Rudi. *Aquinas on God*. Aldershot: Ashgate, 2006.

Thomasius, Gottfried. *Christi Person und Werk*. Third edition. 2 vols. Erlangen: A. Deichert, 1886–88.

Torrell, Jean-Pierre. "Apologétique et Théologie de la Résurrection du Christ." In *Le Verbe Incarné en ses Mystères*, 4:363–74. Paris: Cerf, 2005.

———. "La Science du Christ." In *Le Verbe Incarné*, 2:415–39. Paris: Cerf, 2002.

———. *Le Christ en ses mysteres: la vie et l'oeuvre de Jesus selon saint Thomas d'Aquin*. Vol. 2. Paris: Desclée, 1999.

———. "Le savoir acquis du Christ selon les théologiens médiévaux." *Revue Thomiste* 101 (2001): 355–408.

———. "Nature and Grace in Thomas Aquinas." In *Surnaturel: A Controversy at the Heart of Twentieth-Century Thomistic Thought,* edited by Serge-Thomas Bonino, translated by Robert Williams, translation revised by Matthew Levering, 155–90. Naples, Fla.: Sapientia Press, 2009.

———. "S. Thomas d'Aquin et la science du Christ." In *Saint Thomas au XXe siècle,* edited by S.-T. Bonino, 394–409. Paris: Éditions St. Paul, 1994.

Tschipke, Theophil. *Heilsorgan der Gottheit. Unter Besonderer Berücksichtigung der Lehre des Heiligen. Thomas von Aquin*. Freiburg im Breisgau: Herder, 1940. French translation by P. Secrétan. *L'humanité du Christ comme instrument de salut de la divinité*. Fribourg: Academic Press Fribourg, 2003.

Turner, Denys. *Faith, Reason and the Existence of God*. Cambridge: Cambridge University Press, 2004.

Vacant, A. "Angé. D'Après Les Scholastiques." In *Dictionnaire de Théologie Catholique,* Tome I, part 2, col. 1228–39. Paris: Letouzey et Ané, 1903.

Vall, Gregory. "Psalm 22: Vox Christi or Israelite Temple Liturgy?" *The Thomist* 66 (2002): 175–200.

Vanhoye, Albert. *Old Testament Priests and the New Priest*. Translated by Bernard Orchard. Petersham, Mass.: St. Bede's Press, 1986.

Wallace, William A. *The Modeling of Nature. Philosophy of Science and Philosophy of Nature in Synthesis*. Washington, D.C.: The Catholic University of America Press, 1996.

Wasserman, Tommy. "The 'Son of God' Was in the Beginning (Mark 1:1)." *Journal of Theological Studies* 62, no. 1 (2011): 20–50.

Wawrykow, Joseph. *Grace and Human Action: Merit in the Theology of Thomas Aquinas*. Notre Dame, Ind.: University of Notre Dame Press, 1996.

Weber, Edouord-Henri. *Le Christ selon saint Thomas d'Aquin*. Paris: Desclée, 1988.

Weinandy, Thomas. "The Beatific Vision and the Incarnate Son: Furthering the Discussion." *The Thomist* 70 (2006): 605–15.

———. *Does God Change?* Still River, Mass.: St. Bede's Press, 1985.

———. *Does God Suffer?* Notre Dame, Ind.: University of Notre Dame Press, 2000.

———. "Jesus' Filial Vision of the Father." *Pro Ecclesia* 13 (2004): 189–201.

Weiss, Johannes. *Die Predigt Jesu vom Reiche Gottes*. Göttingen: Vandenhoeck & Ruprecht, 1892.

Welch, Claude. *God and Incarnation in Mid-Nineteenth Century German Theology*. Oxford: Oxford University Press, 1965.

White, Thomas Joseph. "The Crucified Lord: Thomistic Reflections on the Communication of Idioms and the Theology of the Cross." In *Thomas Aquinas and Karl Barth: An Unofficial Catholic-Protestant Dialogue*, edited by Bruce L. McCormack and Thomas Joseph White, 157–89. Grand Rapids, Mich.: Eerdmans, 2013.

———. "Dyotheletism and the Instrumental Human Consciousness of Jesus." *Pro Ecclesia* 17, no. 4 (2008): 396–422.

———. "On the Universal Possibility of Salvation." *Pro Ecclesia* 17, no. 3 (2008): 269–80.

———. "Von Balthasar and Journet on the Universal Possibility of Salvation and the Twofold Will of God." *Nova et Vetera* (English Edition) 4, no. 3 (2006): 633–66.

———. *Wisdom in the Face of Modernity: A Study in Thomistic Natural Theology.* Naples, Fla.: Sapienta Press, 2009.

Wicks, Jared. "Christ's Saving Descent to the Dead: Early Witnesses from Ignatius of Antioch to Origen." *Pro Ecclesia* 17, no. 3 (2008): 281–309.

Wiles, Maurice. *Archetypal Heresy: Arianism through the Centuries.* Oxford: Oxford University Press, 2001.

———. *The Remaking of Christian Doctrine.* Philadelphia: Westminster Press, 1978.

Witherington III, Ben. *The Christology of Jesus.* Minneapolis, Minn.: Fortress Press, 1990.

———. *John's Wisdom.* Louisville, Ky.: Westminster John Knox Press, 1995.

Wright, N. T. *The Climax of the Covenant: Christ and the Law in Pauline Theology.* Minneapolis, Minn.: Fortress, 1993.

———. *Jesus and the Victory of* God. Minneapolis, Minn.: Fortress, 1996.

———. *The Resurrection of the Son of God.* Minneapolis, Minn.: Fortress, 2003.

Yerkes, James. *The Christology of Hegel.* Albany: State University of New York Press, 1983.

Yocum, John. "A Cry of Dereliction? Reconsidering a Recent Theological Commonplace." *International Journal of Systematic Theology* 7, no. 1 (2005): 72–80.

REFERENCE WORKS

Catechism of the Catholic Church. English Edition. New York: Doubleday, 1995.

Decrees of the Ecumenical Councils. Translated and edited by N. Tanner. London / Washington, D.C.: Sheed and Ward / Georgetown University Press, 1990.

The Sources of Catholic Dogma. Translated by R. J. Deferrari from the Thirteenth Edition of Henry Denzinger's *Enchiridion Symbolorum.* Fitzwilliam, N.H.: Loreto Publications, 1955.

Vatican Council II, Vol. I: The Conciliar and Post Conciliar Documents. Edited by A. Flannery. Northport, N.Y. / Dublin: Costello Publishing / Dominican Publications, 2004.

Index

accidental union, 42–43, 49, 63–65, 79–86, 90, 101–16

Aertsen, Jan, 217n28

Alfeyev, Hilarion, 391n34, 410n108

analogia entis, 46, 65, 171–73, 176, 182, 184, 203–8, 229n40, 231, 384

analogia fidei, 176, 205, 231

Anselm, 349–52, 356, 359, 371, 434

apokatastasis panton, 143, 392, 411, 424n142, 428

Aristotle: on analogical knowledge of being, 65, 184–86, 222n33, 230; on dialectic, 486; on four causes, 186; on hylomorphism, 450, 498–99; on philosophy of nature, 156, 159, 491, 498–99; on primary and secondary actuality, 62; on principle of non-contradiction, 488, 490; on sophism, 156–58, 487–90; on theory of forms, 156n67

Ashley, Benedict, 163n87, 504n77

Athanasius: on analogy of the Word, 213, 291–94; on body-soul analogy, 83; on creative agency of the Logos, 211; on cry of dereliction, 314n19; on filial adoption, 18n46; on procession of the Word, 291–94; on soteriology, 299, 348–49, 352; on unity in the Trinity, 291–97, 346–47

Augustine: on analogy of the Word, 208–11, 213; on Christ preaching in hell, 411–12; on Christ's obedience to himself, 265n54; on Limbo, 415–16; on

nature and grace, 155, 165; on predestination, 385, 387; on sacrifice, 356

Balthasar, Hans Urs von: on Christ's descent into hell, 28, 278–79, 351n27, 380–95, 411, 422–36; on cry of dereliction, 309n5; ecumenical concerns, 388–92, 434–36; on kenosis and Trinity, 27, 343, 345n12, 349n23, 350n25, 392–95, 417, 419, 429–34; on natural theology, 26, 62n58, 203; on nature and grace, 127, 135, 203; on the resurrection of Christ, 374–76, 442–47; on universal possibility of salvation, 382–88, 423–28

Bañez, Domingo, 396nn50–51, 398n59, 403n81, 404n82

Barnes, Corey, 118n89

Barrett, C. K., 324n41, 326n46

Barth, Karl: and *analogia fidei*, 205, 227; on analogy of being, 25–26, 45–51, 61–62, 66, 171–202, 438; and analogy of the Word, 208; on Apostles' creed, 221; on Chalcedonian Christology, 45–51, 61–62, 65–70, 279; on Christ's descent into hell, 388–91, 411, 422, 435; on communication of idioms, 285, 393–94; compared to Schleiermacher, 24, 32–68; criticisms of Aquinas, 178–79, 181–92; on cry of dereliction, 308; on divine obedience, 288–300, 369, 432; on election and reprobation, 351n27, 383–91; and *extra Calvinisticum*, 211;

Gardeil, Ambroise, 3n3, 55–58, 61
Garrigou-Lagrange, Reginald, 57n49,
   136–42, 145, 165n91, 177n16, 336n66, 471
Garrigues, Jean-Miguel, 237n1, 239, 246,
   249n23, 251–54, 262, 264n50, 272n67
Gathercole, Simon J., 10n19, 11n26, 11n28,
   117n88
Gavrilyuk, Paul L., 80n8, 109n81, 342n4,
   346n14
Geffré, Claude, 483–84
Geiger, L.-B., 212n13
Gilson, Étienne, 177n16
Gonet, Jean-Baptiste, 396n52
grace: extrinsicism, 128, 133, 140, 143, 150,
   154, 159, 165, 228, 231n48, 449, 454–55;
   final end of man, 127, 135, 159–66;
   obediential potency, 144, 150; original
   justice, 138–40, 143, 162n84, 165; state
   of pure nature, 131–42, 164–68; universal possibility of salvation, 382–88,
   395–405, 423–26
Gramsci, Antonio, 150n59
Gregory Nazianzus, 119, 211
Griffiths, Paul, 381n2
Grillmeier, Aloys, 17n44, 75, 468
Guardini, Romano, 348n19

habitus theory, 84–86, 93
Harnack, Adolf von, 6–7, 35, 236
Hart, David Bentley, 49n32, 159n76, 199,
   209n7, 411n109
Hegel, G. W. F., 45, 195, 342, 433n155
Heidegger, Martin, 5n9, 33, 177, 442, 447,
   474–75, 484, 493
Heidler, Fritz, 446n15
Hengel, Martin, 10n17, 59
Heraclitus, 488n45, 491
hermeneutics, 470–98
Hick, John, 77, 101–5, 112, 148–49, 166
homo assumptus theory, 43, 84–86, 88,
   109, 113
Humbrecht, Thierry-Dominique, 177n17
Hunsinger, George, 45n25
Hurtado, Larry W., 11n23, 14n34, 15n36,
   21n51, 117n88
Hütter, Reinhard, 161n78, 193n50, 205n4
hylomorphism, 399–402, 450–55

Ignatius of Antioch, 12n29
incarnation: and accidental union,
   42–43, 49, 63–65, 79–86, 90, 101–16;
   and Christological nihilism, 85; and
   grace of union, 84–87; habitus theory,
   84–86; homo assumptus theory, 43,
   84–86, 88, 109, 113; and instrumentality
   of humanity of Christ, 83–84, 112–16,
   119–21, 256–62, 266, 286n15, 359–64,
   371–72, 431, 459, 461; and kenotic theology, 340–53; and natural theology,
   203–35; and nature/mode distinction,
   251–56; subsistence theory, 84–86,
   112–16, 247–51
Irenaeus of Lyon, 314n19, 347n17, 390

Jesus Christ: beatific vision of, 236–74,
   329–39; and communication of idioms,
   19–21, 79–81, 109, 285, 393–94, 419–20;
   as creator, 9–14; cry of dereliction,
   308–39; death of, 340–79; descent
   into hell, 380–437; habitual grace of,
   84–91; human consciousness of, 26,
   37, 41–44, 48–50, 60, 63, 65, 67–68,
   70, 76n2, 94–96, 99, 101–22, 236–74,
   329, 333, 338–39, 344–45, 348, 368n77;
   human nature of, 16–19, 126–70; human obedience of, 17–18, 23, 26–27, 48,
   50, 63, 65–66, 99, 108, 119, 121, 123, 239,
   246, 262–67, 273–74, 277–307, 310–11,
   313, 316, 319, 332, 334, 343, 349–51, 356,
   369, 371, 374–75, 418, 423, 434; and
   hypostatic union, 73–125; kenosis
   of, 340–79; Lordship, 14–16; prayer
   of, 267–74; pre-existence, 9–14, 20,
   77, 207, 210n9, 218, 220, 292n31; and
   pure nature, 164–68; resurrection of,
   364–67, 438–64; suffering of, 270–72,
   304–5, 308–39; theandric acts, 23, 120,
   251, 259, 262, 274, 286n15, 304, 357n51,
   370, 459–60, 503n75; two natures of,
   171–202, 295–96; two wills of, 256–63
John Damascene, 125, 200n65, 213, 246–53,
   260n44, 264n50, 267, 269n61, 272n67,
   302n52, 318n28, 331n56, 387
John of the Cross, 334n63
Johnson, Luke Timothy, 38n13

CPSIA information can be obtained
at www.ICGtesting.com
Printed in the USA
FFHW021249140819
54328417-60003FF